Leggetts' Antiques Atlas™

West
2000 Edition

by Kim and David Leggett

Foreword by Ralph and Terry Kovel

THREE RIVERS PRESS
NEW YORK

Published by Three Rivers Press, 201 East 50th Street, New York, New York 10022. Member of the Crown Publishing Group.

Random House, Inc. New York, Toronto, London, Sydney, Auckland
www.randomhouse.com

THREE RIVERS PRESS is a registered trademark of Random House, Inc.

Originally published in different format by Rainy Day Publishing, Inc. in 1997 and by Three Rivers Press in 1999. Copyright © 1997, 1999 by Kim and David Leggett.

Printed in the United States of America

Library of Congress Catalog Card Number: 98-34759

ISBN 0-609-80492-8 (pbk.)

10 9 8 7 6 5 4 3 2 1

Revised Edition

Dedication

This book is dedicated to all of those special people who put forth their time, money and talents to make a project of this size happen. A special thanks to Linda Miller, David and Jo Brandon, Frank Bertelt, Kimberly Poland of Mollyockett Antique Market for her hard work in updating the state of Maine, Kitty and Tony Ables, Heart of Country Antiques Shows, the Baird Texas Marketing Alliance, Antique Associations and Chamber of Commerce organizations across America, our editor PJ Dempsey at Crown for her patience and hard work, and Terry Kovel for recommending such a fabulous publisher. We thank you and love you all.

Contents

Foreword

Of course, we are always looking for that out-of-the-way shop filled with unrecognized treasures, that $1,000 vase priced at $75. But when does it pay to leave the turnpike and go off into a small town to visit the shops? Local dealers often have brochures listing nearby antiques stores, the farm papers sometimes include a section on shopping for antiques, and the dealers are usually happy to direct us to the next area with stores. But we need more.

The *Leggetts' Antiques Atlas* is the first large national guidebook that recognizes the problems of the out-of-state shopper searching for antiques. It has maps, places to stay, to eat, and a town-by-town guide to the shops and malls. We like to photocopy the pages about the states we plan to be in. That way we have some of the town history, detailed directions, and maps. There are also antique show schedules so we can try to arrive in a town when the big show is on.

Thank you, Kim and David, for writing this book that helped us out of a very scary night. We were driving in a rural area, no houses in sight, when the fog made it almost impossible to see. Once in a while a street sign was visible. The book listed a phone number for a nearby shop. We hoped the owner lived there and was awake as we called from the car phone to explain our problem. Antiques people are the best! The shop owner talked us along the road and through the fog telling us where to turn. Thirty minutes later we were at a motel.

We know it is impossible to ever do a complete listing of antiques shops. They open and close daily. The *Leggetts' Antiques Atlas* is as complete as any we have used.

Ralph and Terry Kovel
Kovels' Antiques & Collectibles Price List

Introduction

Even as a child I loved to go "antiquing." Every Friday night my aunt and grandmother would take me along to a little country auction at "Peppermint Pond," where they often purchased incredible antiques at next to nothing prices. To this day my aunt still sleeps in a gorgeous six-foot-long oak bed which she purchased for $20. Not one to be left out of a bargain-hunting shopping excursion, I too purchased a fair amount of jumble and junk along with some "good stuff" (or so I thought). My room became the envy of cousins and friends who came to admire the long, sparkling strands of hippie beads, peace signs, strange-looking incense burners and other '60s memorabilia. Today, 30 years later, I prefer early American painted pieces over the "Partridge Family Does Dixie" look, but one thing has never changed — the intense desire to search and find "pieces of the past."

I was convinced that there were plenty of antique establishments all across America worth seeking out, but there was simply no handy way to find them. Because I could not find a book which provided such a listing, I resolved to research and write one myself. I am happy to say that most businesses were thrilled to be included in this book. Their personal stories are a testimony to their love and devotion to their business. Within these pages you will find a great mix of "antiquing" possibilities, from the offerings of exclusive antiques markets and group shops to the diverse selections of traditional antiques and collectibles shops and malls. All the antiques shows listed in this book represent only the finest in antique furnishings and very early collectibles. Many of the bed and breakfasts, country inns, and hotels are listed on the National Register of Historical Places and offer exceptional overnight accommodations. You'll also find information on historical towns and suggestions for some very interesting "in-town" side trips to add to your "antiquing" adventures. Should all this shopping make you hungry, I have thrown in a few select dining establishments as well.

If in your travels you happen upon a shop/mall/market/show/auction, etc., that is not included, please call us. We would love to include them in our year 2001 edition. And most important, when visiting any of these businesses, please let them know you read about them in *Leggetts' Antiques Atlas*.

Happy Hunting!
Call us anytime — we would love to hear from you!
(615) 599-5406
Kim and David Leggett

How to Use This Book

1. The listings following the maps are in alphabetical order. Consequently, the numbers appearing on the maps will not be in numerical order.

2. The purpose of the maps is to direct you to a general location using major highways or interstates as references. Secondary highways and streets are intentionally omitted.

3. The directions in this book were submitted to *Leggetts' Antiques Atlas* by the listed business. Neither *Leggetts' Antiques Atlas* nor Crown Publishing Group accepts responsibility for incorrect directions.

4. At the time of publishing, the information in this book was verified to be correct. However, the publisher cannot be responsible for any inconvenience due to outdated or incorrect information.

NOTE: *At the time of printing, we were experiencing a large volume of area code changes. If you should reach a number which appears to be disconnected, call the operator to verify if there has been an area code change.*

Arizona

0 Mileage 30

- 15
- 93
- 40
- 4 Flagstaff
- 40
- 89
- 16 Sedona
- Jerome
- 2 Cornville
- 7
- 3 Cottonwood
- 89A
- 8 Lake Havasu City
- 93
- 14 Prescott
- 69
- 12 Pine
- 89
- 10 Payson
- 13 Pinetop-Lakeside
- 17
- 19 Wickenburg
- 60
- 60
- 87
- 60
- 10
- Glendale 5
- 15 Scottsdale
- 95
- 11
- Phoenix
- Goodyear 6
- 9 Mesa
- 60
- 70
- 85
- 10
- 8
- 20
- Yuma
- 18 Tucson
- 10
- 19
- 90
- 80
- 191
- 17 Tombstone
- 80
- 1 Bisbee

Arizona

1 BISBEE

Arizona's most interesting town — a place where you can read history in the ornate facades of turn-of-the-century buildings, or hear first hand from veterans of the copper mining days. It's a walker town with networks of tiny streets which remind one of a European village. Bisbee is jammed with antiques, boutiques, quaint inns, art galleries and live theater. Be sure to tour the authentic copper mine. Bisbee boasts the best year-round climate on earth.

To stop in Bisbee is to stop in time. Nestled in the mile high Mule Mountains of southern Arizona, Bisbee has maintained an Old World charm seldom found anywhere in the United States. The fine collection of well-preserved turn-of-the-century Victorian structures are full of old west history and copper mining lore. Old miners' boarding houses have been refurbished into many charming small bed and breakfast establishments, of which no two are alike. Former saloons are now quaint shops, antique stores or art galleries, cafes and restaurants.

A popular activity is Bisbee's excellent self-guided fully-illustrated Walking Tour, which details each historic structure and guides the visitor with a map. Included in the Walking Tour is world-famous Brewery Gulch, which in its heyday boasted upwards of 47 saloons and was considered the "liveliest spot between El Paso and San Francisco."

On Consignment in Bisbee

100 Lowell Traffic Circle
520/432-4002
Open: Tues.–Sat. 10:30–5:30 and 1st Sun. each month 12–5
Directions: Located ¼ mile south of the Lavender Pit Mine on the Traffic Circle (the only building right on the circle)

Antiques and glass, tools and brass, vintage kitchenware, jewelry and lots of ???. On Consignment boasts of having something for every taste and budget. With over 600 consignors, the store has been described as "The Attic of Cochise County." Within its 12,000 sq. ft., this shopper's paradise is jam-packed with an amazing mix of old, new and the unusual. Strange things have been known to happen at On Consignment in Bisbee. A woman customer came in and recognized, high on the wall, a seascape painted by her husband's long-deceased great-aunt, who never left San Francisco. Like most of the great-aunt's paintings, it had been sold at a gallery. The family had only a few of her works and the woman was thrilled to find one for $25.

Bisbee Antiques & Collectibles
3 Main St.
520/432-4320

Pentimento
29 Main St.
520/432-2752

Johnson's Antiques & Books
45 Main St.
520/432-2736

Good Goods
54 Brewery Gulch
520/432-2788

Main Street Antiques
67 Main St.
520/432-4104

Crystal Moon
76 Main St.
520/432-0988

Atalanta Music & Books
38 Main St.
520/432-9976

Far Out Ranch
78 Main St.
520/432-2912

Flying Saucers Antiques & Cllbls.
26A Brewery Ave.
520/432-4858

Acorn Gift Shoppe & Antiques
924 Hwy. 80, 1 Mile E. of Tunnel
520/432-7314

Horse Hotel Antiques
69 Main St.
520/432-9050

Timeless Treasures
2 Copper Queen Plaza
520/432-5888

Cruceros
23 Erie
520/432-1299

Johnson Gallery
28 Main St.
520/432-2126

Great Places to Stay

Hotel La More/The Bisbee Inn

45 OK St.
1-888-432-5131 or 520/432-5131
Email: Bisbeeinn@aol.com
Alfred & Elissa Strati, Proprietors
Directions: For specific directions to The Bisbee Inn from your location, please call the Innkeepers.

Originally built in 1917 as a miner's hotel, today the inn is a certified historic restoration containing 20 guest rooms, most with private baths, original oak and period furnishings, and a charming dining room serving complimentary country breakfasts. It is located in the Downtown Historic District in close proximity to Brewery Gulch and other Bisbee points of interest.

Interesting Side Trips

Bisbee boasts the oldest golf course in Arizona, live repertory theaters, numerous art galleries, pottery studios, jewelry, craftsmen and gem and mineral stores.

Bisbee Mining and Historical Museum

Located in Downtown Historic Bisbee
Open: Daily 10–4, fee charged, senior discount
520/432-7071

Queen Mine Tours

Hwy. 80 interchange entering Old Bisbee
520/432-2071

2 CORNVILLE

Eight Ball Antiques
1050 S. Page Springs Road
520/634-1479
Open: Wed.–Sun. 10–5, Mon. & Tues. by chance
Directions: Located 80 miles north of Phoenix or 45 miles south of Flagstaff. Take I-17 to McGuireville Exit #293. Travel west 9 miles on Cornville Road to Page Springs Road. Turn right on Page Springs Road. Go ¼ mile, building is on left.

"If you build it, they will come" — a commonly heard phrase originally coined by several "claim to fame" baseball teams. I borrowed it because it is so appropriate for Eight Ball Antiques. Nestled away in the sleepy little community of Cornville, Jim and his wife, Kristin, have successfully attracted collectors of the unusual from all over the U.S. You will understand this curious following the minute you enter the 4,500-square-foot building filled to the rafters with oddities such as service station memorabilia, wagon wheels, large games, pedal toys, Lincoln Log building sets, old tools, primitives and lots more. If one of the antique cars offered for sale won't fit into your trunk, you can opt for a scaled-down version. Jim has quite an assortment of collectible cars from which to choose.

Not your traditional antique "stop," I figured Jim must have some "highly guarded" sources for acquiring such offerings. He clarified my misconception by explaining that his forte for gathering this hodge-podge of gizmos and gadgets was a result of his 30 years of collecting. Looks like Jim and Kristin had one heck of a spring cleaning when they decided to open up shop!

3 COTTONWOOD

Home Sweet Home
303 S. Main St.
520/634-3304

J & J Antiques & Things
796 N. Main St.
520/639-1732

Old Town Antiques
712 N. Balboa St.
520/634-5461

4 FLAGSTAFF

Carriage House Antique Mall
413 N. San Francisco St.
520/774-1337

Golden Memories
101 S. Milton Road
520/774-5915

Collection Connection
901 N. Beaver
520/779-2943

Incahoots
9 E. Aspen Ave.
520/773-9447

Mountain Christmas
14 N. San Francisco St.
520/774-4054

Old Highway Trading Post
698 E. Route 66
520/774-0035

Lightning Antiques
1926 N. 4th St. #8
520/527-4444

Great Places to Stay

The Inn at 410 Bed & Breakfast
410 N. Leroux St.
520/774-0088

Turn-of-the-century home — eight guest rooms with private baths.

5 GLENDALE

Known as Arizona's "Antique Capital," Historic Glendale offers more than 80 antique and specialty shops, plus unique eateries and tea rooms in the Historic Downtown area.

Directions: Downtown Glendale is located at 59th and Glendale Avenues, just 4 miles west of I-17. Take the Glendale Avenue exit and drive approximately 20 minutes from downtown Phoenix, 40 minutes from Scottsdale Road and Lincoln Drive, and 30 minutes from downtown Tempe.

Boasting the greatest concentration of antique shops in Arizona, this charming Historic District is much more than just a lot of stores—it's an overall experience to all who visit. The more than 90 antique shops, specialty stores and unique restaurants are housed in old storefronts and century-old bungalows in a small town atmosphere that is as American as apple pie. Nestled in a few blocks surrounding shady Murphy Park, 58th and Glendale Avenues, this wonderful pedestrian area features brick sidewalks lined with trees and gas-style lamps and is dotted with comfortable benches that invite one to sit and soak up the ambience.

If you love to antique, are an avid collector, or just have the urge to "go back in time," downtown Glendale is the place for you. The shops are as varied as they are numerous. There are large multi-dealer malls, smaller shops and specialized dealers. This wide variety of establishments offers vintage sports and automobile memorabilia, nostalgic conversation pieces, captivating old books, yesterday's toys and dolls and thousands of other items of gone-by days. From one shop to another, you'll travel through time as you absorb the history of the 1800s, the Victorian era, the wild and roaring '20s, the simple and rustic charm of America's farms, the excitement and adventure of the old west, sports heroes and yesterday's cars, and the quiet elegance and style of a previous generation.

The selection of quality merchandise, the convenience of parking and easy walking to shops, a small-town atmosphere in a picturesque setting, free rides on the town trolley, friendly shopkeepers, great food and

Arizona

hospitality, wonderful special events—these are just some of the reasons that Downtown Glendale was chosen as the "best place to antique in Arizona" by the *Arizona Republic* newspaper.

The Apple Tree
5811 W. Glendale Ave.
602/435-8486
Open: Mon.–Sat. 10–5, Sun. 11–4
Directions: (Phoenix Metro Area) From I-17, exit #205, Glendale Ave., go West 4 miles. From I-10, Exit #138. 59th Avenue, go North 5 miles to Glendale Avenue, turn right (East) on Glendale Ave. Shop is on south side of Glendale Ave. Between 59th and 58th Avenues.

Located in the heart of Historic Downtown Glendale, The Apple Tree is 6,300 square feet of antiques and collectibles. Dealers offer quality merchandise including furniture, pottery, Depression and elegant glass, toys, advertising, china, linens, quilts, lamps and much, much more. Owner Karen Hess-Landes specializes in early country and primitives, devoting more than  half of the shop to this passion. Early pine cupboards, dry sinks, jelly cabinets, harvest tables, benches, chairs, pie safes, wooden bowls, crocks, redware, tin and iron, yellowware—if it's country, you'll find it at The Apple Tree.

Merchandise is beautifully displayed and the staff is friendly, knowledgeable and willing to assist. Dealers and designers are always welcome and considerations are given. This is a full-service shop, accepting all major credit cards, checks, layaway, shipping and customer search service. Now in its eighth year, The Apple Tree was chosen "Best Antiques Shop" in the Phoenix metro Northwest Valley by readers of the *Arizona Republic*.

Shaboom's
5533 W. Glendale Ave.
602/842-8687

Purple Elephant
5734 W. Glendale Ave.
602/931-1991

Ramblin Roads
5747 W. Glendale Ave.
602/931-5084

Antique Arena
5825 W. Glendale Ave.
602/930-7121

Strunk's Hollow
6960 N. 57th Dr.
602/842-2842

Adventures Thru The Looking Glass
5609 W. Glendale Ave.
602/930-7884

Nifties Antiques
5745 W. Glendale Ave.
602/930-8407

Lois Lovables Antiques
5748 W. Glendale Ave.
602/934-8846

Larry's Antiques
7120 N. 55th Dr.
602/435-1133

Old Mill Stream Antique & Cllbls.
7021 N. 57th Dr.
602/939-2545

Now Then & Always Inc.
7021 N. 57th Dr.
602/931-1116

Antique Treasurers
7025 N. 57th Dr.
602/931-8049

Memories Past Antiques
7138 N. 57th Dr.
602/435-9592

Century House Antiques
6835 N. 58th Ave.
602/939-1883

Lamps by Shirley
6835 N. 58th Ave.
602/842-3306

Grandma's House Antiques & Collectibles
7142 N. 58th Ave.
602/939-8874

Hometown Antiques
5745 W. Palmaire Ave.
602/931-8790

ABD/Murphy Park Place
5809 W. Glendale Ave.
602/931-0235

Cooper Street Antiques
5757 W. Glendale Ave.
602/939-7731

House of Gera
7025 N. 58th Ave.
602/842-4631

Remember That? Antiques
5807 W. Myrtle Ave.
602/435-1179

Antique Etc.
5753 W. Glendale Ave.
602/939-2732

Gatehouse Antiques
7023 N. 57th Dr.
602/435-1919

Back To The Classic Antiques
7031 N. 57th Dr.
602/939-5537

Antique Emporium
6835 N. 58th Dr.
602/842-3557

Mr. Peabody's Antiques
6835 N. 58th Ave.
602/842-0003

Glendale Square Antiques
7009 N. 58th Ave.
602/435-9952

Sandy's Dream Dolls
7154 N. 58th Ave.
602/931-1579

Second Debut
5851 W. Palmaire Ave.
602/939-3922

Casa De Lao
5803 W. Glendale Ave.
602/937-9783

Shady Nook Books & Antiques
5751 W. Glendale Ave.
602/939-1462

Arsenic & Old Lace
7157 N. 59th Ave.
602/842-9611

Antique Apparatus Exchange
5802 W. Palmaire Ave.
602/435-1522

6 GOODYEAR

Your Hidden Treasures
100 E. Western Ave.
602/932-9332

7 JEROME

Almost a mile high in the center of Arizona, the town of Jerome is a Historic National Landmark. Once a roaring copper mining camp and a boom town of 15,000 people, Jerome was built on Cleopatra Hill above a vast deposit of copper. The mines, the workers and those who sought its wealth — miners and smelter workers, freighters and gamblers, bootleggers and saloon keepers, storekeepers and assorted Europeans,

Arizona

Latins and Asians, prostitutes and preachers, wives and children — all made Jerome, Ariz., what it was.

Prehistoric Native Americans were the first miners. The Spanish followed, seeking gold but finding copper. Anglos staked the first claims in the area in 1876, and United Verde Mining Operations began in 1883, followed by the Little Daisy chain. Americans, Mexicans, Croatians, Irish, Spaniards, Italians and Chinese added to the increasingly cosmopolitan mix that caused Jerome to grow rapidly from tent city to prosperous company town.

Billions of dollars of copper were extracted from the earth under Jerome. Changing times in the Arizona Territory saw pack burros, mule-drawn freight wagons and horses replaced by steam engines, autos and trucks. Fires ravaged the clapboard town again and again, but Jerome was always rebuilt.

In 1918, underground mining was phased out after uncontrollable fires erupted in the 88 miles of tunnels under the town. Open pit mining brought dynamiting. The hills rattled and buildings cracked. The earth's surface began to shift and sections of the business district slid downward. Jerome's notorious "sliding jail" moved 225 feet and now rests across the road from its original site.

Dependent on the ups and downs of copper prices, labor unrest, depressions and wars, Jerome's mines finally closed in 1953. After the mines closed and "King Copper" left town, the population went from a peak of 15,000 in the 1920s to some 50 hardy souls in the late 1950s. The 1960s and '70s were the time of the counter culture, and Jerome offered a haven for artists, who renovated homes and opened abandoned shops to sell their wares. Soon newcomers and a few remaining Jerome old-timers were working together to bring Jerome back to life.

Today, Jerome is very much alive with writers, artists, artisans, musicians, historians, and families. The town is chock-full of shops and galleries, and about 95% of all the town's remaining buildings date from 1895 to the 1920s.

Collectors Emporium	**Papillon**
301 N. Hull Ave.	410 Main St.
520/639-3321	520/634-7626

Great Places to Stay

Ghost City Inn Bed and Breakfast
541 N. Main St.
520/63GHOST (520/634-4678)
Open: All year
Rates: $75–$95, full breakfast included

Built in 1898, the Historically Registered Ghost City Inn Bed & Breakfast offers a veranda view from each guest room that scans the Verde Valley and the terraced red rocks of Sedona — a view that some say challenges the views of the Grand Canyon in magnificence. All five guest rooms contain an artful blend of Victorian and early American. A full-service breakfast and afternoon tea are provided, as well as a turn-down service with chocolates, and assistance with recreational plans.

■ 8 LAKE HAVASU CITY

Boulevard Mall	**Now & Then**
2137 McCulloch Blvd. N.	2104 McCulloch Blvd. N.
520/855-7277	520/680-1700
Remember When Antiques & Gifts	**Classic Golf & Collectibles**
2026 McCulloch Blvd. N.	2014 McCulloch Blvd.
520/453-9494	520/453-2070
Somewhere in Time Antiques	**Whimsical Antiques**
1535 Marlboro Dr.	1535 Marlboro Dr.
520/453-7778	520/453-2112

■ 9 MESA

Carole & Maxine's Antiques
2353 E. Brown Road
602/964-6006
Email: carol@azantique.com
Web site: www.azantique.com
Open: Tues.–Sat. 11–5
Directions: Traveling Highway 60 east of Phoenix, take Gilbert Rd. Exit north to Brown Road. Turn east ½ mile on south side. Mesa is approximately 18 miles east of Phoenix. The shop is on E. Brown Road in Mesa.

Ms. Augustin has been importing 18th and 19th century pine furniture and accessories from the U.K. for 37 years. The shop and the Augustin home is located on historical property. The farmhouse dates back to 1918 and the antique shop is situated in the two-story barn in back. Ms. Augustin was originally in business with her mother, but today she runs this elegant, "with the feel of country," upscale shop herself. Her knowledge of fine quality antiques is evident in the selections she has displayed throughout the shop. Along with the pine furnishings you'll find a delightful array of flow blue, as well as other fine blue and white pieces, Victorian glass, a sampling of decorative accessories, and "hard to find" exceptional copper and brass items.

Stewart's Military Antiques	**Country Attic**
108 W. Main St.	1941 W. Guadalupe Road
602/834-4004	602/838-0360
Downtown Antiques	**New Again Antiques**
202 W. Main St.	212 W. Main St.
602/833-4838	602/834-6189
Glass Urn	**Almost Anything**
456 W. Main St. #G	3015 E. Main St., #101
602/833-2702	602/924-6260

Treasures From The Past Antiques
106 E. McKellips Road
602/655-0090

Beyond Expressions Antique
3817 E. McKellips Road
602/854-7755

Mesa Antique Mart
1455 S. Stapley, Suite 12
602/813-1909

Pam's Place
1121 S. Country Club Dr.
602/827-9637

Ron & Soph Antiques
1060 W. Broadway
602/964-7437

Antique Plaza
114 W. Main St.
602/833-4844

Interesting Side Trip

The Lost Dutchman
Located in the Superstition Mountains just outside of Mesa

There have been hundreds of reported claims to the Lost Dutchman treasure dating back as far as the 1870s. Perhaps the first recorded claim was made by The Dutchman, a man named Jacob Waltz who was actually of German descent. The gold is believed to be stashed away in the Superstition Mountains somewhere near the landmark known as Weaver's Needle. Additional clues published in the *Phoenix Gazette* during the late 1800s indicate that a lost cabin plays a significant part in the claim's location.

The question of whether this gold is, in fact, from a mine or the remains of some earlier expedition, is as much a mystery as the treasure itself. One of the many legends surrounding the Lost Dutchman indicates that in the 1840s a Mexican cartel unearthed the treasure from the mine. However, the miners were attacked by Apaches and never got out with the gold. Unaware of the importance of the yellow metal, the Indians ripped apart the sacks containing the gold, spreading it across the area.

If this story is true, then the Lost Dutchman isn't a mine at all. This would also mean Jacob Waltz wasn't digging; he was gathering the gold scattered by the Apaches. His claim was merely a cover for protection against other prospectors seeking the lavish bounty. According to Waltz, the same map used by the Mexican expedition led him and another German, Jacob Weiser, to discover the mine. Once again, their extraction of the gold was cut short by an Apache ambush similar to the one staged against the Mexicans in 1840. It is unclear whether Jacob Weiser survived, but Waltz made it out alive.

There is no indication that Waltz returned to collect his fortune prior to the earthquake on May 3, 1887. The gold, whether still in the mine or scattered on the ground, would have disappeared in the shifting of rock and earth. If, in fact, Waltz had located the Lost Dutchman, the identifiable landmarks which served as clues would have been dramatically altered by the quake.

Nevertheless, Jacob Waltz definitely knew something about this mysterious lost treasure — too much of his life was consumed by its existence.

On his deathbed on October 25, 1891, Waltz spoke one last time about the infamous Lost Dutchman. He told his caretaker, Mrs. Julia Thomas, the story of the fabulous mine he had discovered in the Superstition Mountains.

Given all the information reported by Jacob Waltz and countless others who have followed in his footsteps, it seems somewhat reasonable to believe the Lost Dutchman, in whatever form, exists.

10 PAYSON

Country Corner
111 E. State Hwy. 260
520/474-0014

Granny's Attic
800 E. State Hwy. 260
520/474-3962

Star Valley USA Antiques
55293 E. State Hwy. 260
520/472-7343

The Teapot
216 W. Main St.
520/474-0718

Hopi House
102 S. Beeline Hwy.
520/474-4000

Payson Antique Mall
1001 S. Beeline Hwy.
520/474-8988

Hodge Podge Cottage
204 S. Beeline Hwy.
520/472-7752

Pioneer Village Trading Post
1117 N. Beeline Hwy.
520/474-3911

11 PHOENIX

Antique Gems
2305 N. 7th St.
602/252-6288

Spine
1323 E. McDowell Road
602/252-4858

Vintage Classics
2301 N. 7th St.
602/252-7271

Consignment Gallery
330 E. Camelback Road
602/631-9630

Mussallem Fine Arts, Inc.
5120 N. Central Ave.
602/277-5928

Xavier Square Antiques
4700 N. Central Ave.
602/248-8208

Alcuin Books
115 W. Camelback Road
602/279-3031

Antique Gallery
5037 N. Central Ave.
602/241-1174

Central Antique Gallery
36 E. Camelback Road
602/241-1636

Pink Flamingo Antiques
2241 N. 7th St.
602/261-7730

Arizona Historical Cache Antiques
5807 N. 7th St.
602/264-0629

Bobbi's Antiques
3838 N. 7th St.
602/264-1787

Empire Antiques
5003 N. 7th St.
602/240-2320

Second Hand Rose
1350 E. Indian School Road
602/266-5956

Central Outpost
9405 N. Central Ave.
602/997-2253

Antique Gatherings
3601 E. Indian School Road
602/956-8203

Sweet Annie Doodle's
5025 N. 7th St.
602/230-1058

Travel Thru Time
5115 N. 7th St.
602/274-0666

Arizona

Nook & Kranny
4302 N. 7th St.
602/241-0228

Antiquary
3044 N. 24th St.
602/955-8881

Antique Outpost
10012 N. Cave Creek Road
602/943-9594

Nickelodeon
110 W. Seldon Lane
602/943-3512

Pzaz
2528 E. Camelback Road
602/956-4402

Brass Armadillo
12419 N. 28th Dr.
888/942-0030

J & K Furniture
2811 E. Bell Road
602/992-6990

Matlosz & Co. Antique Furniture
2227 N. 24th St.
602/273-7974

Estate Gallery
3157 E. Lincoln Dr.
602/956-8845

Lamp Hospital
1643 E. Bell Road
602/788-1000

Wizard of Odz Antiques
1643 E. Bell Road
602/788-1000

Do Wah Diddy
3642 E. Thomas Road
602/957-3874

Millie's Antiques, Gifts & Cllbls.
5102 N. Central Ave.
602/264-0294

Scott D Gram Arts & Antiques
1837 W. Thunderbird Road
602/548-3498

Antique Accents
2515 E. Bell Road
601/493-1956

Sally's Attic Collectibles
24 E. Mohave St.
602/256-4536

Labriola's Antique Gallery
3311 N. 24th St.
602/956-5370

Eric's Antiques
2539 W. Northern Ave.
602/995-2950

Antique Market
1601 N. 7th Ave.
602/255-0212

Stratford Court Antiques & Interiors
4848 E. Cactus Road
602/788-6300

Interesting Side Trips

The Heard Museum

22 E. Monte Visa Road
602/252-8840 or 602/252-8848 (message)
Open: Mon.–Sat. 9:30–5, Wed. 9:30–8, Sun. noon–5, closed on major holidays. Admission charges.
Directions: One block east of Central Ave., and three blocks north of McDowell Road

Since first opening its doors in 1929, the Heard Museum has earned an international reputation for its outstanding representation of the culture and heritage of Native Americans in the Southwest, plus its unique exhibits and innovative programming. It is internationally recognized for its collections of artifacts and art documenting the history of native cultures, especially Southwestern Native Americans. The Heard Museum was founded in 1929 by Dwight B. and Maie Bartlett Heard, a prominent Phoenix couple who had moved to the Valley of the Sun in the mid-1880's from Chicago. The Heards were avid collectors of Native artifacts

and art, especially those of Southwestern Native American cultures. The couple built the Heard Museum in order to share their collection. More than 250,000 people visit the Heard Museum each year — more than any other museum in Arizona. About 25,000 visitors are school children.

Located in central Phoenix, the Heard Museum is home to more than 35,000 objects, as well as an extensive 24,000-volume reference library. The variety of exhibits contain objects that run the gamut from 800 A.D. to pieces made in the 1990s. The Spanish Colonial Revival building was especially designed on Heard property to house their renowned family collection. Today, visitors can enjoy the Heard's seven exhibit galleries and grounds. Frequently, Native American artists demonstrate beadworking, weaving or carving. Visitors have an opportunity to talk with the artists as they work.

12 PINE

Gingerbread House
Hwy. 87 & Randell Dr.
520/476-3504

Pineberry Antiques & Collectibles
86 Hwy. 87
520/476-2219

Apple Annie's
Hardscrabble Road
520/476-4569

13 PINETOP/LAKESIDE

Harvest Moon Antiques
392 W. Mountain Blvd.
520/367-6973

Billings Country Pine Antiques
103 W. Yaeger Lane
520/367-1709

Pinecrest Lane Antiques
50 E. Pinecrest Lane
520/367-0943

Sherry's Antiques Mall
857 E. White Mountain Blvd.
520/367-5184

The Antique Mercantile Co.
Hwy. 260
520/368-9090

Orchard Antiques
1664 W. White Mountain Blvd.
520/368-6563

Antiques & Stuff
774 W. Woodland Lake Road
520/367-1732

White Mountain Antiques
1691 W. White Mt. Blvd.
520/368-6266

Sweet Corn Antiques
Hwy. 260
520/368-9090

Homestead Antiques & Collectibles
Corner of Homestead/Mt. View
520/368-6592

Wings of Faith Antiques
1687 W. White Mountain Road
520/368-5772

14 PRESCOTT

Historic Prescott, established in 1864, is one of the oldest communities in Arizona. Located nearly a mile high on a pine-covered basin at the base of the Bradshaw Mountains, Prescott was the only United States territorial capital founded in a wilderness. It was spawned from gold fever after mountain man Joseph Reddeford Walker led the first prospectors to the site in 1863. What began as a ramshackle mining camp grew into the central Arizona territory's hub for trading and freighting. Miners, ranchers and cowboys found solace in the gambling halls and saloons that soon peppered the city's streets.

Prescott's first courthouse was built in 1867; its first hanging occurred in 1875 (the doomed man's innocence was proven 60 years later). Twice named territorial capital, it lost the honor first to Tucson in 1867, and finally to Phoenix in 1889. A devastating fire in 1900 all but leveled downtown, razing homes, hotels and businesses along the streets of Gurley, Montezuma and North Cortez. Undaunted, the citizens of Prescott rebuilt their lost structures in much finer fashion than those that had stood before.

Traces of Prescott's earlier days abound throughout the downtown area, from saloons boasting hand-carved mahogany bars to historic hotels, from the Hassayampa Inn to Sharlot Hall Museum. Take a turn up North Cortez, where an entire row of antique emporiums offer collections ranging from the distinctive to the whimsical. Step off the beaten path and you may discover that singular treasure of your dreams tucked inside one of the Alley shops.

The depths of downtown Prescott's commitment to the cultural arts was firmly established with the laying of the cornerstone of the Elks Opera House April 4, 1904. This Grand Lady of Gurley Street has graciously hosted live performances for more than 90 years, echoing with the footfalls of famous vaudeville troupes, distinguished actors from the Royal Shakespeare Company, and Broadway stars. On Gurley Street, the Sharlot Hall Museum opens the door on the color and excitement of the Arizona Territory. The museum bears the name of the first woman to hold public office in Arizona (1909), a local poet and historian whose life was an adventure in itself. Resting gracefully on three acres, Sharlot Hall Museum's historic buildings house a fascinating collection of artifacts which help bridge the span of time between Prescott's modern life and that of the past.

Book Nook
324 W. Gurley St.
520/778-2130

Lil Bit O'Everything
136 S. Montezuma
520/445-6237

Prescott Antiques & Crafts
115 N. Cortez St.
520/445-7156

131 North Cortez Antiques
131 N. Cortez St.
520/445-6992

Merchandise Mart
205 N. Cortez St.
520/776-1728

Collector's Mart
133 N. Cortez St.
520/776-7969

Emporium on Cortez
107 N. Cortez St.
520/778-3091

Pennington's Antiques
117 N. Cortez St.
520/445-3748

Deja Vu
134 N. Cortez St.
520/445-6732

Arizona Territory Antiques
211 W. Aubrey St.
520/445-4656

Young's Antiques & Collectibles
115 W. Willis St.
520/717-1526

Antique Bulldog
711 Miller Valley Road
520/717-1484

Keystone Antiques
127 N. Cortez St.
520/445-1757

Second Hand Man, Inc.
535 S. Montezuma St.
520/445-6007

A Hidden Treasure
140 N. Cortez St.
520/776-4268

Atteberry's Antiques
126 N. Cortez St.
520/778-6565

Old Firehouse Antiques
334 S. Montezuma St.
520/778-2969

Great Places to Stay

Mount Vernon Inn
204 N. Mount Vernon Ave.
520/778-0886

1900s Greek Revival, located in Arizona's largest Victorian neighborhood.

15 SCOTTSDALE

The Song of the Balladeer

Back in the 1880s Chaplain Winfield Scott heard the siren song of the unexplored. The irresistible melody, which had already lured thousands to the California gold mines, called him to travel. Gazing at a vast stretch of undeveloped country, Scott proclaimed it "unequaled in greater fertility or richer promise." What would soon become an agricultural community, christened Scottsdale, recorded its first official historic moment.

That strong tie to a frontier past still exerts itself, with great charm and persistence, in modern Scottsdale. Cowboys, horses, a reverence for the land, and a respect for Western tradition are very much a part of the contemporary scene. Visitors come here today, as they did years ago, to explore the possibilities.

So what's the most direct way to experience the Old West? A guided horseback ride or jeep tour over desert trails, the snug fit of your cowboy hat's brim, the drowsy warmth of the sun, or the brilliant streaks of vermilion reddening the Western horizon, evoke a deeply nostalgic response. A mesquite campfire carrying the aroma of sizzling steaks, and the lonesome melodies of a cowboy balladeer will beckon you back in time and in spirit.

The ultimate immersion in life on the trail, however, is the dude ranch. Straying from authenticity just enough to keep guests happy, the ranch experience embraces the rowdy fun of haywagon rides, songfests, cookouts, trap and skeet shooting and, of course, daily horseback excursions.

Most unusual, though, may be an overnight pack trip in the nearby Superstition Mountains. Here you can pan for gold and search like

Arizona

thousands of wild-eyed prospectors before you, for the legendary Lost Dutchman's Mine. (See #9 Mesa for more information on the Lost Dutchman's Mine.)

Scottsdale's truest, proudest passion, however, is reserved for the arts. This glorious environment inspired master architects Frank Lloyd Wright, Paolo Soleri and Bennie Gonzales, whose studios and works have helped to create the aesthetic appeal of the city.

With more than 120 galleries, studios and museums, Scottsdale shines as an internationally known art center. You'll want to plan an evening around the Scottsdale Art Walk held in downtown Scottsdale every Thursday night, year-round. The galleries stay open late, serve refreshments, and encourage you to meet their guests — artists, art critics, writers, musicians, dancers, and performers of all types.

Antiques Super-Mall
(formerly Arizona Antique Gallery)
1900 N. Scottsdale Road
602/874-2900
Open: Mon.–Sun. 10–6, Thurs. 10–8

Antique Centre
2012 N. Scottsdale Road
602/675-9500

Antique Trove
2020 N. Scottsdale Road
602/947-6074

Why drive all over town looking for unique antiques and collectibles when you can visit Arizona's premier "Antique Destinations" in Scottsdale. Always a favorite stop for the two of us, Antiques Super Mall, Antique Trove and Antique Centre offer over 600 dealers within three large stores spanning a whopping 120,000 square feet! The best part is the malls are all located within a one-block area and are open faithfully from 10 a.m. to 6 p.m. daily. If you are passing through late on Thursdays, all these fine stores are open until 8 p.m.

Brown House Antiques
7001 E. Main St., #4
602/423-0293

J. H. Armer Co.
6926 E. Main St.
602/947-2407

Gray Goose Antiques
7012 E. Main St.
602/423-5735

Rose Tree Antiques
7013 E. Main St.
602/949-1031

Carriage Trade Antiques, Inc.
7077 E. Main St.
602/970-6700

J. Scott Antiques
7001 E. Main St.
602/941-9260

Richard II Antiques
7004 Main St.
602/990-2320

Irontiques
7077 E. Main St., #4
602/947-9679

Collectors' Finds Antiques, Inc.
7077 E. Main St.
602/946-9262

Christopher's Galleries
7056 E. Main St.
602/941-5501

Music Box Shop, Inc.
7236 E. 1st Ave.
musicbox@getnet.com

Bradbury's Antique Bazaar
6166 B Scottsdale Road #603
602/998-1885

Pewter & Wood Antiques
10636 N. 71st Way
602/948-2060

Impeccable Pig
7042 E. Indian School Road
602/941-1141

Ye Olde English Antiques Co.
6522 E. Mescal St.
No Phone # Available

Estate Gallery
7077 E. Main St., Suite 5
602/423-8023

Accents to the Max
7140 E. 6th Ave.
602/947-3070

Circa Galleries
7056 E. Main St.
602/990-1121

Mollard's
7127 E. 6th Ave.
602/947-2203

Gallery 10, Inc.
34505 N. Scottsdale Road
602/945-3385

Rustique Collections
23417 N. Pima Road, Suite 165
602/473-7000

John C. Hill Antique Indian Art
6962 E. 1st Ave., Suite 104
602/946-2910

Bishop Gallery
7164 E. Main St.
602/949-9062

Great Places to Stay

The Phoenician Resort
6000 E. Camelback Road
602/941-8200 or 1-800-888-8234 (U.S. and Canada)
(a property of the ITT Sheraton Luxury Collection)

An all-encompassing, international luxury resort harmoniously covering 250 acres at the base of Camelback Mountain. The Phoenician has only been in operation eight years, yet has garnered every possible award in all categories offered by national and international ratings surveys. An elegant vacation retreat, it offers an unparalleled combination of luxury accommodations, appointments, amenities and service.

16   SEDONA

Greentree Stocks
2756 W. Hwy. 89A
520/282-6547

Compass Rose Gallery
671 State Route 179
520/282-7904

Claire's Sweet Antiques
251 Hwy. 179
520/204-1340

Sedona Antique Mall
6586 State Route 179
520/284-1125

Arizona

17 TOMBSTONE

How Tombstone Came To Be

Tombstone, Ariz., is one of the most recognizable names in American history. About 70 miles southeast of Tucson and 30 miles from the Mexican border in southeastern Arizona, Tombstone is one of the most famous of the silver boomtowns of the Old West. But it was actually named in ironic humor of a man's impending death!

With a prospector's outfit and $30, Edward Schieffelin headed for Apache country, east of Fort Huachuca, Arizona, to look for silver. When soldiers at the fort heard of his folly, they laughed and told him all he would find in those hills would be his tombstone...meaning that the Indians would surely get him. In late August, 1877, Schieffelin made his first of many silver strikes and named his rich vein "The Tombstone." He realized around $1 million from his claims in the early 1880s, and soon the town of Tombstone arose, the mightiest city between El Paso and San Francisco. Some reports go as far as to state that the population in the 1880s reached nearly 15,000 — larger than Los Angeles or San Francisco at the time! But the silver mines closed in 1889 and the population disappeared. Today about 1,600 people live in Tombstone, but hundreds of thousands of tourists visit each year.

On May 14, 1896, Schieffelin died in Oregon. In accordance with his wishes, he was buried in Tombstone, covered by a monument three miles west of town. On this monument is a marker inscribed, "This is my Tombstone."

Interesting Side Trips

The Bird Cage Theatre
Downtown Tombstone, Arizona
Admission charged

The last of a bygone era of western history, the Bird Cage was the most famous honky-tonk in America between 1881 and 1889. The *New York Times* referred to it in 1882 as the wildest, wickedest night spot between Basin Street and the Barbary Coast! Tombstone was in its prime mining boom during the 1880s. At the same time, the Bird Cage was making a reputation for the town that would never be forgotten. In nine years this lusty den of iniquity never closed its doors 24 hours a day. Before its operation would end in 1898, it would be the sight of 16 gunfights. The 140 bullet holes that riddle the walls and the ceilings are mute evidence of these happenings.

The Bird Cage was named for the 14 bird cage crib compartments that are self-suspended from the ceiling overhanging the gambling casino and dance hall. It was in these compartments that the prostitutes (or ladies of the night, as they were called) plied their trade. The refrain from the song "She's Only A Bird In A Gilded Cage" became one of the nation's most popular songs. These bird cages remain today with their original red velvet drapes and trimmings.

The entertainment on stage at the Bird Cage ranged from its nightly French circuit cancan dancers to risqué performances for the male gender, to national headliners such as Eddie Foy, Lotta Crabtree and a host of others. The ladies of the town, and there were some, never entered the Bird Cage — or, for that matter, even walked on the same side of the street. The hand-painted stage, with its original curtain, retains its faded luster today, as in 1881.

Directly below the stage are the wine cellar, the dressing rooms and the poker room. Here the longest poker game in western history occurred. It was a house game and players had to buy $1,000 minimum in chips for a seat in the game.The game ran continually for eight years, five months and three days! Today that poker table still stands as it was left, with its chairs on the dirt floor. Some of the most famous characters of western history came to the Bird Cage to gamble, drink and be entertained by its lovely ladies. Wyatt Earp met his third wife, Sadie Marcus, at the Bird Cage. Red-coated bartenders poured nothing but Tombstone's best at a custom-made cherrywood bar and back bar. The bar is flanked by a dumb-waiter that sent drinks upstairs to the ladies of the night and their men friends. Today it exists as Tombstone's only remaining bar of the 1880s in its original building.

When you look into the original French mirror of the back bar, you see the famous bar painting of Fatima, who has been hanging in the same location since 1882. She carries the scars of six bullet holes and stands nine feet high. When disaster struck Tombstone by the folding of the mines, the Bird Cage was sealed and boarded up with all its fixtures and furnishings intact. For almost 50 years it stood closed, its contents touched only by the passing of time. In 1934 the Bird Cage Theatre became a historic landmark of the American West, when it was opened for the public to visit. The Bird Cage stands today as an adolescent old maid in her infancy for all to see and to feel the nostalgia of the past. It is Tombstone's only historic landmark in its original state, preserved from its beginning in 1881, maintaining its lighting fixtures, chandeliers, drapes and gambling tables on the casino floor. Its massive grand piano is still in the orchestra pit. The coin-operated jukebox still plays today as in 1881. You also see Tombstone's most valuable individual antique — The Black Moriah. This original Boothill hearse is trimmed in 24K gold and sterling silver.

A big draw today for the Bird Cage is its ghosts — dozens, maybe even hundreds of them — that manifest themselves on a daily basis to just about everyone who comes to town. It seems that the paranormal is the "normal" order of modern Tombstone, complete with sights, sounds, smells, ghostly appearances, and objects that mysteriously and inexplicably appear and disappear. Bill Hunley (whose family built, owned and operated the Bird Cage), his family and friends, plus hundreds of tourists, have all documented these strange but (to Tombstone residents) normal occurrences. So have numerous parapsychologists, psychics and professional photographers. Some years ago, Duke University even sent a team of parapsychologists to conduct research at the Bird Cage, where they counted 27 spirits and even took their photographs! So when people

Arizona

say that the past comes back to haunt us, they mean it literally in Tombstone!

Third Street Antique Mall
109 S. 3rd St.
520/457-9219

18 TUCSON

American West Primitive Art
363 S. Meyer Ave.
520/623-4091

Antiques Warehouse
3450 E. 34th St.
520/326-9552

Antiques & Old Things
2549 E. Broadway Blvd.
520/325-4554

Treasure Shop
24 E. 15th St.
520/622-5070

A Treasure Chest
4041 E. Grant Road
520/327-9001

Eisenhut Antiques
2229 N. Country Club Road
520/327-9382

Medicine Man Gallery
7000 E. Tanque Verde Road, Suite 7
520/722-7798

Antique Mini-Mall
3408 E. Grant Road
520/326-6502

Cat House Collectibles
2924 E. Broadway Blvd.
520/795-2181

Primitive Arts Gallery
3026 E. Broadway Blvd.
520/326-4852

Camille's
2930 N. Swan Road, #127
520/322-9163

Saguard Moon Antiques Co-op
45 S. 6th Ave.
520/623-5393

Hammerblow Mining Museum
1340 W. Glenn St.
520/882-7073

Firehouse Antiques Center
6522 E. 22nd St.
520/571-1775

Christine's Curiosity Shop
4940 E. Speedway Blvd.
520/323-0018

Antique Center of Tucson
5000 E. Speedway Blvd.
520/323-0319

Antique Mall
3130 E. Grant Road
520/326-3070

Arizona Mall
3728 E. Grant Road
520/770-9840

Country Trading Post
2811 N. Country Club Road
520/325-7326

Sunland Antiques Inc.
2208 N. Country Club Road
520/323-1134

Phyliss' Antiques
1918 E. Prince Road
520/326-5712

Country Emporium Antiques
3431 N. Dodge Blvd.
520/327-7765

Colonial Frontiers
244 S. Park Ave.
520/327-7765

Morning Star Antiques
2000 E. Speedway Blvd.
520/881-3060

Unique Antiques
5000 E. Speedway Blvd.
520/323-0319

19 WICKENBURG

An Antique Store
272 E. Wickenburg Way
520/684-3357

Treasures N Trashe
1141 W. Wickenburg Way
520/684-7445

Head-West Barber & Antique Shop
605 W. Wickenburg Way (Hwy. 60)
520/684-3439

20 YUMA

Packrat's Den
1360 S. 3rd Ave.
520/783-4071

Bargain Spot
385 S. Main St.
520/783-5889

Antique Presidio
3024 E. Grant Road
520/323-1844

B & T Antique Mall
5602 E. 22nd St.
520/745-3849

Elegant Junque Shop
4932 E. Speedway Blvd.
520/881-8181

Antique Center
5000 E. Speedway Blvd.
520/323-0319

Vintage Treasures & Antiques
2351 N. Elvernon, Suite J
520/795-7475

Antique Village
280 E. Wickenburg Way
520/684-5497

Quarter-Horse Rancho Antiques
30220 U.S. Hwy. 60 89
520/684-7445

Gila Gallery Antiques
195 S. Gila St.
520/783-6128

Britain's Antiques
4330 W. Riverside Dr.
520/783-4212

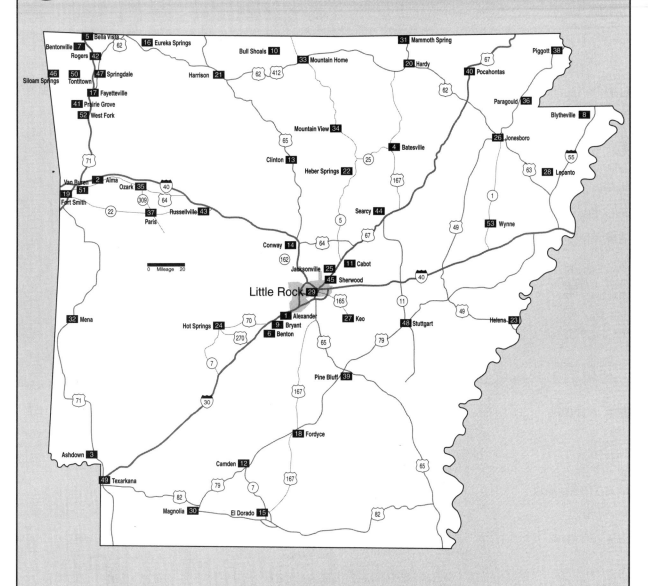

Arkansas

1   ALEXANDER

Blackwell Antiques
23650 I-30
501/847-2191

Large selection of English antique furniture.

Partain's Antique Mall
25014 I-30
501/847-4978

Specializing in leather bound books and fine antique furniture.

Wornock's Antiques
12590 I-30
501/847-8222

Robeson's Antiques & Collectibles
25608 I-30
501/847-4720

2   ALMA

Days Gone By
400 Heather Lane
501/632-0829
Open: Jan.–1st Mon. in Apr., Mon.–Sat. 9–6, Sun. 1–5; 1st Mon. in
Apr.–Dec., Mon.–Sat. 9–9, Sun. 1–5

Sisters 2 Too Antique Mall
702 Hwy. 71 N.
501/632-2292

3   ASHDOWN

The Castle
120 Rankin St.
870/898-9080

Country Store Antiques #1
73 E. Main St.
870/898-5741

Country Store Antiques #2
330 Keller St.
870/898-5741

Memories on Main
69 E. Main St.
870/898-8112

Memory Lane Antiques
34 E. Commerce
870/898-8301

Sandy's Collectibles
370 Keller St.
870/898-5381

4   BATESVILLE

Back In Time Antiques
217 E. Main St.
870/793-6445

Specializing in antique lighting.

AARON's Antiques
1382 Bates St.
870/793-7233

Country Girl Antiques
1981 Batesville Blvd.
870/251-2710

Diamann's Antiques
4401 Heber Springs Road
870/251-9151

Patterson Antique Shop
535 White Dr.
870/793-1139

Ramsey Mt. Treasures
553 Batesville Blvd.
870/793-5714

5   BELLA VISTA

The Bella Vista Flea Market
130 The Plaza - Hwy. 71
501/855-6999

Treasures at Wishing Springs
Wishing Springs Road
501/271-1991

6   BENTON

Saugey's Antique Mall
18325 I-30
501/778-9532

Upscale antiques, American country primitives.

Jerry Van Dyke's Den & Attic Antiques
117 S. Market St.
501/860-5600

7   BENTONVILLE

Sunshine Glassworks & Antiques
206 Hwy. 72 E.
501/273-9218

Oldies But Goodies Antiques
305 N.W. 5th St.
501/273-6921

8   BLYTHEVILLE

Sisters
524 N. 6th St.
870/763-2520

Mike's Antiques
6416 N. County Road 761
870/762-5013

Discount Warehouse-Blytheville
812 N. 6th St.
870/763-2709

9   BRYANT

Collector's Market
22430 I-30
501/847-6899

Galarena Antique Mall
22430 I-30, Exit 123
501/847-6173

Finders Keepers Flea Market
23650 I-30
501/847-4647

Blue Moon Antiques
25608 Hwy. 30
501/847-7144

Arkansas

10 BULL SHOALS

Interesting Side Trip

Bull Shoals Caverns and Mountain Village 1890
Located just off Hwy. 178 in Bull Shoals
501/445-7177 or 1-800-445-7177

In north central Arkansas you can see what life was like for turn-of-the-century settlers back to prehistoric man. Mountain Village 1890 is an authentically restored Ozark town that was retrieved from neglect and decay and completely resurrected as a living tribute to a hardy, resourceful and gentle people — the Ozark mountain folk. See life as it was over 100 years ago, then move to Bull Shoals Caverns, and visualize how prehistoric man, then indigenous Native Americans, and finally Ozark mountaineers lived in some of the world's oldest caverns. You'll see natural formations, underground rivers, a miniature lake and an underground waterfall, while learning how the caverns were formed.

11 CABOT

Simpler Times Antiques
114 Financial Dr.
501/941-1306

Specializing in antique furniture, Victorian, pottery and advertising.

Cruse Antiques
1212 S. Second St.
501/843-8713

Specializing in furniture, pottery, glassware.

Ole South Antiques & Collectibles
105 Commercial Hwy. 167/67
501/605-8526
Directions: Exit 16 to 367 N., left at Citgo.

Specializing in antique furniture, primitives, advertising, vintage clothing, '50s kitchen.

12 CAMDEN

Downtown Antique Mall
131 S. Adams St. S.E.
870/836-4244
Open: Mon.–Sat. 10–5, Sun. 1–5

18,000 square feet, featuring Carmark and Roseville pottery, antique furniture, paintings, glassware and a large selection of Grapette items.

Tate's Bluff Antique & Collectibles
112 Washington N.E.
870/836-3495

Specializing in sports memorabilia and advertising.

Margaret's Gifts and Collectibles
2925 Hwy. 24 W.
870/863-2539

13 CLINTON

Antique Warehouse of Arkansas
Hwy. 65 N. & 110
501/745-5842

Large selection of English antiques, graniteware, and stained glass.

14 CONWAY

Gray's Antiques
1711 Bruce St.
501/329-5760

Specializing in silver and vintage linens.

Rara Avis
405 Acklin Gap Road
501/450-7966

Specializing in Fire King and kitchen collectibles.

Antiques in the Red Barn IH-40 at Hwy. 64 501/329-9608	**Front Street Antiques** 910 Front St. 501/327-2185
Carmen's Antiques 1017 Van Ronkle St. 501/327-6978	**Bobbie's Antiques** 1015 Oak St. 501/327-7125
Honey Hole Antiques 382 Hwy. 65 N. 501/336-4046	**Quattlebaum Antiques** 1010 Van Ronkle St. 501/329-8671
Sybella's 286 Hwy. 65 N. 501/329-8847	**Treasure Hunt** 5 D Gapview Road 501/329-6007
Conway Antique Mall 925 Oak St. 501/450-3909	**Antiques Plus** 1014 Oak St. 501/450-7656

15 EL DORADO

Peggy's Hobby House
2908 Oak Lane
870/863-9553

Marian's Downstairs Attic
301 S. Madison Ave.
870/862-9580

Blewster's Antiques & Gifts
1603 W. Hillsboro St.
870/862-2903

Blann's
320 W. Main St.
870/863-9302

Royal Gallery Antiques & Interiors
114 E. Elm St.
870/862-8783

Main St. Antique Mall
209 E. Main St.
870/862-0028

Friendship District
800 E. Spring St.
870/863-3913

Attic Treasures
520 N. Jackson
870/862-6331

16 EUREKA SPRINGS

The Victorian era of the late 1800s and the Ozark Mountains in northern Arkansas have combined to create a beautifully unique town that has the distinction of having its entire downtown shopping district and residential area listed on the National Register of Historic Places. In Eureka Springs not only will you find hundreds of Victorian buildings, but there are narrow, winding mountain streets and lovely limestone walls built from Arkansas stone. Streets are sometimes hundreds of feet higher or lower than adjacent streets, and no streets cross at right angles. The town grew from belief in the legendary healing powers of its spring waters, as thousands of people traveled to the springs for their health. Today Eureka Springs is a world-famous Victorian resort town of native limestone buildings, gingerbread houses, shaded trails, springs and gazebos. The best way to explore this fascinating town is by trolley and on foot. Six trolley routes service most of the town's lodgings, each designated by a color displayed on a sign in the front window. Just west of town on U.S. 62 W. are two particularly fascinating attractions: the exquisitely beautiful Thorncrown Chapel, an architectural masterpiece, and the 33-acre Eureka Springs Botanical Gardens. Eureka Springs is also home to the nationally famous Passion Play, a spectacular outdoor drama depicting the life, death and resurrection of Christ. And from its roots as an artists' colony in the 1930s and '40s, the town is now one of the most respected fine arts centers for the Mid-South. The Eureka Springs and North Arkansas Railway offers a four-mile excursion (departing hourly) through the Ozarks. A more leisurely tour of the mountains is available by cruise boat on the scenic Beaver Lake.

Old Sale Barn Antiques

Hwy. 23 S. & 62 E.
501/253-5388

Primitives, antiques and collectibles.

Pump & Circumstance

28 Spring St.
501/253-6644

19th-century pine, hunting, fishing, outdoor items.

Forgotten Treasures Antiques

53 Spring St. #B
501/253-9989

Specializing in antique dolls and toys and out-of-print books.

Crystal Gardens Antiques

190 Spring St.
501/253-9586

Specializing in restored lighting.

Bustopher Jones Antiques

5 Van Buren
501/253-6946

Specializing in Victorian, Mission, Nouveau, Deco and Moderne.

Pleasure to Measure

76 Center St.
501/253-5885

Specializing in antique lighting and repair, custom upholstery.

Castle Antiques

16436 Hwy. 62 W.
501/253-6150

Offering true antiques, no reproductions.

Evening Shade Antiques
Hwy. 62 E.
501/253-6264

Garrett's Antique Print
125 Spring St.
501/253-9481

Melinda's Memories
82 Armstrong St.
501/253-7023

Mount Victoria
28 Fairmount St.
501/253-7979

Eureka Emporium
Hwy. 187
501/253-9346

Main St. Traders Gallery
35 N. Main St.
501/253-6159

Memories Past Antiques
Hwy. 62 E.
501/253-5747

Gingerbread House Antiques
183 E. Van Buren
501/253-2299

Arkansas

Jack's Antiques
4762 Hwy. 21 S.
501/253-4945

Country Antiques
Stadium Road
501/253-8731

Springs Antiques
6 S. Main St.
501/253-6025

Treasured Memories Antiques
Hwy. 23 S.
501/253-4900

Mitchell's Folly Antiques
130 Spring St.
501/253-7030

Antiques at 69 Kings Hwy.
69 Kings Hwy.
501/253-8257

Front Porch Antiques
Hwy. 23 N.
501/253-6557

Center St. Antique Mall
78 Center St.
501/253-2239

Yesteryears Antique Mall
Hwy. 62/412 @ Rockhouse Road
501/253-5100

Mr. Haney's Antiques
Hwy. 62 W.
501/253-5752

Great Places to Stay

Crescent Cottage Inn

211 Spring St.
501/253-6022
Web site: www.eureka-usa.com/crescott
Rates: $93–130, includes breakfast
Directions: For specific directions to Crescent Cottage Inn, please call the innkeeper.

Built in 1881 for Powell Clayton, the first governor of Arkansas after the Civil War, Crescent Cottage Inn is a famous historic landmark. This "Painted Lady" with three stories, turned posts, spindlework on front and back porches, a tower capped by a pointed hipped roof, curved topped tall windows, cut-out gable decorations and sunburst, is located at the residential beginning of the historic loop known in Governor Clayton's days as the "Silk Stocking District." It is the most historic and  photographed house in town and appears in the famous book *American Painted Ladies*. Its photograph also graces the pages of *Victorian Express*. The house and guest rooms are filled with European antiques dating from 1770 to 1925. The living and dining rooms are separated by a great arch (the only one remaining by the English architect Bousell) and offers high coffered ceilings. A hand-pressed flower chandelier from 1882 hangs in the living room. There are four guest rooms, all with private baths, Jacuzzi, queen-size beds, TV, VCR and telephones.

Two of the guest rooms, Miss Adaline's Room and Charlotte's Room, have double Jacuzzi spas, refrigerators and beautiful fireplaces along with unique hand-painted ceilings. The doors of the rooms open onto a porch with swings for enjoying the panoramic view while providing access to the lovely English gardens complete with a waterfall. The Sun Room,

named from its origin as a sun porch, includes a Jacuzzi. The Cranberry Suite includes a sitting room and hand-painted ceilings. All guest rooms along with the two back verandas overlook a rare, largely unobstructed view of a valley and totally forested mountain range.

A great full breakfast is served on the upper porch when possible (usually April through October), or in the dining room. Fresh local fruits, berries and melons, baked bananas, Belgian waffles, salsa soufflé, oven-baked puff pancakes, smoked ham, bacon, sausages, juices, rich coffees, teas and hot chocolate are a part of the menu offered at the inn.

Crescent Cottage Inn is a short walk to historic downtown attractions. A trolley stop is located across from the inn for those who prefer to tour the city by trolley. The area is known for two large lakes offering great swimming, boating and fishing, hiking trails, summer opera, art galleries, shops, restaurants, folk art and craft fairs and is home to *The Great Passion Play*. The town swells with tourists in the fall, mainly in October, for a glimpse of the beautifully colored leaves. Crowds gather again in spring for the wild flowering dogwood and redbud trees.

The inn, featured in *Country Living, Southern Living, Country Inns* and numerous newspapers throughout the U.S., has a three-diamond AAA rating, is Mobil quality rated and is also a member of and inspected by The Association of B&Bs of Arkansas. For more information on Crescent Cottage Inn, visit their web site at www.eureka-usa.com/crescott or call 501/253-6022 for a color brochure.

17 FAYETTEVILLE

Home Place
701 North St.
501/443-4444

Gift House
525 Mission Blvd.
501/521-4334

Long Ago Antiques
304 W. Meadow
501/443-5173

Sara Kathryn's
600 Mission Blvd.
501/444-9991

Dickson Street Bookshop
325 W. Dickson St.
501/442-8182

Long Ago Antiques
102 N. School Ave.
501/521-3459

Heritage House Antiques
351 N. Highland Ave.
501/582-5653

Feather Your Nest
17 N. Block
501/443-3355

18 FORDYCE

From a Civil War battleground and cemetery and vintage trains to antiques, Paul "Bear" Bryant, and a bakeshop/deli of national renown, Fordyce, Ark., is an intriguing little town in southern Arkansas. Although its present claim to fame is a vast pine forest, resources for Georgia-Pacific Industries, Fordyce has preserved a good portion of its colorful past. The town was named after Civil War Colonel Samuel Fordyce, who later built the Fordyce Bath House in Hot Springs. Even the first direct-dial long-distance telephone call in the U.S. was made from Allied Telephone Company in Fordyce in 1960! There's a large historic district and a great many antique shops. The Dallas County Museum features the county's history and includes displays and memorabilia of one of its famous sons: the late, legendary Paul "Bear" Bryant, football coach for decades at the University of Alabama. The Wynne Phillips House Bed & Breakfast, a National Historic Register listing, is still owned and operated by one of the children whose parents bought the house in 1914. Hampton Springs Cemetery, near Carthage, is the only segregated burial site in the state, with graves dating back to 1916 and bearing primitive markings and accents of African heritage. And, of course, there's Klappenbach Bakery, offering a full menu of baked goods and a terrific sandwich shop next door. Then there's the annual Fordyce on the Cotton Belt Festival, a full week of fun in April with a parade, arts and crafts, food, antique cars and vintage trains on display.

Main Street Antiques & Collectibles

219 Main St.
870/352-7467

20 booths offering books, glassware, pottery, furniture.

Great Places to Stay

Wynne Phillips House Bed & Breakfast

412 W. Fourth St.
870/352-7202
Rates: $55–$60, including full breakfast

This rambling, pale apricot-colored clapboard home, set in isolated splendor in the middle of an immaculately manicured lawn, is one of the most impressive bed & breakfasts you will encounter. It is surrounded by a complete walkaround porch — a veranda of incredible size and style. The second story is completely ringed with a balcony that follows the perimeter of the veranda, making the entire second story as accessible for strolling and sitting as the ground floor!

Built around 1904, this Colonial Revival style home was purchased in 1914 by Colonel Thomas Duncan Wynne, an attorney and three-time mayor, for his wife and the seven children who would be born there. The youngest of those seven children — Agnes Wynne Phillips — owns the house today with her husband, Colonel James H. Phillips, and operates it as a B & B. Agnes inherited the house in 1985 and turned it into a B&B because it was so large. It took her and Jim three years to restore the huge property. Drawing on the original house plans from archives in the Old State House in Little Rock, old photographs, newspaper clippings, and the memories of family and friends, Agnes and Jim have recreated the ambience of the home's earlier years.

There are five guest rooms with private baths, a glass-enclosed game room at the back of the house, and a 60-foot lap pool. The house is furnished from all different eras and styles, and includes antiques and family heirlooms. The downstairs boasts Chippendale chairs with needlepoint seats in the dining room, gas fireplaces in the parlor and a Mission-furnished library, with a scattering of Asian rugs and interesting pieces from the Phillips' travels (during Jim's army career they were posted in Pakistan and Germany, and moved 30 times). Upstairs each guest room is named after one of Agnes' siblings, and each is decorated with treasures from their childhood. Breakfast is prepared for guests by Walter, the house butler, who formerly was an army cook. Two types of grapes found only in the South are grown in the inn's arbor, and are offered in the inn's breakfast jelly.

19 FORT SMITH

Remember When Antique Mall

4407 Burrough Road
501/646-2200
Open: Mon.–Sat. 9:30–6, Sun. 12:30–5

30,000 square feet, several dealers specializing in Jade-ite, Jewel Tea, old bottles, Santa Clauses, sports memorabilia.

Coming Home
809 S. Greenwood Ave.
501/782-4438

Phoenix Village Antique Mall
4600 Towson Ave.
501/648-9008

Packrat's Antiques
319 Rogers Ave.
501/783-3330

Century Plaza
3702 Century Dr.
501/646-8500

Old Vogue Vintage Clothiers
820 Garrison Ave.
501/783-1369

Eva Gotlib Antique Galleries
1110 Garrison Ave.
501/783-1711

Now & Then Shoppe, Inc.
115 Lecta Ave.
501/783-8022

Steve's Antiques
4700 Towson Ave.
501/646-1121

Collection Connection
403 Garrison Ave.
501/782-3302

Great Places to Stay

Beland Manor B&B

1320 S. Albert Pike
501/782-3300 or 1-800-334-5052
Web site: www.bbonline.com/ar/belandmanor/
Rates: $75–$150

Colonial mansion — 8 guest rooms.

Arkansas

20 HARDY

Donnie's Antiques
4 Mi. East, Hwy. 62 & 63 E.
870/856-4358

Specializing in American country primitives and formal furnishings. The shop caters to dealers.

Old Hardy Town Mall 710 E. Main St. 870/856-3575	**Rain Barrel Antiques** Main St. 870/856-2242
Steele's Antiques Main St. 870/856-3247	**Sugar Creek Antiques** Shows/Mail Order 870/856-2909
Memory Lane Mall 621 Main St. 870/856-4044	

21 HARRISON

Lake Harrison Antique Market
108 E. Stephenson
870/743-4287

Antique furniture, china, early glassware.

Post Oak Antiques 1629 N. Hwy. 62 & 65 870/741-7766	**65 Treasures Antique Market** 4721 Hwy. 65 S. 870/743-4004

22 HEBER SPRINGS

If you like beautiful lakes and rivers, scenic mountains, all kinds of water sports and outdoor activities, antiques, and general exploring, then Heber Springs, Ark., is tailor-made for you. The town hugs the eastern end of shimmering Greers Ferry Lake, a 40,000-acre U.S. Corps of Engineers facility. Just below the dam at Heber Springs is the Little Red River, one of America's best trout fishing streams. All around the lake and river are parks, resorts, accommodations and full-service marinas for all sorts of water-related activities.

The Heber Springs area is noted for its numerous antique, gift and collectibles shops, ranging from Depression glassware to 19th century European furniture. In addition to the antiques, there are Ozark crafts that represent an era when the Arkansas hill people had to produce the things necessary for survival in this isolated and primitive frontier. In October each year, Heber Springs hosts craftsmen from a wide geographical area for a three-day show and sale. Art is also an important aspect of the offering to tourists coming to this mountain community.

Heber Springs is also home to two nationally known producers of potpourri and fragrances, as well as another famous firm that sells framed prints of original paintings and decorative accessories. These companies supply gift shops all over the country and, to some extent, internationally. And there are festivals every year, from April through December. Nearby attractions to Heber Springs include the Ozark Folk Center in Mountain View, Blanchard Springs Caverns (just up the road from the Ozark Folk Center), Batesville (the state's oldest surviving town), and Little Rock.

Antique Market Place Mall 306 W. Main St. 501/362-2111	**Vintage Collection** 1105 S. 7th St. 501/362-7992
Somewhere in Time 304 W. Main St. 501/362-9429	**Virginia's Antiques** Hwy. 25 N. 501/362-3282
Browsing Post 1103 S. 7th St. 501/362-5560	**Timeless Treasures** 419 W. Main St. 501/362-9944

Nearby Antique Shopping (Rose Bud)

Cothren's Antiques
2820 Little Rock Road
501/556-5292
Directions: Located on Hwy. 5, 10 miles south of Heber Springs.

Cothren's offers a general line of antiques as well as country primitives.

Rose Bud Antiques
By appointment only
501/556-5365

Specializing in American country and Stangl pottery.

23 HELENA

Antique Mall of Helena 428 Cherry St. 870/338-8612	**Sue Mathews Gifts & Antiques** 430 Cherry St. 870/338-6071
Between Friends 517 Cherry St. 501/338-3150	**On the Levee Antiques & Gifts** 107 Cherry St. 501/338-8500
Magnolia Antiques 322 Cherry St. 870/338-7991	**This Little Pig Antiques** 105 Cherry St. 870/338-3501

Arkansas

Great Places to Stay

Foxglove B&B
229 Beech
870/338-9391

Stunning antiques abound in this nationally registered inn — 10 guest rooms.

24 HOT SPRINGS

Deco & Dolls
103 Glenridge Court
501/321-1474

Featuring deco, '50s furniture and vintage Barbies.

Seller's Showcase Antique Mall 2138-E Higdon Ferry Road 501/525-2098	**Antique & Collector's Showroom** 1100 Malvern Ave. 501/623-6278
Three Sisters Antiques 821 Hobson Ave. 501/623-1909	**Kathern's Antiques** 2230 Malvern Ave., Suite E 501/624-4781
Arkansas Minuteman 821 Hobson Ave. 501/624-6420	**Adele's Antiques & Yesteryear** 1704 Albert Pike 501/623-3573
Shepard's Old Time Shop 1 Carmona Center 501/922-3215	**Country Cupboard Antiques** 1003 Park Ave. 501/623-8224
Tillman's Antiques 118 Central Ave. 501/624-4083	**Historic District Antiques** 514 Central Ave. 501/624-3370
Yum-Yum Antiques 1313 Central Ave. 501/624-7046	**Shaw's Antiques** 1526 Central Ave. 501/624-0163
Morris Antique Mall 1700 Central Ave. 501/623-4249	**Watson Antiques** 1819 Central Ave. 501/623-6061
Central Ave. Antiques 2025 Central Ave. 501/623-9003	**Lee's Antiques** 1704 Albert Pike Road 501/623-3573
Heirlooms 366 Central Ave. 501/318-0226	**Quilt House Antiques** 5841 Central Ave. 501/525-1567
Papa's Antiques 308 Whittington Ave. 501/624-4211	**Jay's Uniques** 309 Whittington Ave. 501/623-5911
Bath House Row Antiques 202 Spring St. 501/623-6888	**Old South Antique Mall** 5444 Central Ave. 501/525-6623

Oldies & Goodies
2002 Higdon Ferry Road
501/525-5783

Ouachita Antiques
336 Ouachita
501/624-1665

Antiqueland
2375 E. Grand Ave.
501/623-0155

Gilbert's Antiques
3310 Central Ave.
501/623-0044

Utopia Antiques
801 Hobson Ave.
501/318-1192

Great Places to Stay

The Gables Inn
318 Quapaw Ave.
501/623-7576 or 1-800-625-7576

Experience the romance and charm of this beautifully restored 1905 Victorian home, where turn-of-the-century quality of life comes alive with period decor and antiques. The Gables Inn Bed and Breakfast is the perfect setting for a wedding or a romantic get-away. The inn is just blocks from Historic Downtown Hot Springs, Bathhouse Row, fine dining, antique shops, museums and entertainment.

The Gables offers four lovely rooms, each individually decorated and each with a private bath. A full breakfast is served on fine china and crystal. Rates begin at $65.

Wildwood 1884 B&B
808 Park Ave.
501/624-4267

1884 Victorian - 5 guest rooms.

Great Places to Eat

Hamilton House
Hwy. 7 S. at Lake Hamilton
501/525-2727 or 501/525-1717
Open: Daily 5:30, reservations recommended

If you truly love sumptuous, cosmopolitan dining, there's a place in Little Rock you don't want to miss! Hamilton House offers a menu that rivals many topnotch restaurants in the major metropolitan cities of the U.S. and Western Europe. Here they specialize in seafood, politically incorrect grain-fed and aged prime beef, poultry, and decadent desserts, heavy on the sinful chocolate dishes, with a wide selection of wines for dining and dessert. Worth a trip!

Arkansas

Interesting Side Trips

Hot Springs National Park

Hot Springs is America's favorite spa, a world-famous resort built around the thermal waters from the Ouachita Mountains. In this beautifully restored National Park area, you'll experience bathhouses, Victorian buildings, antique shops, art galleries, and interesting and educational museums and attractions.

Hot Springs has always been a special place. President Andrew Jackson made Hot Springs the first Federal Reservation in 1832, the first piece of America protected for future generations. Hot Springs was, in essence, America's first National Park.

The Hot Springs Experience

Historic 1901 Short-Dodson House, 755 Park Avenue, 501/624-9555, was designed and built by Joseph G. Horn. This stunning Victorian mansion was placed on the Register of Historic Places in 1976. Here you'll see impressive and highly detailed oak and maple woodwork and flooring, along with stained glass.

You can actually hold a piece of the Berlin Wall, read Dunham Short's love letter to Corala, stand face-to-face with Karla Parker's portrait of Moses and touch the world famous "Fainting Couch." Truly a "must see" in Hot Springs.

The Witness: A Dramatic Musical Passion Play
501/623-9781

The Witness is the story of the birth, life, death and resurrection of Jesus Christ, as told and sung by the Apostle Peter. Everyone can see a little of themselves in this common fisherman, whose life was changed by the miraculous events he witnesses. You, too, will find yourself caught up in the struggles, human doubts and eventual great faith of the disciples, as each panoramic scene unfolds.

The Witness is performed outdoors in the Mid-America Amphitheatre, nestled in a beautiful wooded area of the Ouachita Mountains. Call for dates and times.

Bathhouse Row

(Located in the Heart of Hot Springs)

Visit the Fordyce Bathhouse Museum to experience the grandeur of the golden age of spas.

Enjoy a luxurious bath for yourself in one of several bathhouses located on Bathhouse Row. You'll be relaxed and ready to "antique" in the many shops located adjacent to the bathhouses.

Buckstaff Bathhouse

Bathhouse Row
501/623-2308

Only in Hot Springs can you take a whirlpool bath and get a massage courtesy of the U.S. National Park Service! Buckstaff Bathhouse, a

tradition on world-famous Bathhouse Row in Hot Springs, is operated under the regulation of the U.S. Dept. of the Interior, National Park Service. So relax and enjoy the ultimate bathing experience. Buckstaff has served bathers since 1912. A top-flight staff offers outstanding service, top facilities and famous Hot Springs thermal mineral water baths — an unbeatable combination for therapeutic bathing or just plain relaxing. Placed on the National Register of Historic Places in 1974, and declared a National Historic Landmark in 1987, Buckstaff offers massages, bathing packages, bathing supplies, separate men's and women's departments, and men's and women's sun decks.

25 JACKSONVILLE

Decorators Bizzare
100 Municipal Dr.
501/985-9842

Betty Dipasquales Antiques
2112 Lancelot Lane
501/982-6273

Uniques by Frances
820 Stone St.
501/982-7060

Vince Cole Antiques & Auction
7711 John Hardin Dr.
501/985-8687

26 JONESBORO

Branding Iron Antiques & Grill

305 S. Main St.
870/972-9444

Antiques, collectibles, fine dining.

Easter's Auction
6614 Stadium Blvd.
870/932-8966

Edwina's Antiques
600 Southwest Dr.
870/935-1358

Granny's Prettys
980 Freeman St.
870/931-9277

Glass Concepts
322 S. Main St.
870/972-0282

Nettleton Antiques
4920 E. Nettleton Ave.
870/932-8580

Tymes Past Antiques
305 S. Main St.
870/972-9444

Forty Niner Antiques
3105 Southwest Dr.
870/972-8536

Collectors Corner
4914 E. Nettleton Ave.
870/972-9659

Yesterdays Antique Mall
4109 E. Highland Dr.
870/933-8615

Arkansas

27 KEO

Morris Antiques
306 Hwy. 232 W.
P.O. Box 127
501/842-3531
Open: Mon.–Sat. 9–5, Sun. 12–5
Directions: Take I-440 to Exit 7. Follow Hwy. 165 South towards England. Go 13 miles to Keo. Turn right on Hwy. 232 at the flashing caution light. Go 3 blocks and turn right behind the Methodist Church.

Known as "a place to look and look again," Morris Antiques offers 55,000 square feet of antique paradise. With 8 buildings full of American, English, French, and Austrian furniture, you can easily spend a whole day browsing.

If you are interested in the very "big stuff" with lots of carvings and intricate inlays, this is the place to shop. Merchandise ranges from Victorian teester beds, massive sideboards, large ornate dining room sets, over 100 armoires, beautiful bedroom sets, to dainty parlor chairs, delicate end tables, practical halltrees, and durable oak pub tables.

Customers are welcome to wander through unusual things from the past such as old cars, farm implements, and a horse-drawn hearse to name a few. There are even a variety of animals the children enjoy seeing, such as miniature horses and a llama.

Lemon's Antiques
350 Main St.
501/842-2442

28 LEPANTO

Victorian Rose
244 Greenwood Ave. S.
870/475-2568
Email: vrose@eritter.net

A little off the beaten path, but well worth the trip. Lepanto not only has some fabulous places to shop and an auction house too, but here at Victorian Rose you will find yourself in a "glass" house. Beautiful displays of glassware from floor to ceiling are evident in this shop owned by the nicest and  friendliest lady in town. She will open up for you after the auction, even if it is midnight and 2 inches of snow and ice on the ground.

Southern Charm
239 Greenwood Ave.
870/475-6122
Open: Mon.–Sat. 9–6

Specializing in vintage clothing with a sprinkling of antiques and collectibles. Southern Charm serves teas from around the world.

This and That Shop
231 Greenwood Ave.
870/475-2665

29 LITTLE ROCK, NORTH LITTLE ROCK

Adams House
109 N. Van Buren (LR)
501/663-5533

Painted furniture, dolls, general line of antiques and collectibles.

Faded Fables
2919 Kavanaugh Blvd. (LR)
501/664-4646

Books, history, and genealogy.

Great American Inventions Co.
1020 Rock St.
501/375-8000

Parts, maintenance, installation of restored antique lighting.

Crystal Hill Antique Mall
5813 Crystal Hill Road (NLR)
501/753-3777

Early glass and china, Victorian, Depression, Flow Blue, ironstone, pottery, Watt, Shawnee, early American antiques.

New Town Antique Shoppes
5913 Crystal Hill Road (NLR)
501/753-3460

Early pottery, hunting, fishing, Fiesta, Shawnee, Majolica.

Pflugrad Antiques
5624 R St. (LR)
501/661-0188

American and European furniture, leather books.

Train Station Antiques
1400 W. Markham St. (LR)
501/376-2010

50 dealers offering a large selection of antiques and collectibles.

Bowman Curve Antiques
11600 Mara Lynn Road (LR)
501/228-4898

American and European antiques.

I-40 Antique Mall
Exit 142 @ Longfisher Road (NLR)
501/851-0039
Open: Mon.–Sat. 10–5, Sun. 1–5

40 dealers, paintings, lamps, European antiques.

Kavanaugh's Antiques
2622 Kavanaugh (LR)
501/661-0958

Early American country furniture, willow furniture, large selection of smalls.

Twin City Antique Mall
5812 Crystal Hill Road (NLR)
501/812-0400

Large mall offering elegant glassware, art, pottery, Depression glass, Fiesta, Wagner, Griswold, primitives.

Vince Cole Antiques
8901 Faulkner Lake Road (NLR)
501/988-2146

Abingworth
5327 Sherwood Road (LR)
501/663-5554

Antique Lighting Sales
316 E. Eleventh St. (LR)
501/375-8000

Marshall Clements Corp.
1509 Rebsamen Park Road (LR)
501/663-1828

Pasha Bass Antiques
5811 Kavanaugh Blvd. (LR)
501/660-4245

Dauphine
5819 Kavanaugh Blvd. (LR)
501/664-6007

Cottage Collection
701 N. Ash St. (LR)
501/664-0883

Cantrell Design Center
7619 Cantrell Road (LR)
501/225-0002

Grand Finale
1601 Rebsamen Park Road (LR)
501/661-9242

My Husband's Treasures
4401 Camp Robinson Road (NLR)
501/791-3628

Lorenzen & Co. Booksellers
7509 Cantrell Road (LR)
501/663-8811

Old Stuff Store
4811 Jones Loop Road (LR)
501/821-3178

Jordan's Antiques
4705 Frazier Pike, College Station
501/490-1391

Collector's Haven Antiques
12109 Macarthur Dr. (NLR)
501/851-2885

English Antiques Gallery
5500 Landers Road (NLR)
501/945-6004

Capital View Antiques
3515 Old Cantrell Road (LR)
501/661-0666

Classic Collections
301 N. Shackleford E-1 (LR)
501/219-2527

Needful Things
21115 Arch St. (LR)
501/888-4882

Private Collections
400 N. Bowman Road (LR)
501/228-0228

Second Chance Collectibles
10 Office Park Dr. (LR)
501/224-5792

Mark's Nostalgia Land
3719 Harold St. (NLR)
501/758-2086

Pike Plaza Antiques & Flea Market
2657 Pike Ave. (NLR)
501/771-4877

Hogan's Antique Furniture
14600 Cantrell Road (LR)
501-868-9224

Fabulous Finds Antique Mall
1521 Merrill Dr. (LR)
501-224-6622

General Store Antiques
12227 Macarthur Dr. (NLR)
501/851-6202

Homestead Antiques
4823 Rixie Road, #B (NLR)
501/833-8676

LaVien Rose
5800 R St., Suite 101 (LR)
501/661-1620

Antiques By The Wharf
2310 Cantrell Road (LR)
501/376-6161

Argenta Antique Mall
201 E. Broadway (NLR)
501/372-7750

Lady I's Specialty Shoppe
7706 Cantrell Road (LR)
501/228-4860

Perdue's Antiques & Accents
5711 Kavanaugh Blvd. (LR)
501/7663-4888

Potential Treasures Antiques
700 N. Van Buren St. (LR)
501/663-0608

Z Gallery
15607 Cantrell Road (LR)
501/868-6066

Great Places to Stay

Dr. Witt's Quapaw Inn
1868 Gaines
501/376-6873 or 1-800-732-5591
Check-in between 5–10, exceptions by prior arrangement
Reservations requested but not always necessary
Directions: From I-30 take I-630 to the Broadway-Central Exit (IB).
Follow the access road to Broadway. Turn left onto Broadway, go 8 blocks to 18th St., go 2 blocks to Gaines, turn left onto Gaines. The inn is 1¹/₂ blocks from where you turned onto Gaines.

Guests at Dr. Witt's Quapaw Inn not only get a good night's rest, but can also get the "inside scoop" on America's first family! Innkeeper Dottie Woodwind says that since Bill, Hillary and Chelsea were their neighbors during President Clinton's tenure as governor of Arkansas, the Woodwinds have dozens of Clinton family stories to tell, even some about Socks, the First Cat! Guests at Little Rock's original bed and breakfast can also get information on boarding the family horse, making theater and dinner reservations, and getting directions to the best places to visit. Breakfast at the inn is served to guests only.

30 MAGNOLIA

This 'n' That Antiques
205 W. Main St.
870/234-2076

Fostoria, American furnishings, pottery.

Auld's Antiques
1517 E. Main St.
870/234-3774

Imperial Antique Mall
114 S. Washington St.
870/234-7059

Jenning's Trading Post
1519 E. Main St.
870/234-1170

Needful Things
1511 E. Main St.
870/234-6820

Seasons Design
101 S. Jefferson
870/234-6469

31 MAMMOTH SPRING

Country Store Antiques
314 Main St.
870/625-3844

Michael's Variety
304 Main St.
870/625-3254

Ozark Heritage
301 Main St.
870/625-7303

32 MENA

Depot Antiques Mall
519 Sherwood
501/394-1149

Mena Street Antique Mall
822 Mena St.
501/394-3231

Bird's Nest Antiques
Hwy. 88 E.
501/394-3033

Architectural Salvage
2309 Hwy. 71 S.
501/394-2438

33 MOUNTAIN HOME

Located in north central Arkansas, Mountain Home is cradled in the gentle slopes of the Ozark Mountains.

With each moderate but distinct season, the Ozarks unfold to present a new panorama of color and beauty. Winter's light blanket of snow covers the forest floor during its brief hibernation. Although much of the plant life will temporarily succumb to winter's presence, the pines and cedars remain evergreen throughout the year. After a two- to three-month winter reprieve, the hills spring to life with pinks and whites of blossoming redbuds and dogwood trees and colorful wildflowers. Set against a new pale green cover, spring's blooms remind us of a water color palette of subtle, pastel colors.

Under a sky of intense blue, summer brings its own plethora of color to the forest — deep greens of the cedar glades complement the various greens of the hardwoods. The cool temperatures of autumn drastically change the color scheme of the mountains, and the forest bursts into the fire-like colors of red, orange and gold.

The Ozarks offer miles of natural beauty any time of the year. You can wander the past while contemplating the present and dreaming of the future. It all combines to give you a wonderful time and place for "antiquing" in the picturesque setting of Mountain Home.

Then & Now Antiques
Hwy. 5 S. to Brough Road
870/491-5719

Antiques, collectibles, German teapots.

Ozark Antique Mall
1330 Hwy. 62 E.
870/425-7149

Earl's Antiques
3348 Hwy. 62 W.
870/425-8578

Dolls of Yesteryear
6601 Hwy. 62 E.
870/492-4010

Antique Mall of Mt. Home
686 Hwy. 62 E.
870/424-2442

Magnolia House Antiques
6417 Hwy. 62 E.
870/492-6730

Once upon a Time Antiques
625 Hwy. 62 E.
870/425-1722

Ox Yoke Antiques
4689 Hwy. 62 & 412 E.
870/492-5125

Char's Place
4588 Hwy. 62 E.
870/492-6644

Remember When
5655 Hwy. 62 E.
870/492-4551

Back In Time
Tracy Ferry County Road 53
870/425-7570

Five South Antiques
Hwy. 5 S.
870/425-3553

34 MOUNTAIN VIEW

Interesting Side Trips

The Ozark Folk Center

Spur 382 off AR Hwy. 5
501/269-3851 (information)
501/269-3871 or 1-800-264-FOLK (lodging and conference facilities)

Instead of buying antiques, here's the chance of a lifetime to see just how those antiques you love were crafted and to make some heirlooms yourself! A one-of-a-kind place, the Ozark Folk Center is America's only facility that works at preserving the heritage and way of life of the Ozark mountain people. There is such an incredible array of things to do, see, hear, and experience that visitors really should plan to spend at least a few days at the Center. Not only are there dozens of things going on at the Center from early morning to very late at night, but you can also see the awesome Blanchard Springs Caverns just a few miles away, or go trout fishing in some of the best waters in the country, picnic and hike in the Ozarks, and then rest a day or two at Greers Ferry Lake before returning home.

The Center offers a full season of events, and hands-on activities, and Dry Creek Lodge offers comfortable rooms right at the facility. You can also design your own custom crafts workshops and enroll for private or group lessons in such old-time arts as: broom making, corn shuckery, natural dyes, spinning, weaving, herb gardening, blacksmithing, needlework, quilting, photography, pottery, hominy making, lye soap making, sorghum making, woodstove cookery, basket making, bowl carving, coopering, chair making, chair seat weaving, hickory bark peeling, shingle making, spoon carving, and woodcarving.

Rainbow Antique Mall

99 W. Main St.
870/269-3261

Flow Blue, Jade-ite, Niloak.

Dottie's Antiques	**Mellon Patch**
Hwy. 66 W.	Hwy. 5 N.
870/269-8427	870/269-3354
Sweet Caroline's Antiques	
Hwys. 5, 9 & 14	
870/269-2621	

35 OZARK

Located in the picturesque mountain area known as the Ozarks and surrounded by beautiful lakes and countryside, the little town of Ozark was established in 1835. It got its name from French explorers who called this area "aux arc," meaning "big bend," a likely reference to the 19-mile bend in the Arkansas River on which this town is bordered.

A quaint little town, Ozark's history is rich with Civil War happenings. Originally built in the 1800s, the beautiful Franklin County Courthouse played host during the Civil War to Union troops who captured the courthouse, built gun ports in its walls and used it for supply storage. A Confederate raid destroyed its beauty and, in fact, when the last smoke cleared, all the houses in Ozark were burned except three. The structure was rebuilt in 1945 and is now listed on the Register of Historic Places.

There are several excursion possibilities in Ozark, a town which is a veritable "old attic" of discoveries for the collectibles and antiques enthusiast. Its charming square has shops to be explored and interesting spots to get a bite to eat. A "must see" is the old jail, built in 1914 out of locally quarried stone cut in random size blocks. Five public hangings, viewed by thousands, took place near this building — all hanged for murder.

36 PARAGOULD

Faulkner County Place	**Paragould Antique Mall**
6205 W. Kingshighway	6312 W. Kingshighway
870/239-3301	870/239-4485
Williams Glass Barn	**Reba Mack's**
330 Greene Road 796	222 S. Pruett
870/236-3610	870/236-6795

37 PARIS

Miller's Antiques	**Kountry Store**
State Hwy. 22	State Hwy. 22 W.
501/963-2627	501/635-2762
Bullock's Antiques	**Red Barn Antiques**
State Hwy. 22 W.	State Hwy. 22 W.
501/963-1300	501/934-4466

38 PIGGOTT

Sugar Creek Antiques

126 S. 2nd St.
870/598-3923

Majolica, Watt, Shawnee, art glass, Victorian silver.

Victorian Ribbons & Roses

127 W. Main St.
870/598-2514

Victorian furniture, linens, glassware, antique dolls.

Enchanted Forrest	**Mother's Victorian Memories**
193 W. Main St.	188 W. Main St.
870/598-3663	870/598-5606

Arkansas

39 PINE BLUFF

Amo's Antiques & Things
1323 S. State St.
870/535-7500

Specializing in Victorian.

Sissy's Log Cabin
2319 Camden Road
870/879-3040

Victorian jewelry and antiques.

White House Antiques
4005 Camden Road
870/879-1336

Jo-Be's Antiques
402 Portea Circle
870/534-1362

Caroline's Victorian Country
9404 Hwy. 270
870/247-4258

Hart's Desire Trunk & Treasures
7606 Hwy. 54
870/879-4461

Francesca Antiques
426 Main St.
870/535-3632

Memories and More
2603 S. Cherry St.
870/536-3116

Abby's Attic
811 W. Fifth Ave.
870/535-2006

Chapel Plaza Antique Mall
1 Chapel Plaza Hwy. 79 S.
870/879-4402

Drake's Antiques & Jewelry
3811 W. 4th Ave.
870/536-5321

40 POCAHONTAS

Antiques Only
304 McDonald St.
870/892-7410
Open: Mon.–Sat. 10–6, Sun. 12–6

Architectural elements, glassware, large selection of furniture, 10,000 square feet.

Nearby Antique Shopping (Biggers)

Green Gables Antiques
Hwy. 67
870/769-2424

Large mall, glassware, pottery, architectural elements.

41 PRAIRIE GROVE

Our Place
124 S. Mock St.
501/846-3200
Open: Tues.–Sun. 10–6

4,000 square feet of antiques, part of a '50s diner serving old-fashioned plate lunches. Restaurant hours: 6–2, dinner hours 6–10.

Country Charm Antiques
16781 W. Hwy. 62
501/846-2689

Keep It Country Antiques
15746 Prairie View Road
501/846-3565

Antique Emporium
107 E. Buchanan
501/846-4770

Hidden Treasures
116 N. Mock St.
501/846-4540

Remember When Antiques
311 E. Buchanan
501/846-3622

42 ROGERS

Yesteryears Antique Mall
3704 Walnut St.
501/636-9273
Open: Mon.–Sat. 10–6, Sun. 12–5

General mix of antiques and collectibles, especially primitives.

The Rose Antique Mall
2875 W. Walnut St.
501/631-8940

Shelby Lane Mall
719 W. Walnut St.
501/621-0111

Clark's Depression Glass
1003 N. 8th St.
501/636-4327

Country House
1007 N. 2nd St.
501/631-9200

Homestead Antique Mall
3223 Hudson Road (Hwy. 102)
501/631-9003

Vintage Antique Mall
108 W. Walnut St.
501/631-3930

Miss Judi's Passion
103 W. Walnut St.
501/636-7758

Ozark Antique Outlet
1620 E. Hwy. 12
501/621-6360

McGregor's Antiques
2143 W. Olive St.
501/636-6829

Arkansas

43 RUSSELLVILLE

Buford Smith's Finer Things
418 E. Fifth St.
501/968-3820

Victorian glass, oil lamps, porcelain.

Shellen's Antiques
Shows and mail order
501/967-4618

Sterling silver matching service.

PJ's Corner
903 W. Main St.
501/968-1812

6,000 square feet of silver, china, glassware, mahogany furniture.

This N That & Something Else
519 S. Arkansas Ave.
501/968-5356

Specializing in elegant and Depression glassware, old Carnival glass and pottery.

Emporium
214 W. Main St.
501/968-1110

Civil War items, jewelry, furniture, glassware.

Antique Mall
1712 N. Arkansas Ave.
501/968-3449

Treasure House Antiques
Hwy. 7
501/968-3652

Sweet Memories Antique Mall
212 W. Main St.
501/967-5354

All Our Treasures
3018 N. Arkansas Ave.
501/967-2920

Dubois Antiques
2614 W. Second Lane
501/968-8370

Bradley's Antiques
155 W. Gumlog Road (Hwy. 124)
501/967-2225

Clopton's Antiques
355 Humphrey Road (Dover)
501/331-2842

44 SEARCY

Archer's Antiques
505 E. Moore
501/268-9566
Open: By chance or appointment

Specializing in Depression glass, Fenton, and collector books.

Frances Antiques
701 W. Race Ave.
501/268-2154

Three large buildings full of oak, walnut and mahogany.

Room Service Antique Mall
2904 E. Race Ave.
501/279-0933

15,000 square feet of antiques and collectibles.

Memory Lane Antiques
1006 S. Main St.
501/268-2439

Bob's Antiques
3317 Hwy. 36 W.
501/268-3198

Jessica Ray Antiques
410 N. Oak St.
501/279-0611

Searcy Emporium
3015 E. Race Ave.
501/279-7025

Family Memories
1509 W. Pleasure
501/305-4380

45 SHERWOOD

Hidden Treasures Flea Market
9107 Hwy. 107
501/833-0200
Open: Daily 9–8

45 vendors, general line of antiques.

The English Antiques Gallery
5500 Landers Road
501/945-6004

Featuring English antiques.

Kiehl Avenue Antique Mall
902 E. Kiehl Ave.
501/834-6314

Arkansas

46 SILOAM SPRINGS

Washington Street Antiques
1001 S. Washington St.
501/524-9722

The French Hen
120 S. Broadway
501/524-3788

Fantasy Land Flea Market
1490 Hwy. 412 W.
501/524-6681

Classic Antique Mall
Hwy. 412-W. Siloam Springs
918/422-5676

Has Been Flea Market
100 E. University
501/549-3315

47 SPRINGDALE

Famous Hardware Antique Mall

113 W. Emma Ave.
501/756-6650

Famous Hardware offers the area's largest selection of antiques and collectibles reference books. Several dealers specialize in Country, Empire, Victorian, Art Deco, and Fifties furnishings.

Barker's Antiques
Elm Springs & Oak Grove Roads
501/750-2305

Jennifer's Antique Mall
824 S. 48th St.
501/750-4646

Magnolia House Flea Market Inc.
312 S. Thompson
501/751-1787

Discount Corner Flea Market
418 E. Emma Ave.
501/756-0764

Pat's Antiques
2500 Melody Lane
501/751-6703

48 STUTTGART

Antiques on Park Avenue

1703 S. Timber
870/673-1179
Open: Mon.–Sat. 10–5; Sun 1–5
Directions: From I-40 take the Hazen exit (#193). Travel South 2 to 3 miles on Hwy. 11 until the highway T's into Hwy. 70. Take a left at the T, travel 2 miles to Hwy. 11 S., continue South on Hwy. 11 into Stuttgart. To get to Antiques on Park Avenue, turn left at the red light when you come into Stuttgart which is Hwy. 79. Go through the next light to the 2nd light which is 165 and Park. Take a right, travel approximately 3 miles, Antiques on Park Avenue is located on the right across from the car wash on the left.

Although not a large city, the town of Stuttgart is bustling with activity. Probably best noted, by those living outside of town, as the home of The World's Championship Duck Calling Contest, Stuttgart has other attractions as well.

The Agricultural Museum provides its visitors with an understanding of the tools and methods of farming, as well as a glimpse of the lifestyle of days gone by; after all Stuttgart *is* the Rice Capital. A recent expansion documents the agricultural and transportation equipment that was used by local farmers in the past,  and another addition records the history of duck hunting in the area. Stuttgart boasts an Art Center which provides year-round exhibits and related activities, such as classes. The duck-calling contests draw visitors to the area several times a year, but Stuttgart also has a national miniature art show with representatives from more than a dozen states.

Stuttgart is also home to Antiques on Park Avenue. Earleen and Dwight were the first to open an antique mall in Stuttgart, which grew out of Earleen's love for collecting old things. After she had furnished two old homes with antiques, she found herself with lots of wonderful things, but nowhere to put them. That's when she convinced Dwight to renovate a portion of this truck repair shop to accommodate an antique mall. The entrance to the two-story shop is around and behind the building which houses the truck shop. She, along with several other dealers, carries a general line of antiques, but includes the unusual as well.

Antiques on Park Avenue offers after-hours showings by calling the mall at 870/673-1159 during open hours, or calling Dan at 870/673-1364 or Hotsey at 870/673-6640 after 5 p.m.

Walt Krisell
502 E. Second St.
870/673-3558

Carol's Country Collectibles
316 S. Main St.
870/673-6593

Ponders Auction
1504 S. Leslie
870/673-6551

49 TEXARKANA

Sweet Temptations
6707 E. Ninth St.
870/772-9687

Yesterday's Rose
6705 E. Ninth St.
870/772-2394

Garden Gate Antiques
6703 E. Ninth St.
870/773-1147

M & M Antique Mall
401 E. Broad St.
870/773-1871

Collectors Corner
309 East St.
870/779-1188

Antiques Plus
401 E. 3rd St.
870/772-6510

Oak Tree Antiques
123 E. Broad St.
870/773-1588

State Line Antique Mall
1104 N. State Line Ave.
870/772-8434

Arkansas

50 TONITOWN

Tonitown Flea Market & Antique Mall
Hwy. 412 W.
501/361-9902
Open: Mon.–Sat. 9–5, Sun. 12–5

The flea market features 90 vendors.

Historic Mercantile Flea Market
136 Henri De Tonti Blvd.
501/361-2003

Located in what was once the town mercantile store, this historic building holds the wares of 72 dealers offering a wide selection of antiques and collectibles.

Yesteryears
Hwy. 412 W.
501/361-5947

The 412 Flea Market
Hwy. 412 W.
501/361-9118

51 VAN BUREN

Just across the river from Ft. Smith, Ark., and right at the Oklahoma state line, Van Buren is an antique lover's dream. Its restored Victorian Main Street is a smorgasbord of tiny shops and warehouses filled with furniture, including the largest importer of European antique furniture in the Southwestern U.S. The shops are also filled with rare glass treasures, vintage hats and clothing, Coca-Cola and other trademark collectibles, antique toys, porcelain and china dolls, Victorian prints, and old tins and canisters. And since it's one of the original entryways to the Southwest, you can also shop for anything "southwestern," including turquoise and sterling silver jewelry, Navaho rugs and blankets, hand-thrown pottery, and western art of all kinds.

If you tire of shopping, you can take the "scenic route" and enjoy Ozark beauty from the Ozark Scenic Railway vintage train, or the Frontier Bell excursion river boat that travels along the Arkansas River. Top it all off with a couple of nights at the Old Van Buren Inn on Main Street, and you've got a great little vacation!

Antique Mall of Van Buren
415 Main St.
501/474-7896

Bridgewater's Antiques
616 Main St.
501/474-8616

T J's Treasures & Bevie's
715 Main St.
501/474-7678

Victoria's Antiques
514 Main St.
501/474-5299

Maria's Treasures
624 Main St.
501/471-0018

Antique Warehouse of Arkansas
402 Main St.
501/474-4808

Grapevine Shoppe, Inc.
615 Main St. #A
501/474-5800

Aunt Jenny's
700 Main St.
501/474-4465

Carter's Trading Post
412 Main St.
501/471-7182

Spinning Wheel Antiques
620 Main St.
501/410-1410

Great Places to Stay

Old Van Buren Inn
633 Main St., corner of 7th and Main
501/474-4202

Built in 1889, Victorian — outstanding restaurant — 3 guest rooms.

52 WEST FORK

West Fork Antiques
34 McGee Road
501/839-8202

53 WYNNE

Ageless Antiques & Collectibles
111 Merriman Ave. E.
870/238-5992

Joyce Ann-Tiques
428 Hwy. 64
870/238-2734

South Falls Emporium & Antique
111 Maryman St.
870/238-6562

Front Street Flea Market
142 County Road 392
870/238-7274

Two Sisters
717 Hamilton Ave. E.
870/238-7198

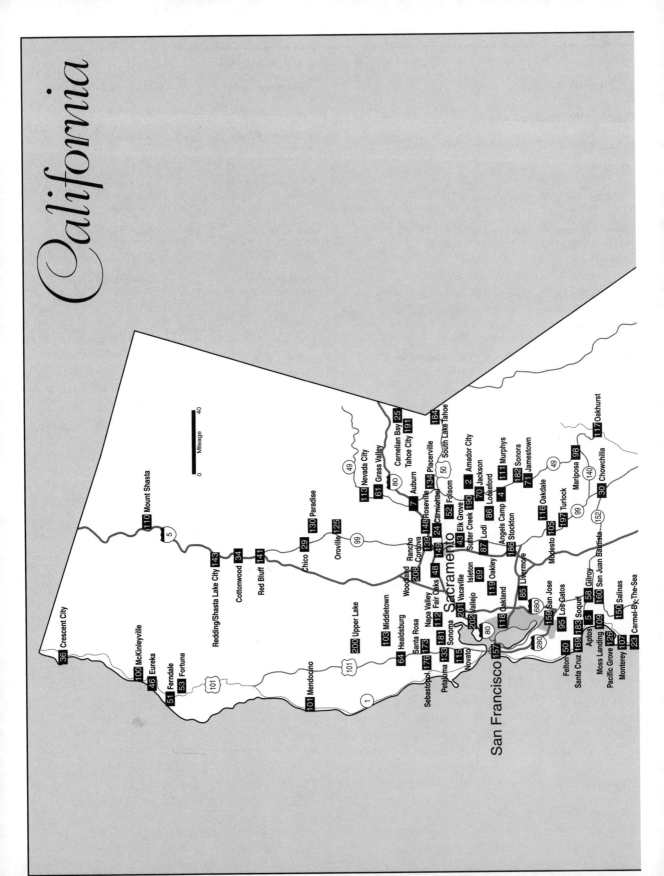

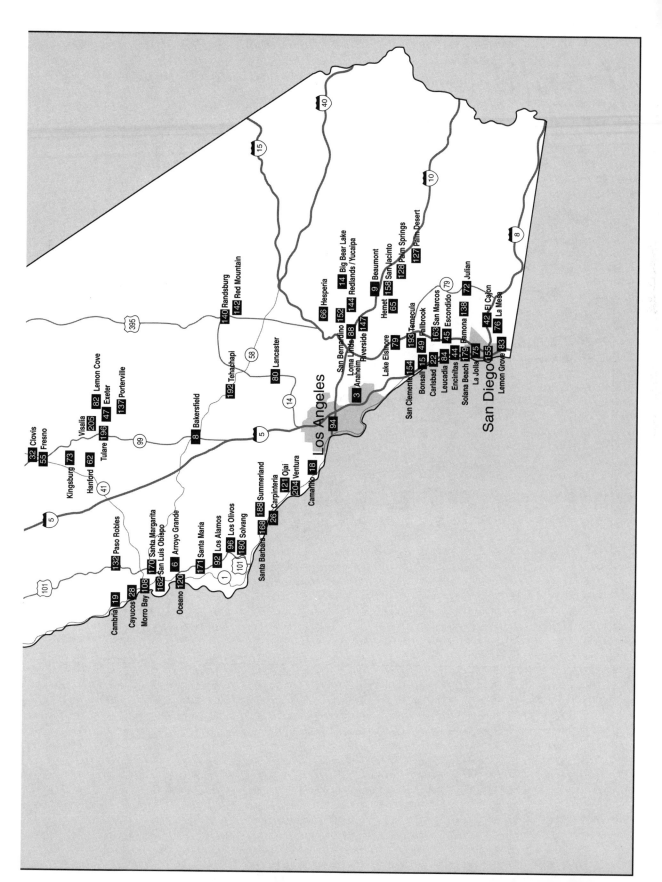

California
Los Angeles Area

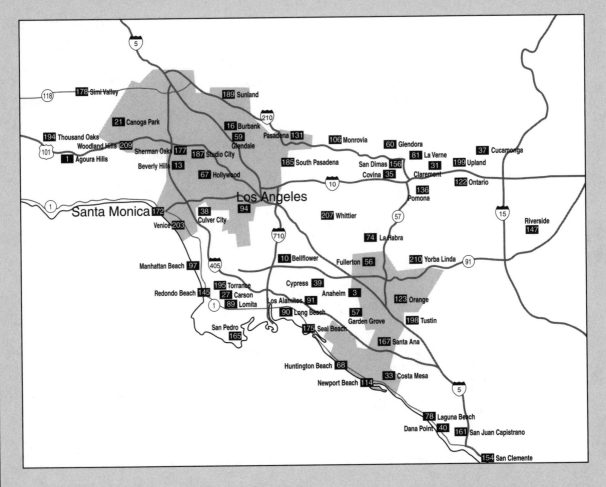

California
San Francisco Area

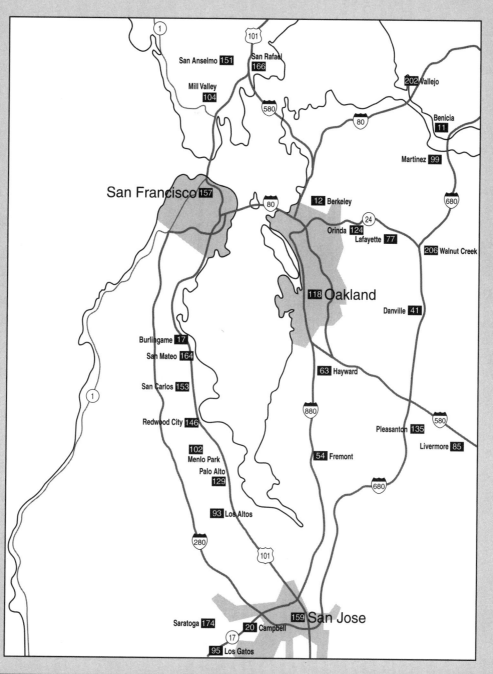

San Anselmo 151 · San Rafael 166

Mill Valley 104

202 Vallejo

Benicia 11

Martinez 99

San Francisco 157

12 Berkeley

24

Orinda 124

Lafayette 77

206 Walnut Creek

118 Oakland

Danville 41

Burlingame 17

San Mateo 164

63 Hayward

San Carlos 153

Redwood City 146

Pleasanton 135

Livermore 85

102 Menlo Park

54 Fremont

Palo Alto 129

93 Los Altos

159 San Jose

Saratoga 174 · 20 Campbell

95 Los Gatos

1 AGOURA HILLS

Agoura Antique Mart
28863 Agoura Road
818/706-8366

Sandy Lane Antique Mall
28878 Roadside Dr.
818/991-0229

Victoria's Antique Mall
28912 Roadside Dr.
818/879-8626

Showcase Antiques
5021 Kanan Road
818/865-8268

Antique Mall
28826 Roadside Dr.
818/991-8541

2 AMADOR CITY

Sherrill's Country Store
14175 State Hwy. 49
209/267-5578

Jensen's Antique Dolls Bears
14227 State Hwy. 49
209/267-5639

Victorian Closet
14170 State Hwy. 49
209/267-5250

Miller's Antiques & Collectibles
14183 State Hwy. 49
209/267-1582

Mac Clan Antiques
14215 State Hwy. 49
209/267-1032

Roth Van Anda Antiques
14461 W. School
209/267-5411

Country Living
Hwy. 49
209/267-0874

3 ANAHEIM

Len & Kathy's Collectible Toys
1215 S. Beach Blvd., Suites E & F
714/995-4151

Lincoln Antique Mall
1811 W. Lincoln Ave.
714/778-2522

Treasure Cliff
1783 W. Lincoln Ave.
714/491-2830

Antique Alley
10351 Magnolia St.
714/821-1576

4 ANGELS CAMP

Calaveras Coin & Collectibles
1255 S. Main St.
209/736-2646

Grandmother's Antiques
1273 S. Main St.
209/736-0863

Nellie Lou's
Main St.
209/836-6728

Angels Camp Mercantile
1267 S. Main St.
209/736-4100

Orphan Annie's Emporium
1284 Main St.
209/736-9086

Mystic Hollow
1219A S. Main St.
209/736-0826

5 APTOS

Village Fair
417 Trout Gulch Road
408/688-9883

Twenty individual shops under one roof.

6 ARROYO GRANDE

Rich Man-Poor Man Antiques
106 W. Branch St.
805/489-8511

Village Antique Mart
126 E. Branch St., #A
805/489-6528

Creekside Antiques
122 E. Branch St.
805/473-2505

Branch St. Antique Mall
126 E. Branch St.
805/473-3276

Glance at the Past
410 E. Branch St.
805/489-5666

7 AUBURN

Fine's Antique Mall & Gallery
337 Commercial St.
916/888-7607

Sweet Sue Old & New
345 Commercial St.
916/885-5537

Betty Nelson Antiques
1586 Lincoln Way
916/823-2519

Serendipity
135 Sacramento St.
916/885-1252

Pauline's Antiques of Auburn
301 Commercial St.
916/885-6828

Wild Horse Antiques
923 Lincoln Way
916/823-7870

Old West Trail Antiques
343 Commercial St.
916/823-2784

Antiques International
4035 Grass Valley Hwy.
916/888-0324

Mercantile Antiques
875 Nevada St.
916/888-8740

As Time Goes By
321 Commercial St.
916/823-7723

Oshay's Flowers & Antiques
1280 Grass Valley Hwy.
916/823-1169

8 BAKERSFIELD

Renaissance
168 H St.
805/327-2902

Edison Antiques
2227 Edison Hwy.
805/322-6174

Antique Loft
6 H St.
805/325-2402

Cleo's Attic Antiques
1888 S. Chester Ave.
805/832-8202

Collectorium
2414 Edison Hwy.
805/322-4712

Fond Memories
151 H St.
805/322-9326

Season's
166 H St.
805/323-7673

Childhood Memories Antiques
1106 H St.
805/326-0346

Betty's Barn of Antiques
4811 Morro Dr.
805/366-5620

Central Park Antique Mall
701 19th St.
805/633-1143

Somewhere in Time
1312 19th St.
805/326-8562

Five & Dime Antiques
1400 19th St.
805/323-8048

Johnny Crow's Garden
5635 Taft Hwy.
805/836-9828

Aatelier Antiques & Art
612 18th St.
805/326-1922

Bow-Tique Furn. & Accessories
1420 19th St., Suite A
805/322-8500

Harvey's Antiques & Gifts
230 Bernard St.
805/322-8676

Cottage Gardens
30 H St.
805/322-6254

Golden West Antiques
500 E. 18th St.
805/395-1174

Good Brother's Antiques & Gifts
332 Hwy. 43 (F St.)
805/758-2663

Peabody's Books-Records
2315 Edison Hwy.
805/322-8382

Sam's
2491 Edison Hwy.
805/323-3798

Chris Vanderlei
3031 H St.
805/323-0742

Pidgeon Hill
167 H St.
805/323-1226

Grandma's Trunk
1115 H St.
805/323-2730

Great American Antiques
625 19th St.
805/322-1776

Nothin' New
1310 19th St.
805/327-9664

Timeless Treasures
1320 19th St.
805/327-5052

Curiosity Shop Antiques
1607 19th St.
805/324-7112

Old World Emporium
731 16th St.
805/861-0940

A-Plus Pak-Rats
10711 Rosedale Hwy.
805/588-1212

Consign It Stores, Inc.
H Street at Brundage
805/325-2401

Memory Lane Antique Mall
1810 R St.
805/327-8232

Estate of American Heritage
1420 Suite C 19th St.
805/325-3132

Gone Junkin'
1703 N. Chester
805/393-5251

Goodies from the Past
1610 19th St.
805/636-0368

Peaches 'n' Cream
159 H St.
805/634-9704

Timeless Dreams
316 State St.
805/746-6764

9 BEAUMONT

Larry Nelson's Antiques
136 E. 6th St.
909/769-1171

Beaumont Antique Mall
450 E. 6th St.
909/845-1397

Browning's
504 W. 6th St.
909/845-8608

Legacy Antiques
442 E. Sixth St.
909/845-5600

Toys In The Attic
200 E. 6th St.
909/769-0011

R & R Antiques & Collectibles
273 E. 6th St.
909/845-2787

Nelson's Antique Mall
630 California
909/769-1934

10 BELLFLOWER

Fischer Antiques
17041 Lakewood Blvd.
310/633-6718

11 BENICIA

This That 'n' Whatever
129 1st St.
707/745-8706

Kindred Spirits
632 1st St.
707/745-6533

Consigntiques
917 1st St.
707/746-6675

Lottie Ballou Vintage Clothing
130 W. E St.
707/747-9433

Possessions of the Past
435 1st St.
707/748-4487

12 BERKELEY

Lorne Gay Antiques
2990 Adeline St.
510/649-8550

Chatterbox
350 E. 6th St.
909/769-1071

Decorating Addict Antiques
480 E. 6th St.
909/845-5856

L & M Coins & Collectibles
725 A Beaumont Ave.
909/769-2800

Wholesale Antique Mall
320 E. 6th St.
909/845-0155

Parson's Cottage Antiques
402 E. 6th St.
909/845-2523

Jacqueline's Antique Mall
626 Beaumont
909/769-0023

Memories Antiques
280 E. 6th St.
909/845-6255

Vic Clar Antiques Juke Boxes
9313 Rose St.
562/866-7106

Benicia Antique Shop
305 1st St.
707/745-0978

Jeanie's
727 1st St.
707/746-8464

Lundin House of Antiques
Corner 1st & J St.
707/745-1554

Discover Yesterday
364 1st St.
707/747-0726

Golden Horseshoe Antiques
415 1st St.
707/745-2255

Jack's Antiques
3021 Adeline St.
510/845-6221

California

Betty Jane's Collectibles
3192 Adeline St.
510/652-4586

Military Artifacts & Collectibles
1601 Ashby Ave.
510/841-2244

Berkeley Collectibles Shop
2280 Fulton
510/848-3199

June Kadish Antiques
1878 Solano Ave.
510/52802785

It's Her Business Junque Funk
2508 San Pablo Ave.
510/845-1663

Laurent Bermudez Primitive Arts
1859 Solano Ave., #B
510/527-1042

Asiantique
933 Parker St.
510/843-7515

Behm-Powell Collection
1347 Martin Luther King Jr. Way
510/526-7227

Craftsman Home
3048 Claremont Ave.
510/655-6503

Fenton MacLaren
1325 San Pablo Ave.
510/526-5377

Lundberg Haberdashery
396 Colusa Ave.
510/524-3003

Eugene's Antiques
2001 Milvia St.
510/548-5954

Reliance Antiques
830 Gilman St.
510/525-7003

Von Homert Antiques
1989 Ashby Ave.
510/548-1327

13 BEVERLY HILLS

Sherwood's Spirit of America
325 N. Beverly Dr.
310/274-6700

Roth & Co.
9511 Brighton Way
310/271-5485

Trout Farm Antiques
2179 Bancroft Way
510/843-3565

Louis A Capellino Antiques
1987 Ashby Ave.
510/845-5590

Grove Antiques (Sat. Only)
1417 Martin Luther King Jr. Way, #A
510/525-9120

Brent's Unique Shop
1824 San Pablo Ave.
510/841-9051

Rosebud Gallery
1857 Solano Ave.
510/525-6454

Antiques by Tony
3017 Adeline St.
510/649-9016

Aura Jewelers
2122 Vine St., #A
510/644-1487

Continental Art Shop
2490 Telegraph Ave.
510/843-2957

Carol-Davis Antiques
2808 Adeline St. #A
510/843-7582

Lacis
2982 Adeline St.
510/843-7290

Moe's Books
2476 Telegraph Ave.
510/849-2087

Nomad's Gallery
2548 Telegraph Ave.
510/841-5622

People's Bazaar
3258 Adeline St.
510/655-8008

Zentrum Antiques
1085 Ashby Ave.
510/841-1808

Auntie Barbara's Antiques
238 S. Beverly Dr.
310/285-0873

Barakat Antiques Gallery
9876 Wilshire Blvd.
310/859-0676

Royal-Athena Galleries
9478 W. Olympic, Suite 304
310/277-0133

Krono's
421 N. Rodeo Dr.
310/205-0766

Chait Gallery Beverly Hills
9330 Civic Center Dr.
310/828-8537

14 BIG BEAR LAKE/BIG BEAR CITY

M & B Antiques
40143 Big Bear Blvd.
909/866-4200

Weber's Thrift & Save
39998 Big Bear Blvd.
909/866-2758

Village Antiques
40671 Village Dr.
909/866-6115

Dinky's & Ruthy's
40629 Lakeview Dr.
909/866-1729

Boulevard Antiques
41114 Big Bear Blvd.
909/866-4086

Fox Farm Antique Mall
42146 Fox Farm Rd.
909/866-0618

A Sign of the Times
525 W. Big Bear Blvd.
909/585-4208

Way Out There
1107 Baldwin Lake
909/585-5145

Amphora Arts & Antiques
308 N. Rodeo Dr.
310/273-4222

Jake's Antiques
8668 Wilshire Blvd.
310/360-0416

Soltani Rugs & Antiques
267 N. Canon Dr.
310/858-1770

Boulder Bay Antiques
39209 Big Bear Blvd.
909/866-4293

Big Bear Thrift & Treasures
40074 Big Bear Blvd.
909/866-4336

Harris House Antiques & Cllbls.
579 Paine Road
909/866-0491

Joanie's Attic
40747 Lakeview Dr.
909/584-2468

Myers Old & New Antiques
41578 Big Bear Blvd.
909/866-4149

Yours, Mine & Ours
612 W. Big Bear Blvd.
909/584-2675

Fowler's
212 E. Big Bear Blvd.
909/585-7522

Fox Den Antiques
39434 N. Shore Dr.
909/866-3196

Great Places to Stay

Gold Mountain Manor Historic B&B
1117 Anita
1-800-509-2604

Built in 1928, Gold Mountain Manor is Big Bear's only historic bed & breakfast. This 7,000-square-foot historic log mansion sits on an acre of forested pine trees in a quiet residential area. The estate is within walking distance of the national forest and is a 10-minute drive from all of Big Bear's recreational activities. It is a getaway for romance and relaxation! Decorated in antiques, the six rooms have queen-sized beds and wood-burning fireplaces. Featured in the books *Best Places to Kiss* and *Fifty Most Romantic Places in Southern California*.

California

15 BONSALL

This Old House
30158 Mission Road
760/631-2888

16 BURBANK

Tower Trading Co.
1314 W. Magnolia Blvd.
818/848-3950

Renaissance Antiques
3317 W. Magnolia Blvd.
818/567-0935

Victorian Rose Antiques
3421 W. Magnolia Blvd.
818/842-3201

Antique Attic
4005 W. Riverside Dr.
818/566-7155

Best of Times
2918 1/2 W Magnolia Blvd.
818/848-5851

Napolean Gifts & Antiques
2912 W. Burbank Blvd.
818-566-1958

AARS
2926 W. Magnolia Blvd.
818/558-1033

Madrid Antiques
3416 W. Magnolia Blvd.
818/845-9028

White Elephant
3422 W. Magnolia Blvd.
818/842-0721

Magnolia House Antiques & Cllbls.
3910 W. Magnolia Blvd.
818/843-8750

Five Sisters
2524 W. Magnolia Blvd.
818/566-6897

17 BURLINGAME

Burlingame Antiques
915 Howard Ave.
650/344-4050

Whistling Swan Antiques
359 Primrose Road
650/343-1419

Heirloom's Antique Mall
783 California Dr.
650/344-8800

Period Hardware
1499 Bayshore Hwy. #104
650/697-4972

Fat Cat Antiques
247 California Dr.
650/348-1119

Wood Duck Antiques
363 Primrose Road
650/348-0542

Kern's Fine Jewelry
235 Park Road
650/348-7557

18 CAMARILLO

Unique Antiques
65 Palm Dr.
805/484-4100

Ingersoll's Antiques
62 Palm Drive
805/482-9936

Abagail's Attic Antiques
2633 Ventura Blvd.
805/388-0334

The Antique Mall of Camarillo
58 Palm Dr.
805/484-7710

Augusta's Showroom
2280 Ventura Blvd.
805/987-9883

Savannah West
2235 Ventura Blvd.
805/383-6836

The Yellow House Antiques
2369 Ventura Blvd.
805/482-0330

Window Box Antiques
72 Palm Dr.
805/987-8191

Antique Corner
92 Palm Dr.
805/484-5913

19 CAMBRIA

Morning Song
4210 Branch St.
805/927-7101

Granny Had One Antiques
712 Main St.
805/927-7047

Urban Roots
768 Main St.
805/927-7234

Antiques on Main
2338 Main St.
805/927-4292

Moonstone Antique Emporium
5620 Moonstone Beach Dr.
805/927-5624

Once Upon A Time
555 Main St.
805/927-5554

Fairey's Antiques
715 Main St.
805/927-3665

Cambria Antique Center Mall
2110 Main St.
805/927-2353

Country Collectibles
2380 Main St., #A
805/927-0245

Great Places to Stay

Sylvia's Rigdon Hall Inn
4022 Burton Dr.
805/927-5125

Rigdon Hall Inn (Sylvia's) is located on Historical Burton Drive, in the heart of Cambria's original village, just six miles south of the famous Hearst Castle. The recently renovated inn features eight elegant, quiet, spacious suites. They are individually decorated and impeccably maintained. Each of the deluxe suites includes a large sitting room with luxurious furnishings. Bedrooms feature a king-sized bed.

The J. Patrick House
2990 Burton Dr.
1-800-341-5258

The J. Patrick House is an authentic log cabin bed and breakfast nestled in the woods. There are eight spacious and romantic rooms, all with woodburning fireplaces and private baths. Each guest room is uniquely decorated in country charm. At 5:30 each day, enjoy the company of guests with hosts Barbara and Mel as you gather around the fireplace with your selection of wine or hors d'oeuvres.

20 CAMPBELL

Donna's Antiques
301 E. Campbell Ave.
408/866-1252

Woodworks Antiques
841 Union Ave.
408/377-9778

Second Time Around
327 E. Campbell Ave.
408/379-7240

All Things Past & Present
313 E. Campbell Ave.
408/378-3605

21 CANOGA PARK

Collector's Eye
21435 Sherman Way
818/347-9343

Antique Cottage
21513 Sherman Way
818/347-8778

Sadie's Corner Antiques
21515 Sherman Way
818/704-7600

Old Country Road
21529 Sherman Way
818/340-3760

Kingston Galleries, Inc.
8573 Canoga Ave.
818/885-7694

West Hills Antique Center
6633 Fallbrook Ave.
818/888-1362

Courtyard Antiques
7207 Alabama
818/992-5189

Now & Then
21501 Sherman Way
818/340-4007

Claudia's Collectibles
21511 Sherman Way
818/702-6261

Jeanne's Antiques & Collectibles
21523 Sherman Way
818/702-9266

Affordable Antiques
21612 Sherman Way
818/348-2909

Turn of the Century Antiques
21531 Sherman Way
818/704-7711

Zulia's Antiques
21525 Sherman Way
818/888-6660

22 CARLSBAD

AANTEEK AAVENUE MALL

2832 State St.
760/434-8742
Open: Daily 11–5, closed major holidays only.
Directions: Take I-5 to Carlsbad Village Drive, then turn west and go 5 blocks to State Street. Turn north (right) and go 1 full block, cross over Grand Avenue, and count 6 stores on the right (east) side of State Street.

AANTEEK AAVENUE MALL is one of our favorite shops within a three-block walk of 22 antique stores in Carlsbad. The shop consists of 5,000 square feet of exceptionally organized antiques and collectibles.

There are several reasons why this shop is among our favorites. The selections and the price ranges  offer something for everyone. From $1 to $25,000, no one should leave empty-handed from this incredible shop. The owner is a jewel himself and particularly loves to work with dealers to offer the best prices possible.

Dresden, flow blue, Roseville, Bauer, cut glass, sterling, art, Hummels, Royal Doulton, stained glass lamps, estate jewelry, California pottery, pens, Franciscan and exceptional furnishings are just a sampling of the selections you'll find at AANTEEK AVENUE MALL.

From Clara's Attic
561 Carlsbad Village Dr.
760/720-9384

Carlsbad House of Antqs. & Doll Houses
2752 State St.
760/720-1061

De Witt's Antiques
2946 State St.
760/720-1175

Mulloy's Estate Jewelry
2978 State St.
760/729-5774

Antiques Junction
457 Carlsbad Village Dr.
760/434-2332

Byrnes Antiques Restoration Co.
2698 State St.
760/434-7800

US Antiques
2525 El Camino Real
760/720-5254

Antique Crossroads
3021 State St.
760/434-3355

Hattie P's Treasures
2921 Roosevelt St.
760/729-5010

Lisa's Miniatures, Collectibles, Gifts
3077 State St.
760/434-1358

Black Whale Lighting & Antiques
562 Carlsbad Village Dr.
760/434-3113

Olde Ivy Antiques
2928 State St.
760/729-8607

Roseboro House
2971 State St.
760/729-3667

Backroads Antiques
2988 State St.
760/729-3032

Country Treasures
4901 El Camino Real
760/730-7474

Postal's Antiques
2825 State St.
760/729-7816

Sunflower Cottage
2525 El Camino Real
760/434-7643

Gallery of Miniatures
2763 State St.
760/729-3231

A&E Antiques & Estate Jewelry
2802 State St.
760/434-6400

Great Places to Eat

Neiman's
2978 Carlsbad Blvd.
760/729-4131

Dine luxuriously in the elegant home of German immigrant Gerhard Schutte, one of the driving forces behind the development of Carlsbad. From 5 p.m. every evening enjoy the pasta, salad, soup and shrimp buffet, or prime rib, steaks and fresh fish. A cafe menu is served daily from 11:30 a.m. to 11 p.m., and Sunday champagne brunch from 8:30 a.m. -2 p.m.

California

23 CARMEL/CARMEL VALLEY

Nestled in a pine forest above a spectacular white sand beach, the one-square-mile village of Carmel is reminiscent of European charm. There is no mail delivery: homes are known only by name and have no addresses. Winding streets, secluded alleyways, courtyards and arcades are highlighted by 70 art studios and galleries, numerous antique shops, specialty boutiques and small cafes.

Carmel is also the home of Mission Ranch Restaurant, owned by actor and two-term Carmel mayor, Clint Eastwood. Clint bought the historic Mission Ranch property in 1986. The ranch, built in the mid-1880s, was a dairy farm until the '20s. What is now the restaurant was once the dairy's creamery.

The dining room has a cozy ranch decor, complete with checkered tablecloths and a large stone fireplace. For views of the scenic pastoral grounds, one can eat outside on a wide deck with umbrella tables.

The basic menu is ranch-style: prime rib, steaks and BBQ ribs. If this doesn't arouse your tastebuds, Chef Craig Ling offers other house specialties from which to choose: loin of lamb, salmon, fresh seafood, roasted chicken, beef brochette and meatless lasagna for vegetarians. Dinners include soup or salad, twice-baked potatoes and fresh vegetables. The restaurant offers an appetizer, a la carte and a homemade dessert menu as well.

Mission Ranch Restaurant

26270 Delores
408/625-9040
Hours: dinner, 4:30–10 daily; lunch, 11:30–3 Sat. only; Sunday brunch, 9:30–2:30

Anna Beck Antiques
26358 Carmel Rancho Lane
408/624-3112

Langer's Antiques
Delores (Between Ocean & 7th)
408/624-2102

Trappings
W. Juniper between 5th & 6th
408/626-4500

Robt Cordy Antiques
Lincoln & 6th
408/625-5839

Great Things Antiques
Ocean Ave.
408/624-7178

Antiques Francais
3742 The Barnyard
408/624-7444

Maxine Klaput Antiques
Mission & 7th
408/624-8823

Robertson's Antiques
Delores & 7th
408/624-7517

Anderle Gallery
Lincoln, Ocean & 7th
408/624-4199

Magpie Antiques
Ocean Ave. & Lincoln
408/622-9341

Hildegunn Hawley Antiques
Delores (Between 5th & 6th)
408/626-3457

Keller & Scott
Delores near 5th St.
408/624-0465

Carmel Valley Antiques
7151 Carmel Valley Road
408/624-3414

Mid Valley Antiques
312 W. Carmel Valley Road, #320
408/624-0261

Off The Wall
Lincoln (Between 5th & 6th)
408/624-6165

T. B. Scanlon Antiques
Carmel Valley
408/659-4788

Luciano Antiques
San Carlos St.
408/624-9396

Laura's Antiques & Collectibles
3724 The Barnyard
408/625-6480

Sandy's Antiques
1 Esquiline Road
408/659-2629

Teeleet Antiques
25 Pilot Road
408/625-2134

Great Places to Stay

Candle Light Inn

P.O. Box 1900
1-800-433-4732

This Tudor-style inn offers charm and warmth with a friendly staff who provides good old-fashioned service. Rooms have king beds, wood-burning fireplaces and full kitchens or standard rooms with one king bed and two double beds. Rates include a picnic basket breakfast and the morning newspaper delivered to your door. Located in the heart of the village, within walking distance to all the shops, galleries and restaurants.

The Stonehouse Inn

8th below Monte Verde
408/624-4569 or 1-800-748-6618
Open: Daily 10–9
Rates: $99–$199
Directions: Traveling Hwy. 1 south or north, take Ocean Avenue Exit. Travel Ocean Avenue to Junipero, turn left, proceed to 8th, turn right, travel five blocks to Monte Verde. Located on the left side (south side) of block between Monte Verde and Casanova.

This charming inn has a complete stone exterior, hand-shaped by local Indians when it was built in 1906. Through the years, Mrs. "Nana" Foster, the original owner, often invited notable artists and writers from the San Francisco Bay area to stay in her Carmel home. Sinclair Lewis, Jack London and Lotta Crabtree were among these guests. Rooms are named in their honor.

A glass-enclosed front porch provides the entrance and sets the mood for the warmth and ambiance you are soon to experience.

Guests often gather in the living room in front of the large stone fireplace to enjoy not only the warmth of the fire, but the pleasure of meeting new friends from around the world.

The restful bedrooms are light and airy, some having a view of the ocean through the trees. Each room is decorated in soft colors and features antiques, cozy quilts, fresh flowers, fruit and special touches.

California

A generous breakfast is served each morning in the sunny dining room, the peaceful garden or before the fire.

Tally Ho Inn
Monte Verde & 6th
1-800-652-2632
Web site: www.tallyho-inn.com

Secluded and tranquil, the 1920 Tally Ho Inn offers a true English countryside atmosphere. Only half a block from the heart of Carmel, the Tally Ho is an idyllic retreat of flowers, gardens, fireplaces and a soothing view of the ocean. Take a short picturesque stroll to Carmel's famous white sandy beach and revel in the fabulous views of the Pacific Ocean, Pebble Beach and Point Lobos. Accommodates fourteen guests.

24 CARMICHAEL

Queen Anne Cottage
2633 El Camino Ave.
916/481-4944

For Olde Tyme Sake
6030 Fair Oak Blvd.
916/978-9818

Antiques Unlimited
6328 Fair Oaks Blvd.
916/482-6533

Hovis Antiques
7800 Fair Oaks Blvd.
916/944-4736

The White House
6210 Fair Oaks Blvd.
916/979-9742

The Elegant Antique Barn
6443 Fair Oaks Blvd.
916/973-8590

25 CARNELIAN BAY

The Meadows Collection
By appointment only
530/546-5516

26 CARPINTERIA

Angels
4846 Carpinteria Ave.
805/684-8148

Magpie Collections
961 Linden Ave.
805/684-6034

Antique Delights
771 Linden Ave.
805/684-2717

27 CARSON

Memory Lane Antique Mall
20740 S. Figueroa St.
301/538-4130

28 CAYUCOS

Cayucos Antiques
151 Cayucos Dr.
805/995-2206

Cayucos Trading Post
98 N. Ocean Ave.
805/995-3453

Rich Man — Poor Man Antique Mall
146 N. Ocean Ave.
805/995-3631

Remember When
152 N. Ocean Ave.
805/995-1232

American Pie
890 S. Ocean Ave.
805/995-0832

29 CHICO

Country Squyres' Antiques
164 E. 3rd St.
916/342-6764

Trends & Traditions
126 W. 3rd St.
916/891-5622

American Antiques
1355 Guill St.
916/345-0379

Soot & Shine Shed Antiques
11708 Butte Creek Island Road
916/342-8806

8th & Main Antiques Center
745 Main St.
916/893-5534

Antique Annex
1421 Carnaby St.
916/893-8823

Hidden Treasure Antiques
2234 Park Ave.
916/893-5773

Voses Shopping Center
9145 Cohasset Road
916/342-5214

30 CHOWCHILLA

While driving through Central California, look for the quaint agricultural town of Chowchilla, an easy and convenient exit off of State Freeway 99 and State Hwy. 152, where you and your family can park your R.V. and rest and relax in a palm-shaded park. Adjacent is a cluster of seven antique shops within a four-block area located on the main street through town. Enjoy this low-key pioneering atmosphere where you can take your time to shop and browse among friendly small town people. There are also numerous restaurants and sandwich shops with a variety of cuisines available.

Chowchilla has an unusual history in its development. This small city named after an Indian tribe, did not explode in population as did most early California settlements. However, it sits in the geographical center of the state and requires only a short drive west to the ocean front attractions and a short drive east to the high Sierra Nevada Mountains and to the entrance of the beautiful Yosemite Valley. (The Sierras offer many scenic routes that include Redwood forests, mountain lakes, streams and camping.) It is located in the most productive agricultural area in the world. The Central Valley boasts the production of 250 agricultural commodities.

The Parrott Shop
535 Robertson Blvd.
209/665-4311
Open: Daily 10:30–5

Harvey & Geri Parrott, owners of The Parrott Shop, have been antique collectors for 25 years. Their shop on Robertson St. is filled with over

California

10,000 items within its 4,000 square feet. A large selection of prints, glassware (including carnival and depression), crystal, china, pottery such as Roseville, Weller, Hull, Bauer, Fiesta and McCoy can be found among this eclectic offering of antiques. Military items, costume jewelry, tools, kitchen ware, fishing items, books, cookie jars, decanters, bird cages, musical instruments, lighting, furnishings of several periods and styles are also available. They even have a section devoted to oriental pieces, along with a special area for quilters.

Frontier Towne

521 Robertson Blvd.
209/665-3900
Open: Daily 10:30–5, closed Thurs.
Owner: Sandy Batey

Frontier Towne opened its doors in 1985 as one of the first collectives in the San Joaquin Valley. The interior resembles the main street of an old western town, complete with settings of an old general store, bank, saloon, boarding house and blacksmith shop. This 5,000-square-foot shop offers a huge variety of antiques and collectibles. Western collectibles are a specialty of the owner as she is a ranch-raised cowgirl and still rides and competes in rodeos (in her spare time!). A very interesting stop on your antique trail.

The 2nd Frontier

529 Robertson Blvd.
209/665-3900
Open: Daily 10:30–5, closed Thurs.

The 2nd Frontier, which opened in 1997, is the sister shop to Frontier Towne. Specializing in retro furniture and large items, the shop has a quickly changing inventory — mostly due to its exceptionally low prices.

His & Hers Antiques

527 Robertson Blvd.
209/665-1911
Open: Daily 11–5

Noted as one of the fun places to shop in Chowchilla, His & Hers Antiques offers something for everyone from primitive to formal. Twelve dealers from Fresno to San Francisco supply the wares which make up this eclectic inventory.

Village Antiques

510 Robertson Blvd.
209/665-1487
Open: Thurs.–Mon., 9–5, Tues. 9–2

For the past 10 years, Brigette Brooks has offered her customers a

unique blend of antiques and collectibles. In addition to the usual and the unusual, she also carries old paper items.

The Glasstique Shoppe

331 Robertson Blvd.
209/665-5676
Open: Daily, 10–5, closed Wed.

This shoppe, which is 1,700 square feet in size, specializes in flow blue porcelain, beautiful furniture, and a general line of antiques and collectibles.

The owners have been collecting antiques for thirty-five years and have operated The Glasstique Shoppe for ten years at this location.

Gray Duck Antique Mall

216 Robertson Blvd.
209/665-3305
Email: grammy@madnet.net
Open: Daily 10–5, closed Wed.

Gray Duck Antique Mall has established itself over the past fifteen years as a special place to shop. This 3,000-square-foot showcase mall specializes in advertising, war memorabilia, toys and western tack along with a general line of antiques and collectibles.

31 CLAREMONT

Cat In The Window
206 W. Bonita Ave.
909/399-0297

Barbara Cheatley Antiques
215 Yale Ave.
909/621-4161

Cambridge Row Antiques
206 W. Bonita Ave.
909/625-1931

32 CLOVIS

Osterberg's Mercantile
Fifth St.
209/298-4291

Old Town Antiques
410 Clovis Ave.
209/325-1208

Olde Time Antique Mall
460 Clovis Ave.
209/299-2575

Treasured Memories
460 Clovis Ave.
209/299-4266

Donnie Lu's Gfts & Treas
320 Pollasky Ave.
209/299-5538

Clovis Antique Mall 1&2
530 & 532 Fifth St.
209/298-1090

Peacock Alley Antiques
614 Fifth St.
209/299-1186

Melton's Carousel World
425 Pollasky Ave.
209/298-8930

4th Street Antique Mall
461 Pollasky Ave.
209/323-1636

33 COSTA MESA

Panier De Fleurs
2915 S. Bristol
714/979-1819

Jack & Gloria's Antiques
1304 Logan Ave., #E,F,G
714/546-5450

Greenville Station
1685 Tustin Ave.
714/642-0218

Heirloom Galleries
369 E. 17th St.
714/631-4633

Cottage Company
1686 Tustin Ave.
714/722-0777

The Country Inn
130 E. 17th St., Unit P
714/722-1177

Musket & Sabre Antique Arms
446 W. 19th St.
714/645-0036

Old Stones
Appointment Only
714/574-8033

Richard Felch Antiques
120 Virginia Place
714/642-8911

Castle Antiques
112 E. 18th St.
714/722-6779

Fanfare Tiffany Lamps
1765 Newport Blvd.
714/642-6692

Zazy Goona Antique Mall
1770 Orange Ave.
714/646-4561

Crofton Antiques
670 W. 17th St.
714/642-4585

Treasures on Consignment
2220 Fairview Road
714/645-5477

Consignment Gallery
270 E. 17th St.
714/631-2622

Stix & Stones
333 E. 17th St., Unit b-12
714/646-7233

Normandy Metal
1603 Superior Ave.
714/631-5555

Jack & Gloria's II
2981 Fairview Road
714/751-3809

34 COTTONWOOD

Country Lane Antiques
20839 Front St.
916/347-5598

Cottonwood Antiques
3306 Main St.
916/347-0692

Abbey Gayle's Fine Things
20840 Front St.
916/347-9669

35 COVINA

Signs of the Times Antiques
110 N. Citrus Ave.
818/966-7101

Collector's Alley
225 N. Citrus Ave.
818/858-9964

Looking Back
316 N. Citrus Ave.
818/966-8842

Nostalgia Nook Antiques
112 N. Citrus Ave.
818/339-8699

Vestige Antiques
312 N. Citrus Ave.
818/967-8970

Ivy & The Rose
113 W. College St.
818/967-1171

Old Covina Antique Emporium
514 N. Citrus Ave.
818/859-9972

36 CRESCENT CITY

Antiques Etc.
280 U.S. Hwy. 101 S.
707/464-9012

Eclectic
305 U.S. Hwy. 101 S.
707/464-7907

Sylvia's Attic
285 L St.
707/464-9466

37 CUCAMONGA

A's Antiques
8078 Archibald
909/989-8017

38 CULVER CITY

Beaded Bird
3811 Bagley Ave.
310/204-3594

39 CYPRESS

Cora & Mac's Glass Antiques
5012 Ball Road
714/229-8325

40 DANA POINT

The Landmark Antiques
34241 Coast Hwy.
714/489-1793

41 DANVILLE

Antiques Du Coeur
391 Hartz Ave.
510/837-5049

Danville Antiques
111 Town & Country Road
510/837-4784

Sweet Ivy
3470 Blackhawk Plaza Circle
510/736-0949

42 EL CAJON

Antique Mercantile Co.
161 E. Main St.
619/441-8804

G & L Collectibles
332 N. Citrus Ave.
818/966-6829

Sunset House Antiques
1060 Sunset Circle
707/464-6631

Shrader Antiques
2025 U.S. Hwy. 199
707/458-3525

Aunt Iris's Antiques
10762 Washington Blvd.
310/838-5349

Anne Michael's
5917 Cerritos Ave.
714/821-7990

Traditions Tea Room
34241 Pacific Coast Hwy. #101
714/248-7660

Rue 137
398 Hartz Ave.
510/837-1148

Menagerie Antiques
105 Town and Country Dr.
510/837-3929

French Country
398 Hartz Ave.
510/837-1148

Main Street Antique Mall
237 E. Main St.
619/447-0800

California

The Doll Den
231 W. Douglas
619/44-2198

Flinn Springs Country Store
14860 Olde Hwy. 80
619/443-1842

Antique Blvd. Mall
799 El Cajon
619/447-8057

43 ELK GROVE

Dalin Jewelers
8765 Elk Grove Blvd.
916/685-6530

Bells Cookie Jar
9086 Elk Grove Blvd.
916/685-7810

Remember When
9116 Elk Grove Blvd.
916/685-6776

44 ENCINITAS

Simply Nostalgia
162 S. Rancho Sante Fe Road
619/943-1328

Paris Flea Market
N. Coast Hwy. 101
760/633-1373

45 ESCONDIDO

Victorian Garden Antiques
115 W. Grand Ave.
760/737-9669

Escondido Antique Mall
135 W. Grand Ave.
760/743-3210

In The Cave
227 E. Grand Ave.
760/739-9117

Cornucopia Antiques
317 E. Grand Ave.
760/745-9792

Grab Bag Antiques
150 E. Grand Ave.
760/480-1861

Stuff Your Mom Throughout
144 E. Main St.
619/440-2440

Magnolia Antique Mall
456 N. Magnolia Ave.
619/444-0628

The Beehive
1258 Broadway
619/444-4837

Country Blend
9084 Elk Grove Blvd.
916/686-8223

Country Grove Antiques
9098 Elk Grove Blvd.
916/685-2082

Antique Crossroads
765 S. Coast Hwy. 101
760/753-0292

Coastal Consignment Connection
850 S. Coast Hwy. 101
760/943-1199

121 Grand Antiques
121 W. Grand Ave.
760/489-0338

Memory Lane Antiques
158 E. Grand Ave.
760/480-1215

Art's Antiques & Collectibles
252 E. Grand Ave.
760/746-7104

Hidden Valley Antique Emporium
333 E. Grand Ave.
760/737-0333

Lionheart Consignment
262 E. Grand Ave.
760/746-8636

46 EUREKA

Antiques and Goodies
1128 3rd St.
707/442-0445
Open: Mon.–Sat.10–5, Sun. during the summer.
Directions: Traveling south on U.S. 101 turn right on M Street, left on 3rd; shop is on the left. Traveling north on U.S. 101 turn left on L Street, right on 3rd; shop is on the right.

Located among the grand Victorian homes of Eureka, Antiques and Goodies will quickly become one of your favorite antiquing experiences. It's one of those nice places where quality is still affordable. The shop offers seven full rooms (5,000 sq. ft.) of exceptional imported 19th-century furnishings and smalls. The owners take great pride in their ability to find the best bargains, which is evidenced in the hand-selected inventory from Great Britain and throughout the continent.

The shop specializes in English, French and Japanese furniture, Victorian housewares, tools and clocks. You will also find a large selection of Quimper, Mottoware, Majolica and British commemoratives.

Antique Annex
208 F St.
707/443-9113

Eureka Antique Mall
533 F St.
707/445-8835

The Hose Company
1401 3rd St.
707/445-4673

Empire Furniture Antiques
111 5th St.
707/442-1871

Kit-N-Kaboodle
527 3rd St.
707/442-5760

Old Town Antiques
318 F St.
707/442-3235

Hexagram Antiques
426 3rd St.
707/443-4334

Antique Bottles & Relics
2235 Broadway St.
707/442-2667

Antique Arcade
501 3rd St.
707/442-3895

Great Places to Stay

Abigail's Elegant Victorian
1406 C St.
707/444-3144
Rates: Begin at $85

In a town full of historic buildings (nearly 1,600, in fact) this inn stands as one of the finest examples of Eastlake cottage-style architecture along the West Coast. Though it looks like a mansion, the structure is classified as a "cottage" because of its one-and-a-half stories, two flanking bay windows, and ornate barge boards that festoon the gables.

William S. Clark, twice the mayor of Eureka, lived here for over 50

California

years. Because his family figured prominently in Eureka's history (and literally owned half the town), Clark entertained many famous guests, such as Lily Langtry and Ulysses S. Grant, at his home during the turn of the century.

After 100 years of private ownership, the home was recently turned into a bed and breakfast inn. Its name is derived from the 1888 newspaper description, "An elegant Victorian mansion." New owners, Doug and Lily Vieyra, a spirited couple, love playing their roles to the hilt. They also operated The Chalet of France, an unusual Swiss-style mountain retreat, complete with Tyrolean costumes. The motto for their new inn is, "Come to where history lives." Doug says, "We want to relive that exciting transition period from the horse to the automobile." They greet their guests in vintage costumes, and enjoy staging mystery weekends, classical concerts, and guided tours of Eureka in antique cars.

Elaborate ceilings, painted chandelier medallions, wall coverings by Bradbury & Bradbury, and carved fireplaces enhance the original splendor of the two parlors, dining room and library. An enclosed porch wraps around the back of the house, where a Finnish sauna is concealed. (Belgian born Lily also offers Swedish massages.) A formal garden of over one hundred roses beckons guests to step outside, and go back to a gentler era of croquet and afternoon tea.

A Weaver's Inn

1440 B St.
Web site: www.humboldt1.com/~weavrinn
1-800-992-8119

A Weaver's Inn provides an atmosphere reflecting warmth and the elegance of the Victorian era. Your stay will be in a gracious Queen Anne home surrounded by a cottage-style, fenced garden and spacious lawn (for playing croquet or quiet contemplation). Three lovely guest rooms and the two-room Pamela Suite are furnished with many antiques, down comforters and fresh flowers from the garden. Each room reflects the genteel elegance of a by-gone era, including two with fireplaces. Located only ten blocks from historic Old Town. From the inn you can easily access a tour of the harbor or a carriage ride along the waterfront.

Carter House Victorians

301 L St.
Web site: www.carterhouse.com
1-800-404-1390

Welcoming travelers since 1981, The Carter House is an enclave of three magnificent Victorians perched alongside Humboldt Bay at the gateway to Eureka's Historic District. Guest rooms feature antiques, private baths and luxurious amenities soothe the soul and delight the senses.

Dinner at Restaurant 301 is truly a celebration of the senses. The gardens provide herbs and fresh vegetables for the chefs.

Old Town Bed & Breakfast Inn

1521 Third St.
1-800-331-5098

This 1871 Victorian in the seaport of Eureka is the quintessence of world-class B&B. Six guest rooms are available.

47 EXETER

Exeter Antiques
216 E. Pine
209/594-4221

By The Water Tower
141 S. B St.
209/594-4060

Antique's & More
275 E. Pine
209/592-5697

Heritage Plaza
196 E. Pine
209/592-8101

Olde Town Exchange
117 E. Pine
209/592-5858

Tumbleweeds
400 Rock Hill Dr.
209/592-2565

Greenleave's Antiques
277 E. Pine
209/592-1880

Pine Street Relics
201 E. Pine
209/592/4170

Snazzy Antiques
228 E. Pine
209/592-9606

48 FAIR OAKS

Mary Scott Antiques
10211 Fair Oaks Blvd.
916/967-2493

Blue Eagle Antiques
10201 Fair Oaks Blvd.
916/966-4947

49 FALLBROOK

Jewelry Connection
113 N. Main St.
760/723-4629

Country Elegance
3137 S. Mission Road, #B
760/723-3417

Tin Barn Antiques
3137 S. Mission Road, #D
760/723-1609

Thomas Antiques
2809 S. Mission Road
760/728-5156

Millies Antique 'n' Old Lace
3137 S. Mission Road, #A
760/723-9206

Ivy House Antiques
3137 S. Mission Road, #B
760/728-7038

Kirk's Antiques
321 N. Orange Ave.
760/728-6333

50 FELTON

Carousel Gallery Antique Dolls
6931 Hwy. 9
408/335-3076

OJ's American Antiques
135 Valhalla Way
408/335-5590

Huckleberry House
Antiques by appointment
408/335-1395

51 FERNDALE

Foggy Bottoms
563 Main St.
707/786-9188
Open: Mon.–Sat. 12–5, Sun. 12–4
Directions: Take the Ferndale Exit from Hwy. 101. Cross over Fernbridge Drive into Ferndale. Foggy Bottoms is in the first block of the business district on Main St. near Shaw Ave.

Foggy Bottoms Antiques, named for the foggy veil which often descends upon this quaint valley town, is located in a State Historic Landmark town, on a National Historic Landmark street.

The shop, housed in a 1,000-square-foot turn-of-the-century building, may be small but is richly blessed with notable charm. "It's all I can handle," says Jacque Ramirez, who is both shopkeeper and owner of Foggy Bottoms. She is also co-owner (with her husband, Richard) of Grandmother's House Bed and Breakfast located just seconds away from the shop at 861 Howard St.

Foggy Bottom's "claim to fame" is its offering of many old radio program cassettes. The shop stocks a hodge-podge of unusual smalls; china, porcelains, a nice selection of salt and pepper shakers, early rolling pins, pottery and just about anything old that Jacque finds interesting.

For some unknown reason, Ferndale happens to be the home to many avid sweater knitters, and for that reason Foggy Bottoms offers an ample selection of yarns, patterns and accessories for the genteel looper.

After a long day of antiquing and sight-seeing in this "picture postcard" valley, you're always welcome to stay at Grandmother's House. Built in 1901, this bed and breakfast offers gracious accommodations with all the romance and charm of the turn of the century. The three guest rooms are decorated with antique furnishings, as is the rest of the house. The dining room provides a parlor with wood-burning fireplace.

Enjoy the peaceful back porch while watching buffalo graze in a nearby pasture. Located in a quiet residential neighborhood.

Golden Gait Mercantile
421 Main St.
707/786-4891

Aunt Jane's Collectibles
Main St.
707/786-4903

Cream City Mall
1400 Main St.
707/786-4997

Great Places to Stay

Gingerbread Mansion Inn
400 Berding St.
707/786-4000
Rates: $100–$205

Located in a well-preserved Victorian Village, the Four-Diamond rated Gingerbread Mansion Inn is one of northern California's most photographed homes. The inn is a striking display of superior Victorian architecture surrounded by immaculately groomed English gardens.

52 FOLSOM

As Time Goes By Antiques
306 Rile St.
916/985-6206

Thistle & Rose Scottish Antiques
722 Sutter St.
916/353-1936

Williams Carriage House Antiques
728 Sutter St.
916/985-7416

Curiosity Shoppe
801 1/2 Sutter St.
916/985-0534

Colonies
813 Sutter St.
916/985-3442

Setnik's In Time Again
815 Sutter St.
916/985-2390

Folsum Mercantile Exchange
726 Sutter St.
916/985-2169

Sheepish Grin Antique Market
625 Sutter St.
916/885-0257

Dal Bello Antiques Collective
727 Sutter St.
916/985-3772

Emily's Antique Corner
732 Sutter St.
916/985-6222

Olde Towne Antiques
809 Sutter St.
916/985-2853

Cottage in the Mall
813 Sutter St.
916/985-0496

A-Arts Antiques
707 Sutter St.
916/985-6429

53 FORTUNA

Fernbridge Antique Mall
597 Fernbridge Dr.
707/725-8820

Antique Depot
1122 Main St.
707/725-5503

Rundells Antiques & Collectibles
569 Main St.
707/725-9175

Fortuna Art & Old Things
1026 Main St.
707/725-3003

54 FREMONT

Cherished Memories/Dodi's Dolls
37390 Niles Blvd.
510/792-2559

My Friends & I
37521 Niles Blvd.
510/792-0118

The Clock Man
120 J St.
510/794-5928

With a Little Help My Friends
37313 Niles Blvd.
510/797-2088

Morning Glory Antiques
37372 Niles Blvd.
510/790-3374

The Store
37415 Niles Blvd.
510/797-8471

Ma Mere Intl.
37501 Niles Blvd.
510/793-8043

Bite & Browse
37565 Niles Blvd.
510/796-4537

Old and New
37675 Niles Blvd.
510/792-4757

Side Street Antiques
37581 Niles Blvd.
510/795-9005

Timeless Treasures
37769 Niles Blvd.
510/795-7755

Niles Antique Co-op
37759 Niles Blvd.
510/744-1602

55 FRESNO

Treasure of Sierra Madre
463 E. Belmont Ave.
209/264-9343

Chesterfield Antiques
5092 N. Blackstone Ave.
209/225-4736

Lina's Antiques
1918 N. Echo Ave.
209/497-9767

Fulton's Folly Antique Mall
920 E. Olive Ave.
209/268-3856

Collectique
140 E. Olive Ave.
209/441-1252

It's About Time
1526 N. Van Ness Ave.
209/264-3529

Antiques Junction
37312 Niles Blvd.
510/793-3481

Niles Blvd. Antique Center
37825 Niles Blvd.
510/790-1221

Woodhaven
37396 Niles Blvd.
510/745-7666

Shades of the Past
37495 Niles Blvd.
510/791-2415

Les Belles Antiques
37549 Niles Blvd.
510/794-4773

Lost in the Attic
37663 Niles Blvd.
510/791-2420

East Bay Dolls & Bears
37721 Niles Blvd.
510/792-2559

Jean & Bea's Toys U-NU
37769 Niles Blvd.
510/793-2848

S & H Antiques
130 J St.
510/792-7792

Dug O' Vic's European Antiques
1310 N. Blackstone Ave.
209/442-8494

Bell Antiques
3265 E. Belmont Ave.
209/485-8381

Alice's Palace
22 E. Olive Ave.
209/485-4408

Antiques & Favorite Things
444 E. Olive Ave.
209/497-0217

Fellini's
836 N. Fulton St.
209/498-3321

Marcel's Antiques
834 N. Van Ness Ave.
209/266-3040

Valentino's Altern. Appraisal
814 E. Olive Ave.
209/233-6900

56 FULLERTON

Krypton
101 E. Commonwealth Ave., #C
714/446-0592

George's Antiques
201 W. Commonwealth Ave.
714/871-4347

Doll Trunk
531 W. Commonwealth Ave.
714/526-1467

Susan Herpel Antique Quilts
By appointment only
714/870-8989

Amerage Avenue Antiques
122 N. Harbor Blvd., Suite 110
714/525-6383

Antique Companion
204 N. Harbor Blvd.
714/525-2756

Harbor Antique Mall
207 N. Harbor Blvd.
714/680-0532

Ashley Rose Antique
213 N. Harbor Blvd.
714/871-4656

Eclectic Antiques
108 E. Amerige Ave.
714/871-7373

57 GARDEN GROVE

Private Collections
12931 Main St.
714/539-4419

L C & Sally's Antiques
12951 Main St.
714/530-3035

58 GILROY

Final Frontier
7411 Monterey St.
408/847-1050

Monterey St. Antiques
7511 Monterey St.
408/848-3788

Yosemite Coins & Antiques
4568 N. 1st St.
209/229-5672

Antique Mine
124 E. Commonwealth Ave.
714/526-2200

Back Home Antiques
509 W. Commonwealth Ave.
714/526-3553

Jones Mercantile
531 W. Commonwealth Ave.
714/879-3501

Antique Gallery
110 N. Harbor Blvd.
714/871-3850

Kindred Co.
202 N. Harbor Blvd.
714/879-2324

Old Towne Fullerton Antiques
206 N. Harbor Blvd.
714/447-9046

Apropos Antiques
112 E. Amerige Ave.
714/871-8920

David's Antiques & Clocks
201 N. Harbor Blvd.
714/447-4308

Silver Lining
122 N. Harbor Blvd. #109
714/871-8760

Garden Grove Mercantile
12941 Main St.
714/534-1857

Sleepy Hollow Antique Mall
12965 Main St.
714/539-9187

Gilroy Antiques
7445 Monterey St.
408/842-1776

Serendipity
7515 Monterey St.
408/842-0399

was said to be "the most modern and scientific of its time." Eight guest accommodations.

Holbrooke Hotel & Purcell House
212 W. Main St.
916/273-1353

The Holbrooke Hotel invites guests to indulge in the elegance of a bygone era. Established in 1851, the hotel is located in the heart of the scenic Sierra Nevada Motherlode, and is a California Registered Historical Landmark. The hotel has hosted many luminaries from four of America's most famed Presidents — Ulysses S. Grant, Benjamin Harrison, James A. Garfield and Grover Cleveland — to boxers Gentleman Jim Corbett and Bob Fitzsimmons.

Murphy's Inn
318 Neal St.
916/273-6873

Built in 1866 by a gold mine owner for his new bride, Murphy's Inn is a beautifully restored Greek Revival home. All rooms are beautifully decorated with antiques. A 130-year-old sequoia tree overlooks a wonderful deck for relaxing and reading. All rooms have private baths. Some rooms have fireplaces. A full hot breakfast is served. Chocolate chip cookies and soft drinks are always available.

Garbos Antiques & Collectibles
7517 Monterey St.
408/848-6722

Littlejohn's Fine Jewelry
8220 Monterey St.
408/842-1001

Hampton Court Antiques
7542 Monterey St.
408/847-2455

Lindsey & Friends Antique Mall
7888 Monterey St.
408/842-5586

59 GLENDALE

Fiona's
3463 N. Verdugo Road
818/249-6776

About Antiques
3533 Ocean View Blvd.
818/249-8587

60 GLENDORA

Millie's Dolls
140 N. Glendora Ave.
818/963-8311

Country Village Antiques
163 N. Glendora Ave.
818/914-6860

Anything Goes Emporium
218 N. Glendora Ave.
818/963-3939

Old Packing House
243 S. Vermont Ave.
818/963-8171

Orange Tree Antiques
216 N. Glendora Ave.
818/335-3376

61 GRASS VALLEY

Grass Valley Antique Emporium
150 Mill St.
916/272-7302

Al's Attic Antiques
11671 Maltman Dr.
916/272-1777

The Rubaiyat
151 Mill St.
916/272-4844

Young's Olde Treasures
101 S. Church St.
916/274-1917

Duck Soup
160 Mill St.
916/477-7891

Auntie's Attic
504 Whiting St.
916/273-1095

Granny's Treasure Chest
132 E. Main St.
916/272-5129

The Palace Antiques & Collectibles
138 E. Main St.
916/273-6043

Great Places to Stay

Elam Biggs Bed & Breakfast
220 Colfax Ave.
530/477-0906

The Elam Biggs Home was built in 1892 by one of Grass Valley's foremost successful merchants. This beautiful Queen Anne Victorian is set amid a large yard surrounded by tall old shade trees and a rose-covered picket fence.

All this is just a short stroll to Historic Downtown. This grand home is a perfect setting for that special time away, or a steppingstone to the history of the Gold Rush Era. When Elam Biggs built this house for his family, it

62 HANFORD

Country Bazaar
7090 N. Douty St.
209/584-8798

Corner
102 E. 6th St.
209/584-7097

Livery Stable Shops
113 S. Douty St.
209/582-0356

Hanford Antique Emporium
108 E. 8th St.
209/583-8202

63 HAYWARD

Hayward Faire Antiques
926 B St.
510/537-7823

Jeannie's Antiques
1013 B St.
510/582-1773

Antique Connection
1033 B St.
510/889-8608

Creative Cottage
938 B St.
510/728-7644

Incurable Collector
944 B St.
510/733-5122

Ryan's Country Farm Antiques
1028 B St.
510/881-7755

B Street Antiques
1025 B St.
510/889-8549

California

64 HEALDSBURG

Antique Harvest
225 Healdsburg Ave.
707/433-0223

Healdsburg Classic Antiques
226 Healdsburg Ave.
707/433-4315

Vintage Antiques Etc.
328 Healdsburg Ave.
707/433-7461

Irish Cottage Antiques
112 Matheson St.
707/433-4850

Going Vintage Antiques & Collectibles
44 Mill St.
707/433-4501

Vintage Plaza Antiques
44 Mill St.
707/433-8409

Great Places to Stay

Bergerie
5325 Eastside Road

Bergerie is a romantic, private bed and breakfast in the heart of Sonoma County wine country in Northern California. Located on an estate of ten acres, nestled in a forest of redwood trees, there are hiking trails, a trout pond and lots of wildlife to enjoy.

Camellia Inn
211 North St.
Web site: www.camellia.com
1-800-727-8182

An 1869 Italianate Victorian townhouse on half-acre grounds. Antiques fill nine spacious bedrooms, each with private bath. Double parlors with twin marble fireplaces and a dining room with a massive mahogany mantel return you to the elegance of yesteryear. Several rooms have double whirlpool tubs, gas fireplaces or private entrances. Afternoon refreshments are served in the parlor or by the swimming pool.

George Alexander House
423 Matheson St.
1-800-310-1358

The George Alexander House, built in 1905, is noted for its exuberant ornamental details and its many quatrefoil windows. As an inn, it is ideally situated a few blocks from Healdsburg's Plaza, where visitors may taste wine, dine in wonderful restaurants, or browse in unique shops. The inn has four guest rooms, each with its own bath, two large parlors for guest use, many books, good art, and Oriental rugs.

65 HEMET

Hermitage Antiques
910 E. Florida Ave., #B2
909/925-1968

Fond Memories
123 N. Havard St.
909/652-2511

Second Time Around
699 N. San Jacinto St.
909/652-6798

Charlotte's Antiques
41171 Crest Dr.
909/658-4870

Buyers Inn
123 Harvard Ave.
909/652-2727

Jamie's Junque
25760 New Chicago Ave.
909/927-7090

Rusty Relics
135 N. Harvard St.
909/766-7784

66 HESPERIA

Carousel Faire
15800 Main St.
760/244-2336

Antiques by Janie
15885 Main St., #220
760/244-9797

Apple Pie Antiques
15885 Main St.
760/947-4474

Miss Jenny's
15885 Main St., #170
760/947-4020

Sonja's Treasures
15885 Main St.
760/947-6642

Eufemia's Antiquery
11605 Mariposa Road
760/244-4828

Silvia's Boutique
15885 Main St.
760/244-0796

Making Memories
15885 Main St., #160
760/947-6259

Cobblestone Square Antiques
15885 Main St.
760/244-5301

Miss Jenny's II
15885 Main St., #260
760/947-2229

67 HOLLYWOOD/WEST HOLLYWOOD

Rye Byers Antiques
8424 Melrose Ave.
213/655-2095

City Antiques
8444 Melrose Ave.
213/658-6354

Villa Medici
8687 Melrose Ave.
310/659-9984

Papillion Gallery
8818 Melrose Ave.
310/659-9984

W Antiques
8925 Melrose Ave.
310/275-5099

Antiques & Design
610 N. Robertson Blvd.
310/659-0946

Ashby's Antiques
638 N. Robertson Blvd.
310/854-1006

John Alan Antiques
644 N. Robertson Blvd.
310/854-5438

Gregory's Country Home
8747 Sunset Blvd.
310/652-7288

Last Moving Picture Co.
6307 Hollywood Blvd.
213/467-0838

California

Great Places to Stay

Radisson Hollywood Roosevelt Hotel

7000 Hollywood Blvd.
213/466-7000 or for reservations 1-800-833-3333

Situated right in the heart of Hollywood, the Radisson Hollywood Roosevelt Hotel is a stylish property built in 1927 as the centerpiece of the film world — a role it still fulfills. Always the place to see and be seen, it staged the first-ever Academy Awards ceremony in its Blossom Ballroom in 1929, and it has hosted a variety of major movie premieres and opening night galas during the following four decades. Today the hotel features 335 beautifully appointed rooms, including 20 luxury suites.

68 HUNTINGTON BEACH

Way Back When
8901 Atlanta Ave.
714/960-5335

Back In Tyme Antiques
517 Walnut Ave.
714/536-2194

Country Cottage
18211 Enterprise Lane, #B
714/842-5959

69 ISLETON

Country Cupboard
15 Main St.
916/777-6737

Windmill Antiques, Etc.
15041 State Hwy. 160
916/777-6112

Junk & Treasures
112 2nd St.
916/777-4828

70 JACKSON

Amador Antique Emporium
12311 Martell Road
209/223-2030

National Hotel Antiques
2 Water St.
209/223-3447

Sisters
5 Main St.
209/223-2930

Water Street Antiques
11101 State Hwy. 88
209/223-4189

Specialty Shop
5 Main St.
209/223-3036

71 JAMESTOWN

Main St. Mercantile
18138 Main St.
209/984-6551

Butterfield House Country Gifts
18158 Main St.
209/984-3068

Bear Essentials Antiques
18145 Main St.
209/984-5315

Over The Hill Antiques
18205 Main St.
209/984-3237

Crackel & Co.
18210 Main St.
209/984-4080

Jamestown Mercantile Antiques
18255 Main St.
209/984-5148

Daisy Tree II
18280 Main St.
209/984-0661

Pine Tree Peddlers
18211 Main St.
209/984-3647

Mostly Pennsylvania
18278 Main St.
209/984-0533

Now & Then Antiques
17775 State Hwy. 108
209/984-4224

72 JULIAN

Wynola Timeless Treasures
4355 Hwy. 78, #C
760/765-3113

Applewood & Co.
2804 Washington
760/765-1185

Antique Boutique
2626 Main St.
760/765-0541

Great Places to Stay

Butterfield Bed and Breakfast

2284 Sunset Dr.
760/765-2179

An added treat to your visit to the tiny hamlet of Julian is a memorable stay at Butterfield Bed and Breakfast. Four guest rooms (French Bedroom, Country Rose, Feathernest, Apple Cellar Sweet), each with private bath and two with a fireplace, and Rose Bud Cottage all create a weekend to remember.

Julian White House B&B Inn

3014 Blue Jay Dr.
1-800-948-4687

Recommended by K-ABC's Elmer Dill, "The innkeepers, Alan & Mary Marvin, are the perfect hosts for your romantic escape to the past." This petite colonial mansion is located in the mountainous countryside of Julian. Secret Garden of Roses lends itself to afternoon relaxation or evening star gazing. All guest rooms are appointed with authentic antiques, private baths and queen-size beds.

73 KINGSBURG

Swedish Village Antiques
1135 Draper St.
209/897-4419

Granny's Attic
1513 Draper St.
209-897-4203

Apple Duplin Antiques
1440 Draper St.
209/897-5936

California

74 LA HABRA

Su Casa Antiques
310 E. Whittier Blvd.
562/694-3108

Clockworks
2204 W. Whittier Blvd.
562/694-5608

Ragtime Antiques
901 W. Whittier Blvd.
562/694-5414

75 LA JOLLA

McGee's Antiques of La Jolla
7467 Cuvier St.
619/459-1256

Antiques of Europe
7437 Girard Ave.
619/459-5886

Silver Store
7909 Girard Ave.
619/459-3241

Bird Rock Antiques
5623 La Jolla Blvd.
619/459-4091

Alcala Gallery
950 Silverado St.
619/454-6610

La Jolla Consignment & Mall
7509 Girard
619/456-0936

Renaissance Art & Antiques
7715 Fay Ave.
619/454-3887

Glorius Antiques
7645 Girard Ave.
619/459-2222

Circa
7861 Herschel Ave.
619/454-7962

Angelique's
1237 Prospect St., Suite U
619/459-5769

Taylor Antique Gallery
1000 Torrey Pines Road
619/456-1041

Early American Numismatics
P.O. Box 2442
619/459-4159

76 LA MESA

Antique Elegance
8363 Center Dr., #5B
619/697-8766

Country Loft
8166 La Mesa Blvd.
619/466-5411

Time & Treasures
8290 La Mesa Blvd.
619/460-8004

La Mesa Village Antiques
8371 La Mesa Blvd.
619/461-7940

Boulevard Antiques
8362 La Mesa Blvd.
619/698-8555

Norma Jean's Antiques
8341 La Mesa Blvd.
619/466-6640

Grossmont Antique Mart
8379 Center Dr.
619/466-2040

Rocking Horse Antique Mall
8223 La Mesa Blvd.
619/469-6191

Bloom 'n' Antiques
8360 La Mesa Blvd.
619/462-7100

Image Maker
8219 La Mesa Blvd.
619/461-9490

Mesa Verde
8295 La Mesa Blvd.
619/462-7630

Finders Keepers
8371 La Mesa Blvd.
619/698-6777

77 LAFAYETTE

Antiquary
1020 Brown Ave.
510/284-5611

Clocks Etc.
3401 Mount Diablo Blvd.
510/284-4720

Brown Ave. Collective
1030 Brown Ave.
510/284-7069

78 LAGUNA BEACH

Laguna Antiques & Consign
330 N. Coast Hwy.
714/497-9744

Ruins Antiques
1231-33 N. Coast Hwy.
714/376-0025

Antiqua
1290 N. Coast Hwy.
714/494-5860

Family Jewels
490 S. Coast Hwy.
714/494-2436

Antique Boutique
1432 S. Coast Hwy.
714/494-1571

Redfern Gallery
1540 S. Coast Hwy.
714/497-3356

Consignment Corner
888 Glenneyre St.
714/497-1010

Jerry's Antiquities N Things
1295 Glenneyre St.
714/494-0019

Gallery One of Laguna
1220 N. Coast Hwy.
714/494-4444

Melange
1235 N. Coast Hwy.
714/497-4915

Antiques & Interiors
448 S. Coast Hwy.
714/376-2005

Richard Yeakel Antiques
1099 S. Coast Hwy.
714/494-5526

Iron Maiden
1524 S. Coast Hwy.
714/497-0414

Kaehler's Fine Arts
332 Forest Ave.
714/494-3864

Roberta Gauthey Antiques
1166 Glenneyre St.
714/494-9925

79 LAKE ELSINORE

Antique Corner
106 W. Graham Ave.
909/674-7989

Grand Antique Mall
18273 Grand Ave.
909/678-5095

Enchanted Treasures
169 N. Main St.
909/674-8336

Chimes
201 W. Graham Ave.
909/674-3456

Antique Emporium
101 S. Main St.
909/245-3977

80 LANCASTER

Antiques & Things
44625 Sierra Hwy.
805/945-0504

Buffy's Antiques & Collectibles
3606 E. Ave. I
805/946-0335

81 LA VERNE

Generations
2343 D St.
909/593-4936

Sweet Memories
2336 D St.
909/596-2944

Yesterday's Antiques
2320 D St.
909/593-4456

Ken's Olden Oddities
1910 White Ave.
909/593-1846

82 LEMON COVE

Walker House Antiques
33513 Sierra Dr., Hwy. 198
209/597-2361

Great Places to Stay

Mesa Verde Plantation Bed & Breakfast
33038 Sierra Hwy. 198
209/597-2555 or 1-800-240-1466
Web site: www.psnw.com/~mvpbb
Email: mvpbb@psnw.com
Rates: $70–$125
Directions: Take Hwy. 99 to the town of Visalia. Go 23 ½ miles east on Hwy. 198.

Scott and Marie Munger operate their bed & breakfast at an old citrus plantation in the foothills of the Sierra Nevada Mountains. To carry out the plantation theme, Scott and Marie have named and decorated all eight guest rooms after characters from *Gone With the Wind*. There's the Melanie, the Scarlett O'Hara, the Belle Watling, the Rhett Butler, the Ashley Wilkes, Mammy's Room, Prissy's Room, and the Aunt Pitty Pat. From the descriptions of the rooms they sent us, they are right on the mark for matching decor to personalities!

The Mesa Verde also offers guests orange groves for meandering, a spa, heated pool, gazebo, hammocks under the trees, verandas and fireplaces. Guests can also enjoy a gourmet breakfast in the elegant dining room or outside in the courtyard garden, where you can dine with the hummingbirds.

83 LEMON GROVE

Years of Yesterday Antiques
7895 Broadway
619/464-3892

Broadway Antique Mall
7945 Broadway
619/461-1399

Lemon Grove Antique Mall
7919 Broadway
619/461-1361

Vivian's
7968-7970 Broadway
619/461-2728

84 LEUCADIA

Collectors Cottage
1786 N. Coast Hwy. 101
760/436-7937

Caldwell's Antiques
1234 N. Coast Hwy. 101
760/753-2369

Acanthus Fine Antiques
1010 N. Coast Hwy. 101
760/633-1515

Grandpa's Antiques
1240B N. Coast Hwy 101
760/942-5202

ABC Trading Co.
1240 N. Coast Hwy. 101
760/753-5160

Antique Clock Shop
1340 N. Coast Hwy. 101
760/753-8844

85 LIVERMORE

Livermore Trading Post
250 Church St.
510/443-2822

Adams Family Antiques
2047 1st St.
510/443-9408

Anne Marie's Antiques & Things
2074 1st St.
510/454-9870

Bill's Antiques & Collectibles
2339 1st St.
510/449-9002

Cleo's Memory Lane Antiques
2041 1st St.
510/443-2536

Yesterday's
2053 1st St.
510/373-1817

Forget Me Not
2187 1st St.
510/606-6330

Blue Door Antiques
321 N. L St.
510/449-2111

86 LOCKEFORD

Foxglove Antiques
13333 Hwy. 88
209/727-3008
Open: Mon.–Sun. 10–5, closed Tues.
Directions: Traveling south from Sacramento on Hwy 99 to Lodi (or traveling north from Stockton on Hwy 99), take Hwy 12 east, travel approximately 6 miles to Hwy 88, follow Hwy 88 northeast to Lockeford. Located next to Post Office.

It will come as no surprise that Foxglove Antiques offers a nice selection of Roseville pottery. The owner, Gloria Mollring, is the author of *Roseville Pottery Collector's Price Guide*. If pottery is not your fancy, Gloria and her husband, Jim, provide an eclectic selection for any curious shopper. Exceptional period pieces, jewelry, books, dolls, and paper collectibles are just a few of the many antiques available at this shop.

87 LODI

Old Friends Antiques
225 N. California St.
209/367-0607

Grave's Country Antiques
15 N. Cherokee Lane
209/368-5740

Grand J D Antiques
440 E. Kettleman Lane
209/334-1140

Victoria — 1894 Victorian House
861 E. Pine St.
209/333-1762

88 LOMA LINDA

Loma Linda Antique Mall
24997 Redlands Blvd.
909/796-4776

89 LOMITA

A & D Antiques
2055 1/2 Pacific Coast Hwy.
310/326-2434

Gloria's Antiques
2032 Pacific Coast Hwy.
310/530-5060

90 LONG BEACH

Quick's Antiques
2545 E. Broadway
562/433-8038

Outré Antiques
2747 E. Broadway
562/439-0339

Antique Clock Gallery
2122 E. 4th St.
562/438-5486

Kathy's Antiques
1340 E. Market St.
562/422-6987

Sleepy Hollow Antique Mall
5689 Paramount Blvd.
562/634-8370

Redondo House
274 Redondo Ave.
562/434-5239

Village Vault Antiques
5423 E. Village Road
562/425-7455

91 LOS ALAMITOS

Whiskers & Co. Antiques
10670 Los Alamitos Blvd.
562/493-4700

Estate Store
10899 Los Alamitos Blvd.
562/430-8819

Moehring's Antiques
440 E. Kettleman Lane
209/369-1818

Mickey's Antiques & Cllbls. Mall
14 N. School St.
209/369-9112

Anna Vocka's Antiques
1856 Pacific Coast Hwy.
310/325-2574

William J Hossack Antiques
2720 E. Broadway
562/439-4195

Kelly's Place
412 Cherry Ave.
562/438-2537

Millie's Place
144 Linden Ave.
562/435-8566

Long Beach Antique Mall
3100 E. Pacific Coast Hwy.
562/494-2526

Antiques & More
327 Pine Ave.
562/432-1173

Antique Adoption
4160 N. Viking Way
562/420-1919

Julie's Antique Mall
1133 E. Wardlow Road
562/989-7799

Los Alamitos Antique Shop
10702 Los Alamitos Blvd.
562/493-5911

Coliseum Antiques
10909 Los Alamitos Blvd.
562/598-0811

92 LOS ALAMOS

Gussied Up
349 Bell St.
805/344-2504

Krall Antiques
515 Bell St.
805/344-6311

Los Alamos Depot Mall
515 Leslae
805/344-3315

93 LOS ALTOS

Patrician Antiques
197 1st St.
415/948-5218

Maria's Antiques of Los Altos
288 1st St.
415/948-1965

Maria's Antiques of Los Altos
393 Main St.
415/941-9682

94 LOS ANGELES

Art Spectrum
2151 Ave. of the Stars
310/788-0720

Fainting Couch
7260 Beverly Blvd.
213/930-0106

Futurama
7956 Beverly Blvd.
213/651-5767

Marc Navarro Antiques
8840 Beverly Blvd.
310/285-9650

Antiquarius Center
8840 Beverly Blvd.
310/274-2363

European Antiques
8840 Beverly Blvd.
310/274-3089

London Imports
8840 Beverly Blvd.
310/858-7416

Catchell Five
1740 Colorado Ave.
213/256-0114

General Store Antiques
458 Bell St.
805/344-2123

The Prop Shop
Bell St.
805/344-3121

Oriental Corner
280 Main St.
415/941-3207

Geranium House Antiques
371 1st St.
415/941-2620

Bus Stop
5273 1/2 E. Beverly Blvd.
213/728-6720

Houle Rare Books & Autographs
7405 Beverly Blvd.
213/937-5858

Beverly Hills Antiquarian
8840 Beverly Blvd., #32
310/278-0120

918 Antique Gallery
8840 Beverly Blvd.
310/271-0404

Angele Hobin
8840 Beverly Blvd.
310/276-4449

Excalibur Antique Jewelry
8840 Beverly Blvd.
310/859-2320

Lief
8922 Beverly Blvd.
310/550-8118

Circa Antiques
3608 Edenhurst Ave.
213/662-6600

Farmer's Market Arts & Antiques
140 S. Fairfax Ave., #N
213/931-4804

Menyea's Decor
3113 W. Florence Ave.
213/752-9326

Caravan Book Store
550 S. Grand Ave.
213/626-9944

Rosetta Gallery
1958 Hillhurst Ave.
213/913-0827

Fat Chance
162 N. La Brea Ave.
213/930-1960

Iron N' Antique Accents
342 N. La Brea Ave.
213/934-3953

Virtue
149 S. La Brea Ave.
213/932-1789

Consignment Collections
355 N. La Cienega Blvd.
310/657-2590

Gregorius-Pineo
653 N. La Cienega Blvd.
310/659-0588

Quatrian
700 N. La Cienega Blvd.
310/652-0243

Remains to be Seen Antiques
735 N. La Cienega Blvd.
310/659-3358

Blackman Cruz
800 N. La Cienega Blvd.
310/657-9228

Ralf's Antiques
807 N. La Cienega Blvd.
310/659-1966

Abraham Larry Antiques
810 N. La Cienega Blvd.
310/651-4834

Chateau Allegre
815 N. La Cienega Blvd.
310/657-7259

Baldacchino Antiques
919 N. La Cienega Blvd.
310/657-6810

Showcase Gallery
140 S. Fairfax Ave.
213/939-7403

Penny Lane
2820 Gilroy St.
213/667-1838

La Maison Du Bal
705 N. Harper Ave.
213/655-8215

Simply Unique Collectibles
1903 Hyperion Ave.
213/661-5454

Repeat Performance
318 N. La Brea Ave.
213/938-0609

Retro Gallery
524 1/2 N. La Brea Ave.
213/936-5261

Francesca Dona
665 S. La Brea Ave.
213/933-0433

Dagmar
514 N. La Cienega Blvd.
310/652-1167

Blake's Antiques
665 N. La Cienega Blvd.
310/289-0970

Therien & Co.
716 N. La Cienega Blvd.
310/657-4615

Pat McGann Antiques
748 N. La Cienega Blvd.
310/358-0977

Nina Schwimmer Antiques
804 N. La Cienega Blvd.
310/657-4060

Richard Gould Antiques
808 N. La Cienega Blvd.
310/657-9416

Christianne Carty Antiques
814 N. La Cienega Blvd.
310/657-2630

Evans & Gerst Antiques
910 N. La Cienega Blvd.
310/657-0112

Smith & Houchins
921 N. La Cienega Blvd.
310/652-0308

Antique Rug Co.
928 N. La Cienega Blvd.
310/659-3847

Lifetime Arts & Crafts Gallery
7111 Melrose Ave.
213/939-7441

Denny Burt Modern Antiques
7208 Melrose Ave.
213/936-5269

Pictorial Antiques
7965 Melrose Ave.
213/951-1060

Pine Mine
7974 Melrose Ave.
213/852-1939

Burke's Country Pine Inc.
8080 Melrose Ave.
213/655-1114

Thanks for the Memories
8319 Melrose Ave.
213/852-9407

Recollections II
8377 W. Melrose Ave.
213/655-6221

French Antiques
8404 Melrose Ave.
213/653-5222

Marshall Galleries
8420 Melrose Ave.
213/852-1964

Empire Gallery
8442 Melrose Ave.
213/655-9404

French Antique Clock
8465 Melrose Ave.
213/651-3034

Charles Gill, Inc.
8475 Melrose Ave.
213/653-3434

Dassin Gallery
8687 Melrose Ave., #B131
310/652-0203

Rosh Antique Galleries
8400 Melrose Place
213/655-6969

B Nagel Antiques
8410 Melrose Place
213/655-0115

Niakin Gallery
935 N. La Cienega Blvd.
310/652-6586

Circa 1910 Antiques
7206 Melrose Ave.
213/965-1910

Off The Wall Antiques
7325 Melrose Ave.
213/930-1185

Grumps Antiques & Collectibles
7965 1/2 Melrose Ave.
213/655-3564

Napolean Antiques
8050 Melrose Ave.
213/658-7853

Hays House of Wicker
8253 Melrose Ave.
213/653-2999

Archipelago
8323 Melrose Ave.
213/653-7133

Marshall Galleries
8401 Melrose Ave.
213/852-6630

J.F. Chen Antiques
8414 Melrose Ave.
213/655-6310

Blue House
8440 Melrose Ave.
213/852-0747

CBH Antiques
8452 Melrose Ave.
213/653-3939

J P Hemmings Antiques USA
8471 Melrose Ave.
213/655-7823

Cota's Antiques
8573 Melrose Ave.
310/659-1822

Deanna Yohanna Antiques
8908 Melrose Ave.
310/550-0052

Mehran Antiques
840 Melrose Place
213/658-8444

Museum Antiques
8417 Melrose Place
310/652-3023

La Maison Francaise Antiques
8420 Melrose Place
213/653-6534

Licorne Antiques
8432 Melrose Place
213/852-4765

R. Tallow Antiques
8454 Melrose Place
213/653-2122

Connoisseur Antiques
8468 Melrose Place
213/658-8432

Charles Pollack Antiques
8478 Melrose Place
213/651-5852

Recollections I
140 S. Orlando Ave.
213/852-7123

Blagg's
2901 Rowena Ave.
213/661-9011

Camille Chez Antiques
513 N. Robertson Blvd.
310/276-2729

Gazebo Antiques
120 S. Robertson Blvd.
310/275-5650

Acquisitions
1020 S. Robertson Blvd.
310/289-0196

Paladin Antiques
7356 Santa Monica Blvd.
213/851-8222

Ramon's Antique Store
8250 Santa Monica Blvd.
213/848-2986

Antiques Plus
11914 1/2 Santa Monica Blvd.
310/826-1170

Ragtime
11715 San Vincente Blvd.
310/820-3599

Westchester Faire
8655 S Sepulveda Blvd.
310/670-4000

Stephen Hilliger Antiques
8655 S. Sepulveda Blvd.
310/670-9306

Karl the Twelfth Swedish Antiques
8428 Melrose Place
213/852-0303

Sabet Antiques
8451 Melrose Place
213/651-5222

Villa Medici
8460 Melrose Place
213/951-9172

Tent Antiques
8469 Melrose Place
213/651-1234

R.M. Barokh Antiques
8481 Melrose Place
213/655-2771

Other Times Books
10617 W. Pico Blvd.
310/475-2547

Hideaway House Antiques
143 N. Robertson Blvd.
310/276-4319

Chelsea Antiques
117 S. Robertson Blvd.
310/859-3895

Collection
315 S. Robertson Blvd.
310/205-3840

An Antique Affaire
2600 S. Robertson Blvd.
310/838-2051

Big White Elephant
7974 Santa Monica Blvd.
213/654-1928

Antique Way
11729 Santa Monica Blvd.
310/477-3972

Portabella
11715 San Vincente Blvd
310/820-3599

Family Tree
8655 S. Sepulveda Blvd.
310/641-2122

London Bridge Antiques
8655 S. Sepulveda Blvd.
310/216-7677

Rose Antiques
8655 Sepulveda Blvd.
310/641-6967

Rubbish
1627 Silver Lake Blvd.
213/661-5575

Minnette's Antiques Etcetera
2209 W. Sunset Blvd.
213/413-5595

Arts & Antiques
2211 W. Sunset Blvd.
213/413-5964

China House Funky Junk
5652 W. 3rd St.
213/935-9555

Electica
8745 W. 3rd St.
310/275-1004

High Noon
9929 Venice Blvd.
310/202-9010

Antique Guild
3225 Helms Bakery Bldg.
310/838-3131

95 LOS GATOS

Main Street Antiques
150 W. Main St.
408/395-3035

Curious Book Shoppe
23 E. Main St.
408/354-5560

Antiquarium
98 W. Main St.
408/354-7878

Main St. Antiques
150 W. Main St.
408/395-3035

96 LOS OLIVOS

Linrich Antiques & Collectibles
2879 Grand Ave.
805/686-0802

Maria Tatiana Gallery
2920 Grand Ave.
805/688-9622

97 MANHATTAN BEACH

Once Upon a Quilt
312 Manhattan Beach Blvd.
310/379-1264

Arthur Green
2201 W. Sunset Blvd.
213/413-3427

Wells
2209 Sunset Blvd.
213/413-0558

Peron Antiques & Collectibles
2213 W. Sunset Blvd.
213/413-7051

Giermo Antique Lighting
8405 W. 3rd St.
213/653-3450

Harry Studio Antiques Warehouse
8639 Venice Blvd.
310/559-7863

Joe's Antiques
3520 1/2 Washington Blvd.
213/737-4267

Maria's Antiques
112 N. Santa Cruz Ave.
408/395-5933

Patterson's Antiques
88 W. Main St.
408/354-1718

Jean Newhart Antiques
110 W. Main St.
408/354-1646

Les Poisson Antiques
25 N. Santa Cruz Ave.
408/354-7937

Haywire
2900 Grand Ave.
805/688-9911

California

98 MARIPOSA

Downtown Mariposa offers a historic glimpse of the gold rush days. Many buildings evident of the era now house antiques, art galleries and fine dining establishments. Mariposa is the home of the oldest continuously operating courthouse west of the Rocky Mountains.

Jailhouse Square Gifts/Antiques
5018 Bullion St.
209/966-3998

Correia's Antiques
5031 B Hwy. 140
209/966-5448

Anita's Antiques
Corner Hwy. 140 & 4th
209/966-2433

Fabled Kottage
5029 State Hwy., #C
209/742-7075

Chocolate Soup/Jailhouse Too
Corner 6th & Bullion
209/966-5683

Campbell's Antiques
Corner 4th & Hwy. 140
209/966-4660

Princeton Empor Antiques
4976 Mt. Bullion Cutoff
209/966-2372

Great Places to Stay

Restful Nest Bed & Breakfast Resort

4274 Buckeye Creek Road
209/742-7127
Web site: www.yosemite.net/mariposa/mhotels/restful/
Directions: From Merced (37 miles); from Hwy. 99 take I-40 East. Make a right on Yaqui Gulch Road. Go about 3^1/$_2$ miles, Yaqui Gulch turns into Buckeye Road. Follow Buckeye Road for approximately 1 mile. Make a left on Buckeye Creek Road. The Restful Nest is ^{3}/$_{10}$ mile on the right. From Fresno & Oakhurst: From Fresno, take 41 North to Oakhurst. From Oakhurst, take 49 North. Go 30 miles to Ben Hur. Make a left on Ben Hur. Follow Ben Hur to Buckeye Road. Make a right to Buckeye Creek Road. The Restful Nest is ^{3}/$_{10}$ mile on the right.

Nestled in the beautiful foothills of the Sierra Nevada mountains in the heart of California Gold Country, the Restful Nest offers an experience of olden California hospitality with the flavor of Provence.

Three tastefully appointed guest rooms promise pleasant relaxation and refreshment. Each room has a private entrance, a private bath and fresh air windows, overlooking majestic oaks and rolling hills.

The aroma of freshly baked brioche and other breads (rated tops by visitors from France and Belgium) will lure you to the country dining room where, along with these delicious breads, you will enjoy homemade sausages, luscious California fruits, country jams, preserves, juice, freshly brewed coffee and a variety of teas.

99 MARTINEZ

Antique Connection
817 Arnold Dr.
510/372-8229

Nature's Way Doll Center
917 Alhambra, Suite A
510/228-5263

Ferry Street Antiques
413 Ferry St.
510/370-9091

Olde Towne Antiques
516 Ferry St.
510/370-8345

Asilee's Victorian Antiques
608 Ferry St.
510/229-0653

Crance's Antiques
605 Main St.
510/229-2775

First Street Antiques
613 Main St.
510/228-7560

Shannon's Olde & Goodies
623 Main St.
510/372-6045

B J's Antiques & Collectibles
627 Main St.
510/228-1202

Molly's Collectibles
718 Main St.
510/370-7466

Bayol's Antiques & Collectibles
728 Main St.
510/372-3398

Family Traditions
810 Main St.
510/229-4331

Another Time
911 Alhambra Ave.
510/229-5025

Cobweb Antiques
735 Escobar St.
510-229-9038

Antique Corner
500 Ferry St.
510/372-9330

Our Shoppe
606 Ferry St.
510/228-9919

Sheila a Grilli Bookseller
610 Ferry St.
510/228-6422

Bill & Mike's Antiques
609 Main St.
510/229-3664

Lipary Sports Collectibles
617 Main St.
510/370-6032

The Military Store
625 Main St.
510/372-5897

Attic Child Antiques
653 Main St.
510/228-3072

Martinez Antiques & Collectibles
724 Main St.
510/335-0939

Plain & Fancy Antiques
802 Main St.
510/229-4288

Annie's Unique Antiques
814 Main St.
510/228-0394

100 McKINLEYVILLE

Almost All Antiques
2764 Central Ave.
707/839-0456

101 MENDOCINO

Golden Goose
45094 Main St.
707/937-4655

Primrose Lane
44770 Larkin Road
707/937-2107

Great Places to Stay

Blackberry Inn
44951 Larkin Road
707/937-5281

Blackberry Inn has adopted the theme of a western frontier town in order to tap the nostalgia of this myth. Each room is entirely different and represents a well-known establishment associated with a frontier town. There is the Sheriff, Livery Stable, General Store, Barber Shop, The Bank, and of course the town fancy house known as Belle's Place, which is truly one of the most beautiful rooms on all the Mendocino Coast. All rooms have separate, private entrances and private baths.

Joshua Grindle Inn
44800 Little Lake Road
Web site: www.joshgrin.com
1-800-474-6353

New England charm in coastal California? Situated on two acres in the historic village, this lovely home was built in 1879 by Joshua Grindle, the town banker. The rooms (all private baths) are located in the Main House, the Cypress Cottage, and the Watertower and are furnished with Early American and Shaker antiques. Each room has comfortably arranged sitting areas, and some have ocean views, others have fireplaces. A full gourmet breakfast is served. AAA Three Diamond property.

Stanford Inn by the Sea
Coast Hwy. & Comptcheukiah Road
Web site: www.stanfordinn.com
1-800-331-8884

A rustic, yet elegant, inn with beautifully landscaped grounds on ten acres with swans, llamas, horses, and organic farm. The lodge sits atop a meadow overlooking the ocean and historic Mendocino. Guest rooms are furnished with antiques and four poster beds with designer comforters. Work from local artists, plants, woodburning fireplaces, books, and plush towels enhance the persona of this special coastal retreat. Country wines are provided daily, as is the Stanford's special blend of locally roasted gourmet organic coffee for each room's drip maker. Breakfast is served in the inn's dining room featuring organic foods prepared to order.

Whitegate Inn
P.O. Box 150
Web site: www.whitegateinn.com
1-800-531-7282

The Whitegate Inn, built in 1883, lies in the heart of Mendocino. An English garden sets off the pristine white exterior. Originally the home of the town's first doctor, today it remains an elegant Victorian lady offering six professionally decorated bedchambers filled with antiques and fresh flowers. A full breakfast is served in the sunny dining room on fine china and sterling silver.

102 MENLO PARK

Millstreet Antiques
1131 Chestnut St.
415/323-9010

Mary J. Rafferty Antiques
1158 Chestnut St.
415/321-6878

Conversation Piece
889 Santa Cruz Ave.
415/327-9101

103 MIDDLETOWN

Middletown Antiques Collective
21207 Calistoga
707/987-2633

Cobb Mountain Antiques
17140 Hwy. 175
707/928-5972

Dorothy's Antiques
21304 Hwy. 175
707/987-0325

104 MILL VALLEY

Luck Would Have It
14 Locust Ave.
415/380-8625

Nellus Antiques
357 Miller Ave.
415/388-2277

Via Diva Antiques
27 Throckmorton Ave.
415/389-0911

Capricorn Antiques
100 Throckmorton Ave.
415/388-1720

Dowds Barn
157 Throckmorton Ave.
415/388-8110

105 MODESTO

Chelsea Square Antiques
305 Downey Ave.
209/578-5504

Hatch Road Antique Mall
2909 E. Hatch Road
209/538-0663

Crow Trading Company
707 I St.
209/579-2173

The March Hare
321 Downey Ave.
209/524-8336

Retro Antiques
502 Scenic Dr.
209/522-2959

Looking Back Antiques
1136 Tully Road
209/523-1443

Antique Emporium
1511 J St.
209/579-9730

Antique Emporium
1208 Ninth St.
209/527-6004

M. L. & Co.
2308 McHenry Ave.
209/491-0340

McCoy's Antiques
503 Scenic Dr.
209/549-9827

California

Austin Antiques
204 Sylvan Ave.
209/526-2509

Kay's Collectibles
530 14th St.
209/522-6562

Sarah Frances Antiques
1208 J St.
209/523-4937

106 MONROVIA

Patty's Antiques
109 W. Foothill Blvd.
818/358-0344

Kaleidoscope Antiques
306 S. Myrtle Ave.
818/303-4042

Frills
504 S. Myrtle Ave.
818/303-3201

107 MONTEREY

Alicia's Antiques
835 Cannery Row
408/372-1423

Pieces of Olde
868 Lighthouse
408/372-1521

And Another Thing
317 Downey Ave.
No phone listed

Melrose Place
1700 McHenry Ave.
209/525-8981

Sticks & Stones Collection
3338 Oakdale Road
209/551-9540

Monrovia West Antique Mall
925 W. Foothill Blvd.
818/357-5235

Through the Years
401 1/2 S. Myrtle Ave.
818/305-5259

Treasure Bay
801 Lighthouse Ave.
408/656-9303

Cannery Row Antique Mall
471 Wave St.
408/655-0264

Great Places to Stay

Victorian Inn
487 Foam St.

The Victorian Inn — Monterey's inviting hideaway. All guest rooms have marble fireplaces, honor bars and private patios, balconies or window seats. Guests can enjoy the outdoor garden hot tub, complimentary continental breakfast and afternoon wine and cheese served in the parlor. Walk to the Aquarium, Fisherman's Wharf and Cannery Row.

108 MORRO BAY

Antiques Et Cetera
1141 Main St.
805/772-2279

Wits End
257 Morro Bay Blvd.
805/772-8669

Madam & The Cowboy
333 Morro Bay Blvd.
805/772-2048

Glass Basket
245 Morro Bay Blvd.
805/772-4569

O Susanna
325 Morro Bay Blvd.
805/772-4001

Scruples Antiques
450 Morro Bay Blvd.
805/772-9207

Woody's Antiques
870 Morro Bay Blvd.
805/772-8669

109 MOSS LANDING

Then & Now
Moss Landing Road
408/633-4373

Moss Landing Antique Co.
Moss Landing Road
408/633-3988

Harbor House Antiques
7092 Moss Landing Road
408/633-8555

Moss Landing Merc Antiques
7981 Moss Landing Road
408/633-8520

Little Red Barn Antiques
8045 Moss Landing Road
408/633-5583

Waterfront Antiques
7902F Sandholdt Road
408/633-1112

110 MOUNT SHASTA

Mount Shasta Black Bear Gallery
201 N. Mount Shasta Blvd.
916/926-2334

Antiques Etc.
612 S. Mount Shasta Blvd.
916/926-2231

111 MURPHYS

D.E.A. Bathroom Machineries
495 Main St.
209/728-2031 or 1-800-255-4426

Cindi's Antiques
820 Morro Bay Blvd.
805/772-5948

Potter Palmer Antiques
Moss Landing Road
408/633-5415

Life In The Past Lane
Moss Landing Road
408/633-6100

Zyanya Collectibles
7981 Moss Landing Road, #A
408/633-4266

Up Your Alley
8011 Moss Landing Road
408/633-5188

Paul Messer Antiques
8461 Moss Landing Road
408/633-4361

Halfords Antiques
407 N. Mount Shasta Blvd.
916/926-3901

Porcelain glistens from five showrooms in the former Odd Fellows Hall. You will find antique bathroom fixtures from soap dishes to sitz baths, bathroom scales to bathroom sinks, lighting fixtures, wash basins, clawfoot tubs, drinking fountains, brass hooks to brothel tokens. Showrooms are filled with spittoons, wooden toilet tanks, steam radiators, antique mail boxes, medicine cabinets, rib-cage showers (bigger than some bathrooms), and toilets. Toilets made back when toilet making was an art. Gorgeous toilets with sculptured tanks and bowls, gracefully and flowing bulbous, some hand-painted, some with raised ornamentation.

The most decorative bowl, called "The Deluge," is the rarest of the collection. Sorry, it's not for sale. It's an original, manufactured by

California

Thomas Twyford, who worked in Victorian England for the most renowned toilet maker of them all, Thomas Crapper.

If you can't make it to the showroom, D.E.A. offers two mail order catalogues featuring their supply of the above plus much, much more in antique and reproduction fixtures and accessories. Video catalogues are also available to provide clients a better idea of their hundreds of antique products.

The company boasts a rather impressive client list: Ted Turner, Mark Harmon, Sally Jesse Raphael, Lloyd Bridges and Ralph Lauren have all purchased fixtures from D.E.A. museums. Bed and breakfasts, public and private restoration projects from all over the country have also looked to D.E.A. for their architectural needs.

The store has become quite a tourist attraction over the past 20 years. Sightseers have been known to wander into the store just for a peek at the unusual "stuff" offered there. And more unusual "stuff" is always on the way. The owner, Tom Schellar, travels across the United States looking for deals on all kinds of antiques. Anything interesting, he buys it — and in his delightful store, he'll probably sell it.

All That Glitters	Sue's Antiques
434 Main St.	466 Main St.
209/728-2700	209/728-9148

112 NAPA VALLEY

There are approximately 184 wineries dotting the picturesque countryside known as the Napa Valley. Many were established well over 100 years ago and are still operating today. Most offer samplings in the tasting rooms located in the elegant mansions once owned by the founding winemakers.

One such estate is the Beringer Vineyards. Established in 1876 by Jacob and Frederick Beringer, it is the oldest continuously operated winery in the Napa Valley. The tasting room is located in Frederick's mansion (The Rhine House) and is elegantly decorated with stained glass, carved oak wainscoting, slate roof and wood floors. The excellent guided tour of the St. Helena Winery leads you through the wine caves tunneled deep into the hillside where Beringer vintages age in oak cooperage.

California's first three-story stone gravity-flow winery, Far Niente, was completed in 1885 and the words "Far Niente" were carved into its stone face. A loose translation from the Italian phrase "In Dolce Far Niente" suggests "life without a care." The winery's operation ceased with prohibition and Far Niente lay sleeping for 60-odd years until it was purchased and renovated by the present owners.

Winemaking at Freemont Abby in St. Helena dates from the fall of 1886 when Josephine Tychson, the first woman to build a winery in California, began operating on the site. The present owners began their enterprise in 1967. The wines, Chardonny, Merlot, Cabernet Sauvignon,

Cabernet Bosche and Johannisberg Riesling, have won international acclaim. The tasting room is furnished with antiques and Oriental rugs.

It was in the stone cellar of St. Clement Vineyards' historic Rosenbaum House that the eighth Napa Valley winery was established before the turn of the century. It is in that same hundred-year-old cellar that St. Clement wines are aged today.

The Rosenbaum House, a landmark Victorian, has been meticulously restored and is now open to visitors for the first time since 1878. The parlor now serves as an intimate tasting room. The porch swing on the veranda, picnic tables on the shaded patio and the expansive gardens offer a nostalgic vantage from which to view the valley.

Established in 1890, Sutter Home has been owned since 1947 by the Trinchero family. It is renowned for its rich, robust Amador County Zinfandel and its pale pink White Zinfandel, the best-selling premium wine in America. Sutter Home also produces a full line of high-quality varietal wines sold under the Sutter Home Fre brand name.

The Sutter Home Victorian house and gardens are landmarks in Napa Valley-featuring over 800 varieties of plant life, including 100 varieties of roses, 50 different daylilies, a dazzling array of camellias, lupines, columbines, begonias, century-old palm and orange trees and an extensive herb garden. Sutter Home's Visitor's Center, housed in the original winery building, features special exhibits evoking 19th century Napa Valley, as well as complimentary tastings.

NOTE: For a complete listing of Napa Valley wineries and tour information, contact Napa Valley Visitors Bureau at 1-800-651-8953.

Antiquing in the Napa Valley

CALISTOGA

The Tin Barn Collective
At the Gliderport
1510 Lincoln Ave.
707/942-0618
Open: Daily, 10–5

Offers a distinctive array of antiques and collectibles including china and crystal, vintage lighting, art pottery, prints and paintings, silver and linens, wicker and wrought iron, jewelry, arts and crafts, country primitives, French antiques, Orientalia, art deco and a new garden center.

NAPA

Antiques Etc.
3043 California Blvd. off Trancas
707/255-4545
"The Estate Shop" Open: Tues.–Sat. 11–5 or by appointment

Thousands of collectibles, memorabilia, paintings, textiles, musical instruments, Indian baskets, rugs, art glass, cut glass, dolls, furniture, lamps, clocks, jewelry, pottery and more in a warehouse setting. Appraisal service.

Gullwigg & Thacker Antiques
1988A Wise Dr.
707/252-7038
Open: Daily 10–5

Not a "My grandmother had one of those" shop (unless, of course, she was 200 years old). Decidedly different. Varied in content. Compassionately priced, 17th, 18th, 19th, 20th century antiques.

The Irish Pedlar
1988A Wise Dr.
707/253-9091
Open: Daily 10–5

Offers an extensive selection of one-of-a-kind, old country pine and a large variety of accessories to accent the pine—linens, quimper, French wine related items, decoys.

Napa Coin Gallery
3053 Jefferson (Sam's Plaza)
707/255-7225
Open: Tues.–Fri., 11–5, Sat. 11–4, closed Sun. and Mon.

"The One Stop Shop" for gold and silver coins and all supplies. Estate jewelry as well as coin jewelry items. Small antiques. Old postcards and other interesting historical items.

Red Hen Antiques
5091 St. Helena Hwy.
707/257-0822
Open: Daily 10–5

Situated in the vineyards on Hwy. 20 between Napa and Yountville, Red Hen Antiques houses more than 65 quality antique dealers. It features an extensive array of well-displayed collectibles, antiques and gifts. A landmark antique showplace.

Riverfront Antique Center
805 Soscol Ave. below 3rd St.
707/253-1966
Open: Daily 10–5:30

75-plus dealers, 24,000 square feet. Napa's newest multidealer antiques mall offers a large selection of unique and affordable antiques and collectibles.

ST. HELENA

Elrod's Antiques
3000 St. Helena Hwy.
707/963-1901
Open: Daily 11–5

European Country Antiques
1148 Main St.
707/963-4666
Open: Mon.–Sat. 10–5, Sun. 12–4

Specializes in German pine wood antiques.

St. Helena, St. Helena Antiques
1231 Main St.
707/963-5878
Open: Daily 11–5 and by appointment

Rare and unusual antiques, antiquities and collectibles. Tools, rugs, corkscrews, quilts, primitives, garden appointments, ethnic objects, masks, furniture, clocks, china, decanters, guns, paintings. Buy and sell.

YOUNTVILLE

Antique Fair
6412 Washington St.
707/944-8440
Open: Daily 10–5
Web site: www.antiquefair.com

An impressive selection of French furniture and accessories.

Bed & Breakfasts in the Napa Valley

ANGWIN

Forest Manor
415 Cold Springs Road
707/965-3538 or 1-800-788-0364

Secluded 20-acre English Tudor estate tucked among forest and vineyards above St. Helena. Described as "one of the most romantic country inns . . . a small exclusive resort," the three-story Manor features high vaulted ceilings, massive hand-carved beams, fireplaces, verandas. The romantic honeymoon suite has a fireplace and a private jacuzzi for two.

CALISTOGA

Brannan Cottage Inn
109 Wapoo Ave.
707/942-4200

Delightful gardens surround this quiet 6-room gingerbread Victorian, winner of the 1985 Napa Landmarks Award for historic preservation in Napa County. Known for its original wild flower stencils, the Inn offers a sunny courtyard & parlor with fireplace. Listed on the National Register of Historic Places, this is the only guest house left on its original site built for the "Calistoga Hot Springs Resort" in 1860.

Calistoga Country Lodge
2883 Foothill Blvd.
707/942-5555

Secluded lodge in the western foothills of Calistoga. Beautifully decorated with American antiques, bleached pine, lodgepole furniture and Indian artifacts.

Calistoga Inn/Napa Valley Brewing Co.
1250 Lincoln Ave.
707/942-4101

A landmark building built at the turn of the century, the Calistoga Inn is located on the main street of town. The Inn features a fine restaurant, an outdoor patio-grill and beer wine garden, and an in-house pub brewery where Calistoga Lager is brewed and served fresh.

Calistoga Wayside Inn
1523 Foothill Blvd.
707/942-0645

A 1920s Spanish style home situated in a secluded park-like setting on half acre with decorative gardens. Relax in the hammock.

Calistoga Wishing Well Inn
2653 Foothill Blvd. (Hwy. 128)
707/942-5534

A three-story farmhouse, situated among vineyards on four acres with a breathtaking mountain view.

Christopher's Inn
1010 Foothill Blvd.
707/942-5755

Original 1930s cottages have been transformed into intimate rooms, interiors by Laura Ashley and antique furnishings, many with fireplaces. Some rooms have patio gardens.

Culver's, a Country Inn
1805 Foothill Blvd.
707/942-4535

This completely restored country Victorian home, circa 1875, is a registered historical landmark. Each of the bedrooms has period furniture, including a uniquely designed quilt. Living room with fireplace, porch with view of Mount St. Helena.

The Elms
1300 Cedar St.
707/942-9476 or 1-800-235-4316

A three-story French Victorian built in 1871 and on the National Register of Historic Places, The Elms offers charm and elegance within walking distance of Calistoga. Located on a quiet street next to a park, it has antique-filled rooms with fireplaces, feather beds, down comforters, and bathrobes.

Falcons Nest
471 Kortum Canyon Road
707/942-0758

A secluded hilltop estate nestled on 7 acres. Panoramic views overlooking the Napa Valley. Just minutes to the wineries and spas. All rooms have Country French decor with queen beds, and you can enjoy the spa under the stars. Breakfast is served on the balcony.

California

Fanny's

1206 Spring St.
1-888-942-9491

Built in 1915 as a comfortable family home, Fanny's has now been renovated and named for Robert Louis Stevenson's bride. The exterior of the house has a full length porch ready with rocking chairs and a swing. Inside, bedrooms feature plank floors, feather comforters and window seats that will take you back to grandma's attic. The living room and dining room are rich with charm. An old fireplace, numerous soft quilts, sofas and an array of nooks and crannies are perfect for hiding away or meeting new people.

Foothill House

3037 Foothill Blvd.
707/942-6933 or 1-800-942-6933

Nestled among the western foothills just north of Calistoga, the Foothill House began as a simple farmhouse at the turn of the century. The cozy yet spacious rooms are individually decorated with country antiques, and a queen or king four poster bed. Gourmet breakfast, complimentary wine; hors d'oeuvres served in the evening.

Hill Crest B&B

3225 Lake County Hwy.
707/942-6334

Located near the base of Mt. St. Helena, this rambling country home is filled with cherished family heirlooms. Antique silver, china, oriental rugs, books and other furnishings are the legacy of the Tubbs and Reid families. There's a small lake for fishing, and you may hike on 36 hilly acres, take a dip in the pool or relax in the sun and take in the breathtaking view.

Meadowlark Country House

601 Petrified Forest Road
707/942-5651

Built in 1886 and situated on 20 forested acres, this two-story country home has been remodeled for modern comfort and retains its relaxed country atmosphere. Each room has queen bed and view of forest, gardens or meadows. California breakfast included.

The Pink Mansion

1415 Foothill Blvd.
707/942-0558

Painted pink in the 1930s by Aunt Alma, this 120-year-old Calistoga landmark offers a combination of Victorian elegance and modern luxury.

The formal living room with fireplace, as well as the dining room and game room, are for guests' use. Each room has a postcard view of the hills and local landmarks, and downtown Calistoga is within walking distance. Full gourmet breakfast. Three acres of landscaped gardens and wooded escapes. For those who enjoy a late night swim, the indoor heated pool and jacuzzi are a must.

Quail Mountain Bed & Breakfast

4455 North St. Helena Hwy.
707/942-0316

A secluded, luxury romantic estate located on 26 acres, 300 ft. above Napa Valley on a heavily forested mountain range with a vineyard and orchard on the property. Full breakfast is served in the sunny solarium common room or formal dining room in winter months.

Scarlett's Country Inn

3918 Silverado Trail
707/942-6669

Three exquisitely appointed suites set in the quiet mood of green lawns and tall pines overlooking the vineyards. Breakfast under the apple trees or in your own sitting room. Close to wineries and spas.

Scott Courtyard

1443 2nd St.
707/942-0948

Just two blocks from downtown Calistoga, Scott Courtyard resembles a Mediterranean villa with latticed courtyard and private gardens. The large social room has been described as "tropical Art Deco" with a bistro kitchen where a full breakfast is served pool side.

Silver Rose Inn

351 Rosedale Road
707/942-9581

Located near the end of picturesque Silverado Trail at Rosedale Road, high on a rocky outcropping and surrounded by centuries-old live oak trees, this lovely retreat has a panoramic view of the upper Napa Valley with its spreading vineyards and the towering Palisade mountains. All nine tastefully decorated guest rooms have private baths and some have balconies, fireplaces and whirlpool tubs. The Silver Rose has recently added a new hot springs spa. For the exclusive use of guests staying at the inn, the new spa includes mud, seaweed, herbal baths, hydro massage, facials and massage services.

Stephen's Wine Way Inn
1019 Foothill Blvd.
707/942-0680 or 1-800-572-0679

A restored 1915 home where the atmosphere is casual and the innkeepers are like old friends. You can enjoy a glass of wine on the spectacular multi-level deck or by the fire in the parlor. Enjoy a full gourmet breakfast from an ever-growing collection of recipes. Each room is individually decorated in antiques and quilts. A cottage offers privacy for those who prefer it.

Trailside Inn
4201 Silverado Trail
707/942-4106

This charming 1930 farmhouse in the country has three suites, each with private entrance, porch-deck, bedroom, kitchen, bath and living room with fireplace. Complimentary wine, mineral water, fresh baked bread and breakfast fixings provided.

Triple S Ranch
4600 Mt. Home Ranch Road
707/942-6730

Rustic cabins and a homey atmosphere make this mountain hideaway a pleasant place to relax and unwind. There's a swimming pool, restaurant and cocktail lounge and many scenic mountain trails to hike. Nearby are the Old Faithful Geyser of California and the Petrified Forest.

Zinfandel House
1253 Summit Dr.
707/942-0733

A private home located in a wooded setting above the valley floor between St. Helena and Calistoga. The 1,000-square-foot deck offers a spectacular view of the valley. Two tastefully decorated rooms. Wine is offered and a lovely breakfast is served in the morning.

NAPA

Arbor Guest House
1436 G St.
707/252-8144

This 1906 Colonial transition home and carriage house have been completely restored for the comfort of guests. Rooms are beautifully appointed with antiques. Two rooms have spa tubs. For guests seeking privacy and seclusion, the carriage house bed/sitting rooms, both with fireplaces, are most fitting. A charming garden motif is featured throughout the Inn, with the wallpaper, window coverings and the medley of period furniture in brass, iron, oak, mahogany, wicker and carved and beveled glass.

Beazley House
1910 First St.
1-800-559-1649

Napa's first bed and breakfast is located in central Napa in a fine old neighborhood. The shingle style/colonial revival mansion of over 4,400 square feet was built in 1902. It has six guest rooms, all with private baths. Behind the mansion the carriage house has been reproduced and has five rooms, all with private baths, fireplaces and private, two-person spas. A full breakfast of home-baked muffins, fresh fruit and crustless cheese quiche is served in the mansion's formal dining room. In the spacious living room, complimentary tea is available to guests each afternoon.

The Blue Violet Mansion
443 Brown St.
707/253-BLUE

A large, elegant 1886 Queen Anne Victorian, the mansion was built for Emanuel Manasse, an executive at the Sawyer Tannery. Lovingly restored, and winner of the 1993 Landmarks Award of Merit for historical restoration. Located in the historic district of Old Town Napa, it is within walking distance of downtown shops and restaurants. The home now offers large, cheerful rooms with queen or king beds, fireplaces, balconies, spas and private baths. Outside is a garden gazebo with a swing, a shaded deck and rose garden. Full country breakfast and afternoon and evening refreshments are included.

Brookside Vineyard
3194 Redwood Road
707/944-1661

This gracious country bed and breakfast is also a picturesque working vineyard. A tree-shaded lane leads you to the serene creek setting of this comfortable California mission-style inn. The three spacious guest rooms each have adjoining baths, and are tastefully furnished with antiques and collectibles. One room has a private patio, fireplace and sauna. Guests enjoy complimentary afternoon wine on the deck with a glorious view, or in the living room next to the fireplace. After dinner cordials are available in the cozy library. A full breakfast is served in the gazebo overlooking a stand of Douglas fir and the natural beauty of a creek lined with oak and bay trees.

The Candlelight Inn
1045 Easum Dr.
707/257-3717

This English Tudor, built in 1929 on one park-like acre in the city of Napa, has nine romantic rooms, one with its own sauna. The elegant living room features high contoured ceilings and a fireplace, and the innkeepers serve an exquisite breakfast and provide an afternoon social hour in the dining room, where the view through the French doors into the garden will delight you.

Cedar Gables Inn
486 Coombs St.
707/224-7969

Built in 1892, Cedar Gables is styled after 16th Century English Country homes. Six beautifully appointed guest rooms are furnished with antiques — some have whirlpool tubs and fireplaces. All have private baths. Each evening, innkeepers Margaret and Craig Snasdell welcome you with a spread of fruit, cheeses and wine. A bountiful breakfast is served in the cheerful sunroom.

Churchill Manor
485 Brown St.
707/253-7733

An 1889 National Landmark, Churchill Manor is the largest home of its time in the Napa Valley. The mansion rests amid lush grounds and is surrounded by an expansive veranda with 22 gleaming white columns. Entering through leaded-glass doors, guests are surrounded by magnificent woodwork, fixtures, and antique furnishings. While lavish in appointments, Churchill Manor is also warm and inviting. Guests enjoy afternoon fresh-baked cookies and refreshments, and a two-hour wine and cheese reception in the evening, and gourmet breakfast in the marble-tiled solarium.

Country Garden Inn
1815 Silverado Trail
707/255-1197

Situated on 1 1/2 acres of mature woodland riverside property, the inn was built in the 1850s as a coach house on the Silverado Trail. The building is surrounded by trees and flowers, brick and stone pathways, a garden terrace, and there's a circular rose garden with a lily pond, fountain and large aviary. Each spacious room is furnished with antiques. Several have private jacuzzis and fireplaces. Full breakfast, afternoon tea and evening hors d'oeuvres are included.

Cross Roads Inn
6380 Silverado Trail
707/944-0646

Offering unparalleled views and complete privacy from its 20-acre vantage point high in the eastern hills of the Napa Valley, Crossroads Inn has spacious, individually decorated suites with wine bars and jacuzzi spas. Breakfast can be served in your suite or on your private deck. Afternoon tea, wine and cocktails are served around the native stone fireplace, and brandies are offered before retiring.

The Hennessey House
1727 Main St.
707/226-3774

This Eastlake-style Queen Anne Victorian was once the residence and office of Dr. Edward Zack Hennessey, an early, prominent Napa County physician. The house is now listed on the Register of Historic Places. Rooms have private baths, and some have canopy or feather beds, fireplaces and whirlpool tubs. The house is furnished with English or Belgian antiques, and the dining room features a hand painted, stamped ceiling.

Hillview Country Inn
1205 Hillview Lane
707/224-5004

Enjoy the country life at Hillview Country Inn, a spectacular 100-year-old estate where you can stroll the beautifully manicured grounds amid fruit trees, herb garden, lavish lawns and the Old English Rose Garden. In the inn's gracious parlor, you can start your morning with a sumptuous country breakfast. Each guest suite is distinctly decorated, and includes a fruit and wine basket upon arrival and a sweeping view of the Napa Valley.

Inn on Randolph
411 Randolph St.
707/257-2886

A showcase for area artists, every room in this restored 1860 Gothic Revival has been embellished with original designs — from handpainted murals and faux finishes to a distinctive willow canopy bed. Each generously proportioned guest room offers a sitting area, private bath and robes. Some feature a double or deep soaking whirlpool tub, gas fireplace or private deck. Comfortable sitting areas have marble fireplaces. The one-half acre of landscaped grounds provides a sundeck, gazebo and hammock.

California

La Belle Epoque
1386 Calistoga Ave.
707/257-2161

A Queen Anne Majesty built in 1893, with its multi-gabled dormers and high-hipped roof, La Belle Epoque is one of the finest examples of Victorian architecture in the wine country. Decorative flat and molded carvings can be seen in the gables and bays, and the original stained glass windows remain in the transoms and semi-circular windows. Guest rooms are decorated with fine period furniture, and several have fireplaces. Generous gourmet breakfast. Complimentary wine and hors d'oeuvres served in wine tasting room.

La Residence
4066 St. Helena Hwy.
707/253-0337

A French barn and 1870 mansion in its own 2-acre park-like setting, beautifully restored and furnished. The spacious rooms and suites have private baths, fireplaces, French doors, verandas or patios, and are luxuriously appointed. A spa and heated pool are framed by heritage oaks and towering pines. Full breakfast in sun-filled dining room with classical piano and fireplace included, as are sunset wine and hors d'oeuvres.

The Napa Inn
1137 Warren
707/257-1444 or 1-800-435-1144

A three-story Queen Anne Victorian located on a quiet tree-lined street in a historic section of the town of Napa, the inn is furnished with turn-of-the-century antiques in each of the six guest rooms, parlor and formal dining room.

Oak Knoll Inn
2200 E. Oak Knoll Ave.
707/255-2200

A romantic, elegant, all-stone French country inn secluded within an expansive vineyard preserve. Features pool and hot tub and rooms with Italian marble fireplaces, private baths, vaulted ceilings, king-size brass beds and separate French door entrances, providing views of Stag's Leap Palisades and the surrounding oak-studded hillsides. A full breakfast in the morning, and wine and hors d'oeuvres in the evening are served on the deck overlooking the vineyards, or in front of the fireplace in the dining room.

The Old World Inn
1301 Jefferson
707/257-0112

A unique and memorable Victorian, decorated in the bright Scandinavian colors of artist Carl Larsson. Afternoon tea and cookies, nightly hors d'oeuvres, and an evening gourmet dessert buffet are offered.

Stahlecker House Bed & Breakfast, Country Inn & Garden
1042 Easum Dr.
707/257-1588

A secluded, quiet country inn, Stahlecker House is located just minutes from the wineries. Canopy beds, antique furnishings and a comfortable gathering room with fireplace, contribute to a relaxed, homey atmosphere. A quiet, restful deck overlooks lawns, gardens and shade trees. Complimentary lemonade, coffee, tea and cookies.

Trubody Ranch
5444 St. Helena Hwy.
707/255-5907

Built in 1872, Trubody Ranch is a Gothic Revival Victorian home with water tower. Surrounded by 120 acres of family-owned vineyard land, the ranch is located in the center of Napa Valley. Rooms are furnished in family antiques of the period. Guests enjoy garden and vineyard strolls. There are views from both rooms. Breakfast is freshly baked breads, home-grown fruit in season, fruit juice, tea and coffee.

ST. HELENA

The Ambrose Bierce House
1515 Main St.
707/963-3003

Ambrose Bierce, famous witty author of *The Devil's Dictionary* and many short stories, lived in this house on the main street of St. Helena until 1913, when he mysteriously vanished into Mexico. His former residence, now a luxurious bed and breakfast inn, was built in 1872. Like Bierce himself, the inn is an intriguing blend of ingredients—luxury, history and hospitality. Bedroom suites are furnished with antiques, including comfortable queen-sized brass beds and armoires. Bathrooms have brass fittings, clawfoot tubs and showers. Suites are named for the historical figures whose presence touched Bierce and the Napa Valley in the late 1800s: Ambrose Bierce himself; Lillie Langtry, the era's most scandalous woman; Edward Muybridge, acclaimed "father of the motion picture," and Lillie Hitchcock Coit, the legendary "Belle of San Francisco." Complimentary gourmet breakfast of coffee, juice, fruits and pastries.

California

Asplund Conn Valley Inn
726 Rossi Road
707/963-4614

Nestled in lush garden surroundings with views of the vineyards and rolling hills, the inn is truly in the country, yet just five minutes away from Main Street, St. Helena. Antique furnishings, garden views, library and fireplace. Complimentary fruit, cheese and wine and a full breakfast. Country roads for strolling. Fishing nearby.

Bartels Ranch and Country Inn
1200 Conn Valley Road
707/963-4001

Peaceful, romantic, 60-acre country estate with 10,000 acre views amid vineyards! Award-winning "3 star" accommodations feature 3 guest rooms and one champagne suite with spa, sauna, and fireplace. Private baths include robes. Full breakfast served til noon in choice view settings. Unique entertainment room offers fireside billiards, chess, piano and library. Evening social hour, dessert, tea, coffee & cookies served 24 hrs.

Bylund House Bed & Breakfast Inn
2000 Howell Mtn. Road
707/963-9073

Secluded country estate in the tradition of the Northern Italian Villa just minutes from downtown St. Helena. Two very private rooms with private baths, balconies and custom appointments. Complimentary wine, hors d'oeuvres and lavish continental breakfast.

Chestelson House
1417 Kearney St.
707/963-2238

Victorian home in a quiet residential neighborhood away from the busy highways. Gracious hospitality, delicious full breakfast and afternoon social hour. View of the mountains from the wide veranda.

The Cinnamon Bear
1407 Kearney St.
707/963-4653

This charming bed & breakfast home is just a 2-block walk to St. Helena's Main St. shops and restaurants. Antiques, quilts and teddy bears fill the rooms. Afternoon refreshments and dessert in the evening are followed by a full gourmet breakfast. Read by the fireplace or relax on the spacious porch of this quaint place to stay.

Creekside Inn
945 Main St.
707/963-7244

Located in the heart of St. Helena, yet sheltered from the hustle and bustle of town by ancient oaks and by the murmurs of White Sulphur Creek rippling past its secluded rear garden patio, Creekside offers three guest rooms furnished in a Country French theme. There's a fireplace in the common room, and a full breakfast is served in the sunroom or on the creekside patio.

Deer Run
3995 Spring Mtn. Road
707/963-3794

A truly secluded, peaceful mountain, four-acre retreat, Deer Run is nestled in the forest on Spring Mountain above the valley vineyards, affording the quiet serenity of a private hideaway. All units have fireplaces and antique furnishings. And there's a heated swimming pool. A full breakfast is served in the dining area.

Erika's Hillside
285 Fawn Park
707/963-2887

This hillside chalet, just two miles from St. Helena, has a peaceful, wooded country setting and a view of vineyards and wineries. The grounds are nicely landscaped. The rooms are spacious, bright and airy with private entrances and bath, fireplace and hot tub. Continental breakfast is served in the solarium. The structure has been remodeled and personally decorated by German-born innkeeper, Erika Cunningham.

Glass Mountain Inn
3100 Silverado Trail
707/963-3512

In the midst of the Napa Valley's vineyards, yet snuggled among century-old redwoods, pines and oaks, proudly stands the majestic Victorian Glass Mountain Inn. Towers, turrets and stained glass enhance the inn, where amenities include hand carved oak fireplaces, whirlpool and Roman soaking tubs. A full breakfast is served in a stone dining room viewing a candlelit wine cave built in the 1800s.

Harvest Inn
1 Main St.
707/963-9463

This elegant AAA Four Diamond English Tudor-style inn has spacious and secure cottages furnished with original antiques. Many cottages also

include elaborate brick fireplaces, wet bars and vineyard views. Deluxe spa suites are available. 24-hour pool and Jacuzzi, wine bar and conference rooms with cobblestone fireplaces and stained glass windows are available.

Hilltop House
9550 St. Helena Road
707/963-8743

Just minutes from St. Helena, Hilltop House is a peaceful mountain hideaway on 135 acres of unspoiled wilderness on the Napa County line, which offers a hang glider's view of the historic Mayacama Mountains.

Hotel St. Helena
1309 Main St.
707/963-4388

Victorian hotel located on St. Helena's Main Street. Offers richly furnished antique-filled rooms with private or shared baths. The hotel is within walking distance of St. Helena's many fine restaurants and wineries.

Ink House
1575 St. Helena Hwy.
707/963-3890

A traditional Italianate Victorian built by Theron H. Ink in 1884. This historic valley home offers four charming guest bedrooms complete with era furnishings with private baths. In the parlor, guests are invited to read or play the antique pump organ. a glass-walled observatory features a 360-degree view of the vineyards.

Judy's Ranch House
701 Rossi Road
707/963-3081

At Judy's country-style bed and breakfast, surrounded by a 3-acre Merlot vineyard, you can enjoy the oak trees and seasonal creek that run through the seven acres, or take a walk down a peaceful country road.

La Fleur B&B
1475 Inglewood Ave.
707/963-0233

This Victorian, nestled among the vineyards, features three beautifully appointed rooms, all with fireplaces and private baths. A deluxe full breakfast is served in the solarium overlooking the surrounding vineyards. A private tour of Villa Helena Winery comes with your stay.

Oliver House Bed & Breakfast
2970 Silverado Trail
707/963-4089

A Swiss chalet nestled in the hills with a panoramic view of the Napa Valley. There are four bedrooms with antiques; one has a 115-year-old brass bed. Another bedroom has its own private fireplace. The focal point of the cozy living room parlor is a large stone fireplace. Breakfast of muffins, fruit and pastries is served. Visitors are welcome to stroll around the lovely grounds of the four-acre estate.

Rustridge Ranch
2910 Lower Chiles Valley Road
707/965-9353

A family-owned and operated estate where grapes and horses grow together, Rustridge Ranch and Winery is seven miles east of the Silverado Trail in the picturesque rolling hills of the Chiles Valley. Thoroughbred racehorses graze among the oak trees and along the hillsides, while vineyards envelop the valley. The rambling Southwestern ranch-style house has been remodeled and converted into a gracious, contemporary Bed and Breakfast Inn.

Shady Oaks Country Inn
399 Zinfandel Lane
707/963-1190

Old-fashioned elegance and warm hospitality welcome you to this country inn. Secluded and romantic on 2 acres and nestled in the vineyards among some of the finest wineries and restaurants in the Napa Valley. The guest rooms and their country comforts are housed in a 1920s home and a winery built in the 1800s. The rooms are furnished with antiques, fine linens and private baths. A full champagne gourmet breakfast is served fireside, in bed or on the garden veranda. Wine and cheese are served each evening.

Spanish Villa Inn
474 Glass Mountain Road
707/963-7483

Nestled in a wooded valley on Glass Mountain Road, the villa is a short scenic drive from St. Helena and Calistoga. Each room includes a king-size bed, private bath and Tiffany lamps. Breakfast is served in the galleria. Neatly manicured grounds with ancient oak trees, palms and flower gardens surround the villa.

California

Sutter Home Winery B&B
277 S. St. Helena Hwy.
707/963-3104

Situated on the beautifully landscaped grounds of this historic old winery, Sutter Home's guest rooms offer Victorian elegance and a central location convenient for fine dining, shopping and relaxed wine country touring. Accommodations include antique furnishings, fireplaces, as well as an expanded continental breakfast featuring freshly baked goods, fruit juices, cereals and coffee.

Vigne Del Uomo Felice
1871 Cabernet Lane
707/963-2376

Situated on the west side of Napa Valley surrounded by the peace and quiet of the vineyards, Vigne del Uomo Felice is, appropriately translated, Ranch of the Happy Man. The completely furnished stone cottage with bedroom, bath and studio offers guests the opportunity to shed their cares.

Villa St. Helena
2727 Sulphur Springs Ave.
707/963-2514

A grand Mediterranean-style villa located in the hills above St. Helena. This secluded 20-acre wooded estate combines quiet country elegance with panoramic views of beautiful Napa Valley. Built in 1941 to accommodate elaborate entertaining with its spacious courtyard and view-filled walking trails, the Villa has a comfortable interior featuring period-style furniture.

White Sulphur Springs Resort
3100 White Sulphur Springs Road
707/963-8588

California's first resort, established 1852, White Sulphur Springs has two small inns and nine cottages, outdoor sulphur soaking pool, massage, mud wraps and jacuzzi, and hiking trails. It is a rustic old-world retreat with 330 acres of redwood, fir and madrone forests — secluded, yet only 3 miles from St. Helena.

Wine Country Inn
1152 Lodi Lane
707/963-7077

Perched on a knoll overlooking manicured vineyards and nearby hills, this country inn offers 24 individually decorated guest rooms. The Smiths used local antiques and family-made quilts to create an atmosphere of warmth and comfort. Fireplaces and balconies add charm.

Wine Country Victorian and Cottages
707/963-0852

This classic Victorian beauty is situated amid majestic oaks, elms and pines. In the adjoining gardens the estate also offers WINE COUNTRY COTTAGE, originally guest quarters for the main residence, now a cozy self-contained unit. You'll find "country quiet" here, as well as many delightful surprises in Napa Valley's oldest Bed & Breakfast.

Zinfandel Inn
800 Zinfandel Lane
707/963-3512

Burgundy House
6711 Washington
707/944-0889

A stone two-story brandy distillery built in 1891 of local fieldstone and river rock now houses the country inn. Five comfortable and cozy rooms, each with private bath, welcome you, as does a decanter of local wine. Antique country furniture and period furnishings complement the rugged masonry. A full breakfast is served in the "distillery."

Maison Fleurie
6529 Yount St.
707/944-2056 or 1-800-788-0369

The Maison Fleurie, Four Sisters Inns newest inn, is a luxurious haven of French country romance. Two-foot-thick brick walls, terra cotta tile and paned windows are reminiscent of a farmhouse in Provence. The inn has 13 beautifully decorated guest rooms, a swimming pool and outdoor spa, spacious landscaped grounds and a cozy dining room serving a gourmet breakfast to each guest. Wine tastings, dinner reservations, balloon rides, spa services and sightseeing itineraries are carefully planned by the inn's attentive staff. In the afternoon, wine and hors d'oeuvres are served, as well as cookies, fruit and beverages throughout the day.

Napa Valley Railway Inn
6503 Washington St.
707/944-2000

Rekindling the nostalgia evoked by names like Burlington Route, Great Northern RR and Southern Pacific, the inn consists of nine turn-of-the-century railroad cars — three cozy cabooses and six spacious railcars restored to their original glory. Interiors are furnished to suggest the opulence of the era, with the added comfort of contemporary amenities. Each suite has a brass bed, sitting room with a loveseat for relaxing, and a full bath. Adjacent to Vintage 1870, Yountville, with its restaurants, shops and galleries.

California

Oleander House
7433 St. Helena Hwy.
707/944-8315

Comfortable, elegant, sun-drenched and carefree, this Country French two-story B&B combines old-world design with modern amenities. Guests enjoy spacious rooms with queen-size beds, high ceilings, private bath, balcony, fireplace, antiques and Laura Ashley decor. Landscaped patio garden. A full gourmet breakfast is served. Knowledgeable innkeepers assist with advice on the valley's best attractions. Within walking distance of Mustards Restaurant.

Vintage Inn, Napa Valley
6541 Washington St.
707/944-1112

Created by California artist Kip Stewart, the inn features spacious, exquisitely appointed guest rooms, each with wood-burning fireplace, refrigerator, whirlpool bath spa, in-room brewed coffee and terry robes. An elaborate California champagne breakfast is included, along with afternoon tea and nightly turn-down service. Recipient of AAA's prestigious Four Diamond Award. Walk to Vintage 1870 and many fine restaurants.

The Webber Place
6610 Webber St.
707/944-8384

Surrounded by a white picket fence, the Webber Place is a red farmhouse built in 1850. It is now a homey and affordable bed and breakfast inn decorated in Americana Folk Art style. Artist Diane Bartholomew bought the place seven years ago, and she has her studio next door. On sunny afternoons she serves sun tea and cookies on the front porch, and in the morning the farmhouse kitchen smells of coffee, biscuits and bacon as she sets to work making a real country breakfast. Guest rooms have ornate iron and brass beds covered with antique quilts. Two rooms share a deep old-fashioned tub with brass fixtures, and the other two rooms have tub alcoves right in the room. The Veranda suite is much larger, with a hammock on its own sheltered veranda and entrance.

Great Places to Eat

Spring Street
1245 Spring St. — St. Helena
707/963-5578

This bungalow-turned-restaurant on Spring Street, St. Helena, was the home for nearly 50 years of opera singer Walter Martina and his wife, Dionisia, who moved to St. Helena in 1915 to manage the popular William Tell Hotel. The Martinas loved to entertain. Their guests gathered for gourmet cooking, fine wine and music in the lush adjoining garden with its vine-covered trellis beside the oval fountain. Spring Street Restaurant carries on the tradition of good food and wines, serving Saturday and Sunday brunch that features fresh baked biscuits, sweet rolls, muffins, special omelettes and homemade preserves; weekday lunches featuring special sandwiches, salads and homemade desserts, and delicious, American fare dinners daily. Everything is available for takeout and may be ordered ahead by calling the restaurant.

Trilogy
1234 Main St.
707/963-5507

You enter this small, intimate restaurant through an iron gate and a courtyard off St. Helena's Hunt Street and find yourself in a quiet dining room with gracious furniture, elegant chandeliers, flowers on cloth-covered tables and classical stereo music. The California French cuisine of chef Diane Pariseau is delicious to the palate and delightful to the eye. Trilogy's wine list is exciting and cosmopolitan and goes far beyond the choices you find in many larger wine country restaurants. Local produce and fresh fish and poultry, never frozen, are featured and the sauces — French — are prepared in the restaurant's own kitchen. People watchers will enjoy watching the passing parade on St. Helena's quaint Main Street from the dining room, and those who enjoy outdoor dining will find the courtyard a pleasant place in fair weather.

Triple S Ranch
4600 Mt. Home Ranch Road — North of Calistoga
707/942-6730

A ranch and restaurant operated by the Schellenger family for more than 30 years. Triple S Ranch serves up nostalgia along with mouth-watering meals. Perched high in the Sonoma Mountains near Petrified Forest, The Triple S Restaurant was converted from the ranch's original redwood barn built more than a century ago. Thick homemade soup or large salads with plenty of French bread accompany each dinner, and there's a choice of delicious country specialties. The portions are generous. Onion rings at Triple S are legendary, and the ranch has become famous for them. They also have french fried frog legs! After dinner, you might enjoy a game of bocci ball or horseshoes.

113 NEVADA CITY

Nevada City Warehouse
75 Bost Ave.
916/265-6000

Assay Office Antiques
130 Main St.
916/265-8126

La Cache
218 Broad St.
916/265-8104

Shaws' Antiques
210 Main St.
916/265-2668

California

Main Street Antique Shop
214 1/2 Main St.
916/265-3108

Tinnery
205 York St.
916/265-0599

2nd Time Around
548 Searls Ave.
916/265-8844

Great Places to Stay

Emma Nevada House
528 E. Broad St.
1-800-916-EMMA

Nineteenth Century Opera Star Emma Nevada would be proud of the inn bearing her name. This completely restored and decorated 1856 Victorian sparkles like a jewel from an abundance of original, water-float glass windows, one of many marvelous architectural details. The six guest rooms are a mix of grand, high-ceilings, and cozy intimate settings, all with private baths (some jacuzzi tubs), queen beds, and fluffy down comforters.

Flume's End Bed and Breakfast Inn
317 S. Pine St.
1-800-991-8118

The Gold Country's most unique bed and breakfast, Flume's End rests on a picturesque hillside sloping down to the natural waterfalls of a famous creek meandering through three wooded acres of natural beauty. In the 1800s the historic flume beside the inn brought Sierra Mountain gold miners "waters of good fortune." The ambiance you will experience at Flume's End will make your visit equally bountiful.

114 NEWPORT BEACH

Vallejo Gallery
1610 W. Coast Hwy.
714/642-7945

Antiques 4 U
312 N. Newport Blvd.
714/548-4123

A Secret Affair
3441 Via Lido, Suites A & B
714/673-3717

Jeffries Ltd.
852 Production Place
714/642-4154

Jane's Antiques
2811 Lafayette Road
714/673-5688

Old Newport Antiques
477 N. Newport Blvd.
714/548-8713

Grandma's Cottage
400 Westminster Ave.
714/645-9258

115 NOVATO

Consignment Shop
818 Grant Ave.
415/892-3496

Now & Then
902 Grant Ave.
415/892-0640

Black Pt. Antiques Collectibles & Gifts
35 Harbor Dr.
415/892-5100

116 OAKDALE

Past & Present Antiques
219 E. F St.
209/847-1228

Two Gals Trading Post
1725 E. F St.
209/847-3350

Twice Treasured
231 E. F St.
209/848-2750

Peddler's Attic
223 S. Sierra Ave.
209/847-4710

117 OAKHURST

Good Oldaze
Hwy. 41 & 426
209/683-6161

Collectors Mall
40982 N. State Hwy. 41
209/683-5006

Oakhurst Frameworks
49027 Road 426
209/683-7845

118 OAKLAND

Tim's Antiques & Collectibles
5371 Bancroft Ave.
510/533-7493

Deerfield's Collectibles
5383 Bancroft Ave.
510/534-6411

Rockridge Antiques
5601 College Ave.
510/652-7115

Garcia's Antiques
2278 E. 14th St.
510/535-1339

Lost and Found Antiques
4220 Piedmont Ave.
510/654-2007

Williamsburg Antiques
5375 Bancroft Ave.
510/532-1870

Good The Bad & The Ugly
5322 & 26 College Ave.
510/420-1740

Avenue Antiques
6007 College Ave.
510/652-7620

Richard a Pecchi Antiques
30 Jack London Square, #110
510/465-9006

119 OAKLEY

Lena's Antiques
3510 Main St.
510/625-4878

Country Courthouse
3663 Main St.
510/625-1099

Norcross Timeless Treasures
3639 Main St.
510/625-0193

120 OCEANO

A Pier at the Past
368 Pier Ave.
805/473-1521
Open: During summer 10–6 Wed.–Sun., during winter 11–5 Wed.–Sun., Mon. & Tues. by chance.
Directions: From Hwy. 101 North: Take Los Barros Road exit to Oceano. From Hwy. 101 South: Take 4th Street exit to Grand, right to Hwy. 1, left to Pier Avenue, right to the shop and the beach. A Pier at the Past is on State Hwy. #1, 3 miles south of Pismo Beach and 2 miles north of Nipomo.

I don't know which you'll love the most — the antique shop or George Kiner himself. He is the epitome of the "laid back" California lifestyle. George set up shop on the beach at Oceano in 1994, but he has been in business in California for 35 years. Starting out in the 1960s, before the major rekindling of interest in antiques took hold, George was one of the early Union Street dealers. He owned several shops in various San Francisco locations — one of which was the ever-popular Varietorium. It was dubbed "the" place to shop for antiques, and George, with his myna bird Susie, became quite well known.

George opened two more shops in California, one in the San Fernando Valley and one in Studio City. Both were destroyed by earthquakes. These events prompted his move to Oceano, where he opened a fun little shop call A Pier at the Past.

It is, according to George, right at the entranceway for the tricycles and A.T.V.s heading for the Oceano Dunes, "the only place on the West Coast where you can drive down and find 1,000 campsites." There used to be a pier at the beach years ago, but it was lost in a storm. The gutted building that houses A Pier at the Past had been a building block restaurant. George rented it, put up temporary walls for his paintings, hung some lighting and was in business. He knows how temporary things can be, having weathered the earthquakes and lost stores over the years. George also lives in the shop, which visitors often don't realize as they browse. He keeps everything open. "You can walk through into the living room and on into the bedroom," says George. "If someone wants to buy my bed, I'll sell it and sleep on a futon until I find something I like."

Besides his bed, George carries lots of cups and saucers, paintings from all periods, costume jewelry and accessories, beaded purses, compacts and barber bottles, Indian pottery, unusual furniture pieces, lots of little tables, Oriental decorative items, English Bristol china, German Royal Bonn porcelain and kitchen items to the 1930s.

If you know you're going to stop by, you might want to call first — George is often out on the beach taking a walk.

Central Coast Outdoor Antique & Collectible Market
Oceano Airport
561 Air Park Dr.
805/481-9095 (Dealer Information)
Open: 2nd Sat. of each month, 7–2
Directions: Off Hwy. 1, South of Pismo Beach.

On the second Saturday of every month, the Oceano Airport parking lot is transformed into an antique mecca. This open air market is only one and a half blocks from Pismo Beach and is part of the beautiful tourist area of San Luis Obispo County. The Market features free admission and parking.

The Hangar Antiques & Collectibles
Oceano Airport
561 Air Park Dr.
805/481-9095
Open: Fri., Sat., & Sun. or by appointment

This unusual setting for antiques was once an old airplane hangar. Today, it is packed with quality antiques and collectibles ranging from gas and oil memorabilia, airplane related items, many big boy toys, as well as wonderful items for the ladies. Constantly changing inventory.

121 OJAI

Gracies Antique Mall
238 E. Ojai Ave.
805/646-8879

Treasures of Ojai
110 N. Signal St.
805/646-2852

Antique Collection
236 W. Ojai Ave.
805/646-6688

122 ONTARIO

Ontario Antiques Annex
127 W. B St.
909/391-8628

Inland Empire Antiques
216 W. B St.
909/986-9779

Golden Web
235 N. Euclid Ave.
909/986-6398

Ontario Antiques
203 W. B St.
909/391-1200

Martha's Antique Mall
326 N. Euclid Ave.
909/984-5220

Treasures 'N' Junk
215 S. San Antonio
909/983-3300

123 ORANGE

Listed on the National Register of Historic Places, Old Towne Orange is home to more than 50 antique shops, 10 antique malls and over 10 art galleries. The antique capital of Southern California, the Orange Plaza offers vintage furniture and memorabilia, as well as unique gifts.

Among an eclectic array of fine restaurants, pubs and casual eateries you will find just about any food you desire. No matter what ambience suits you — breakfast (all day) at the "fifties" soda fountain inside Watson Drug, high tea in a historic setting, fresh and healthy authentic Thai cuisine at Bebe's Cafe, a snack and freshly brewed beer at a microbrewery in the historic train depot, coffee or a fine meal at P.J.'s Abbey Restaurant, a beautifully restored Victorian-era church built in 1891, or outdoor dining in Old Towne — you will find it in Orange. For a sampling of culinary delights, plan on visiting during the International Street Fair held every Labor Day weekend for food and entertainment from every continent on earth.

Happy Time Antiques Mall

109 W. Chapman Ave.
714/538-3844

Most of the locals know Happy Time Antiques Mall for its award winning window displays, but that is only a small sampling of what is inside this fabulous store. Fine glass and pottery abound throughout the store with sprinklings of Roseville, Hull, vaseline, purpled glass, cut glass, pressed glass and much, much more. The shop also offers a nice selection of Victorian purses and jewelry with an added array of fine furnishings. Throughout the year owner Pat Kelly hosts antique fairs. These special events provide customers with the opportunity to shop for bargains and to attend seminars with guests such as expert porcelain restorer, Joan Walton.

Today's Memories
129 N. Glassell
714/516-1860

S & E Gallery
227A E. Chapman Ave.
714/532-6787

Daisy's Antiques
131 W. Chapman Ave.
714/633-6475

Tony's Architectural & Garden
123 N. Olive
714/538-1900

Mulherin & O Dell's Antiques
106 N. Glassell St.
714/771-3390

George the Second
114 N. Glassell St.
714/744-1870

Wheels 'n' Wings Collectibles
115 N. Orange
714/538-0242

American Roots
105 W. Chapman Ave.
714/639-3424

Country Roads Antiques
204 W. Chapman Ave.
714/532-3041

Treasures from the Past
611 W. Chapman Ave.
714/997-9702

Anthony's Fine Antiques
114 N. Glassell St.
714/538-1900

Rocking Chair Emporium
123 N. Glassell St.
714/633-5206

Happiness by the Bushel
128 N. Glassell St.
714/538-3324

Grand Avenue Antiques
140 N. Glassell St.
714/538-3540

Encore Presentations
144 N. Glassell St.
714/744-4845

Mr C's Rare Records
148 N. Glassell St.
714/532-3835

A & P Collectibles
151 N. Glassell St.
714/997-1370

Lucky Find Antiques
160 N. Glassell St.
714/771-6364

Woody's Early Misc.
169 N. Glassell St.
714/744-8199

Rick Sloane Antiques
2055 N. Glassell St.
714/637-1257

Antique Annex
109 S. Glassell St.
714/997-4320

Orange Circle Antique Mall
118 S. Glassell St.
714/538-8160

Someplace In Time
132 S. Glassell St.
714/538-9411

Nick Schaner Antiques
136 S. Glassell St.
714/744-0204

Plaza 42 Antiques
141 S. Glassell St.
714/633-9090

Victoria Co.
146 S. Glassell St.
714/538-7927

Ruby's Antique Jewelry
84 Plaza Square
714/538-1762

Willard Antiques
143 S. Olive St.
714/771-7138

It's About Time
131 N. Glassell St.
714/538-7645

Antique Place
142 N. Glassell St.
714/538-4455

Jim & Shirley's Antiques
146 N. Glassell St.
714/639-9662

Antiques & Me
149 N. Glassell St.
714/538-7044

Attic Delights
155 N. Glassell St.
714/639-8351

Antiques Antiques
165 N. Glassell St.
714/639-4084

Le Chalet Antiques & Doll Shop
277 N. Glassell St.
714/633-2650

Watch And Wares
108 S. Glassell St.
714/633-2030

Partners Eclectic Antiques
110 S. Glassell St.
714/744-4340

Uncle Tom's Antiques
119 S. Glassell St.
714/538-3826

Muff's Antiques
135 S. Glassell St.
714/997-0243

Just For Fun
140 S. Glassell St.
714/633-7405

Summerhill Limited
142 S. Glassell St.
714/771-7782

Antique Station
178 S. Glassell St.
714/633-3934

Old Towne Orange Antique Mall
119 N. Olive St.
714/532-6255

Rothdale's Fine Antiques
40 Plaza Square
714/289-6900

California

J & J Antiques
55 Plaza Square
714/288-9057

China Terrace Antiques
1192 N. Tustin Ave.
714/771-4555

124 ORINDA

The Family Jewels
572 Tahos Road
510/254-4422

Orinda Village Antiques
107 Orinda Way
510/254-2206

Karla's Antiques
83 Orinda Way
510/254-0964

125 OROVILLE

Day Dreams
1462 Myers St.
916/534-8624

Lock Stock & Barrell
2061 Montgomery St.
916/534-7515

Miners Alley Collective
1354 Myers St.
916/534-7871

Old Town Emporium
2034 Montgomery St.
916/533-7787

Carousel Antiques
2421 Montgomery St.
916/534-8433

126 PACIFIC GROVE

Patrick's
105 Central
408/372-3995

Antique Warehouse
2707 David Ave.
408/375-1456

Trotter's Antiques
301-303 Forest Ave.
408/373-3505

Front Row Center
633 C Lighthouse Ave.
408/375-5625

Woodenickle
529 Central
408/646-8050

Camden & Castleberry Antiques
2711 David Ave.
408/375-0701

Antique Clock Shop
489 Lighthouse Ave.
408/372-6435

Interesting Side Trips

Point Pinos Lighthouse
Asilomar Ave. off Ocean View Blvd.
408/648-3116

Built in 1856, oldest continuously operating lighthouse on the West Coast.

Tea Leaf Cottage
60 Plaza Square
714/771-7752

127 PALM DESERT

Treasure House
73199 El Paseo, Suite C & D
760/568-1461

128 PALM SPRINGS

Palm Springs Art Gallery
170 E. Arenas Road
760/778-6969

Irene's Antiques
457 N. Palm Canyon Dr.
760/320-6654

Campbell's Estate Gallery
886 N. Palm Canyon Dr.
760/323-6044

Pars Gallery
353 S. Palm Canyon Dr., #A
760/322-7179

Robert Kaplan Antiques
469 N. Palm Canyon Dr.
760/323-7144

Carlan Collection
1556 N. Palm Canyon Dr.
760/322-8002

Great Places to Stay

Casa Cody Bed & Breakfast Country Inn
175 S. Cahuilla Road
760/320-9346
Rates: Vary by season

A romantic, historic hideaway nestled against the spectacular San Jacinto Mountains in the heart of Palm Springs Village, Casa Cody is the oldest operating hotel in Palm Springs. It was founded in the 1920s by the beautiful Hollywood pioneer, Harriet Cody, cousin to the legendary Buffalo Bill. The inn has 23 single-story accommodations in five early California hacienda-style buildings, all decorated in Santa Fe decor, and surrounding bougainvillaea and citrus-filled courtyards. Guests have a choice of single or double rooms, studios, and one or two bedroom suites, each with private baths and entrances. There's a one-bedroom cottage and a historic two-bedroom adobe for those who desire even more seclusion. The inn also offers two pools and a tree-shaded whirlpool spa.

Ingleside Inn & Melvyn's Restaurant & Lounge
200 W. Ramon Road
Web site: www.prinet.com/ingleside

Favorite Hideaway of the Biggest Names in Show Business, Industry and Politics. Featured as "One of the Ten Best" — *Lifestyles of the Rich and Famous*. Experience the beauty and old world charm that place the historic Ingleside Inn at the top of every Traveler's "Wish List." An oasis where quiet elegance reigns in a setting of unequaled serenity, sunshine and personalized service by European-trained staff. The world-famous Melvyn's Restaurant is still a Palm Springs tradition.

California

129 PALO ALTO

Antique Emporium
4219 El Camino Real
415/494-2868

Kimura Gallery
482 Hamilton Ave.
415/322-3984

Hilary Thatz, Inc.
38 Stanford Shopping Center
415/323-4200

Alan Jay Co.
14 Town & Country Village
415/462-9900

Adele's Antiques
231 Hamilton Ave.
415/322-7184

Antiques Unlimited
542 High St.
415/328-3748

Di Capi Ltd.
10 Town & Country Village
415/327-1541

Cotton Works
500 University Ave.
415/327-1800

130 PARADISE

19th Century Antique Shop
5447 Skyway
916/872-8723

Penny Ante Antiques
5701 Skyway
916/877-0047

Attic Treasures
7409 Skyway
916/876-1541

Time Was
5610 Skyway
916/877-7844

Patti's Snoop Shoppe
7357 Skyway
916/872-4008

Deloris' Antiques & Collectibles
7639 Skyway
916/872-2828

131 PASADENA

Carol's Antiques
1866 N. Allen
818/798-1072

Jay's Antiques
95B N. Arroyo Pkwy.
818/792-0485

Carlson-Powers Antiques
1 W. California Blvd., Suite 411
818/577-9589

On The Twentieth Century
910 E. Colorado Blvd.
818/795-0667

Tiffany Tree
498 Del Rosa Dr.
818/796-4406

Georgene's Antiques
448 S. Fair Oaks Ave.
818/440-9926

Pasadena Antique Center
480 S. Fair Oaks Ave.
818/449-7706

Chuck's Antiques
23 N. Altadena
818/564-9582

Jane Warren Antiques
832 E. California Blvd.
818/584-9431

Dovetail Antiques
1 W. California Blvd., Suite 412
818/792-9410

Time Recyclers
2552 E. Colorado Blvd.
818/440-1880

Antiques & Objects
446 S. Fair Oaks Ave.
818/796-8224

Marc's Antiques
460 S. Fair Oaks Ave.
818/795-3770

Blackwelders Antiques & Fine Art
696 E. Colorado Blvd.
818/584-0723

Oliver's Antiques Fine Arts
597 E. Green St.
818/449-3463

Green Dolphin St Antiques
985 E. Green St.
818/577-7087

Pasadena Antique Mall
44 E. Holly St.
818/304-9886

Marco Polo Antique Shop
62 N. Raymond Ave.
818/356-0835

A Matter Of Taste
328 S. Rosemead Blvd.
818/792-2735

Kelley Gallery
770 E. Green St., #102
818/577-5657

J & N Antiques
989 E. Green St.
818/792-7366

Showcase Antiques
60 N. Lake Ave.
818/577-9660

Design Center Antiques
70 N. Raymond Ave.
213/681-6230

Novotny's Antique Gallery
60 N. Lake Ave.
818/577-9660

132 PASO ROBLES

Antique Emporium
1307 Park St.
805/238-1078

Homestead Antiques & Collectibles
1320 Pine St.
805/238-9183

Heritage House Antique Gallery
1345 Park St.
805/239-1386

Great American Antiques
1305 Spring St.
805/239-1203

Sentimental Journey
1344 Pine St.
805/239-1001

133 PETALUMA

R & L Antiques
3690 Bodega Ave.
707/762-2494

Waddles 'n' Hops
145 Kentucky St.
707/778-3438

Doris's Antiques
152 Kentucky St.
707/765-0627

Chanticleer Antiques
145 Petaluma Blvd. N.
707/763-9177

Antique Market Place
304 Petaluma Blvd. N.
707/765-1155

Vintage Bank Antiques
101 Petaluma Blvd.
707/769-3097

Kentucky Street Antiques
127 Kentucky St.
707/765-1698

Dolores Hitchinson Antiques
146 Kentucky St.
707/763-8905

Fraley's Antiques
110 Petaluma Blvd. N., #A
707/763-4087

Chelsea Antiques
148 Petaluma Blvd. N.
707/763-7686

Antique Collector
523 Petaluma Blvd. S.
707/763-7371

California

134 PLACERVILLE

Jennings Way Antiques
3182 Center St.
916/642-0446

Empire Antiques
420 Main St.
916/626-8931

Olde Dorado Antique Emporium
435 Main St.
916/622-4792

Beever's Antiques & Books
462-464 Main St.
916/626-3314

Treasure Tent Antiques
376 Main St.
916/626-9364

The Loft
420 Main St.
916/626-8931

Placerville Antiques & Collectibles
440 Main St.
916/626-3425

Memory Lane Antiques
460 Main St.
916/626-9207

135 PLEASONTON

Olde Towne Antiques
465 Main St.
510/484-2446

Main St. Antiques & Collectibles
641 Main St.
510/426-0279

Clutter Box
99 W. Neal St.
510/462-8640

B J Gardner Fine Period Furniture
531 Main St.
510/484-5456

Cattelan's Antique Furniture
719 Main St.
510/485-1705

136 POMONA

Swan Song
197 E. Second St. (Antique Row)
909/620-5767 or 562/433-1033 (appt.)
Open: By appointment

Swan Song is an exceptional, upscale antique shop with a unique setting. Primitives and country furnishings fill the basement of what once was the old department store. The main floor is reserved for oil paintings, art glass, silver, oriental, and fine china. The second story is filled (over 100 pieces) with Victorian furniture, vintage clothing, along with American and Indian pottery. The third and final floor of this shop features quilts, traditional antique furnishings along with designer pieces. If you're not in the market to purchase these exquisite items, you can rent them. Everything in the store is available for rental. Sounds like a great place to plan a wedding or party.

Pfeiffer's Collectibles
147 E. 2nd St.
909/629-8860

Jack's Antiques
161 E. 2nd St.
909/633-5589

Girl's Antiques
151 E. 2nd St.
909/622-5773

Pomona Antique Center
162 E. 2nd St.
909/620-7406

My Way Antiques
175 E. 2nd St.
909/620-6696

Ralph's Inland Empire Antiques
185 E. 2nd St.
909/622-0451

Grandpa's Antiques
205 E. 2nd St.
909/629-5854

Collector's Choice
104 S. Locust
909/865-7110

Kaiser Bill's Military Shop
224 E. 2nd St.
909/622-5046

Empire House Antiques
237 E. 2nd St.
909/622-9291

McBeth's Antiques
263 E. 2nd St.
909/622-0615

Harries General Store
269 E. 2nd St.
909/629-1446

Sanders Antiques
279 E. 2nd St.
909/620-8295

Southwest Antiques
198 E. 2nd St.
909/620-8334

137 PORTERVILLE

Now & Then Country Mall
19230 Ave. 152
209/783-9313

Sandie's
32 W. Mill Ave.
209/781-6740

J. Fox Antiques
40 W. Mill Ave.
209/784-1737

Downing Antiques
1522 W. Putnam Ave.
209/784-1465

138 RAMONA

Ye Olde Curio Shoppe
738 Main St.
760/789-6365

Persnickity Antiquity
180 E. 2nd St.
909/620-8996

Robbins Antique Mall
200 E. 2nd St.
909/623-9835

Grandma's Goodies
211 E. 2nd St.
909/629-3906

Dragon Antiques
216 E. 2nd St.
909/620-6660

Lila's Place
233 E. 2nd St.
909/620-7270

Olde Towne Pomona Mall
260 E. 2nd St.
909/622-1011

Nothing Common Antiques
265 E. 2nd St.
909/620-1229

Hobbs & Fried Mercantile
275 E. 2nd St.
909/629-1112

China Closet
290 E. 2nd St.
909/622-2922

Jerico Antique Emporium
134 N. Main St.
209/784-2211

Junk N Tique
36 W. Mill Ave.
209/783-2448

Irene's Antiques
33 W. Putnam Ave.
209/782-8245

Cotton Center Trading Post
15366 Road 192
209/784-4012

Old Town Antiques
760 Main St.
760/788-2670

California

Ramona Antiques & Collectibles
872 Main St.
760/789-7816

Peterson's Antiques & Collectibles
2405 Main St.
760/789-2027

139 RANCHO CORDOVA

Antique Plaza
11395 Folsom Blvd.
916/852-8517

140 RANDSBURG

Cottage Hotel Bed & Breakfast & Antiques
130 Butte Ave.
760/374-2285
Open: Thurs.–Mon. 11–5, closed Tues.–Wed. (sometimes) and during Christmas/New Year.

This is the place to go to be pampered — a quiet getaway with an enclosed Jacuzzi for all-season use. Hidden away in the California High Desert in the historical gold mining town of Randsburg, the Cottage Hotel Bed & Breakfast began at the turn of the century with the gold boom in Randsburg. Today all the rooms have been restored to reflect that era, with period furnishings being the key. There are common areas for relaxing and viewing the desert, and even accommodations in the Housekeeping Cottage next door for families with small children. Located conveniently between Highways 14 and 395, the Cottage Hotel Bed & Breakfast is also listed in the Auto Club (AAA) tour book for California and Nevada, and the Bed & Breakfast Guide *Gateway To Death Valley*. According to innkeeper Brenda Ingram, Randsburg is called "The Living Ghost Town," but she assures us that all the ghosts are very friendly!

141 RED BLUFF

Antiques 'n' Things
339 Ash St.
916/527-7098

Stelle's Main St. Antiques
623 Main St.
916/529-2238

Hunt House Antiques
718 Main St.
916/527-6104

Washington St. Antiques
610 Washington St.
916/528-1701

Great American Antiques
613 Main St.
916/529-4340

Kramer's Antiques
644 Main St.
916/527-1701

Kelco Antiques & Collectibles
1445 Vista Way
916/529-3245

142 RED MOUNTAIN

Old Owl Inn Cottages, a Bed & Breakfast
Cottontail Antiques, Collectibles & Gifts
701 Hwy. 395
760/374-2235 or 1-888-653-6954 (toll free)
Antique shop open daily except Wed. from 10–5
Bed and Breakfast open daily
Directions: 25 miles north of intersections Hwy. 395 and 58. Twenty miles south of Ridgecrest.

The Old Owl Inn, originally owned by Slim Riffle, was at one time a library in the town of Atolia. Slim moved it to Red Mountain in 1918. He then added on to the building and turned it into a bar, brothel and gambling salon.

The Owl witnessed many shoot-outs, bar-room brawls and two-fisted poker games. Legend has that the ladies of the evening along with illegal booze were hidden in tunnels below and out of sight of the watchful eye of the local sheriff.

Today, The Owl Cottages is a bed and breakfast decorated with antiques throughout. Guests can stay in Slim's Cottage, a spacious two-bedroom with kitchen, living room and old-fashioned bath, which was the private home of Slim Riffle. Bessie's Honeymoon Cottage is also available for that special romantic night or weekend, with kitchen and private bath.

The newly expanded Cottontail Antiques is located on the property, providing antiquers with treasures to take home as a memento of their stay at the Old Owl Inn, including Fenton, angels and needlework items.

143 REDDING/SHASTA LAKE CITY

Absolutely Wonderful Antiques
2948 Cascade Blvd.
916/275-4046

Antiques & Accents
3266 Cascade Blvd., #12
916/275-2619

I-5 Antique Mall
3270A Cascade Blvd.
916/275-6990

Barbara's Antiques
3266 Cascade Blvd.
916/275-6879

Hollibaugh Antiques
3266 Cascade Blvd.
916/275-2990

California

144 REDLANDS/YUCAIPA

Ila's Antiques and Collectibles
215 East Redlands Blvd.
(located in the Packing House Mall, in "The Cellar")
909/793-8898
Open: Mon.–Sun., 11–5:30
Directions: Traveling I-10, exit at Orange Street and go south 3 blocks, turn left to 7th and Redlands Blvd.

Ila's Antiques is located in "The Cellar" of the old Banner Packing House. In the early days of the 1900s, this historic building housed a citrus packing company which shipped sweet California oranges to markets all across the U.S.

To get to Ila's, you must first pass through the Packing House Mall (a separate business) which houses 80 dealers offering a wide variety of antiques and collectibles. Once inside, take the stairs to "the cellar," where you'll discover 3,000 square feet of the finest antiques in the area. This shop undoubtedly has one of the largest costume jewelry collections in the U.S. — over 5,000 pieces! In addition, you'll find silver, crystal, Czechoslovakian glass, china, antique dolls and some select furniture pieces.

Laurel Jones China
409 N. Orange
909/793-8611

Carriage Barn Antiques
31181 Outer Hwy. 10 S.
909/794-3919

Sandlin's Antiques
31491 Outer Hwy. 10
909/794-4311

Fiddler's Cove
31567 Outer Hwy. 10, #1
909/794-6102

Raney's Freeway Antiques
31597 Outer Hwy. 10
909/794-4851

Antique Gallery
31629 Outer Hwy. 10, Unit E
909/794-0244

Cathy's Cottage Antiques
31843 Outer Hwy. 10
909/389-9436

Last Stop Antique Shop
32019 Outer Hwy. 10 S.
909/795-5612

Precious Times Antiques
1740 W. Redlands Blvd.
909/792-7768

Emma's Trunk
1701 Orange Tree Lane
909/798-7865

Antique Exchange Mall
31251 Outer Hwy. 10
909/794-9190

Marion Side Door Antiques
31567 Outer Hwy. 10
909/794-1320

Cripe's Antiques
31583 Outer Hwy. 10 S.
909/794-5355

Out Back Antiques
31599 Outer Hwy. 10
909/794-0530

Ellen's Antiques
31629 Outer Hwy. 10, Unit F
909/794-9340

Keepsake Antique Mall
31933 Outer Hwy. 10
909/794-1076

The Packing House
215 E. Redlands Blvd.
909/792-9021

Eclectic Art Gallery
516 Texas St.
909/793-7016

Paul Melzer Rare Books
12 E. Vine St.
909/792-7299

The Blues
114 E. State St.
909/798-8055

Antique Arcade
31159 Outer Hwy. 10 S.
909/794-5919

Chandlers Cove
Brookside Plaza — 1512 Barton Road
909/307-0622

Memory Lane Antiques
31773 Outer Hwy. 10 S.
909/794-3514

Anne's Yesteryear's
31663 Outer Hwy. 10 S.
909/795-5446

Gatherings
330-a N. Third St.
909/792-1216

C.B. Antiques
316 E. Citrus Ave.
909/792-0017

Vintage Clothing & Books
31629 Outer Hwy. 10, B
909/794-1785

Olde Hollow Treet
38480 Oak Glen Road
909/797-5032

Antiques Unlimited
31567 Outer Hwy. 10 S.
909/794-4066

145 REDONDO BEACH

Patina
1815 ¹/₂ S. Catalina Ave.
310/373-5587

Le Grange Country Furniture
719 S. Pacific Coast Hwy.
310/540-7535

Antique Doll Closet
1303 S. Pacific Coast Hwy.
310/540-8212

Antique Corral
145 S. Pacific Coast Hwy.
310/374-0007

Vicki's Antiques & Collectibles
1221 S. Pacific Coast Hwy.
310/540-6363

146 REDWOOD CITY

Athena Antiques Inc.
926 Broadway St.
415/363-0282

Finders Keepers Antiques
837 Main St.
415/365-1750

Eclectric Antiques
1101 Main St.
415/364-1549

Palace Market Antiques
825 Main St.
415/364-4645

Redwood Cafe & Spice Co.
1020 Main St.
415/364-1288

147 RIVERSIDE

Abbey's Antiques
3671 Main St.
909/788-9725
Open: Mon.–Sat.10–5:30, Sun. by chance.

Offering 2,000 square feet of fine antiques, vintage clothing, linens, jewelry, silver and more.

Mission Antiques
4308 Lime St.
909/684-5639

Katy's Collectibles
6062 Magnolia Ave.
909/369-9030

Amazing Grace Antiques
3541 Main St.
909/788-9729

Darlene Nemer
3596 Main St.
909/684-9010

Seventh Heaven Antiques
3605 Market St.
909/784-6528

Beasley's Antiques
3757 Mission Inn Ave.
909/682-8127

The Gas Pump
9637 Magnolia
909/689-7113

Mr. Beasley's Auction
3878 6th St.
909/682-4279

Cinnamon Lane Antique Mall
6056 Magnolia Ave.
909/781-6625

Karen's Antiques
9631 Magnolia Ave.
909/358-0304

R.R. Antiques
3583 Market St.
909/781-6350

Mrs. Darling
4267 Main St.
909/682-0425

Petey's Place
4212 Market St.
909/686-4520

Crystal's Antique Mall
4205 Main St.
909/781-9922

Victorian Rose Antique Mall
3784 Elizabeth St.
909/788-5510

148 ROSEVILLE

Roseville Antique Mall
106 Judah St.
916/773-4003

Terri Andrus' Treasures
1304 Buttercup Court — Section D #5
916/782-6158

Pepper Tree
223 Vernon St.
916/783-1979

Home Passage Antiques
229 Vernon St.
916/782-5111

Antique Trove
238 Vernon St.
916/786-2777

Julie's Antique Mall
625 Vernon St.
916/783-3006

Around Again Antiques
342 Lincoln St.
916/783-8542

Tin Soldiers
222 Vernon St.
916/786-6604

Antique Store
226 Vernon St.
916/774-0660

Velvet Purse Antiques
230 Vernon St.
916/784-3432

This 'n' That
243 Vernon St.
916/786-7784

Memories Past Antiques
801 Vernon St.
916/786-2606

149 SACRAMENTO

Historic Old Sacramento

The Old Sacramento historic area, a registered national landmark and state historic park, is a 28-acre site on the banks of the Sacramento River. It is a vital historic, business, residential, shopping, and dining district with a fascinating past and the greatest concentration of historic buildings in California.

John Sutter arrived in 1839 and founded the first permanent settlement in the area. After the gold discovery in 1848, businesses sprang up along the riverfront in what is now Old Sacramento. There were hotels, saloons, bathhouses, the first theatre in California, and a variety of shops where would-be miners could outfit themselves for the gold fields.

Transportation has always figured prominently in Sacramento's history. The city was the western terminus of the short-lived Pony Express and the transcontinental railroad. Today, Old Sacramento is home to the largest interpretive railroad museum in North America — the California State Railroad Museum. The 100,000-square-foot museum displays 21 meticulously restored locomotives and cars, and over 40 one-of-a-kind exhibits tell the fascinating story of railroad history from 1850 to the present. Historic equipment and exhibits on the transcontinental railroad and 19th-century rail travel are housed in the reconstructed 1876 Central Pacific Railroad Passenger Station.

About one mile from the California State Railroad Museum, just on the edge of Old Sacramento, is another spectacular facility dedicated to transportation — the Towe Ford Museum. The world's most complete antique Ford automobile collection includes every year and model produced by Ford between 1903 and 1953. There are more than 150 cars and trucks, with many in excellent original condition and others that have been beautifully and authentically restored. The collection also includes an array of original and restored cars from the late '50s, '60s, and '70s.

Other museums include the California Military Museum, the Discovery Museum and the Crocker Art Museum. Explore historic Old Sacramento with a self-guided "Walking Tour," which is available from the Visitor Information Center at 2nd and K streets. One hundred unique shops and 20 eclectic restaurants will satisfy even the most discerning visitor. Numerous special events take place here year-round including the Sacramento Jazz Jubilee, Festival de la Familia, Pacific Rim Festival and a couple of collectors' fairs.

Haulbaurs Timeless Treasures
3207 Marysville Blvd.
916/924-1371
Open: Mon.–Sat. 10–5:30
Directions: Traveling business 80 from San Francisco to Sacramento, take the Marconi exit, head West. Marconi becomes Arcade, Arcade takes you to Marysville Blvd. Located near the corner of Arcade and Marysville Blvd.

Haulbaurs Timeless Treasures has been in operation for four years. It is amazing how that many treasures can be up for grabs in 1,700 square feet of space. The shop is literally filled to the brim with some of the most unusual collectibles west of the Mississippi.

California

Do you collect antique fishing gear? They have it—lots of it! What about old telephones? Yes, they have those, too. Cookie jars, bird cages, books, musical instruments, tools? — yes, all there. European army collectibles, European beer steins — (you won't be bored). Oh, and did I mention German pencil sharpeners and German toys? — Got 'em! It's one of those "It's no telling what you'll find in here" kind of shops.

Anna's Collectibles
1905 Capitol Ave.
916/441-1310

Antiques Etc.
4749 Folsom Blvd.
916/739-1483

Closet
1107 Front St.
916/442-3446

Lovell's Antique Mall
2114 P St.
916/442-4640

Slater Antiques & Collectibles
609 N. 10th St.
916/442-6183

Wee Jumble Shop
1221 19th St.
916/447-5643

Grandpa's Antiques
1423 28th St.
916/456-4594

Discovery Antiques
855 57th St.
916/739-1757

Gravy Boat Antiques
855 57th St.
916/457-1205

Elaine's Jewel Box
866 57th St.
916/451-6059

Sullivan's Antiques
866 57th St.
916/457-9183

57th Street Antique Mall
875 57th St. (off H St.)
916/451-3110

Old World Antiques
6313 Elvas Ave.
916/456-9131

Memory Lane
1025 Front St.
916/488-0981

River City Antique Mall
10117 Mills Road
916/362-7778

Bookmine
1015 2nd St.
916/441-4609

Antique Tresors Legacy
1512 16th St.
916/446-6960

Swanberg's Antiques & Collectibles
2673 21st St.
916/456-5300

Chez Antique
855 57th St.
916/455-7504

Windmill Antiques
855 57th St.
916/454-1487

Every Era Antiques
855 57th St.
916/456-1767

Bagwell's Antiques
866 57th St.
916/455-3409

Fifty-Seventh St. Antiques
875 57th St.
916/451-3110

Great Places to Stay

Amber House
1315 22nd St.
Web site: www.amberhouse.com
1-800-755-6526

Just eight blocks from the state capitol, Amber House offers a quiet sanctuary for a romantic interlude or a special hideaway for the business traveler. Each room has its own special appeal. Seven rooms have Jacuzzi bathtubs for two. Included in the rates is a full gourmet breakfast, served in the guest's room, dining room or on the veranda.

Hartley House B&B Inn
700 22nd St.
1-800-831-5806

Hartley House is a stunning turn-of-the century mansion, built in 1906 and surrounded by the majestic elm trees and stately homes of historic Boulevard Park in midtown Sacramento. Exquisitely appointed rooms are conveniently located near the State Capitol, Old Sacramento, the Sacramento Community Convention Center, and the city's finest restaurants, coffee cafes and dessert shops. They even have a cookie jar filled with freshly baked cookies!

Inn at Parkside
2116 Sixth St.
Web site: www.innatparkside.com
1-800-995-7275

This stunning Mediterranean Revival grand mansion is furnished with museum quality antiques and stained glass throughout. Neoclassic art adorns walls and ceilings, with faux painting and original murals. A full gourmet breakfast is served in the dining room, garden or guestroom. There is a ballroom and garden area for small weddings, receptions, meetings or other special events. Inn at Parkside is the winner of the 1996 Sacramento Old City Association award for best commerical historic renovation and the 1997 award for best front entry.

Riverboat Delta King Hotel
1000 Front St. (on the Sacramento River)
Old Sacramento
916/444-5464

This magnificently restored dockside paddlewheeler has been entertaining guests since 1927. Spend the night in one of 44 elegant staterooms on the shores of the Sacramento River.

If murder and suspense intrigue you, you will enjoy the Suspects Murder Mystery Dinner Theatre on the Delta King Friday and Saturday evenings. Match wits with a master detective searching for clues and interrogating guests. Look out, you may be a suspect yourself!

Interesting Side Trips

Exploring Gold Country

Sacramento was the original jumping off point for the goldminers, and today it's the perfect base for exploring the Gold Country, an area so rich in lore that you may easily find yourself transported back to that era. Remnants of this exciting time in California history are still visible all around. To reach the northern mines, take Interstate 80 east from Sacramento toward the town of Auburn, a quaint gem with great antique stores and a variety of restaurants. From here head north on Hwy. 49 to the Empire State Mine in Grass Valley. From Auburn you may also head south on Hwy. 49 to Coloma, the original gold discovery site in 1848. Continue south on 49 through Placerville and stop at one of the many El Dorado or Amador County wineries for a taste. On to Calaveras County and Angels Camp, home to the Jumping Frog Jubilee during the third week in May. Other well-preserved Gold Rush era towns include Murphys, San Andreas, Mokelumne Hills and Copperopolis. Don't miss Calaveras Big Trees State Park with its giant sequoias. Have you every tried spelunking? Moaning, California and Mercer Caverns are just the places for it. There're dozens of eclectic art galleries, quaint antique shops and excellent eateries all around the area. Take an hour to ride the train in the breathtaking foothills scenery at Railtown State Park near Jamestown, or pan for gold in a clear mountain stream. Sonora, Columbia State Park and Groveland are other draws for Gold Country visitors.

Heading south on Hwy. 49 stop in Coulterville, one of the best-preserved Gold Rush towns in the Sierra foothills. Enjoy boating and fishing at Lakes McClure and McSwain, and visit the oldest continuously operating courthouse west of the Rocky Mountains in the quaint town of Mariposa. At the end of a long day relax in the pine-covered community of Fish Camp located at the southern entrance to Yosemite National Park.

150 SALINAS

Echo Valley Antiques
849 Echo Valley Road
408/663-4305

Lily's Odds & Ends
10 W. Gakilan St.
408/757-4562

Generation Gap
338 Monterey St.
408/751-6148

Bonanza Antiques
467 El Camino Real
408/422-7621

Hall Tree Antique Mall
202 Main St.
408/757-6918

Country Peddler Antiques
347 Monterey St.
408/424-2292

151 SAN ANSELMO

Greenfield Antiques
8 Bank St.
415/454-4614

C. Fetherston Antiques
10 Bank St.
415/453-6607

Center Market
Center Blvd. & Saunders
415/454-3127

Oveda Maurer Antiques
34 Greenfield Ave.
415/454-6439

Roger Barber Asian Antiques
114 Pine St.
415/457-6844

Michael Good Fine & Rare Books
35 San Anselmo Ave.
415/452-6092

Vintage Flamingo
528 San Anselmo Ave.
415/721-7275

Second Hand Land
703 San Anselmo Ave.
415/454-5057

Legacy Antiques
204 Sir Francis Drake Blvd.
415/457-7166

Aurora Gallery
306 Sir Francis Drake Blvd.
415/459-6822

San Anselmo Country Store
312 Sir Francis Drake Blvd.
415/258-0922

Pavillion Antiques
610 Sir Francis Drake Blvd.
415/459-2002

Antique Habit
10 Greenfield Ave.
415/457-1241

Antique World
216 Greenfield Ave.
415/454-2203

Modern I Gallery
500 Red Hill Ave.
415/456-3960

Shadows
429 San Anselmo Ave.
415/459-0574

Yanni's Antiques
538 San Anselmo Ave.
415/459-2996

Dove Place Antiques
160 Sir Francis Drake Blvd.
415/453-1490

Sanford's Antiques
2 Tunstead Ave.
415/454-4731

Kisetsu & The French Garden
310 Sir Francis Drake Blvd.
415/456-9070

Collective Antiques
316 Sir Francis Drake Blvd.
415/453-6373

152 SAN BERNARDINO

Mueller's Vintage Collectibles
363 S. Arrowhead Ave.
909/384-8110

Old Fashion Shop West
1927 N. E St.
909/882-5819

A Touch of Class
214 W. Highland Ave.
909/883-1495

Treasure Mart Antiques.
293 E. Redlands Blvd.
909/825-7264

The Heritage Gallery
1520A S. E St.
909/888-3377

AEL Antique Mall
24735 Redlands Blvd.
909/796-0380

153 SAN CARLOS

Antiques Trove
1119 Industrial Road
650/593-1300

Antique Collage Collective
654 Laurel St.
650/595-1776

Felicity's Collectibles
600 Laurel St.
650/593-9559

Laurel Street Antiques
671 Laurel St.
650/593-1152

California

154 SAN CLEMENTE

Plum Precious Antiques
101 Avenida Miramar
714/361-0162

San Clemente Antiques
214 Avenida Del Mar
714/498-2992

Three Centuries Antique Gallery
408 N. El Camino Real
714/492-6609

Patrice Antiques
1602 N. El Camino Real
714/498-3230

Garden Antiques
109 S. El Camino Real
714/492-8344

Antiques & Collectibles
159 Avenida Del Mar
714/369-7321

Forgotten Dreams
1062 Call Del Cerro Bldg. #1226
714/361-0054

Stanford Court Antiques
106 Avenida Del Mar
714/366-6290

Zachery's Crossing
307 N. El Camino Real
714/498-1148

Pacific Trader
1407 N. El Camino Real
714/366-3049

Victoria's Antiques
101 N. El Camino Real
714/366-6232

Penny N' Sues
218 Avenida Del Mar
714/492-6027

Blue Moon Antiques
111 W. Avenida Palizada, #10A
714/498-4907

155 SAN DIEGO

Adams Avenue Antique Row and Park Blvd.

Adams Ave. Consignment
2873 Adams Ave.
619/281-9663

Alouette Antiques
2936 Adams Ave.
619/284-9408

Mary's Finest Collectibles
3027 Adams Ave.
619/280-6802

Hunter's Antiques
2602 Adams Ave.
619/295-1994

Resurrected Furniture
2814 Adams Ave.
619/283-3318

TMH Antiques & Art
4615 Park Blvd.
619/291-1730

What Mama Had
4215 Park Blvd.
619/296-7277

Country Cousins
2889 Adams Ave.
619/284-3039

Antique Seller
2938 Adams Ave.
619/283-8467

Gledhill's Vintage Furniture
2610 Adams Ave.
619/296-8272

Refindery
3463 Adams Ave.
619/563-0655

Virtu Garden & Home Antiques
4416 Park Blvd.
619/543-9150

Alessandria
2606 Adams Ave.
619/296-4662

Miscellanea
4610 Park Blvd.
619/295-6488

Rocky's Antiques, Books, Collectibles
4608 Park Blvd.
619/297-1639

Downtown-Gas Lamp Area

Palace Antiques
363 5th Ave., #104
619/234-4004

5th & J Antique. Mall
501 J St.
619/338-9559

Empire Enterprises
704 J St.
619/239-9216

Third Floor Antiques
448 W. Market (Cracker Factory)
619/238-7339

Unicorn Antiques
704 J St.
619/232-1696

Second Floor Antique. Mall
448 W. Market (Cracker Factory)
619/236-9484

Burton's Antiques
448 W. Market (Cracker Factory)
619/236-9484

LaRosa Family Antiques Center
445 8th Ave.
619/234-1970

Gaslamp Books, Prints & Antiques
413 Market
619/237-1492

Memories Antiques
448 W. Market (Cracker Factory)
619/231-9133

Bobbie's Paper Dolls
448 W. Market (Cracker Factory)
619/233-0055

Elite Antiques
448 W. Market (Cracker Factory)
619/238-1038

Lincoln Roberts Gallery
411 Market
619/702-5884

Legacy's Antiques
448 W. Market (Cracker Factory)
619/232-7236

Bert's Antiques
448 W. Market (Cracker Factory)
619/239-5531

Ocean Beach Antique District

Vignettes-Antiques
4828 Newport Ave.
619/222-9244

Mallory & Sons Antiques
4926 Newport Ave.
619/226-8658

Newport Avenue Antiques
4836 Newport Ave.
619/224-1994

Ocean Beach Antique Mall
4878 Newport Ave.
619/222-1967

Newport Ave. Antique Center
4864 Newport Ave.
619/222-8686

Cottage Antiques
4882 Newport Ave.
619/222-1967

Antiques & Stuff by Ruth
4051 Voltaire, Suite B
619/222-2232

Old Town Area

Circa a.d.
3867 4th Ave.
619/293-3328

Antique Alley Mall
1911 San Diego Ave.
619/688-1911

Country Craftsman
2465 Heritage Park Row
619/294-4600

Hillcrest Area

Papyrus Antiques & Unusual Shop
116 W. Washington St.
619/298-9291

Mission Gallery
320 W. Washington St.
619/692-3566

House of Heirlooms
801 University Ave.
619/298-0502

The Private Collector
800 W. Washington St.
619/296-5553

North Park District

St. Vincent De Paul Center Shoppe
3137 El Cajon Blvd.
619/624-9701

El Cortes District

Paper Antiquities
1552 5th Ave.
619/239-0656

Additonal shops in San Diego

Beverlee's Antiques
1062 Garnet Ave.
619/274-1933

Lost Your Marbles Too
3933 30th St.
619/291-3061

Whooping Crane Antiques
1617 W. Lewis St.
619/291-9232

Antique Castings
8333 LaMesa, Suite B
619/466-8665

English Garden
4140 Morena Blvd. #B
619/456-1793

T & R Antiques Warehouse
4630 Santa Fe St.
619/272-2500

Great Places to Stay

Carole's Bed and Breakfast

3227 Grim Ave.
619/280-5258

Built in 1904 by Mayor Fray, this historic site has the handsome style and craftsmanship of its time. It has been restored by the present owners who live on site giving it constant loving care. The decor is of its period, with antiques and comfort as the focus. There are five guest accommodations. Amenities include a black bottom pool, spa and a rose garden. Location is within walking distance to Balboa Park, and many small shops and restaurants.

Heritage Park Inn

2470 Heritage Park Row
Email: innkeeper @heritageparkinn.com
1-800-995-2470

Unique lodging for discriminating travelers ... far from ordinary ... yet central to everything. Nestled in a quiet Victorian park, lined with cobblestone walkways in the heart of historic Old Town. This award winning Queen Anne mansion is only minutes from the San Diego Zoo, shops, beaches and restaurants. Twelve guest accommodations.

156 SAN DIMAS

Just Us Antiques
120 W. Bonita Ave.
909/599-0568

Old Towne Antique Mall
125 W. Bonita Ave.
909/394-1836

Jabberwocky Antiques
138 W. Bonita Ave., #101A
909/394-0084

Heart of the Village Antique
155 W. Bonita Ave.
909/394-0628

Annie's Antiques & Collectibles
161 W. Bonita Ave.
909/592-2616

Two Eager Beavers Antiques
165 W. Bonita Ave.
909/592-3087

Frontier Village Antiques
115 N. Monte Vista Ave.
909/394-0628

157 SAN FRANCISCO

Clyde & Eva's Antique Shop
3942 Balboa St.
415/387-3902

Antique Traders
4300 California St.
415/668-4444

Browsers Nook
530 Castro St.
415/861-2216

Brand X Antiques
570 Castro St.
415/626-8908

Lovejoy's Antiques & Tea Room
1195 Church St.
415/648-5895

Schlep Sisters
4327 18th St.
415/626-0581

Grand Central Station Antiques
595 Castro St.
415/863-3604

Homes of Charm
1544 Church St.
415/647-4586

Alley Cat Jewels
1547 Church St.
415/285-3668

Old Stuff
2325 Clement St.
415/668-2220

Garden Spot
3029 Clement St.
415/751-8190

Mureta's Antiques
2418 Fillmore St.
415/922-5652

Other Shop
112 Gough St.
415/621-1590

Deco to 50s
149 Gough St.
415/553-4500

California

Decodence
149 Gough St.
415/553-4500

Vintage Modern
182 Gough St.
415/861-8162

J.C.'s Collectibles
564 Hayes St.
415/558-6904

Jekyll's on Hyde
1044 Hyde St.
415/775-3502

Thomas Livingston Antiques
414 Jackson St.
415/296-8150

Lotus Collection
434 Jackson St.
415/398-8115

Dora Mauri Antichita
455 Jackson St.
415/296-8500

Challiss House
463 Jackson St.
415/397-6999

Sen's Antiques Inc.
200 Kansas St.
415/487-3888

D. Carnegie Antiques
601 Kansas St.
415/641-4704

North Beach Antiques & Collectibles
734 Lombard St.
415/346-2448

Browsers Nook
1592 Market St.
415/861-3801

Isak Kindenauer Antiques
4143 19th St.
415/552-6436

Four Corners Antiques
90 Parnassus Ave.
415/753-6111

Russian Hill Antiques
2200 Polk St.
415/441-5561

Lupardo
3232 Sacramento St.
415/928-8662

Modern Era Decor
149 Gough St.
415/431-8599

Henry's Antiques & Art Gallery
319 Grant Ave.
415/291-0319

Foster-Gwin Antiques
38 Hotaling Place
415/397-4986

Hyde & Seek Antiques
1913 Hyde St.
415/776-8865

Louis D. Fenton Antiques
432 Jackson St.
415/398-3046

Edward Marshall Antiques
441 Jackson St.
415/399-0980

Daniel Stein Antiques
458 Jackson St.
415/956-5620

Hunt Antiques
478 Jackson St.
415/989-9531

Antiques Antiques
245 Kansas St.
415/252-7600

Willmann Country Pine
650 King St.
415/626-6547

Golden Gate Antiques
1564 Market St.
415/626-3377

Grand Central Station Antiques
1632 Market St., #A
415/252-8155

In My Dreams
1300 Pacific Ave.
415/885-6696

La Belle Antiques
2035 Polk St.
415/673-1181

Alexander Collections
309 W. Portal Ave.
415/661-5454

Woodchuck Antiques
3597 Sacramento St.
415/922-6416

Every Era Antiques
3599 Sacramento St.
415/346-0313

Sixth Ave. Antiques
189 6th Ave.
415/386-2500

Biscuit Jar Antiques
2134 Taraval St.
415/665-4520

Tampico
2147 Union St.
415/563-3785

Upstairs/Downstairs
890 Valencia St.
415/647-4211

San Francisco Antique Design Mall
701 Bayshore Blvd.
415/656-3530

Harvey Antiques
700 7th St., 2nd Floor
415/431-8888

Quality First
608 Taraval St.
415/665-6442

Telegraph Hill Antiques
580 Union St.
415/982-7055

Collective Antiques
212 Utah St.
415/621-3800

Decorum
1400 Vallejo St.
415/474-6886

Great Places to Stay

A Country Cottage
#5 Dolores Terrace
415/479-1913

A cozy country style bed and breakfast in the heart of San Francisco. The four guest rooms are comfortably furnished in country antiques and brass beds. The house is located at the end of a quiet street away from the city noise.

Archbishop's Mansion
1000 Fulton St.
1-800-543-5820

The Archbishop's Mansion, which opened as a bed and breakfast in 1982, was built in 1904 as the residence for the Catholic Archbishop of San Francisco. It is a beautifully restored belle epoque mansion that is furnished throughout with European antiques. Each individually decorated guestroom has a private bath and many have a working fireplace. There are two romantic rooms with double Jacuzzi tubs and five spacious suites. Guests enjoy a generous continental breakfast.

Bock's Bed and Breakfast
1448 Willard St.
415/664-6842

Opened in 1980 as a bed and breakfast, this lovely 1906 restored Edwardian residence is the family home of your host and her Scottish Terrier, Rosie. Two blocks from the Golden Gate Park and an easy walk to shops and restaurants.

Subtleties: Carol's Cow Hollow Inn

2821 Steiner St.
Web site: www.subtleties.com
1-800-400-8295

The former President of ABC wrote: "Without a doubt, this is the best B&B we have ever stayed in, and there have been many. Lots of space, good beds, great food, wonderful advice and computer printouts for visiting the city, and the cheerful, smiling and generous faces of Carol and Sacha. We are recommending it to all our friends."

Located in the heart of Pacific Heights/Cow Hollow, Carol's Cow Hollow Inn is within walking distance from delightful Union Street Victorian architecture, sidewalk cafes, fun boutiques, and delicious, inexpensive restaurants that locals prefer. Fisherman's Wharf, Chinatown, cable cars, and Golden Gate Park are easy to get to and you don't need a car. Each of the three rooms is spacious, decorated with original oil paintings and views of the bay make for a memorable stay.

The Garden Studio

1387 6th Ave.
415/753-3574

Tired of tourist hotels? Want to mingle with the natives and be minutes from all the famous San Francisco sights? Then we have the place for you. A quiet studio apartment opening onto your own private garden. The Inner Sunset is a safe, urban neighborhood filled with excellent restaurants. Two blocks from Golden Gate Park (the Arboretum and Aquarium), and twenty minutes to Chinatown, cable cars, Fisherman's Wharf, etc.

The Spencer House

1080 Haight St.
415/626-9205

The Spencer House is a splendid Queen Anne Victorian mansion built in 1887 that evokes the luxurious, classic mood of a fine European house. Its original graciousness meticulously restored, the home brims with European and Oriental antiques and fabrics, draperies and linens. There are six guest rooms, each with private bath, in this 8,000 square foot private home. Guests are offered feather beds and down duvets in an atmosphere enriched by oriental rugs and exquisite antiques.

The Willows B&B Inn

710 14th St.
415/431-4770

The Willows Inn is located within the Gay and Lesbian Castro neighborhood. The rustic country decor is a beautiful combination of handcrafted bentwood willow furnishings, antique dressers and armoires,

plantation shutters, cozy comforters, and plants. Kimono bathrobes are provided along with fine English soaps and shampoo. A continental plus breakfast is served in bed with the morning newspaper and an evening port and chocolate bed turndown service is available. Twelve guest rooms are available.

Victorian Inn on the Park

301 Lyon St.
1-800-435-1967

Lisa and William Benau have been the innkeepers at this "truly" family owned business since it opened in 1981. Both Lisa and Willie love food and wine and know all the best restaurants and local food hangouts. They collect wine and cook as well so they can lead you to the best wine stores and specialty food shops. Willie is also a true sports fan and knows all the local sports arenas and game schedules. Everything from bookstores, clothing shops, antique shops to theater and nightclubs are interests of the Innkeepers. Lisa's mom, Shirley Weber, is responsible for most of the decorating and remodeling at the Inn. Lisa and Willie's two children, Cassandra and Zachary, often help guests as well. Many Saturday and Sunday mornings they are assisting in serving breakfast.

158 SAN JACINTO

Country Heritage Antiques
2385 S. San Jacinto Ave.
909/658-8468

Corner Antiques
2525 S. San Jacinto Ave.
909/925-1799

Ann's Attic
2547 S. San Jacinto Ave.
909/925-0272

Yellow House Antiques
410 E. Main St.
909/487-7879

159 SAN JOSE

Time Tunnel Vintage Toys
532 S. Bascom Ave.
408/298-1709

William B. Huff Antiques
999 Lincoln Ave.
408/287-8820

Past & Presents
1324 Lincoln Ave.
408/297-1822

Willow Glen Collective
1349 Lincoln Ave.
408/947-7222

Gold Street Antiques
2092 Lincoln Ave.
408/266-9999

Ancora Ancora
751 W. San Carlos St.
408/977-1429

Antique Village
1225 W. San Carlos St.
408/292-2667

San Carlos St. Antiques
1401 W. San Carlos St.
408/293-8105

Laurelwood Antiques & Collectibles
1824 W. San Carlos St.
408/287-1863

Briarwood Antiques & Collectibles
1885 W. San Carlos St.
408/292-1720

Annette's Antiques
1887 W. San Carlos St.
408/289-1929

Antique Colony
1915 W. San Carlos St.
408/293-9844

California

Antique Dreams
1916 W. San Carlos St.
408/998-2339

Antique Memories & Collectibles
2314 Steven Creek Blvd.
408/977-1758

Antique Decor/A Treasure of Joy
1957 W. San Carlos St.
408/298-5814

Rosewood Antiques
1897 W. San Carlos St.
408/292-1296

Interesting Side Trips

The Winchester Mystery House
525 S. Winchester Blvd.
408/247-2000

Was widowed heiress, Sarah Winchester, a few bricks shy of a full load, believing she'd ward off the spirits of hostile Indians and others by the continuous thirty-eight-year construction of what eventually became her 160-room, $5.5 million mansion? Or was she merely a frustrated architectural genius, the first to discern the value of many late nineteenth-century innovations, who, rather than using a blueprint, sketched as the "spirits" moved her? Her home was among the first in the country to have elevators, wool insulation, gas lights and stove, an "annunciator" intercom with which she could page her many servants from anywhere in the house, and built-in scrub boards and soap holders, which she patented.

This is the puzzle posed to visitors of the Winchester Mystery House in San Jose, Calif., which was built and rebuilt from 1884 until practically the moment after Sarah Winchester's death in 1922. At 24,000 square feet, it has 10,000 windows, 2,000 doors, 52 skylights, 47 fireplaces (one of which is hand carved), 40 staircases and bedrooms, 13 bathrooms, six kitchens, three elevators, two basements, and one shower.

Only the best was used, and this Victorian home boasts parquet floors with multifaceted inlaid patterns of precious hardwoods; gold and silver chandeliers; exquisite art glass windows, and doors with hinges and designs of silver, bronze, and gold. Storerooms still contain tens of thousands of dollars worth of Tiffany doors and windows, as well as precious silks, satins, linens, and other fabrics. A glass-lined conservatory not only guaranteed sunlight but also had a metal sub-flooring that could be drained to the garden below whenever the servants watered the plants. An acoustically balanced ballroom that cost the then-outrageous sum of $9,000 was put together using carpenter's glue and wooden pegs, with tiny nails used only in moldings and floorings.

But the mansion, which rambles over nearly six acres and is four stories (down from seven before the San Francisco earthquake), brims with oddities. Stairways lead to ceilings, and doors open into walls. Pillars on fireplaces are installed upside down, ostensibly to confuse evil spirits. One $1,500 Tiffany window will never see the light of day because it's blocked off by a wall. Skylights shoot up from the floor, and a five-foot door, just right for the diminutive (four feet, ten inches, one hundred pounds) Sarah, stands next to a normal-sized one that leads nowhere. One cabinet opens up to one-half inch of storage space, while the closet

across from it reveals the back thirty rooms of the home.

The number thirteen abounds. Several rooms have thirteen panels with the same number of windows, which, in turn, have "guess how many" panes. A baker's dozen can be found in the lights in the chandeliers, in the cupolas in the greenhouse, and in the palms that line the front driveway. Sarah's last will and testament consisted of thirteen parts and was signed thirteen times, and legend has it that when she dined, it was on a gold service set for herself and twelve invisible guests. To further encourage ghost busting, the house had only two mirrors.

In order to better understand the house, one needs to delve into the enigma that was Sarah Pardee Winchester. Born in 1839, in New Haven, Connecticut, she married William Winchester in 1862. He was the son of Oliver Winchester, inventor and manufacturer of the repeating rifle that allegedly won the West. According to several accounts, Sarah was an attractive, cultured musician who spoke four languages.

But her life was far from normal. Her only daughter, Anna, died in infancy, and a few years later in 1881 her husband succumbed to pulmonary tuberculosis. "Sarah had never fully recovered from the first loss, so this further intensified her anguish," states Shozo Kagoshima, director of marketing for the museum. Sarah was now incredibly wealthy, thanks to the invention that had the dubious honor of having killed more game, Indians, and U.S. soldiers than any other weapon in American history. She inherited $20 million and nearly 50 percent of the stock in the Winchester company, the latter of which gave her a tax-free (until 1913) stipend of about $1,000 a day. So money was no object.

To ease her grief, Sarah went to a "seer" in Boston, who told her that "the spirits of all those the Winchester rifles had killed sought their revenge by taking the lives of her loved ones," relates Kagoshima. "Furthermore, they'd placed a curse on her and would haunt her forever." But Sarah could construct her own escape hatch, the medium said, by "moving West, buying a house, and continually building on it as the spirits directed." That way, she could escape the hostile ones (particularly Indians), while providing a comfortable respite for friendly ghosts (including perhaps Casper), and possibly guaranteeing eternal life.

So Sarah traveled to San Jose and plunked down nearly $13,000 in gold coins to buy an eight-room farmhouse from a Dr. Caldwell. Thus an exquisite behemoth was born.

Renovated in 1973, the rambling structure has 110 rooms open to the public, about 20 more than were in use when Sarah was alive. "The rest were damaged by the 1906 earthquake or are offices," explains Kagoshima. Other than normal restoration to maintain the status quo "the house is to remain the same as when she died."

"Sarah was an eccentric, although she had many good ideas about building and modern conveniences," sums up Kagoshima. The Winchester Mystery House may never be solved, but it—and everyone connected with it—has had a long, strange trip.

From *America's Strangest Museums*
© 1996 by Sandra Gurvis
Published by arrangement with Carol Publishing Group, a Citadel Press Book

California

160 SAN JUAN BAUTISTA

Lillian Johnson Antiques
405 3rd St.
408/623-4381

Gerrie's Collectibles Etc.
406 3rd St.
408/623-1017

Golden Wheel Antiques
407 3rd St.
408/623-4767

161 SAN JUAN CAPISTRANO

Old Mission San Juan Capistrano

There is one historic place in Southern California where visitors gather, only to return again and again. It is the famous old Spanish Mission at San Juan Capistrano, the quaint little town located above the shores of the Pacific, halfway between San Diego and Los Angeles along the old Camino Real.

Mission San Juan Capistrano is beautiful, old and romantic. You can hear the tolling of its centuries-old bells and walk down its time-worn paths. Its serenity and peace amid lush gardens and cool fountains, cloistered by old adobe walls, offers visitors seclusion from the sounds and sights of a busy world.

Founded over two centuries ago, the Mission is a monument to California's multi-cultural history, embracing its Spanish, Mexican, Native American and European heritage. Originally built as a self-sufficient community by Spanish padres and Indian laborers, the Mission was a center for agriculture, industry and education. The spiritual and cultural heritage of the Mission is owed to the legendary Fr. Junipero Serra, who founded over eight missions in California and earned heroic stature as the "Father of California," becoming its first citizen in July of 1769.

Today, you'll discover many areas of interest within the Mission walls, including the museum, founding documents, early soldiers' barracks, friars' quarters, an olive millstone, cemetery, and an aqueduct system. Then, continue with a walk through the renowned gardens to the majestic ruins of the great Stone Church, and along the path to beautiful little Serra Chapel, oldest building in California.

You can see the little adobe church, "Father Serra's Chapel," the oldest building still in use in California. Constructed in 1777, it houses a magnificent Baroque altar which is over 350 years old. The famous "Golden Altar" was shipped from Spain to California in 10 large crates containing 396 pieces. Originally intended for use in the Los Angeles Cathedral, the altar piece was given to the Mission in 1922. Crafted of Spanish cherry wood covered with gold leaf, the 22 feet high and 18 feet wide golden altar features 52 carved angels who watch over visitors today.

The setting is very spiritual. Light falls on it from a long narrow window above. Viewed through the 100-foot nave, which is usually in semi-darkness, the shimmering golden sight is one not easily forgotten.

There are many romantic legends about the Mission. The most popular are about the swallows of Capistrano. Swallow's Day is celebrated annually on March 19. Visitors from all over the world come to witness the return of the swallows to Capistrano. Legend says the swallows, seeking sanctuary from an innkeeper who destroyed their nests, took up residence at the old Mission. They return to the site each year to nest, knowing their young can be safe within the Mission walls.

You'll also learn about the legend of Magdalena, whose penance was to walk up and down the church aisle with a lighted candle to atone for disobeying her father, who had forbidden her from courting a man beneath her station in life. On her first day of penance, December 8, 1812, an earthquake destroyed the great Stone Church and buried her in the ruins. It is said that on certain nights in December her candlelight can still be seen shining out of the church ruins.

General Information: The Mission is open from 8:30 a.m. to 5 p.m. daily except on Thanksgiving, Christmas and Good Friday afternoon. Admission is $5 for adults and $4 for seniors and children. Members free. There is usually no extra charge for exhibitions or special events.

Location: The Mission is conveniently located one block from the Ortega exit off the 5 freeway, at the corner of Camino Capistrano and Ortega Hwy.

Visitors Center: To book a guided tour or arrange a special event, call 714/248-2049. To write for information, please send inquiry to P.O. Box 697, San Juan Capistrano, CA 92693.

Yesterday's Paper

31815 Camino Capistrano, Suite C11
714/248-0945
Open: Daily 11–5
Directions: From the I-5 exit (Ortega Hwy. 74) to W. 2 blocks to Camino Capistrano St., turn left, shop is on right. Located in the Historic District.

Yesterday's Paper provides over 25 years of experience and an extensive inventory in providing everything old made of paper to their customers. Whether for the collector, for the historian, or for the customer who wants a piece of nostalgia from their childhood; a tour through their 3 large rooms of wall and case displays plus neatly organized inventory bins allows you to find items quickly and easily.

The shop offers additions for your collection or decorating needs whether it's books, magazines, illustrations, maps, movie material, posters, documents, postcards, advertising cards, calendars, menus, photos, comics, sheet music, catalogs, labels, railroad paper, aviation paper, sports paper, stock certificates, checks, valentines, pin-ups and more.

Mail service is available both for in-store, call-in, or mail order customers as well.

Majorca of San Juan
31815 Camino Capistrano
714/496-7465

Durenberger & Friends
31531 Camino Capistrano
714/240-5181

California

Old Barn Mall
31792 Camino Capistrano
714/493-9144

Just Perfect Antiques
31815 Camino Capistrano
714/240-8821

Decorative Arts Villa
31431 Camino Capistrano
714/488-9600

Gifts For The Home International
31681 Camino Capistrano
714/443-3913

Grand Avenue Antiques
33208 B Paseo Cerveza
714/661-1053

Sentimental Journey West
31843 Camino Capistrano
714/661-4560

Encore Antiques
31815 Camino Capistrano
714/661-3483

Curiosity Antiques
31107 Rancho Viejo Road, #B2
714/240-1553

Studio Five Design
31511 Camino Capistrano
714/240-1474

Ye Old Collector Shop
31815 Camino Capistrano
714/496-6724

Wild Goose Chase
31521 Camino Capistrano, #A
714/487-2720

Great Places to Eat

Capistrano Depot
26701 Verdugo Street-Amtrak Station
714/488-7600

Ramos House Cafe
31752 Los Rios Street-Historic District
714/443-1342

L'Hirondelle French Cuisine
31661 Camino Capistrano
714/661-0425

Sidewalk Cafe
31882 Del Obispo-Plaza Del Obispo
714/443-0423

162 SAN LUIS OBISPO

Treasure Island Antiques
645 Higuera St.
805/543-0532

Showroom
1531 Monterey St.
805/546-8266

Great Places to Stay

Apple Farm Inn

2015 Monterey St.
1-800-255-2040

The comforts of a first-rate hotel and atmosphere of a turn-of-the-century bed and breakfast, blend to create the charming Apple Farm Inn. On a creekside setting surrounded by shady sycamores and beautiful gardens, this country-Victorian inn is an elegant peaceful retreat. Rich decor, distinctive beds and a fireplace that conveys warmth and hospitality, give each room its own identity. Accommodates 69 guests.

Heritage Inn B&B

978 Olive St.
805/544-7440

Heritage Inn is located at the crossroads of Hwy. 101 and Hwy. 1, midway between Los Angeles and San Francisco. This gorgeous turn-of-the-century Victorian home is within walking distance of quaint downtown and San Luis Obispo Mission. Just minutes from beautiful beaches for sunbathing and sport fishing, natural hot springs, horseback riding and of course, the famous Hearst Castle. Hiking, picnicking and very popular winery tours are a wonderful way to enjoy the wildflowered countryside. Each room has its own special touch, a cozy fireplace, old-fashioned window seat, or a walk-out terrace with views of the mountain and creek. Peaceful creekside gardens abound with playful kitties and guests are often delighted to find ducks and deer sharing this natural area.

163 SAN MARCOS

San Marcos Antique Village
983 Grand Ave.
760/744-8718

Burdock Victorian Lamp Co.
757 N. Twin Oaks Valley Road, #5
760/591-3911

Vicki Harman, Antiques-Estates
1440 Grand Ave.
760/591-4746

164 SAN MATEO

Hoosier-Town Antiques
726 S. Amphlett Blvd.
650/343-3673

Camelot Antiques & Art
714 S. B St.
650/343-7663

Ellsworth Place Antiques
115 S. Ellsworth Ave.
650/347-5906

Shawn's
2218 Palm Ave.
650/574-2097

Come C Antiques
159 South Blvd.
650/344-5899

Memory House Antiques
74 E. 3rd Ave.
650/344-5600

B Street Collective
710 S. B St.
650/342-0993

Come C Interiors
807 S. B St.
650/344-5899

Canterbury Antiques
1705 Gum St.
650/570-7010

Albert's Antiques
310 S. San Mateo Ave.
650/348-2369

Look What I Found
168 South Blvd.
650/573-7113

165 SAN PEDRO

South Bay Antiques
100 W. 1st St.
310/833-2578

166 SAN RAFAEL

English Country Pine & Design
2066 4th St.
415/485-3800

Bargain Box Sunny Hills
508 Irwin St.
415/459-2396

Collier Lighting
3100 Kerner Blvd.
415/454-6672

Twenty Ross Common
20 Ross St.
415/925-1482

167 SANTA ANA

Steven-Thomas Antiques
800 E. Dyer Rd.
714/957-6017

Lyman Drake Antiques
2901 S. Harbor Blvd.
714/979-2811

Charles Wallace Antiques, Inc.
2929 S. Harbor Blvd.
714/556-9901

Second Season
2380 N. Tustin
714/835-0180

168 SANTA BARBARA

Collector's Corner
701 Anacapa St.
805/965-8915

Adobe Antiques
707 Anacapa St.
805/966-2556

A Walk in the Woods
15 E. Anapamu
805/966-1331

Peregrine Galleries
508 Brinkerhoff Ave.
805/963-3134

Elders
512 Brinkerhoff Ave.
805/962-0933

Hightower & Russell
528 Brinkerhoff Ave.
805/965-5687

Mary's on the Avenue
529 Brinkerhoff Ave.
805/962-8047

Robert Livernois Art
533 Brinkerhoff Ave.
805/962-4247

Corner Cottage
536 Brinkerhoff Ave.
805/962-7010

Peregrin
1133 Coast Village Road
805/969-9671

Main Antiques
39 E. DeLa Guerra St.
805/962-7710

Moriarty's Lamps
305 E. Haley St.
805/966-1124

Mackey Antiques/Pine Trader
410 E. Haley St.
805/962-0250

State St. Antique Mall
710 State St.
805/965-2575

Mingei
736 State St.
805/963-3257

Indigo
1323 State St.
805/962-6909

Amphora Arts & Antiques
1321 State St.
805/899-2122

Great Places to Stay

Casa Del Mar Inn

18 Bath St.
1-800-433-3097

A unique Mediterranean-style family inn with lush gardens year round, located one-half block from the beach. Walk to excellent shopping, fine restaurants, and all beach activities. A variety of room types offer

accommodation options ranging from one or two-room bungalow-style family suites with full kitchens and fireplaces to cozy rooms with one king or queen size bed. All rooms feature private entrance and private bath. Amenities include a garden courtyard spa and sun deck.

Cheshire Cat Inn

36 W. Valerio St.
Web site: www.cheshire@chesirecat.com
805/569-1610

A 17-room inn, the Cheshire Cat is comprised of two 100-year-old Queen Anne side-by-side Victorians, three cottages and a coach house, surrounded by romantic flower gardens, a spa-filled gazebo, brick patios, decks with private sitting areas and fountains. The guest rooms, which are decorated in a Laura Ashley–Alice in Wonderland theme with English antiques, all have phones and baths.

Glenborough Inn Bed & Breakfast

1327 Bath St.
1-800-962-0589

Private, Romantic, Intimate … the inn with its three homes, reflecting Victorian and California Craftsman eras, is surrounded by gardens on a quiet tree-lined street just three blocks from downtown and 14 blocks from the seashore. Luxuriate in the privately-reserved garden spa and pamper yourself with a hot breakfast served to your room or in the gardens. Relax around the parlor fireplace or in the gardens as you enjoy a refreshment or quiet moment. The inn is located in the heart of historic downtown Santa Barbara.

Laguna Garden Inn

909 Laguna St.
1-888-770-8880

A quiet, very private Victorian era cottage (c.1874). A peaceful getaway with old-fashioned front porch, spacious tree-shaded sunny deck with award-winning flower gardens and enchanting mountain views. Two blocks to popular downtown restaurants, quality shopping and theatres. Open-air tram to the beach and Stearn's Wharf from this central location.

Montecito Inn

1295 Coast Village Road
Web site: www.montecitoinn.com
1-800-843-2017

The Montecito Inn is unique among Santa Barbara landmarks. Located two blocks from the beach, the hotel is a product of Hollywood's Golden Era, built in 1928 by silent screen legend Charlie Chaplin as a haven for tinsel town celebrities.

Today's red tile roof and white plaster walls pay homage to the original construction.

During its renovation, the wishing well that inspired composer Richard Rodgers to write his memorable love song, "There's a Small Hotel" (1936) was lost. A replica of that well now sits in the highly acclaimed Montecito Cafe. Magnificently restored, the Inn's sixty rooms include seven one-bedroom luxury suites featuring spacious Italian marble bathrooms with Jacuzzi tubs and custom fireplaces. Cinema buffs will delight in the Inn's complete library of Chaplin films.

Secret Garden Inn and Cottages

1908 Bath St.
1-800-676-1622

The Secret Garden is one of Santa Barbara's oldest inns, formerly called the Blue Quail. The inn consists of a main house and four cottages set in a lush jasmine, jacaranda and camellia-filled garden. The intertwined branches of the persimmon, avocado and pecan trees, combined with the high hedges and private lawns, add to the secrecy of the garden while hummingbirds, blue jays and the trickling of fountains add peace and tranquillity. All nine rooms and cottages have private bathrooms with showers.

Simpson House Inn

121 E. Arrellaga St.
Web site: www.simpsonhouseinn.com
1-800-676-1280

North America's only 5-diamond AAA B&B. Nestled in an acre of English gardens in downtown Santa Barbara, the Simpson House Inn offers fourteen luxurious guest accommodations. The original 1874 Eastlake Victorian house contains six antique-filled guest rooms, along with a formal dining room, and elegant living room with fireplace. The renovated barn features four suites, each with a king-size bed, sitting area, fireplace, and wet bar. Three individual private cottages come with Jacuzzi spa-tubs, stone-faced fireplaces, private garden patios and queen-size canopied featherbeds.

The Tiffany Inn

1323 De La Vina St.
1-800-999-5672

Classic antiques and period furnishings welcome you throughout this lovingly restored 1898 Victorian home. Guest rooms all have queen or king beds, garden or mountain views and most have fireplaces. The three suites also feature whirlpool spas. Tiffany is a short walk from exclusive downtown shops, restaurants, galleries, theaters and museums. A sumptuous breakfast is served on the garden veranda. Enjoy wine and cheese in front of the main fireplace in the afternoon.

169   SANTA CRUZ

The Santa Cruz area, a popular antique destination, has designed a way for visitors to preview the area's antique and collectible stores. Their on-line directory (www.santacruzantiques.com) contains a complete listing of the antique stores to visit.

The web site includes a master list of every store from the San Lorenzo Valley to Aptos. Each store's listing consists of their address and phone number along with a link to a map on which they appear. Some of the shops have an expanded listing of their merchandise and some have links to their own web pages.

A visitor to the site can also go directly to the maps page to locate all the stores in a different shopping area such as Soquel Village or San Lorenzo Valley. The maps can then be printed out and used for travel.

There is a resource page on the web site which also includes antique resources such as furniture refinishing and china repair services as well as links to various Santa Cruz sites.

There is also a calendar of events which lists Northern California and Central California antique shows for 1998. A special attraction to the site is a live spy cam positioned above the famous Santa Cruz Boardwalk so visitors can check the day's weather before they plan their trip. Look in the near future for a complete list of restaurants and lodging available.

By Jayne Skeff, Antiques & Collectibles

Modern Life
925 41st Ave.
408/475-1410

Lovejoy's
2600 Soquel Ave.
408/479-4480

Possibilities Unlimited
1043 Water St.
408/427-1131

Mr Goodie's
1541 Pacific Ave.
408/427-9997

Hall's Surrey House Antiques
708 Water St.
408/423-2475

Great Places to Stay

Chateau Victorian

118 First St.
408/458-9458
Open: Daily
Rates: $110–$140
Directions: Hwy 17 drops onto Ocean St./Beaches. Go to the end of Ocean St. which forms a "T" at the light. Right on San Lorenzo to next light; left on Riverside, go over bridge through the light to the next stop sign; right on 2nd St., next stop sign left on Cliff St.; go one block; right on 1st St.; just past the first building on the left is parking. House is on the right. From Hwy 1, coming from the north. Coming in on Mission St., go to 4th stop light; right on Bay St. to the end, forming a "T"; left on West Cliff Dr., which drops onto Beach St.; bottom of small hill is a stop sign; continue straight to next stop sign; left on Cliff St.;

California

go one short block; left on First St. From Hwy 1, coming from the south; ends in a fish hook and drops onto Ocean St./Beaches, and as above.

Replete with decorative cornices, bay windows and gingerbread trim, Chateau Victorian was built around 1885. It was turned into an elegant bed & breakfast in 1983. The inn was originally a single-family residence for a family that obviously enjoyed the beach and the ocean. Within a block of Chateau Victorian is a beautiful beach, stretching for nearly a mile from the San Lorenzo River to beyond the wharf.

Wood-burning fireplaces adorn all seven rooms and each room offers its own special touch of Victorian-styled themes. The Garden Room contains an original Victorian bay window and a four-poster canopy bed. The Bay Side Room has a marble fireplace and a clawfoot tub. The Pleasure Point Room has a bay window seat overlooking a garden of flowers. Old-fashioned armoires, and private entrances to The Patio Room and Sunrise Room, provide an intimate "home away from home" atmosphere. There is a Lighthouse Room and a Natural Bridges Room with high ceilings and redwood crossbeams. From this room guests will also enjoy a small view of Loma Prieta Mountain.

A breakfast of fresh fruits, croissants, muffins, preserves, juices, coffee and teas are available from 9-10:30 a.m. in the lounge, on the secluded deck or the patio.

170 SANTA MARGARITA

Gasoline Alley Antiques
2200 El Camino Real
805/438-5322

Faded Glory Antiques
2719 El Camino Real
805/438-3770

Little Store Antiques
22705 El Camino Real
805/438-5347

Kathy's Antiques
2324 El Camino Real
805/438-3542

Carriage House Antiques
22302 El Camino Real
805/438-5062

171 SANTA MARIA

Little Store Antiques
22705 El Camino Real
805/438-5347

Antique Mall
1573 Stowell Center Plaza
805/922-6464

Golden Retriever Antiques
111 W. Main St.
805/349-1038

172 SANTA MONICA

Santa Monica Antique Market
1607 Lincoln Blvd.
310/314-4899
Open: Daily Mon.–Sat., 10–6, Sun., 12–5
Free valet parking

Santa Monica Antique Market is located on Los Angeles' fashionable West Side and houses over 150 dealers and 20,000 square feet of merchandise. The inventory comes from all over the world and includes all types of furnishings and collectibles. Rediscover the Age of Romance with distinctive antique and custom-made decorative accessories from the Victorian through the Art Deco periods. You'll find exquisite lamps and chandeliers, signature jewelry, figurines, cherubs, pottery, and assorted items of uncommon beauty reminiscent of Victorian times.

Create the pleasure of outdoor living in your garden room or terrace with gilded wooden columns, statues, fountains, handsomely crafted wrought iron pieces and neo-classical accents. If you enjoy and cherish America's textile arts, accessories and furnishings, then you're in for a treat. The Market offers lovely antique quilts dating from 1870-1940, stunning iron and brass beds, a 1910 white wicker chair, bird houses from 1920-1940, and many fine and unusual folk art pieces. You'll also find a superb representation of country primitives such as Shaker and Mennonite shutters, mantels, pie safes, windows and old watering cans.

The Market displays some wonderful American arts and crafts movement pieces. Furniture bearing the distinctive names of Stickley, Limberts, Lifetime and Harden can be found along with hand-hammered copper lighting and metalwork by Roycroft and Dirk Van Erp.

Travel through American modernism to Italian Baroque with architectural fragments, pediments, finials and columns, Palladian mirrors, tin work, mercury glass, paintings, iron work and Latin American furniture.

One of the Market's greatest successes has been the ability to tailor services to the different needs of its diverse customer base. Santa Monica Antique Market offers a layaway plan, 48-hour at home trial period, delivery, international shipping, item searches, restoration and appraisal referrals, bridal registry, gift certificates, free gift wrapping and off-hours shopping, popular among celebrity clientele. Other bonuses include a book section, an espresso bar, and free valet parking.

California

House of Yorke
549 11th St.
310/395-2744

Main Street Antiques
2665 Main St.
310/392-4519

British Collectibles Ltd.
1727 Wilshire Blvd.
310/453-3322

Rosemarie McCaffrey
1203 Montana Ave.
310/395-7711

Montana Country
1311 Montana Ave.
310/393-3324

Country Pine & Design
1318 Montana Ave.
310/451-0317

Blue House
1402 Montana Ave.
310/451-2243

Caswell Antiques
1322 2nd St.
310/394-3384

Clifford Antiques
1655 Lincoln Blvd.
310/452-7668

Raintree Antiques
2711 Main St.
310/392-7731

Quilt Gallery
1025 Montana Ave.
310/393-1148

Brenda Cain Store
1211 Montana Ave.
310/395-1559

Prince of Wales
1316 Montana Ave.
310/458-1566

Twigs
1401 Montana Ave.
310/451-9934

Federico's
1522 Montana Ave.
310/458-4134

Great Places to Stay

Channel Road Inn
219 W. Channel Road
310/459-1920

Originally the home of Thomas McCall, a pioneering Santa Monica businessman, this house was moved from a hilltop site to its current location tucked in a hillside of Santa Monica Canyon, one block from the beach. With the help of the local historical society, innkeeper Susan Zolla saved the Colonial Revival building from demolition and turned it into a gracious inn, one of the only within view of the beach in Los Angeles County. The house is sheathed in blue shingles, a rarity in Los Angeles. Room rates are slightly lower Sunday through Thursday. The inn accommodates 14 guests.

173 SANTA ROSA

Antiques Apples & Art
105 3rd St.
707/578-1414

Whistle Stop Antiques
130 4th St.
707/542-9474

Marianne Antiques
111 3rd St.
707/579-5749

Blue Goose Antiques
60 W. 6th St.
707/527-8859

C & H Antiques
204 Wilson St.
707/527-7421

Treasure House
700 Wilson St.
707/523-1188

Great Places to Stay

Pygmalion House
331 Orange St.
707/526-3407
Open: Year round
Directions: For specific directions from your location, please call the innkeepers.

If you're looking for the perfect romantic getaway that won't cost you a fortune, you need look no further than Pygmalion House in Santa Rosa, California. Pygmalion House is nestled in a quiet neighborhood just a couple of blocks from Santa Rosa's Old Town. It is within walking distance to the various antique shops as well as some wonderful restaurants and coffee houses.

Pygmalion House, one of Santa Rosa's historical landmarks, is a fine example of Victorian Queen Anne architecture. This charming home was built in the 1800s on land owned by one of the city's leading developers, Mr. Thomas Ludwig. This house withstood the great earthquake and fire of 1906 which devastated much of Santa Rosa's heritage.

Pygmalion House derives its name from an ancient Greek myth, which was the basis for George Bernard Shaw's play *Pygmalion* and the musical *My Fair Lady*. The name reflects the transformation, brought about by painstaking renovation, from an old dilapidated house to the grand lady it is today.

You'll find this gracious Bed and Breakfast full of antiques from the collection of the famous stripper Gypsy Rose Lee and the famous madam and past Sausalito mayor, Sally Stanford. Each of the guest rooms are quiet and nicely decorated, including private bath, and a queen or king-size bed. The main room, or "double parlor," includes a beautiful fireplace as well as an offset sitting area that looks out from octagon-shaped windows.

Each morning you'll feast on the full breakfast that is served from 8:00 a.m. to 9:30 a.m. Breakfast includes fresh fruit or melon, fresh baked muffins and croissants, and eggs with either ham, bacon, or sausage. Fresh squeezed orange juice is also served as well as Pygmalion House's fresh ground blend of five different kinds of coffee, including Kona coffee from Hawaii.

With all of these special touches that Pygmalion House offers you would think that a night's stay would be expensive. Well, the best thing about this B&B is their prices. You can get a room with a queen-sized bed for only $75 per night and a king-sized bed for $85. Considering that B&Bs can run as much as $100–$200 a night, Pygmalion House offers its guests true value for their money as well as a wonderful experience that is sure to bring you back time and time again.

California

174 SARATOGA

Carol's Antique Gallery
14455 Big Basin Way
408/867-7055

Bit O Country
14527 Big Basin Way
408/867-9199

Front Window
12378 Saratoga Sunnyvale Road
408/253-2980

M E Benson's Antiques
14521 Big Basin Way
408/741-0314

McKenzie House Antiques
14554 Big Basin Way
408/867-1341

Blue Candlestick
14320 Saratoga Sunnyvale Road
408/867-3658

175 SEAL BEACH

Audrey's Antiques
132 Main St.
562/430-7213

Finders Keepers Unlimited
406 Marina Dr.
562/493-4952

Antique Gallery
217 Main St.
562/594-4985

176 SEBASTOPOL

Carol's Curios
961 Gravenstein Hwy.
707/823-8334

Antique Society
2661 Gravenstein Hwy.
707/829-1733

Willow Tree Antiques
2701 Gravenstein Hwy.
707/823-3101

Llano House Antiques
4353 Gravenstein Hwy.
707/829-9322

Country Cottage Antiques
1235 Gravenstein Hwy.
707/823-4733

Ed's Antiques
2661 Gravenstein Hwy.
707/829-5363

Lone Pine Antiques
3598 Gravenstein Hwy.
707/823-6768

Sebastopol Antique Mall
755 Petaluma Ave.
707/829-9322

177 SHERMAN OAKS

Outer Limits
13542 Ventura Blvd.
818/906-8133

Piccolo Pete's
13814 Ventura Blvd.
818/990-5421

Aunt Teeks
4337 Woodman Ave.
818/784-3341

Marilyn Hirsty Antiques
13627 Ventura Blvd.
818/995-4128

Sherman Oaks Antique Mall
14034 Ventura Blvd.
818/906-0338

178 SIMI VALLEY

A Collectors Paradise - Penny Pinchers
4265 Valley Fair St.
805/527-0056
Web site: www.city.411
Open: Mon.–Sat. 10–5 and Sun. 11–5
Directions: From the 405 Freeway: Take Hwy. 118 West to the Tapo Cyn. exit, make a left to Cochran, make another left and go three blocks to Winifred, make a right and go about 10 blocks to Valley Fair. OR from Hwy. 101, take 23 North, which changes into the 118 East. Go to Tapo Cyn. exit, make a right, go to Cochran, make a left, go three blocks to Winifred, make a right and go about 10 blocks to Valley Fair.

In business for 32 years, Penny Pinchers offers Empire furniture and Depression glass, plus all types of nostalgic antiques and collectibles. They also offer the very hard, but not frequently found, services of furniture repair, jewelry repair and custom work, and appraisals. Also a full antique and collectible book library is available for the customers' use.

Memories Antiques
4325 Valley Fair St.
805/526-6308

Antiques at Willie's
4345 Valley Fair St.
805/584-2580

Pine Haven Antiques
4371 Valley Fair St.
805/520-3801

179 SOLANA BEACH

Antique Warehouse
212 S. Cedros Ave.
619/755-5156

Geissmann Rudolf Oriental Carpet
143 S. Cedros Ave.
619/481-3489

Appleby International Art
143 S. Cedros Ave.
619/259-0404

180 SOLVANG

California is noted for having a little bit of everything in the state, but what about the title of "Danish Capital of America"? In the gently rolling Santa Ynez Valley, Solvang (which means sunny field in Danish) was founded in 1911 by Danes from the Midwest seeking to establish a West Coast Danish colony and folk school. Over the years the town began to look more and more Danish as the townspeople, perhaps encouraged by visits from Danish royalty, turned increasingly to Danish-style architecture.

Today, visiting Danes say the town looks more like Denmark than the original country, with buildings of timber-framed white stucco, sloping green copper or wood shingle roofs, gables, dormer and towers, cobblestone sidewalks, outdoor cafes, and shops with leaded-glass windows. There are even four windmills — one still turns.

Specific Danish sites in Solvang include a half-scale replica of the Little Mermaid (the original sits in the Copenhagen harbor), and the Bethania Lutheran Church, a typical rural Danish church with hand-carved pulpits and a scale model of a Danish sailing ship hanging from the ceiling. The Elverhoy Museum preserves the history of Solvang with old photographs, crafts, period rooms, and other exhibits, and the Hans Christian Andersen Museum honors the life and work of the father and master of the modern fairy tale.

But Solvang's most historic site is, ironically, not Danish. It is the beautifully restored adobe Mission Santa Ines, established in 1804 as the 19th of the 21 missions built in California by Spanish Franciscan priests. The chapel, in continuous use since 1817, is decorated with murals by Indian artists and masterpieces of Moorish art and architecture.

But for the shopper, Solvang is Valhalla! There are 350 shops, noted for their antiques, paintings and Danish goods (pastries, music boxes, porcelain figurines, knotted sweaters, folk art, handmade lace, and Danish costumes). After shopping, visitors can tour the town by carriage or on the Honen, a replica of a turn-of-the-century Copenhagen streetcar pulled by a pair of Belgian draft horses. And to tour the picturesque valley, hang gliders and bicycles are the only way to go!

Solvang Antique Center

486 First St.
805/686-2322
Open: Daily 10–6
Cafe/Bistro in same building, open daily 11–9
Directions: *From the south* (Los Angeles, Santa Barbara): Hwy. 101 North to Buellton. Take Solvang Exit (Hwy. 246) east into Solvang (3 miles). Just past Solvang Park in the center of the village turn right onto First Street. The Solvang Antique Center is on the left in the middle of the block or Hwy. 101 North to Santa Barbara. Take Hwy. 154 Exit (San Marcos Pass) past Lake Cachuma. Take Solvang Exit (Hwy. 246) west into Solvang. Once in the Solvang village, go one block past the stop light at Alisal Road. The Solvang Antique Center is on the left in the middle of the block. One route is a divided highway; the other is scenic. *From the north* (San Francisco, Hearst Castle): Hwy. 101 South to Buellton. Take Solvang Exit (Hwy. 246) east into Solvang (3 miles). Just past Solvang Park in the center of the village turn right onto First Street. The Solvang Antique Center is on the left in the middle of the block.

Solvang Antique Center is California's finest multiple-dealer gallery featuring an overwhelming selection of high-quality antiques, making for a unique resource for collectors, designers and dealers.

The open floor plan with over 100 well-lit galleries and showcases

creates a delightful museum-like shopping environment. Sixty-five quality dealers from around the world present European carved furniture, quality American oak, porcelain, sterling silver, cut glass, estate jewelry, paintings, sculpture, pianos, clocks, music boxes, watches, scales, tools and lighting. In addition, the gallery offers expert in-house restoration of antique furniture, clocks, watches, music boxes and scales. Solvang Antique Center provides worldwide delivery and a "hard to find items" locator service.

Home Ranch
444 Atterdag Road
805/686-0069

Frogmore House Antiques
1676 Oak St.
805/688-8985

181 SONOMA

Buffy Antique
414 1st St.
707/996-5626

Antique Center of Sonoma
120 W. Napa St.
707/996-9947

D Tenenbaum Antiques
128 W. Napa St.
707/935-7146

Cat & The Fiddle
153 W. Napa St.
707/996-5651

Curry & I Antiques
17000 Sonoma Hwy.
707/996-8226

182 SONORA

Antique Passions
8 S. Washington St.
209/532-8874

Antiques Etcetera
18 S. Washington St.
209/532-9544

Carriage Trade Antiques
36 S. Washington St.
209/532-0282

Castagnola's Empor. Antiques
93 S. Washington St.
209/533-8443

Baer's 1851 Antiques
105 S. Washington St.
209/533-2460

Pine Tree Peddlers
107 S. Washington St.
209/533-2356

183 SOQUEL

Wayne's Antiques
2940 S. Main St.
408/462-0616

Crawford Antiques
4401 Soquel Dr.
408/462-1528

Frank's Antiques
4900 Soquel Dr.
408/462-3953

Country Garden Antiques
4904 Soquel Dr.
408/462-5188

After Effects
4920 Soquel Dr.
408/475-5991

Edward & Sons Antiques
5025 Soquel Dr.
408/479-7122

Vintage Textiles
4631 Soquel Dr.
408/476-9007

Trader's Emporium
4940 Soquel Dr.
408/475-9201

Tiffany's Antiques
3010 Center St.
408/477-9808

Front Porch Antiques
5320 Soquel Dr.
408/475-1108

Baker & Co.
5011 Soquel Dr.
408/479/4404

Wisteria Antiques and Design
5870 Soquel Dr.
408/462-2900

184 SOUTH LAKE TAHOE

Auntie Q's 2nd Hand Treasures
800 Emerald Bay Road
916/542-2169

Hannifin's Antiques
868 Emerald Bay Road
916/544-6769

Hannifin's Art & Antiques
855 Emerald Bay Road
916/542-4663

Sierra Bookshop
3445 Lake Tahoe Blvd.
916/541-4222

185 SOUTH PASADENA

Isn't It Romantic
950 Mission St.
818/441-4824

Mission Antiques
1018 Mission St., #3
818/799-1327

Yoko
1011 Mission St.
818/441-4758

And Etc
1110 Mission St.
818/799-6581

186 STOCKTON

Buckeye Appliance

714 W. Fremont
209/464-9643
Directions: Going North on I-5 take the Pershing Street exit. Make a left at bottom of ramp. Go 2 blocks to stop light (Fremont Street), make a left. Store is approximately 10 blocks down on right side of street. Going South on I-5 take Oak Street/Fremont exit. Make a left at bottom of ramp (Fremont Street). Go approximately 11 blocks. Located on the right side of the street.

A visit to Buckeye reminds you of Grandma's kitchen. Remember the heavy '50s stoves that had the deep well? You can find them here. The shop carries '50s chrome dinettes, porcelain top tables, Hoosier cabinets and tons of kitchen collectibles. Everything you need for a Retro kitchen.

This shop specializes in the sales, service, parts and restoration of antique gas stoves.

Ivy
209 Dorris Place
209/466-6652

Peckler's Antiques
220 W. Harding Way
209/462-7992

House of Clocks
311 Lincoln Center
209/951-1363

A & B Antiques
216 W. Harding Way
209/946-4337

Lions Den Antiques
230 W. Harding Way
209/547-0433

Memory's Antiques & Collectibles
2220 Pacific Ave.
209/462-5258

Trotting Horse Antiques
9177 Thornton Road
209/477-0549

Mardel's Antiques
926 N. Yosemite St.
209/948-8948

Mardel's Antique Annex
917 N. Yosemite St.
209/546-0926

187 STUDIO CITY

The Cranberry House

12318 Ventura Blvd.
818/506-8945
Open: Daily 11–6
Directions: Take Hwy. 405 North to Hwy. 101 East (to Los Angeles). Exit at Coldwater Canyon, turn right to Ventura Blvd., then turn left. Cranberry House is on the right about 2 miles. OR take Hwy. 5 North to Hwy. 134 West, take Hwy. 134 West to Hwy. 101 West, take Hwy. 101 West to Laurel Canyon, turn left onto Ventura Blvd., then right and go about 3 blocks. Cranberry House will be on the left. Look for the 100-foot cranberry awning on the front!

Designers, prop masters, serious collectors, flea market fanatics and avid antique perfectionists all declare The Cranberry House as their source for the best in treasure hunting. One hundred forty dealers in 15,000 square feet offer Americana, fine and costume jewelry, linens and quilts, smoking collectibles, vintage accessories and silver, toys and the  best in furniture of domestic and European heritage from Roccoco to Modern. Still can't find it? Register for the "Wish List" and their friendly, knowledgeable staff will assist with a no obligation search and notify you when your "wish" arrives. Worldwide shipping, layaway, bridal registry, custom gift wrap, 24-hour approval program, and gift certificates are all a part of the excellent customer service.

Be sure to attend the annual Birthday Sale the third weekend in May with discounts up to 50%. Also not to be missed is the Holiday Open House the second weekend in December. The breathtaking holiday decor, free gourmet eats and 10% off everything sales create an unforgettable shopping experience. Get your personal invitation to both events by adding your name to the guest registry.

Ivy Cottage
12206 Ventura Blvd.
818/762-9844

Mother of Pearl & Sons
12328 Ventura Blvd.
818/505-8057

Pearl River
13031 Ventura Blvd.
818/986-5666

Fables Antiques
12300 Ventura Blvd.
818/506-2904

Ferret
12334 Ventura Blvd.
818/769-2427

Kings Cross
13059 Ventura Blvd.
818/905-3382

California

188　SUMMERLAND

Mary Suding Fine Antiques
2173 Ortega Hill Road, 2nd Floor
805/969-4324

Summerland Antique Collective
2194 Ortega Hill Road
805/565-3189

Urban Hunter
2272 Lillie Ave.
805/969-7987

Summerhill Antiques
2280 Lillie Ave.
805/969-3366

Heather House Antiques
2448 Lillie Ave.
805/565-1561

Christian-Tevis Antiques
2173 Ortega Hill Road
805/969-0966

Summerland Antique Annex
2240 Lillie Ave.
805/565-5226

Antico II
2280 Lillie Ave.
805/565-4899

Lillie Antiques & Accessories
2560 Lillie Ave.
805/565-1271

Gentlemen Antiquarians
2560 Lillie Ave.
805/565-1271

189　SUNLAND

Adventure In Postcards
8423 Foothill Blvd.
818/352-5663
Open: Wed.–Sat. 10–5, unless out of town buying or selling.
Directions: Located just ½ mile east of the #210 Freeway at the
Sunland Blvd. offramp (Sunland becomes Foothill one block east of
the freeway).

If you are looking for a very small, portable, inexpensive piece of
Americana, Lee Brown's emporium in Sunland may have just what you
need. The shop is truly an adventure in postcards.

With something like a quarter of a million postcards in stock, covering
everything imaginable, most of Lee's cards are in the $1-5 range and are
dated pre-World War I.

Although some signed cards can pull $100 or so, and a few rare ones
can fetch $1,000 at an art auction, thousands of the little pictures sell for
just 20 cents, making postcards one of the most affordable and interesting
collectibles available.

The Sunland shop stocks everything from depictions of natural
disasters, like the 1906 San Francisco earthquake, to one-eyed cows and
nudes reading books. Other paper ephemera and some miscellaneous
smalls are also offered.

Interesting Story

It was three years ago that Brown discovered a very special holiday
card that stood out among the thousands she was sorting. "I seldom
read the backs of postcards, there's just not time; but I noticed some
handwriting that I recognized," Brown said. "Then I spotted my
grandmother's name, Mabel Holdefer, on a card dated 1908. She had

sent it to a relative." Her grandmother raised her, so finding the card was
a real treasure. I'm sure that's one postcard that will never be sold.

Antiques Etc.
7906 Foothill Blvd.
818/352-3197

Cathy's Cottage
8417 Foothill Blvd.
818/353-7807

190　SUTTER CREEK

Klima's Antiques
94 Boston Alley
209/267-5318

Alicia's
26 Main St.
209/267-0719

Columbian Lady
61 Main St.
209/267-0059

Water Street Antiques
78 Main St.
209/267-0585

Cobweb Collection Antiques
83 Main St.
209/267-0690

Jackson Antiques
28 Main St.
209/223-0188

Creekside Shops
22 Main St.
209/267-5520

Somewhere In Time
34 Main St.
209/267-5789

Old Hotel Antiques
68 Main St.
209/267-5901

Arnolds Antiques
80 Main St.
209/267-0603

O'Neill's Antiques
84 Main St.
209/267-0450

191　TAHOE CITY

Girasole
319 W. Lake Blvd.
916/581-4255

192　TEHACHAPI

Mom & Apple Pie Antiques
798 Tucker Road, #2
805/822-8765
Open: Tues.–Fri. 10–5, Sat. 10–5:30, Sun. 12–5, closed Mon.
Open late or open early if needed for you out-of-towners!

Mom & Apple Pie Antiques began business September 1, 1996. Courtney
Kearnes, owner, decided to open up shop after the antique store she
managed closed in July of 1996. With the help of husband Brent, son
Jarred (3) and daughter Taylor (1), Mom got the store up and running
in a month. The business is now a REAL family affair, as her moms and
dads (2 of each) are involved in the business with her!

The 2,000-square-foot shop is home to 12 dealers from all around the
area. Most of the dealers have 20+ years of experience in the business
and deal in QUALITY, QUALITY, QUALITY merchandise. The shop
specializes in vintage jewelry (Victorian through '60s), timepieces, vintage

linens & lace, quilts, sewing implements, Victorian smalls of all kinds, country primitives including furniture, and so much more! They dabble in just about everything and will do mail order business on most items. Visit their website for a firsthand look.

The atmosphere is inviting, with fresh hot coffee or apple cider in the cool months, and refreshing iced tea in the summer. They offer special presentations for local clubs or groups on request. Come see it to believe it - Mom would love to show you some down home hospitality!

Kathy's Mini Mall
104 W. Tehachapi Blvd.
805/822-6691

Apple Country Antiques
114 W. Tehachapi Blvd.
805/822-7777

Grace's Antiques
20300 Valley Blvd., #E
805/822-5989

193 TEMECULA

Across the River Antiques
28418 Felix Valdez Ave.
909/699-9525

Granny's Attic
28450 Felix Valdez Ave., #C
909/699-9449

Always Wanted Antiques
28545 Felix Valdez Ave.
909/695-1136

Chaparral Antique Mall
28465 Front St.
909/676-0070

A to Z Antiques
28480 Front St.
909/699-3294

Loft
28480 Front St.
909/676-5179

Old Town Antique Faire
28601 Front St.
909/694-8786

Mr. R's Antiques
28635 Front St.
909/676-2002

Gramma Audrey's Antiques Too
28636 Front St.
909/699-9338

Shire Limited
28656 Front St.
909/676-9233

Nana's Too
28677 Front St., #C
909/699-5292

Country Seller & Friends Antiques
42050 Main St.
909/676-2322

Treasures You'll Cherish
42012 Main St.
909/694-6990

Timeless Treasures
28475 Front St., Suite A
909/695-2926

Nancy's Antique Mall
42030 Main St., #BF
909/699-3889

Packards Antiques
42031 Main St., #C
909/693-9442

Gramma Audrey's Antiques
42031 Main St.
909/699-9139

Morgan's Antiques
42049 Main St.
909/676-2722

Temecula Trading Post
42081 Main St.
909/767-5759

Juliet's Collectibles
44060 Margarita Road
909/693-1410

194 THOUSAND OAKS

2nd Edition
368 E. Thousand Oaks Blvd.
805/497-9727

Antique Suites Mall
783 E. Thousand Oaks Blvd.
805/373-0366

Maggie & Me Antiques
783 E. Thousand Oaks Blvd.
805/496-1603

Antiques of Tomorrow
3075 E. Thousand Oaks Blvd.
805/494-4095

195 TORRANCE

Kasden's Antiques
24548 Hawthorne Blvd.
310/378-8132

Dunk Antiques
4164 Pacific Coast Hwy.
310/375-6175

Janson & Son Antiques
1325 Sartori Ave.
310/787-1670

Collector's Gallery
833 Torrance Blvd.
310/532-2166

Pieces of the Past Antique Mall
19032 S Vermont Ave.
310/324-6767

196 TULARE

Old Town Emporium
207 S. K St.
209/688-8483

197 TURLOCK

Yesterday's Expressions
116 S. Center St.
209/669-7003

Trinkets to Treasures
125 S. Center St.
209/667-4988

J.B.'s Antiques
1237 N. Golden State Blvd.
209/632-8220

Johnson's Flowers & Collectibles
417 E. Main St.
209/634-4467

Main Street Antiques
208 E. Main St.
209/669-7000

198 TUSTIN

Tustin Consignments
474 El Camino Real
714/730-5037

Angels Garden
486 El Camino Real
714/669-1337

Bruce Cole Noland Antiques
500 El Camino Real
714/730-5502

Step Back in Time
528 El Camino Real
714/734-9093

Not Just Antiques
546 El Camino Real
714/731-8813

Gerda's Antiques
550 El Camino Real
714/832-4932

Olde Town Tustin Antique Mall
650 El Camino Real
714/838-1144

Van Dorens Consignments
17321 17th St.
714/505-3141

California

Schafer's Antiques
171 N. Tustin Ave.
714/541-5555

199 UPLAND

Calico Reflections
130 E. 9th St.
909/981-2135

Antique Alley
257 E. 9th St
909/985-5563

Carriage House Antiques
152 N. 2nd Ave.
909/982-2543

Alphenaar's Antiques
251 N. 2nd Ave.
909/949-7978

Classic Collectibles
136 E. 9th St.
909/985-9543

Upland Ole Town
270 N. 2nd Ave.
909/981-2408

Collectors Cottage
243 E. 9th St.
909/920-1136

Myra's Antiques
139 N. 2nd Ave.
909/981-7002

Kiosk Corner
188 N. 2nd Ave.
909/981-2876

Sideboard
170 N. 2nd Ave.
909/981-7652

The Art Room Antiques
291 N. 2nd Ave.
909/946-8160

200 UPPER LAKE

Vintage Store
375 N. Hwy. 2
707/275-0303

First & Main
9495 Main St.
707/275-3124

201 VACAVILLE

Bygone Shoppe Antiques
143 McClellan St.
707/449-3575

Past & Presents
333 Merchant St.
707/449-0384

Vasquez Antiques & Collectibles
357 Merchant St.
707/447-9434

202 VALLEJO

Yesteryear's Marketplace

433 Georgia St.
707/557-4671
Open: Mon.–Sat. 10–5, Sun. by chance — knock if light is on.
Directions: From I-80 take Georgia St. exit west to Old Town. 30 yards past Sonoma Blvd. (Hwy 29). Parking front and rear.

With 9,500 square feet of almost everything in antiques and collectibles the shop is located in the Redman's Hall which housed the National Dollar store in the 1930s.

Since 1990 it has been the home of a wonderful shop filled to the brim with a wide variety of crystal, art glass, china, pottery, lamps, prints, paper goods, vintage small appliances, costume jewelry and furniture — ranging from kitsch to elegant.

Interesting Side Trips

St. Peter's Chapel at Mare Island

328 Seawind Dr.
707-557-1538

Famous for its 29 stained glass windows, most designed by the Tiffany Studios of New York.

203 VENICE

Revival
1356 Abbot Kinney Blvd.
310/396-1360

Bountiful
1335 Abbot Kinney Blvd.
310/450-3620

Neptina
1329 1/2 Abbot Kinney Blvd.
310/396-1630

204 VENTURA

Antique Alley
263 S. Laurel St.
805/643-0708

Heirlooms Antique Mall
327 E. Main St.
805/648-4833

Antiques Etc. Mall
369 E. Main St.
805/643-6983

Nicholby Antique Mall
404 E. Main St.
805/653-1195

Times Remembered
467 E. Main St.
805/643-3137

Red House Antiques
1234 E. Main St
805/643-6787

Garden Angel Collective
1414 E. Main St.
805/643-1980

Bid Time Return
1920 E. Main St.
805/641-2003

Curio Cottage
64 S. Oak St.
805/648-5508

Antique Accents
315 E. Main St.
805/643-4511

Attic Treasures
337 E. Main St.
805/641-1039

Main Street Antique Mall
384 E. Main St.
805/648-3268

My Last Hurrah/Attic Trunk
451 E. Main St., #9
805/643-6510

Sevoy Antiques
494 E. Main St.
805/641-1890

Sherlock's Antique Lighting
8672 N. Ventura Ave.
805/649-4683

Park Place Collectibles
1416 E. Main St.
805/652-1761

Oak Street Antiques
27 S. Oak St.
805/652-0053

Sevoy Antiques
1501 Palma Dr.
805/642-8031

America Antiques
2459 Palma Dr.
805/650-6265

205 VISALIA

Planning Mill Mall
515 E. Center Ave.
209/625-8887

Cottage
15472 E. Mineral King
209/734-8996

White's House Antiques
4628 W. Mineral King
209/734-2128

Antiques at the Works Showcase Mall
26644 S. Mooney
209/685-1125

Stuff 'n' Such
1214 E. Houston
209/734-4114

Carriage House Antiques
15484 E. Mineral King
209/635-8818

Spit 'n' Polish Antiques
15361 Ave. 280
209/247-3558

206 WALNUT CREEK

Sundance Antiques
2323 Boulevard Circle
510/930-6200

Quail Country Antiques
1581 Boulevard Way
510/944-0930

Our Showroom Antiques
2363 Boulevard Circle
510/947-6844

Walnut Creek Antiques
2050 N. Broadway
510/947-4900

207 WHITTIER

Virginia's Antiques
6536 Greenleaf Ave.
562/696-2810

Uptown Antiques
6725 Greenleaf Ave.
562/698-1316

Yellow Pipe Antiques
13309 Philadelphia St.
562/945-2362

Elegant Elephant
6751 Washington Ave.
562/698-7037

All The Kings Toys
12323 Whittier Blvd.
562/696-3166

Treasure Chest Antiques
6718 Greenleaf Ave.
562/696-6608

Yesterdays Memories
12310 Penn St.
562/696-6124

Pepe's Antiques
13310 Philadelphia St.
562/945-1676

King Richards Antique Mall
12301 Whittier Blvd.
562/698-5974

208 WOODLAND

Bee's Antiques & Collectibles
1021 Lincoln Ave.
916/662-3246

Tinkers Antiques & Collectibles
338 Main St.
916/662-3204

Old Depot Antiques
1021 Lincoln Ave.
916/662-1215

House Dresser
518 Main St.
916/661-9596

Antiques on Main
528 Main St.
916/668-1815

209 WOODLAND HILLS

Affordable Antiques
4870 Topanga Canyon Blvd.
818/888-2568

Antique Frames & Furniture
22845 Ventura Blvd.
818/224-4845

Joseph Wahl Arts
5305 Topanga Canyon Blvd.
818/340-9245

210 YORBA LINDA

C.P. McGinnis & Co.
4887 Main St.
714/777-8990

Dixie Lee's Antiques
4900 Main St.
714/779-3905

Susan Tanner Antiques
4884 Main St.
714/693-1913

Gifts N Treasures
4897 Main St.
714/777-8371

Colorado

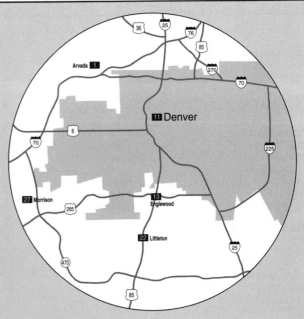

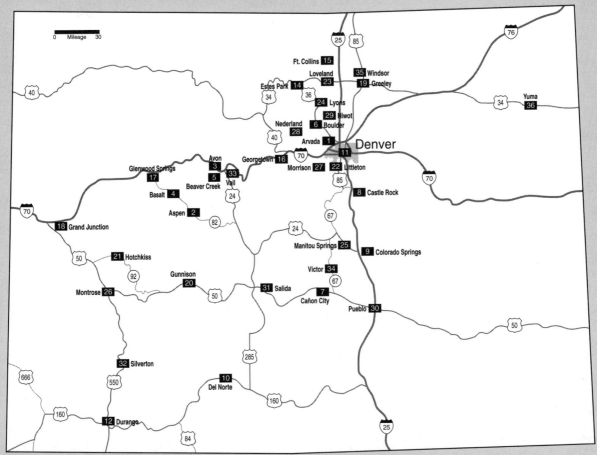

Colorado

1 ARVADA

Penny's
5713 Olde Wadsworth Blvd.
303/403-0290

Cabin Antiques
7505 Grandview Ave.
303/467-7807

Foxhaven Farms Antiques
7513 Grandview Ave.
303/420-2747

Olde Wadsworth Antiques
7511 Grandview Ave.
303/424-8686

Arvada Antique Emporium
7519 Grandview Ave.
303/422-6433

Elegant Glass Antiques
7501 Grandview Ave.
303/424-9330

House of Rees
7509 Grandview Ave.
303/424-0663

2 ASPEN

Alderfer's Antiques
309 E. Main St.
970/925-5051

MC Hugh Antiques
431 E. Hyman Ave.
970/925-5751

Fetzers
308 S. Hunter
970/925-5447

Cooper St. Art & Antique
316 S. Mill St.
970/925-1795

Country Flowers
433 E. Cooper St.
970/925-6522

Katie Ingham Antique Quilts
257 Glen Eagles Dr.
970/925-2595

Morocco
616 E. Hyman Ave.
970/925-9275

Curious George
426 E. Hyman Ave.
970-925-3315

3 AVON

Shaggy Ram
1160 W. Beaver Creek Blvd.
970/949-4377

Grammy's Attic
Hwy. 6 & 24
970/949-6099

4 BASALT

Basalt Antiques
132 Midland Ave. Mall
970/927-3326

Old Paint & Memories
50 Sunset Dr.
970/927-8096

Double D Lazy T Trading Co.
22826 Hwy. 82
970/927-9679

Little Bear Antiques & Uniques
402 C Park Ave.
970/927-8091

5 BEAVER CREEK

Note: Below is a wonderful story submitted by the Vail Valley Tourism & Convention Bureau.

A bear in Beaver Creek was yearning for a spa vacation. Earlier, he'd secretly watched vacationers soaking, enjoying wine and sharing stories of mountain hikes and river rafting adventures, Swedish massages and mud treatments. Long after they departed, he climbed atop the floating cover of a bubbling hot tub and swatted at the delicious-looking hummingbird feeders above.

Locals in the valley like to enjoy the good life, too, you know.

Grammy's Attic
41131 U.S. Hwy. 6 & 24
970/949-6099

Shaggy Ram
1060 W. Beaver Creek Blvd.
970/926-4663

6 BOULDER

8th & Pearl Antiques
740 Pearl St.
303/444-0699

Indochine
2525 Arapahoe Ave. E31
303/444-7734

Candy's Vintage Clothing
4483 Broadway St.
303/442-6186

Rosetree Cottage
2525 Arapahoe Ave., #E34
303/442-5794

Bargain Store Antiques
1949 Pearl St.
303/443-0671

Classic Facets
2010 10th St.
303/938-8851

Sage Gallery Antiques
5360 Arapahoe Ave.
303/449-6799

Crystal Galleries Ltd.
1302 Pearl St.
303/444-2277

American Heritage Antiques
1412 Sunshine Canyon Dr.
303/939-8890

Great Places to Stay

Inn on Mapleton Hill
1001 Spruce St.
1-800-276-6528
Email: maphillinn@aol.com

The Inn on Mapleton Hill is a 100-year-old home welcoming visitors to Colorado in the tradition and warm hospitality of its early settlers. It all started in 1899 when Emma Clarke, a widowed dressmaker and daughter of a Canadian sea captain, first opened the three-story red brick building for boarders, many of which were school teachers. Situated in what is now known as the Mapleton Hill Historic District, it continues to serve as a haven of hospitality.

7 CAÑON CITY

Sherrilyn Antiques
202 Main St.
719/275-5849

Lone Tree Antiques
429 S. 9th St.
719/275-0712

Greenhorn Enterprises
1434 Pine St.
719/275-1444

Colorado

8 CASTLE ROCK

Auntie Lisa's Antiques
1647 Park St.
303/688-7552

9 COLORADO SPRINGS

It was in 1870 that Civil War hero and retired army general, William Jackson Palmer, caught his first glimpse of what is now Colorado Springs. After the war, the rapidly growing railroad industry had captured his interest, and he had come to the Pikes Peak region to investigate the possibilities of expansion.

In 1871, enchanted by the beauty of the region, Palmer began laying out the city of his dreams. He fancied to build a tourist resort on the region's reputation as a healthful climate. He dubbed the town Colorado Springs, although the closest mineral springs were six miles away in Manitou Springs, several hours by buggy.

In the 1800s only the very wealthy could afford to tour, so Palmer saw to it that the finest hotels and private mansions were built. Attracting Europeans in droves, Colorado Springs earned the nickname "Little London."

In 1893, an eastern school teacher making her first visit to the young city was captivated, as General Palmer had been, by the area's grandeur. After a trip to the top of Pikes Peak, teacher and poet, Katharine Lee Bates, wrote what would become her most famous work. Later set to music, "America the Beautiful" has become perhaps the nation's most beloved patriotic anthem.

In the years that followed the founding of Colorado Springs, thousands of others have been inspired by the beauty of the region. From that inspiration the citizens of the Pikes Peak region have grown to appreciate their rich cultural heritage. Today the city boasts many fine historical homes, museums, a living history farm and some of the most spectacular views in the world.

Antique Gallery
21 N. Nevada Ave.
719/633-6070

McIntosh Weller Antiques
1013 S. Tejon St.
719/520-5316

Jug & Basin Antiques
1420 W. Colorado Ave.
719/633-9346

Villagers Antiques & Collectibles
2426 W. Colorado Ave.
719/632-1400

Antique Legacy
2624 W. Colorado Ave.
719/578-0637

Antique Merchants
14 S. Tejon St.
719/442-6928

Kaya Gaya
1015 S. Tejon St.
719/578-5858

Dean & Co. Antiques
2607 W. Colorado Ave.
719/635-3122

Avenue Antiques & Collectibles
2502 W. Colorado Ave.
719/520-9894

Adobe Walls
2808 W. Colorado Ave.
719/635-3394

My Mother's Attic Antiques
207 W. Rockrimmon Blvd., #F
719/528-2594

NuNN Art & Antiques
717 N. Union Blvd.
719/473-4746

Antiques Unique on 8th Street
1515 S. 8th St.
719/475-8633

Iron Pump Antiques
1024 S. Royer St.
719/636-3940

Antique Mart
829 N. Union Blvd.
719/633-6070

Lace Chest
101 S. 25th St.
719/632-1770

Country Pines Antiques
6005 Templeton Gap Road
719/596-4004

Nevada Avenue Antiques
405 S. Nevada Ave.
719/473-3351

Legend Antiques
2165 Broadway St.
719/448-9414

Colorado Country Antique Mall
2109 Broadway St.
719/520-5680

Consignment of Collectibles
5681 N. Academy Blvd.
719/528-5922

Korean Antique Gallery
1788 S. 8th St., #A
719/386-0305

Great Places to Stay

Room at the Inn
618 N. Nevada Ave.
1-800-579-4621
Call the innkeepers for specific directions

Ideally located in the Historic Center of Colorado Springs, Room at the Inn retains the charm, romance and gracious hospitality of the Victorian Era. A wealthy mine investor and his wife built the house in 1896 in classic Queen Anne style. The inn features original hand-painted murals, four Italian tiled fireplaces, fish scale siding, a wrap-around veranda and a three-story turret overlooking a wide tree-lined avenue. Room at the Inn has been carefully restored to its former elegance with the added history and comfort of modern amenities.

The five guest rooms in the Main House offer private baths, queen size beds, period antiques and oriental rugs. Each room has distinguishing characteristics such as fireplaces. whirlpool or soaking tubs for two and a turret sitting area.

The Carriage House has two guest rooms with private baths.

Interesting Side Trips

Van Briggle Art Pottery
600 S. 21st St.
719/633-7729
Tours: Mon.–Sat., call for times
Directions: Five minutes west of downtown Colorado Springs at 21st
Street and Highway 24.

Van Briggle Art Pottery has been mixing clay, water and fire with the potter's magic since 1899. It is one of the oldest active art potteries remaining in the United States. The company was founded by acclaimed potter and sculptor Artus Van Briggle, together with his wife, Anne, who was also an accomplished artist. The Van Briggles designed their creations by incorporating flowing floral motifs, carefully patterned to enhance the graceful shapes of the pottery, and then finishing the pieces with the soft "matte" glazes which have come to represent the Van Briggle style. These beautiful glazes grace a variety of designs, from Art Nouveau to current Southwestern styles. You will also find figurines, distinctive lamp shades, bowls, vases and lamps made at the studio.

Rock Ledge Ranch
1805 30th St.
719/578-6777
Call for hours June-August

Located near the Gateway Rocks to the Gardens of the Gods, the Rock Ledge Ranch, formerly the White House Ranch, provides a living history of an early Colorado Springs ranch, with exhibits and demonstrations of old-time ranching.

Ghost Town Museum
Hwy. 24
719/634-0696
Open: Year-round

Ghost Town Museum is an authentically reconstructed Old West town built from the very buildings abandoned after the Pikes Peak Region's gold mining era. Explore the boardwalk that connects the saloon, jail, blacksmith and merchants of "Main Street" to the livery (which houses stagecoaches, buggies, carriages of the day, and turn-of-the-century automobiles) and the Victorian Home. Each exhibit displays a fascinating array of valuable collectibles such as those actually used by our ancestors – your great-grandparents!

North Pole
Santa's Workshop
North Pole, Colo.
719/684-9432

Open: Mid-May–December
Directions: Drive 10 miles west of Colorado Springs on Highway 24 to Cascade (Exit 141 from I-25) and follow the signs.

Imagine a place where every day is Christmas. Where your children can meet and talk to Santa Claus himself. Where your family can ride a mountaintop ferris wheel, a swinging space shuttle, an antique carousel, an aerial tram through the treetops, a miniature train and more.

Where you can enjoy tasty foods and snacks, and picnic in an evergreen forest. Where your kids can feed live deer, create their own colorful candle, watch a magician perform and play in a game-packed arcade. Where you can mail cards postmarked "The North Pole."

You don't have to imagine such a place because it really exists...at the North Pole, home of Santa's Workshop...at the foot of Pikes Peak. Call for exact days and times.

Great Places to Eat

Giuseppe's Old Depot Restaurant
10 S. Sierra Madre
719/635-3111
Directions: Downtown, 1 block west of Antlers/Doubletree.

On October 26, 1871, the first passenger train from Denver stopped at the site of the soon-to-be Denver & Rio Grande Western Railroad Station in the infant city of Colorado Springs. The history of Colorado can hardly be considered without the history of the railroad. Rich in timber and minerals, the new territory attracted adventurous souls filled with optimism as well as foresight.

Perhaps nothing reflects the courage and glamour of those times more than this Denver Rio Grande Western Railroad Station. Constructed of "glass stone" found near Castle Rock, Colorado, the Depot still shakes to the freight and coal trains of today. The last passenger train pulled out of the Depot in 1966, but the memories have been preserved in the many photographs and memorabilia gracing the walls of the station. The original oak doors still open wide to welcome today's guests. The floor of the main Dining Room still bears the original tiles that have been polished smooth by millions of feet since 1887. Colorado Spruce was used for the twenty-foot ceiling in the former passenger waiting room. The cherubim overlooking the north and south ends of this room have been preserved from a less fortunate structure, The Burns Theater.

The Depot has provided a whistle stop for former presidents, Theodore and Franklin Roosevelt, as well as Harry Truman during campaigns for the presidency.

Today the customers inside this 107-year-old historically restored station aren't passengers. They are diners feasting upon such specialties as stonebaked pizza and lasagna, savory ribs and steak, prime rib, spaghetti, or one of the many other scrumptious choices offered by Giuseppe's Old Depot Restaurant.

Colorado

10 DEL NORTE

Great Places to Stay

La Garita Creek Ranch
38145 County Road 39-E
719/754-2533
Directions: 17 miles south of Sayuache or 18 miles north of Monte Vista on Hwy. 285 – turn west at La Garita sign (Road G). Continue approximately 6 miles past La Garita Store to fork in road. Take left fork. Continue approximately 4 miles to the next fork. You will see La Garita Creek Ranch sign. Take right fork for 1 mile. Turn right at sign onto the property.

If you're feeling energetic after all that antique shopping, you've come to the right place. La Garita Creek Ranch offers plenty of activities for further explorations. You might try horseback riding along the scenic trails or fishing in a nearby creek. The true adventurists can test their skills in Penitente Canyon, the world renowned rock climbing area. Then end your perfect day in a quiet mountain cabin, complete with fireplace and hot tub. The ranch offers a full bar and restaurant.

11 DENVER

Antique Market
1212 S. Broadway
The Antique Guild
1298 S. Broadway
303/744-0281

The Antique Market and The Antique Guild offer the wares of over 250 vendors in one block at the top of Denver's Antique Row on South Broadway just two blocks south of Interstate 25. The Market at 1212 S. Broadway has the most entertaining inventory of antiques and collectibles in the region. Known for its eclectic mix of merchandise and its reasonable prices, the Market offers free off-street parking and a delightful cafe with home-cooked baked goods and sandwiches to make for a complete shopping experience. The mall specializes in oak and primitives as well as a large selection of '50s furniture. There is not much that the collector cannot find at the Antique Market from cowboy collectibles to fine china.

The Antique Guild, a cooperative of individual businesses a half a block down from the Market, shows off gorgeous antique furnishings. Specialists in rare books, glassware and old radios are a feature.

The Antique Market and The Antique Guild are the anchor stores for a four-block area known as Antique Row in Denver. This is the most extensive collection of antiques in the Rocky Mountain Region, one that should not be missed for the aficionado or the family looking for a fun afternoon of entertainment.

Antique Row is easily accessible from the Interstate and Denver's Light Rail, originating near downtown hotels, arriving only two blocks from the Antique Market. Check Antique Row's web page at http://www.webolutions.com/antiquerow.

Architectural Salvage, Inc.
1215 Delaware St.
303/615-5432
Open: Mon.–Sat. 10–5, Sun. 12–5
Directions: Traveling I-25, take exit 210 A (Colfax exit), east 1 mile, south on Delaware 2½ blocks. (Delaware runs south only from Colfax between Rocky Mountain News Building and The Denver Mint.)

No reproductions here. For 10 years, Architectural Salvage has provided customers with outstanding antique doors, lighting, windows, leaded glass, clawfoot tubs, shutters, gates, columns and more. Everything is neatly arranged indoors for your convenience.

The Gallagher Collection Books and Antiques at the Antique Guild
1298 S. Broadway
303/756-5821
Email: gallabks@dimensional.com
Open: Mon.–Sat. 10–5:30, Sun. 12–5
Directions: Take I-25, exit 207, 4 blocks south to the corner of Louisiana and South Broadway.

Located in the old potato chip factory amidst Denver's Antique Row, The Gallagher Collection offers an outstanding array of unusual books in all fields. You'll find significant selections in Western, Americana, Children's, Illustrated, Leather and Decorative Bindings, History, Biography, Natural History, Birds, Hunting and Fishing, and Cookbooks, plus additional books in other fields. They even offer antiques for the library and a significant selection of original World War I and II posters.

In addition to authors to read, they offer authors to play. Remember when you used to play the Authors Card Game. Now you can play it again and share it with your children and grandchildren. Also available, and played the same way: Childrens Authors, Women Authors, American Authors, Civil War Series, and Baseball.

The Gallagher Collection also buys books and provides a book search service. As members of the Rocky Mountain Antiquarian Booksellers Association, they adhere to the highest standards of the book trade. You'll enjoy perusing the wonderful antique cast iron bookshelves for that special book in a friendly, comfortable setting.

Maggie May's Sandbox
212 S. Broadway
303/744-8656

Antique Mercantile
1229 S. Broadway
303/777-8842

Antique Alcove
1236 S. Broadway
303/722-4649

Denver Antique Guild
1298 S. Broadway
303/722-3359

Rosalie McDowell Antiques
1400 S. Broadway
303/777-0601

Hooked on Glass
1407 S. Broadway
303/778-7845

Al's Collectibles & Antiques
1438 S. Broadway
303/733-6502

Stuart-Buchanan Antiques
1530 15th St.
303/825-1222

Aspen Antiques
1464 S. Broadway
303/733-6463

Glass Roots Antiques
27 E. Dakota Ave.
303/778-8693

Wazee Deco
1730 Wazee St.
303/293-2144

Foxy's Antiques
1592 S. Broadway
303/777-7761

Times Shared
1160 E. Colfax Ave.
303/863-0569

Decorables & Antiques Best
5940 E. Colfax Ave.
303/399-8643

Country Club Antiques
408 Downing St.
303/733-1915

Artifact Room
2318 S. Colorado
303/757-2797

Gateway Antiques & Art
357 Broadway
303/744-8479

Antique Center on Broadway
1235 S. Broadway
303/744-1857

Talisman Antiques
1248 S. Broadway
303/777-8959

Antiques by Corky
1449 S. Broadway
303/777-8908

Warner's Antiques
1401 S. Broadway
303/722-9173

Uniquittes
1415 S. Broadway
303/777-6318

Calamity Jane Antiques
1445 S. Broadway
303/778-7104

Cravings/Upland Interiors
1460 S. Broadway
303/777-1728

Antique Exchange Co-op
1500 S. Broadway
303/777-7871

Antiques of Denver
1534 S. Broadway
303/733-9008

Sleepers Antiques
1564 S. Broadway
303/733-8017

Packrat Antiques
1594 S. Broadway
303/778-1211

Reckollections Indoor
5736 E. Colfax Ave.
303/329-8848

Treasured Scarab
25 E. Dakota Ave.
303/777-6884

East West Designs
600 Ogden St.
303/861-4741

Antique Zoo
1395 S. Acoma St.
303/778-9191

Buckboard
3265 S. Wadsworth Blvd.
303/986-0221

Wayside Antiques
3795 S. Knox Ct.
303/783-3645

Borgman's Antiques & Things
1700 E. 6th Ave.
303/399-4588

Mountain Man Antiques
3977 Tennyson St.
303/458-8447

Country Line Antiques
1067 S. Gaylord St.
303/733-1143

Victoriana Antique Jewelry
1512 Larimer St. #39R
303/573-5049

Red's Antique Galleries
5797 E. Evans Ave.
303/753-9187

Sandpiper Antiques
1524 S. Broadway
303/777-4384

Sheptons Antiques
389 S. Broadway
303/777-5115

American Vogue Vintage Clothing
10 S. Broadway
303/733-4140

Antique Brokers
1388 S. Broadway
303/722-3090

Collector's Choice Antiques
2920 E. Colfax Ave.
303/320-8451

Belleli Antiques & Fine Arts
210 Clayton St.
303/355-2422

Finders Keepers Antiques
1451 S. Broadway
303/777-4521

Frontier Gallery
1500 S. Broadway
303/733-4200

Hampden Street Antiques
8964 E. Hampden Ave.
303/721-7992

Collectible Chair Co.
2817 E. 3rd Ave.
303/320-6585

Starr Antiques
2940 E. 6th Ave.
303/399-4537

Feathered Nest
935 E. Cedar Ave.
303/744-6881

Railroad Memories
1903 S. Niagara St.
303/759-1290

APIRY
585 Milwaukee St.
303/399-6017

Denver Doll Emporium
1570 S. Pearl St.
303/733-6339

Queen City Architectural
4750 Brighton Blvd.
303/296-0925

Sixth Avenue Antiques
2900 E. 6th Ave.
303/322-5773

And Etcetera Antiques
1065 S. Gaylord St.
303/744-0745

Broadway Antiques & Auction
511 Broadway
303/825-7533

Collectors Corner
10615 Melody Dr.
303/450-2875

Eron Johnson Antiques Ltd.
451 Broadway
303/777-8700

French Country Antiques Ltd.
2906 E. 6th Ave.
303/321-1977

Metropolitan Antique Gallery
1147 Broadway
303/623-3333

Colorado

La Cache
400 Downing St.
303/871-9605

Amsterdam Antiques
1428 S. Broadway
303/722-9715

Mer-Sadies Antiques
1345 S. Broadway
303/765-5440

Great Places to Stay

Capitol Hill Mansion
1207 Pennsylvania St.
1-800-839-9329

The Capitol Hill Mansion is located in the most architecturally outstanding area of the City, surrounded by historic houses of pioneers, governors, financiers, mining magnates and other families of wealth and power. Built in 1891, it is one of the last splendid homes erected before the Great Silver Crash. The elegant exterior of ruby sandstone is expressed in a Richardsonian Romanesque style: high turrets, balconies, soaring chimneys and a grand curved porch. The entry interior of meticulously-crafted patterned plaster and golden oak paneling opens to a dramatic sweeping staircase, punctuated by an exquisite stained and beveled glass window. Inviting public parlors in rich green tones and exceptional guest rooms, each individually decorated, complete the appointments to this truly grand mansion.

Interesting Side Trips

Byers-Evans House
Corner of 13th Ave. & Bannock St.
303/620-4933

The Byers-Evans House was built in 1883 by *Rocky Mountain News* publisher William Byers. It was sold in 1889 to the family of William Gray Evans, an officer of the Denver Tramway Company. Guided tours take visitors through this elegant residence, richly filled with original family furnishings.

12 DURANGO

Southwest Book Trader
175 E. 5th St.
970/247-8479

Wildflowers Antiques
742 Main Ave.
970/247-4249

Treasures by Therese
111 E. 30th St.
970/259-5034

Time Traveler
131 E. 8th St.
970/259-3130

Comstock Mercantile
638 Main Ave.
970/259-5069

Appaloosa Trading Co.
501 Main Ave.
970/259-1994

Great Places To Stay

Blue Lake Ranch
16000 Hwy. 140 (Hesperus)
970/385-4537
Email: bluelake @frontier.net
Web site: www.frontier/nbluelake
Rates: $65–$245
Reservations taken Mon.–Sun. 8–8
Directions: Blue Lake Ranch is 15 minutes west of Durango. To protect the guests' privacy, there is no highway signage for Blue Lake Ranch. Use your odometer to find the gravel driveway. From the north, east or west: Take Highway 140 south at Hesperus. Go 6½ miles to find the driveway to the right. From the south: Take Highway 170 in New Mexico north, which turns into Colorado Highway 140 at the state line. Continue north and note the junction of Highway 141 and Highway 140. Blue Lake Ranch is 1³/₁₀ miles north of this junction on the left.

Blue Lake Ranch has evolved from a simple 1910 homestead into a luxurious European-style Country Estate. From the elegantly appointed Main Inn to the secluded garden cottages, there are unsurpassed views of Blue Lake, and the gardens of the 13,000-foot La Plata Mountains. A year-round destination acclaimed for its spring and summer gardens, the ranch offers spectacular fall color and becomes a winter wonderland with the first snowfall. There is absolute privacy and quiet without another house in sight. Guests enjoy fishing for trophy trout in the lake, strolling in the gardens, where over 10,000 iris bloom annually, and exploring the ranch's private wildlife preserve.

The Main Inn is the original restored homestead house and serves as Ranch headquarters. In the summer a European-style breakfast buffet is served in the dining room and on the garden patios. The buffet offers a delicious selection of cheeses, meats, cereals, fruits, seasonal berries, pastries, juices, Southwestern dishes and fresh roasted coffee or tea. Afternoon tea is served at 5 p.m. on the garden patios.

The four guest rooms in the inn are all comfortably separated from one another. The Garden Room entered through the library hall has a window seat, fireplace and private deck in a garden overlooking the lake. The Oriental-style bath has a shower room with a deep-soaking tub. Situated at the top of a circular staircase, The Rose Room provides 360-degree views of the lake, gardens and mountains through dormer windows, has a queen bed and sitting area. The Victorian Room is furnished with an 1850s handcarved four poster canopied double bed and has a Dutch door to the garden. The private unattached bath has a six-foot-long claw footed tub.

In addition to the four rooms in the inn, Blue Lake Ranch has a 3 bedroom, 3 bath log cabin on the lake, a cottage in the woods, two suites in a renovated barn and a turn of the century homestead house on the banks of the La Plata River.

Note: Dr. Shirley Isgar, Innkeeper at Blue Lake Ranch, delights in

Colorado

recounting this amusing tale. At the Country Inn, an elusive trout lured a first-time fisherman physician in waders a bit too far out into the lake. While concentrating on landing an incredible rainbow trout, he didn't realize he had sunken into the soft mud up to his thighs. Meanwhile, a guest (a malpractice lawyer) was watching from the cabin directly on the lake. Finally the physician, not being able to move, cried for help and the lawyer pulled him into shore...minus his boots. Who gets the bill?

The Historic Strater Hotel
699 Main Ave.
970/247-4431 or 1-800-247-4431
Open: Year round

Built in 1887 and furnished throughout with authentic Victorian antiques, the Strater Hotel has been catering to travelers for 108 years. Selected by *Diversion Magazine* as " Colorado's finest Victorian Hotel," the Strater offers 93 beautiful guest rooms, a restaurant, and a saloon all set in the melodramatic aura of the 1800s gold rush days.

Interesting Side Trips

Durango & Silverton Narrow Gauge Railroad
479 Main Ave./Durango & Silverton Train Depot
970/247-2733
Call for schedule & tickets

When you ride the Durango & Silverton Narrow Gauge Railroad, you'll experience a legacy of mountain railroading history that has remained virtually unchanged for over a century.

This historic steam-powered train once carried food, provisions and silver. Today the Silverton takes visitors on a spectacular scenic trip through the San Juan Mountains. Witness relics of the 1800s that line the railroad's tracks, or even catch a glimpse of bears, elk, bald eagles, and many other species of Rocky Mountain wildlife. It's one train ride you won't soon forget.

Animas Museum
31st St. & W.2nd Ave.
970/259-2402
Open: Mon.–Sat. 10–6 May through Oct.

Located in the residential neighborhood in the old Animas City section of town, Durango's only history museum is somewhat out of the public eye. But what surprises are in store for those who venture off the beaten path of north Main to visit the museum! Cloistered within the sandstone walls of the 90-year-old museum building are untold treasures of the San Juan Basin's rich and colorful heritage. Does an 1880s hand-crafted saddle made in Animas City intrigue you? Perhaps a porcelain Victorian

doll, a D&RG railroad lantern, a pair of Buckskin Charlie's beaded moccasins or a Zuni polychrome olla is more to your liking. These objects and many more can be seen in the museum's exhibits.

13 ENGLEWOOD

Van Dyke's Antiques
3663 S. Broadway
303/789-3743 or 303/973-0110 for after-hour appointments
Open: Mon.–Sat. 10–5, Sun. 1–4
Directions: Denver Metro Area – Take I-25 to Hwy. 285 (Hampdon Ave.) west to Broadway, exit south on Broadway, 1½ blocks on west side of street.

For those interested in flow blue china, Van Dyke's Antiques has one of the largest selections to be found. In addition, the shop is filled with magnificent selections of other quality antiques such as Victorian glass, pocket watch holders, pickle casters, brides baskets, epergnes, scent bottles and lusters. You'll also find American and European furniture, silver, paintings, prints, perfume bottles, lighting, lamps, crystal and more.

QMyan's Popourri Antiques
3665 S. Broadway
303/781-7724

Rocky Mountain Clocks & Repair
2739 S. Broadway
303/789-1573

14 ESTES PARK

Bountiful
125 Moraine Ave. #B
970/586-9332

Cottage & Gardens
7461 County Road 43
970/586-0580

Little Victorian Attic
157 W. Elkhorn Ave.
970/586-8964

15 FORT COLLINS

Nostalgia Antiques
2216 Northridge Court
970/221-5139

Bell Tower Antiques
2520 N. Shields St.
970/482-2510

Happenstance
136 W. Mountain Ave.
970/493-1668

Collins Antique Mart
6124 S. College Ave.
970/226-3305

Front Range Antique Mall
6108 S. College Ave.
970/282-1808

Yesterday's Treasures
272 N. College Ave.
970/493-9211

Colorado

Windswept Farm
5537 N. County Road 9
970/484-1124

Bennett Antiques & Accessories
1220 S. College Ave.
970/482-3645

Never Open Antiques
1746 E. Mulberry St.
970/495-0401

Foothills Indoor Flea Market
6300 S. College Ave.
970/223-9069

Nesch Brass & Antiques
201 N. Link Lane
970/221-0787

Create Antiques
2200 Reservoir Road
970/353-1712

Foster's Antiques & Clock Shop
1329 9th Ave.
970/352-9204

16 GEORGETOWN

Antique Emporium
501 Rose St.
303/569-2727

Nora Blooms's Antiques
614 6th St., #B
303/569-0210

Stuff & Such
601 14th St.
303/569-2507

Cobweb Shoppe of Georgetown
512 6th St.
303/569-3112

Powder Cache Antiques
612 6th St.
303/569-2848

17 GLENWOOD SPRINGS

Anita's Antiques & Elegant
1030 Grand Ave.
970/928-9622

Glenwood Books & Collectibles
720 Grand Ave.
970/928-8825

Strange Imports
291 County Road 119
970/945-1484

Forever Elegant
815 Grand Ave.
970/928-0510

Antiques Etc.
212 6th St.
970/945-6129

First Class Trash
3330 S. Glen Ave.
970/945-0533

18 GRAND JUNCTION

Guy Kelly Washburn Antiques
600 White Ave.
970/241-6880

American Heritage Antiques
117 N. 6th St.
970/245-8046

Finders Trove
558 Main St.
970/245-0109

Antique Emporium
140 W. Main St.
970/242-1563

Great American Antiques Store
439 Main St.
970/242-2443

19 GREELEY

Antiques at Lincoln Park
822 8th St.
970/351-6222

Blossom Tyme Gifts & Antiques
1201 11th Ave.
970/352-4379

20 GUNNISON

Chars
119 S. Main St.
970/641-2494

Great Places to Stay

Eagle's Nest Bed and Breakfast
206 N. Colorado
970/641-4457
Open: Daily
Directions: Take Hwy. 50 to the Holiday Inn in Gunnison. Located directly behind the Holiday Inn on the corner of Colorado and Virginia.

Hugh and Jane McGee are retired school teachers from a northern Chicago suburb. They now enjoy their new vocation as proprietors of the Eagles Nest B&B in Gunnison.

The upstairs of the McGee home has a large suite, private bath and breakfast nook or reading room for relaxing. The front porch beautifully displays Hugh's own works of art — stained glass. Hugh's superb culinary masterpieces — Western Eggs Benedict, Vegetable Omelets and French Toast "keeps folks raving!" Jane also finds time to be a Mary Kay cosmetics consultant. It is advisable to call well ahead for reservations.

21 HOTCHKISS

Beulah B's
1091 A Hwy., #133
970/872-3051

The Ark II
101 W. Bridge St.
970/872-2226

Olde Town Hall Antiques
503 N. 2nd St.
970/872-3500

Cowboy Collectibles
448 Bridge St.
970/872-3025

Country Home Store
264 W. Bridge St.
970/872-4647

Colorado

22 LITTLETON

Colorado Antique Gallery
5501 S. Broadway
303/794-8100
Open: Mon.–Sat. 10–6, Thurs. 10–8, Sun. 12–6

The Colorado Antique Gallery, located in Littleton, is Colorado's largest antiques mall with over 50,000 square feet and 200 of Colorado's best antique dealers. The variety of merchandise is unlimited – a great selection of fine china, Depression glass, estate jewelry, RS Prussia, Royal Bayreuth, and much, much more. Since opening in 1992, the Gallery has become a favorite stop, not only for Colorado's antiques enthusiasts, but also for collectors from across the country. A combination of quality merchandise as well as friendly and helpful salespeople has earned the Colorado Antique Gallery a reputation for being top notch.

Creamery
2675 W. Alamo Ave.
303/730-2747

Olde Littleton Antique Co-op
2681 W. Alamo Ave.
303/795-9965

Olde Towne Antiques & Vintage
2500 W. Main St.
303/347-9258

Remember When Antiques
2569 W. Main St.
303/798-2989

23 LOVELAND

Lynn Allee Down Antiques
1220 Langston Lane
970/667-9889

Bonser Antique Mall
315 E. 4th St.
970/669-8005

Canyon Collectibles
5641 W. U.S. Hwy. 34
970/593-9227

Country Shed Antiques
136 E. 4th St.
970/667-9448

Country Wishes & Wants
120 E. 4th St.
970/635-9132

Diamonds & Toads
137 E. 4th St.
970/667-9414

Grandma's Attic
214 E. 4th St.
970/667-1807

Kottage
333 Cleveland Ave.
970/667-1110

Nostalgia Corner
140 E. 4th St.
970/663-5591

Rocky Mt. Antiques, Inc.
3816 W. Eisenhower Blvd.
970/663-7551

Bill's Antiques & Flea Market
339 E. 4th St.
970/663-4355

Ed's Antique Furniture Sales
1400 Falls Court
970/669-3545

North Fork Antique Flea Market
3121 W. Eisenhower Blvd.
970/203-1522

24 LYONS

Left-Hand's Antique & Western
228 E. Main St.
303/823-5738

Ralston Brothers Antiques
426 High St.
303/823-6982

Left-Hand Trading Co.
401, 405 & 228 Main St.
303/823-6311

25 MANITOU SPRINGS

Nothing New
116 Canon Ave.
719/685-9353

Interesting Side Trips

Miramont Castle
Capitol Hill Ave. off Ruxton Ave.
719/685-1011

Are you fascinated by old buildings? Do you love history? Are you interested in the unusual? If so, tour Miramont Castle! The world-famous "castle" was constructed in 1895, and currently hosts more than 42,000 visitors annually. The four-story structure has 46 rooms (28 of them open to the public), two-foot-thick stone walls, and incorporates nine distinctly different styles of architecture over 14,000 square feet of floor space!

Miramont Castle has played an important role in the history of Manitou Springs. Originally built by a wealthy French priest, over the years the castle has been both a sanitarium and an apartment house.

Today you can tour the historic Miramont Castle and marvel at the Drawing Room with its gold ceiling and 200-ton Peachblow sandstone fireplace. You can enjoy a quiet moment in the eight-sided Montcalm Chapel, visit the new miniature museum, or take in the grandeur of the 400-square-foot Marie Francolon bedroom. Relax in the Queen's Parlor enclosed tearoom, which offers tasty menu items and striking views of the surrounding mountains.

26 MONTROSE

Black Bear Antiques
62281 Hwy. 90
970/249-5738

C & D Antiques
1360 Townsend Ave.
970/249-6155

Colorado

27 MORRISON

El Mercado
120 Bear Creek Ave.
303/697-8361

Morrison Antiques
307 Bear Creek Ave.
303/697-9545

Little Bits of Yesterday
309 Bear Creek Ave.
303/697-8661

Western Trail Antiques & Gifts
205 Bear Creek Ave.
303/697-9238

28 NEDERLAND

Off Her Rocker Antiques
4 E. First St.
303/258-7976

29 NIWOT

Lockwood House Antiques
198 2nd Ave.
303/652-2963

Wise Buys Antiques
190 2nd Ave.
303/652-2888

Niwot Antique Emporium
136 2nd Ave.
303/652-2587

Niwot Trading Post
149 2nd Ave.
303/443-0184

30 PUEBLO

Silver Lining Antiques
27050 U.S. Highway 50 E.
719/545-3575

Mid 30s Glass Shop
225 S. Union Ave.
719/544-1031

Oldies But Goodies Antique Shop
113 W. 4th St.
719/545-4661

A Touch of the Past
3369 S. I-25
719/564-1840

Quilt Shop Antiques
111 E. Abriendo Ave.
719/544-4906

Silver Lining Antiques
27050 U.S. Hwy. 50 E.
719/545-3575

Abriendo Antiques
130 W. Abriendo Ave.
719/543-3036

Highlander Antiques
330 S. Union Ave.
719/544-6040

Blazing Saddle Antiques
118 S. Union Ave.
719/544-5520

Cardinelli's Antiques
525 N. Santa Fe Ave.
719/544-9016

Victorianna's
213 S. Union Ave.
719/583-8009

Lane's House of Glass, Inc.
111 Colorado Ave.
719/542-2210

Trail Antiques
28018 E. U.S. Hwy. 50
719/948-2001

Why Not Antiques
1240 Berkley Ave.
719/544-4104

Because You Love Antiques
118 W. 3rd St.
719/544-5567

Trolley Stop Antiques
818 W. 4th St.
719/543-1261

31 SALIDA

Carriage House Antiques
148 N. F St.
719/539-4001

Old Log Cabin Antiques
225 E. Rainbow Blvd.
719/539-2803

Jacobson's Antiques
7535 W. U.S. Hwy. 50
719/539-2093

Hartman's Furniture & Antqiues
11384 W. U.S. Hwy. 50
719/539-4083

32 SILVERTON

Silverton, Colo., and its surrounding countryside are a playground where the scenery uplifts the spirit and sends energy levels climbing. The town is a National Historic Landmark, representing the Victorian era.

Having never suffered the catastrophic fires that most old mining towns have endured, Silverton is one of the best preserved, with most of its original homes and businesses still standing. Among the original buildings to explore is the San Juan County Historical Society Museum, a 1902 structure that once housed the county jail. The museum provides an excellent introduction to the town and its history.

On the "wilder" side of town is Blair Street, infamous for once offering Silverton and its visitors 40 saloons and brothels. These businesses appeared in abundance in mining and railroad towns at the turn of the century. Now serving as a location for many western movie shots, the street has earned an additional reputation since the heyday of its original activities.

Tantalized by the history and the longing for gold that the town and its premises encourage, you should be well prepped for the Old Hundred Gold Mine Tour. Local miners have established this one-hour train ride tour into an authentic gold mine deep within a mountain. Experienced miners guide the tours.

For the adventurous, a trip can be planned aboard a coal-fired, steam-operated train of the Durango & Silverton Narrow Gauge Railroad, which has served Silverton since 1882. Part of the year a railroad-operated bus shuttles passengers from Silverton to Durango for return the same day by rail, allowing a new perspective of the fabulous views offered by the surrounding landscape. Another option is to make the complete Durango-Silverton-Durango loop, stopping over for one or more nights in Silverton.

Great Places to Stay

Alma House
220 E. 10th St.
970/387-5336
Open: Year-round

European style.

Great Places to Eat

The French Bakery
1250 Greene St.
970/387-5423
Directions: From Denver, take I-70 West to exit 37 (before Grand Junction), CO 141 South to U.S. 50 South to U.S. 550 (at Montrose), U.S. 550 South to Silverton. Located on the first floor of Teller House Hotel.

The French Bakery is located on Greene Street, which just happens to be the main fairway through the tiny town of Silverton. Along this street, attractive Victorian period buildings and homes patiently pass the years.

The building housing the bakery is also home to the Teller House Hotel, which is on the second floor of the two-story brick building. Built by Silverton Brewery owner, Charles Fischer, the upstairs has been a hotel since its construction in 1896. It is listed as a National Historic Landmark and retains its original woodwork, high ceilings and many of its original Victorian furnishings.

The French Bakery, on the first floor below, serves a hearty southwestern breakfast, soup, deli sandwich or gourmet pizza for lunch. The bakery has long been hailed as a favorite dining spot by hotel guests and drop-ins.

33 VAIL

Englishman Fine Art & Antiques
143 E. Meadow Dr., #205
970/476-3570

Finishing Touch of Vail, Inc.
122 E. Meadow Dr.
970/476-1656

Lodge & Cabin Dry Goods Co.
100 E. Meadow Dr.
970/476-1475

34 VICTOR

Assay Office Antiques
113 S. Third St.
719/689-2712
Open: Daily from end of May to September 15, 11–5; open by appointment in the winter
Directions: Take Highway 67 to Victor. At the corner of Victor Avenue and 3rd Street, turn right. The shop is situated in the middle of the block on the west side.

Assay Office Antiques gets its name from the building's younger days as an assayer's office. For those of you who haven't a clue what an assayer is, here's an explanation. Back in the gold rush days, Victor was the largest gold mining district in the United States. The miners, speculators, the hopeful and the lucky, would bring their samples to the local assayer's office where it was tested for its true gold content.

Today within the walls of this turn-of-the-century building, trades of the past can still be found (and offered for sale). The shop carries a nice selection of gold mining gear, such as picks, pans, weights and measuring devices. Apart from the relics related to the history of the town, you can turn up old railroad items, some nice primitives, old toys, glassware and other interesting collectibles.

35 WINDSOR

Memory Lane Antiques
426 Main St.
970/686-7913

36 YUMA

The Farmstead
46999 County Road E.
970/848-2643

Albany Street Antique & Gift
203 S. Albany St.
970/848-5214

Kaliko Kreations
419 S. Houston
970/848-0807

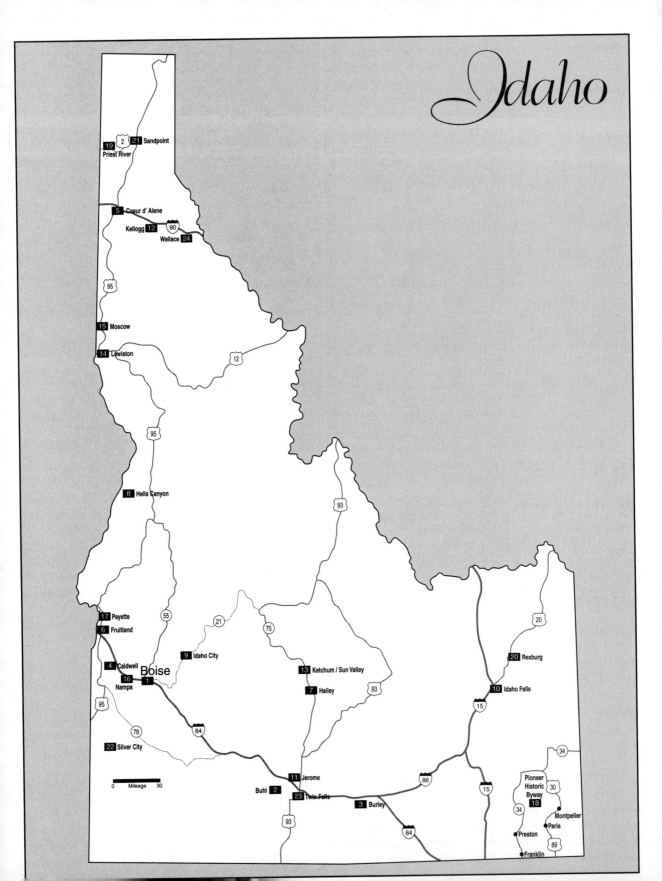

Idaho

19 2 21 Sandpoint
Priest River

5 Coeur d' Alene
Kellogg 12 90
Wallace 24

95

12

15 Moscow

14 Lewiston

95

8 Hells Canyon

93

17 Payette
6 Fruitland

55

21

75

20

9 Idaho City

13 Ketchum / Sun Valley

20 Rexburg

4 Caldwell
Boise
16 1
Nampa

7 Hailey

93

10 Idaho Falls

15

95

78

22 Silver City

84

34

11 Jerome

86

15

Pioneer
Historic
Byway 30
18

Buhl 2
23 Twin Falls

3 Burley

34

Montpelier
Paris

0 Mileage 30

93

84

Preston

89

Franklin

Idaho

1 BOISE

Acquired Again
1306 Alturas St.
208/338-5929

Perkins & Perkins Antiques
1516 Vista Avenue
208/344-6153

American Nostalgia Antiques
1517 N. 13th St.
208/345-8027

Early Attic
2002 Vista Ave.
208/336-7451

Antiques Hub
2244 Warm Springs Ave.
208/336-4748

Collector's Choice
5150 Franklin Road
208/336-2489

Elliott's Great Stuff
1006 Main St.
208/344-9775

Boise Antique & Unique
350 N. Milwaukee St.
208/377-3921

Victoria's Antiques
9230 Ustick Road
208/376-8016

Memory Lane Antiques
5829 Franklin Road
208/384-0074

Forget Me Not Antiques
1603 N. 13th St.
208/344-0678

Collection Connection
1612 N. 13th St.
208/343-6221

Antique Village
944 Vista Ave.
208/342-1910

Hobby Horse Antiques
231 Warm Springs Ave.
208/343-6005

Carol's Antiques & Collectibles
10670 Overland Road
208/322-5059

Collector's Choice Too
5284 Franklin Road
208/336-3170

Nifty 90s Antique Shop
2422 Main St.
208/344-3931

5th Street Antiques
225 N. 5th St.
208/344-7278

Wild Hare Bookshop
3397 N. Cole Road
208/377-5070

Great Places to Stay

Idaho Heritage Inn

109 W. Idaho
208/342-8066
Open: Year-round. Reservations requested.
Directions: Exit I-84 at Broadway in Boise; then follow north to Idaho Street.

The Idaho Heritage Inn was built in 1904 for one of Boise's early merchants, Henry Falk. It remained in the Falk family until it was purchased in 1943 by then governor Chase A. Clark. Lovingly restored by its present owners, the Inn is now listed on the National Register of Historic Places.

All rooms at the Inn have been comfortably and charmingly provided with private baths, period furniture and crisp linens. The spacious main floor common rooms include a formal dining room, living room and

sun room, featuring diamond-paned French doors, oak flooring and Oriental carpets.

Guests of the Inn enjoy a complimentary breakfast of fresh-squeezed juice, choice of beverage, fresh fruit in season, and a delectable entree which may include baked German pancakes, apricot cream cheese stuffed French toast, or apple skillet cake.

Surrounded by other distinguished turn-of-the-century homes, the Inn is conveniently located within walking distance of downtown, 8th Street Marketplace and Old Boise (a historic shopping district).

J J Shaw House Bed & Breakfast Inn

1411 W. Franklin St.
208/344-8899

This beautiful three-story brick and sandstone residence is accented with original leaded glass and interesting bay windows. Architectural details reminiscent of the 1900s include columns, decorative moldings and french doors. A variety of living areas are available to guests. Gourmet breakfasts are served in the dining room or sun porch. J J Shaw is within walking distance to fine restaurants, Hyde Park and Idaho's State Capitol. The Boise River offers unlimited outdoor activities and snow skiing just sixteen miles away.

2 BUHL

Claudia's Country Cabin
3917 N. 1500 E.
208/543-5315

Granny's Drawers
219 Broadway Ave. N.
208/543-6736

3 BURLEY

South of Burley is an eerie and dreamlike landscape where people have been doing a double-take for centuries. It's called City of Rocks and it's now a national reserve.

There's little warning of what is to come as you drive the gravel road over rolling hills of desert sage. Suddenly, huge granite columns loom up 60 stories high!

The area has a poignant history that can still be glimpsed. Here is where would-be Californians parted from the Oregon Trail and headed southwest over desert plains and high mountain passes. The impressive spires became a memo board of hope, fear and determination; many of the inscriptions written in axle grease can still be read.

Rumor has it that there's gold among the mammoth rocks. On his deathbed, a stagecoach robber confessed to burying his treasure at the City of Rocks. It has never been found.

The City of Rocks is a bit out of the way, but well worth the effort. Oakley, a village en route, is listed on the National Register of Historic Places because of its many intricate stone and wood structures built before the turn of the century. No other town in Idaho has such a concentration of old buildings.

A good starting point is the Oakley Co-op Building on the corner of Main and Center Streets. Near the city park is a jail cell that once held the noted outlaw, "Diamondfield" Jack Davis.

Golden Goose
1229 Overland Ave.
208/678-9122

4 CALDWELL

Alan Vulk Auction Service
523 Main St.
208/454-2910

Caldwell Auction
4920 Cleveland Blvd.
208/454-1532

5 COEUR D'ALENE

Coeur D'Alene Antique Mall
3650 N. Government Way
208/667-0246

Coeur D'Alene Antique Mall
408 W. Haycraft Ave., #11
208/664-0579

Good Things
204 N. 3rd St.
208/667-6958

Crow's Nest Antiques
416 E. Sherman Ave.
208/667-1679

Lake City Antique Mall
401 N. 2nd St
208/664-6883

Sherman Antiques & Collectibles
415 E. Sherman Ave.
208/666-1809

Worthington's Fine Antiques
210 Sherman Ave., #103
208/765-7753

Timeless Treasures Antiques
823 N. 4th St.
208/765-0699

Wiggett Marketplace
119 N. 4th St.
208/664-1524

Ciscos-Hunters of the Past
212 N. 4th St.
208/769-7575

Dicker-N-Swap Secondhand
810 N. 4th St.
208/666-9042

One of a Kind
413 Sherman Ave.
208/664-5145

Ciscos - II
317 Sherman
208/765-7997

Great Places to Stay

Amors Highwood House

1206 Highwood Lane
1-888-625-3470
Web site: www.amors.com

"Highwood House" is nestled in towering Ponderosa Pines, half a mile from Coeur d'Alene National Forest and five minutes from Lake Coeur d'Alene and Fernan Lake.

The home features a newly decorated master suite with king size bed with a down comforter and private bathroom. For your enjoyment the inn offers mountain bikes or table tennis, then relax in the Gazebo covered spa.

Awaken to the aroma of fresh brewed coffee and look forward to a hearty full breakfast in the dining room or the adjoining deck.

Baragar House Bed and Breakfast

316 Military Dr.
1-800-615-8422
Web site: www.baragarhouse.com

This charming Craftsman-style bungalow in historic Fort Sherman was built by a lumber baron. The spacious common area, comfortably furnished, has an antique parlor furnace, a victrola, and a lovely piano. The beautiful neighborhood viewed through the exquisite antique beveled, leaded windows shows the lovely, mature trees native to this area. The rooms are decorated in themes: The "Country Cabin" is delightful with its decor of mountain stream and cloud murals. The "Garden Room" is floral, with a canopied window seat and unique antique vanity. The "Honeymoon Suite" in Victorian decor is especially appealing with its over-sized bathroom offering a claw-foot tub under a bay window and curved glass shower. All rooms have private use of indoor spa/sauna, and "sleep under the stars" of a professionally applied solar system. Wonderful "wreck your diet" breakfasts.

Berry Patch Inn

1150 N. Four Winds Road
208/765-4994
Web site: www.bbhost.com/berrypatchinn

The Berry Patch Inn offers a restorative atmosphere for the guest who needs to "get-away-from-it-all," whether for an evening or an extended stay. Your hostess, Ann Caggiano, a world traveled proprietress, offers her beautiful mountaintop chalet home, nestled in a forest of tall pines, for that perfect diversion to everyday life.

Only three miles from the center of the town, the Berry Patch has private road access and is very serene and quiet, ideal for a fabulous honeymoon escape. Guests are invited to take a walk on the two acres, and stop by the seasonal fruit orchard, berry patches and green gardens to take in the sounds of nature and munch on the sun-warmed berries. For those who enjoy the more quiet wonders of nature, this mountain is a bird watcher's paradise, and occasionally you will hear the call of the wild.

An authentic Sioux tepee on the property offers a place for quiet contemplation and communication with nature. Nordstrom's Store (Spokane) praised this bed and breakfast in their "Rediscover the Northwest" 1993 promotion, while *Country Magazine* gave national acclaim in "Perfect Place to Stay while Touring America's Countryside" (1994) and just recently it was hailed as one of the top 20 inns of the Rockies by *National Geographic Traveler* (March 1997).

Idaho

Gregory's McFarland House Bed and Breakfast
601 E. Foster Ave.
208/667-1232
Web site: www.bbhost.com/mcfarlandhouse

In 1989, McFarland House won a Special Heritage Preservation Award presented by the Cranbrook Archives, Museum and Landmark Foundation for the preservation and restoration of this circa 1905 home. It was also the featured bed and breakfast in the August 6, 1989 travel section of the *Los Angeles Times*, in which Jerry Hulse, Travel Editor, wrote, "Entering Gregory's McFarland House is like stepping back 100 years to an unhurried time when four posters were in fashion and lace curtains fluttered at the windows and the notes of a vintage piano echoed through the house." A perfect romantic and peaceful getaway.

The Roosevelt Inn
105 Wallace Ave.
208/765-5200
Open: Year-round
Directions: Call ahead.

The Roosevelt Inn, named after the 26th president, Theodore Roosevelt, was built in 1906. Included in the National Register of Historic Places, this beautiful red brick building with its steeple shaded by maple trees, offers traditional elegance and Hungarian hospitality.

Two charmingly furnished parlors and dining area featuring lovely leaded glass windows and a hand-painted mural welcome you on the main floor. Each of the cozy guest rooms is decorated with antiques and provides a view of the lake.

The Roosevelt Inn is located within a short walking distance to area restaurants, shops and boutiques. The nature trails of beautiful Tubbs Hill are also within easy access.

6 FRUITLAND

Now & Then
7190 Elmore Road
208/452-5500

Suzy's Nu-2-U
200 S.W. 3rd
208/452-5878

Riverview Antiques & Collectibles
1125 N.W. 16th St.
208/452-4365

Great Places to Stay

Elm Hollow Bed & Breakfast
4900 Hwy. 95
208/452-6491
Open: Year-round
Directions: Traveling I-84, take Exit 3. Drive toward Parma. Elm Hollow is at the bottom of the dip between Glenway and Fairview. Make

a left onto the driveway, just before milepost 58. Only 2½ miles south of I-84; makes for a convenient stop-over for travelers.

Nestled against a hillside overlooking fertile Idaho farms and orchards, Elm Hollow Bed & Breakfast gives the weary traveler a true taste of home. Guests to this country retreat experience the relaxing atmosphere of old-fashioned hospitality and good Dutch cooking.

The Guest Room offers spacious comfort with queen-size beds and loveseat, and a full bookcase provides the touches of home for a cozy evening.

For a romantic getaway, the Barn (a renovated section of the old dairy barn) offers privacy and a great view of the countryside.

Mornings at Elm Hollow start with a choice of Continental breakfast with home-baked breads and sweet rolls, or a full and hearty country meal, served family style in the dining room.

7 HAILEY

Hailey's Antique Market
P.O. Box 1955
208/788-9292
Locations: Inside—Hailey Armory; Outside—Roberta McKercher Park

Call for July and September show dates.

Lone Star Designs
109 S. Main St.
208/788-9158

8 HELLS CANYON

Seven Devils and a Hell of a Canyon
Over one mile deep, Hells Canyon is North America's deepest river gorge, deeper even than the Grand Canyon. Walls of black, crumbling basalt thrust straight up, forcing boaters and fishermen on the Snake River to crane their necks for blue sky. Looking down upon the canyon are the mighty Seven Devils, an awe-inspiring mountain range that crests over 1½ miles above the river.

9 IDAHO CITY

Idaho City was, at one time, the largest city in the Northwest — a rough and tumble, rip-roaring mining town that epitomized the "boom or bust" lifestyle of Gold Rushers. Gold often took precedence over human life. It's said that of the 200 men and women buried in picturesque Boot Hill, only 28 died of natural causes.

Idaho

One Step Away Bed and Breakfast and Antique Shop
112 Cottonwood St.
208/392-4938

Nestled on a quiet little street on the south side of town, One Step Away is a quaint bed and breakfast with an exquisite antique shop adjoining it. Rooms are tastefully furnished in 1800s elegance and named after early settlers of Idaho City. The Jenny Lind Chamber is dedicated to the famous lady of the Nightingale Theater; the Miner's Room is named in honor of all the men who left their native homes in search of fortunes and were the first to settle in the area, and the Beth Parkinson Suite serves as a tribute to the previous owner of the house.

A gourmet breakfast is served on antique china and silver pieces of the era. The antique-filled dining room is available for meals, or room service is provided if you prefer.

Idaho City Hotel
Corner of Montgomery and Walulla
208/392-4290

In 1929, the Idaho City Hotel was a boarding house run by Mrs. Mary Smith. Since that time it has been completely renovated to retain its quaint charm and rustic flavor. Five guest rooms are available. The hotel has a wonderful wraparound porch and a tin roof.

10 IDAHO FALLS

A spectacular waterfall provides the scenic centerpiece for Idaho Falls, a growing city surrounded by gold and green croplands and rustic barns.

This community of 50,000 people is further blessed by 39 parks ranging from small corner parks, where business people stop to chat and eat lunch, to large parks such as Tautphaus Park which houses a nationally renowned zoo.

The Rotary International Peach Park located along the greenbelt features granite lanterns, gifts to the city from its sister city in Japan.

Cross Country Store
4035 Yellowstone Hwy.
208/529-0766

Scavenger Shop
202 1st St.
208/523-7862

Country Store Boutique
4523 E. Rire Hwy.
208/522-8450

Antique Gallery
341 W. Broadway St.
208/523-3906

A Street Village
548 Shoup Ave.
208/528-0300

11 JEROME

Frontier Antiques
149 W. Main St.
208/324-1127

Antiques & Things
137 E. Main St.
208/324-8549

Vintage Vanities
921 S. First St.
208/324-3067

Rose Antique Mall
130 E. Main St.
208/324-2918

12 KELLOGG

Driving east on I-90 from Coeur d'Alene, you'll find yourself in the Silver Valley, the largest silver producing area in the world and a bonanza for history buffs.

Silver Valley has been transformed not once but twice, first by the ambition and sacrifice of intrepid miners. Today, Kellogg offers different treasures—a Bavarian-theme village, murals, statues, a mining museum, and unique events.

Willow's Antiques
119 McKinley Ave.
208/556-1022

13 KETCHUM/SUN VALLEY

Antique Peddlers' Fairs
Location: Warm Spring Resort
208/344-6133
Directions: At the base of Bald Mountain
Call for specific dates

Antiques, Etc.
431 Walnut Ave. N.
208/726-5332

Polly Noe Antiques
471 Leadville Ave. N.
208/726-3663

Charles Stuhlberg Gallery
511 East Ave. N.
208/726-4568

Legacy Antiques & Imports
491 10th St.
208/726-1655

Angel Wings
320 Leadville Ave. N.
208/726-8708

14 LEWISTON

Bargain Hunter Mall
1209 Main St.
208/746-6808

Marsh's
1105 36th St. N.
208/743-5778

Somewhere in Time
628 Main St.
208/746-7160

Yesturday's Antiques & Florist
925 Preston Ave.
208/743-0345

15 MOSCOW

Second Hand/First Hand
107 S. Main St.
208/882-5642

Now & Then
321 E. Palouse River Dr.
208/882-7886

Bill's Antiques
5010 Harden Road
208/882-4812

Idaho

16 NAMPA

Old Towne Antique Mall-Coffee House
1212 1st St. S.
208/463-4555
Open: Mon.–Sat. 10–6, Sun. 10–3 (seasonal)
Coffee House: Mon.–Fri. 8–6, Sat. 10–6, Sun. 10–3 (seasonal)
Directions: Traveling I-84 Exit 36. Travel South on Franklin Blvd. to stop sign. Turn right on 11th Avenue. Drive approximately 1½ miles, then under railroad overpass. Immediately turn left on 1st Street south at light. Located 1½ blocks on left (Historic Downtown). We are 25 miles east of Boise, Idaho.

Located in historic downtown Nampa, Old Towne Antique Mall is more than just an antique shop. It has a coffee shop inside serving delicious espresso. The dealers who display their wares are usually on hand to answer any questions you may have.

A wide variety of merchandise is available such as nostalgic paper goods, vintage clothing, china, pottery, along with a complete line of furnishings from early country to Victorian to depression.

Yesteryear Shoppe
1211 1st St. S.
208/467-3581

Victorian Shoppe
911 12th Ave. S.
208/465-7565

Village Square Antiques
1309 2nd St. S.
208/467-2842

17 PAYETTE

Lambsville Collectibles
101 S. 16th St., Hwy. 95
208/642-1727

Yesterdays Cupboard
220 N. Main St.
208/642-3711

18 PIONEER HISTORIC BYWAY

Southeast Idaho's Pioneer Historic Byway gives motorists a nostalgic glimpse, through rustic ranches and roadside communities, of a West long past. The route begins in Franklin, Idaho's oldest white settlement, and retraces the steps of Idaho's earliest pioneers. Franklin's center is now designated by the state as a historic district, and two buildings are on the National Historic Register—the Franklin Co-op Building built in the 1860s, and the Hatch home, a classic of pioneer architecture.

Nearby are the remnants of Idaho's first flour mill and one of the oldest homes in the state, a two-story edifice built almost entirely of rock.

After passing through the rustic town of Preston, you'll come to the Bear River Massacre Site, now a national landmark. More Indians were killed here in one battle than in any other in the United States.

The byway continues on to Montpelier, home of the fascinating Rails and Trails Historical Museum. Just south of Montpelier is the small town of Paris. The Romanesque Mormon Tabernacle, complete with intricate wood ceilings and stone carvings, was built in 1889 of red sandstone snow-sledded to Paris from a quarry 18 miles away.

Between Montpelier and the Utah border, Butch Cassidy made a quick but impressive visit by robbing the local bank.

Another astounding drive is the Bear Lake-Caribou Scenic Byway running through Paris. It begins on Highway 89 at the Utah state border and passes mammoth Bear Lake.

The Scenic Byway continues at Montpelier on Highway 30 and at Soda Springs on Highway 34. The drive, in its entirety from the Utah border to the Wyoming border, is 111 miles or 2 ½ hours. Along the way are numerous attractions—Bear Lake State Park, the Paris Museum, the Cache National Forest, the Caribou Forest, the carbonated waters and spouting geysers of Soda Springs and the Blackfoot Reservoir.

19 PRIEST RIVER

Mercer's Memories
221 Main St.
208/448-1781

Joodle Bug's
120 Wisconsin
208/448-2442

20 REXBURG

North of Idaho Falls on Highway 20 is the historic and charming town of Rexburg, home to several diverse and noteworthy attractions.

Just a block off Main Street you'll find a gray stone Tabernacle now listed on the National Register of Historic Places. At Porter Park is the only restored authentic wooden carousel in Idaho.

But Rexburg is probably best known for a nearby, unusual tourist site: a dam which collapsed in June 1976, dumping eight billion gallons of roaring flood water into the unsuspecting valley below. A visit to the dam site on the Teton River will give you an idea of the power that was unleashed. An understanding of the flood's effect on local people, and their ability to rebuild their fertile valley, can be gained at a unique museum outside Rexburg.

Rexburg is also home to the Idaho International Folk Dance Festival. The week-long event features dance groups from around the world. Dancers and musicians gather here from Europe, Asia, South America and the south Pacific to share the vibrant and expressive spirit of their homelands. Perhaps no other event in Idaho boasts such international flavor. The dancing begins July 26th and concludes August 3rd each year.

Country Keepsakes
12 E. Main St.
208/359-1234

Mainstreet Antiques Mall
52 E. Main St.
208/356-5002

21 SANDPOINT

Antique Arcade
119 N. 1st Ave.
208/265-5421

Antique Collective
504 W. Oak St.
208/263-6499

Idaho

Great Places to Stay

Angel of the Lake Bed & Breakfast
410 Railroad Ave.
1-800-872-0816

A century ago Sandpoint's first mayor built a beautiful home on the shores of Lake Pend Oreille in North Idaho. Today this very special place is a step back in time as you feel the romance of another era. Take a short scenic walk to the many shops and restaurants in downtown Sandpoint or a leisurely stroll along the lake. In winter, world class Schweitzer Mountain, rated 7th in North America, is a 20-minute drive away.

Schweitzer Mountain Bed and Breakfast
110 Crystal Court
1-888-550-8080

Even if you're not a skier, there's something very cool about staying at a mountain resort. The first thing you notice about the new bed and breakfast at Schweitzer — the only on-mountain bed and breakfast — is the silence. At night, it's interrupted only by the sound of the wind or the occasional rumbling of a snowplow. With the lack of noise, getting a good night's sleep is a cinch. It also makes it easy to concentrate on a good book, if you opt not to battle the elements on the ski hill. The Schweitzer Mountain Bed and Breakfast sits high on the mountain, at the end of a road that at certain times of the year is accessible only by four-wheel drive. Or, it might be reached by a determined driver of a front-wheel drive. The feeling of being up where the birds fly only increases after you climb the stairs to the guest quarters on the third and fourth floor of the 5,000 sq. ft. gorgeously decorated home. There are five rooms, all with private baths, all named for the area's ski runs. A "must" stay over on your antique trail.

22 SILVER CITY

Silver City, high in the Owyhee Mountains, is an evocative ghost town chock-full of historic buildings and atmosphere. This "Queen of Idaho Ghost Towns" appears just as she was during her boom times with over 70 rustic buildings remaining intact.

23 TWIN FALLS

The Oregon Trail pioneers, who trudged through South Central Idaho on their way to Oregon, would be astounded at the sight of present-day Twin Falls. Poised near the edge of spectacular Snake River Canyon, the city is the commercial center of scenic Magic Valley, one of America's most productive agricultural areas.

Driving down inside the canyon is an experience, a world apart from the terrain high above. The Perrine Bridge spanning the canyon is 1,500 feet long and 486 breathtaking feet above the river. This is the location of Evil Knievel's attempted jump across the canyon in a rocket cycle.

In town are two museums of note. The Herrett Museum on the College of Southern Idaho campus has in its collection over 3,000 North and Central Native American artifacts, ranging from 12,000-year-old relics to contemporary Hopi Kachina Dolls.

Anne Tiques, Etc.
325 Main Ave. E.
208/736-0140

Snow's Antiques & Sleigh Works
136 Main Ave. N.
208/736-7292

Back Door Antiques
195 Washington St. N.
208/733-7639

Dudley Studio
1062 Blue Lakes Blvd.
208/733-7110

Second Time Around
689 Washington St. N.
208/734-6008

Treasures from the Past
227 Main Ave. E.
208/733-2976

Every Blooming Thing
266 Blue Lakes Blvd.
208/733-8322

24 WALLACE

The Wallace Corner
525 Cedar St.
208/753-6141

Wallace Antiques
506 Bank St.
208/752-2011

Great Places to Stay

Beale House Bed and Breakfast
107 Cedar St.
1-888-752-7151
Rates begin at $75

The Beale House, a prominent turn-of-the-century dwelling, has many unique features and impressive architectural details. This stately 1904 Colonial Revival home is listed on the National Register of Historic Places, as is the entire town of Wallace. Original parquet floors, antique furnishings, and memorabilia contribute to an atmosphere of comfortable elegance reminiscent of bygone days. A massive Palladian  window in the library area provides a scenic view of the grounds and mountains. Each of the five second-floor guest rooms has its own distinctive charm—one with a fireplace, another with a balcony, still another with two full walls of windows. Guests are invited to peruse the collection of historic photographs acquired from prior owners, as well as from the renowned Barnard-Stockbridge Photographic Collection housed at the University of Idaho.

The Jameson

304 6th St.
208/556-1554

The Historic Jameson Restaurant and Saloon opened its doors in 1900 as a small-town hotel and traditional saloon. It is now restored to its former elegance, offering guests the charm of the Victorian era. The bedrooms are on the third floor, and are very Victorian in appearance with heavy wooden furniture, chunky hand-carved wooden headboards and carpets in Victorian patterns. It is in room three that Maggie, who once stayed at the hotel as a long-term guest in the early part of the century, often returns for a visit. The hotel staff knew very little about Maggie except that she often received letters from New York and London. The letters arrived frequently for years until one day, early in the 1930s, Maggie checked out of the hotel headed for the East Coast. A few weeks later, word was received that she had either been murdered in a train robbery or died violently in an accident.

Several months later the staff noticed room fans and lights were turned off by an invisible hand. Hot showers turned cold and guests found themselves locked in their rooms with the key on the outside! Strangest of all, someone was using the sheets and towels in room three, despite the fact that it was locked and empty.

The puzzled owners decided to consult a psychic who agreed there was a spirit at the hotel: a woman who had died violently and who, because she had no home of her own, had "checked back in." To this day, Maggie makes her presence known. She still steals keys, turns off the water and joins guests for social gatherings. She is always friendly and welcomed by the current owners and their guests.

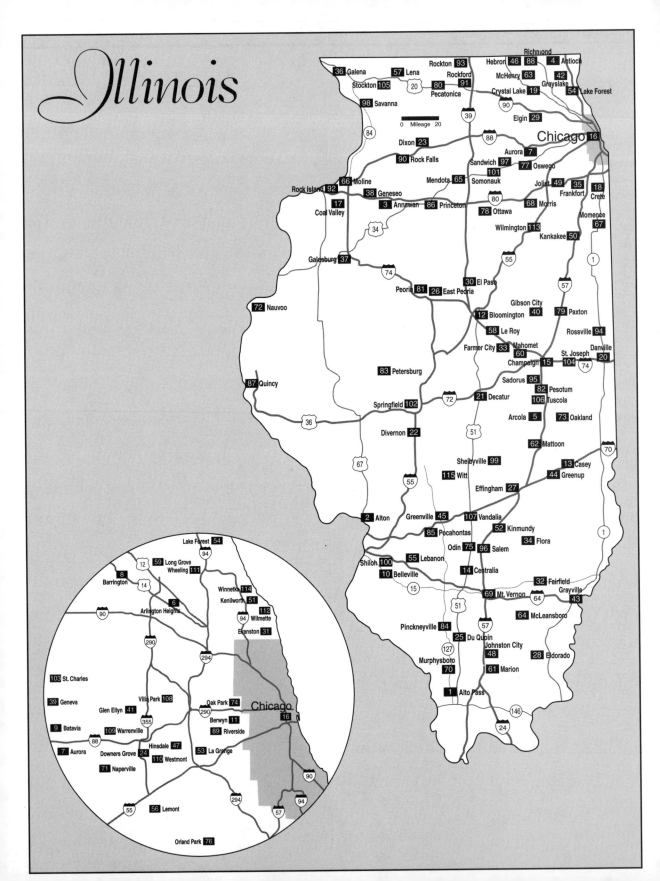

1 ALTO PASS

Austin's of Alto Pass
Route 127 and Alto Pass Road
618/893-2206
Open: Sat. 10-5; Sun. 1-5; other times, call for appointment.
Directions: Alto Pass, Ill., is located on Illinois Highway 127. Travel 16 miles south from Murphysboro, Ill., or 8 miles north from Jonesboro, Ill., on Highway 127. To reach Alto Pass from Carbondale, Ill., take Route 51 south to Makanda Road; turn right; then make a quick left onto Old Highway 51 South. Travel approximately 5 miles to Alto Pass Road and turn right to stop sign at Skyline Drive. Turn right onto Skyline and follow through town to old grade school building on the left.

This one-owner shop is located in a beautifully restored brick grade school built in 1927. A large selection of hand-picked, restored furniture and lots of unusual old wares are available to the discriminating shopper.

2 ALTON

Carol's Corner
318 E. Broadway
618/465-2606

Glass, china, lace, quilts, art and clocks.

1900s Antique Company
9 E. Broadway
618/465-2711

Furniture, primitives, books, paper, paintings and rugs.

Alton Antique Center
401 E. Broadway
618/463-0888

American, European and Oriental antiques.

Heartland Antiques
321 E. Broadway
618/465-6363
Open: Mon.–Sun. 11–5

Furniture, art, quilts, pottery and glassware.

Old Post Office Mall
300 Alby St.
618/462-8204

Dormann's Gifts & Interiors
330 Alby St.
618/462-2654

Broadway Antiques
217 E. Broadway
618/465-0423

Golden Time Treasures
302 E. Broadway
618/465-9275

Cracker Factory Mini Mall
203 E. Broadway (2nd Floor)
618/466-9008

Country Meadows
401 E. Broadway
618/465-1965

Simple Treasures
301 E. Broadway
618/462-3003

River Bend Replicas
301 E. Broadway
618/462-8206

Unusual Place
301 E. Broadway
618/474-2128

Mississippi Mud Pottery
310 E. Broadway
618/462-7573

Jack's Collectibles/Jeanne's Jewels
319 Broadway
618/463-0451

Jan's Antiques
323 E. Broadway
618/465-2250

Old Bridge Antique Mall
435 E. Broadway
618/463-9907

Debbie's Decorative Antiques
108 George & Broadway
618/465-6018

Sloan's Antiques
401 E. Broadway
618/463-0808

Alton Landing Antiques
110 Alton St.
618/462-0443

Prairie Peddler
200 State St.
618/465-6114

Thames on Broadway
205 E. Broadway (Lower Floor)
618/462-1337

Antiques & Collectibles
301 E. Broadway
618/462-3656

Jim's Attic
301 E. Broadway
618/463-7699

The Second Reading
301 E. Broadway
618/462-2361

Wildwood
301 E. Broadway
618/465-4012

Granny's Time
319 Broadway
618/462-5440

Plain & Fancy Emporium
112-114 E. Broadway
618/465-0742

Steve's Antiques
323 E. Broadway
618/465-7407

Rubenstein's Antiques
724-26 E. Broadway
618/465-1306

River Winds
117 Market St.
618/465-8981

Illinois

3 ANNAWAN

Annawan Antique Alley
309 N. Canal St.
309/935-6220
Open: Jan.–March Mon.–Sat., 10–5; Sun. 12–4; April–Dec., Mon.–
Sat., 9–5:30; Sun., 12–4
Directions: From Interstate 80, take Exit 33. Go south on Illinois 78.
The first left driveway (about 1 block from Exit 33).

Tucked away in the quiet, small town of Annawan, Ill., the Annawan
Antique Alley adopted its name from its former life as a bowling alley.
Located just one block from I-80 the "alley" is a convenient "antique
stop." This multidealer antique mall offers furnishings, quilts, Tiffany
and Tiffany-style lamps, statuary, and a lot more of the items you would
expect to find in a quality antique mall.

4 ANTIOCH

Green Bench Antiques
924 Main St.
847/838-2643

Furniture, glass, linens, paper and jewelry.

Williams Brothers Emporium
910 Main St.
847/838-2767
Open: Mon.–Sat. 10–5, Sun. 12–5

Stained glass and a large furniture selection.

Another Man's Treasure
25218 Route 173
847/395-8513

Collection Connection
400 Lake St.
847/395-8800

Past & Presents
345 Park Ave.
847/838-2600

Park Avenue Antique Mall
345 Park Ave.
847/838-1624

Channel Lake School Mall
Lake Ave.
847/395-0000

5 ARCOLA

Green Barn Antiques
111 N. Locust St.
217/268-4754

Emporium Antiques
201 E. Main St.
217/268-4523

6 ARLINGTON HEIGHTS

All My Treasures
7 E. Miner St.
847/394-2944
Open: Wed. & Sat. 10–5, Thurs. & Fri. 10–6:30

Antiques, collectibles, small furniture & accessories.

Arlington Antiques Etc.
208 N. Dunton
847/788-1481
Open: Wed.–Sat. 10–5, Thurs. & Fri. til 7

World's Fair memorabilia, rugs, lamps, glass, furniture, costume
jewelry & glassware.

Cobblestone Antiques
17 E. Miner St.
847/259-4818
Open: Tues. & Sat. 10–5, Thurs. 10–7

Specializing in sterling silver.

Collage Antiques
1005 S. Arlington Heights Road
847/439-5253
Open: Mon.–Fri. 10–5:30, Sat. 10–5, Sun. 12–5

Forgotten Times Ltd.
104 N. Evergreen
847/259-8641
Open: Mon.–Tues. & Thurs.–Fri. 8–6, Thurs. til 8, Sat. 9–3

Restoration, sales and service of vintage and contemporary timepieces.

Museum Country Store
112 W. Fremont St.
847/255-1450
Open: Thurs.–Sat. 10–4, Sun. 1–4

Consignment shop of the Historical Society of Arlington Heights.
Antiques and collectibles.

PJ's Antiques & Collectibles
116 N. Evergreen
847/259-7130
Open: Tues.–Sat. 10–5, Thurs. til 8, Fri. til 6

Bottles, Depression glass, advertising, postcards, furniture and collectibles.

7 AURORA

Sue Keyes Antiques
903 Garfield Ave.
630/892-8524
Open: By appointment only

18th & 19th Century American furniture, paintings, prints, textiles, stoneware, pottery, glass, metals and folk art.

8 BARRINGTON

Estate Jewelers
118 W. Main St.
847/382-8802
Open: Thurs.–Sat. 11–5

Vintage and antique jewelry

Hypoint American Antiques & Folk Art
847/540-0615
Open: By appointment only

American country furniture and folk art.

Romantiques
118 W. Main St.
847/304-9421
Open: Mon.–Fri. 10–5, Sat. 10:30–4:30

Direct importers of European furniture.

Silk'n Things
308 W. Main St.
847/381-3830
Open: Mon.–Fri. 10–5:30, Sat. 10–5, Sun. 12–4

Antiques, linens and furniture.

9 BATAVIA

Yesterdays
115 S. Batavia Ave.
630/406-0524

Just Good Olde Stuff, Inc.
8 E. Wilson St.
630/879-2815

Village Antiques
416 E. Wilson St.
630/406-0905

Savery Antiques
14 N. Washington
630/879-6825

Pedals, Pumpers & Rolls
240 E. State St.
630/879-5555

10 BELLEVILLE

Antiques & Things
704 N. Douglas Ave.
618/236-1104

Eagle Collectibles, Inc.
22 E. Main St.
618/257-1283

Ben's Antique Mall
225 E. Main St.
618/234-0904

Traditional Manor
1101 N. Illinois St.
618/235-4683

Belleville Antique Mall
208 E. Main St.
618/234-6255

11 BERWYN

BBMM Antiques
6710 Cermak Road
708/749-1465

Antique Treasure Chest
6746 16th St.
708/749-1910

Josie's Antiques & Collectibles
2135 Wisconsin Ave.
708/788-3820

Silver Swan Antiques
6738 16th St.
708/484-7177

Past Time Antiques
7100 16th St.
708/788-4804

12 BLOOMINGTON

Bloomington Antique Mall
102 N. Center St.
309/828-1211

A. Gridley Antiques
217 E. Front St.
309/829-9615

Antique Mart/Joce Williams, Inc.
907 S. Eldorado Road
309/662-4213

Illinois

Great Places to Stay

The Burr House
210 E. Chestnut St.
1-800-449-4182

A Civil War Era brick home constructed in 1864, situated near downtown Bloomington in central Illinois. The Burr House B&B is located in the city's historic district across from Franklin Park. Six rooms are available, including one suite with a private bath and sitting room, three rooms with private bath and two with a shared bath. The home has three marble fireplaces, ornate plaster ceilings, inlaid wood floors and a formal dining room where breakfast is served. A variety of stately trees and an outdoor private terrace are all surrounded by a wrought-iron fence. Attractions within walking distance include antique shops, fine dining, retail shops and the community's museum and historic sites.

13 CASEY

Perisho's Antiques
104 E. Colorado Ave.
217/932-4493

14 CENTRALIA

Kim Logan
1829 Gragg St.
618/532-8495

Cedar House Antiques & Collectibles
I-57 & Hwy. 161 (Exit 109)
618-533-0399

Lofty Affair
Walnut Hill Road
618/532-0186

J & M Resales
1180 Medlin Road
618/532-6031

15 CHAMPAIGN

First Street Antiques
206 S. 1st St.
217/359-3079

Carrie's
204 N. Neil St.
217/352-3231

Capricorn Antiques
720 S. Neil St.
217/351-6914

Vintage Antiques
117 N. Walnut St.
217/359-8747

Good Time Antiques
1519 N. Highland Ave.
217/359-6234

Partners in Time Antiques
311 S. Neil St.
217/352-2016

Gray's Antiques & Collectibles
723 S. Neil St.
217/351-9079

16 CHICAGO

Salvage One Architectural Artifacts
1524 S. Sangamon St.
312/733-0098
Open: Tues.–Sat., 10–5; Sun., 11–4
Directions: From O'Hare Airport, downtown Chicago, north and west suburbs, take Dan Ryan Expressway, 90/94 east; exit 18th Street Exit and turn right (west); right (north) on Halsted; left (west) on 16th Street; go three blocks and right (north) on Sangamon Street.
From Midway, Indiana, Michigan, and South Chicago, take Dan Ryan Expressway 90/94 West; exit Canalport/Cermak Road Exit; proceed north on access road (Ruble Street); left (west) on 16th Street, go five blocks and right (north) on Sangamon Street.

Salvage One was founded in 1980 and purchased in 1986 by Leslie Hindman Auctioneers, the Midwest's leading auction house. It has since grown to be the largest architectural salvage company in the country. "Today the popularity of using salvaged architectural materials is not limited to people restoring vintage homes or even choosing to construct a historically accurate design. The vast majority of people buying architectural elements are adding them to enhance their homes or surroundings," says Anne McGahan, of Salvage One.

The staff at Salvage One travels the continent in search of the finest architectural treasures available. At the time of this printing the group had purchased a stunning collection of 13, 14th-century Italian pink marble columns and capitals, a late 17th-century Chinese pottery water carrier, an early French pine butcher's table, a pair of cast iron garden urns with elaborate rococo designs and a Chinese teakwood lantern with hand-painted glass panels.

Salvage One offers over 6,000 interior and exterior doors, an enormous selection of vintage hardware, stained, leaded and beveled glass windows and doors, garden ornaments, fabricated furniture, bathroom fixtures, lighting, and one of the nation's largest inventories of period American and Continental fireplace mantels and accessories, acquired from across the U.S., England, and France.

Brochures, photographs, condition reports and worldwide shipping are available for Salvage One customers.

Turtle Creek Antiques
850 W. Armitage Ave.
773/327-2630

Daniels Antiques
3711 N. Ashland Ave.
773/868-9355

Ray's Antiques
1821 W. Belmont Ave.
773/348-5150

Armitage Antique Gallery
1529 W. Armitage Ave.
773/227-7727

Lincoln Antique Mall
3141 N. Lincoln Ave.
773/244-1440

Antique House
1832 W. Belmont Ave.
773/327-0707

S & F Johnson Antiques
1901 W. Belmont Ave.
773/477-9243

Kristina Maria Antiques
1919 W. Belmont Ave.
773/472-2445

Phil's Antique Mall
2040 W. Belmont Ave.
773/528-8549

Father Time Antiques
2108 W. Belmont Ave.
773/880-5599

Good Old Days
2138 W. Belmont Ave.
773/472-8837

Belmont Antique Mall West
2229 W. Belmont Ave.
773/871-3915

Quality Antiques & Gifts
6401 N. Caldwell Ave.
312/631-1134

Wrigleyville Antique Mall
3336 N. Clark St.
773/868-0285

Camden Passage Antiques Market
5309 N. Clark St.
773/989-0111

Michael Fleming Antiques
5221 N. Damen Ave.
773/561-8696

Wallner's Antiques
1229 W. Diversey Pkwy.
773/248-6061

Stanley Antiques
3489 N. Elston Ave.
773/588-4269

Aged Experience Antiques
2034 N. Halsted St.
773/975-9790

Hyde-N-Seek Antiques
5211 S. Harper Ave., #D
773/684-8380

Portals Limited
230 W. Huron St.
312/642-1066

Tompkins & Robandt
220 W. Kinzie St., 4th Floor
312/645-9995

Nineteen Thirteen
1913 W. Belmont Ave.
773/404-9522

Belmont Antique Mall
2039 W. Belmont Ave.
773/549-9270

House of Nostalgia
2047 W. Belmont Ave.
773/244-6460

Danger City
2129 W. Belmont
773/871-1420

Kaye's Antiques
2147 W. Belmont Ave.
773/929-8187

Olde Chicago Antiques
2336 W. Belmont Ave.
773/935-1200

Stanley Galleries Antiques
2118 N. Clark St.
773/281-1614

Acorn Antiques & Uniques Ltd.
5241 N. Clark St.
773/506-9100

Collectables on Clybourn
2503 N. Clybourn
773/871-1154

Shop Front Antiques
5223 N. Damen Ave.
773/271-5130

International Antiques
2300 W. Diversey Ave.
773/227-2400

Pilsen Gallery Arch
540 W. 18th St.
312/829-2827

Silver Moon
3337 N. Halsted St.
773/883-0222

Sandwich Antiques Market
1510 N. Hoyne Ave.
773/227-4464

Antiques Centre at Kinzie Square
220 W. Kinzie St.
312/464-1946

Griffins & Gargoyles Ltd.
2140 W. Lawrence Ave.
773/769-1255

Haily's Antiques & Collectibles
5508 W. Lawrence Ave.
773/202-0555

Steve Starr Studios
2779 N. Lincoln Ave.
773/525-6530

Urban Artifacts
2928 N. Lincoln Ave.
773/404-1008

Red Eye
3050 N. Lincoln Ave.
773/975-2020

Gene Douglas Antiques
3419 N. Lincoln Ave.
773/561-4414

Lake View Antiques
3422 N. Lincoln Ave.
773/935-6443

Benkendorf Antique Clocks
900 N. Michigan Ave.
312/951-1903

U.S. #1 Antique
1509 N. Milwaukee Ave.
773/489-9428

Crossings Antiques Mall
1805 W. 95th St.
773/881-3140

Malcolm Franklin, Inc.
34 E Oak St
312/337-0202

David McClain Antiques
2716 W. 111th St.
773/239-4683

Decoro
224 E. Ontario St.
312/943-4847

Architectural Artifacts, Inc.
4325 N. Ravenswood Ave.
773/348-0622

Garrett Galleries
1155 N. State St.
312/944-6325

Sara Breil Designs
449 N. Wells St.
312/923-9223

Pimlico Antiques Ltd.
500 N. Wells St.
312/245-9199

Gibell's & Bits
5512 W. Lawrence Ave.
773/283-4065

Time Well
2780 N. Lincoln Ave.
773/549-2113

Chicago Antique Center
3045 N. Lincoln Ave.
773/929-0200

Harlon's Antiques
3058 N. Lincoln Ave.
773/327-3407

Zigzag
3419 N. Lincoln Ave.
773/525-1060

Lincoln Ave. Antique Co-op
3851 N. Lincoln Ave.
773/935-6600

Antiques on the Avenue
104 S. Michigan Ave., 2nd Floor
312/357-2800

Modern Times
1538 N. Milwaukee Ave.
773/772-8871

Little Ladies
6217 N. Northwest Hwy.
773/631-3602

Russell's Antiques
2404 W. 111 St.
773/233-3205

Therese Chez Antiques
3120 W. 111th St.
773/881-0824

Time Square, Ltd.
6352 S. Pulaski Road
773/581-8216

Gallery 1945
300 N. State St.
312/573-1945

First Arts & Antiques
7220 W. Touhy Ave.
312/774-5080

Rita-Bucheit, Ltd.
449 N. Wells St.
312/527-4080

O'Hara's Gallery
707 N. Wells St.
312/751-1286

Illinois

Chicago Riverfront Antique Market
2929 N. Western Ave.
773/252-2500

Penn Dutchman Antiques
4912 N. Western Ave.
773/271-2208

Memories & More
10143 S. Western Ave.
773/238-5645

Grich Antiques
10857 S. Western Ave.
773/233-8734

An Antique Store
1450 W. Webster Ave.
773/935-6060

Rich Oldies & Goodies
4642 N. Western Ave.
773/334-7033

A & R
8024 S. Western Ave.
773/434-9157

Cluttered Cupboard
10332 S. Western Ave.
773/881-8803

R.J. Collectibles
11400 S. Western Ave.
773/779-8828

Jazz'e Junque
3831 N. Lincoln Ave.
773/472-1500

17 COAL VALLEY

Country Fair Mall

504 W. 1st Ave. (Hwy. 6)
309/799-3670
Open: Mon. & Thurs. 10–6, Tues., Fri., & Sat. 10–5, Sun. 12–5, closed Wed.
Directions: Traveling I-280 west to Exit 5B (Moline Airport) to Highway 6 east. Mall is 1³/₄ miles on the north side of the highway.

No one goes away emptied handed at Country Fair Mall. Kent Farley, the owner, has created a two-star attraction for antiquers. For the discriminating shopper, one location provides upscale antiques; no reproductions, no sifting through the ordinary. The second location houses 150 to 170 booths of a "Shopper's Haven." Treasure hunters should be prepared to dig!

18 CRETE

Third Generation Antiques
831 W. Exchange
708/672-3369

Season's
1362 Main St.
708/672-0170

Gatherings
1375 Main St.
708/672-9880

Village Antiques and Lamp Shop
595 Exchange
708/672-8980

Woodstill's Antiques
610 Gould St. (Beecher)
708/946-3161

Farmer's Daughter
1262 Lincoln St.
708/672-4588

Indian Wheel Co.
1366 Main St.
708/672-9612

The Marketplace
550 Exchange
708/672-5556

The Finishing Touch
563 Exchange
708/672-9520

19 CRYSTAL LAKE

Way Back When Antiques
4112 Country Club Road
815/459-1360

Railroad Street Market
8316 Railroad St.
815/459-4220

Carriage Antiques & Collectibles
8412 Railroad St.
815/455-0710

Carriage's Antiques
5111 E. Terra Cotta Ave.
815/356-9808

Penny Lane Antiques
6114 Lou St.
815/459-8828

Aurora's Antiques
8404 Railroad St.
815/455-0710

Country Church Antiques
8509 Ridgefield Road
815/477-4601

20 DANVILLE

Queen Ann's Cottage
407 Ann St.
217/443-5958

Bob's Antiques
53 N. Vermilion St.
217/431-3704

Treasures Unique
1327 Main St.
217/443-4280

Two's Company
109 N. Vermilion St.
217/446-7553

21 DECATUR

China House Antiques
801 W. Eldorado St.
217/428-7212

Nellie's Attic Antique Mall
3030 S. Mount Zion Road
217/864-3363

Collector's Shop
2345 S. Mount Zion Road
217/864-3000

Calliope House
560 W. North St.
217/425-1944

Great Places To Stay

Younker House Bed and Breakfast

500 W. Main St.
217/429-9718

The Younker House is a beautiful Victorian brick home located in the historic district of downtown Decatur. The home was once the residence of Dr. William Barnes, who was well known for housing the largest butterfly collection in North America. The home has won several awards for historical preservation and is on the historic register.

Illinois

22 DIVERNON

Lisa's I & II Antique Malls
I-55 and Route 104
217/628-1111 or 217/628-3333
Open: Daily 10–6, closed Thanksgiving and Christmas
Directions: Both Lisa's I & II Antique Malls are located on Interstate 55 at Route 104 (Exit 82), 10 miles south of Springfield, Illinois.

Promising 40,000 square feet of rambling room, these two malls exhibit a full array of antiques and collectibles. No crafts are to be found among the quality selection of antiques which includes: furniture (oak, cherry, walnut, pine, mahogany), early American, glassware, old toys, jewelry and much, much more.

If you are looking for something "large" to take home, the old Stagecoach is for you. It's quite a showpiece and it's FOR SALE! Delivery is available at Lisa's I & II (I wonder if that means the Stagecoach, too?).

Country Place Antiques
RR1 Frontage Road
217/628-3699

23 DIXON

Brinton Ave. Antique Mall
725 N Brinton Ave.
815/284-4643

Dixon Antique Station
1220 S. Galena Ave.
815/284-8890

E & M Antique Mall
1602 S. Galena Ave.
815/288-1900

24 DOWNERS GROVE

Mr. Chips Crystal Repair
743 Ogden Ave.
630/964-4070

Asbury's
1626 Ogden Ave.
630/769-9191

Country Cellar
2101 Ogden Ave.
630/968-0413

25 DUQUOIN

Main Street Antiques Mall
211 E. Main St.
618/542-5043

Mulberry Tree Antqs., Cllbls. & Gifts
24 S. Mulberry St.
618/542-6621

26 EAST PEORIA

Charley's
1815 Meadows Ave.
309/694-7698

Pleasant Hill Antique Mall
315 S. Pleasant Hill Road
309/694-4040

Southern Knights
125 E. Washington St.
309/694-4581

Cowboy Antiques
1107 E. Washington St.
309/699-3929

Antiques Inclusive
2469 E. Washington St.
309/699-0624

27 EFFINGHAM

Antik Haus
915 N. Henrietta St.
217/342-4237

Red Coach Antiques
608 W. Fayette Ave.
217/342-6280

28 ELDORADO

Eldorado Antique Mall
935 4th St.
618/273-5586

Little Egypt Antiques
1212 State St.
618/273-9084

29 ELGIN

Antique Corner
475 Walnut Ave.
847/931-0310

State Street Market
701 N. State St.
847/695-3066

The Antique Emporium at The Milk Pail
Route 25 (½ mi. north of I-90 – Dundee)
847/468-9667

30 EL PASO

Century House Antiques
11 & 2nd St./I-39 Exit 14
309/527-3705

El Paso Antique Mall
I-39 & Route 24
309/527-3705

31 EVANSTON

Eureka!
705 W. Washington
847/869-9090
Open: Tues.-Sat. 11-5
Directions: From Chicago, take any main artery north to Evanston. Evanston is the first suburb north of Chicago along the lake. When going north or south along the Tri-State (Route 294) or on the Edens Expressway (Route 94), exit at Dempster (east). Go east 15-20 minutes to Ridge Avenue in Evanston (stoplight). Turn right (south); go 1 street past Main Street. Turn left onto Washington, and go 3 blocks to 705. Located 1 block south of Main, 1 block west of Chicago Avenue, 3 blocks east of Ridge.

Now, this shop could quite possibly be a first — "No Repros" in the way of collectibles. The owner claims "this is the best nostalgia shop in Chicagoland! Early advertising, paper ephemera, world's fair collectibles, black memorabilia, and oddball items can all be found throughout this fun shop. Men will love it!"

Harvey Antiques
1231 Chicago Ave.
847/866-6766

Another Time Another Place
1243 Chicago Ave.
847/866-7170

Illinois

Pursuit of Happiness
1524 Chicago Ave.
847/869-2040

Village Bazaar
503 Main St.
847/866-9444

Rusty Nail
912 1/2 Sherman Ave.
847/491-0360

32 FAIRFIELD

Riverside Antiques
Hwy. 15 E.
618/842-3570

Dickey's Antiques
Hwy. 15 E., Route 5
618/842-2820

33 FARMER CITY

Main Street Antiques
115 S. Main St.
309/928-9208

Salt Creek Emporium
120 Main St.
309/928-2844

Renaissance Art Studio
211 S. Main St.
309/928-2213

34 FLORA

Eileen's Antiques
526 E. Fourth St.
618/662-6171

35 FRANKFORT

Antiques Unique
100 Kansas St.
815/469-2741

36 GALENA

Directions: From Chicago, travel I-90 (Northwest Tollway) to U.S. 20 at Rockford. Follow U.S. 20 west to Galena: also from Chicago, take I-88 to I-39. Travel I-39 north to U.S. 20 at Rockford. Go U.S. 20 west to Galena.

Once mired in decay and forgotten river routes, Galena, Illinois, has been revived. Some of America's most enticing countryside surrounds this small town of historic manor houses, handsome brick mercantile and business buildings, and churches accented with the craft and love

Sarah Bustle Antiques
821 Dempster St.
847/869-7290

Edward Joseph Antiques
520 Main St.
847/332-1855

Robinson's Antiques
Route 15
618/842-3626

La Jean's Country Antiques
U.S. 45 S.
618/847-4525

Margaret's Attic to Basement
117 S. Main St.
309/928-3023

Farmer City Antiques Center
201 S. Main St.
309/928-9210

The Junction
E. Route 150 & 54
309/928-3116

Wallace Antiques
504 E. North Ave.
618/662-8252

The Trolley Barn
11 S. White St.
815/464-1120

shown in hand-carved altars and pulpits. The enchanting qualities of Galena are echoed in the fact that many leading Chicago CEOs have chosen to retire to this spot.

Galena and Jo Daviess County swell with more than 50 antique shops (making this the main Midwestern antiquing center), 50 bed and breakfasts, 12 galleries, 25 private studios, along with 150 specialty shops. Billed and living up to fame, Galena is one of the most popular destinations in the Midwest. Weekends find bed and breakfasts booked, so travelers should make reservations early. November and March are the only reliably slow months during the year.

Glick Antiques
112 N. Main St.
815/777-0781

Hawk Hollow
103 S. Main St.
815/777-3616

My Favorite Things
116 S. Main St.
815/777-3340

Karen's
209 S. Main St.
815/777-0911

Sparrow
220 S. Main St.
815/777-3060

Village Mercantile
225 S. Main St.
815/777-0065

Tin-Pan Alley
302 S. Main St.
815/777-2020

Belle Epoque
306 S. Main St.
815/777-2367

A Peace of the Past
408 S. Main St.
815/777-2737

Reds Antiques & Collectibles
11658 W. Red Gates Road
815/777-9675

Galena Shoppe
109 Main St.
815/777-3611

Touch-Banowetz Antiques
117 S Main St.
815/777-3370

Cedar Chest
213 S. Main St.
815/777-9235

J G Accent Unlimited
221 S. Main St.
815/777-9550

Beneath The Dust
302 S. Main St.
815/777-3202

EGK Collectibles
305 S. Main St.
815/777-0180

Crickets
404 S. Main St.
815/777-6176

Galena Antique Mall
8201 State Route 20 W.
815/777-3440

Great Places to Stay

Avery Guest House Bed & Breakfast
606 S. Prospect St.
815/777-3883

This 1848 pre-Civil War home is beautifully decorated in period decor. It was once owned by Major George Avery, who served with General Grant during the Civil War. Located just two and one half blocks from Galena's Historic Main Street.

Bielenda's Mars Ave. Guest Home
515 Mars Ave.
815/777-2808

The Bielenda's Mar Ave. Guest House was built in 1855 in the Federal style by J. C. Packard, owner of the town's dry good store. During 1930 the home served as Maybelle's Tea Room (first tea room in town). The three guest rooms are large with queen sized beds and private baths. Relax on the porch in a swing and enjoy the scenery.

Brierwreath Manor Bed & Breakfast
216 N. Bench St.
815/777-0608

The elegant Brierwreath Manor Bed & Breakfast is listed on the National Historic Register. The home was built in 1884 and has antique furnishings to reflect that era. The Mayor's Room, named for former mayor Frank Einsweiler, who once owned the home, is a rose-colored two-room suite with gas log fireplace. The Heirloom Suite is a Victorian splendor featuring two beds and a claw-foot tub.

Craig Cottage
505 Dewey Ave.
815/777-1461

Craig Cottage, named after Captain Nathan Boone Craig, who married Daniel Boone's granddaughter, built this brick and limestone house in 1827. It has since been restored and featured in *Country Living* magazine, Hallmark Christmas cards and a tour of homes in Galena. The house is very quaint, private, peaceful and well equipped. It overlooks a wooded valley and is within walking distance of Historic Galena.

Park Avenue Guest House
208 Park Ave.
1-800-359-0743

This Queen Anne Victorian "Painted Lady" features original ornate woodwork, pocket doors, transoms, 12 foot ceilings, and an open staircase. Three guest rooms feature private baths, queen-size beds, fireplaces, and antique decor. During the summer, enjoy the extensive perennial gardens alongside a unique gazebo, or sip a cool drink on the screened wrap-around porch. Experience an old-fashioned opulent Christmas — you'll find a miniature Dickens Village with over 70 houses, 12 full-sized trees, and yards of beautiful garlands with while lights glowing softly. Take a short stroll to Grant Park or across the footbridge to Main Street, where you'll find plenty of shopping and fine restaurants.

Victorian Mansion
301 S. High St.
1-888-815-6768

Higher Ground Victorian Mansion is an elegant Italianate Victorian home set amidst an acre of trees and gardens. Accommodations include eight bedrooms with beautiful ornate Victorian beds and marble-topped dressers. All bedrooms have a private bath and two have marble fireplaces. Relaxing comes easily in two large parlors and library with a fireplace. The music parlor has a turn-of-the century Victrola and an antique pump organ. Old-time movies are availabe in the TV/movie parlor. A full breakfast is served in a lovely dining room that seats fourteen people around four tables. The Mansion is located on a hilltop that provides a commanding view of the countryside from the second-floor porch. Downtown Historic Galena is two blocks away, accessed by a flight of stairs known as the school house stairs.

Great Places to Eat

American Old-Fashioned Ice Cream Parlor
102 N. Main St.
815/777-3121

An 1846 soda fountain with 50 flavors of ice cream and yogurt, sherbet, shakes, floats, sodas, sandwiches, snacks. Coke memorabilia. Trolley tickets. '50s music.

Backstreet Steak & Chophouse
216 S. Commerce
815/777-4800

Dinner nightly: fine steaks, pork and lamb chops, veal and seafood. BBQ ribs a specialty.

Boone's Place
305 S. Main St.
815/777-4488

Lunch and dinner daily, breakfast on weekends, in an 1846 historic building with antique decor. Full espresso bar. Specializing in "made from scratch" gourmet sandwiches, stuffed potatoes, soups, salads, homemade deep dish pie, ice cream and cheesecakes.

Grant's Place
515 S. Main St.
815/777-3331

Civil War theme restaurant on second floor over winery. Lunch and dinner daily. Gourmet sandwiches, seafood and steaks.

Fried Green Tomatoes
1031 Irish Hollow Road
815/777-3938

Upscale country Italian dining in an historic brick farmstead two miles southeast of Galena just off Blackjack Road. Black Angus steaks, chops, fresh seafood. Full bar, detailed wine list.

Jakels' Backerei Cafe & Break Shop
200 S. Main St.
815/777-0400

European bakery. Breakfast and lunch daily. Hearth-baked breads, Danish, tortes.

37 GALESBURG

East Main Antiques
125 E. Main St.
309/342-4424

Highway Antique Shop
224 E. Main St.
309/343-1931

Antique Corporation
674 E. Main St.
309/342-9448

Attic Antique Shop
169 E. Water St.
309/342-7956

Galesburg Antique Mall
349 E. Main St.
309/343-9800

Rug Beater Antiques
137 E. Main St.
309/343-2001

Rail City Antiques
665 E. Main St.
309/343-2614

General Store Antiques
940 E. North St.
309/342-2926

Ziggy's Antiques
674 E. Main St.
309/342-9448

38 GENESEO

Geneseo Antique Mall
117 E. Exchange
309/944-3777

Heartland Antique Mall
4169 S. Oakwood Ave.
309/944-3373

39 GENEVA

Findings of Geneva Antiques
307 W. State St. (Route 38)
630/262-0959
Email: findingsg@aol.com

"Findings" has been open approximately 2 years at the busy intersection of Route 38 (State St.) And Third St., in Geneva's beautiful downtown shopping district. It is owned by Marv and Jan Barishman, who operate it on a daily basis from 10:30 to 6 p.m. Tuesday through Saturday, 12 to 5 p.m. on Sunday, and closed on Mondays.

The shop has become well known for its finer and unusual older books, covering a wide range of collectible topics. Sharing the spotlight is collectable glass, pottery, sterling and finer linens. It is not unusual to find prints by collected artists hanging on the walls; as well as a wide selection of older postcards, world's fair items, paper collectibles, magazines, pocket knives, and toys.

The customer is always dealing with the owners in this shop, and has an opportunity to source information, as well as friendly discussion surrounding the items displayed here. Buying and selling items is a daily occurrence in this old-fashioned environment, and one can hear a pleasant interchange of price negotiating during many of the purchase and sale transactions. The store is actively buying many items regularly. The most sought-after items are pre-1900 leather bound and "marbelized" books, fancy cutwork tablecloths, whitework bed linens, table scarves and damask napkins. Active buying is always taking place in Franciscan Pottery's "Desert Rose," "Ivy" and "Apple" dinnerware; Hall China's "Crocus" pattern, and McCoy Pottery, Fostoria, Heisey, and Cambridge glass; and illustrated children's books like "Little Black Sambo" and those illustrated by N. C. Wyeth or Jessie Wilcox Smith.

A Step in the Past
122 Hamilton St.
630/232-1611

Geneva Antique Market
227 S. 3rd St.
630/208-1150

Geneva Antiques, Ltd.
220 S. 3rd St.
630/208-7952

Fourth Street Galleries
327 Franklin
630/208-4610

40 GIBSON CITY

Wil E Makit Antiques
305 E. 1st
217/784-4598

The Silver Lion
107 N. Sangamon
217/784-8220

Red Barn Antiques
620 E. 11th St. (Route 54 & 11th)
217/784-8752

41 GLEN ELLYN

Patricia Lacock Antiques
526 Crescent Blvd.
630/858-2323

Finders Keepers
558 Crescent Blvd.
630/469-5320

Royal Vale View Antiques
388 Pennsylvania Ave.
630/790-3135

Stagecoach Antiques
526 Crescent Blvd.
630/469-0490

Marcia Crosby Antiques
477 Forest Ave.
630/858-5665

Pennsylvania Place
535 Pennsylvania Ave.
630/858-1515

42 GRAYSLAKE

Grayslake Trading Post
116 Barron Blvd.
847/223-2166

Duffy's Attic
22 Center St.
847/223-7454

Yesterday Once More
299 W. Belvidere Road
847/223-4944

Antique Warehouse
2 S. Lake St.
847/223-9554

43 GRAYVILLE

Antiques & More
1 Mile N. Of I-64
618/375-4331

Prairie Town Antiques
101 N. Main
618/375-7306

44 GREENUP

Cumberland Road Collectibles
100 W. Cumberland
217/923-5260

Western Style Town Antique Mall
113 E. Kentucky St.
217/923-3514

45 GREENVILLE

County Seat Mall, Inc.
105 N. Third St.
618/664-8955

46 HEBRON

Prairie Avenue Antiques
9936 Main St.
815/648-4507

Grampy's Antique Store
10003 Main St.
815/648-2244

Nancy Powers Antiques
12017 Maple Ave. (Route 173)
815/648-4804

Back in Time Antiques
10004 Main St.
815/648-2132

Hebron Antique Gallery
10002 Main St.
815/648-4080

Lloyd's Antiques & Restoration
10103 Main St.
815/648-2202

Scarlet House
9911 Main St.
815/648-4112

Watertower Antiques
9937 Main St.
815/648-2287

47 HINSDALE

Yankee Peddler
6 E. Hinsdale Ave.
630/325-0085

Griffin's in the Village
16 E. 1st St.
630/323-4545

Aloha's Antique Jewelry
6 W. Hinsdale Ave.
630/325-3733

Fleming & Simpson Antiques, Ltd.
53 S. Washington St.
630/654-1890

48 JOHNSON CITY

Little Shop in the Woods
Corinth Road
618/982-2805

Shamrock Antiques
306 W. Broadway
618/983-6661

Seagle's Creative Collectibles
Liberty School Road
618/983-8130

Some Things Special Antiques
1805 Benton Ave.
618/983-8166

49 JOLIET

Joliet is home to four Riverboat Casinos, the historic Rialto Theatre and is situated on the Heritage Corridor of the I&M Canal that runs from Chicago to La Salle-Peru, Illinois. There are numerous restaurants in the area that run the gamut from fast food to fine dining. There are a large number of motels at the Houbolt Road and Larkin Ave. exits off of I-80 and at the Route 30 exit off of I-55.

The largest and best antique show in the Midwest is the Sandwich Antiques Market, about 30 miles from Joliet. There is one show a month from May to October; you can call the Chicago office for the 1998 show dates (773/227-4464) or contact them on the internet at this address: http://www.antiquemarkets.com

Uniques Antiques, Ltd.
1006 W. Jefferson St.
815/741-2466

Uniques Antiques, Ltd. at 1006 W. Jefferson Street in Joliet is conveniently located near two interstates. You can reach it from I-55 at the Route 52 east exit 253 and go straight east for 4.8 miles; Route 52 is W. Jefferson St. as it goes through Joliet. You can also reach it from I-80 at the Larking Ave. North exit 130B. Take Larkin Ave. North, turn right (east) at the 3rd stoplight and go 1.5 miles to Uniques.

Uniques Antiques, Ltd. is a single-owner shop that has 3,000 square feet of a wide variety of clean, quality, and well-displayed antiques and collectibles. Everything is guaranteed to be what it is represented as; 99% of the merchandise is 30 years old or older. The owner, Ron Steinquist, stands behind the authenticity of his merchandise. You will find everything from smalls to furniture: advertising items and signs, china, clocks, cameras, crocks, dolls, glassware, jugs, lamps, mirrors, military items, milk bottles, phonographs, pocket watches, pottery, prints, political pins, radios, sheet music, toys, telephones, vases, wristwatches from the

'40s, World's Fair items, and much more. In addition there is one room of "Boys Toys" that specializes in auto-related items, hunting, fishing, etc. You can almost smell the testosterone in this room!

Special services that are available at Uniques Antiques, Ltd. are: clock and watch repair, chair caning, radio repair, and stain removal from porcelain and pottery. China repair will be available in the near future.

50 KANKAKEE

Kankakee Antique Mall
145 S. Schuyler Ave.
815/937-4957

Blue Dog Antique
440 N. 5th Ave.
815/936-1701

Bellflower Antique Shop
397 S. Wall St.
815/935-8242

Indian Oaks Antique Mall
N. Route 50 & L. Power Road (Bourbonnais)
815/933-9998

51 KENILWORTH

Smith & Ciffon
626 Green Bay Road
847/853-0234

Federalist Antiques
515 Park Dr.
847/256-1791

Kenilworth Antique Center
640 Green Bay Road
847/251-8003

Indian Oaks Antique Mall
N. Route 50 & L. Power Road (Bourbonnais)
815/933-9998

52 KINMUNDY

Buckboard Antiques
253 S. Madison
618/547-3731

Lil's Antiques
301 E. Third St.
618/547-3604

53 LA GRANGE

Corner Shop
27 Calendar Court
708/579-2425

Victorian Vanities
19 W. Harris Ave.
708/354-1865

Antiques & More
2 S. Stone Ave.
708/352-2214

Patterns of the Past
15 W. Harris Ave.
708/579-5299

Rosebud Antiques
729 W. Hillgrove Ave.
708/352-7673

Another Time Around
10 S. Stone Ave.
708/352-0400

54 LAKE FOREST

Country House
179 E. Deerpath Road
847/234-0244

Samlesburg Hall Ltd. Antiques
730 Forest Ave.
847/295-6070

Lake Forest Antique, Inc.
950 N. Western Ave.
847/234-0442

Lake Forest Antiquarians
747 E. Deerpath Road
847/234-1990

Spruce Antiques
740 N. Western Ave.
847/234-1244

Anna's Mostly Mahogany
950 N. Western Ave.
847/295-9151

On Consignment Ltd. Antiques
207 E. Westminster Road
847/295-6070

Snow-Gate Antiques, Inc.
234 E. Wisconsin Ave.
847/234-3450

55 LEBANON

General Store Antique Mall
112 E. St. Louis St.
618/537-8494

Grandma's Attic
119 W. St. Louis St.
618/537-6730

The Cross Eyed Elephant
201 W. St. Louis St.
618/537-4491

Peddler Books
209 W. St. Louis St.
618/537-4026

Heritage Antiques
218 W. St. Louis St.
618/537-2667

The Shops at 111
111 W. St. Louis St.
618/537-4162

Mom & Me
200 W. St. Louis St.
618/537-8343

Town & Country
205 W. St. Louis St.
618/537-6726

And Thistle Dew
210 W. St. Louis St.
618/537-4443

Owings Antiques
326 W. St. Louis St.
618/537-6672

56 LEMONT

Thirty minutes southwest of Chicago, Lemont has over 40 dealers in 8 antique stops. Specialty stores display the works of local craftsmen and artisans. A cookie jar museum and historical museum are located nearby.

Antiques On Stephen Street

Carroll & Heffron Antiques & Collectibles
206 Stephen St.
630/257-0510
Open: Mon.–Sat., Sun. 12–4

Proud to be a part of the little international village of Lemont, the store has an always-changing inventory of almost everything: furniture, toys, glassware, books, artwork, and more.

Myles Antiques
119 Stephen St.
630/243-1415
Open: Daily 10–4

Affordable elegance with a fine selection of European and American furniture, quality home decorating accessories, and Fenton art glass. Discover treasures from the past or that special something for that special someone.

Illinois

Bittersweet Antiques & Country Accents
111 Stephen St.
603/243-1633
Open: Daily 10–4

Located in an 1885 Limestone building filled with country primitives, painted furniture, decoys, fishing lures and woodenware. In addition they offer antique country decorator items, candles, lamps, wreaths, silks, etc. Sourcing available to find your special "wants."

Pacific Tall Ships
106 Stephen St.
1-800-690-6601

Unique maritime gallery specializing in handcrafted museum quality sailing ships of the world. Included with the ships are your choice of several different custom-built cases to enhance the decor of your home or office.

Antiques On Main Street

Greta's Garrett
408 Main St.
603/257-0021
Open: Tues.–Sat. 11–4

Antiques, collectibles, art pottery, fine glass, jewelry, Lenox china, linens, jewelry, old books, etc. Specializing in appraisal service and estate sales. We buy. Free estimates.

Lemont Antiques
228 Main St.
630/257-1318
Open: Daily usually 10–5 or by appointment

Set in the restored 1862 Gerharz Funeral Store. Restoration and referral service, clock repair, antiques & collectibles, furniture, china, glass, clocks, dolls, jewelry, salt and pepper shakers, linens, lamps, cookie jars, collector plates, Russian curios and primitives.

Main Street Antique Emporium
220 Main St.
630/257-3456
Open: Mon.–Fri. 11–8, Sat. 10–5, Sun. 11–5

Two stores in one, filled with antiques, collectibles, stamps, postcards, lamps, toy trains, and unique things. We also refurbish lamps. Multi-dealer shop.

Antiques On Canal Street

Antique Parlour
316-318 Canal St.
630/257-0033
Open: Tues.–Sun. 11–5

Set in the 2400-square-foot 1928 Dodge Car Showroom. Engraved with the "Bicentennial Mural" wall. Victorian & Country fine furniture and homethings, 1840s to 1940s, antique guide books, plate holders, Victorian paper goods, silk lampshades.

Great Places to Eat

Lemont's Famous Christmas Inn
107 Stephen St.
630/257-2548
Open: Tues.–Sat. starting at 11 a.m., Sun. 9–2

Lunch and dinner in a Christmas atmosphere. Featured in "Best Decorations in Chicagoland." Sunday's breakfast buffet is a great way to start your antiquing day in Lemont.

Old Town Restaurant
113 Stephen St.
630/257-7570
Open: Tues.–Sun 11–8, closed Mon.

Lunch, dinner, family-style European cuisine, including Polish, Lithuanian, Hungarian, German. Carry-outs. Homemade bakery the specialty. Sunday brunch.

The Strand Cafe & Ice Cream Parlor
103 Stephen St.
630/257-2112
Open: Weekdays 11–10, weekends 8–10

Fantastic food, breakfast, lunch or dinner! Serving the best Cajun food outside New Orleans. Best ice cream parlor in the U.S.A. and the best chocolate soda in the world. Bob Gerges plays the concert piano, honky tonk piano and accordion Fri.–Sun., 6 p.m. to closing. Tony Price plays the concert piano and sings every day for lunch.

Illinois

Nick's Tavern
221 Main St.
630/257-6564
Open: Mon.–Sat. 11–10:30

An antique in its own right, Nick's Tavern has been serving Lemont for more than 50 years. Home of "The Best Biggest Cheeseburger" in the state.

Interesting Side Trip

The Cookie Jar Museum
111 Stephen St.
708/257-2101

In 1975, Lucille Bromberek successfully completed a treatment program for alcoholism. Although she had no idea what to do with her life now that she'd recovered, she bolted up in bed one night "because a little voice inside my head told me to start collecting cookie jars." Four years later, she opened the only known cookie jar museum in the civilized world.

"I traveled throughout the country and found them at garage sales, antique shows, and flea markets," she remembers. As her reputation grew, people began sending her C-jars, as she fondly calls them, from all over the United States and abroad. Soon her home was overflowing, not unlike one of her overfilled collectibles.

Today the museum is in an office building and boasts a Wedgewood jar that's over a century old; rare Belleek china shamrock-and-pineapple containers from Ireland; a Crown Milano jar worth $3000 and petite, hand decorated biscuit jars, some of which have gold filigree, and others of which are made of exquisite cranberry glass.

"Most C-jars cost from $1 to $2,000, although prices have risen dramatically since I started. Jars I paid $5 for are now worth at least $125." For instance, those made from Depression glass, which was cheap in the thirties, can now fetch up to $8,000. "A few go for as high as $23,000, such as the McCoy 'Aunt Jemima' that belonged to Andy Warhol." That's a lot of dough for something that holds empty calories. Most in the two-thousand-plus collection are from twenty to fifty years old.

But the real fun of the museum is the perusal of Bromberek's piquant groupings. In the Pig Sty, Miss Piggy shares shelf space with peers dressed in black tie, chef's togs, and a nurse's uniform. There's even a jar depicting a farmer giving slop to the porkers.

Other cookie jar menagerie members include dogs, owls, turkeys, bears, camels, cows, fish, and a whale. "The lambs and the lions and the cats and mice are shelved together and get along beautifully." One of Bromberek's favorites is the "Peek-a-Boo" jar, a ceramic rabbit in pajamas. "They made only a thousand."

The museum has cookie jar trolleys, ships, trains, cars, airplanes, and even a gypsy wagon and a spaceship to help visitors along on their journeys. And, of course, there are the usual seasonal themes: a jack-o'-lantern, a Santa Claus, and a jar commemorating the annual downfall of many a dedicated dieter, Girl Scout cookies.

Nursery rhyme characters range from the old woman who lived in the shoe to the cow who jumped over the moon, and visitors will find Dennis the Menace, Howdy Doody, and W.C. Fields as well. Bromberek has devoted three shelves to a Dutch colony and its population. Some of her arrangements tell a story, such as the one in which Cinderella is followed by a castle and then a pumpkin coach. "Turnabouts," with different faces on each side, include Mickey/Minnie Mouse, Papa/Mama Bear, and Pluto/Dumbo.

No cookie jar museum would be complete without homage paid to the treats they hold. A giant Oreo and a Tollhouse cookie, bags depicting Pepperidge Farm and Famous Amos munchies, and the Keebler elf are all represented here. Other enterprising containers include the Quaker Oats box, a Marshall Field's Frango Mint bag, the real-estate logo for Century 21, and an Avon lady calling on a Victorian-style house. For the health conscious, there are strawberry and green-pepper-shaped jars (at least the *container's* nonfattening). And you can really get caught with your hand in cookie jars that play music when opened.

Although Bromberek collects cookie cutters, cookie cookbooks, cookie plates, and measuring spoons that work for other comestibles besides cookies, the jars remain her true passion. "If they could talk, the stories they'd tell!" she half-jokes. "They come alive when I'm not there. The chefs and grannies stir up their favorite recipes for a grand gala affair. They come out of their little house C-jars, go to the barn, turn on the radio C-jar and dance up a storm." She claims she sometimes finds them in different spots in the morning. Well, okay.

Leave the appetite at home, however. "There's not a cookie on the premises."

From *America's Strangest Museums*
Copyright 1996 by Sandra Gurvis
Published by arrangement with Carol Publishing Group, a Citadel Press Book

57 LENA

St. Andrew's Antiques
12075 W. Oak St.
815/369-5207

Cubbies Bull Pen
211 N. Schuyler St.
815/369-2161

Rebecca's Parlor Antiques
208 S. Schuyler St.
815/369-4196

Raccoon Hollow Antiques
7114 U.S. Route 20 W.
815/233-5110

58 LE ROY

On The Park Antiques Mall
104 E. Center St.
309/962-2618

Party Line Antiques
301 W. Oak
309/962-8269

59 LONG GROVE

Mrs. B & Me
132 N. Old McHenry Road
847-634-7352

Curiosity Shop
350 N. Old McHenry Road
847-821-9918

Emporium of Long Grove
227 Robt Parker Coffin
847-634-0188

Especially Maine Antiques
231 Robt Parker Coffin
847-634/3512

Carriage Trade
427 Robt Parker Coffin
847-634-3160

60 MAHOMET

Country Crossroads
103 S. Lincoln St.
217/586-5363

Olde Town Gallery
401 E. Main St.
217/586-3211

Victorian House
408 E. Main St.
217/586-4834

Tin Rabbit
415 E. Main St.
217/586-4178

Willow Tree Antiques
421 E. Main St.
217/586-3333

61 MARION

Collector's Choice
500 S. Court St.
618/997-4883

Old Homeplace
112 E. Deyoung St.
618/997-2454

Treasure Trove
1616 Emory Lane
618/993-2213

Kerr's Antiques
213 N. Hamlet St.
618/993-6389

Spotlight Antiques
1301 Interprise Way
618/993-0830

Oldies But Goodies
503 N. Madison St.
618/993-0020

Guesswhat & Co.
103 N. Market St.
618/997-4832

Jenny Lee Antiques
314 Red Row
618/993-5054

B & A Collections & Antique Clock Repair
1420 Julianne Dr.
618/997-2047

62 MATTOON

Country Charm Antiques
816 Charleston Ave.
217/235-0777

Mattoon Antique Mart
908 Charleston Ave.
217/234-9707

Patti Re's Artistic Creations
Route 4 Box 11A
217/235-4857

Maple Tree Corner Antiques
1316 Lafayette Ave.
217/235-4245

63 McHENRY

The Crossroad Merchant
1328 N. Riverside Dr.
815/344-2610

64 McLEANSBORO

Melba's Antiques
601 S. Washington St.
618/643-3355

Southfork Antique Mall
105 E. Broadway
618/643-4458

65 MENDOTA

Prairie Trails Antique Mall
704 Illinois Ave.
815/539-5547

Apple Tree Junction
701 Illinois Ave.
815/539-5116

Heartland Treasures
714 Illinois Ave.
815/538-4402

Little Shop on the Prairie
702 Illinois Ave.
815/538-4408

66 MOLINE

Mostly Old Stuff
1509 15th St.
309/797-3580

Victorian House Antiques
1925 6th Ave.
309/797-9755

Mississippi Manor Antique Mall
2406 6th Ave.
309/764-0033

67 MOMENCE

Cal-Jean Shop
127 E. Washington
815/472-2667

Days of Yesteryear
Hwy. I-17
815/472-4725

68 MORRIS

Judith Ann's
117 W. Jackson St.
815/941-2717

Morris Antique Emporium
112 W. Washington St.
815/941-0200

69 MT. VERNON

Darnell's Antiques
Route 148
618/242-6504

Flota's Antiques
901 S. 10th St.
618/244-4877

Olde World Antiques
2515 Broadway
618/242-7799

Variety House Antiques
410-412 S. 18th St.
618/242-4344

70 MURPHYSBORO

Virginia's Antiques
1204 Chestnut St.
618/687-1212

Old & In The Way
1318 Walnut St.
618/634-3686

Phoebe Jane's Antiques
1330 Walnut St.
618/684-5546

71 NAPERVILLE

Nana's Cottage
122 S. Webster
800/690-2770

72 NAUVOO

Country Cottage Antiques
1695 Knight St.
217/453-6478

Rita's Romantiques
2592 N. Sycamore Haven Dr.
217/453-6480

Old Nauvoo Antique Mall
1265 Mulholland St.
217/453-6769

Great Places to Stay

The Ancient Pines
2015 Parley St.
217/453-2767

Surrounded by orchards, a winery, herb gardens, perennials, and old roses, this stunning home has ornate brick details, stained glass windows, pressed metal ceilings, and carved woodwork. The rooms are furnished with antiques. Within walking distance of antique shops.

73 OAKLAND

Outback Antique Store
2 E. Main St.
217/3462584

74 OAK PARK

Treasures 'n' Trinkets
600 Harrison St.
708/848-9142

Antiques Etc. Mall
125 N. Marion
708/386-9194

75 ODIN

Lincoln Trail Antiques
U.S. Hwy. 50
618/775-8255

Vernon's Antiques
Box 57, Route 50
618/775-8360

76 ORLAND PARK

Beacon Hill Antique Shop
14314 Beacon Ave.
708/460-8433

Emporium Antique Shop
14320 Beacon Ave.
708/460-5814

Old Bank Antique Shop
14316 Beacon Ave.
708/460-7979

Favorite Things
14329 Beacon Ave.
708/403-1908

Olde Homestead Ltd.
14330 Beacon Ave.
708/460-9096

General Store
14314 S. Union Ave.
708/349-9802

Cracker Barrell Antiques
9925 W. 143rd Place
708/403-2221

Station House Antique Mall
12305 W. 159th St. (Lockport)
708/301-9400

77 OSWEGO

Bob's Antique Toys
23 W. Jefferson St.
630/554-3234

Oswego Antiques Market II
78 S. Main St.
630/554-9779

Oswego Antiques Market
72 S. Main St.
630/554-9779

Old Oak Creek Shoppes
4025 U.S. Hwy. 34 #B
630/554-3218

78 OTTAWA

Gramma's Attic Antique Mall
219 W. Main St.
815/434-7332
Open: Mon.-Sat. 9:30-5
Directions: From Interstate 80, take the Ottawa Exit south on Highway 23 to Main St. Located south of Downtown courthouse, go right (west) ½ block, south side of the street.

From the name given to this establishment, one might come to the conclusion that it is a cozy little place filled with great "old things." But you can't judge a book by its title! This building swells to four floors and is a restored 150-year-old former hotel. That would date its existence back to 1847, when Illinois was the Pioneer West in still young America. It was a time when gunbelts were slung over bedposts, "ladies of the night" were escorted upstairs, whiskey flowed and bar-room brawls extended out into the streets. Today, thanks to the restoration efforts of Woody Jewett, Gramma's Attic, one of Ottawa's newest antique malls, is a "gem" of a place to shop. Thirty-four dealers present a large selection of antique glassware, furniture, quilts, dolls, jewelry, collectibles, books and more.

79 PAXTON

Cheesecloth & Buttermilk
124 S. Market St.
217/379-3675

Antique Mall & Tea Room
931 S. Railroad Ave.
217/379-4748

80 PECATONICA

Antiques at Hillwood Farms
498 N. Sarwell Bridge Road
815/239-2421

Illinois

81 PEORIA

Mia's Antiques & Uniques
1507 E. Gardner Lane (Heights)
309/685-1912

Whaley's Clock Shop
218 W. McClure Ave.
309/682-8429

Backdoor Antiques & Collectibles
725 S.W. Washington
309/637-3446

U Name It
3205 W. Harmon Hwy.
309/677-6710

Abe's Antiques
2001 N. Wisconsin Ave.
309/682-8181

The Illinois Antique Center
308 S.W. Commercial St.
309/673-3354

82 PESOTUM

Wildflower Antique Mall
511 S. Chestnut
217/867-2704
Open: Mon.–Sat. 9–6, Sun. 10–5
Directions: Exit 220 - I-57 & Route 45

Stepping into Wildflower Antique Mall gives you a feeling of nostalgia. This true "sense for the past" is created by 55 dedicated and experienced dealers whose quality merchandise is displayed throughout this 5,300-square-foot mall. Selections are nicely diverse and neatly arranged; showcased in such a way as to provide you with unique decorating ideas. A convenient stop for travelers, the mall is located just off I-57, Exit 220 in Pesotum.

83 PETERSBURG

Salem Country Store
Route 97 S.
217/632-3060

Fezziwig's
110 E. Sheridan St.
217/632-3369

Stanis Sayre Antique Store
511 S. 6th St.
217/632-7016

Petersburg Peddlers
113 S. 7th St.
217/632-2628

Estep & Associates
320 N. 6th St.
217/632-4154

84 PINCKNEYVILLE

Great Places to Stay

Oxbow Bed & Breakfast
Route 1, Box 47
618/357-9839
Open: Year-round from 7–11
Directions: Oxbow is located on Highways 13/127, 1¾ miles south of Perry County Courthouse. If traveling I-64, take Exit 50 (Highway 127), and drive approximately 23 miles south. If driving I-57, take Exit 77 (Highway 154), then go 28 miles east.

A true vision of craftsmanship, Oxbow Bed & Breakfast was created by taking old barns and silos and turning them into perfect retreats for anyone in search of the more relaxed life. The barns were moved from various sites throughout the area to the present property, then painstakingly reconstructed and restored.

An older barn (settled behind the main house) is a retreat for honeymooners or others wanting to escape the crowds. During the summer months, take a dip in the swimming pool creatively constructed from old silo staves.

85 POCAHONTAS

Annabelle's Antiques Academy
Academy & National
618/669-2088

Wagon Wheel Antiques
202 National St.
618/669-2918

T G Antiques Mall
IH 70 & Hwy. 40
618/669-2969

Village Square Antiques
202 State St.
618/669-2825

86 PRINCETON

Midtown Antique Mall
I-80 Exit 56
815/872-3435

Sherwood Antique Mall
1661 N. Main St.
815/872-2580

87 QUINCY

Broadway Antique Mall
1857 Broadway
217/222-8617

R & W Antiques
117 N. 4th St.
217/222-6143

Old Town Antiques
2000 Jersey St.
217/223-2963

Yester Year Antique Mall
615 Maine St.
217/224-1871

Pawnee
501 Hampshire St.
217/222-8090

June's Antiques
121 N. 4th St.
217/223-9265

Brock's Antiques
516 Main St.
217/224-7414

Carriage House Antiques
805 Spring St.
217/228-2303

Vintage Home Furniture
208 S. 10th
217/224-5166

88 RICHMOND

A Little Bit Antiques
5603 Broadway
815/678-4218

Once Upon a Time
5608 W Broadway
815/678-6533

Hiram's Uptown Antiques
5613 Broadway
815/678-4166

Cat's Stuff
5627 Broadway
815/678-7807

Antiques on Broadway
10309 N. Main St.
815/678-7951

Marilyn's Touch
10315 N. Main St.
815/678-7031

Happy House Antiques
5604 Broadway
815/678-4076

Old Bank Antiques
5611 Broadway
815/678-4839

A Step Above
5626 Broadway
815/678-6906

Serendipity Shop
9818 Main St.
815/678-4141

Emporium-1905
10310 N. Main St.
815/678-4414

Ed's Antiques
10321 N. Main St.
815/678-2911

89 RIVERSIDE

Riverside Antique Market
30 East Ave.
708/447-4425

Arcade Antiques & Jewelers
25 Forest Ave.
708/442-8110

J P Antiques
36 East Ave.
708/442-6363

Arcade Antiques & Furniture
7 Longcommon Road
708/442-8999

90 ROCK FALLS

Rock River Antique Center
2105 E. Route 30
815/625-2556

91 ROCKFORD

Homestead Antiques
3712 N. Central Ave.
815/962-7498

Houtkamp Art Glass Studio
120 N. Main St.
815/964-3785

Eagle's Nest Antiques
7080 Old River Road
815/633-8410

East State St. Antique Mall #2
5301 E. State St.
815/226-1566

Peddler's Attic
2609 Charles St.
815/962-8842

Krenek's Clock Haven
2314 N. Main St.
815/965-4661

Forgotten Treasures
4610 E. State St.
815/229-0005

East State St. Antique Mall
5411 E. State St.
815/229-4004

92 ROCK ISLAND

Rock Island Antique Mart
1608 2nd Ave.
309/793-6278

Iron Horse Antiques & Gifts
533 30th St.
309/793-4500

Old Hat Antiques
1706 3rd Ave.
309/794-9089

Jackson's Antiques
1310 30th St.
309/793-1413

Great Places to Stay

The Potter House
1906 7th Ave.
1-800-747-0339

Stay in either the main house or the adjacent cottage at this turn-of-the-century home listed on the National Register of Historic Places. Look for the old-fashioned details, from brass doorknobs to embossed leather wallcovering and stained and leaded glass windows. Even the bathrooms are distinctive. One has its original nickel-plated hardware. You'll notice other historic homes in the area which you can tour on foot, by carriage or by trolley.

The Victorian Inn
702 20th St.
1-800-728-7068

Nestled in the Heart of Old Rock Island on nearly an acre of wooded gardens is the gracious Victorian Inn Bed and Breakfast. The Broadway Historical Area begins at the Victorian Inn where old-fashioned trolley and walking tours crisscross the neighborhood. The inn, built in 1876, offers five guest rooms with private baths.

93 ROCKTON

Big D's Antiques
110 N. Blackhawk Road
815/624-6300

Nichols Antiques
212 W. Main St.
815/624-4137

94 ROSSVILLE

Fife & Drum
15 E. Attica St.
217/748-4119

Hall Closet
103 S. Chicago St.
217/748-6766

Market Place
106 S. Chicago St.
217/748-6066

Scarce Glass
101 S. Chicago St.
217/748-6352

Heritage House
104 S. Chicago St.
217/748-6681

Smith's Antiques & Collectibles
107 S. Chicago St.
217/748-6728

Freeman's Folly
110 S. Chicago St.
217/748-6720

95 SADORUS

Antique & Curiosity Shop
101 S. Vine St.
217/598-2200

This 'n' That Shop
119 E. Market St.
217/598-2462

96 SALEM

Freeman Creek Antiques
3242 Hotze Road
618/548-6677

Little Lulu's
216 E. Main St.
618/548-0219

97 SANDWICH

Sandwich Antique Market
2300 E. Route 34, Village East Plaza
815/786-6122

Quackers Country Accents
127 S. Main St.
815/786-6429

Sandwich Antiques Mall
108 N. Main St.
815/786-7000

98 SAVANNA

Pulford Opera House Antiques Mall/J.T. Bradley's
324 Main St.
815/273-2661
Open: Mon.–Thurs. 10:30–5:30, Fri.–Sat. 10:30–8, Sun. 11–6
Memorial Day through Labor Day: Mon.–Sat. 9:30–8, Sun. 11–6
Directions: Highway 84, "Great River Road," is a major highway running north/south along the Mississippi River. (Savanna is mid-distance between the Quad cities and Dubuque, Iowa.) Route 84 is called Main Street in downtown Savanna. The mall is located on Main Street.

The Pulford Opera House Antique Mall was built at the turn of the century and is the largest antique mall in northwestern Illinois. In 1905, the Opera House was the site of the murder of a local attorney, followed by the suicide of the Opera House owner, Botworth Pulford, a week later. Some folks attribute the occasional strange noises and occurrences throughout the house to their "ghosts." Apart from the spiritual visitors that frequent the Pulford Opera House are thousands of antique enthusiasts who flock to this 27,000-square-foot establishment, noted for its quality antiques. Located four doors south is J. T. Bradley's, the mall's companion store. This restored 1880s eatery offers soups, sandwiches, a salad bar, pastries and many entrees along with 30 more booths of antiques. a total of 120 dealers from Illinois, Iowa and Wisconsin provide the fine antiques displayed for purchase throughout both locations.

99 SHELBYVILLE

Hidden Antiques at the Hub
111 E. Main St.
217/774-2900

Pat's Antiques
133 E. Main St.
217/774-4485

Wooden Nickel Antiques
140 E. Main St.
217/774-3735

Auntie Darling's Daydreams
225 N. Morgan St.
217/774-5510

Jake's Antiques
W. Route 16
217/774-4223

Kinfolk
RR 1
217/774-2557

Jake's Warehouse
1501 W. S. 8th St.
217/774-4201

100 SHILOH

Mueller's Antiques & Collectibles
522 N. Main St.
618/632-4166
Open: Thurs.–Sun. 1–5
Directions: Traveling Interstate 64, exit at #19 B (S.R. 158). Go north to traffic lights (Old S.R. 50). Turn left, and go approximately 1/4 mile to Shiloh Road (Main Street). Turn left going 1/4 mile to shop on the left.

Some of us collect antique glassware, linens, primitives, etc. but the owners at Mueller's Antiques collects buildings. Not necessarily buildings of a historic nature, but buildings full of history. On the main street of town in Shiloh, Ill., you'll find six farm buildings filled to the rafters with antiques. Everything imaginable can be found in here, so bring a big truck and a hefty wallet — you won't go away empty-handed.

101 SOMONAUK

House of 7 Fables
300 E. Dale St.
815/498-2289
Open: Daily 10–5, but call ahead to avoid disappointment.
Directions: Somonauk is on U.S. Route 34 (Ogden Avenue) which runs parallel to and between Interstates 80 and 88, approximately 22 miles east of Interstate 39. The shop is at the corner of North Sagamore and Dale Streets, 1/2 block north of Route 34. The shop is a red house with white trim, white letters "ANTIQUES."

House of Seven Fables is, itself, one of those treasures that collectors love to find. The half dozen or more buildings that make up the shop are all painted brick red with white trim and are rescued antiques themselves.

Owner Merwin Shaw got hooked on antiques back in the 1930s, when he "dusted, polished and steel-wooled antiques for a lady here in

Somonauk." as he tells it.

Not only is the store, with all its items for sale, crammed to the rafters with finds in just about every category, but the repair areas — yes, repair areas — are just as interesting, because much of the repair work done here is a lost or dying art. There are hobby horse and toy restoration workshops, a wicker repair workshop, and an antique picture framing area. The shop handles vintage lighting, but they also do restoration and wiring of old pieces.

Inside one of the buildings, stuffed among the Windsors and firkins stacked in front of a window area, are several moonshine jugs, and green glass sits on the window ledge. Another window holds pink and red glass, with rockers, tables and baskets in front.

Antique chandeliers and bird cages hang from the ceiling in another corner over a hodgepodge of furniture covered with paintings and potted plants. Another corner, with shelves and cabinets running floor to ceiling, holds hundreds of vintage tins: coffee, tea, milk, liquor, all shapes, sizes, colors, configurations. Another wall is more elegant in tone, with framed pictures of all kinds hung in an orderly arrangement over a few choice pieces of furniture. Then there are the showcases — antiques themselves — filled with colored pressed glass cruets, rose bowls, toothpick holders, butter molds, complete sets of dishes, and perfume bottles, all arranged by color. It's a visual feast!

Bigger pieces of early American furniture that shoppers will find include Colonial pine cupboards, Shaker rockers, and hutch-top dry sinks decorated with accessories like salt glaze pottery, apothecary items and Norwegian tins.

There's usually something for everyone, and more importantly, there is a place to bring your treasures when they need tender loving care.

102 SPRINGFIELD

Old Georgian Antique Mall
830 S. Grand Ave. E.
217/753-8110

AAron's Attic Antiques
1525 W. Jefferson St.
217/546-6300

Silent Woman Antique Shop
2765 W. Jefferson St.
217/787-3253

House of Antiques
412 E. Monroe St.
217/544-9677

Springfield Antique Mall
3031 Reilly Dr.
217/522-3031

Ruby Sled Antiques & Art
1142 S. Spring St.
217/523-3391

Antiques Antiques
2851 Green Valley Road
217/546-1052

Renaissance Shop
2402 W. Jefferson St.
217/787-8125

Eastnor Gallery of Antiques
700 E. Miller St.
217/523-0998

Antiques Unique
617 E. Monroe St.
217/522-0772

Barrel Antique Mall
5850 S. 6th St.
217/585-1438

Pastime Antiques
6279 N. Walnut St.
217/487-7200

Murray's Oxbow Antiques
2509 S. Whittier Ave.
217/528-8220

103 ST. CHARLES

Riverside Antiques
410 S. 1st St.
630/377-7730

Brown Beaver Antiques
219 W. Main St.
630/443-9430

Studio Posh
17 N. 2nd Ave.
630/443-0227

Memory Merchant Antiques
15 S. 3rd St.
630/513-0340

Antique Market II
303 W. Main St. (Route 64)
630/377-5798

Consign-Tiques
214 W. Main St.
630/584-7535

Antique Market III
413 W. Main St.
630/377-5599

Market
12 N. 3rd St.
630/584-3899

Antique Market I
11 N. Third St.
630/377-1868

104 ST. JOSEPH

Peach's Antiques
228 E. Lincoln
217/469-8836

The Village Shoppe
228 E. Lincoln
217/469-8836

Pine Acres Trees & Herbs
E. of Sidney on 2300 E.
217/688-2207

105 STOCKTON

Grandpa & Grandma Antiques
118 W. Front Ave.
815/947-2411

Tredegar Antique Market
208 E. North Ave.
815/947-2360

Cornerstone Creations
101 N. Main St.
815/947-2358

Glick's Antiques
3602 E. Woodbine St.
815/858-2305

106 TUSCOLA

Wood Tin & Lace
604 S. Main St.
217/253-3666

Prairie Church Antique Mall
568 36th E.
217/253-3960

Prairie Sisters Antique Mall
102 W. Sale St.
217/253-5211

107 VANDALIA

Back When Antiques
118 N. Elm
No number listed

Cuppy's Antique Mall
 & Old Fashioned Soda Fountain
618/283-0080

Treasure Cove Antique Mall
302 W. Gallatin
618/283-8704

Wehrle's Antiques
Route 51
618/283-4147

108 VILLA PARK

Astorville Antiques
51 S. Villa Ave.
630/279-5311

Memories from the Attic
119 S. Villa Ave.
630/941-1517

109 WARRENVILLE

Lil' Red Schoolhouse Antiques and Collectibles
3 S. 463 Batavia Road
630/393-1040
Open: Mon.–Sat. 10–5, Sun. 11–5
Directions: From Chicago, take 290 (Eisenhower Expressway) west to I-88. Continue on I-88; exit at Winfield Road. Travel north to second stoplight (Amoco and Mobile stations); turn left, go 2 blocks to STOP sign. Turn right, 4th building on the right (opposite the fire station). Coming on Route 59, turn east on Butterfield Road, to Batavia Road. Turn right (south) to shop on left-hand side.

Settled among a grove of wonderful trees which give way to a lawn tumbling down to the Du Page River, sets the Lil' Red Schoolhouse. It was built in 1836 when teachers were required to be single ladies. There are ten rooms and two porches which make up the schoolhouse's construction. The desk, the chalkboard, the pencils and the rulers have all been replaced with quality antiques and collectibles. You'll find tables, chairs (many dating to the early 1900s and beyond), lamps, glassware, early tools and a hodgepodge of other wonderful things.

The Lil' Red Schoolhouse schedules outdoor sales and special events during each season (dealers take note).

Rt. 59 Antique Mall
3 S. 450 Route 59
630/393-0100
Open: Mon.–Sat. 10–6, Sun. 11–4:30
Directions: 1 mile north of I-88, Just South of Butterfield Road, 1 mile from Cracker Barrel.

Rt. 59 Antique Mall is the premier mall in Chicago's Western Suburbs. Featuring the wares of over sixty quality dealers, you will enjoy browsing through an excellent selection of furniture, home accents, primitives, glassware, architectural items, art deco, '50s items, and much more. In their two years of existence the owners are frequently complimented for the ever-changing variety of items and pleasant shopping atmosphere. Stop and see why Rt. 59 Antique Mall is a favorite spot for local antiquers and treasure hunters just passing through.

110 WESTMONT

Tony's Collectibles
141 S. Cass Ave.
630/515-8510

Elite Repeat
123 E. Ogden Ave.
630/960-0540

Old Plank Road Antiques
233 W. Ogden Ave.
630/971-0500

Zeke's Antiques & Leo's Lamps
135 W. Quincy St.
630/969-3852

111 WHEELING

Kerry's Clock Shop
971 N. Milwaukee Ave.
847/520-0335

Lundgren's
971 N. Milwaukee Ave.
847/541-2299

The Crystal Magnolia
971 N. Milwaukee Ave.
847/537-4750

Shirley's Dollhouse
971 N. Milwaukee Ave.
847/537-1632

My Favorite Place
971 N. Milwaukee Ave.
847/808-1324

O'Kelly's Antiques
971 N. Milwaukee Ave.
847/537-1656

County Faire Antiques
971 N. Milwaukee Ave.
847/537-9987

Antiques of Northbrook
971 N. Milwaukee Ave.
847/215-4994

Coach House Antiques
971 N. Milwaukee Ave.
847/808-1324

Antiques Center of Illinois
1920 S. Wolf Road
847/215-9418

112 WILMETTE

Shorebirds
415 1/2 4th St.
847/853-1460

Buggy Wheel
1143 Greenleaf Ave.
847/251-2100

Collected Works
1405 Lake Ave.
847/251-6897

Raven & Dove Antique Gallery
1409 Lake Ave.
847/251-9550

Heritage Trail Mall
410 Ridge Road
847/256-6208

Josie's
545 Ridge Road
847/256-7646

113 WILMINGTON

Wilmington Antique Dealers Association
Wilmington offers days of treasure hunting in the century old buildings of N. Water Street. There are 3 multilevel antique malls and 9 additional antique shops featuring over 100 dealers with a wide variety of antiques and collectibles. These shops along with a diner and "The best burgers in Will County" at RTM's, specialty shops with bakery, coffee, teas and ice cream make N. Water Street an enjoyable and rewarding adventure.

Snuggled within 20 minutes of three major interstate routes on the Kankakee River, Wilmington is easily accessible. From I-80 take the I-55 exit south to sixth 238, then left on Strip Mine Road. to Route 53, left again to second light then left on Water St. From I-57 take the Peotone/

Wilmington exit 327 to Route 53 then left to second light, and left on Water St.

Mill Race Emporium
110 N. Water Street
815/476-7660

Multilevel, multidealer antiques and collectibles.

Water Street Mall
119-121 N. Water St.
815/476-5900

Multilevel, multidealer. Full line-Fenton-Heisey-carnival-pottery-toys. Discover, Visa, MasterCard.

Abacus Antiques
113-115 N. Water St.
815/476-5727

Art Deco-'50s items, furniture, more.

The Opera House Antiques
203 N. Water St.
815/476-0872

Antiques, collectibles, primitives. Discover, Visa, MasterCard.

R. J.'s Relics
116-118-120 N. Water St.
815/476-6273

Multilevel, multidealer. Space and showcase rental. Knives, military, books, sports cards, jewelry, vintage clothing, furniture and much more. Discover, Visa, MasterCard.

Paraphernalia Antiques
112-114-124 N. Water St.
815/476-9841

Jewelry, Irish pine, European imports.

Stuff 'n' Such
815/476-0411

Antiques, collectibles, crafts.

O'Koniewski's Treasures
815/476-1039

General line, anything unusual and interesting.

114 WINNETKA

Jack Monckton Gallery
1050 Gage St.
847-446-1106

Arts 220
895 1/2 Green Bay Road
847/501-3084

Antique Heaven
982 Green Bay Road
847/446-0343

Pied a Terre
554 Lincoln Ave.
847/441-5161

Robertson-Jones Antiques
569 Lincoln Ave.
847/446-0603

Country Shop
710 Oak St.
847/441-8690

West End Antiques
619 Green Bay Road
847-256-2291

Knightsbridge Antiques
909 Green Bay Road
847/441-5105

M Stefanich Antiques Ltd.
549 Lincoln Ave.
847/446-4955

Heather Higgins Antiques
567 Lincoln Ave., #A
847/446-3455

Stuart Antiques
571 Lincoln Ave.
847/501-4454

115 WITT

Hole in the Wall
3 E. Broadway
217/594-7132

Mystique Antiques
510 N. Main St.
217/594-2802

Country Store Antiques
411 E. Ford St.
217/594-7275

Iowa

Mileage
0   20

- 38 Spirit Lake
- 36 Sioux City
- 29
- 4 Aurelia
- 16 Fort Dodge
- 169
- 20
- 18
- 59
- 71
- 41 Walnut
- 22 Kimballton
- 10 Council Bluffs
- 29
- 80
- 9 Clear Lake
- 27 Mason City
- 35
- 218
- 63
- 2 Ames
- 26 Marshalltown
- 11 Creston
- 39 Thayer
- 46 Winterset
- 13 Des Moines
- 45 West Des Moines
- 35
- 31 Newton
- 35 Pella
- 23 Knoxville
- 2
- 8 Centerville
- 34
- 33 Oskaloosa
- 15 Ottumwa
- 34 Eldon
- 40 Villages of Van Buren County
- 63
- 29 Mount Pleasant
- 17 Fort Madison
- 21 Keokuk
- 5 Burlington
- 28 Mediapolis
- 30 Muscatine
- 61
- 20 Kalona
- 18 Hills
- 19 Iowa City
- 218
- 1 Amana
- 80
- 44 West Branch
- 12 Davenport
- 24 Le Claire
- 7 Cedar Rapids
- 25 Marion
- 3 Anamosa
- 380
- 14 Dubuque
- 20
- 32 Oelwein
- 42 Waterloo
- 6 Cedar Falls
- 43 Waverly
- 18
- 37 Spillville
- 63

Let's take a trip through history and celebrate the 10th anniversary of "Main Street" Iowa. Over the past decade, the preservation-based downtown revitalization program of the National Trust for Historic Preservation has helped Iowa not only to preserve, but celebrate and share its heritage and culture through the "Main Street" program. All across the state each year, "Main Street" towns keep their pasts alive. Annual heritage festivals help Iowans and visitors appreciate the lifestyles of our ancestors with food, costumes, events and music of times past. Visiting these "Main Street" communities is like an annual vacation in a time machine! You'll see unique shops intermingled with historic buildings...festivals, food and fun from America's Heartland...pride, personality and friendliness of hearty, happy people. Consider this your special invitation to stop by, stay a while and catch the spirit on "Main Streets" all across Iowa.

1 AMANA

Iowa's Amana Colonies are seven closely situated villages that comprise a unique settlement running along the Iowa River valley, through lush farming country. Amana's early settlers left Germany in 1842 seeking religious freedom. They settled near Buffalo, N.Y., but in 1855 they moved to Iowa and established seven villages known as the Amana Colonies on 26,000 acres of wooded hills. There they lived under a religious communal system, sharing work, meals, worldly goods and religious services. In 1932 the villagers voted to end the communal way, and they created the Amana Church Society to direct their faith, which is now known as the Community of True Inspiration. They created the Amana Society to operate the 26,000 acres of land and businesses that were formerly held by the commune. All the villagers became stockholders in the Society, bought their own homes, and some founded their own businesses.

The first village to be settled was named "Amana," from the Song of Solomon (4:8), which means "to remain true." There were seven villages in the original Colonies; today there are a total of nine. Visitors may recognize the name Amana from an appliance they may own. Amana Refrigeration was founded by Amana people and is located in the village of Middle Amana! Just 93 miles east of Des Moines, the other villages are West Amana, East Amana, South Amana, High Amana, and Homestead. There is also a section of South Amana called Upper South, and another village called Little Amana, that were not part of the original colony.

Colony villagers have all remained true to a simpler way of life that still revolves around old-world craftsmanship and handcrafted furniture, clock-making, blacksmithing, world-famous cooking, and locally manufactured goods. These items are sold in numerous stores and shops, including the many quality antique shops that are an added attraction of the Colonies. For the past 150 years, Amana residents have quarried their own sandstone, made their own bricks, and cut their own timber for more than 400 buildings that cover the villages. They farmed, built woolen and calico mills for clothing and fabric, established cabinet shops to build furniture, and craft shops to supply daily necessities. Today they

still produce products at the furniture factories, the woolen mill, and in most of the craft shops, where artisans make baskets, brooms, candles, ironwork, pottery and more.

Community life called for community kitchens, and the Amana Colonies have become well-known for superb food, wines and beer. In the tradition of communal kitchens, food is served family style. German specialties include Wienerschnitzel and Sauerbraten, as well as traditional Midwestern food. The bakeries are known for breads and pastries, the many wineries for their fruit wines, and the brewery for award-winning "German style" beer.

The Colonies remain Iowa's leading visitor attraction because of their heritage and hospitality. People come from around the world to see the historic villages and to buy their products, to tour the museums and to enjoy a piece of Germany in the American colonies.

Great Places to Shop
(Antiques in the Amana Colonies)

Main Amana

Antiques and Things
F St. (next to Colony Cone)
319/622-6461
Open: Daily 9–5

Antiques, collectibles, doll houses and crafts

Carole's
4521 220th Trail (Main St.)
319/622-3570
Open: Daily summer 9–6, winter 10–5

Upstairs: old-new-used-abused

Erenberger Antiques
4514 F St.
319/622-3230
Open: Mon.–Sat. 11–5, Sun. 12–5

Primitives and pine furniture are the main items featured in this original Amana home built in 1856. Early pine and painted furniture are displayed, along with small primitive antique accessories including greenware, pottery, tin, copper, pewter, stickware, baskets, decoys, quilts and more.

Renate's Antique Gallery
4516 F St.
319/622-3859
Open: Mon.–Sat. 10–5, Sun. 12–5

Eight rooms of exploring fun are in this original, two-story Amana home built in 1870. Each room displays something different. In the entry room Renate has her loom where she makes rag rugs (some days visitors can watch). There's china and glass in the dining room, bowls in the kitchen, furniture in the bedroom and primitives in the family room. Renate's specializes in pottery and antiques from the Amana Colonies.

Smokehouse Square Antiques
4503 F St.
319/622-3539
Open: Mon.–Sat. 10–5, Sun. 11–5; summer 9:30–5:30, Sun. 11–5

Smokehouse Square Antiques has added a new dimension to antiquing in the Colonies. The mall is home to more than 29 of eastern Iowa's finest antique dealers. The inventory is constantly changing, but you will always find furniture, glassware, china, pottery, stoneware, graniteware, silver, jewelry, quilts and linens, books and paper, pictures and mirrors, and many advertising items, plus toys and children's collectibles, primitives, folk art, tools, decoys, fishing collectibles, 1950s memorabilia and railroad items.

Tick Tock Antiques
220th Trail (across from Amana General Store)
319/622-3730

Collectibles, glassware, primitives

West Amana

Cricket on the Hearth Antiques
404 6th Ave. W.
319/622-3088
Open: Wed.–Sun. 10–5 May–Oct.

Unique country gifts, collectibles and antiques

West Amana General Store
511 F St.
Located on top of the hill
319/622-3945
Open: Daily 10–5, summer 9–5

Antiques, furniture and a nice line of gifts

South Amana

Fern Hill Gifts and Quilts
103 220th Trail
Located at the corner of Hwy. 6 and 220
319/622-3627
Open: Mon.–Sat. 9:30–5, Sun. 12–4

Antiques, quilts, supplies, dolls, bears and everlastings

Granary Emporium
1063 4th Ave.
319/622-3195
Open: Daily 10–5

Antiques, glassware, furniture, primitives

High Amana

High Amana Store
1308 G St.
Located on Hwy. 220 (Amana Colonies Trail, 4 miles west of Main Amana)
319/622-3797
Open: Daily

Built in 1857 of sandstone quarried at the edge of High Amana, the High Amana Store was the original "one stop" shopping center of its time for local residents and area farmers. Over the years it has sold everything from fabric and notions to bicycles and appliances to kerosene, and even served as the local post office. In a setting of original pressed tin ceilings, glass display showcases and comb-painted drawer fronts, the store today offers traditional Amana Colonies arts and crafts, quilts, products of Iowa, glassware, unique toys and books, cards, gourmet food products, herbs, spices and more.

Great Places to Stay in the Amana Area

Babi's B & B
2788 Hwy.
South Amana
319/662-4381

Corner House B & B
404 F St.
West Amana
319/622-6390 or 1-800-996-6964

Dusk To Dawn B & B
2616 K St. Box 124
Middle Amana
319/622-3029

Baeckerei B & B
6 Trail, Box 127
South Amana
319/622-3597 or 1-800-391-8650

Die Heimat Country Inn
Box 160, 4430 V St.
Homestead
319/622-3937

Rawson's B & B
Box 118
Homestead
319/622-6035 or 1-800-637-6035

Iowa

Interesting Side Trip

Herbert Hoover Presidential Library and Birthplace
Located in West Branch just 30 miles east of Amana Colonies a short
distance from I-80
319/643-5301
Open: Daily

Kalona: Amish and Mennonite community that offers an opportunity
to see the differences between the Amanas (not Amish) and Kalona, which
is "Amish-land."
Located about 30 miles south and east of the Amana Colonies.
319/656-2519

2 AMES

Memories on Main Antique Mall
& Old-Fashioned Ice Cream Parlor
203 Main St.
515/233-2519
Open: Daily, Memorial Day–Labor Day 10–8;
Labor Day–Memorial Day 10–6, Mon. til 8, special Christmas hours
Directions: Located 3 miles from I-35. From Exit 111 B: Take
Hwy. 30 west, Duff Ave. north, then left on Main St. From Exit 113:
Take 13th St. west, Duff Ave. south, right on Main St.

Great ice cream, great antiques and collectibles, an unbeatable
combination! You get both at M.O.M.'s, as it's known in Ames. The 1940s
soda fountain serves great ice cream treats made the old-fashioned way,
while Fancy That Lamp Shop features fine fabric and glass shades suitable
for antique and vintage lamps. The mall itself offers a constantly changing
array of items, from fine furniture to fun collectibles like lamps, glass,
china, dinnerware, linens, pottery, figurines, decorative accessories,
kitchen collectibles, primitives, crocks, cast iron, dolls, children's items,
vintage clothing, records, books, sheet music and more!

Pak-Rat
110 S. Hyland Ave.
515/296-0230

Coin Castle II, Inc.
236 Main St.
515/232-7527

Victorian Showcase Mall
26772 241st St.
515/232-4818

3 ANAMOSA

This Old Farm Antiques
110 S. Elm St.
319/462-2856

Country Creek Cove
110 E. Main St.
319/462-3788

Antiques of Anamosa
122 E. Main St.
319/462-4195

Memory Shoppe
203 E. Main St.
319/462-6085

4 AURELIA

C & M Antiques
Highway 7 W.
712/434-2217

Brown's Antiques
116 Main St.
712/434-2337

Forgotten Favorites
128 Main St.
712/434-2069

Vogt's Antiques & Toys
141 Main St.
712/434-5380

Cedars Antiques
2235 W. 9th St.
712/434-2244

5 BURLINGTON

A-1 Antiques & Uniques
1234 Agency St.
319/752-5901

Privy Antiques
2500 Division St.
319/752-8320

Call & Haul Antiques
401 N. Front St.
319/754-6389

Antique Mall
800 Jefferson St.
319/753-6955

Antiques & Things
806 Jefferson St.
319/753-5096

Casey's World Antiques
6212 Summer St.
319/752-3265

5th St. Antique Mall & Collectibles
211 N. 5th St.
319/752-0498

6 CEDAR FALLS

Jackson's
2229 Lincoln St.
319/277-2256

Gilgen's Consignment Furniture
115 W. 16th St.
319/266-5152

Cellar Antiques
4912 University Ave.
319/266-5091

7 CEDAR RAPIDS

Antique Wicker & Collectibles
1038 3rd Ave. S.E.
319/362-4868

Wellington Square Antique Mall
1200 2nd Ave. S.E.
319/368-6640

Gingerbread
92 16th Ave. S.W.
319/366-8841

Cellar Door-Stable on Alley
2900 1st Ave. N.E.
319/366-1638

8 CENTERVILLE

Summer Antiques
1099 N. 18th St.
515/856-2680

Taste of Country
300 W. State St.
515/856-5705

Iowa

9 CLEAR LAKE

Yesteryear House of Antiques
112 N. 8th St.
515/357-4352

Good Olde Days
809 5th Pl. N.
515/357-6575

Antiques on Main
309 Main Ave.
515/357-3077

Jo's Antiques
311 Main Ave.
515/357-8120

Antique Alley
19 S. 3rd St.
515/357-7733

Whispering Oaks Antiques
2510 S. 8th St.
515/357-5094

Keepsake Antiques
308 Main Ave.
515/357-7553

Jada Consignment Shop
309 Main Ave., #B
515/357-2555

Legacy Antiques
315 Main Ave.
515/357-4000

Cornerstone Antiques
22 S. 3rd St.
515/357-3899

10 COUNCIL BLUFFS

Collins Antiques
607 S. Main St.
712/328-2598

Jantiques
729 S. Main St.
712/323-6624

11 CRESTON

Jessie's Antique Gems
1481 130th St.
515/782-5366

Timeless Treasures Antiques
1313 U.S. Hwy. 34
515/782-6517

Two Bricks Shy Antiques
Hwy. 34 E.
515/782-2725

12 DAVENPORT

Trash Can Annie Antiques
421 Brady St.
319/322-5893

Raphael's Emporium
628 N. Harrison St.
319/322-5053

Lampsmith Antique
5102 W. Locust St.
319/391-8552

Antiques By Judy
401 E. 2nd St.
319/323-5437

Riverbend Antiques
425 Brady St.
319/323-8622

Upper Level Antiques
321 E. 2nd St.
319/324-2133

Bird in Hand
1121 Mound St.
319/322-1082

Antique America
702 W. 76th St.
319/386-3430

13 DES MOINES

Brass Armadillo, Inc.
701 N.E. 50th Ave.
515/282-0082

R & S Enterprises
1601 E. Grand Ave.
515/262-9384

Soda City Collectibles
1244 2nd Ave.
515/282-0345

Christine's
309 E. 5th St.
515/243-3500

Emily's Attic/Emily's Closet
4800 Maple Dr.
515/262-3933

Majestic Lion Antique Center
5048 N.W. 2nd St.
515/282-5466

Time Passages Ltd.
980 73rd St.
515/223-5104

Bartlett's Antiques
820 35th St.
515/255-1362

Corner Collectors
1903 46th St.
515/274-4106

Madaline's Gifts & Antiques
3000 E. 9th St.
515/266-0204

Murray's Antiques
1805 Army Post Road
515/285-8840

14 DUBUQUE

Bob's Antiques
3271 Central Ave.
319/583-6061

Harbor Place Antiques
98 E. 4th St.
319/582-6224

Old Towne Shoppe
163 Main St.
319/583-1962

Collector's Corner
340 W. 5th St.
319/588-0886

Antiques at the Schoen's
144 Locust St.
319/556-7547

Antiques on White
902 White St.
319/557-2141

15 ELDON

American Gothic Antiques & Tearoom
408 Elm St.
515/652-3338

For a nostalgic antiquing experience American Gothic Antiques & Tearoom offers antiques in the front 1500 square feet of the store, and a restaurant and ice cream shop in the back. Homemade pies are the house specialty. Everything is housed in an historic old hardware store that is over 100 years old — a true antique itself!

16 FORT DODGE

Antique Emporium
Crossroads Mall
515/955-4151

Downtown Antiques Mall
102 S. 14th St.
515/573-3401

Pine Cupboard
25 S. 12th St.
515/576-7463

Old Harvester Gifts & Antiques
1915 1st Ave. N.
515/955-6260

Michehl's Memory Furniture
1731 Paragon Ave.
515/576-0148

Young's Antiques & Collectibles
814 1st Ave. S.
515/576-4733

Iowa

17 FORT MADISON

For an old army post, Fort Madison is a swinging, adventurous place even today! It was the site of the first outpost west of the Mississippi River, when flintlock rifles and cannons were the main armaments. Today visitors can take the narrated Olde Towne Express and buy antiques galore in the Downtown Riverfront district. You can watch — and maybe walk — the world's longest double-deck swingspan bridge in action, or take your chances on firmer ground at the Catfish Bend Casino.

Sixth & G Antique Mall
602 Ave. G
319/372-6218

Memory Lane Antique Mall
820 Ave. G
319/372-4485

Wishing Well Antiques
3510 Ave. L
319/372-5237

Devil's Creek Antiques
2495 Hwy. 61
319/372-7101

Great Places to Stay

Mississippi Rose & Thistle Inn
532 Ave. F
319/372-7044
Open: Daily 8–10
Rates: $70–$90
Directions: Fort Madison is easily reached by U.S. 61, a major connection to I-80 and I-70. The inn is located between Burlington, Iowa (18 miles north) and Keokuk, Iowa (20 miles south). Both are reached by U.S. 61, and the inn is located 2 blocks north of the highway. Turn on 5th St., go 2 blocks, turn left on Avenue F (a one-way street). Go 1 block and the inn is on the left side at the corner of Avenue F and 6th St.

This lovely, historic brick Italianate mansion was built in 1881 by Dennis A. Morrison, a partner in Morrison Plow Works. The Morrison family owned the first automobile in Fort Madison, a 1902 Stanley Steamer. Today, the inn has been carefully restored to its past splendor, extravagance and elegance. Guests can gaze upon ornate woodwork and marble fireplaces, walk on Oriental carpets, and enjoy period antiques. After a day exploring, riverboat gambling, antiquing, golfing, and picnicking, guests can return to the inn for afternoon wine and hors d'oeuvres in the parlor or on the wraparound porch, then choose a book from the library and retire with a glass of sherry from your own private stock! Candlelight dinners and gourmet picnic baskets are available with advance notice.

Each bedroom has its own distinctive charm and decor. The Lillian Austin Room is furnished with an old-fashioned brass bed, antique oak dresser and clawfoot tub. The Celsiana Room holds an old-fashioned white and brass bed, antique walnut dresser and clawfoot tub. The Mary Rose Room offers a clawfoot tub, white and brass bed and antique Eastlake

dresser. And the Tara Allison Room charms guests with a white and brass bed, sitting alcove, balcony and whirlpool.

18 HILLS

Antiques in the Old White Church
120 Oak St.
319/679-2337

19 IOWA CITY

Granny's Antique Mall
315 E. 1st St.
319/351-6328

Antique Mall of Iowa City
507 S. Gilbert St.
319/354-1822

Watt's Antiques & Collectibles
1603 Muscatine
319/337-4357

Ackerman's Newton Road Antiques
814 Newton Rd.
319/338-8449

Antique Christmas Shop
1600 Sycamore St.
319/679-2337

European Vintage Lace Shop
5011 Lower West Branch Road S.E.
319/351-2801

Sweet Livin'
224 S. Linn St.
319/337-5015

Avenue B Antiques
511 B Ave.
319/656-2500

20 KALONA

Kalona Antique Co. Plus
Antique Furniture Warehouse
Corner of 4th & C
211 4th St.
319/656-4489 Days
319/656-5157 Evenings
Open: Mon.–Sat. 9–5, closed Sun. & Major Holidays
Directions: Located just 18 miles south of Iowa City, Iowa on Hwy. 1, or 9 miles west of Hwy. 218 (The Avenue of the Saints) on Hwy. 22.

The Kalona Antique Company is housed in an old 1890s Baptist Church in downtown Kalona, Iowa, the home of the largest Amish settlement west of the Mississippi River. The Kalona Antique Co. showcases the wares of 19 dealers on 2 floors offering a quality selection of antiques, quilts and collectibles. Ken and Brenda Herington own and operate the Kalona Antique Co. and Furniture Warehouse. They specialize in oak, pine and walnut furniture. The Furniture Warehouse, just one block south of the Kalona Antique Co. features original finish furniture. The shop offers wholesale prices to dealers and will open after hours for dealers traveling through the area.

Main Street Antiques
413 B Ave.
319/656-4550

Courtyard Square
417 B Ave.
319/656-2488

Iowa

Woodin Wheel Antiques & Gifts
515 B Ave.
319/656-2240

Heart of the Country Antiques
203 5th St
319/656-3591

Yoder's Antiques
435 B Ave.
319/656-3880

Fifth Street Antiques
303 5th St.
319/656-2080

Weathervane
411 5th St.
319/656-3958

Avenue B Antiques
511 B Ave.
319/656-2500

Eckhart's Antique Furniture
560 10th St.
319/377-1202

Harmening Haus
915 10th St.
800/644-3874

Sanctuary Antique Center
801 10th St.
319/377-7753

Cooper's Antiques
997 10th St.
319/377-3995

21 KEOKUK

Showcase Antique Mall
800 Main St.
319/524-1696

Treasures & Trash
1803 S. 7th St.
319/524-1112

26 MARSHALLTOWN

Charley's Antiques
3002 S. Center St.
515/753-3916

Main Street Antique Mall
105 W. Main St.
515/752-3077

Marshall Relics
14 E. Main St.
516/752-7060

Granny's Country Mall
3201 Village Circle
515/752-6966

22 KIMBALLTON

Attic Antiques
114 N. Main St.
712/773-3255

Mercantile
122 N. Main St.
712/773-3777

D Johnson Antiques
209 N. Main St.
712/773-3939

Mama Bear
117 N. Main St.
712/773-2430

Country Corner
200 N. Main St.
712/773-2300

27 MASON CITY

Olde Central Antique Mall
317 S. Delaware Ave.
515/423-7315

Cobweb Corners Antiques
715 N. Federal Ave.
515/423-2160

Wilson Antiques
317 S. Delaware Ave.
515/423-5811

North Federal Antique
1104 N. Federal Ave.
513/423-0841

23 KNOXVILLE

Antiques or Others
1253 Hwy. 14
515/842-4644

28 MEDIAPOLIS

Patriot Antiques
Hwy. 61
319/394-9137

Lamp Post Antiques
318 Wapello St. N.
319/394-3961

Heirloom Antiques
Hwy. 61 S.
319/394-3444

24 LE CLAIRE

Riverview Antiques
510 Cody Road
319/289-4265

Memory Lane
110 S. Cody Road
319/289-3366

Rare Find Antiques
114 N. Cody Road
319/289-5207

29 MOUNT PLEASANT

Iris City Antique Mall
Hwy. 34 W.
319/385-7515

Lori's Loft
2001 E. Washington St.
319/986-9980

Old & New Things Plus
110 S. Main St.
319/385-7311

25 MARION

Country Corner Antiques
786 8th Ave.
319/377-1437

Antiques of Marion
1325 8th Ave.
319/377-7997

Park Place Hotel Antiques
1104 7th Ave.
319/377-2724

Remember When Antiques
847 8th Ave.
319/373-3039

Scott's Antiques Furniture
1060 7th Ave.
319/377-6411

Marion Center Antique Mall
1150 7th Ave.
319/377-9345

30 MUSCATINE

River Bend Cove
418 Grandview Ave.
319/263-9929

Melon City Antique Mart
200 E. 2nd St.
319/264-3470

Manley's Antiques
417 E. 2nd St.
319/264-1475

Market Place
1919 Grandview Ave.
319/263-8355

River's Edge Antiques
331 E. 2nd St.
319/264-2351

Lost Treasures
419 E. 2nd St.
319/262-8658

Iowa

Old Blue Bldg. Antiques
821 Park Ave.
319/263-5430

Koosli Antiques
208 E. 2nd St.
319/264-8625

31 NEWTON

Pappy's Antique Mall
103 1st Ave. W.
515/792-7774

Tripp thru the Past
3928 N. 4th Ave. E.
515/792-5514

Skunk Valley Antique Mall
7717 Hwy. F 48 W.
515/792-2361

32 OELWEIN

Amish Settlement
Rural Buchanan County
319/283-1105
Open: Mon.–Sat. 8–5 year-round, closed New Year's, Epiphany, Good
Friday, Ascension Day, Thanksgiving Day and Christmas Day

Visitors to the Amish Settlement are given a glimpse of the life that
fascinates most Americans. The Amish teach separation from the world,
which includes living without modern conveniences, something most
Americans find unbelievable. The Amish till the soil with horse-drawn
equipment, and their doctrine forbids the use of electricity and telephones.
They make most everything they need on a daily basis, and they sell
baked goods, quilts, and handmade furniture at their farm homes in the
Settlement.

West Charles Antiques
17 W. Charles St.
319/283-3591

33 OSKALOOSA

Rock & Shell Shop
117 A Ave. W.
515/673-3816

Tyme & Again
113 High Ave. E.
515/673-5857

Antique Shop
117 High Ave. E.
515/673-0895

Old Friends Antiques
123 N. Market
515/673-0428

34 OTTUMWA

Phil Taylor Antiques
224 Fox Sauk Road
515/682-7492

Nancy's Unique Antiques
510 E. Main St.
515/682-8661

35 PELLA

When you drive into Pella, Iowa, you'll probably double check the
map, because you'll feel like a giant wind has blown you across the ocean

to Holland! It looks and sounds like Holland, with windmills and wooden
shoes, Dutch pastries and Klokkenspel, courtyards and sunken gardens,
and acres and acres of tulips! In Pella the Old and New worlds combine
completely every May and December at the Tulip Time Festival and
Sinterklass (Santa Claus) Day. And the recently renovated and reopened
Pella Opera House, built in 1900, provides year-round musical and
theatrical performances by nationally known performers.

Beekhuizen Antiques
913 W. 8th St.
515/628-4712

Country Lane Antqs. & Collectibles
752 190th Ave.
515/628-2912

Red Ribbon Antique Mall
812 Washington St.
515/628-2181

36 SIOUX CITY

Red Wheel Furniture & Antiques
By Appointment Only
712/276-3645

Old Town Antiques & Collectibles
1024 4th Hwy.
712/258-3119

Heritage House Antiques
3900 4th Ave.
712/276-3366

Gas Light Antiques
1310 Jennings Hwy.
712/252-2166

Collectors Cupboard
500 S. Lewis Blvd.
712/258-0087

Shirley's Stuff & Antiques
1420 Villa Ave.
712/252-1565

Antiques Sioux City, Inc.
1014 4th St.
712/252-1248

Dealin Antiques & Collectibles
509 8th St.
712/252-1060

37 SPILLVILLE

Great Places to Stay

Taylor-Made Bed & Breakfast
330 Main St.
319/562-3958

Built in 1890, this Victorian home featuring four antique filled guest
rooms is located across the street from the world-reknown Bily Clock
Museum.

38 SPIRIT LAKE

Spirit Lake Antique Mall
2015 18th St.
712/336-2029

Heritage Square Antiques
1703 Hill Ave.
712/336-3455

Rubarb Antiques
2009 Hill Ave.
712/336-2154

Ardie's Attic
1612 Ithaca Ave.
712/336-4233

Iowa

39 THAYER

L & H Antique Mall

301 S. 3rd Ave. (mailing address)
Hwy. 34 (shop location)
515/338-2223 or 1-888-338-7178
Open: Tues.–Sat. 10–5, Sun. 12–5, closed Mon., holidays and the week between Christmas and New Year's.
Directions: Located on Hwy. 34, 14 miles west of Osceola and 17 miles east of Creston.

Lee and Helen Spurgeon, the owners of L & H Antique Mall, celebrate their seventh anniversary in their shop this year. They started out with 3,200 square feet and 20 dealers. Last year they added 1,100 square feet and eight more dealers. Who knows how high they'll go? And if you look closely in the shop, among the Depression glass, Hull pottery, furniture, tools, black memorabilia, Fox and Parrish prints and country crafts, you'll see an engraved walnut plaque congratulating Helen on her selection to the National Directory of Who's Who in Executives and Professionals. Congratulations to the Spurgeons!

40 VAN BUREN COUNTY

The Villages of Van Buren County

1-800-868-7822
Email: Villages@netins.net
Web site: www.netins.net/showcase/villages

These former riverboat ports, located along the Des Moines River in the southeast corner of Iowa just north of the Missouri border, are quaint, quiet villages that still maintain the atmosphere and relaxed lifestyle of the past century. Populated today with resident artists and craftspeople, antiques sellers and history buffs, these villages offer visitors relaxation and renewal in a setting that preserves and illuminates our history.

The villages in Van Buren Country include Selma, Birmingham, Stockport, Douds, Leando, Kilbourn, Lebanon, Pittsburg, Milton, Cantril, Keosauqua, Bentonport, Vernon, Mount Sterling, Bonaparte and Farmington, plus several lakes and state parks.

Bentonport National Historic District

Scenic Byway J-40 in Van Buren County
319/592-3579
Open: Tues.–Sun. 10–5, April–October. Some businesses open daily or for longer season

This 1840s river town, with its 100-year-old bridge and walkway, was already thriving when Iowa became a state. Mormon craftsmen, on their western trek to Utah, helped construct some of its buildings; the ruins of old mills along the Des Moines River are evident even today. Visitors can stroll through shops in historic buildings that feature antiques, locally made handcrafted items from working artisans, and American Indian artifacts. Then they can camp at riverside parks and campgrounds or stay at the historic bed and breakfast, eat at the cafe, view the rose garden, or launch into the river at the boat ramp and dock that are available.

Great Places to Shop, Eat and Stay in Bentonport

Greef General Store

Downtown Bentonport
319/592-3579

Antique mall features quality furniture, primitives, etc., plus art and a collection of Indian artifacts.

Country Peddlers

Downtown Bentonport
319/592-3564

Specializes in originally designed folk art.

The Hot Pot Cafe

Downtown Bentonport
319/592-3579

Sandwich shop serves soup and sandwiches, drinks, homemade goodies, ice cream and Dutch treats.

Mason House Inn and Antique Shop of Bentonsport

Route 2, Box 237
1-800-592-3133
Rates: $54–$74

The Mason House Inn was built by Mormon craftsmen on their way to Utah in 1846, the year Iowa became a state. It remains the oldest steamboat river inn in the Midwest still serving overnight guests, quite a record when you consider that it has been in continual service to travelers for 150 years! With the state's only fold-down copper bathtub (that really raises questions, doesn't it!), it has, according to local legend, hosted such notables as John C. Fremont, Abraham Lincoln and Mark Twain. The inn offers nine guest rooms, five with private bath.

Outback Antiques is also located on the premises.

Bonaparte National Historic Riverfront District

The history of Iowa's riverboat era is predominant in Bonaparte. The historic buildings in its downtown district have been carefully preserved and restored in a renaissance of cultural revival. Two of the 1800s mills are still in existence. The old flour and grist mill of 1878 is now the

Iowa

location of one of southeast Iowa's finest restaurants, The Bonaparte Retreat. Bonaparte Mill Antiques is next door in the former Meek's Woolen Mill, and other historic buildings in the district house a variety of businesses. The Aunty Green Museum is just down the street, where visitors can see a collection of historic memorabilia.

Great Places to Shop and Eat in Bonaparte

Bonaparte Mill Antiques
319/592-3274
Open: Tues.–Sun. 11–7

Antiques and collectibles

Bonaparte Retreat Restaurant
319/592-3339
Open: Lunch served 11-1 every day except holidays; dinner served at 5 every day except holidays and Sundays.

Located in a restored grist mill.

Milton, Cantril, Lebanon Triangle
Van Buren County

Another opportunity for people to see firsthand the simple but beautifully crafted life of the Amish and Mennonites is available in the villages of Milton, Cantril and Lebanon, a triangular area in the western end of Van Buren County. Mennonites have settled in the Cantril community, offering several businesses that are open to visitors, including a general store that features bulk groceries and yard goods. In the Milton and Lebanon areas, visitors can watch the Amish practice the trades of horseshoeing, blacksmithing, buggy and harness making, furniture making, sawmill work, and other old world crafts that are a daily part of the Amish lifestyle. Candy and dry goods stores are open to visitors in the Milton area.

Daughtery's Coffee Shop
Cantril
319/397-2100
Open: Mon.–Fri. 7–5

Antiques, lunch, coffee and donuts

Great Places to Shop and Eat in Farmington

Borderline Antiques
103 Elm
319/878-3714
Open: Thurs.–Sat. 10–4:30

Bridge Cafe and Supper Club
319/878-3315
Open: Mon. & Tues. 6–4, Wed.–Sat. 6–9, Sun. 7–2

"Traditional Iowa fare since 1932"

Great Places to Shop, Eat and Stay in Keosauqua

Hotel Manning
100 Van Buren St.
319/293-3232 or 1-800-728-2718
Open: Year-round
Rates $35–$65

Hotel Manning, named for a founder of Keosauqua, was built in 1839 to house a bank and general store. The second and third stories were added in the 1890s and the entire edifice took on a style known as "steamboat gothic," with verandas spanning the width of the first two floors. The grand hotel opened on April 27, 1899 and has been in continuous use as a hotel since then! Guests and visitors can marvel at the lobby's ceilings, original pine woodwork and antique fixtures. The lobby also holds a rare Vose rosewood grand piano, a specially commissioned grandfather clock, and outstanding examples of early pine and oak furniture. The 18 guest rooms, 10 with private bath, are filled with handsome antiques.

Top of the Hill Antiques
319/293-3022

Their antiques can also be found at the Greef Store in Bentonsport.

The Village Creamery
319/293-3815
Open: Daily summer 11–10, daily winter 11–5

Soft ice cream products, sandwiches, etc.

41 WALNUT

Farm Fresh Antiques
200 Antique City Dr.
712/784-2275

Heart of Country
207 Antique City Dr.
712/784-3825

Corn Country Antiques
212 Antique City Dr.
712/784-3992

Antique Furniture Emporium
226 Antique City Dr.
712/784-3839

Simple Pleasures-Antiques
309 Antique City Dr.
712/784-3999

Bear Trap Antiques
608 Highland St.
712/784-3779

Walnut Antique Mall
514 Pearl St.
712/784-3322

Village Blacksmith
610 Pearl St.
712/784-3332

Country Treasures Mall
202 Antique City Dr.
712/784-3090

Everybody's Attic Antiques
210 Antique City Dr.
712/784-3030

Victorian Rose Antiques
216 Antique City Dr.
712/784-3900

Walnut Mercantile Co.
230 Antique City Dr.
712/784-2225

Don's Antiques
310 Antique City Dr.
712/784-2277

Barn Mall
615 Highland St.
712/784-3814

Granary Mall
603 Pearl St.
712/784-3331

Forget-Me-Nots
209 Antique City Dr.
712/784-3040

42 WATERLOO

Calico Hen's House
1022 Alabar Ave.
319/234-1266

Grandpa Harry's
620 Commercial St.
319/232-5900

Pilot House Antiques
1621 Falls Ave.
319/232-5414

Black's Antiques
501 Sycamore St.
319/235-1241

Buehner's Antiques
627 Sycamore St.
319/232-5710

Tovar's Hidden Treasures
1642 Burton Ave.
319/232-0769

Toad's Treasures
622 Commercial St.
319/233-6506

Pink Pig (Washburn)
7114 Laporte Road
319/296-3000

Antique Galleries
618 Sycamore St.
319/235-9945

Gathering
1910 Forest Ave.
310/236-3352

43 WAVERLY

Apple Cottage Gifts & Antiques
103 Bremer Ave.
319/352-0153

Round Barn Antiques
R.R. 2
319/352-3694

44 WEST BRANCH

Memories Restored
111 E. Main St.
319/643-7330

Main Street Antiques & Art
110 W. Main St.
319/643-2065

45 WEST DES MOINES

Antique Jamboree
Location: Valley Junction, 5th Street area
Call for dates.

For more than eighteen years, important antique dealers from across the Midwest have presented their wares at the West Des Moines Antique Jamboree. The show promoters insist upon exceptional antiques; no reproductions or crafts. Therefore, the discriminating shopper will be delighted to find nice porcelains, art glass, period to formal furnishings and more.

Valley Junction
Directions: Take I-235 to the 63rd Street exit. Go south and follow the Valley Junction signs.

In 1893 Valley Junction bustled with horse-drawn traffic, a trolley line, eight-foot wooden sidewalks, and dirt streets lined with three banks, three drug stores and several "boarding houses" of questionable character! By 1900 the Chicago, Rock Island and Pacific Railroad made Valley Junction a popular stop, with 26 passenger trains arriving and departing daily. Today visitors can enjoy more than 120 specialty stores, art galleries, antique shops and restaurants, each with a unique historic character.

One of the places in Valley Junction that is an absolute "must see" for anybody, any age, is the Valley Junction Train Station and Toy Train Museum. Centerpiece of the museum is the colossal 1,000 square foot toy train layout, designed by renowned Broadway set designer Clarke Dunham, and built in New York by Dunham Studios. Eleven Lionel trains, powered by state-of-the-art electronics, run on four different elevations where viewers of all sizes can watch and discover minute details at every eye level.

There's the candy factory with its arteries of pipes, valves, tanks and Life Saver watertower. There are animated figures working and playing in a four-season wonderland, concrete arch viaducts, tunnels through spectacular mountains, towns and villages where tiny figures recreate daily life and fun all across America. Over 2,000 feet of track, connected by bridges and viaducts, loop through a scale-model of America's rural and urban landscapes. You'll see freight trains hauling grain and delivering goods to industrial areas; passenger trains carrying workers and tourists to the layout's metropolitan cities. Surrounding the central layout are dozens of custom-built oak and glass showcases where museum owner Doug DuBay displays his personal, extensive collection of antique trains, tiny houses and railroad memorabilia.

Iowa

From there visit the Valley Junction Toy Train Station — a collector and hobbyist shopping paradise! Shelf after shelf of Lionel equipment and layout accessories are there for viewing, dreaming and buying. After seeing the museum and its fantastic possibilities, it's no wonder that most visitors don't leave the Toy Train Station empty-handed! The museum and Toy Train Station are open Mon.-Sat. 10-5 and Sun. 12-5. The address is 401 Railroad Place, 515/274-4424.

Fifth Street Mall
115 5th St.
515/279-3716

Fifth Street Mall presents quality antiques and collectibles with showcases full of great merchandise. They also have a 1940s original soda fountain.

Elinor's Wood 'n' Wares
102 5th St.
515/274-1234

Station
104 5th St.
515/255-6331

Antique Mall
110 5th St.
515/255-3185

Cherry Stone
111 5th St.
515/255-6414

David Meshek Antique Lighting
115 5th St.
515/277-9009

Especially Lace
202 5th St.
515/277-8778

Pegasus Gallery
218 5th St.
515/277-3245

Lanny's
404 5th St.
515/255-0700

A Okay Antiques
124 5th St.
515/255-2525

"Prezzies"
513 Elm St.
515/255-1915

Joy's Treasures
108 5th St.
515/279-5975

Diane's Antiques
110 5th St.
515/255-3185

Country Caboose Antiques
113 5th St.
515/277-1555

Time Passages, Ltd.
980 73rd St.
515/223-5104

Alverda's Antiques
211 5th St.
515/255-0931

Valley Junction Mall
333 5th St.
515/274-1419

Antique Collectors Mall
1980 Grand Ave.
515/224-6494

Century Shop
333 5th St.
515/255-9449

46 WINTERSET

Madison County Mercantile
58 W. Court Ave.
515/462-4535

East Coast Connection
116 S. 1st Ave.
515/462-1346

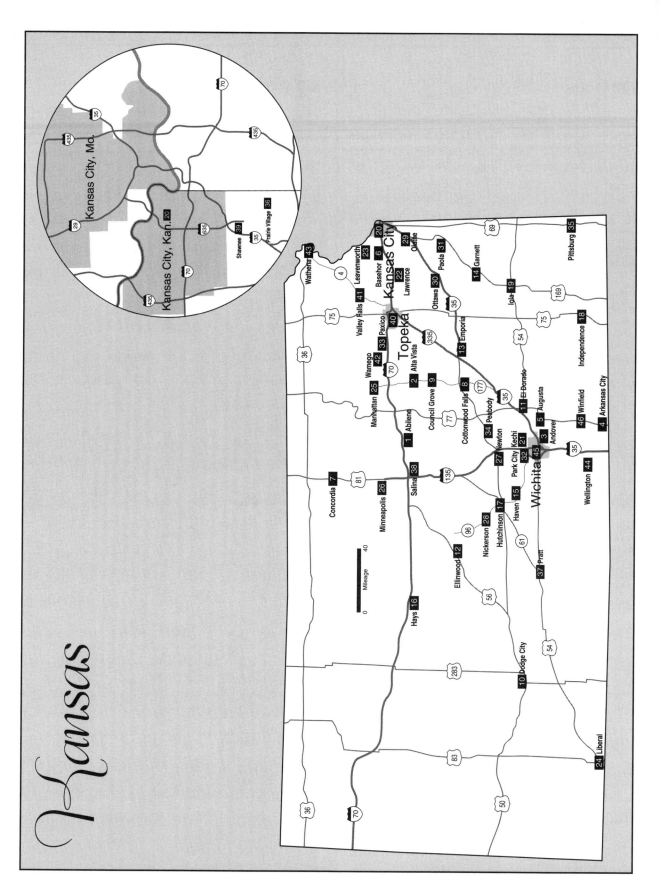

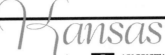

Kansas

1 ABILENE

If you "like Ike," you're in the right place. After he returned from World War II, General Dwight D. Eisenhower told a hometown crowd "the proudest thing I can claim is that I am from Abilene." At the Eisenhower Center in Abilene, visit the home, library and final resting place of the former president and five-star general.

And don't miss Kirby House, a fully restored 1855 gingerbread mansion that is now a wonderful family restaurant, and the Seelye Mansion, a twenty-five room Georgian mansion built in 1905.

Downtown Antique Mall
313 N. Buckeye Ave.
913/263-2782

Liddle Shoppe
306 N. Cedar St.
913/263-0077

Family Antiques
1449 2700th Ave.
913/598-2356

Chicken Crossing Antiques
1975 Hawk Road
913/263-3517

Prairie Antiques
301 N. Cedar St.
913/263-1119

Chisholm Trail Antiques
1020 S. Buckeye Ave.
913/263-2061

Abilene Antique Plaza
418 N.W. 2nd St.
913/263-4200

Buckeye Antique Mall
310 N. Buckeye Ave.
913/263-7696

5th & Cedar Antiques, Etc.
421 N. Cedar St.
913/263-3919

Splinters & Rags
612 S. Buckeye Ave.
913/263-4615

2 ALTA VISTA

Alta Vista Antiques
902 N. Main St.
785-499-5375
Open: Thurs., Fri., Sat., 10–5, Sun. 1–5
Directions: Sixteen miles south from I-70

Located in a little Victorian house decorated in room settings.

3 ANDOVER

Andover Antique Mall
656 N. Andover Road
316/733-8999

4 ARKANSAS CITY

Antiques Plus Mall
120 N. Summit St.
316/442-5777

Mylissa's Garden Antiques
309 S. Summit St.
316/442-6433

Summit Antique Mall
208 S. Summit St.
316/442-1115

5 AUGUSTA

White Eagle Antique Mall
10187 S.W. U.S. Hwy. 54
316/775-2812
Open: Mon.–Sat., 10–9; Sun. 12–7
Directions: Located 2 ½ miles west of Augusta on the south side of U.S. Hwy. 54. Travelers on U.S. Hwy. 77 take U.S. Hwy. 54 west at Walnut Street stoplight in Augusta.

White Eagle Antique Mall, billed as "A Collector's Dream Come True," is no disappointment. The mall features that hard-to-find, early petroleum and gas station memorabilia. With over 100 dealers, this place is attractively filled to the brim with high quality glassware, primitives, vintage clothing, old books, jewelry, lamps, old toys, pottery, tools, large and small furniture and other exceptional antiques.

Like A Rose
343 Main St.
316/775-5860

Two Fools Antiques
429 State St.
316/775-2588

Serendipity
529 State St.
316/775-6117

Circa 1890
10257 S.W. River Valley Road
316/775-3272

Pigeons Roost Mall
601 State St.
316/775-2279

6 BASEHOR

Great Places to Stay

Bedknobs & Biscuits
15202 Parallel
913/724-1540
Rates: $50–$70

A little bit of country close to Bonner Springs and Kansas City. A warm, inviting beamed gathering room; walls covered in hand-painted vines. Stenciling throughout the house, lovely quilts, lace curtains and colorful stained glass to enjoy. Complimentary cookies in the evening and a huge country breakfast in the morning.

7 CONCORDIA

General Store Antiques
317 W. 5th St.
913/243-7280

Chapter I Books
120 E. 6th St.
913/243-1423

Dan's Antiques
101 E. 6th St.
913/243-3820

Antique Mall
128 E. 6th St.
913/243-2313

Kansas

8 COTTONWOOD FALLS

Great Places to Stay

Grand Central Hotel
215 Broadway
316/273-6763 or 1-800-951-6763

Most of us rarely think of hills in connection with Kansas, but hidden among the state's Flint Hills is an elegant hotel that is a luxurious surprise when you stumble across it. The Grand Central Hotel bills itself as "very exclusive, very distinctive, very, very special." Located one block west of National Scenic Byway 177 in historic Cottonwood Falls, the hotel was built in 1884 and has been fully restored to its original grandeur. It offers ten suites, each beautifully appointed and oversized, and decorated with a western flair. In fact, each suite is "branded" with historic brands of the area's local ranchers! It offers full dining and complete catering services, and is often the suite of choice for weddings, receptions, small board and business conferences, corporate outings, and, of course, private accommodations. It caters to the business trade with concierge and room service, plus V.I.P. robes and a business center; but the hotel also offers hunting trips, bicycle tours, horseback riding, and tours of the surrounding Flint Hills.

1874 Stonehouse Bed & Breakfast on Mulberry Hill
Rural Route 1, Box 67A
316/273-8481
Rates $75

If you've ever wondered about the landscape that nurtured Dorothy and Toto, here's your chance to spend some time at one. The 1874 Stonehouse on Mulberry Hill offers three lovely rooms with private baths on the second floor, with two common rooms and a stone fireplace. But that's not nearly all. On its 120 acres guests can spend all day, or several days, exploring old stone fences, a river valley that crosses the property, acres of woods (more than 10 acres), a pond, the ruins of an old stone barn and corral, an abandoned railway right-of-way, and a decrepit "hired hands place." The inn and its grounds are a magnet for fishermen and hunters, equestrians and naturalists, antiquers and photographers, cyclists and hikers, bird watchers and historians, and maybe even a little girl in pigtails and her funny little dog.

9 COUNCIL GROVE

Council Grove was the last outfitting post between the Missouri River and Santa Fe on the Santa Fe Trail. In 1825, the U.S. government negotiated with the Osage Indians for a passage across their lands. The stump of Council Oak still stands where the treaty was signed. At the Last Chance Store, you can still visit the last supply stop on the Santa Fe Trail.

And if you're hungry, try some tasty family recipes at the Hays House Restaurant, the oldest continuously operated restaurant west of the Mississippi.

Prairie Pieces	**Faded Roses**
217 W. Main St.	307 E. Main St.
316/767-6628	316/767-5217

Great Places to Stay

The Cottage House Hotel
25 N. Neosho St.
1-800-727-7903

Flint Hills B&B
613 W. Main St.
316/767-6655

Flint Hills Bed and Breakfast is located on the Santa Fe Trail in Historic Council Grove. The house is an American Four Square built in 1913 by the Jacob Rhodes family. It still has its original yellow pine and oak woodwork and hardwood floors. Each room is antique-filled and has a personality of its own. Get acquainted with other guests in the sitting room furnished with TV, coffee pot, and refrigerator, or relax outside on the porch swing. In the morning you will join other guests in the main dining room where you will be served a full country breakfast. Afterwards you may want to tour one of Council Grove's eighteen Registered Historic Sites or enjoy one of the two beautiful lakes.

Great Places to Eat

Hays House 1857 Restaurant
112 W. Main St.
316/767-5911
Open: Summer 7–9, winter: 7–8

Oldest restaurant west of the Mississippi; National Register Historic Landmark; nationally acclaimed restaurant featured in many magazines and newspapers; outstanding steaks, breads and dessert made from scratch daily.

10 DODGE CITY

Ole Jem's	**Collectors Cottage**
212 S. 2nd Ave.	106 E. Wyatt Earp Blvd.
316/227-6162	316/225-7448
Curiosity Shoppe	
1102 W. Wyatt Earp Blvd.	
316/227-3340	

Kansas

Interesting Side Trip

Relive the 1870s heyday of the rip-snortin', gun-slingin' Wild West at Dodge City's Boot Hill Museum and Front Street complex. More than five million Texas longhorn cattle were driven to the "Cowboy Capital." Miss Kitty still runs the Longbranch Saloon, gunslingers have "high noon" shootouts and an authentic stagecoach still boards passengers for a ride along Front Street.

11 EL DORADO

North Ward Junction Antiques
518 North Star
316/321-0145 or 1-800-286-0146
Open: Mon.–Sat. 10–5:30, Sun. 1–4
Accepts all major credit cards — offers dealer discounts.
Directions: *From I-35 exit 71* (East); turn left on Central, go 2 ½ miles into El Dorado. Turn left at the courthouse onto Star. Go five blocks north. *From Highway 54* east of El Dorado, come into town on Central heading west, turn right at the courthouse; go five blocks north.

This shop began life in 1884 as the North Ward School. No longer catering to the educational concerns of fidgety boys and girls, this 4,000-square-foot shop provides fifteen quality antique dealers the opportunity to display their wares in decorated room-like settings. A large selection of furniture is available along with accent pieces of porcelain, china, glassware, elegant table settings, linens, prints and much, much more.

Cinnamon Tree
1417 W. Central Ave.
316/321-0930

Blast from the Past
527 N. Washington St.
316/321-3434

Silver Bell Antiques
204 W. Carr
316/321-3913

Leather Works
1630 W. Central Ave.
316/321-7644

Haverhill Antiques
811 S. Haverhill Road
316/321-3199

12 ELLINWOOD

James J. Elliott Antiques
1 N. Main St.
316/564-2400

Starr Antiques
104 E. Santa Fe
316/564-2400

Our Mother's Treasures
14 N. Main St.
316/564-2218

13 EMPORIA

Emporia is a city with over 130 years of history as an agricultural and railroad community. It still maintains its small town Middle American charm, exemplified by brick streets, tree-lined avenues and many beautiful old Victorian homes.

Emporia was also the home of two-time Pulitzer Prize winner, William Allen White, owner of *The Emporia Gazette*. White became famous overnight for his opposing editorial reviews against the Populist Party.

Wild Rose Antique Mall
1505 E. Road 175
316/343-8862
Open: Tues.–Sat. 11–5, Sun. 1–5, closed Mon.
Directions: 3 miles East of Emporia on I-35 at exit #135 (Thorndale exit)

Terry McCracken, owner and shopkeeper at the Wild Rose Antique Mall, has collected antiques since her childhood. Up until seven years ago, she had never sold a one of them. When she decided to retire as a real estate broker (she added that she's not that old); she opened a booth at a mall in Topeka. Her success prompted her to open her own shop in Emporia where she presented high-end antique glassware, quilts, jewelry, china, pottery, linens, primitives and furnishings. Today, thanks to all the folks who enjoyed shopping at Wild Rose, Terry has expanded. Her new shop allows space for more dealers with a broader selection of antiques. Three dealers specialize in items from the Victorian era. Congratulations, Terry!

Great Places to Stay

Plumb House Bed and Breakfast
628 Exchange St.
316/342-6881
Rates $35–$75
Directions: Call from your location.

Built in 1910 and once the home of George and Ellen Plumb, this bed and breakfast offers classic Victorian charm. Its original beveled glass windows and pocket doors are still intact, and the home is furnished throughout with Victorian era antiques.

Guests may choose from the Horseless Carriage with large windows overlooking a garden; the Garden Suite offering views from a balcony; the Rosalie Room, the Loft, or Grannie's Attic filled with over 250 dresses, hats, gloves, shoes, and jewelry. Everything you need for dress-up tea parties.

14 GARNETT

Country Peddler
146 E. 5th Ave.
913/448-3018

Corner Stone Antiques
146 E. 5th Ave.
913/448-3737

Goodies Antiques
121 E. 4th Ave.
913/448-6712

Emporium on the Square
415 S. Oak St.
913/448-6459

15 HAVEN

The Home Place Antiques
7619 S. Yoder Road
316/662-1579
Open: Tues.–Sat. 10–5
Directions: 4 ¹⁄₂ miles south of Highway 50; 1 ¹⁄₂ miles north of Highway 96.

The Home Place Antiques is located in a barn built in 1909 and sets on a fourth-generation farm, thus creating the perfect atmosphere for selling antiques. The "old barn" is full of antiques, from furniture (lots of it) to dishes, to pottery, to a little of everything.

16 HAYS

Antique Mall
201 W. 41st St.
913/625-6055

Littles Antiques
717 Vine St.
913/628-3393

Interesting Side Trip

Old Fort Hays was built to protect military roads, guard the mails and defend construction gangs on the Union Pacific Railroad. See the original blockhouse, guardhouse and officers' quarters. "Buffalo Bill" Cody supplied the fort with buffalo meat, and General Custer's ill-fated 7th cavalry was stationed here.

17 HUTCHINSON

Antique Memories
25 E. 1st St.
316/665-0610

Unique Antiques
1831 E. 4th Ave.
316/669-8678

Yesterdays Treasures
436 Hendricks St.
316/662-0895

Cow Creek Antiques
127 S. Main St.
316/663-1976

Nu-Tu U
201 S. Main St.
316/662-4357

Book Collector
404 N. Main St.
316/665-5057

Finders Keepers II
412 N. Main St.
316/663-5457

Brokers Antiques
820 S. Main St.
316/665-7040

GAI Marche Ltd.
2528 N. Main St.
316/662-6323

Armstrong's Antiques
121 S. Main St.
316/664-5811

Bluebird Antiques
112 S. Main St.
316/663-1519

Old Tyme Things
129 S. Main St.
316/665-6024

Jim's Antique Bottles
1310 13th Terrace
316/662-7784

The Antique Connection
419 N. Poplar
No phone listed

The Shoppe
1000 S. Main St.
316/663-7789

Wild Horse Primitives & Antiques
123 S. Main St.
316/662-6773

Wood N Horse
15 E. 1st St.
1-800-293-6607

18 INDEPENDENCE

If you're a fan of "Little House on the Prairie," visit a replica of the house where Laura Ingalls Wilder lived and found inspiration for her books. The cabin was rebuilt where it originally stood near Independence.

Attic Treasures
211 E. Main St.
316/331-6401

Southwest Wood Shop
1813 W. Main St.
316/331-1400

Susie's Vintage Villa
2919 W. Main St. (Hwy. 160)
316/331-6811

Great Places to Stay

The Rosewood Bed and Breakfast
417 W. Myrtle
316/331-2221
Rates: $50–$60
Directions: Located 1 block north of Hwy. 75/169 at 11th Street and Myrtle.

This stately home was built in 1915 for William Gates, general manager of Prairie Oil and Gas. Leaded glass windows and wrap-around porches still embrace the home. Decorated throughout in period antiques, the Victorian Rose room creates a picture of a romantic time gone by. A white iron bed piled high with pure white and soft pink dressings is the focus of the room, with a large bay window providing the morning sun. The Royal Orchid, preferred by honeymooners, has a black canopy bed. The Desert Blossom is the whimsical room, decorated in a Southwestern flair.

Breakfast is served in the dining room near the bay windows and fireplace.

Kansas

19 IOLA

Great Places to Stay

Northrup House Bed & Breakfast
318 East St.
316/365-8025
Rates: $60–$70

The Northrup House, a Queen Anne Victorian, was built in 1895 by Lewis Northrup, a prominent Iola businessman and community leader. The interior features stained glass windows, beautiful oak woodwork, crystal chandeliers and pocket doors. The house is furnished with elegant antiques. The guests are welcome to use the parlors, dining room and porches.

20 KANSAS CITY

Palmers Antique
761 Central Ave.
913/342-8299

Happy House Antiques
1712 Central Ave.
913/321-8909

Antique & Craft City Mall
1270 Merriam Lane
913/677-0752

Andersons General Store
1713 Minnesota Ave.
913/321-3165

Show Me Antiques
4500 State Line Road
913/236-8444

Collectors Emporium
3412 Strong Ave.
913/384-1875

Glenn Books
1710 Central Ave.
913/321-3040

Treasures From Granny's Attic
6000 Leavenworth Road
913/334-0824

Adventure Antiques
1306 Merriam Lane
913/831-6005

Old World Antiques
4436 State Line Road
913/677-4744

State Line Antique Mall
4510 State Line Road
913/362-2002

Past Renewed
4356 Victory Dr.
913/287-2817

21 KECHI

Country Antiques Kechi
201 E. Kechi Road
316/744-0932

Cherishables
311 E. Kechi Road
316/744-9952

Jo's Antiques
210 E. Kechi Road
316/744-1581

Daisy Patch Antiques
134 E. Kechi Road
316/744-1144

Anderson Antiques
309 E. Kechi Road
316/744-8482

Primitives Plus
127 Foreman
316/744-1836

Aunt B's
130 E. Kechi Road
316/744-3505

Rememberings
132 E. Kechi Road
316/744-3400

The Five Little Ladies
128C E. Kechi Road
316/744-8874

22 LAWRENCE

Quantrill's Antique Mall & Flea Market
811 New Hampshire St.
913/842-6616
Open: Daily 10–5:30
Directions: Located 3 miles south of the I-70 East Kansas Turnpike Exit. One block east of Massachusetts Street. Two blocks from Riverfront Outlet Mall.

Quantrill's is the oldest antique mall in the state of Kansas. This massive 3-story natural limestone structure dates back to 1863. With 150 dealers covering 20,000 square feet, their inventory list is just as impressive. You'll find furniture, toys, jewelry, glassware, pottery, books, lunch boxes, dolls, advertising memorabilia, buttons, crocks and Fiesta. From their list of the unusual, they offer retro '60s and '70s items, tobacco, military and '50s dinettes and other nostalgic items.

Topiary Tree, Inc.
15 E. 8th St.
913/842-1181

B & S Antiques
1017 Massachusetts St.
913/843-9491

Antique Mall
830 Massachusetts St.
913/842-1328

Strongs Antiques
1025 Massachusetts St.
913/843-5173

23 LEAVENWORTH

Caffee's Leavenworth Antique Mall
505 Delaware
913/758-0193
Open: Mon.–Sat. 10–6
Directions: Located in Historic Downtown Leavenworth.

Caffee's Antique Mall occupies 7,900 square feet in the old J.C. Penney building at 505 Delaware St. in Downtown Historic Leavenworth. Renovation began Jan. 1, 1998, to add 900 square feet to the first level. A total of ten new booths, three new shelf units, a larger showcase area, and a combination consignment/ dance floor area were created. A total of 60 vendors rent space on three levels at Caffee's Antique Mall, therefore, new antiques and collectibles arrive daily. The first floor is home to The Tea Room, where lunch is served Monday

through Saturday, and the site of many special parties and functions. Caffee's Antique Mall and The Tea Room host meetings and other functions in a separate meeting area.

Within walking distance of Caffee's Antique Mall are four other quality antique shops, a new flea market, and an "everything" shop. Just two blocks to the east, visitors will find the historic Leavenworth Landing shopping area and the new Riverside Park.

Bob's Antiques
511 Delaware St.
913/680-0101

Carol's Cupboard
207 S. 5th St.
913/651-0400

River Front Antique Shop
401 S. 2nd St.
913/682-3201

June's Antiques
612 Cherokee
913/651-5270

Ginny's Antiques
206 S. 5th St.
913/651-8426

Weakley's Antique Furniture
1433 Kingman St.
913/682-5816

Trumpet Vine
1700 2nd Ave.
913/651-8230

24 LIBERAL

Randy's Antiques
1 S. Kansas Ave.
316/624-0641

Yesterdays Treasure
406 E. Pancake Blvd.
316/624-1683

Interesting Side Trip

Take a stroll along Dorothy's Yellow Brick Road in Liberal. See the original miniature farmhouse used in the 1939 classic film *The Wizard of Oz*, or go through a full-size replica of Dorothy's house. Liberal also is the home of Kansas' largest aviation museum, the Mid-America Air Museum. There are more than 80 vintage aircraft on display. And the world-famous International Pancake Race is held in Liberal each Shrove Tuesday.

25 MANHATTAN

Pop's Collectibles
315 S. 4th St.
785/776-1433

On The Avenue
405 Poyntz Ave.
785/539-9116

Under The Avenue Antique Mall
413 Poyntz Ave.
785/537-1921

Tuttles Antique Market
2010 Tuttle Creek Blvd.
785/537-4884

Gumbo Hill Antique Shop
6590 Gumbo Hill Road
785/539-5778

Antique Emporium of Manhattan
411 Poyntz Ave.
785/537-1921

Zeandale Store
R.R. 3
785/537-3631

Time Machine Antique Mall
4910 Skyway Dr.
785/539-4684

26 MINNEAPOLIS

Griffin's Antiques & Collectibles
703 E. 10th
913/392-2821

Blue Store Emporium
307 W. Second St.
913/392-3491

27 NEWTON

Wharf Road
413 N. Main St.
316-283-3579

The Curiosity Shop
106 W. Broadway
316/283-5555

Stuart's Antique Gallery
709 N. Main St.
316/284-0824

28 NICKERSON

Johnson's Antique Warehouse
#2 Nickerson St.
316/442-3225

Great Places to Stay

Hedrick Exotic Animal Farm/Bed and Breakfast
7910 N. Roy L. Smith Road
316/422-3245 or 1-800-618-9577
Open: Daily 8–10
Directions: 50 miles NW of Wichita on Highway 96; 8 miles west of Hutchinson on Highway 96. From I-70, go south on 135 at Salina to McPherson. Take Highway 61 to Hutchinson, Take Highway 96 west 8 miles. Located on the north side of Highway 96.

Looking for a little bit out of the ordinary place to stay? Then book your reservations here. Hedrick's Bed and Breakfast offers a relaxing, country atmosphere in a picturesque Old West town front nestled in the midst of a farm. But cows and horses aren't the only animals you'll find here. It wouldn't be out of the ordinary to find camels, zebras, llamas, kangaroos, and ostriches. And Jeffrey, the tallest animal found on the farm, will practically kiss you for an apple slice. In case you haven't guessed, Jeffrey's a giraffe.

You can arrange for the staff to take you on a guided tour where you can actually touch and feed the animals. Camel rides, pony rides, hayrack rides and campfire wiener roasts can also be arranged.

The decor of each guest room depicts an animal on the farm, with personal touches such as zebra sheets, rugs from Peru and much more. True to the western heritage of Kansas, the Inn reflects the image of Main Street in the Old West, complete with swinging "bar" doors. An outside balcony which completely surrounds the Inn is accessible from each room. A great place to bring the kids.

Kansas

29 OLATHE

Rosebriar Limited
11695 S. Black Bob Road
913/829-3636

Aggies Attic Antiques
301 1/2 W. Park St.
913/768-0058

Heirloom Antiques
2135 N.E. 151 St.
913/780-3478

Flutterby
1313 E. Santa Fe St.
913/780-1644

30 OTTAWA

Over The Hill Collectibles
120 S. Main St.
785/242-8016

Gables Antiques
503 N. Main St.
785/242-7144

Silver Arrow Trading Post
1630 S. Main St.
785/242-0019

Down Home Antiques
202 S. Main St.
785/242-0774

Outback Antiques
534 N. Main St.
785/242-1178

Ottawa Antique Mall & Restaurant
202 S. Walnut St.
785/242-1078

31 PAOLA

Park Square Emporium
18 S. Silver St.
913/294-9004

Special Occasions
23 W. Wea St.
913/294-8595

Magdelena's Antiques & Collectibles
8 S. Silver St.
913/294-5048

32 PARK CITY

Recollections
1530 S. 61st St.
316/744-8333

Teddy's Antiques & Collectibles
1550 E. 61st St.
316/685-0435

Howe's Homestead
8416 N. Broadway
316/755-0371

Poor House Antiques
1542 N. 61st St.
316/744-9935

Annie Antiques & Collectibles
1600 S. 61st St.
316/744-1999

Park City Antique Mall
6227 N. Broadway
316/744-2025

33 PAXICO

Paxico Variety Shop
203 Main St.
913/636-5292

Time Warp Antiques
207 Main St.
913/636-5553

Paxico Antiques
111 Newbury Ave.
913/636-5426

Main Street Antiques
204 Main St.
913/636-5200

Mill Creek Antiques
109 Newbury Ave.
913/636-5520

34 PEABODY

This little town of 1,400 probably has preserved its architectural heritage better than any other community in the state. Gutted by two fires in its first 14 years of existence, Peabody was rebuilt in 1885 with limestone fire walls between the buildings.

"That's what saved our town," said the town historian, Koni Jones. "You can see that the buildings are still the way they were in the 1880s. One of our slogans is 'It really is a step back in time.'"

The town was named for a railroad executive who donated a library to the fledgling community in 1874. It was the first free library in Kansas, and today the original building is the Peabody Historical Museum.

Visitors downtown can also browse an antique store, try a Phosphate at a 1920s soda fountain, enjoy flavored coffees and teas at the Jackrabbit Hollow Bookstore, or dine in restaurants that once were a bank in 1887 and a chicken hatchery in 1885.

Tumbleweed Antiques
101 N. Walnut St.
316/983-2200

Turkey Red Restaurant
101 S. Walnut St.
316/983-2883

Sharon's Korner Kitchen
128 N. Walnut St.
316/983-2307

Jack Rabbit Hollow Books
113 N. Walnut St.
316/983-2600

35 PITTSBURG

Marilyn's Ceramics Crafts
710 W. Atkinson Road
316/231-4131

Treasure Village Antiques
212 S. Broadway St.
316/231-4888

Friday's Child
615 N. Broadway St.
316/235-0403

George's Antiques
210 S. Broadway St.
316/232-6340

Browsery-Collector Antiques
216 S. Broadway St.
316/232-1250

Antique Shop
2305 N. Broadway St.
316/231-4090

36 PRAIRIE VILLAGE

Mission Road Antique Mall
4101 W. 83rd St.
913/341-7577
Open: Mon.–Sat. 10–7, Sun. 11–5

Simply the best! Experience one of the largest, most impressive antique malls in the country. See thousands of antiques (furniture, crystal, pottery, jewelry, silver, books and collectibles) creatively displayed throughout 50,000 square feet of individual showrooms and unique vignettes. The unique landmark locations has been home to 250 of the area's finest antique dealers since 1994. A distinctive reputation for quality and selection attracts shoppers, designers and collectors from all over the world.

Kansas

Treat yourself to a delicious lunch at The Bistro. Enjoy creative cuisine, made from family recipes. Indulge in an array of homemade desserts and pastries. Great care is taken to insure that customers receive the freshest food and friendliest service.

37 PRATT

Peggy's Antiques
208 S. Main St.
316/672-5648

Brick Street Antique Mall
212 S. Main St.
316/672-6770

Mom's Attic
607 S. Main St.
316/672-7656

Higgin's Antiques
617 Champa
316/672-6655

38 SALINA

Auld Lang Syne & Auld Lang Syne, too
1-101 N. Santa Fe
too-110 N. Santa Fe
913/825-0020 or 913/827-4222
Open: Mon.–Sat. 10–5, Sun. 1–5
Directions: Corner of Santa Fe and Iron

Two shops to double your antiquing pleasure. Auld Lang Syne is located in the former First National Bank Building complete with a center courtyard for relaxing. Auld Lang Syne, too is across the street. Both shops display the wares of ninety dealers offering a selection of antiques and collectibles of various styles and periods

Treasure Chest of Salina
N. Broadway
913/827-9371

Furniture Clinic
405 S. Clark St.
913/827-5115

Stan & Junes Heirlooms
201A S. 5th St.
913/823-6627

Fourth Street Mini Mall
127 S. 4th St.
913/825-4948

Forever & Ever Antiques & Collectibles
108 N. Santa Fe Ave.
913/827-4222

Daddy & Me
116 S. Santa Fe Ave.
913/452-9976

39 SHAWNEE

O'Neill's Classics — Antiques & Uniques
11200 Johnson Dr.
913/268-9008
Open: Tues.–Fri. 10–5:30, Sat. 10–4:30, closed Sun. & Mon.
Directions: One mile from I-35, on the north side of Johnson Drive, just a block west of its intersection with Nieman Road.

Located in the historic town of Shawnee, O'Neill's carries a general line of antiques and collectibles. Antique chairs, tables, dressers, pictures,

elegant glassware and the such are just a few of the items one may find in this quaint 1,400-square-foot store. The oldest piece in the store dates to around 1830 with collectibles up through 1960s.

Local residents frequent the store often, but the owners, Mike & Cyndee Bohaty, love meeting new antique friends who stop in while traveling. Cyndee grew up around antiques and was once a member of Questers, a national association of people interested in antiquing. When Cyndee and Mike were married they loved going to auctions — Cyndee jokingly laughs that they couldn't afford anything else. Today, they still love auctions as evidenced by the wonderful pieces available in their store.

Gene Switzer Antiques
6711 Antioch Road
913/432-3982

Consignment Shop
4740 Rainbow Shop
913/384-2424

Armoires & More
12922 W. 87th St.
913/438-3868

Mission Road Antique Mall
4101 W. 83rd St.
913/341-7577

Memory Lane Antiques
5401 Johnson Dr.
913/677-4300

Lincoln Antiques
5636 Johnson Dr.
913/384-6811

Past & Present Antiques
5727 Johnson Dr.
913/362-6995

Drake's Military Antiques
8929 Johnson Dr.
913/722-1943

Peterson's Antiques
7829 Marty St.
913/341-5065

Antiques & Oak
10464 Metcalf Ave.
913/381-8280

J & M Collectables
7819 W. 151st St.
913/897-0584

Zohner's Antiques
10200 Pflumm Rd.
913/894-5036

June's Antiques
612 Cherokee
913/651-5270

Interesting Side Trips

Old Shawnee Town
As visitors pass through the gates into Old Shawnee Town, they are enveloped by the 1880s atmosphere of the town. From the blacksmith's shop to the sod house, the setting makes visitors become a part of life on the Kansas frontier.

Furniture, tools and household items are just a few of the goods to see on the walk through town. The original Shawnee jail — the first in Johnson County — stands in Old Shawnee Town for people of all ages to explore.

For those who decide to make it a day at the site, the central grassy area serves as an ideal spot for picnics and group gatherings.

Johnson County Historical Museum
From pioneer trail utensils to the coming of the television, the Johnson County Historical Museum brings the area's history to life.

The experiences of prairie pioneers come alive at the Hands-on History display in the museum. After donning the traditional attire of calico dresses or overalls, kids can try their hand at mixing pretend biscuits or discovering how to harness an oxen team.

40 TOPEKA

Shade Tree Antiques
1300 S.W. Boswell Ave.
913/232-5645

Cobweb
2508 S.W. 15th St.
913/357-7498

Antiques Unique
1222 S.W. 6th Ave.
913/232-1007

Packrat Antiques
3310 S.W. 6th Ave.
913/232-6560

Reflections Antiques
2213 S.W. 10th Ave.
913/232-4619

Antique Plaza of Topeka
2935 S.W. Topeka Blvd.
913/267-7411

Darla's World Antiques & Collectibles
3688 S.W. Topeka Blvd.
913/266-4242

Topeka Antique Mall
5247 S.W. 28th Court
913/273-2969

Dickerson Antiques
5331 S.W. 22nd Place
913/273-1845

B & J Antique Mall
1949 S.W. Gage Blvd.
913/273-3409

Antique Elegance
2900 S.W. Oakley Ave.
913/273-0909

Pastense
3307 S.W. 6th Ave.
913/233-7107

Kansan Relics & Old Books
3308 S.W. 6th Ave.
913/233-8232

History House
215 S.W. Topeka Blvd.
913/235-1885

Rose Buffalo Antiques & Cllbls.
3600 S.W. Topeka Blvd.
913/267-7478

Wheatland Antique Mall
2121 S.W. 37th St.
913/266-3266

Washburn View Antique Mall
1507 S.W. 21st St.
913/234-0949

Saltbox
507 S.W. Washburn Ave.
913/233-6264

41 VALLEY FALLS

Valley Falls Antiques
423 Broadway
913/945-3666
Open: Tues.–Sat. 10–5, Sun. 12–5, closed Mon.
Directions: Located halfway between Topeka and Atchison, Kan., 30 miles either direction, via Highway 4. In Valley Falls, go downtown. The store is easily found at the corner of Walnut and Broadway.

Halfway between Topeka and Atchison, Kansas, sits Valley Falls, "Antique Capital of Jefferson County." Among the three established shops and the one opening this year, Valley Falls Antiques presents its shoppers the expected assortment of goods, in addition to some not-so-usual items.

The shop is housed in a historic bank building built in 1872, and

within its walls you can shop for antique furniture, primitives, glassware and collectibles. Delores Werder, owner and shopkeeper, admits that original artwork is a passion for her. She prefers to purchase pieces with some unusual quality. Among her display of art, you will find prints, paintings and block prints.

42 WAMEGO

Carriage House Antiques & Collectibles
210 Lincoln St.
913/456-7021

Antique Emporium of Wamego
511 Lincoln St.
913/456-7111

Wagon Wheel Antiques
409 Lincoln St.
913/456-8480

Fulkerson's Antiques
206 Maple St.
913/456-9175

43 WATHENA

Great Places to Stay

Carousel Bed & Breakfast
Route 1
913/989-3537
Open: Year-round 7–10
Directions: Approximately 15 miles west of I-29 and Highway 36 interchange. The B&B driveway comes off of Highway 36 three miles west of Wathena and 4 miles east of Troy, Kan. (60 miles north of Kansas City and 9 miles west of St. Joseph, Mo.)

Located on a country hillside with a gorgeous panoramic view of the glacial hills, the Carousel Bed and Breakfast has been beautifully restored to its 1917 splendor by innkeeper Betty Price, her husband, and her sister, Ginnie. The trio was the restoration crew responsible for the Victorian elegance evident throughout the home. Ginnie was the painter, Betty hung all the wallpaper while Mr. Price ran all the errands. If you look closely at the stairway spindles, you might observe a rather heavy coating of paint on them. It seems that Ginnie, in her efforts to perform the perfect task, got carried away and painted them five times! That night she dreamed that the stairway reached all the way to heaven and that she was painting every one of them.

This labor of love is especially evident in the Victorian parlor where personal touches have created a soothing environment for guests to relax. Victorian furnishings are placed throughout the home, further enhancing its aura.

Breakfast is served beginning at 7 a.m. for early birds who are eager to venture out into the beautiful surroundings that embrace The Carousel.

Kansas

44 WELLINGTON

Antiques Plus Mall
1112 E. Hwy. 160
316/326-5700

Dianne Wagoner's Antqs. & Cllbls.
Hwy. 81, 1 mi. north of Wellington
316/326-2665

Pastime Treasures Antique Mall
221 N. Washington
316/326-3440

45 WICHITA

In 1865, Jesse Chisholm and James Mead established Wichita near a village of grass lodges built by the Wichita Indians. The settlement around their trading post soon attracted passing drovers along the Chisholm Trail, and Wichita boomed into a wide-open cowtown. Today you'll find remnants of Western history almost everywhere you look. Step back to the early years of the booming cattle town at Old Cowtown Museum. The 44 restored buildings and authentic characters will give you a true sense of Wichita in the 1870s. Visitors can see Wichita's first jail, a fully stocked general store, a one-room school, a saloon, a railroad depot, and also watch a blacksmith demonstrate his craft.

Across town is the Historic Old Town District. It's one part of town you won't want to miss. This newly renovated warehouse district is packed full of antique shops, a variety of delightful restaurants, galleries and great night spots. And from May through October enjoy the Wichita Farm and Art Market, an open-air market of fresh produce, arts, and crafts.

Wooden Heart Antiques
141 S. Rock Island St.
316/267-1475
Open: Daily, evenings by appointment
Directions: 7 blocks off I-135 in the old town business district.

Wooden Heart Antiques & Refinishing occupies a large two-story warehouse in Wichita. The two floors of antique oak, walnut and mahogany furniture as well as a large selection of wonderful old architectural items invites visitors to a wonderland of history. Items range from very rough to fully restored. Special services include furniture stripping, repairing and refinishing. For more information you can visit Wooden Heart's web site at www.feist.com/-woodenheart.

White Eagle Antique Mall
10187 S.W. U.S. Hwy. 54
316/775-2812
Open: Mon.–Sat. 10–9, Sun. 12–7
Directions: Travelers through Wichita on I-135 should take the East 54 (Kellogg) exit. Go east on U.S. Hwy. 54 (Kellogg) 16 miles. The mall is located on the south side of U.S. Hwy. 54.
Travelers on I-35 (Kansas Turnpike) use exit 50 and go east on U.S. Hwy. 54 (Kellogg) 11 miles. The mall is located on the south side of U.S. Hwy. 54.

White Eagle Antique Mall, billed as "A Collector's Dream Come True," is no disappointment. The mall features that hard-to-find, early petroleum and gas station memorabilia. With over 100 dealers, this place is attractively filled to the brim with high quality glassware, primitives, vintage clothing, old books, jewelry, lamps, old toys, pottery, tools, large and small furniture and other exceptional antiques.

Green Dragons Books
2730 Boulevard Plaza
316/681-0746

Park City Antique Mall
6227 N. Broadway St.
316/744-2025

River City Basket Co.
509 E. Douglas Ave.
316/265-1068

Santa Fe House & Old Town Gallery
630 E. Douglas Ave.
316/265-4736

Legacy Antiques
105 S. Emporia St.
316/267-2730

Paradise Antique Mall
430 E. Harry St.
316/269-4441

A & A Antique Mall
2419 Maple St.
316/945-4250

A Little Everything Antiques
2301 S. Meridian Ave.
316/945-3150

Ice House Antiques
136 S. Oliver Road (Kechi)
316/744-2331

Dorothy's Antiques & Collectibles
1515 E. Pawnee St.
316/265-6035

Gay '90s Antique Shop
1303 N. Broadway St.
316/263-7421

M Ballard & Co.
920 Buffum St.
316/267-7831

Douglas Avenue Antiques
517 E. Douglas Ave.
316/263-6454

S A Phillip Company
1109 E. Douglas Ave.
316/267-5730

Variety Plus & Mills Stream
110 W. Harry St.
316-262-4299

KIS Antiques
724 N. Main St.
316/267-1357

Hewitt's Antiques
228 N. Market St.
316/264-2450

Reflections
550 N. Rock Road
316/267-7477

Somewhere in Time
30 N.W. Pkwy.
316/681-1007

Yesterdays
535 N. Woodlawn St.
316/684-1900

Vanderkellen Galleries
701 E. 2nd St. N.
316/264-0338

Hephner Antiques
737 S. Washington St., #3
316/264-3284

Country Sentiments
200 S. 61st St.
316/744-9403

Granny's Shanty
405 N. West St.
316/942-6222

Great Places to Stay

The Castle Inn Riverside

1155 N. River Blvd.
316/263-9300 or 1-800-580-1131

Salve:

This Latin message greets all guests to the Castle Inn Riverside. Carved in stone over the drive, it is one of the many details that will speak to you during your stay. Built in 1888 by Burton Harvey Campbell, this architectural masterpiece was  fashioned after a castle located in the foothills of Scotland. It is more than mortar and limestone, it is the result of one man's dream and several architects' expertise.

The stonework is known as "rough rock face," a style that presents the roughest natural surface of the gray limestone, which came from the Butler Country quarry. Materials also came from farther away. The original floors were created in Chicago by Behl and Company; the hardware was ordered directly from the factory in New York, and the stairwell, fireplaces, lamps and fixtures were imported from Europe.

For 20 years, the mansion remained the property of Campbell. In 1910, Walter Morris purchased the estate for less than a third of what it cost to build.

Fifty years later it became the property of Maye Crumm, who began calling it Crumm Castle. For a time it housed the Belle Carter High School, an institution begun and operated by Crumm.

In April 1973, the castle was entered on the National Register of Historic Places as "a building of architectural significance."

In the '70s, the upkeep of the castle became a constant struggle. To raise funds for its survival, the 19-room mansion was opened to the public for tours of all but the rooms occupied by the Crumm family.

In 1994, the castle, a historic and beloved member of the Wichita community, was existing on borrowed time. It was then that Terry and Paula Lowry purchased the property. Out of respect for Campbell and his vision, they returned his name to the castle.

They invested all their time, energy and resources into restoring this majestic structure to its original beauty. Damaged stones were painstakingly taken apart and replaced with pieces created by expert masons. The woodwork and floors have been brought back to their original luster. The roof has been re-slated with tiles from Vermont. The plumbing was replaced with safer materials and the upstairs ballroom has been converted to luxurious suites.

Like many before them, the Lowrys had a dream of making the castle their home, but their dream is much larger. They want to share its beauty with the rest of the world.

This luxury inn features 14 uniquely appointed guest rooms, each a distinctive theme based on the heritage of the castle. Amenities include Jacuzzi tubs for two (six rooms), complimentary wine and hors d'oeuvres, and an assortment of homemade desserts and gourmet coffees served each evening.

Salve...the castle bids you welcome!

46 WINFIELD

B & B Antiques
1102 E. 5th
316/221-0457

Antique Mall of Winfield
1400 Main St.
316/221-1065

Jennys Treasures
919 Manning St.
316/221-9199

Virginia Jarvis Antiques
701 Main St.
316/221-1732

Antiques Plus Mall
1820 Main St.
316/221-6699

Louisiana

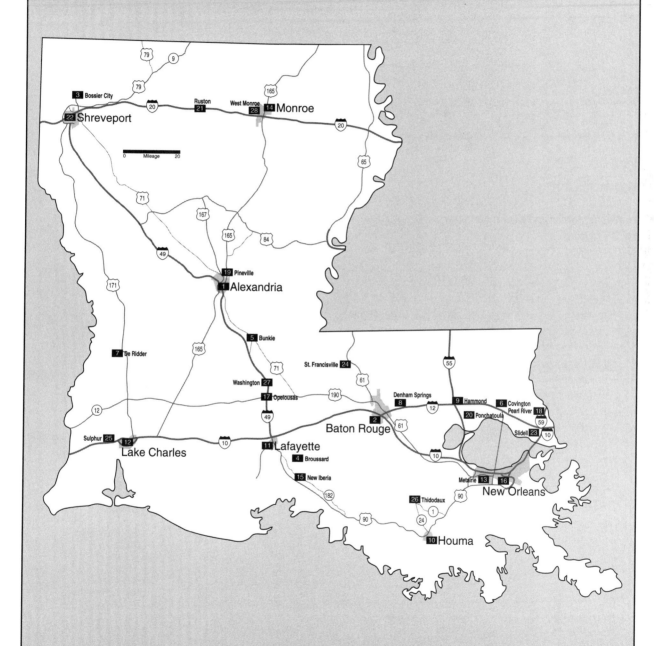

- 79
- 9
- 79
- **3** Bossier City
- 20
- Ruston **21**
- West Monroe
- 165
- **28**
- **14** Monroe
- **22** Shreveport
- 20
- Mileage
- 0   20
- 20
- 65
- 71
- 167
- 165
- 84
- 49
- **19** Pineville
- **1** Alexandria
- 171
- **5** Bunkie
- **7** De Ridder
- 165
- St. Francisville **24**
- 55
- 71
- 61
- Washington **27**
- **17** Opelousas
- 190
- Denham Springs
- **8**
- 12
- **9** Hammond
- **6** Covington
- Pearl River
- **18**
- 12
- 49
- **2**
- 61
- Baton Rouge
- **20** Ponchatoula
- 59
- Slidell **23**
- 10
- Sulphur **25**
- **12**
- 10
- **11** Lafayette
- Lake Charles
- **4** Broussard
- 10
- Metairie **13** **16**
- **15** New Iberia
- New Orleans
- 182
- **26** Thibodaux
- 90
- 24
- 1
- 90
- **10** Houma

Louisiana

1 ALEXANDRIA

Ancient Slots
3609 N. Bolton Ave.
318/473-2184

Eclectic
5528 Jackson St. Ext.
318/487-1728

Eclectic II
5416 Masonic Dr.
318/487-1728

B & N Collectibles Antiques
2000 Rapides Ave.
318/487-8910

Hirsch House Antiques
1216 Jackson St.
318/442-7764

Dantzlers Flea Market
5416 Masonic Dr.
318/443-1589

Miss Lily's
1900 Rapides Ave.
318/448-0186

Sally Foster Designs
1307 Windsor Place
318/445-5480

2 BATON ROUGE

Louisiana Purchases Auction Company
637 St. Ferdinand St.
504/346-1803

The company specializes in on-site estate auctions and tag sales. Clients should call for the next auction date because, as owner Wayne Welch says, "We never know when it will be!" He never knows what customers will do, either, as this story he tells proves:

"I once had a lady wanting to buy a piece of stained glass. At the time I had over 180 pieces. She arrived around 10 a.m. and by 2 p.m. she finally decided on one. She really wanted this piece, knowing full well it would not fit. But she bought it anyway. About 20 minutes later she came back, crying like a baby. 'It just won't fit,' she sobbed. As everyone knows, all sales are final, but this lady had already bought more glass from me than she had windows, so I asked her if she had brought the piece back. She said 'no' because of our policy. I then asked if she would be home after I closed the shop that day. After work I went over to her house and looked at the space she wanted to use the newly purchased piece of glass in. I told her to come by the store the next afternoon and I took the piece back and cut it down to fit. She came that afternoon, got it, took it home, and it fit perfectly. She is now my greatest advertisement!"

Cavalier House
8655 Bluebonnet Blvd.
504/767-9007

Jean Petit Antiques
3280 Drusilla Lane
504/924-3801

Kornmeyer Furniture Co. Inc.
7643 Florida Blvd.
504/926-0137

Merchant's Landing
9800 Florida Blvd.
504/925-1664

Lagniappe Antiques
2175 Dallas Dr.
504/927-0531

Great Heritage Antiques
5905 Florida Blvd.
504/923-1861

AAA Antiques
9800 Florida Blvd.
504/925-1664

Country Time Clocks & Gifts
11242 Florida Blvd.
504/272-4663

Guillot's Furniture Repair
1906 N. Foster Dr.
504/357-6033

Aladdins Lamp Resale Shop
2714 Government St.
504/338-1933

The Antique Group
2963 Government St.
504/387-5543

Estate Auction Gallery
3374 Government St.
504/383-7706

Shades of the Past Antiques
3374 Government St.
504/383-6911

The Decorator's Gallery
3378 Government St.
504/383-7708

Blue Pearl Antiques
3875 Government St.
504/346-8508

Atkinson Antiques
8868 Greenwell Springs Road
504/924-1941

Potluck Antiques
10044 Hooper Road
504/262-8311

Best Kept Secrets
5425 Highland Road
504/763-9066

Farm and Village
6636 Florida Blvd., Suite 10
504/924-7555

Absolutely Genius
7317 Jefferson Hwy.
504/929-9862

Keepsake Antiques & Collectibles
10912 Joor Road
504/261-3540

Wayside House Antiques, Inc.
1706 May St.
504/344-2633

Goudeau Antiques
1284 Perkins Road
504/383-7307

Stewart's Inessa Antiques
8630 Perkins Road
504/769-9363

I M Causey and Co., Inc.
501 Government St.
504/343-3421

Confederate States Military Antqs.
2905 Government St.
504/387-5044

Audubon Station & Co.
3153 Government St.
504/383-3599

River City Books
3374 Government St.
504/383-1003

Westmoreland Antique Gallery
3374 Government St.
504/383-7777

Lynns Antiques & Collectibles, Inc.
3582 Government St.
504/334-9048

Designers Custom Lamps
4375 Government St.
504/344-4674

Hearth & Home Antiques & Cllbls.
10136 Greenwell Springs Road
504/272-7544

Collectors Choice
13612 Hooper Road
504/261-1835

Highland Road Antiques
16257 Highland Road
504/752-8446

Fetzer's Interiors & Fine Antiques
711 Jefferson Hwy.
504/927-7420

Barkers Antique Jewelry
7565 Jefferson Hwy.
504/927-4406

Dixon Smith Interiors
1655 Lobdell Ave.
504/927-4261

Classic Jewelers, Inc.
7610 Old Hammond Hwy.
504/927-6299

Antique Emporium
4347 Perkins Road
504/344-5856

Sylvia's
12648 Perkins Road
504/769-7143

Country Bumpkin Antiques
13166 Perkins Road
504/769-5138

Eagles Nest Antiques
15127 Perkins Road
504/753-4748

Grandpa's Cellar
832 St. Phillip St.
504/344-7030

Country Emporium
10349 Sullivan Road
504/261-6959

3 BOSSIER CITY

Cajun Crafters Junction
1882 Airline Dr.
318/747-6555

4 BROUSSARD

Great Places to Stay

La Grande Maison
302 E. Main St.
318/837-4428
Open: Year-round
Directions: 10 miles south of I-10 or 5 miles south of the airport, exit at Broussard, turn left at light. It is the large Victorian building on the right.

Built in 1911, the La Grande Maison was once the residence of the Paul and Lawrence Billeaud family. This Victorian style home features several lovely porches and is situated on a beautifully landscaped lot with large oak trees.

The home was purchased in 1994 by Norman and Brenda Fakier. It has been completely restored to its current grand style and is listed on the National Historic Register.

The bed and breakfast offers several lovely rooms, all with private bath. A full breakfast is included.

5 BUNKIE

By-Gone Days Antiques
105 W. Magnolia St.
318/346-4940

Griffins Antiques
228 S.W. Main St.
318/346-2806

6 COVINGTON

French House Antiques
735 E. Boston at Lee Lane
504/893-4566

Antiques on Consignment
315 N. Columbia St.
504/898-0955

Fireside Antiques
14007 Perkins Road
504/752-9565

Plank Road Antiques
11728 Plank Road
504/778-0280

Landmark Antique Plaza, Inc.
832 St. Phillip St.
504/383-4867

Lums Place
7607 Tom Dr.
504/923-0745

Antique Obsession
421 N. Columbia St.
504/898-3667

Country Corner Shop
205 Lee Lane
504/892-7995

A Few of My Favorite Things
316 Lee Lane
504/867-9363

Claiborne Hill Antiques
72022 Live Oak St.
504/892-5657

Countryside
828 E. Rutland
504/893-7622

Homespun Antiques
204 W. 21st Ave.
504/892-3828

7 DE RIDDER

Secret Attic
109 S. Washington St.
318/463-4649

Uptown Deridder
113 N. Washington St.
318/463-7200

8 DENHAM SPRINGS

Louisiana Purchases Antique Mall
239 N. Range Ave.
504/665-2803
Open: Mon.–Sat. 10–5, Sun. 12–5
(after hours appointments available by calling 504/346-1803)
Directions: Located off of I-12 in Denham Springs. Take I-12 to Exit #10 and go north about 2 miles. When you cross a railroad track, you will be in "Antique Village." The mall is the last shop on the left at the traffic light.

Louisiana Purchases is one of two malls and a restaurant located under one roof, and shoppers can walk through each shop to get to the other one. In all there are 27 dealers, with several specializing in different items such as antique copper, primitives and antique stained glass. The other mall is La Maison Antique Mall, and the Brass Lantern Restaurant serves the biggest burger in town.

Romantique
104 N. Range Ave.
504/667-2283

Live Oak Antiques
111 N. Range Ave.
504/665-0488

Benton Brothers Antique Mall
115 N. Range Ave.
504/665-5146

Enchanted Attic
123 N. Range Ave.
504/664-3655

Merlyn Fine Antiques
609 E. Gibson
504/892-6099

Walker House Ltd.
221 Lee Lane
504/893-4235

Lee Lane Antique Mall
326 Lee Lane
504/893-4453

Chocolate Tulips
714 E. Rutland St.
504/893-5506

Chimes Antiques
125 N. Theard St.
504/8892-8836

Past Restored
2380 W. 21st Ave.
504/892-7475

Louisiana

Diamond Mine
201 N. Range Ave.
504/664-6463

Painted Lady Antiques
215 N. Range Ave.
504/667-1710

La Maison Antiques
235 N. Range Ave.
504/664-4001

Antiques Plus
226 N. Range Ave.
504/664-3643

9 HAMMOND

Dec's Antiques
100 E. Thomas St.
504/345-1960

10 HOUMA

Heritage House
1714 Barrow St.
504/872-3017

Country Antiques
2036 Coteau Road
504/868-4646

11 LAFAYETTE

Gateway Antiques, Inc.
200 Northgate Dr.
318/235-4989
Open: Mon.–Sat. 10–5, closed Sun.
Directions: Traveling I-10: Take Exit #103A to the first traffic light (East Willow). Take a left at the East Willow light and make another left behind Montgomery Ward in the Northgate Mall. This is Northgate Dr. and the shop is in back of the Montgomery Ward parking lot. It can be seen at the East Willow light if you look to your left.

Gateway Antiques concentrates mostly on smalls and glassware, pottery, toys, perfume bottles, jewelry, jars and boxes, pieces of Roseville, Hull and Fiestaware, with some tools added for good measure.

Accent Studios, Inc.
805 W. University Ave.
318/233-0186

Stewart's
1000 Coolidge Blvd.
318/232-2957

Clock House
326 Duhon Road
318/984-1779

Way Back When Antiques
208 N. Range Ave.
504/667-4169

Hart to Heart Antiques
219 N. Range Ave.
504/667-4018

Backwards Glance
222 N. Range Ave.
504/667-9779

Theater Antiques
228 N .Range Ave.
504/665-4666

Bayou Antiques
2011 Bayou Blue Road
504/873-7500

Antq Gallery of Houma, Inc.
3382 Little Bayou Black
504/857-8237

Coin & Treasure Co.
2474 W. Congress St.
318/237-2646

Bouligny Interiors, Inc.
331 Doucet Road
318/984-2030

Fazy's
1416 Eraste Landry Road
318/269-5800

Ole Fashion Things
402 S.W. Evangeline Thruway
318/234-4800

Antiques & Interiors, Inc.
616 General Mouton Ave.
318/234-4776

Auntie Em's
410 Jefferson St.
318/233-9362

Lafayette Antique Market
2015 Johnston St.
318/269-9430

Julia Martha Antiques Et Cie
3601 Johnston St.
318/981-9847

Gala's Unique Antiques & Gifts
922 Kaliste Saloom Road
318/235-7816

Granny's Attic
410 Mudd Ave.
318/237-6418

Renaissance Market
321 Oil Center Dr.
318/234-1116

Graham's Antiques & Accents
1891 W Pinhook Road
318/234-5045

Hallmark Interiors & Antiques
412 Travis St.
318/234-5997

Accent Studios, Inc.
805 W. University Ave.
318/233-0186

Ruins and Relics
900 Evangeline Dr.
318/233-9163

Kings Rowe Antiques
326 Heymann Blvd.
318/261-5934

Gerts Antiques, Etc.
1306 Jefferson St.
318/261-2311

Antiques Et Cie
3601 Johnston St.
318/981-9847

Artisans of Louisiana
3603 Johnston St.
318/988-4280

Treasures
924 Kaliste Saloom Road
318/234-9978

Gateway Antiques, Inc.
200 Northgate Dr.
318/235-4989

La Jolie
1326 W. Pinhook Road
318/233-5319

Crowded Attic
512 N. University Ave.
318/237-5559

Crowded Attic
512 N. University Ave.
318/233-0012

Great Places to Stay

Alida's, A Bed and Breakfast
2631 S.E. Evangeline Thruway
1-800-922-5867

Alida's, A Bed & Breakfast, can best be described as a haven for the weary traveler to relax, unwind and enjoy the gracious, warm and constant attention lavished on its guests by the hosts, Tanya and Douglas Greenwald. From the deep, deep clawfoot tubs, designed for soaking, to the lively conversation during the evening social hour, to the sumptuous breakfast fit for a king, the highlight of your journey will be your stay at this lovely home. The local area features world-famous Cajun restaurants.

Louisiana

12 LAKE CHARLES

Harry's Hodge Podge
701 14th St.
318/436-6219

Chapman Antiques & Collectibles
748 Bank St.
318/436-2726

Curiosity Antique Mall
831 Kirkman St.
318/491-1170

Lacey Jade & Co.
3612 Kirkman St.
318/478-4304

Kelly's Flea Market
332 N. Martin Luther King Hwy.
318/439-0382

Reflections
608 A E Prien Lake Road
318/479-1974

Nantiques
2508 Ryan St.
318/439-0366

Bayou Furniture, Inc.
1104 Alamo St.
318/477-6456

Somewhere in Time
2802 Hodges St.
318-494-0176

Antics & Attics
1908 Kirkman St.
318/436-5265

My Sister's Closet
3735 Kirkman St.
318/474-4733

Yesterday Today & Tomorrow
138 W. Prien Lake Road
318/478-1010

My Favorite Things
216 S. Ryan St.
318/439-1900

13 METAIRIE

Sisters Antiques
114 Codifer Blvd.
504/828-6701

Olde Metairie Antique Mall
1537 Metairie Road
504/831-4514

Unique Galleries & Auction
4040 Veterans Memorial Blvd.
504/885-9000

Rare Bits
800 Metairie Road
504/837-6771

Steve M. Burgamy
2011 Metairie Road
504/831-9265

14 MONROE

B & W Antiques
407 Desiard St.
318/387-9025

Collectiques
815 Desiard St.
318/387-5974

R.J. Wills Antique Shop
1907 S. Grand St.
318/323-6150

Clarence's Old Stuff
424 Desiard St.
318/323-1306

Cottonland Crafters Mall
1119 Forsythe Ave.
318/323-2325

Camille Wood Antiques
217 Hudson Lane
318-323-8979

15 NEW IBERIA

Jaja's Just Things
609 Charles St.
318/367-2141

Rose Antique Ville
2007 Freyou Road
318/367-3000

Magnolia Antiques
203 E. Main St.
318/365-5285

Janie's Vintage Jewelry
105 E. Saint Peter St.
318/365-8323

Lantiques
311 W. Saint Peter St.
318/364-8517

Bo's Attic Antiques
231 Pollard Ave.
318/364-1093

Kimberly Interiors, Inc.
105 E. Saint Peter St.
318/365-8323

16 NEW ORLEANS

Didier, Inc.
3439 Magazine St.
504/899-7749

This exclusive shop on Magazine Street specializes in period American furniture (1800-1840) and the accompanying decorative arts. Primarily the furniture is from Boston, Philadelphia, New York City and Baltimore. Everything is housed in an 1850s period home, completely restored to that era. The shop has clients who have been with them since 1970. Their decorative arts consist of period prints, paintings, glass and porcelain - absolutely no reproductions.

Bienville Antique Shoppe
4600 Bienville St.
504/488-2428

Cass-Garr Company
237 Chartres St.
504/522-8298

Button Shoppe
328 Chartres St.
504/523-6557

Lucullus
610 Chartres St.
504/528-9620

Animal Art Antiques
617 Chartres St.
504/529-4407

O'Suzanna's
1231 Decatur St.
504/581-5006

Legarage Antiques & Clothing
1234 Decatur St.
504/522-6639

Framboyan
624 Dumaine St.
504/558-9241

Antiques by Ruppert
1018 Harmony St.
504/895-6394

Whisnant Galleries
222 Chartres St.
504/524-9766

Blackamoor Antiques, Inc.
324 Chartres St.
504/523-7786

Ray J. Piehet Gallery-Antiques
608 Chartres St.
504/525-2806

Molieres Antique Shop
612 Chartres St.
504/525-9479

Adrian's Antiques
618 Conti St.
504/525-4615

Collectible Antiques
1232 Decatur St.
504-566-0399

Tomato Warehouse
1237 Decatur St.
504/524-2529

Ruebarb Gallery
1101 First at Magazine St.
504/523-4301

Kohlmaier & Kohlmaier
1018 Harmony St.
504/895-6394

Louisiana

Ole Hickory Antique Clock Repair
216 Hickory Ave.
504/737-2937

Stan Levy Imports, Inc.
1028 Louisiana Ave.
504/899-6384

Java Nola
1313 Magazine St.
504/558-0369

Shop of Two Sisters
1800 Magazine St.
504/586-8325

Aaron's Antique Mall
2014 Magazine St.
504/523-0630

Audubon Antiques
2025 Magazine St.
504/581-5704

Dodge-Fjeld Antiques
2033 Magazine St.
504/581-6930

Jim Smiley Vintage Clothing
2001 Magazine St.
504/528-9449

Mr. Anthony's Town & Country Antiques
2049 Magazine St.
504/451-7314

Renaissance Shop
2104 Magazine St.
504/525-8568

Shades of Light
2108 Magazine St.
504/524-6500

Eclectique Antiques
2112 Magazine St.
504/525-4668

Belle Mina Antique
2127 Magazine St.
504/523-3222

Bernard Regenbogen Furniture Store
2208 Magazine St.
504/522-6351

Christopher's Discoveries
2842 Magazine St.
504/899-6226

Susan Taylor Interiors
3005 Magazine St.
504/891-0123

Antiques, Etc.
8400 Jefferson Hwy.
504/737-3503

Charbonnet & Charbonnet Antiques
2929 Magazine St.
504/891-9948

Lee Ali Interiors Unlimited
1800 Magazine St.
504/586-8325

Antebellum Antiques
2011 Magazine St.
504/558-0208

Hands
2023 Magazine St.
504/522-2590

Antiques Magazine
2028 Magazine St.
504/522-2043

Miss Edna's Antiques
2035 Magazine St.
504/524-1897

Attic Treasures
2039 Magazine St.
504/588-1717

Bep's Antiques
2051 Magazine St.
504/525-7726

Mona Mia's
2105 Magazine St.
504/525-8686

Bush Antiques
2109 Magazine St.
504/581-3518

Antique Vault
2123 Magazine St.
504/523-8888

Magazine Antique Mall
2205 Magazine St.
504/524-0100

Dombourian Oriental Rugs, Inc.
2841 Magazine St.
504/891-6601

Antiques & Things
2855 Magazine St.
504/897-9466

Magazine Arcade Antiques
3017 Magazine St.
504/895-5451

As You Like It Silver Shop
3029 Magazine St.
504/897-6915

The Private Connection
3927 Magazine St.
504/593-9526

Grand Antiques
3125 Magazine St.
504/897-3179

Empire Antiques
3420 Magazine St.
504/897-0252

Blackamoor Antiques, Inc.
3433 Magazine St.
504/897-2711

Custom Linens
3638 Magazine St.
504/899-0604

Brass Image
3801 Magazine St.
504/897-1861

Wirthmore Antiques
3900 Magazine St.
504/899-3811

Jean Bragg Antiques
3901 Magazine St.
504/895-7375

Aux Belles Choses
3912 Magazine St.
504/891-1009

C. Susman — Estate Jewelry
3933 Magazine St.
504/897-9144

Judy, A Gallery
3941 Magazine St.
504/891-7018

Country at Heart
3952 Magazine St.
504/891-5412

Dellwen Antiques
3954-56 Magazine St.
504/897-3617

Davis Gallery
3964 Magazine St.
504/897-0780

Gizmo's
4118-4122 Magazine St.
504/897-6868

Shaker Shop
3029 Magazine St.
504/895-8646

Finders Keepers
3118 Magazine St.
504/895-2702

Esfahani Oriental Rugs
3218 Magazine St.
504/895-5550

French Collectibles
3424 Magazine St.
504/897-9020

Didier, Inc.
3439 Magazine St.
504/899-7749

K & K Design Studios
3646 Magazine St.
504/897-2290

Uptowner Antiques
3828 Magazine St.
504/891-7700

Collector Antiques
3901 Magazine St.
504/895-7375

Orient Expressed Imports, Inc.
3905 Magazine St.
504/899-3060

Mimano
3917 Magazine St.
504/895-9436

Anne Pratt
3937 Magazine St.
504/891-6532

Jacqueline Vance
3944 Magazine St.
504/891-3304

The Sitting Duck Gallery
3953 Magazine St.
504/899-2007

Mac Maison, Ltd.
3963 Magazine St.
504/891-2863

Neal Auction Co.
4038 Magazine St.
504/899-5329

Emil Moore & Co., LLC
4119 Magazine St.
504/891-1198

Louisiana

Talebloo Oriental Rugs
4130 Magazine St.
504/899-8114

Sigi Russell Antiques
4304 Magazine St.
504/891-5390

Custom Woodwork & Antiques
4507 Magazine St.
504/891-1664

Carol Robinson Gallery
4537 Magazine St.
504/899-6130

Jon Antiques
4605 Magazine St.
504/899-4482

19th Century Antiques
4838 Magazine St.
504/891-4845

Wirthmore Antiques
5723 Magazine St.
504/897-9727

Enoch's Framing & Gallery
6063 Magazine St.
504/899-6686

Apropos
3806 Magazine St.
504/899-3500

Au Vieux Paris Antiques
7219 Perrier St.
504/866-6677

Diane Genre Oriental Art & Antiques
233 Royal St.
504/525-7270

Dixon & Dixon
237 Royal St.
504/524-0282

Royal Antiques, Ltd.
309 Royal St.
504/524-7033

Jack Sutton Antiques
315 Royal St.
504/522-0555

Keil's Antiques
325 Royal St.
504/522-4552

J. Herman Son Galleries
333 Royal St.
504/525-6326

Berta's and Mina's Antiquities
4138 Magazine St.
504/895-6201

Top Drawer Auction & Appraisals
4310 Magazine St.
504/832-9080

Fraza Framing & Art Gallery
4532 Magazine St.
504/899-7002

Modell's Rostor & Polsg, Inc.
4600 Magazine St.
504/895-5267

Melange Sterling
5421 Magazine St.
504/899-4796

Pettie Pence Antique
4904 Magazine St.
504/891-3353

The Tulip Tree
5831 Magazine St.
504/895-3748

Le Wicker Gazebo
3715 Magazine St.
504/899-1355

Driscoll Antiques & Restorations
8118 Oak St.
504/866-7795

French Antique Shop, Inc.
225 Royal St.
504/524-9861

Brass Monkey
235 Royal St.
504/561-0688

Rothschild's
241 Royal St.
504/523-5816

Robinson's Antiques
313 Royal St.
504/523-6683

Rothschild's
321 Royal St.
504/523-2281

Royal Co.
325 Royal St.
504/522-4552

Waldhorn — Adler
343 Royal St.
504/581-6379

Manheim Galleries
409 Royal St.
504/568-1901

Cynthia Sutton
429 Royal St.
504/523-3377

Gerald D Katz Antiques
505 Royal St.
504/524-5050

Royal Art Gallery, Ltd.
537 Royal St.
504/524-6070

M. S. Rau, Inc.
630 Royal St.
504/523-5660

Regency House Antiques
841 Royal St.
504/524-7507

Barakat
934 Royal St.
504/593-9944

W M Antiques
1029 Royal St.
504/524-1253

Riccas Architectural Sales
511 N Solomon St.
504/488-5524

Harper's Antiques
610 Toulouse St.
504/592-1996

Moss Antiques
411 Royal St.
504/522-3981

Jack Sutton Co., Inc.
501 Royal St.
504/581-3666

Le Petit Soldier Shop
528 Royal St.
504/523-7741

Harris Antiques, Ltd.
623 Royal St.
504/523-1605

L.M.S. Fine Arts & Antiques
729 Royal St.
504/529-3774

Patout Antiques
922 Royal St.
504/522-0582

Sigles Antiques & Metalcrafts
935 Royal St.
504/522-7647

Centuries Old Maps & Prints
517 Saint Louis St.
504/568-9491

Nina Sloss Antiques & Interiors
1001 State St.
504/895-8088

The Westgate
5219 Magazine St.
504/899-3077

Great Places to Stay

Bywater Guest House
908 Poland Ave.
504/949-6381 or 1-888-615-7498
Email: bywatergh@aol.com
Web site: members.aol.com/bywatergh
Directions: A relaxed, comfortable atmosphere in an 1872 Eastlake Victorian home located in the Bywater National Historic District, 1 mile from the French Quarter.

Located on the site of the Audey Plantation, later known as the Faubourg Washington, Bywater Guest House is located one and one-half miles down river from the French Quarter.

The house was built in 1872, in the Victorian style by Michael Darby, an American engineer. The main building construction shows styles influenced by Charles Eastlake. The site also holds the original kitchen, or cookhouse, which by law had to be a separate structure, and one of the first three-car garages in the City of New Orleans. The house is

Louisiana

furnished in antique and reproduction appointments and original artwork.

The innkeepers at Bywater Guest House take pride in providing a relaxed, comfortable environment for their guests. Amenities for the three guest rooms include: comfortable queen-size beds with feather mattresses and down duvets, writing tables and Queen Anne-style chairs. The full breakfast includes a hot entree, fresh fruit and juice, coffee, tea and breads.

Dusty Mansion

2231 General Pershing St.
504/895-4576
Open: Year-round
Rates $50-75

Just six blocks from the St. Charles Ave. streetcar, Dusty Mansion is ideally located for weekend exploration and enjoyment of New Orleans. This is a homey, casual inn on a quiet residential street just on the edge of the Garden District in the Historic Bouligny Plantation District. It's a turn-of-the-century, two-story frame house with wide front porch and porch swing, original hardwood floors and cypress woodwork and doors. The four guest rooms (two with private bath) have romantic ceiling fans and are filled with antiques and reproduction pieces. The four beds are queen-sized and are either brass, canopied, sleigh or white enameled iron. A continental-plus breakfast is served in the dining room, and afterwards you can explore, relax and catch some rays on the sundeck, read or nap on the shaded patio, play pool or table tennis, and later, ease into the hot tub secluded in the gazebo.

17   OPELOUSAS

Doucet's Acadiana Antiques

1665 N. Main St.
318/942-3425
Open: Mon.–Fri. 9:30–5, Sat. 9–3:30, closed Sun.–Mon.
Directions: From I-49 take the Opelousas exit and follow the signs to Hwy. 182 N. (Main is also known as Hwy. 182 N.). The shop is located across from Soileau's Dinner Club.

Doucet's is a well-heeled shop that has been providing superior pieces since 1928. They handle only fine 18th and 19th century antiques, paintings and collectibles from France and England. This is truly a shop to visit if you are looking for high end French or English period pieces.

Opelousas Antique Mall
353 E. Landry St.
318/942-5620

18   PEARL RIVER

Anns Place Antiques
39613 Pecan Dr.
504/641-2754

19   PINEVILLE

Peck's Antiques
706 Pearce Road
318/640-0006

Beaten Path Antiques
6892 Hwy. 28 E.
318/445-9425

Peck's Antiques
706 Pearce Road
318/640-0006

Jessie's Antique Barn
5632 Hwy. 28 E.
318/473-8347

Handmaiden & Friends
318 Maryhill Road
318-640-3727

20   PONCHATOULA

Remember When Antiques

223 W. Pine St.
504/386-6159
Open: Wed.–Sun. 10–5

This large and spacious mall carries everything from Victorian to primitives, but concentrates primarily on furnishings and glassware accessories.

Ponchatoula Antiques

400 W. Pine St.
504/386-7809
Open: Wed.–Sun. 10–5

This mall carries antiques, but their main focus is on fountains and statuary! They handle new fountains (not antique ones) and statuary in a variety of themes, and have at least 200 fountains on display at all times. The statuary is the free-standing yard and garden variety. If you're looking to add a touch of the exotic or a touch of luxury to your yard and garden, look here first.

Alford's General Store
114 E. Pine St.
504/386-0111

Yesteryear Antiques
165 E. Pine St.
504/386-2741

Country Market
10 W. Pine St.
504/386-9580

Memory Lane
105 W. Pine St.
504/386-2812

Oldies and Goodies
138 W. Pine St.
504/386-0150

Layrisson Walker, Ltd.
123 E. Pine St.
504/386-8759

Ellen's Antiques & Collectibles
179 E. Pine St.
504/386-3564

Needful Things
101 W. Pine St.
504/386-2918

Country Carousel Antiques
120 W. Pine St.
504/386-2271

Red Baron Antiques, Inc.
139 W. Pine St.
504/386-8792

Wholesale Antiques
152 W. Pine St.
504/386-8086

Ma Meres
165 W. Pine St.
504/386-0940

Remember When
223 W. Pine St.
504/386-6159

C.J.'s Antiques & Collectibles
160 S.E. Railroad Ave.
504/386-0026

21 RUSTON

Deep South Antiques
Hwy. 167 N.
318/255-5278

Railroad Depot
101 E. Railroad Ave.
318/255-3103

Times Past Antiques
103 N. Trenton St.
318/254-8279

Pot Luck
202 N. Vienna St.
318/254-1331

22 SHREVEPORT

Hudson House Antiques
3118 Gilbert
318/865-2151

Heirloom Antiques
3004 Highland Ave.
318/226-0146

Hudson House Antiques
109 Kings Hwy.
318/868-9579

Kings Ransom
133 Kings Hwy.
318/865-4811

Katie-Beths Antiques
3316 Line Ave.
318/868-5246

Hinton Gallery
3324 Line Ave.
318/868-0018

Then & Now
6030 Line Ave.
318/865-6340

Courtyard Antiques
155 W. Pine St.
504\386-9569

Roussel's Specialty Shop
177 W. Pine St.
504/386-9097

Ponchatoula Antiques, Inc.
400 W. Pine St.
504/386-7809

Roussel's Annex
138 N. 6th St.
504/386-9096

Michael's Furniture Mart
305 W. Mississippi Ave.
318/251-9409

Acorn Creek Antiques
1323 S. Service Road W.
318/255-1831

Park Ave Antique Mall
108 N. Vienna St.
318/255-4866

Bullock's
1723 Highland Ave.
318/226-9168

Caloways Antiques & Bygones
811 Jefferson Place
318/221-5493

D&B Russell — Books
129 Kings Hwy.
318/865-5198

Enchanted Gardens
2429 Line Ave.
318/227-1213

Arrangement
3322 Line Ave.
318/868-6812

Jack Farmer Antiques
6018 Line Ave.
318/869-3297

Corrente Oriental Antiques
6401 Line Ave.
318/868-3833

Golden Pineapple
6104 Line Ave., #5
318/868-3691

Pilgrim's Progress
6535 Line Ave.
318-868-3383

Estate Sale Consignment
2847 Summer Grove
318/687-7525

Gozas Gallery, Inc.
5741 Youree Dr.
318/868-3429

Nigel's Heirloom Antique Gallery
421 Texas St.
318/226-0146

23 SLIDELL

Recollections
2265 Carey St.
504/641-9410

Magnolia House Antiques
228 Erlanger St.
504/641-3776

La Jolie Maison
1944 1st St.
504/649-7055

Vintage Antiques & Collectibles
1958 1st St.
504/649-5968

Little Green House Antiques
1732 Front St.
504/643-5176

Slidell Antique Market
806 Cousin St.
504/649-0579

Something Old/Something New
1929 2nd St.
504/649-8088

The Antique Store
1944 1st St.
504/649-7055

24 ST. FRANCISVILLE

C & D Collectible Now & Then
217 Ferdinand St.
504/635-3606

Something Special
11911 Ferdinand St.
504/635-9804

London Gallery Antiques
6401 Line Ave.
318/868-3691

Red Caboose Antiques
855 Pierremont Road
318/865-5376

Lost & Found Antiques
2847 Summer Grove
318/687-1896

Antique Mall
546 Olive St.
318/425-8786

Barbara's Victorian Closet
124 Erlanger St.
504/641-6316

Bon MeNage Gallery
1922 1st St.
504/646-0488

Wishing Well
1952 1st St.
504/646-0801

First Street Antiques
1960 1st St.
504/643-6727

Slidell Trading Post
40137 Hwy. 190 E.
504/643-1606

Victorian Tea Room
228 Carey St.
504/643-7881

Parc Antique Mall
2019 2nd St.
504/649-0410

Horaist "A Design Experience"
1654 Front St.
504/643-3030

Honeysuckles
11739 Ferdinand St.
504/635-3367

Pretty Things Antiques
11917 Ferdinand St.
504/635-0308

Louisiana

Great Places to Stay

Barrow House
524 Royal St.
504/635-4791

This beautiful, picturesque building is sitting right in the middle of the historic district of St. Francisville, a wonderful location for exploration. The two-story section was built in 1809 in the salt-box style, while the one-story wing and Greek Revival facade were added in 1855. The inn offers guests one suite and four double rooms, three of them with private baths. Antiques from the 1860s fill every nook and cranny of the historic building and guests are served wonderful dinners in the formal dining room.

25 SULPHUR

Miss Peggy's Antiques & Collectibles
208 S. Huntington St.
318/527-5027

Sherry's Antique & Gift Shop
210 W. Napoleon St.
318/528-3346

Costwold
2223 Maplewood Dr.
381/625-3367

Finders Keepers
414 E. Napoleon St.
318/527-7070

26 THIBODAUX

Dodge City Mall
1213 Canal Blvd.
504/447-4411

Sweet Memories
602 Green St.
504/446-1140

Angela's Antiques
517 Jackson St.
504/446-3641

Lafourche Antiques and Co.
424 Saint Mary St.
504/449-1635

Mainstreet
606 W. 3rd St.
504/449-1001

Erwin's Antique Bank
413 W. 4th St.
504/446-5827

Andree's Antiques
416 Jackson St.
504/447-5889

Terry's Antiques
5504 W. Main St.
504/449-1600

Bryson's Angels
511 St. Phillip
504/447-1800

Debbie's Antiques
705 W. Third
504/633-5680

27 WASHINGTON

O'Connor's Antiques School Mall
210 S. Church St.
318/826-3580

Cajun Antiques
400 S. Main St.
318/826-3710

28 WEST MONROE

Anderson Collection
204 Trenton St.
318/388-0366

River Run Antiques
303 Trenton St.
318/324-0517

Martha's Unfinished Furniture
311 Trenton St.
318/323-1454

O'Kelley's Antiques
313 Trenton St.
318/329-9409

Imperial Galleries Antiques & Fine Arts
317 Trenton St.
318/361-9458

Virginia's Antiques
320 Trenton St.
318/324-9885

Sawyer's Antiques
4352 Whites Ferry Road
318/397-1292

Trenton Street Antique Mall
215 Trenton St.
318/325-9294

Memory Lane Antiques
301 Trenton St.
381/323-3188

Trenton Street Gallery
319 Trenton St.
318/329-9200

Cotton's Collectibles
255 Trenton St.
318/322-6479

Sanderson's Antiques
310 Trenton St.
318/325-0089

Trenton Street Images
312 Trenton St.
318/322-2691

Potpourri de Marie Tante
314 Trenton St.
318/325-0103

Chandler's Antiques
318 Trenton St.
318/322-3925

Old Trenton Country Store
323 Trenton St.
318/323-7152

The Side Track
101 Trenton St.
318/323-9501

Marie's Antiques & Glass
224 Trenton St.
318/388-0908

Sanderson's Antique Mall
308 & 310 Trenton St.
318/325-0089

Minnesota

0 Mileage 20

53

2

2 Bemidji

169

17 Hibbing

12 Eveleth

29 Nevis

371

2

Duluth 10

34 Palisade

210

31 Nisswa

9 Crosby

3 Brainerd

28 Motley

210

371

169

35

23

94

St. Cloud

39

10

11 Elk River

8 Chisago City

35 Paynesville

5 Buffalo

1 Anoka

15 Forest Lake

24 Maple Plain

Minneapolis
27

42 Stillwater

19 Hutchinson

13 Excelsior

St. Paul
40

94

12

38

Shakopee

6 Burnsville

16 Hastings

Lakeville 20

25 Marshall

Northfield 32

36 Red Wing

7 Cannon Falls

New Ulm
30

41 St. Peter

14 Faribault

52

26 Mazeppa

61

33 Oronoco

22 Mankato

23 Mantorville

37 Rochester

43 Winona

23

169

90

35

21 Luverne

44 Worthington

90

14

Inset: Twin Cities

35W

4 Brooklyn Center

694

35E

94

94

12 394

Minneapolis
27

40 St. Paul

694

94

94

18 Hopkins

494

35W

35E

494

Minnesota

1 ANOKA

Round Barn
3331 Bunker Lake Blvd. N.W.
612/427-5321

Amore Antiques
2008 2nd Ave.
612/576-1871

Cat's Den of Antiques
2010 2nd Ave.
612-323-3613

Antiques on Main
212 E. Main St.
612/323-3990

Yours Mine & Ours Antiques
2014 2nd Ave.
612/422-4959

2 BEMIDJI

Bargain Junction
3220 Adams N.W./Hwy. 2 W.
218/751-5036

Louise's Antiques
RR 8 #597
218/751-3577

Anntiques
301 3rd St. N.W.
218/751-2144

Back in Time Antiques
1105 15th St. N.W.
218/759-0206

Brier Patch Antiques
RR 3 #546
218/751-8832

Oelrich's Antique Shop
1114 America Ave. N.W.
218/751-5126

3 BRAINERD

Karen's Antiques & Things
Downtown
218/825-7355

Antiques on Laurel
711 Laurel
218/828-1584

Antiques & Accents-Brainerd
214 S. 7th St.
218/828-0724

Hyland Antiques
1466 Hwy. 371 N.
218/828-8838

Bargains on 7th
211 S. 7th St.
218/829-8822

4 BROOKLYN CENTER

Great Places to Stay

Inn on the Farm
6150 Summit Dr. N.
1-800-428-8382

The Inn on the Farm at Earle Brown Heritage Center offers a bed and breakfast experience you'll never forget. Housed in a cluster of historic farm buildings the inn is located on the grounds of a beautifully restored Victorian gentleman's country estate, just 10 minutes from the heart of downtown Minneapolis. You may choose from eleven exquisitely furnished and beautifully decorated bedrooms, each with private whirlpool bath.

5 BUFFALO

Behind The Picket Fence
30 Central Ave.
612/682-9490

Vintage Mall
8 E. Division St.
612/682-0600

Buffalo Nickel Antique Mall
Hwy. 55
612/682-4735

Annie's Attic
1205 State Hwy. 25 N.
612/682-2818

Division Street Antiques
7 Division St.
612/682-6453

Buffalo Bay Antiques
11 E. Division St.
612/682-1825

Waldon Woods Antiques
2612 State Hwy. 55 S.E.
612/682-5667

6 BURNSVILLE

Robinson Cruise O Antiques
1509 W. 152nd St.
612/435-7327
Open: Available all hours and all days, call ahead
Directions: From Minneapolis, go south on Hwy. 35 West to Burnsville, to County Road 42 West. From County Road 42 West, go until exit onto County Road 5. Turn west on 152nd Street.

In Juanita Robinson's backyard in Burnsville, Minnesota, you will find a dry-docked 35-foot cruiser which has become Robinson Cruise O Antiques.

According to Mrs. Robinson, the boat was built in the late thirties by Mr. Olson, a steel worker by trade. It weighs between 12 and 18 tons and is all steel except the after cabin, which was a later addition. It was designed as a paddle wheeler, but with one critical problem: it would not back up! So the boat was hauled to the backyard until Mr. Olson's death.

In the '50s it was sold to Mr. Batcher who modified it, removed the paddle wheel, and built an after cabin. Proving to be too much to handle, the old boat was sold to the Robinson's who used it for weekend recreation.

After 15 years of use the Robinson Cruise O was dry-docked in the Robinson's 2-acre backyard. Time and disuse took their toll until Mrs. Robinson restored the old boat and converted it into an antique shop.

Primitives form a large part of her inventory, but she also displays dolls, hurricane lamps, dish and kitchen goods, as well as brass, stained glass and buttons. This old boat may not be seaworthy any more, but the old Robinson Cruise O is certainly worth seeing.

Hagen's Furniture & Antiques
2041 W. Burnsville Pkwy.
612/894-5500

Touch of Countree
14150 Nicollet Ave.
612/435-3688

Minnesota

7 CANNON FALLS

Schaffer's Antiques Downtown
Downtown
507/263-5200

Country Side Antique Mall
Old Hwy. #525
507/263-0352

Fourth Street Antiques
106 4th St.
507/263-7249

8 CHISAGO CITY

Chisago Antique Co-op
10635 Railroad Ave.
612/257-8325

Glyer Block Antiques
10675 Railroad Ave.
612/257-3043

Kichi-Saga Antiques & Art
10645 Railroad Ave.
612/257-8273

9 CROSBY

Linda's Collectibles
10 W. Main St.
218/546-8233

Den of Antiquity
108 W. Main St.
218/546-5385

Alice's Antiques
22 First St. N.W.
218/546-6685

Crosby Collectible Co-op
Main St.
218/546-5385

Hallett Antique Emporium
28 W. Main St.
218/546-5444

C & H Odds & Ends
425 Mesaba
218/546-5899

Iron Hills Antiques & Gun
128 W. Main St.
218/546-6783

10 DULUTH

Brass Bed Antiques
329 Canal Park Dr.
218/722-1347

Sunset Antiques
2705 E. 5th St.
218/724-8215

Antiques on Superior St.
11 W. Superior St.
218/722-7962

Antique Collectible Emporium
314 E. Superior St.
218/722-1275

Old Town Antiques & Books
102 E. Superior St.
218/722-5426

Antique Centre-Duluth
335 Canal Park Dr.
218/726-1994

Greysolon Arms
1920 Greysolon Road
218/724-8387

Neil Shakespeare Antiques
38 E. Superior St.
218/723-8100

Canal Park General Store
10 Sutphin St.
218/722-7223

Woodland Antiques
1535 Woodland Ave.
218/728-1996

11 ELK RIVER

Art Barn
20700 Hwy. 169
612/441-7959

Antique Clock Doctor
7808 N.E. River Road
612/441-3456

Antiques Downtown
309 Jackson Ave.
612/441-1818

Historical Fragments
7808 N.E. River Road
612/441-5889

12 EVELETH

Wildrose Antiques & Collectibles
616 Grant Ave.
218/744-3053

Garden Cottage
7687 Wilson Road
218/744-4803

13 EXCELSIOR

Antiquity Rose & Dining Room
429 2nd St.
612/474-2661

Excelsior Coin & Collectibles
449 2nd St.
612/474-4789

Collectors Choice
227 Water St.
612/474-6117

Country Look-In Antiques
240 Water St.
612/474-0050

John Ferm Coins
449 2nd St.
612/474-9223

Mary O'Neal & Co.
221 Water St.
612/470-0205

Leipold's Gifts & Antiques
239 Water St.
612/474-5880

14 FARIBAULT

Curiosity Shop Antiques
3052 Cedar Lake Blvd.
507/334-5959

Dimestore Antique Mall
310 Central Ave. N.
507/332-8699

Collectors Antique Gallery
409 Central Ave. N.
507/332-7967

Country Antiques
212 Central Ave. N.
507/332-2331

Keepers Antique Shop
403 Central Ave. N.
507/334-7673

Stoeckel's Antique Clocks & Dolls
615 3rd St. N.W.
507/334-7772

15 FOREST LAKE

Now Showing Antiques & Collectibles
119 Lake St. N.E.
612/464-2286

Signs of the Past
4864 210th St. N.
612/786-4201

Muriel & Friends Antiques
1031 Lake St. S.E.
612/464-1954

Gold-Dusters
143 Lake St. N.E.
612/464-4442

16 HASTINGS

Carroll's Antiques
107 2nd St. E.
612/437-1912

Cherished Treasures
116 2nd St. E.
612/480-8881

Madeline's
205 2nd St E
612/480-8129

Olde Main St. Antiques
216 2nd St. E.
612/438-9265

Hastings Antique Market
375 33rd St. W.
612/437-7412

Village General Antiques
14570 240th St. E.
612/437-8150

Great Places to Stay

Hearthwood Bed & Breakfast
17650 200th St. E.
612/437-1133

Tucked into the bluffs of the Mississippi River Valley between the historic cities of Hastings and Red Wing, this six bedroom home blends a quaint timber facade with Cape Cod architectural influences. A rural setting of oak, paper birch, and other upland plants nestle the visitor into a sense of one with nature. Come and walk the two nature trails on this estate. One is for the adventurous while the other is for a casual romantic stroll.

17 HIBBING

Northland Antiques & Collectibles
11192 Hwy. 37
218/263-4427

C.T. Antiques
Hwy. 37
218/262-1891

Antique Treasure Trove
3798 S. Pintar Road
218/263-7246

Anties Attic Antiques
1621 13th Ave. E.
218/262-3159

18 HOPKINS

K & C Trains
1409 Cambridge St.
612/935-5007

Blake Antiques
1115 Excelsior Ave. E.
612/930-0477

Mary Francis
901 Main St.
612/930-3283

Hopkins Antique Mall
1008 Main St.
612/931-9748

19 HUTCHINSON

Schaffer's Antiques
16457 Hwy. 7
320/587-4321

Main Street Antiques
122 Main St. N.
320/587-6305

Barb's Country Collectibles & Antiques
12634 Ulm Ave.
320/587-9144

20 LAKEVILLE

Hot Sam's Antiques & Furniture
22820 Pillsbury Ave.
612/469-5922

Nampara Farm Antiques
10196 234th St. E.
612/985-5665

21 LUVERNE

Duane's Glassware & Antiques
Brown Church, Estey and Main St.
507/283-2586

Hillside Antiques
County Road 4-RR 3, Box 22B
507/283-2985

Larry's Furniture Refinishing
RR 1 Box 84
507/283-2275

22 MANKATO

Arts & Antiques Emporium
1575 Mankato Place
507/387-6199

Northwind Antiques
110 E. Washington St.
507/388-9166

Antique Mart
529 S. Front St.
507/345-3393

Earthly Remains
731 S. Front St.
507/388-5063

Save Mor Antiques & Jewelry
816 N. 2nd St.
507/345-5508

23 MANTORVILLE

This quaint little town in the picturesque valley of the middle fork of the Zumbro River, with its wealth of architectural heritage, Mantorville, Minn., was named to the National Register of Historic Places in 1975. A visit here opens the door to many historical pursuits.

This tiny town is probably most famous for one of its limestone buildings constructed in 1854, the Hubbell House Hotel. In its early days, the hotel was a 16x24-foot-long structure and was the only building in town having a double roof, thereby allowing room in the chamber for guests.

In 1856, the present three-story structure was built, and it immediately became an important stopping place along the trail from Mississippi to St. Peter. Senator Alexander Ramsey, General Ulysses S. Grant, Dwight D. Eisenhower, American journalist Horace Greeley, Roy Rogers and Mickey Mantle were but a few of the many guests who took relaxation in the pleasant facilities provided at the Hubbell House.

In 1946, Paul Pappas purchased the old hotel and opened its doors as a first-class restaurant. Although times have changed, early American hospitality is still available at the Hubbell House. Excellent food and outstanding service are still provided for the many visitors who happen upon this wonderful little town called Mantorville.

Grand Old Mansion Bed & Breakfast
No address listed
507/635-3231

Carl's Cut Crystal
5th St.
507/635-5690

Minnesota

Pfeifer's Eden Bed & Breakfast
R.R. 1 (7 miles from Mantorville)
507/527-2021

Memorabilia Antiques
5th St.
507/635-5419

The Chocolate Shoppe
5th St.
507/635-5814

24 MAPLE PLAIN

Country School House Shops
5300 U.S. Hwy. 12
612/479-6353
Open: Daily 10–6
Directions: Located 25 miles west of Minneapolis. Go west from
Minneapolis on Interstate 394 (U.S. Hwy. 12) to Maple Plain.

Plan to spend some time here because there is just so much to see. Set
in an old 3-story schoolhouse are 100 dealers who have something for
every shopper.

If collectibles and memorabilia are your forte, you'll find them here:
toys, dolls, games, coins, glassware, china, books—you name it.

There are also antique household furnishings, rugs, clocks, and lamps,
the latter of which can be repaired by their staff.

The Coffee Cabin Cafe located in the shop offers lunch, dessert, and
gourmet coffee when you feel your energy flagging.

Gingerbread House of Antiques
1542 Baker Park Road
612/479-1562

Steeple Antique Mall
5310 Main St.
612/479-4375

25 MARSHALL

Bev's Antiques
107 5th St.
507/537-1933

General Store
349 Main St. W.
507/537-0408

Orphanage Antiques Strawberry
351 Main St. W.
507/532-3998

26 MAZEPPA

Bed and Browse and Robby's Antiques
1st St.
507/843-4317
Open: Year-round, call for reservation information.
Directions: From Minneapolis, head south on Minnesota Hwy. 52 until
south of Zumbrota, Minn., then east on Country Road 60 to Mazeppa.
Turn north on 1st Street to third block.

The Robinsons of Burnsville, Minn., lived a busy life as foster care
givers and were anxious to find a retreat from the visits of social workers,
personal care attendants, and all of the comings and goings associated
with such charitable works. They finally found asylum in an old building
on a street corner in quaint Mazeppa, Minnesota.

Juanita Robinson recalls, "For 6 years of summer weekends, Luke,
our adopted son, played while I hammered and sawed and painted...." It
is a two-story building, the first floor of which is now Robby's Antiques.
The second floor is now the "getaway."

The building, which is on the National Historic Register, has a brick
front with stone walls on the interior, and has been an overnight haven
for treasure hunters and weary travelers for the past three years. Guests
bring their own food, or eat in nearby cafes.

There are some intriguing curiosities upstairs at the Bed and Browse,
including a 100-year-old duck boat that has been converted to a display
cabinet; an old English zinc bathtub that is now used for reading or
napping, and the "in-house outhouse" door made of stained glass
(backed by wood to insure privacy).

Downstairs at Robby's Antiques you'll find more treasures, such as
stained glass, buttons and collectibles galore. Bed and Browse is also a
convenient stopover for antiquing adventures in nearby Red Wing,
Wabasha, Oronoco, Lake City and Rochester.

27 MINNEAPOLIS

Great Northern Antiques & Vintage
5159 Bloomington Ave. S.
612/721-8731

J & H Used Furniture & Antiques
2421 W. Broadway Ave.
612/588-3049

Ross Frame Shop
4555 Bryant Ave. S.
612/823-1421

Euro Pine Imports
4416 Excelsior Blvd.
612/929-2927

Hollywood North
4510 Excelsior Blvd.
612/925-8695

Park Avenue Antiques
3004 W. 50th St.
612/925-5850

Complements
3020 W. 50th St.
612/922-1702

Loft Antiques
3022 W. 5th St.
612/922-4200

Cupboard Collectibles
3840 W. 50th St.
612/929-9244

Illyricun Antiques
430 1st Ave. N.
612/338-3345

Tiques & Treasures Antiques
117 4th St. N.
612/359-0915

Wooden Horse
3302 W. 44th St.
612/925-1148

Durr, Ltd.
4386 France Ave. S.
612/925-9146

A. Anderson
3808 Grand Ave. S.
612/824-1111

Plaza Antiques
1758 Hennepin Ave.
612/377-7331

Finishing Touches Antiques
2520 Hennepin Ave.
612/377-8033

H & B Gallery
2729 Hennepin Ave.
612/874-6436

J. Oliver Antiques
2730 Hennepin Ave.
612/872-8952

Minnesota

Cobblestone Antiques, Inc.
2801 Hennepin Ave.
612/823-7373

Shades on Lake
921 W. Lake St.
612/822-6427

Antiques Minnesota, Inc.
1516 E. Lake St.
612/722-6000

Muzzleloaders Etcetera, Inc.
9901 Lyndale Ave. S.
612/884-1161

Spiderweb Antiques
6525 Penn Ave. S.
612/798-1862

Indigo
530 N. 3rd St.
612/333-2151

American Classics Antiques
4944 Xerxes Ave. S.
612/926-2509

Getchell's Antiques
5012 Xerxes Ave. S.
612/922-6222

Antiques at Anthonies
801 E. 78th St.
612/854-4855

Annabelle's Gifts & Antiques
2907 Pentagon Dr.
612/788-3700

C. W. Smith Antiques
4424 Excelsior Blvd.
612/922-8542

Hazen's Used & Rare Records
3318 E. Lake St.
612/721-3854

Past Present Future
336 E. Franklin Ave.
612/870-0702

Uptown Antique & General Store
2833 Hennepin Ave.
612/879-0019

28 MOTLEY

Wilson House Antiques
Box 315
218/352-6629

Olde Tyme Trading Post
681 Hwy. 10 S.
218/352-6273

Battlefield Military Antiques
3915 Hwy. 7
612/920-3820

Len's Antiques
1108 E. Lake St.
612/721-7211

Theatre Antiques
2934 Lyndale Ave. S.
612/822-4884

Sherry's Old Stuff Antiques
9139 Old Cedar Ave. S.
612/854-5086

Antiques Riverwalk
210 3rd Ave. N.
612/339-9352

Architectural Antiques, Inc.
801 Washington Ave. N.
612/332-8344

Park Ave Antiques
4944 Xerxes Ave. S.
612/922-0887

American Island
3505 W. 44th St.
612/925-9006

Arteffects
13 5th St. N.E.
612/627-9107

Antique Clock Shop
1516 E. Lake St.
612/722-9590

East Lake Antiques & Collectibles
1410 E. Lake St.
612/721-6589

Minneapolis Uptown Antiques
2512 Hennepin Ave.
612/374-4666

Tom's Antiques
3801 Chicago Ave.
612/823-6076

Waldon Woods Antiques
213 Washington Ave. N.
612/338-2545

Pat's Place
Box 173
218/352-6410

29 NEVIS

Danny's Arcade Ice Cream & Antiques
115 Main St.
218/652-3919

30 NEW ULM

New Ulm was established in 1848 by German settlers, and ties to the old country still run deep. Downtown shops sell delicious fudge and traditional German crafts.

In the town square is a 45-foot glockenspiel, one of a few free-standing carillon clocks in the world. Outside of town is Harkin Store, an authentic restoration stocked with the goods, sights and smells of an 1870s general store.

Antiques Plus
117 N. Broadway St.
507/359-1090

Cherry Lane Antiques
1440 Cherry St.
507/354-4870

Neidecker Antiques
1020 N. State St.
507/354-6459

Antique House
327 N. Broadway St.
507/354-2450

Heritage Antiques
16 N. Minnesota St.
507/359-5150

31 NISSWA

International Country Antiques
Nisswa Square
218/963-0311

32 NORTHFIELD

Drive the Outlaw Trail Tour into Northfield, the escape route of notorious bank robbers Frank and Jesse James, who tried to rob Northfield bank but were foiled by alert townsfolk. The restored bank, one of many buildings in the historic downtown district, is now a museum.

Old Stuff Gallery
200 Division St.
507/645-7821

Three Acres Antiques
302 Division St.
507/645-4997

Remember When Antiques
418 Division St.
507/645-6419

Terrell's Antiques
200 Division St.
507/645-5878

Cherubs Cove, Inc.
307 Division St.
507/645-9680

Seven Gables Books & Antiques
313 Washington St.
507/645-8572

33 ORONOCO

The tiny town of Oronoco (population 700) is famous for the large antique show and flea market which comes to town every third week-end

Minnesota

in August. Thirteen hundred dealers from the U.S. and Canada display their wares amongst a crowd of 30 to 40,000 prospective buyers.

Antiques Oronoco
Hwy. 52
507/367-2220

Gordon and Yvonne Cariveau are professionals when it comes to antiques. Of course, it helps to have been in the business for the past twenty years.

Eight years ago, the Cariveaus built a large shop, about 4,000 square feet of showroom space, plus a restoration area. Last year a 1,500-square-foot wholesale outlet was added.

Antiques are displayed in department store style settings; according to colors, catagories, etc. The inventory is pre-1950s, specializing in early 1900s.

Berg's Antique Store
50/420 Minnesota Ave. S.
507/367-4413 or 507/367-4588
Open: Flexible days/hours. Call for appointment. (When possible, main buildings 9–5, Tues.–Sat.)
Directions: Traveling on State Hwy. 52 (6 miles North of Rochester). Exit onto Minnesota Avenue South (Main Street). Berg's is located next to the bridge in the largest (brick) building in town.

Berg's is an original in more ways than one. With the same owner and location since 1963, it specializes in original finishes and rough oak and pine pieces. "Nothing has been redone," boasts owner Mary Lou Berg.

These original finished pieces are exceptional, highly sought after, and hard to find—except here. You'll also find thousands of "smalls" to suit your fancy. What you won't find here are crafts, gifts, or reproductions.

Because the shop is so specialized, the hours vary, and Mary Lou recommends that you call ahead for an appointment. If you feel impulsive enough to just drop by, your best chances are between 9 and 5 Tuesday through Saturday.

Greta's Country Antiques
1005 1st St. S.E.
507/367-2315

Antiques Oronoco
Hwy. 52
507/367-2220

Cathi's Country Store & Antiques
230 S. Minnesota Ave.
507/367-4931

34 PALISADE

Old River Road Antiques
Route 2, Box 190
218/845-2770
Open: By chance or appointment — open most days during the

summer, and open most weekends during the spring and fall.
Directions: 4 miles north of the Hwy. 169 and Hwy. 210 junction toward Grand Rapids, Minn. 12 miles north of Aiken, Minn., on Hwy. 169.

Both this smaller version and the original barn built in 1913 are constructed of the salvaged wood from the old steamboat, Irene, which once traveled along the Mississippi River. It seems fitting that since its reconstruction in 1983, it has sat on the spot where the river road was once located.

The heritage of Old River Road Antiques provides an interesting introduction to the shop which carries many newly restored furnishings. Mr. Hlidek (the "h" is silent) restores the antique furniture, and the shop is a showcase for his work.

Other interesting items listed among what Ms. Hlidek terms her "fun junk" are Wade porcelain animals from England and her extensive button collection.

35 PAYNESVILLE

Koronis Antiques
26753 N. Hwy. 55
320/243-4268

Country Porch Antiques
399th St. - Hwy. 55
310/243-4027

Antique Cellar
104 Washburne Ave.
320/243-7605

Paynesville Antique Mall
104 Washburne Ave.
320/243-7000

Jeanne's Antiques & Collectibles
109 Washburne Ave.
320/243-7381

36 RED WING

In Red Wing shop for antiques, the latest fashions and more in the Pottery District, where Red Wing Stoneware was once made. On a self-guided walking tour, see the restored T.B. Sheldon Auditorium Theatre, a historic hotel and Goodhue County Historical Museum. More sights are visible from the river by excursion boat or from the Red Wing Shoe Company Observation Deck.

Mona Lisa Antiques & Gardens
1228 W. Main St.
612/388-4027

Memories
2000 W. Main St.
612/388-6446

Old Main Street Antiques
2000 W. Main St.
612/388-1371

Al's Antique Mall
1314 Old W. Main St.
612/388-0572

Dorothy's Antiques
1604 Old W. Main St.
612/388-7024

Tea House Antiques
927 W. 3rd St.
612/388-3669

Ice House Antiques
1811 Old W. Main St.
612/388-8939

Hiawatha Valley Ranch
29665 Hwy. 61 Blvd.
612/388-4033

Minnesota

Great Places to Stay

Pratt-Taber Inn
706 W. Fourth St.
612/388-5945

As an elegant reminder of its heritage, the Pratt-Taber Inn serves its guests a taste of Victorian style. Built in 1876, the interior is of fine woods like butternut and walnut. Particular attention was paid to rich details during construction, including the woodwork throughout and the trim on the wonderful porch, which is so representative of the style. Three fireplaces in the parlors are also expressive of such elegance. The richness continues in the inn's furnishings. The six bedrooms boast Renaissance Revival and Victorian style antiques.

Enjoy a gourmet breakfast before taking a walk to nearby downtown Red Wing, or to the banks of the Mississippi River. If you prefer, you can tour the area aboard an old San Francisco cable car that has been mounted to a truck chassis. If your timing is right, you can watch as eagles migrate through the area. An estimated 4,000 were sighted last year.

37 ROCHESTER

Old Stonehouse Antiques
1901 Bamber Valley Road S.W.
507/282-8497

Sentimental Journeys Unlimited
110 W. Center St.
507/281-6616

Timeless Treasures
7 1st Ave. S.W.
507/288-3398

Mayowood Galleries
Kahler Hotel/ 2nd Ave S.W.
507/288-2695

Collins Antique Feed & Seed Center
411 2nd Ave. N.W.
507/289-4844

Just A Little Something
305 6th St. S.W.
507/288-7172

John Kruesel's General Merchandise
22 3rd St. S.W.
507/289-8049

Old Rooster Antique Mall
106 N. Broadway
507/287-6228

Peterson's Antiques & Stripping
111 11th Ave. N.E.
507/282-9100

Iridescent House
227 1st Ave. S.W.
507/288-0320

Mayowood Galleries
3705 Mayowood Road S.W.
507/288-6791

Blondell Antiques
1408 1nd St. S.W.
507/282-1872

Antique Mall on Third
18 3rd St. S.W.
507/287-0684

Broadway Antiques
324 S. Broadway
507/288-5678

38 SHAKOPEE

Lady Di Antiques
126 S. Holmes St.
612/445-1238
Open: Daily 10–5

Downtown Shakopee, Minnesota, offers the discriminating shopper a superb selection at Lady Di Antiques. Owner Diane Sullivan, well known in Minnesota for her expertise in promoting high-end antique shows, has consolidated her sense of style and taste into this versatile shop.

Merchandise runs the gamut from vintage clothing to dolls and toys, to distinctive furnishings and decorative accessories.

Something Olde
120 Holmes St.
612/445-3791

Interesting Side Trip

Historic Murphy's Village
2187 East Hwy. 101
612/445-6900
Directions: On the banks of the Minnesota River, one mile east of Shakopee on Minnesota Hwy. 101 — 30 minutes from the Minneapolis/St. Paul International Airport and 23 minutes from the Mall of America.

In a quiet village nestled along the shores of the scenic Minnesota River, pioneers long ago learned to thrive in a sometimes hostile, sometimes hospitable new world. As they carved a life for themselves in the wilderness, the stories of their determination and dignity, and their spirit and ingenuity filled this new land.

Today, more than 100 years later, the spirit of that time lives on. Historic Murphy's Village is a unique living history museum that preserves and interprets 19th century life in the Minnesota River Valley. Dedicated to the lives of children and adults, both past and present, Historic Murphy's Village is not only a land that remembers time, but a land where history comes alive with each new day.

The idyllic wooded setting that stretches along one and a half miles of scenic river valley brings alive the charm and challenges of life in the 19th century. Families, history buffs and adventurers of all ages can step into this historic village, which features the rich diversity of early American life.

Each homestead, among the 40 different buildings at Murphy's, represents the coming together of the many groups that settled in the Minnesota River Valley between 1840 and 1890—Czech, Danish, English, French, German, Irish, Norwegian, Polish and Scandinavian. In addition, Murphy's Historic Village includes 16 Native American mounds that are estimated to be more than 2000 years old.

Visitors can stroll on their own or ride on horse-drawn trolleys. Their journey will cover the very early days of the fur trade era when people traveled by footpath and canoes, to the bustling village complete with its shops, homes, church, town hall and railroad depot. Throughout the village, costumed interpreters are prepared to spin a tale, demonstrate their craft and explain the daily life of the men, women and children who settled in the valley more than a century ago. Day-to-day activities such as cooking, weaving, spinning and woodworking take place in their homes and on their farmsteads. Visitors will hear how villagers lived and learned together during that rugged pioneer era.

Music and entertainment also often fill the daily Village routine. Musicians and craftspeople are a common sight, while folks gather at the blacksmith shop or general store for a chat with tour guides and costumed interpreters.

39 SAINT CLOUD

Kay's Antiques
713 Germain
320/255-1220

Depot Antique Mall
8318 State Hwy. 23 & I-94
320/253-6573

Paper Collector Art Gallery
26 7th Ave. N.
320/251-2171

Great Places to Stay

Edelbrock House

216 N. 14th Ave.
320/259-0071

Located in Saint Cloud just south of the famous Minnesota lakes and forests, the Edelbrock House offers guests the opportunity to step back in time to an 1880 yellow brick Victorian farmhouse brimming with antiques, collectibles and country decor. Excellent home cooking and personal pampering will make you fall in love with Edelbrock House.

40 SAINT PAUL

Victoria Grande Gardens
818 Grand Ave.
612/228-0228

Anything & Everything, Inc.
1208 Grand Ave.
612/222-7770

Antiques White Bear, Inc.
4903 Long Ave.
612/426-3834

Danny's Antiques
1076 Maryland Ave. E.
612/776-6287

Cottage Interiors
1129 Grand Ave.
612/224-2933

Oxford Antiques
58 Hamline Ave. S.
612/699-1066

Wicker Shop
2190 Marshall Ave.
612/647-1598

Granny Smiths Antiques & Crafts
7600 147th St. W.
612/891-1686

Antique Mart
941 Payne Ave.
612/771-0860

Golden Lion Antiques
983 Payne Ave.
612/778-1977

Grand Old House
517 Selby Ave.
612/221-9191

Able Antiques
226 7th St. W.
612/227-2469

Alladdin's Antique Alley
239 7th St. W.
612/290-2981

Ann & Larry's Antiques
2572 7th Ave. E.
612/773-7994

Taylor & Rose
251 Snelling Ave. S.
612/699-5724

Antiques Minnesota Midway
1197 University Ave. W.
612/646-0037

Robert J. Riesbery
343 Salem Church Road
612/457-1772

Antique Lane on Payne
946 Payne Ave.
612/771-6544

Emporium Antiques
1037 Payne Ave.
612/778-1919

Oldies But Goodies
1814 Selby Ave.
612/641-1728

Wescott's Station Antiques
226 7th St. W.
612/227-2469

John's Antiques
261 7th St. W.
612/222-6131

Nakashian-Oneil, Inc.
23 6th St. W.
612/224-5465

French Antiques
174 W. 7th St.
612/293-0388

Recollections
4754 Washington Square
612/426-8811

J & E Antiques
1000 Arcade St.
612/771-9654

41 SAINT PETER

Collective Memories
216 S. Minnesota Ave.
507/931-6445

Tate Antiques
817 N. Minnesota Ave.
507/931-5678

42 STILLWATER

American Gothic Antiques

236 S. Main St.
612/439-7709
Open: Mon.–Thurs. 10–5, Fri. & Sat. 10–8, Sun. 11–5
Directions: On Interstate 94, 10 miles east of St. Paul, exit onto Hwy. 95 North at the Wisconsin border. Travel 8 miles north along the St. Croix River to Stillwater, Minn.

This 45-plus dealer shop located in a lovely old building on Stillwater's main street was named from Grant Wood's famous 1930s painting entitled "American Gothic."

What's so unusual is the story behind the naming of this shop. The house in the painting's background belonged to Janie (Johnston) Eiklenborg's (the shop owner) great-grandmother. Janie says her great granny sat on the porch and actually watched as Mr. Wood doodled and

Minnesota

sketched the details for this famous painting. The house located in Eldon, Iowa, is still owned by the family, and Janie's sister Mari Beth lives there today. "It's been a fun story to share with customers," says Janie, "and we're so proud to have been a part of it."

Oh, my goodness, I got so carried away with this story that I almost forgot to tell you about the shop. Inside American Gothic Antiques, dealers display exquisite selections of Victorian and oak furnishings, country furniture and accessories, as well as a choice group of primitive items. On a smaller scale, there are generous offerings of vintage clothing and jewelry, glassware and other collectibles. "Thanks for sharing your story with us, Janie."

DeAnna Zink's Antiques
9344 60th St. N.
612/770-1987
Open: Thurs.–Sat. 12–6, other days and hours by chance or appointment. Monday is "dealer day" from approximately 9–6 (discounts on everything).
Directions: Drive Interstate 694 to Hwy. 36 East. Take Hwy. 36 East 1 ¼ miles to Demontreville Trail. Get off to the left (north). Get on service road (60th Street), and continue east ½ mile to the big gray farmhouse on the hill. (From Stillwater: Take Hwy. 36 West to Keats; veer onto 60th Street; continue west for ½ mile.)

Once inside this 1870s farmhouse, you'll be delighted to find, not only what DeAnna refers to as a "general" line of antique furniture and accessories, but a choice selection of fine glassware, prints, and porcelains. Moreover, the display of Victorian and primitive pieces, which are DeAnna's specialty, are not to be missed.

Treat yourself to coffee and munchies while roaming the aisles of this charming shop.

One of a Kind
102 Main St. N.
612/430-0009

Main Street Antiques Stillwater
118 Main St. N.
612/430-3110

River City Antiques & Collectibles
124 Main St. S.
612/439-3889

Stillwater Antiques
101 S. Main St.
612/439-6281

Mulberry Point Antiques
270 Main St. N.
612/430-3630

Gabrielle
114 N. Main St.
612/439-5930

Country Charm Antiques
124 Main St. S.
612/439-8202

Past and Present Antiques
208 Main St. S.
612/439-6198

St. Croix Antiquarian Books
232 S. Main St.
612/430-0732

Antique Radio Company
301 Main St. S.
612/432-3919

Midtown Antique Mall
301 Main St. S.
612/430-0808

Architectural Antiques, Inc.
316 Main St. N.
612/439-2133

Rivertown Antiques
501 Main St. N.
612/439-8188

43 WINONA

Markham's Antiques
1459 W. 5th St.
507/454-3190

R D Cone Antiques Mall
66 E. 2nd St.
507/453-0445

Country Comfort Antiques
79 W. 3rd St.
507/452-7044

44 WORTHINGTON

Hodgepodge Lodge
214 8th St.
507/376-4542

Margaret's Specialty Antiques
802 3rd Ave.
507/372-2239

Remember When
1321 Milton Ave.
507/376-3548

More Antiques
312 Main St. N.
612/439-1110

Mill Antiques
410 Main St. N.
612/430-1816

Battle Hollow Antiques
6148 Osgood Ave.
612/439-3414

A-Z Chair Caning
160 Main St.
507/454-0366

Traveling Treasures
1161 Sugar Loaf Road
507/452-5440

Haviland Matching Service
467 E. 5th St.
507/454-3283

LBJ Antiques
760 W. Shore Dr.
507/376-5004

Martin's Antiques
259 Kragness Ave.
507/372-5678

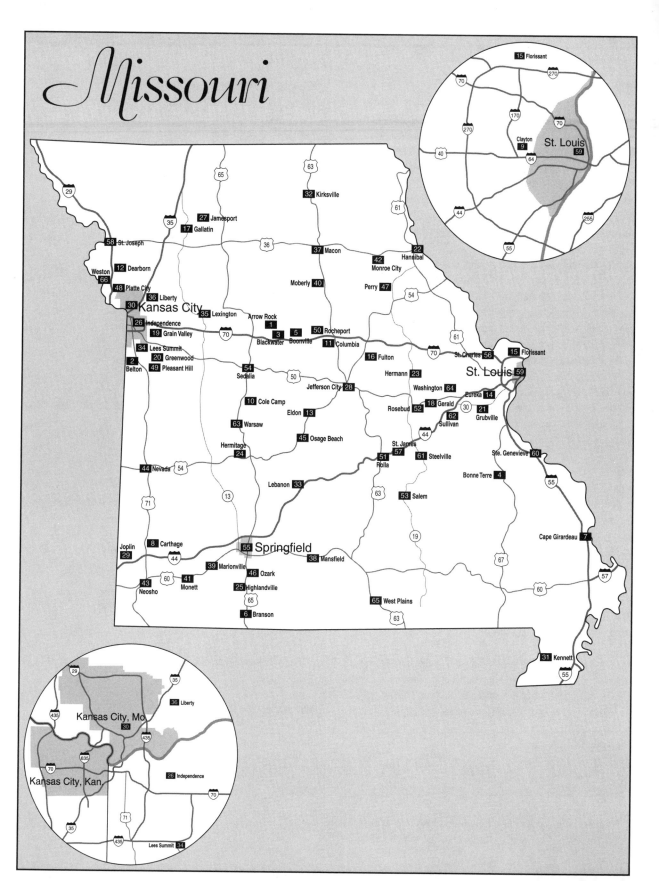

Missouri

15 Florissant

70

270

170

70

270

40

Clayton
9

St. Louis

59

44

255

55

29

65

63

32 Kirksville

61

35

27 Jamesport

17 Gallatin

36

37 Macon

42 Monroe City

22 Hannibal

58 St. Joseph

12 Dearborn

Weston
66

Moberly 40

Perry 47

54

48 Platte City

36 Liberty

30 Kansas City

35 Lexington

Arrow Rock
1

26 Independence

19 Grain Valley

70

3 Blackwater

5 Boonville

50 Rocheport

11 Columbia

61

St. Charles 56

15 Florissant

34 Lees Summit

16 Fulton

St. Louis 59

2 Belton

20 Greenwood

49 Pleasant Hill

Sedalia
54

50

Jefferson City 28

Hermann 23

Washington 64

Eureka 14

10 Cole Camp

Eldon 13

Rosebud 52

18 Gerald

21 Grubville

30

62 Sullivan

63 Warsaw

Hermitage

45 Osage Beach

St. James
57

61 Steelville

Ste. Genevieve 60

24

51 Rolla

55

44 Nevada 54

13

Lebanon 33

63

53 Salem

Bonne Terre 4

19

Joplin

8 Carthage

55 Springfield

38 Mansfield

Cape Girardeau 7

29

44

39 Marionville

46 Ozark

67

57

43 Neosho

60

41 Monett

25 Highlandville

65

67

60

65 West Plains

6 Branson

63

31 Kennett

55

29

35

36 Liberty

435

Kansas City, Mo

30

435

635

70

26 Independence

Kansas City, Kan.

70

71

35

435

Lees Summit 34

Missouri

1 ARROW ROCK

The year was 1804. Lewis and Clark were in the midst of their legendary explorations of the U.S. when they noted the bluff and the nearby salt licks in their journals and maps. Native Americans had for centuries gathered the flint from the bluff for arrowheads, hence the name Arrow Rock. After Lewis and Clark, westbound explorers and traders stopped at Arrow Rock Spring in 1829, some of them settled and founded the town. Today, Arrow Rock is basically untouched by time. The 70 people who currently live in the town are steeped in its history and in the recreation and preservation of its past.

Visitors to Arrow Rock can tour a restored 1834 tavern, a gunsmith's shop and home, the old print shop, frontier artist George Caleb Bingham's home, a museum dedicated to medical doctor John Sappington, who was a pioneer in the treatment of malaria, and more. Then you can experience live entertainment at Arrow Rock's award-winning Lyceum Theatre. Once a church, the theater is now a beautiful 420-seat complex where professional actors from around the country stage Broadway-caliber shows each summer. Also, visit shops filled with antiques, specialty gifts, and old-time crafts. Eat to your heart's content — everything from simple country fare to gourmet delights. Stay at a gracious bed and breakfast, or camp outdoors overlooking the Missouri River Valley.

Great Places to Shop

Arrow Rock Antiques
Located on Main St.
816/837-3333

18th- and 19th-century formal and high country furniture and accessories.

McAdams Ltd.
816/837-3259
Open: Apr.–Dec., Wed.–Sun., 10–5 or by appointment

Once the bank building in a bustling stop on the Sante Fe Trail, this historic building now holds a unique blend of European and American antiques with a distinctive line of new merchandise. Antique, estate and traditional new jewelry have been a McAdams' specialty for 20 years.

Pin Oak Antiques
301 Main St., on the Boardwalk
816/837-3244
Open: Wed.–Sun. or by appointment

A full line of antique country furniture and accessories at reasonable prices. Two floors of antiques, including a basement "rough room."

The Village Peddler Antiques
One-half mile north of Arrow Rock on Hwy. 41
816/837-3392
Open: Wed.–Sun. 10–5 or by appointment

A general line of furniture and smalls.

Great Places to Eat

Arrow Rock Emporium
Located on the Boardwalk
816/837-3364

A tea room atmosphere featuring home-cooked sandwich platters, flavored coffee, and delicious ice cream specialties.

Grandma D's Cafe
One block south of Main St.
816/837-3335

Enjoy dining surrounded by antiques and unique gifts. Sandwiches, salads, homemade soups, pies, and sweet breads.

The Old Arrow Rock Tavern
Located on Main St. one block from the Lyceum Theatre

Built in 1834, The Old Tavern continues to serve the public as it did in the glory days of the Sante Fe Trail. One of the oldest restaurants west of the Mississippi, the Old Tavern fare includes catfish, country ham, and fried chicken, with an ample selection in wine, beer and spirits. Reservations requested.

The Old Schoolhouse Cafe
Located in the Old Schoolhouse
816/837-3331

Enjoy homemade breakfast and lunch specialties located at the Westside basement entrance in The Old Schoolhouse.

The Evergreen Restaurant
Located one block north of Main St. on Hwy. 41
816/837-3251

Enjoy gracious dining with a European touch in a restored 1840s home.

2 BELTON

Dusty Attic Antiques & Collectibles
319 Main St.
816/331-3505

1802
320 Main St.
816/322-7107

Jaudon Antique Mall
20406 S. State Road, #D
816/322-4001

3 BLACKWATER

Rose Hill
21495 Hwy. 41
816/846-3031
Open: Wed.–Sat. 10–5, Sun.–Tues., by chance or appointment
Directions: *From I-70 west*, exit #89. Travel 6 miles north through Blackwater on Route "K" to Hwy. 41, then go ½ mile north on Hwy. 41 to Rose Hill. *From I-70 east*, exit #98. Travel 7 miles north on Hwy. 41 toward Arrow Rock. Rose Hill is ½ mile on the right after you pass Route "K."

Visitors to Rose Hill get a special treat, so take your cameras. The shop of Rose Hill is located behind the Kusgen's home and is set up inside in fashion groupings, by rooms. They have bedrooms decorated with beds, wardrobes, chests and accessories; a living room with antique furniture and accessories; and a kitchen with a working model woodburning stove (not for sale). Kitchen items include old utensils, depression glass, and stoneware bowls.

The special treat is growing on the property at Rose Hill. Its Missouri's largest known sugar maple tree, recognized by the Missouri Department of Conservation. The tree has a circumference of 13 feet 8 inches, soars 62 feet tall, and spreads out 88 feet. The Missouri Forestry Department estimates the tree to be 150 years old. A film about the tree has been televised in Missouri by PBS and a plaque was presented to the Kusgens by the Missouri Department of Conservation, attesting to the claim of the state's largest sugar maple tree.

4 BONNE TERRE

Bonne Terre Antiques
1467 State Hwy. 47
573/358-2235

Great Places to Stay

Victorian Veranda
207 E. School St.
573/358-1134 or 1-800-343-1134
Open: Daily 8–10:30 except Dec. 24–25
Rates: $55–$85
Directions: From St. Louis: Take I-55 South to U.S. 67. Turn south on

U.S. 67 to Bonne Terre exit. Turn right on Hwy. 47, then left on Allen Street in Bonne Terre. Turn right on Main Street, then take an immediate left on East School Street to the inn. Only 45 miles from south St. Louis.

Just one of the unique and historic buildings and homes in Bonne Terre, Victorian Veranda is a large old home with a big wraparound porch and four guest rooms decorated in Victorian and country decor, all with private baths. Victoria's Room has six large windows and Victorian accessories, and a Jacuzzi for two. The Victorian Boot and Lace Room holds a wrought iron queen bed and is filled with Victorian high top boots and Battenburg lace. The Drake Room is furnished in the Mallard duck theme, all greens and burgundies, with a claw-foot tub for playing with your own rubber duckie; The Countryside Room is bursting with Americana and country charm, complete with Charles Wysocki prints and country pine queen bed.

5 BOONVILLE

Itchy's Stop & Scratch Flea Market
1406 W. Ashley Road
816/882-6822

Key to Your Heart Antiques
1420 W. Ashley Road
816/882-8821

Hi-Way 5 Antique Mall
1428 W. Ashley Road
816/882-3341

Reichel and Co.
1436 W. Ashley Road
816/882-3533

Reichel Antique & Auction Corner
1440 W. Ashley Road
816/882-5292

McMillan Ltd. Antiques
417 E. Spring St.
816/882-6337

6 BRANSON

Finders Keepers Flea Market
204 N. Commercial St.
417/334-3248

Apple Tree Mall
Hwy. 76
417/335-2133

Somewhere in Time
Hwy. 76
417/335-2212

Mothers & Mine Antiques
Mutton Hollow
417/334-2588

Apple Pie Ltd.
3612 Shepherd Hill Expressway
417/335-4236

Twin Pines Antiques
1120 W. State Hwy. 76
417/334-5830

Antique City
Hwy. 76 W.
417/338-2673

7 CAPE GIRARDEAU

Annie Laurie's Antique Mall
536 Broadway
573/339-1301
Open: Mon.–Sat. 10–5

Annie Laurie's offers a delightful assortment of country and kitchen collectibles, quality furniture and an amazing selection of paper items from the 1880s and early 1900s.

Campster School Antiques
3892 Bloomfield Road
573/339-1002

Ohaira
1001 Independence St.
573/334-8020

Antique Furniture & Collectibles Mall
18 N. Sprigg St.
573/339-0840

Heartland Antique Emporium
701 William St.
573/334-0102

Attic Treasures
318 S. Sprigg St.
573/335-5445

Doris' Flea Market
631 Good Hope
573/651-1665

Knock on Wood
435 Main St.
573/334-0496

Ross's Place
2044 Broadway
573/339-0001

Antique Center Mall
2127 William St.
573/339-5788

Another Time Another Place
715 Broadway
573/335-0046

Witness Designs
31 N. Main St.
573/334-0333

Peddlers Corner
111 N. Sprigg St.
573/334-1213

A-1 Consignment Center
429 Broadway
573/335-7446

Cooper's Collectibles
225 N. Sprigg St.
573/334-5535

Golden Goose Antiques
2 N. Lorimier
573/243-0762

River City Coins & Jewelry
713 Broadway
573/334-1108

The Stalls
221 Independence St.
573/335-3529

Great Places to Stay

Annie Laurie's Cottage
605 Broadway
573/339-1301
Rates: $55 double

This lovely and quaint two-room brick cottage, circa 1870, is filled with antique books, prints and antique furniture. A delicious breakfast is served to guests.

8 CARTHAGE

Goad Unique Antique Mall
111 E. 3rd St.
417/358-1201

Jerdon Ltd.
311 S. Main St.
417/358-3343

Oldies & Oddities Mall
331 S. Main St.
417/358-1752

Accent Angels & Antiques
342 Grant St.
417/359-5300

Carthage Rt. 66 Antique Mall
1221 Oak St.
417/359-7240

Spring River Antiques
222 Grant St.
417/358-4407

9 CLAYTON

Listed as a part of St. Louis.

10 COLE CAMP

Stone Soup Antiques & Uniques
111 S. Maple St.
816/668-3624
Open: Mon.–Sat. 10–5, Sun. 12–5
Directions: U.S. 65 20 miles south of Sedalia, east Hwy. 52, 1/2 block south of 4-way stop.

Here's a shop that takes its name — Stone Soup — from an old children's story. They offer an eclectic collection of antiques, collectibles, glassware (including depression glass, china and figurines), and country crafts in a "unique" 1906 lumber barn, complete with loft, that began its life as an old mercantile building. They also have a nice selection of furniture, including a bed that belonged to Walt Disney's parents!

Tara Storm
Maple St.
No phone listed

Antiques & Stuff
Hwy. 52
816/668-4720

11 COLUMBIA

Columbia Emporium
810 E. Broadway
573/443-5288
Open: Thurs.–Sat. and Mon. 11–5:30, Tues.–Wed. 11–4, closed Sun.
Directions: Travel west on I-70 (between St. Louis and Kansas City) to Columbia. Exit 126 south on Providence to Broadway. Turn left on Broadway. Columbia Emporium is located in downtown Columbia between 8th and 9th Streets. The shop is a lower level-one. Look for the black and gold sign.

This upscale emporium offers shoppers a large showroom of art, antiques and jewelry; specializing in large "ornate" 100-year-old furniture, and antique and estate jewelry.

Mary Watson Antiques & Interiors
923 E. Broadway Ave.
573/449-8676

Midway Antique Mall
I-70 & Hwy. 40 Exit 121
573/445-6717

Museumscopes Antiques
2507 Old #63 S.
573/449-8523

McAdams, Ltd.
32 S. Providence Road
573/442-3151

Friends Together Antiques
4038 E. Broadway
573/442-6759

Grandma's Treasures
2000 Business Loop
573/499-0883

Gates Antiques
11105 Mexico Gravel Road
573/474-4067

Ice Chalet Antique Mall
3411 Old #63 S.
573/442-6893

Itchys Stop & Scratch
1907 N. Providence Road
573/443-8275

12 DEARBORN

Lickskillet Antique Mall & Shops
214 Main St.
816/992-8776

Yesterday's Memories
110, 112, 114 W. 3rd
816/992-8941

Moore Antiques
108 W. 3rd
816/992-3788

Outpost Trading Co.
201 W. 3rd
816/992-3402

13 ELDON

Red's Antique Mall
Hwy. 52 & Bus 54 S.
573/392-3866

Past & Present
106 S. Maple St.
573/392-2256

14 EUREKA

Remember When Antiques
126 S. Central Ave.
314/938-3724

Firehouse Gallery & Shops
131 S. Central Ave.
314/938-3303

Ice House Antiques
19 Dreyer
314/938-6355

Great Midwest Antique Mall
100 Hilltop Village Center Dr.
314/938-6760

Owl's Nest Antiques
128 S. Virginia Ave.
314/938-5030

Aunt Sadie's Antique Mall
515 N. Virginia Ave.
314/938-9212

Oldys & Goodys Antique Mall
127 S. Central Ave.
314/938-5717

Olde Thyme Shoppe
224 N. Central Ave.
314/938-3818

Eureka Antique Mall
107 E. 5th St.
314/938-5600

Accent on Antiques
120 S. Virginia Ave.
314/938-3200

Gingerbread House
138 S. Virginia Ave.
314/938-5414

Wallach House Antiques
510 West Ave.
314/938-6633

Cherokee Chief Trading Post
529 N. Virginia Ave.
314/772-4433

15 FLORISSANT

Gittemeier House Antiques
1067 Dunn Road
314/830-1133
Open: Daily Mon.–Sat. 10–4, Sun. 12–4
Directions: From Hwy. 270, take Exit 27 (New Florissant Road). Gittemeier House is located on the service road (1067 Dunn Road) behind the Shell Station.

It's always fun to visit an antique shop that is as old, or older, than the merchandise inside! Gittemeier House is a seven room, two-story 1860 Federal style house where the focus inside is on Victorian furniture — lots of impressive, towering wardrobes, marble topped pieces, glassware, all sorts of things from that elegant, extravagant age of Victoria!

Age of Reflection
306 Rue St. Francis
314/972-1700

The Sisters Three
525 Rue St. Francis
314/837-4748

Florissant Treasure House
126 Rue St. Francis
No phone listed

Junkle John's Antiques
525 Rue St. Francis
314/830-0095

Village of the Blue Rose
519 Rue St. Francis
No phone listed

Victorian Country Antiques
1067 Dunn Road
314/921-4606

16 FULTON

Cornerstone Antique Mall
537 Court St.
573/642-6700

King's Row Antiques
Jct. Route F & Hwy. 54
573/642-5335

Lutz & Doters
505 Nichols St.
573/642-9350

Country Clipper Antiques
1225 S. Hwy. 54
573/642-0393

Willing House Antiques
211 Jefferson St.
573/642-7525

17 GALLATIN

Towne Square Antiques
120 W. Grant St.
816/663-2555

Goat Mountain Antiques
Hwy. 6
816/663-2731

18 GERALD

Great Places to Stay

The Bluebird Bed & Breakfast
For more specific information see listing under Rosebud #52.

River House Bed & Breakfast
For more specific information see listing under Rosebud #52.

19 GRAIN VALLEY

Sambo's Antiques
504 S. Main St.
816/224-4981

Primitives Plus
508A Main St.
816/224-3622

Main Street Mall Antiques
518 S. Main St.
816/224-6400

The Collector's Corner
513 Main St.
816/443-2228

20 GREENWOOD

Gate House Antiques & Tea Room
302 Allendale Lake Road
816/537-7313

Country Heritage Antiques
16005 S. Allendale Lake Road
816/537-7822

Greenwood Antiques & Country Tea Room
5th & Main on 150 Hwy.
816/537-7172

Traditions
5th & Main on 150 Hwy.
816/537-5011

Little Blue Antiques
409 W. Main St.
816/537-8688

Greenwillow Farm Antiques
15202 S. Smart Road
816/537-6527

21 GRUBVILLE

Grubville Guitars
314/274-4738
Open: By appointment only
Directions: Located 35 minutes Southwest of St. Louis off Hwy. 30 on State Road. Y between Highways 270 & 44.

A truly interesting shop on your antiquing trek, Grubville Guitars owned by Glenn Meyers, sells and restores used and vintage acoustic and electric guitars, basses, mandolins, banjos, violins and tube type amplifiers.

A musician for most of his life, Glenn thoroughly enjoys his work and has been interested in vintage instruments for 30 years. Most of his business is by word of mouth and his list of clients extends not only from the U.S. but from around the world.

Under Glenn's watchful eye the restoration and repair work is completed by two local guitar builders whose experience allows them to do any work necessary.

Being curious of this unusual fascination of Glenn's, I asked him what

he considered to be a vintage instrument. He explains, "Vintage means certain instruments from the 1960s back to the 1700s. For instance, I recently worked on a style 1-42 Martin guitar that was made in 1898. A beautiful instrument with small body, ivory bridge, ivory tuners, Brazilian rosewood — back and sides — and abalone inlaid around the select spruce top. Martin began building guitars in the early 1800s and to this day builds some of the best instruments available." Glenn also noted that there is a difference in sound between the new and old instruments. "It has to do with the construction techniques used by the best makers, he says. Some of the woods available thirty years ago, are no longer available or are in short supply, such as Brazilian rosewood which is now banned as an import into the United States." Although Glenn prefers the sound of the old instruments, he says there are modern builders today who are reproducing the vintage sound and taking the art to a new level of excellence.

Sounds like Glenn really knows his business. Now we all know who to call the next time we pick up that old mandolin at an auction. You know the one you loved but passed up because it needed repairs.

22 HANNIBAL

Hannibal, Mo., is synonymous with famous author and humorist Mark Twain. Twain's boyhood home, Hannibal, is the setting for the adventures of Tom Sawyer and Huck Finn. Near the riverfront is Twain's childhood home, restored to its exact mid-1800s appearance. The adjacent museum holds manuscripts and memorabilia, including one of his famous white suits. Nearby is the New Mark Twain Museum, featuring original Norman Rockwell paintings. Close by are Judge Clemens' law office, Becky Thatcher's House, and diorama and wax museums depicting Twain's famous characters.

Hannibal is full of interesting shops, and city tours take visitors into two impressive river mansions. The best way to see the sights is by river boat cruise or open-air tram, horse-drawn wagon or trolley. South of town, the Mark Twain Outdoor Theatre recreates some of his best-known works. Visitors can also explore the underground cave named for Twain, or visit the 18,600 acre Mark Twain Lake and the surrounding state park, where Twain's birthplace — a two-room cabin — is preserved.

Mrs. Clemens Antique Mall
305 N. Main St.
573/221-6427
Open: Daily spring–fall 9–5, winter 9:30–4:30
Directions: Enter Hannibal on Route 79, 61, or 36. Mrs. Clemens Antique Mall is located 3 miles from I-72 in the Historic District, 1/2 block from the Mark Twain Home and Museum.

Mrs. Clemens Antique Mall has over 40 dealers displaying a large selection of dolls, advertising items, pottery, cut and pressed glass, period furniture and an electric train booth of 1950s and prior trains and accessories. Mrs. Clemens is also a franchised dealer of Anheuser-Busch collectibles and a member of the Anheuser Busch Collectors Club. When you need to take a break, you have at your fingertips an ice cream parlor and snack bar in the mall, with an old back board and marble top counters. Eight flavors of premium, hand-dipped ice cream, sodas and snacks are served at old ice cream tables with matching chairs.

Mark Twain Antiques
312 N. Main St.
573/221-2568

American Antique Mall
119 S. Main St.
573/221-3395

Market Street Mall
1408 Market St.
573-221-3008

Smith's Treasure Chest, LLC
315 S. 3rd St.
573/248-2955

Cruikshank House Antiques
1001 Hill St.
573/248-0243

Swag-Man Antiques
211 Center St.
573/221-2393

23 HERMANN

Directions: Hermann is located between Hwy. 19 and Hwy. 100. If traveling I-70, Exit Hwy. 19, #175 and travel south for 14 miles to Hermann. If traveling west on I-44, Exit Hwy. 100, #251 (Washington exit) and travel west for 42 miles to Hermann. If traveling east on I-44, Exit Hwy. 19, #208 (Cuba exit) and travel north for 50 miles to Hermann. Hermann is 67 miles from St. Louis and 175 miles from Kansas City, and has daily Amtrak stops.

Hermann is a piece of the Old World in the middle of Missouri. The Germans who founded Hermann wanted a town that was "German in every particular." They carefully chose a site that reminded them of their beloved Rhine Valley and set about creating a city where German culture could flourish in the new world. Their vision was a grand one. Tucked away in the Ozark foothills, Hermann offers world-famous festivals, four thriving wineries, two historic districts, wonderful antique shops and delicious cuisine, served with a generous helping of Old World hospitality.

Great Places to Shop

Ace of Spades
112 E. First St.
573/486-3060

Garden art and handmade copper jewelry.

Antiques Unlimited
117 E. 2nd St.
573/486-2148

Large selection of refinished antique furniture, primitives and collectibles.

Burger Haus
Hwy. 19 and 13th Terrace
573/486-2828
Open: Daily

Furniture reproductions. Also handcrafted and painted items by local woodworker and artist, Os and Va.

Deutsche Schule Arts & Crafts
German School Building
573/486-3313
Open: Daily 10–5

Handmade crafts with 150 artisans from the area. Specializing in quilts. Many other items, including pottery.

Die Hermann Werks
214 E. 1st St.
573/486-2601
Open: Mon.–Sat. 9–5, Sun. 11–4

Specializing in European giftware and Christmas ornaments.

J.H.P. Quilts and Antiques
101 Schiller St.
573/486-3069
Open: Mon.–Sat. 10-4, Sun. 12–4

Specializing in country furniture, primitives, antique quilts, stoneware and accessories.

Jaeger Primitive Arms
415 E. 1st St.
573/486-2394
Open: Mon.–Sat. 9:30–5:30, Sun. 11:30–5

Specializing in black powder guns.

Jewel Shop (Das Edelstein Geshaft)
230 E. 1st St.
573/486-2955
Open: Tues.–Sat. 9–5

Fine jewelry.

Missouri

Pottery Shop
108 Schiller St.
573/486-3552/3558

Handmade porcelain and stoneware by local potter. Special orders accepted for dinnerware, tiles, and mugs.

Rag Rug Factory
113 E. 5th St.
573/486-3735
Open: Daily or by chance or appointment

Rag rugs and other handwoven items.

Sweet Stuff & Shepardson's Antiques
210 Schiller St.
573/486-3903
Open: Thurs.–Mon.

An eclectic blend of gourmet foods and coffees, antiques.

White House Hotel Museum & Antiques
232 Wharf St.
573/486-3200 or 573/486-3493
Open: By chance or appointment

Antique collectibles, dolls.

Wilding's Antiques and Museums
523 W. 9th St.
573/486-5544

Country antiques. Museum houses permanent collection of Clem Wilding's wood carvings.

Wissmath Baskets
Route 1, Box 74
573/486-2090

Mail order or call for information. Specializing in handwoven baskets, deer antler baskets and 1-inch miniature baskets.

Wohlt House
415 E. First St.
573/486-2394
Open: Mon.–Sat. 10–5

Antiques, locally handmade crafts, dried and fresh flower arrangements and wreaths.

Great Places to Stay

Drei Madel Haus
108 Schiller St.
573/486-3552 or 573/486-3558

1840s brick house in old town

Edelweiss B & B
800 18th St.
573/486-3184

Unique house with fabulous view.

Gatzmeyer Guest House
222 E. Second St.
573/486-2635 or 573/252-4380

Circa 1880s in Historic District

German Haus B & B
113 N. Market
573/486-2222

Circa 1840s.

Hermann Hill Vineyard & Inn
711 Wein St.
573/486-4455

Spectacular views and private balconies.

John Bohlken Inn
201 Schiller St.
573/486-3903

American country decor, homemade German pastries for breakfast.

Kolbe Guest House
214 Wharf St.
573/486-3453 or 573/486-2955

Circa 1850 with river view.

Market Street B & B
210 Market St.
573/486-5597

Turn of the century Victorian home.

Missouri

Mary Elizabeth House
226 W. 6th St.
573/486-3281

1890s Victorian House

Meyer's Fourth Street B & B
128 E. Fourth St.
573/486-2917

Circa 1840s. Centrally located.

Mumbrauer Gasthaus
223 W. Second St.
573/486-5246

Circa 1885 in the heart of the Historic District.

Patty Kerr B & B
109 E. Third St.
573/486-2510

Circa 1840. Light breakfast. Outdoor tub.

Pelze Nichol Haus (Santa Haus)
Hwy. 100, 1.3 miles east of Missouri River bridge
573/486-3886

Primitive Christmas decor in 1851 Federalist brick home.

Reiff House B & B
306 Market St.
573/486-2994 or 1-800-482-2994

Circa 1871 in Historic District.

Schau-ins-Land
573/486-3425

Stone home that was once an 1889 winery.

White House Hotel B & B
232 Wharf St.
573/486-3200 or 573/486-3493

1868 historic hotel next to Missouri River with antique shop and ice cream parlor on premises.

Great Places to Eat

Buckler's Deli & Pizza
100 Schiller St.
573/486-1140 or 573/486-3514

See how the Bucklers turned an old bank into a unique deli.

Downtown Deli and Custard Shop
316 E. 1st St.
573/486-5002
Open: Daily til 10 p.m.

Featuring salads, sandwiches served on fresh baked breads and homemade pies. Hand-dipped and soft-serve ice cream.

Vintage 1847 Restaurant
Stone Hill Winery
573/486-3479
Open: Daily, lunch from 11 a.m., dinner from 5 p.m.

Recommended by many food critics as one of America's finest restaurants. Casual dining in the original carriage house of the winery.

24 HERMITAGE

H. Bryan Western Collectables
Located at the corner of Spring St. and Hwy. 54
1-800-954-9911
Open: Daily 9–6
Directions: Hermitage is in southwest Missouri, and H. Bryan Western Collectables is on Hwy. 54 at the corner of Spring Street.

"Real men shop at H. Bryan's Western Collectables," could be the motto at this Midwestern exchange. This home/shop combo was originally established during the 1940s as a watch repair/jewelry store. The present owners spent much of their formative years visiting the shop and learning the trade. It became a full-time profession when they purchased the business in 1995. Through the years, the shop has broadened its specialties to include the buying, selling and trading of vintage watches, collectible cigar lighters, Zippos, as well as antique and new knives for the collector or investor.

25 HIGHLANDVILLE

Tuxedo Cat Antique Mall
8180 Hwy. 160 S.
417/443-5000

Missouri

26 INDEPENDENCE

Country Meadows Antique Mall

4621 Shrank Dr.
816/373-0410
Open: Mon.–Sat. 9–9, Sun. 9–6
Directions: From points North of K.C. Airport: South on I-435 to I-70 E.
To Lees Summit Road. exit. South on Lees Summit Road. To 40 Hwy. &
East to Country Meadows Mall (3 blocks E. of Lee's Summit Road. on
40 Hwy). From points South of Grandview: Take 71 N. to I-470 (this
becomes 291 N.). Exit at 40 Hwy. W. Country Meadows is
approximately 1 mile W. of 291 on 40 Hwy. From points West, by way of
I-70: Take Lees Summit Road Exit S to 40 Hwy E. Country Meadows is
east 3 blocks on 40 Hwy.

Country Meadows Antique Mall offers a stunning array of antiques
and collectibles. This two-story mall is brimming with diverse treasures
from the past and present. Antiques from over 400 dealers fill hundreds
of booths and showcases at Country Meadows, where 40,000 square feet
full of history will keep you shopping for hours. Stop in and enjoy lunch
in the Tea Room, which is open daily. Convenient location, ample parking
and friendly, knowledgeable staff will add to your shopping pleasure.

Sherman's Odds & Endtiques	**Liberty House Antiques**
109 W. Lexington Ave.	111 N. Main St.
816/461-6336	816/254-4494
Black Flag Antiques, Inc.	**Keeping Room**
118 S. Main St.	213 N. Main St.
816/833-1134	816/833-1693
Classic Treasures	**Sermon-Aderson, Inc.**
108 W. Maple Ave.	210 W. Maple Ave.
816/254-5050	816/252-9193
Sermon-Aderson, Inc.	**Adventure Antiques**
10815 E. Winner Road	11432 E. Truman Road
816/252-9192	816/833-0303

Great Places to Stay

Woodstock Inn Bed & Breakfast

1212 W. Lexington Ave.
816/833-2233
Open: Year-round
Rates: $54–$99
Directions: From points north or the K.C. Airport: Take I-435 east (to
St. Louis) to the 23rd Street Exit. Go left 2 ½ miles to Crysler. Be in the
left turn lane and go left 6 blocks. Crylser becomes Lexington and the
Woodstock Inn is on the left at the end of the 6 blocks. From points
west by way of I-70: Follow I-70 east through Kansas City to the I-435
North exit. Follow I-435 North to the first exit (23rd Street exit). Make
a right turn and follow 23rd Street 2 miles to Crysler Street. After

Crysler turns into Lexington, you will see a large auditorium on the
right. The Inn is on the left. From Branson, Springfield and points
southeast: Follow U.S. 30 North to I-70. Turn west on I-70 and follow it
to Exit 12 or Noland Road. Turn right on Noland Road and follow it to
23rd Street (about 1.6 miles). Turn left on 23rd Street and go to Crysler
Street (the first stop light). Turn right on Crysler. After about 7 blocks
Crysler will turn into Lexington. After that, you will see a large
auditorium on the right. The inn is on the left.

Formerly a turn-of-the-century doll and quilt factory, the Woodstock
Inn Bed & Breakfast is situated in the famous Historical District of
Independence. There are 11 guest rooms, each with a distinct personality
and private bath. Guests start the
morning off with the house
specialty—gourmet Belgian
waffles—or another special
breakfast entree. Then it's off to visit
the Truman Home, The Truman
Library and Museum, the National
Frontier Trails Center, the Old Stone Church, the RLDS Temple and
Auditorium, Jackson Square, and all the rest.

But when you get ready for dinner, please ask innkeepers Todd and
Patricia Justice for suggestions, or you might make the same mistake
that some guests did in a story the Justices' tell: "There's a very nice
looking building right up the street from our bed and breakfast. It looks
like a very large house, with nice landscaping and green awnings over
the windows. The sign by the door says 'Speaks.' Early one evening a
pair of hungry and weary guests walked in our door wanting to check in.
After the whole check-in process, the first words out of their mouths were,
'Where can we get something to eat? We are starving!' We suggested a
few places just a couple of miles away, but the lady said right away, 'Oh,
but what about that really nice restaurant on the left, right up the street?'
We looked at each other, then looked at the couple and said, 'We really
don't think you want to eat there!' She then asked, 'Why? It looks really
nice! Have you heard anything bad about the food?' Todd said, 'It's a
nice looking place but...it's a funeral home!' Needless to say our guests
didn't eat dinner, or any other meal, there!"

27 JAMESPORT

The Amish first came to the Jamesport area in 1953, making it the
largest Amish community in Missouri. The town is home to numerous
antique and crafts shops, including Amish stores that specialize in
commodities particular to Amish needs. Other town attractions include
the Harris Family Log Cabin, located in the city park. The cabin was
built in 1836 by Jesse and Polly Harris, one of the first white couples to
settle in the area. Great-grandsons Ray and Herb Harris, both in their
70s now, reconstructed the cabin at its present site.

Great Places to Shop

Antiques Americana
One block north of 4-way stop next to library
660/684-5500 or 660/359-2408

Early American house contains antiques, collectibles, crafts, furniture, vintage clothing, primitives and gift items.

Balcony House Antiques
East of 4-way stop
660/684-6725
Open: Mon.–Sat. year-round, Sun. Apr. 1–Dec. 31.

Features a full line of quality antiques and collectibles: glassware, furniture, Indian artifacts, quilts, etc. In stock there are over 500 titles of reference books (with price guides) on antiques and collectibles.

The Barn Antiques & Crafts
660/684-6711

Large selection of antiques, collectibles, porcelain dolls, willow furniture, quilts, baskets, Christmas shop.

Broadway Pavilion Mall
South of 4-way stop
660/684-6655

Antiques, collectibles, furniture, glassware, pottery, jewelry, large selection of old books.

Carlyles & Pastime Antiques
East of 4-way stop
660/684-6222

Distinguished gifts, collectible items, antique furniture, home decorating ideas.

Colonial Rug and Broom Shoppe
2 ½ blocks west of 4-way stop
1-800-647-5586
Open: Mon.–Sun. 8–6

See hand-woven rugs and brooms made daily. Purchase them already made or have them created to your own needs.

The Country Station
1 block east of 4-way stop
660/684-6454
Open: Mon.–Sat. 10–4

Country furniture, needlework, dolls, doilies, antiques, collectibles and lots more.

Country Treasures
660/684-6338
Open: Mon.–Wed. and Fri.–Sat., 10–4, closed Thurs. and Sun.

Baskets, old spools, Amish pictures, doilies, potpourris, candles, shelves, Amish made furniture, many items one of a kind.

Downtown Oak & Spice
660/684-6526
Open: Mon.–Sat. 9–5

Woodcrafts, teas and spices, oak furniture, hand-dipped ice cream, baskets, Moser glass.

Ellis Antiques
Located at 4-way stop
660/684-6319
Open: Year-round Mon.–Sat., 8–5: Sun. 1–4

Country furniture and accessories, glass, china, jewelry, etc.

Granny's Playhouse Antique Mall
East of 4-way stop
660/684-6599 or 660/359-3021

A unique selection of Jewel Tea, collectible jewelry, porcelain dolls, quilts, wall hangings, chimes, all in 33 booths.

Iris Collectibles
Five blocks west of 4-way stop at corner of South and Elm
660/684-6626

Glassware, pottery, jewelry, and miscellaneous.

Katie Belle's
Two blocks west of 4-way stop
Antiques, collectibles, furniture and country gift items.

Koehn's Country Naturals
855 Hwy. F
660/684-6830

"The Herb Lovers Nook"

Leona's Amish Country Shop
660/684-6628
Open: Daily 9–whenever

Dinner bells, Amish dolls and quilts, antiques and collectibles.

Marigolds
3 blocks west of downtown (The Orange House)
660/684-6122

Retail and wholesale. A house full of primitive country. Birdhouses, benches, mirrors, and lots of folk art.

The Olde Homestead
Two doors south of Post Office
660/684-6870

Rustic, primitive, western folk art.

Pastime Antiques I & II
660/684-6222

Antique furniture, finished and unfinished. Custom birdhouses, old-fashioned candies.

Rolling Hills Store
Hwy. 190
4 ½ miles south of Jamesport

Local made Amish furniture.

Ropp's Country Variety
1 ¼ miles south of Jamesport

Amish shop.

Sherwood Quilts and Crafts
3 miles east on F and one mile south on U

Large selection of handmade quilts, rugs, and baskets. Amish shop.

This 'n' That
S. Broadway
1 block north of 4-way stop
660/684-6594
Open: Mon.–Sat. 9–5

Antique furniture, glassware, jewelry and collectibles.

Warren House Antiques
East of 4-way stop
660/684-6266
Open: Daily 10–5

Antique Mall, 27 booths, antiques and collectibles - dishes, furniture, tools, primitives and more.

Great Places to Stay

Country Colonial Bed & Breakfast
660/684-6711 or 1-800-579-9248

Originally built in the 1800s, this house has been restored to an era past with a veranda and three bedrooms, each with a private bath. Since the B&B is centrally located near the shops, you can spend your day shopping, and at night, relax by playing parlor games, reading one of the 500 antique books in the library, or playing the baby grand piano. In the morning awake to a full country breakfast.

Marigolds Inn
Located 3 blocks west of downtown next to Marigolds Shoppe
660/684-6122

Opening Spring of 1997. Twelve rooms, each individually decorated in folk art themes.

Nancy's Guest Cottage Bed and Breakfast
660/684-6156

The cottage is filled with antique memories of yesteryear. Family style country breakfast is included. Located 2 blocks east of the 4-way stop, 2 blocks north on 190 and 2 blocks east.

Oak Tree Inn Bed & Breakfast
4 miles on Hwy. "F" east of Jamesport
660/684-6250

Relax in an original 3-story Amish-built home set in a wondrous 20 acre grove of tall majestic oak trees.

Missouri

Great Places to Eat

Anna's Bake Shop
Route 1, Box 34A, west end of town (Amish owned)
Open: Mon.–Sat. 8–6, closed Sun., closed from Christmas until Feb.

Fresh baked donuts, pies, breads, cinnamon and dinner rolls, cakes and much more.

Black Crow Soda Fountain
Corner of Main St. & Broadway
660/684-6789

An old-fashioned ice cream parlor. Soup and sandwiches along with their famous "Darla's BBQ beef brisket special."

Country Bakery
Located ½ mile south of Jamesport on Hwy. 190, Route 2, Box 177B
Open: Daily except Thurs. and Sun. (Amish owned)

Large selection of home-made baked goods.

Gingerich Dutch Pantry and Bakery
Located at 4-way stop
Open: Mon.–Sat. 6–9
660/684-6212

(Mennonites owned) Specializing in Amish style meals, homemade pies and baked goods, made fresh daily. Tasty sandwiches to home cooked dinner specials.

28 JEFFERSON CITY

Old Munichberg Antique Mall
710 Jefferson St.
573/659-8494

Twin Maples Collections
1125 Jefferson St.
573/636-2567

Bare Necessities Collectibles
804 E. Hight St.
573-636-5509

Missouri Boulevard Antique
1415 Missouri Blvd.
573/636-5636

29 JOPLIN

Southside Antique Mall
2914 E. 32nd St.
417/623-1000

Uniform Shoppe
1052 S. Main St.
417/624-6650

Connie's Antiques & Collectibles
3421 N. Range Line Road
417/781-2602

Country Heart Village
4901 S. Range Line Road
417/781-2468

Gingerbread House
RR 7
417/623-6690

30 KANSAS CITY

Bella's Hess Antique Mall
715 Armour Road
816/474-4790

Belle Chelsea Antiques
4444 Bell St.
816/561-1056

Estate Pine Gallery
4448 Bell St.
816/931-6661

Olde Theatre Archl. Salvage Co.
2045 Broadway St.
816/283-3740

Cummings Corner Antiques
1703 W. 45th St.
816/753-5353

River Market Antique Mall
115 W. 5th St.
816/221-0220

Molly & Otis O'Conner
1707 W. 45th St.
816/561-6838

Portobello Road & Camel Antiques
1708 W. 45th St.
816/931-2280

Lloyd's Antiques
1711 W. 45th St.
816/931-7922

Elizabeth Gibbs
1714 W. 45th St.
816/561-7355

Joseph's Antiques
1714 W. 45th St.
816/756-5553

Parrin & Co.
1717 W. 45th St.
816/753-7959

Christopher Filley Antiques
1721 W. 45th St.
816/561-1124

Morning Glory Antiques
1807 W. 45th St.
816/756-0117

European Express
1812 W. 45th St.
816/753-0443

Anderson's Antiques
1813 W. 45th St.
816/531-1155

Brown's Emporium
1263 N. 47 St.
816/356-0040

Jewelry Box Antiques
2450 Grand Blvd.
816/472-1760

Mom's Ole Stuff
10939 Hillcrest Road
816/765-6561

Asiatica, Ltd.
4824 Rainbow Blvd.
816/831-0831

J.J. McKee Antiquities
222 W. 7th St.
816/361-8719

Waldo Antiques & Imports
226 W. 75th St.
816/333-8233

Chabineaux's
334 W. 75th St.
816/361-1300

Waldo Galleria
334 W. 75th St.
816/361-2544

Waldo Galleria Antique Annex
336 W. 75th St.
816/361-2396

Remember When Antiques
349 N.W. 69 Hwy.
816/455-1815

Old World Antiques, Ltd.
1715 Summit St.
816/472-0815

Poor Richard's Antiques Object
401 E. 31st St.
816/531-4550

Boomerang
1415 W. 39th St.
816/531-6111

Darlene's Antiques & Collectibles
5502 Troost Ave.
816/361-9901

Town Gallery
3522 N.E. Vivion Road
816/454-3570

Superlatives
320 Ward Pkwy.
816/561-7610

Missouri

Twentieth Century Consortium
1004 Westport Road
816/931-0986

Meirhoff's Antique Stained Glass
210 Wyandotte St.
816/421-4912

Sebree Galleries & Le Picnique
301 E. 55th St.
816/333-3387

5th Street Antique Mall
302 W. 5th St.
816/472-9700

Broyle's Antiques
10605 Blue Ridge Blvd.
816/966-8888

Crestwood Galleries Antiques
301 E. 55th St.
816/333-3387

General Store Antiques
4200 Genessee St.
816/531-7888

Red Room Antiques
232 W. 75th St.
816/361-5933

31 KENNETT

Bank of Antiques & Special Finds
201 First St.
573/888-4663
Open: Mon.–Sat. 10–5, usually open until 8 on Thurs.
Directions: 17 miles from I-55 (Hayti exit) in downtown Kennett.

Bank of Antiques & Special Finds, gets its name from its former life as a bank in downtown Kennett, Mo. Built in 1916, this historical establishment houses a fine selection of glassware, dolls, furniture, jewelry, some collectibles, and more. Within the bookstore located in the shop, you can browse for new books and enjoy a delicious box lunch and a cup of gourmet coffee or hot tea. For those of you interested in "star" memorabilia, music artist Sheryl Crow donates her hand-me-downs to the shop. The proceeds of the clothing and shoe sale supports the local children's home.

The Treasure Chest
211 First St.
573/888-6772

32 KIRKSVILLE

Poor Richards Gifts & Collectibles
713 S. Baltimore St.
816/627-4438

Smith & Burstert
1612 Westport Road
816/531-4772

River Market Antique Mall
115 W. 5th St.
816/221-0220

Antiquities & Oddities
1732 Cherry St.
816/842-4606

Brookside Antiques
6219 Oak St.
816/444-4774

Cheep Antiques
500 W. 5th St.
816/471-0092

Dottie Mae's
7927 Wornall Road
816/361-1505

M & B Antiques
230 W. 7th St.
816/361-7300

Good Ole Days Antiques & Cllbls.
1515 S. Baltimore St.
816/665-3540

Square Deal Antique Mall
Hwy. 63 Route 2
816/665-1686

Potpourri Antiques
106 W. Harrison St.
816/665-8397

33 LEBANON

Treasure Trove Antiques
1231 W. Elm St.
417/532-6945

Jefferson House Antiques
364 N. Jefferson Ave.
417/532-6933

Country Corner Antique Mall
585 N. Jefferson Ave.
417/588-1430

Spring Holler Antiques
15350 Glendale Road
417/532-9453

34 LEES SUMMIT

American Heritage Antique Mall
220 S.E. Douglas St.
816/524-8427

Sandy's Mall
101 S.W. Market St.
816/525-9844

35 LEXINGTON

The Velvet Pumpkin
827 Main St.
816/259-4545

Redgoose Antiques
914 Main St.
816/259-2421

36 LIBERTY

Liberty Square Antiques
2 E. Franklin St.
816/781-7191

Kansas Street Antiques
10 W. Kansas Ave.
816/781-1059

Anna Marie's Antiques Gft & Acces
118 N. Water St.
816/792-8777

Antebellum Antiques
7 N. Missouri St.
816/792-0779

Wood Rail Antique Mall
Hwy. 63 S.
816/665-1555

Pleasant Memories Antique Mall
25999 Hwy. 5
417/588-3411

Jennissa Antiques & Gifts
577 N. Jefferson Ave.
417/588-1029

Griffith House Antiques
115 E. Elm St.
417/532-8211

Annie Sue's Antiques
302 S.W. Main St.
816/246-8082

Exclusively Missouri Gifts & More
200 S.W. Market St.
816/525-5747

Victorian Peddler
900 Main St.
816/259-4533

Liberty Antique Mall
Town Square-1 E Kansas
816/781-2796

Liberty Antique Mall
1005 N. State Route 291
816/781-3190

Sandy's Antiques, Ltd.
131 S. Water St.
816/781-3100

37 MACON

The Weathervane
32429 Juniper Place
816/385-2941

Ugly Duckling Antiques
1144 Jackson-Hwy. 63 N.
816/385-6183

Carousel Antiques
127 Vine St.
816/385-4284

Ednamay's Antiques
203 Jackson St.
816/385-3021

Colonel's Flea Market
312 S. Missouri Hwy. 63
816/385-2497

The Antique Parlor & Coffee Bar
132 Vine St.
816/385-1168

38 MANSFIELD

Laura Ingalls Wilder, the greatly loved and internationally known authoress of the beloved "Little House" books, lived most of her life in Mansfield, Mo. It is here at Rocky Ridge Farm that she wrote all nine of her famous books about her pioneer childhood and later life in Missouri. Her writing desk still stands in the home that Almanzo built for her. The home is on the National Register of Historic Places and is surrounded by apple, walnut and dogwood trees, many of which Laura planted.

Each year the residents of Mansfield relive the times of Laura Ingalls Wilder with their fall festival.

There are costume and beard contests, a kiddie parade, a big parade, an arts and crafts fair, games for the children, surprises, entertainment from the bandstand, lots of good food, and gingerbread made from Laura's recipe. And of course, there are continuous tours all day through the Laura Ingalls Wilder Home and Museum. Call the Friendship House B&B for dates.

Great Places to Stay

Friendship House Bed & Breakfast and Antique Boutique
210 W. Commercial
417/924-8511
Open: Year-round
Directions: For specific directions from your location, please call the innkeepers.

Friendship House is the charming rock home where *Little House* author Laura Ingalls Wilder celebrated birthdays and other special occasions with her close friend, Neta Seals.

Built in 1939, by Mr. and Mrs. Seals, the 16-room home was planned as a rooming house advertising "Modern Rooms." Lovingly preserved by its present owners, the tree-shrouded brownstone wears the soft patina of age and bespeaks the tranquility of days past.

Friendship House is ideally located, one half block from the Mansfield Town Square, and is a five minute drive from the Laura Ingalls Wilder Home and Museum.

Yours hosts, Sharon and Charlie Davis, offer visitors old-fashioned

hospitality and comfortable ambience. Guests may relax with a refreshing iced drink on the charming sun porch or head straight for the swimming pool. Tall fences, stately trees, and a landscaped patio envelop this lush backyard hideaway in peace and privacy.

The living room, with its lace-covered windows and rich blend of antiques and period reproductions, is an inviting place of repose. Breakfast is served in the adjoining formal dining room, where Laura and Neta gathered with their husbands and friends to share meals and celebrations.

Upstairs, visitors are transported in time to the boarding house days of the 1930s. Cozy sleeping rooms open onto the airy central hall. Its restful decor and gleaming woodwork are a welcome change from the sterility of modern day motels. Each room is individually decorated and has its original porcelain sink. A full bath and water closet are shared by the guests.

39 MARIONVILLE

Beautiful Victorian homes and a rare, urban white squirrel population are the hallmarks of Marionville, Missouri. According to town legend, around 1854 a circus came to town and brought rare white squirrels with them (were they part of an act?). When the circus left, their squirrels didn't! Now there are thousands of them. They don't cross the highway; they don't run off to the woods — they like living right in the middle of town!

Ole Mill Around
Hwy. 60
417/463-7423

Kountry Korner Antqs. & Uniques
Hwy. 60 & 265
417/463-2923

Great Places to Stay

White Squirrel Hollow Bed & Breakfast
203 Mill St.
417/463-7626
Open: Daily
Directions: White Squirrel Hollow B&B is located in Marionville at Mill Street and ZZ Hwy., west of U.S. Hwy. 60.

Step back in time when you visit the White Squirrel Hollow Bed and Breakfast. It's a historical, romantic Victorian home built in 1896 by one of the Ozarks first famous families, and it's filled with original antique photos, prints and furnishings. It's also a theme B & B, so its 5,000 square feet are filled with six different atmospheres decorated in antique, purist decor. Guests can choose from the Victorian Honeymoon suite with a full lace canopy bed and private screened balcony; the Gold Coast Room reminiscent of the 1849 California Gold Rush days; the Elizabethan Room, fit for royalty with it's flocked wall paper, satin canopy-covered bed, mink spread and English antiques; Turkish Corners, with a tented canopy bed, fabulous view and exotic touches; the Wild, Wild West Room, with an atmosphere from the days of western adventure; and a cottage

Missouri

that offers a night on African safari. The main house also boasts inlaid hardwood floors, beaded woodwork, a spiral staircase and doorway spandrels that are all original and lavish. The large music room was once a conservatoire, but now houses an antique baby grand and a 600-piece antique book collection. And of course there are the rare white squirrels rambling all across the property for your pleasure!

40 MOBERLY

Reed Street Antiques
303 W. Reed St.
816/263-7878

Moberly Plating & Antiques
512 W. Rollins St.
816/263-5371

Jim's Country Barn Antiques
RR 4
816/263-6714

Kierstle Haus Antiques
Route 1 Box 56
816/263-7828

41 MONETT

V. B. Hall Antiques
201 W. Main St.
417/235-1110
Open: Mon.–Sat. 9:30–5, Sun. 1–5
Directions: From intersection of Highways 60 and 37 in Monett, turn North on 37, 2 blocks turn right, one block - you're there!

The name V.B. Hall Antiques is very well known to the folks of Monett. Four generations of V. B.s have participated in the business community of this Missouri town, with V.B. Sr. even serving as town mayor for a term or two. The store, with 70 to 75 dealers in about 12,000 square feet of space, carries a large variety of items, from primitives to pottery, to glassware and a mixture of furnishings covering several periods and styles. The building itself is vintage 1947, beginning its life as a wholesale produce store.

Banks Antiques
103 N. Lincoln Ave.
417/235-6387

Archer Antiques & Collectibles
119 Commercial
417/235-3523

42 MONROE CITY

Downtown Antique Mall
208 S. Main St.
573/735-4522

Country Mini Mall
Hwy. 24 & 36
573/735-4935

Downtown Antique Mall
Business 36
573/735-3156

Over The Hill Antique Mall
101 S. Main St.
573/735-4966

43 NEOSHO

Neosho Gallery & Flea Market
900 N. College St.
417/451-4675

Four Seasons
322 S. Neosho Blvd.
417/451-3839

44 NEVADA

Crossroads 71/54 Antique Mall
1617 E. Ashland St.
417/667-7775

Louise Fanning Antiques
1231 E. Austin Blvd.
417/667-5903

45 OSAGE BEACH

Osage Beach Flea Market
Hwy. 42 & 54
573/348-5454

Osage River Co. Store
Hwy. 54
573/348-0819

Land of Yesteryear
Hwy. 54
573/348-3855

House of Stewart Antiques
Hwy. 54
573/348-9248

46 OZARK

Most of the thousands of antiquers who come to Ozark, Missouri every summer are, as one antique shop owner puts it, "just coming in to browse, but some people are on a mission." Another says that Ozark is known as "the antique place to come," and that most of the visitors hit every store. There's plenty of stores to be found in Ozark, scattered throughout the city, but most are prominently collected at two sites: Missouri 14 and U.S. 65, and the Riverview Plaza locations on Missouri 14 northeast of the U.S. 65 intersections.

Collectively all these stores contribute significantly to the city's tax revenues and tourism industry. Although the antique shops are not Ozark's only draw, they are important to the city's economy — so much so that the Ozark Chamber of Commerce promotes the shops on billboards and in tourist information mailings. Of course it doesn't hurt that Ozark is on the way to Branson, and picks up a great deal of traffic from that destination. From old dolls and battered school desks to yellowed newspaper front pages and expensive jewelry, any item you are looking for is likely to be somewhere among the booths of old stuff brought in from all over the country.

Antique Emporium
1702 W. Boat St.
Located at 65 & CC (behind Lambert's Cafe)
417/581-5555
Open: Summer Mon.–Sat. 9–9, winter Mon.–Thurs. and Sat. 9–6, Fri. 9–9, Sun. 9–5
Directions: From I-44 exit 65 South. Antique Emporium is located approximately 9 miles south of I-44 on U.S. 65 on route to Branson, 9 miles south of Springfield.

All antiques and no crafts are what you'll find among the 100 dealers in the 12,000-square-foot mall of Antique Emporium. They don't carry a lot of bigger furniture, mostly small period pieces, but shoppers will find a great deal of glass, primitives and collectibles, including Roseville, Fiesta, Candlewick, Fenton, Heisey, china, and ladies artifacts. In addition you'll find clocks, quilts, gas pumps, railroad items, advertising, antique hunting and fishing items and western collectibles.

Ozark Antique Mall and Collectibles

200 S. 20th St.
417/581-5233
Open: Daily summer 9–6, winter 9–5
Directions: At U.S. 65 and Hwy. 14 in Ozark, turn west and take the first left, which is 20th Street. Look for Ozark Antique Mall on the right-hand side — it's the building with all the great old advertising signs and antiques out front in the southwest corner of Highways 65 and 14.

Be prepared to come early and spend plenty of time browing for that special item.

Over 100 dealers have their wares displayed throughout the 17,000 square feet of Ozark Antiques. There is an endless variety of merchandise to choose from, with a very helpful staff happy to aid shoppers as they pore through large collections of primitives, pottery, furniture and thousands of pieces of Depression glass. Other specialty lines include military items, fishing gear, gas pumps, Coca-Cola memorabilia, toys, advertising, architectural salvage items, ball cards, Aladdin lamps, cookie jars, Ertl, radios, trains, tins, Fiestaware, marbles, knives and dolls.

Finley River Heirlooms, Inc.
105 N. 20th St.
417/581-3253

Maine Streete Mall
1994 Evangel St.
417/581-2575

Pine Merchant Antiques
140 N. 20th St.
417/581-7333

Riverview Antique Center
909 W. Jackson
417/581-4426

Scott's-Beckers' Hardware
1411 S. 3rd St.
417/581-6525; 1-800-991-0151

Abbotsford Antiques
200 S. 20th St.
417/581-8445

Crossroads Antique Mall
2004 Evangel St.
417/485-4941

Norman's Antiques
1781 W. Clay St.
417/581-7826

47 PERRY

Huffman Trading Post
Hwy. 19
573/565-3275

Price Emporium
113 W. Main St.
573/565-3159

Packrats Unlimited
124 E. Main St.
573/565-3594

Country Store Antiques
1007 E. Main St.
573/565-2822

Lick Creek Antiques
Main St.
573/565-3422

Miss Daisy's Antique Shop
Main St.
573/565-2737

Elam Antique Shoppe
110 S. Palmyra St.
573/565-2206

Arlington Antiques
Palmyra St.
573/565-2624

Perry Main Street Antiques
S. Palmyra St.
573/565-3246

48 PLATTE CITY

I-29 Antique Mall

Junction I-29 & H. H. Hwy.
816/858-2921
Open: Daily 10–6

I-29 Antique Mall is located in Historic Platte City, Missouri just 30 minutes north of downtown Kansas City on Interstate 29. The Platte City area features some of the best antique shopping in the Midwest, with three large malls offering a wide range of quality furniture, glassware, advertising items and much more. A favorite stop for dealers and collectors from across the country, I-29 Antique Mall is just 6 miles north of K.C. International Airport, with abundant food and lodging close by. Visit the Platte City area and see some of the best antiquing Missouri has to offer!

W.D. Pickers Antique Mall
Exit 20 I-29
816/858-3100

Wellsbrooke Antiques
500 Main St.
816/858-5306

49 PLEASANT HILL

Cookie Jars & More
113 S. 1st St.
816/987-5244

First Street Antiques
121 S. 1st St.
816/987-5432

Sentimental Journey Antiques
100 Wyoming St.
816/987-3661

Downtown Antiques
115 Wyoming St.
816/987-5505

50 ROCHEPORT

Griffith's Antiques
405 Clark
573/698-3503

Richard Saunder's Antiques
Columbia & 2nd St.
573/698-3765

Missouri River Antiques & Books
12851 W. High
573/698-2080

Whitehorse Antiques
12855 W. High
573/698-2088

Farm Road Antiques
370 N. Roby Farm Road
573/698-2206

River City Antique Mall
420 N. Roby Farm Road
573/698-2116

Henderson's Antiques
451 N. Roby Farm Road
573/698-4485

Widow Lister Antiques
405 2nd St.
573/698-2701

51 ROLLA

Antique Corner
606 Lanning Lane
573/368-5579

Totem Pole Trading Post
1413 Martin Spring Dr.
573/364-3519

Mary's Antiques
13458 S. U.S. 63
573/364-5372

Hancock's Used Furniture
102 S. Rucker Ave.
573/364-2665

52 ROSEBUD

Apple Antiques

Hwy. 50
573/764-3148
Open: Thurs.–Mon. 9:30–5, closed Tues.–Wed.
Directions: Apple Antiques is located 50 miles east of Jefferson City on Hwy. 50. From St. Louis, take I-44 west to the Union, Mo. exit, which is Hwy. 50.

Owner Edna Weatherford handles glassware, furniture and collectibles in her store, and tells a very interesting story about the shop's name, Apple Antiques. "The name of my antique shop is very unique, indeed. The customers usually tend to believe 'Apple' is my last name. Actually, it has nothing to do with my name. The last year I taught school, my students made a project of naming my shop. They came up with 'Apple Antiques' — an apple for the teacher, find the apple of your eye, etc. The parts of the apple are all divisions within the shop: the seed — beginning of goodness; the core — innermost and loved; the fruit — no serpents allowed; the peel — delicious value inside; the stem — attached and treasured; and last but not least, the apple orchard — ripe with age.

"There are apples everywhere you look, even on a shoplifting sign, the last line of which says, 'But Eve paid dearly when she stole an apple!' The name 'Apple Antiques' has proven to be very ... fruitful!"

Dinner Bell Antiques

Hwy. 50
573/764-3090
Open: Mon.–Sat. 9:30–5, closed Sun.
Directions: Dinner Bell Antiques faces Hwy. 50 in Rosebud, halfway between St. Louis and Jefferson City.

Dinner Bell Antiques is nestled in a turn-of-the-century building full of antiques, collectibles, old tools, primitives, furniture, glassware and architectural antiques. According to owner Karen Jose, her store was the third building constructed in Rosebud when the railroad came through in 1900. In the past 96 years, the store has housed everything from shoe stores and farm implement stores to a drug store, a grocery, a barber shop, even the town post office.

Quilts by Shirley

249 Hwy. 50 (located at Shirley's House of Beauty)
573/764-2422

Shirley Rice, owner of Quilts by Shirley, is a true artisan, one of a dwindling group of women who still quilt by hand. She began quilting as a little girl, taught by her mother, and they quilted together for years. Shirley didn't really begin quilting part-time until about thirteen years ago, when she lost one of her little girls and went back to quilting as a means of therapy. She is a full-time hairdresser, so she quilts nights, weekends—anytime she has a few spare moments.

Shirley makes all of the tops for her quilts, table runners, baby quilts, Christmas tree skirts and wall hangings herself, and she has a couple of ladies who help her with the actual quilting. She can make most tops in a day's time, she says, but the quilting may take as long as two or three months. Her personal favorite pattern is the Wedding Ring, but she makes them all: Lover's Knot, Lone Star, Dresden Plate, Log Cabin. If customers who come to her shop don't see exactly what they want, Shirley will custom make anything to the exact size and color.

Her husband has gotten into the quilting business with her by making a special quilting frame that is much easier to handle, set up, use and store than the traditional giant frame. Mr. Rice's frame is made from square metal tubing and the frame is 10 feet long but only three feet wide; its special feature is a rolling florescent light that rolls along the edge of the frame, providing shadow-free lighting along the entire frame.

Great Places to Stay

The Wild Rose Bed & Breakfast

Route 1, off Idel Road
573/764-2849
Rates: $55–$65
Directions: The Wild Rose is located off of Idel Road, the first mailbox on the left 1/4 mile east of Rosebud. Rosebud is just one hour west of St. Louis off I-44 on Hwy. 50.

The Wild Rose is a restored farmhouse filled with art and antiques, set on 25 beautifully landscaped acres just outside of Rosebud. The well-stocked lake is surrounded by pines and stately pin oaks, with trails winding through the woods and meadows. There are boats and fishing gear for the fishermen in the group (no license required), while anyone wanting to just unwind and commune with nature can sit by the peaceful Koi and goldfish pond near the house.

The library offers the beauty of stained glass windows, a fireplace and a collection of masks, with an additional fireplace in the cathedral-ceiling living room. Each bedroom has its own unique personality. The Victorian Rose is dominated by a high backed Victorian bed and rose-covered walls. The Rambling Rose combines wicker furniture and whimsical art work, dashed with tropical blues and pastels, plants and seashells. The English

Rose has a wonderful 19th century English brass bed and antique camp table with two large wing chairs.

The Bluebird Bed & Breakfast
5734 Mill Rock Road
573/627-2515
Open: 24 hours daily
Directions: From State Hwy. 50 which runs through Gerald, go south on Route H, eight miles to the Bourbouse River. Go two miles across the river to Mill Rock Road. Turn left onto Mill Rock and the Bluebird is the first drive on the right; approximately ²/₁₀ of a mile. Complete directions are provided with reservations.

The Bluebird Bed & Breakfast offers a peaceful English Country setting for city dwellers in need of a little R & R.

Restful views, the chirping of birds, beautiful trees, flowering gardens and a well-stocked fishing pond provide the perfect escape.

There are four guest rooms, all comfortably appointed, each with its own unique theme. An old fashioned screened porch is ideal for bird watching, fish jumping, or simply cat-napping.

As is customary, continental and full breakfasts are served; gourmet dinners are available with 48 hours notice.

Only minutes from local flea markets, antique shops, caverns, and wine country, the Bluebird Bed & Breakfast can provide an effective reprise from an otherwise hectic world.

River House Bed & Breakfast
5339 Mill Rock Road
573/764-5262
Directions: From Hwy. 50 take Hwy. "H" from Gerald. Go 8 miles and cross the Bourbeuse River. Continue for 2 miles to Mill Rock Road, turn left, River House is 1⁷/₁₀ miles further down.

This bed and breakfast is appropriately named for the Bourbeuse River that flows through the property, with the bedroom window and side deck overlooking the river. The cottage includes a kitchen, full bath, living and dining areas, and bathroom, all completely furnished in antiques, Americana and accessories. The old Franklin wood stove can even be used. A very private, self-contained cozy getaway. Breakfast is served upon request.

53 SALEM

Bargain Barn
506 E. Center St.
573/729-7354

Gunny Sack
306 E. 4th St.
573/729-8797

Antiques & Things
806 E. Center St.
573/729-4062

Nina's Antique & Flea Market
Hwy. 72 N.
573/729-2958

Gateway Antiques
900B S. Main St.
573/729-7766

Gateway Antiques
402 W. 4th St.
573/729-5544

54 SEDALIA

Country Village Mall
4005 S. Limit Ave.
816/827-2877

Millie's Pink Mall
Hwy. 65-5915 Limit
816/826-5894

Downtown Antiques
516 S. Ohio Ave.
816/826-2266

Fourth Street Mall
215 E. 4th St.
573/729-8520

John's Used Furniture & Things
4011 S. Limit Ave.
816/826-7801

Mapleleaf Antique Mall
106 W. Main St.
816/826-8383

Sedalia Antique Shop
804 W. 16th St.
816/826-1472

55 SPRINGFIELD

Park Central Flea Market
429 Boonville
417/831-7516
Open: Mon.–Sat. 10–5, Sun. 12–5
Directions: Traveling I-44 from the west, turn east on Chestnut Expressway, or traveling I-44 from the east, turn south on Glenstone and west on Chestnut Expressway, or exit Hwy. 65, and turn west on Chestnut Expressway. Take Chestnut Expressway to Boonville and turn south to 429 Boonville.

Having been in business for more than 20 years, Park Central Flea Market has lots of antiques and collectibles stashed in its two-story shop. They carry antique glassware, carnival glass, pottery, graniteware, pictures, primitives, toys and lamps.

Aesthetic Concerns, Ltd.
326 N. Boonville Ave.
417/864-4177

Treasure Chest
411 N. Boonville Ave.
417/863-1047

Downtown Furniture Restorations
419 Boonville Ave.
417/865-3230

By-Pass Antiques
535 B N. West Bypass
417/865-4992

Antique Warehouse & Mall
2139 S. Campbell Ave.
417/886-9776

Country Corner Flea Market
351 Boonville Ave.
417/862-1597

Centerfield Sportscards
427 Boonville Ave.
417/831-7675

Fort No. 5
425 N. Boonville Ave., #5
417/865-9966

Bass Country Antique Mall
1832 S. Campbell Ave.
417/869-8255

Auction Barn
1435 W. College St.
417/831-2734

Another Man's Treasure
1700 W. College St.
417/864-2811

G & W Antiques & Collectibles
400 W. Commercial St.
417/869-0061

Century Galleries
1355 E. Commercial St.
417/869-4137

Antique Place
1720A S. Glenstone Ave.
417/887-3800

Cottage & Provence
2744 S. Glenstone Ave.
417/887-1930

Andrew's Collectibles
435 W. Kearney St.
417/831-3577

Touche Designs, Inc.
2009 S. National Ave.
417/883-8633

Furniture Stripping Ozarks, Ltd.
1263 E. Republic Road
417/883-8313

Jerry's Antique Mall
309 South Ave.
417/862-4723

Knight's Stamps
323 South Ave.
417/862-3018

Sunshine Antiques
1342 W. Sunshine St.
417/864-0069

STD East Flea Market
1820 E. Trafficway
417/831-6367

Collections
1112 E. Walnut St.
417/865-0552

56 ST. CHARLES

Saint Charles Antique Mall
1 Charlestowne Plaza
314/939-4178

Fifth Street Antique Mall
520 S. 5th St.
314/940-1862

Royal Antiques
101 N. Main St.
314/947-0537

Nellie Dunn's Antiques
211 E. Commercial St.
417/864-6822

Great Discoveries
416 W. Commerical St.
417/869-9101

Mary II Antiques & Gifts
3747 S. Cox Road
417/888-3099

A Second Time Around Shoppe
1736 N. Glenstone Ave.
417/831-1666

STD East Flea Market
651 S. Kansas
417/831-6331

Coach House Antique Mall
2051 E. Kearney St.
417/869-8008

Apple Barrel Antiques
2104 N. National Ave.
417/862-4635

Viles Swap Shop
3023 E. Republic St.
417/881-4042

South Peer Antique Mall
317 South Ave.
417/831-6558

Springfield Antique Co.
406 South Ave.
417/866-6995

Anastasia & Co.
1700 E. Sunshine St.
417/890-1714

History Antiques
1111 E. Walnut St.
417/864-8147

Class Act Antiques
224 E. Commercial St.
417/862-1370

Log House Antiques
2431 W. Clay St.
314/724-1889

Upstairs Mkt./Aimee B's Tea Room
837 1st Capitol
314/949-9271

Antiques & Oak
319 N. Main St.
314/946-1898

Aladdin's Lamp & Collectibles
321 S. Main St.
314/946-8865

Kuhlmann's Antique Emporium
324 N. Main St.
314/946-7333

Mirabilia Gallery
524 S. Main St.
314/947-9077

Mamie Maples Emporium
825 N. 2nd St.
314/947-0801

Lauree's Vintage Jewelry
827 N. 2nd St.
314/940-1711

Charlestowne Antiques
903 N. 2nd St.
314/946-7134

Pioneer Antiques
1410 N. 2nd St.
314/724-1539

Rachel's Antiques
1601 N. 2nd St.
314/925-1023

57 ST. JAMES

Kracker Barrell Antiques
108 N. Jefferson St.
573/265-3546

Old Mill Store
RR 2
573/699-4423

Treasure Nook
132 W. Washington St.
573/265-7416

58 ST. JOSEPH

Hobbitt's Hole Antiques
323 N. Main St.
314/947-6227

Gina's at the Witt House
426 S. Main St.
314/946-6106

Memories of Yesteryear
806 N. 2nd St.
314/724-2163

French Connection Antiques
826 N. 2nd St.
314/947-7044

Bo's Primitive Peddler
901 N. 2nd St.
314/724-9366

Little Hills Antiques
1125 N. 2nd St.
314/947-1770

Wartimes Memorabilia
1501 N. 2nd St.
314/949-9929

McKinley Antique Mall
1701 N. 2nd St.
314/946-8186

Forest City Popcorn Co.
124 N. Jefferson St.
573/265-3383

Heirlooms Past & Present
107 W. Springfield St.
573/265-7938

No matter where you're bound, St. Joseph is the way to real adventure. Saddle up to glory at the Pony Express National Memorial, where "young, skinny, wiry fellows" like Buffalo Bill Cody and Johnny Fry started their 10-day relay dash to California with the mail. Follow the footsteps of 50,000 '49ers, who left here in the gold rush to "pick up a fortune." Walk in the front door of the house where Jesse James' infamous life came to an end and onto the recreated streets of ol' St. Jo at the Patee House Museum.

St. Jo isn't all rough and ready, though. Turn-of-the-century mansions are open for you to tour and even have high tea. Admire the works of the masters at the Albrecht-Kemper Museum of Art, and discover the secret gardens and stone bridges of the 26 miles of greenway linking the parks.

Hunt through a nearly endless supply of beautiful antiques, and shop to your heart's content.

Located on the scenic river bluffs overlooking the Missouri River, born of the fur trade, nurtured by the "Westward Expansion," and brimming with a spirit of adventure, St. Joseph is a city you will never forget.

Somersby Antiques
501 N. Belt Hwy.
816/390-8864

Horn's Antique Emporium
502 Felix St.
816/364-3717

Jerry's Antiques
2512 Frederick Ave.
816/232-9881

Dakon's Antiques
1801 Garfield Ave.
816/233-2971

Penn Street Square
1122 Penn St.
816/232-4626

Arnold's Antiques
644 S. 6th St.
816/233-4416

Country House Antiques & Crafts
1801 N. Woodbine Road
816/232-4455

Creverling's
1125 Charles St.
816/232-9298

Hatfield's Antique Mall
2028 Frederick Ave.
816/233-9106

Coin-Jewelry-Antique Exchange
3837 Frederick Ave.
816/232-8838

Den of Antiquity
1919 Holman St.
816/279-0942

Corner Shoppe
1503 Penn St.
816/232-0045

A & E Company
1213 S. 22nd St.
816/279-6206

59 ST. LOUIS

Cherokee Antique Row

2014 Cherokee St.
314/664-7916 or 314/773-8810
Open: Daily 11–4
Directions: Take I-55 to Arsenal Street (near the Anheuser-Busch Brewery), turn south on Lemp, go 4 blocks and turn west on Cherokee Street.

Here's your chance to shop from dawn till dusk in one spot! At Cherokee Antique Row you can visit 40 unique shops that sell many different varieties of items in a four-block area. Don't miss it!

Dapple-Gray Antiques
159 W. Argonne Dr.
314/965-0239

John's Furniture & Antiques
7107 S. Broadway
314/351-6745

White Swan Antiques
7006 Bruno Ave.
314/781-7114

Stock Exchange Consignment Shop
2115 S. Big Bend Blvd.
314/645-3025

Phillips Antiques
8473 N. Broadway
314/867-0965

English Garden Antiques
1906 Cherokee St.
314/771-5121

Looking Glass
1915 Cherokee St.
314/773-1912

Neon Lady
1926 Cherokee St.
314/771-7506

Riverside Architectural Antiques
1947 Cherokee St.
314/772-9177

Remember When Antiques
1955 Cherokee St.
314/771-1711

Hartmann's Treasures
1960 Cherokee St.
314/773-5039

Henderson Co.
2020 Cherokee St.
314/773-1021

Odd Shop
2101 Cherokee St.
314/773-8566

Glass Turtle
2112 Cherokee St.
314/771-6779

Nostalgia Shop
2118 Cherokee St.
314/773-4907

Victorian Village Antiques
2125 Cherokee St.
314/773-8810

Antiques by Art of the Ages
2205 Cherokee St.
314/776-0959

Penny's Collectibles
2307 Cherokee St.
314/771-2822

Clayton Antiques
6403 Clayton Road
314/725-9878

Legacy Antiques
7715 Clayton Road (Clayton)
314/725-2209

Finches Consignment & Gifts
7729 Clayton Road
314/725-2622

M.J.'s Consignment Shop
7803 Clayton Road (Clayton)
314/863-8762

Panorama Antiques & Collectibles
1925 Cherokee St.
314/772-8007

Hammonds Books
1939 Cherokee St.
314/776-4737

Lealee Antiques
1950 Cherokee St.
314/772-9030

My Friends Closet
2851 Cherokee St.
314/664-3993

Purple Cow
2018 Cherokee St.
314/771-9400

Haffner's Antiques
2100 Cherokee St.
314/772-6371

Things from the Attic
2110 Cherokee St.
314/865-1552

Southside Antiques
2114 Cherokee St.
314/773-4242

Homemaker Antiques
2124 Cherokee St.
314/776-4267

Frank & Julia's
2201 Cherokee St.
314/865-2995

Debbie Fellenz Antiques
2224 Cherokee St.
314/776-8363

Haffner's Antiques
2847 Cherokee St.
314/771-3173

Shaker Tree Antiques
7713 Clayton Road
314/726-3233

Regent Parade Consignment Shop
7721 Clayton Road (Clayton)
314/727-4959

Davis Place Antqs. & Consignments
7731 Clayton Road
314/727-9850

Matti's Antiques
7805 Clayton Road (Clayton)
314/721-5535

Small World Antiques
9752 Clayton Road
314/997-5854

Antique & Art Appraisers of America
9918 Clayton Road
314/993-4477

Braun Antiques
10315 Clayton Road
314/991-1798

The Original Cast Lighting, Inc.
6120 Delmar Blvd.
314/863-1895

Rothschild's Antiques
398 N. Euclid Ave.
314/361-4870

Kodner Gallery
7501 Forsyth Blvd.
314/863-9366

Books & Collectibles
3196 S. Grand Blvd.
314/771-3196

PSA Presentations
131 W. Jefferson Ave.
314/822-8345

Alamo Military Collectables
716 Lemay Ferry Road
314/638-6505

Ferrari's Consignment Shop
7314 Manchester Road (Maplewood)
314/644-5755

Post Card Shop
12024 Manchester Road (Des Peres)
314/822-7174

Brilliant Antiques
8107 Maryland Ave. (Clayton)
314/725-2526

Clark Graves Antiques
132 N. Meramec Ave.
314/725-2695

Tower Grove Antiques
3308 Meramec St.
314/352-9020

Sambeaus, Ltd.
4724 McPherson Ave.
314/361-4636

West End Antiques Gallery
4732 McPherson Ave.
314/361-1059

Jules L. Pass Antiques, Ltd.
9916 Clayton Road
314/991-1522

Kodner Gallery
9918 Clayton Road
314/993-4477

Ziern Antiques
10333 Clayton Road
314/993-0809

Coyote's Paw Gallery
6388 Delmar Blvd.
314/721-7576

Fellenz Antiques
439 N. Euclid Ave.
314/367-0214

Switching Post
7742 Forsyth Blvd.
314/725-7730

J. Middleton Mid Century Modern
3949 Gravois Ave.
314/773-8096

Shackelford Antiques & More
4519 S. Kingshighway Blvd.
314/832-6508

A Country Place Antiques
2930 Lemay Ferry Road
314/892-6677

European Country Antiques, Ltd.
9621 Manchester Road
314/968-2550

Four Seasons West Antiques
4657 Maryland Plaza
314/361-2929

Tin Roof Antiques
2201 McCausland Ave.
314/647-1049

This 'n' That
3305 Meramec St.
314/353-2365

Alexander Furniture Co.
3309 Meramec St.
314/481-2111

Golden Harvest
4732 McPherson Ave.
314/454-9330

Martin's Galleries
4736 McPherson Ave.
314/361-1202

West Monroe Antiques
132 W. Monroe Ave.
314/821-2931

Designs in Gold
11006 Olive Blvd.
314/567-3530

Now and Then Antiques
6344 S. Rosebury Ave.
314/721-3301

Jack Parker Antiques
4652 Shaw Ave.
314/773-3320

St. Louis Architectural Art
1600 S. 39th St.
314/773-2264

South County Antique Mall
13208 Tesson Ferry Road
314/842-5566

60   STE. GENEVIEVE

Mill Antique Mart
301 N. Main St.
573/883-7333

Sarah's Antiques
124 Merchant St.
573/883-5890

Kaegels Country Collectibles
252 Merchant St.
573/883-7996

Collag
18 S. Third
573/883-9575

Joyce & Choyse's Antiques & Collectibles
58 S. 3rd St.
573/883-2358

Dalton's Treasure Chest
183 S. 3rd St.
573/883-9190

61   STEELVILLE

Nancy's Antique Dolls 'n' Stuff
103 W. Main St.
573/775-3655

Edie's Backwoods Antiques
403 Main St.
573/775-2629

Pierce House Antiques
139 W. Monroe Ave. (Kirkwood)
314/821-5140

Vinegar Hill Antique
107 W. Pacific Ave.
314/962-0375

Remember Me Vintage Clothing
1021 Russell Blvd.
314/773-1930

Tommy T's
3010 Sutton Blvd.
314/645-7471

Harley's Harps
2271 Administration Dr.
314/567-1980 X206

Warson Woods Antique Mall
10091 Manchester Road
314/909-0123

Monia,s Unlimited
316 Market St.
573/883-7874

Mr. Frederic, Ltd.
195 Merchant St.
573/883-2717

Zielinski's
288 Merchant St.
573/883-7004

Odile's Linen & Lace, Etc.
34 S. 3rd St.
573/883-2675

The Summer Kitchen
146 S. 3rd St.
573/883-3498

Willies Moles
105 E. Main St.
573/775-2722

Down Memory Lane
107 W. Main St.
573/775-3131

62 SULLIVAN

Country Collectibles & Early Smithing
5054 Hwy. K
573/468-8170

White Lion Antiques
5 Maple St.
573/468-2437

Sullivan Showcase Antique Mall
201 N. Service Road W.
573/468-3943

63 WARSAW

This Old House Antiques & Crafts
420 Commercial
816/438-3588

Swinging Bridge Antiques & Crafts
Hwy. 7 & Main St.
816/438-7422

Mule Barn
Hwy. 7 & Truman Dam
816/438-3186

Columns Antique Shop
1129 N. Lay Ave.
816/438-6032

Warsaw Antique Mall
245 W. Main St.
816/438-9759

Curiosity Shop
406 W. Main St.
816/438-5034

Molly's Antiques
616 W. Main St.
816/438-6911

Lou's Quilts & Buckley's Antiques
702 W. Main St.
816/438-7853

64 WASHINGTON

Annie-Rose
1110 Clock Tower Plaza
314/239-1970

Waterworks Antiques
1 Elbert Dr.
314/390-2344

Feed Store Antique Mall
101 E. Main St.
314/390-0115

Tamm Haus Antiques
5 W. 2nd St.
314/239-9699

Attic Treasures
100 W. Front St.
314/390-0200

65 WEST PLAINS

Elledge House Antiques
315 Broadway
417/256-2442

Aid Downtown Antique Mall
1 Court Square
417/256-6487

Jefferson St. Flea Market
310 Jefferson Ave.
417/256-4788

Looking Back
712 Porter Wagoner Blvd.
417/256-8586

Antique Corner
313 Washington Ave.
417/256-2193

66 WESTON

J & L Antiques
Hwy. 45 & P
816/386-2456

Tobacco Road
400 Main St.
816/386-2121

J.P.'s Antiques
509 Main St.
816/386-2199

J.P.'s Antiques
523 Main St.
816/386-2828

Painted Lady Antiques
540 Main St.
816/386-5580

Tobacco Patch Country Store
18260 State Route 45 N.
816/640-2627

J.P.'s Antiques
424 Main St.
816/386-2894

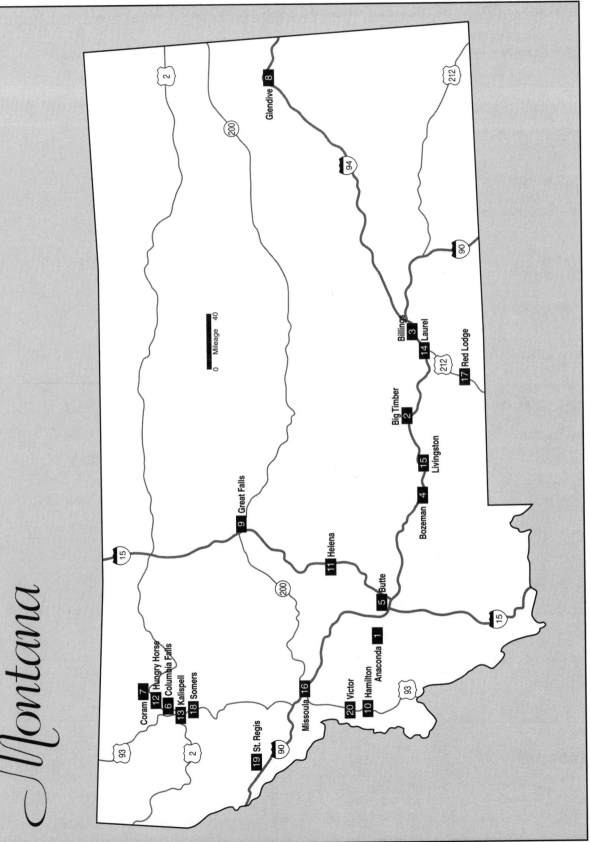

Montana

Mileage
0 — 40

2
200
8 Glendive
212
94
90
Billings
3
14 Laurel
212
17 Red Lodge
2 Big Timber
15 Livingston
4 Bozeman
9 Great Falls
11 Helena
15
200
Butte
5
1 Anaconda
15
93
7 Coram
12 Hungry Horse
6 Columbia Falls
13 Kalispell
18 Somers
20 Victor
10 Hamilton
16 Missoula
19 St. Regis
90
93
2

1 ANACONDA

Founded in 1883, this small town owes its existence to Marcus Daly and the Anaconda Copper Company. Smelting operations were suspended in 1980, but Anaconda has a firm grip on its role in Montana history. The town's landmark and a state park, "The Stack," stands 585 feet 1.5 inches tall. Visit the Copper Village Museum and Art Center for area history and a copper smelter display, and the Hearst Free Library, a classic 1889 period building donated to the city by George and Phoebe Hearst. Self-guided walking tour, brochure and bus tour of historic Anaconda begins at the Anaconda Visitors' Center.

Brewery Antiques
125 W. Commercial St.
406/563-7926

Park Street Antique Mall
113 E. Park St.
406/563-3150

2 BIG TIMBER

Located at the foot of the Crazy Mountains, Big Timber offers a broad range of activities in a beautiful setting. Explore the Boulder Valley, fish blue-ribbon trout streams and stop by the Yellowstone River Trout Hatchery for an appreciation of cut-throat trout. Visit museums, galleries, antique shops and historic sites including Victorian Village, Montana Armory, Shiloh Rifle Manufacturing Co., Sweetgrass and Sage Gallery and the Crazy Mountain Museum.

Crazy Mountain Art & Antiques
14 Anderson
406/932-4797

3 BILLINGS

Montana's largest city, Billings is a regional business hub, as well as a cultural, medical, educational and entertainment center. Museums, art galleries, theaters and shopping are all part of the appeal of this vibrant city. Discover the elegantly restored, turn-of-the-century Moss Mansion providing a glimpse into the life of Preston B. Moss, one of Billings' most prominent early residents. Bordered on the north by distinctive rock formations known as rimrocks, Billings is a gateway to Little Bighorn Battlefield National Monument, Bighorn National Recreation Area, Yellowstone Park, the Yellowstone River and the Abrasroka-Beartooth Wilderness.

Whispering Pines
12 S. Broadway
406/446-1470

Waterwheel Antiques
2339 S. 56th Road
406/656-8350

Antique Peddler
1327 Main St.
406/256-7003

Pickett Fence Antqs. & Collectibles
645 Custer Ave.
406/254-1725

Magic City Floral
1848 Grand Ave.
406/652-6960

Oxford Hotel Antiques
2411 Montana Ave.
406/248-2094

Billings Nursery
2147 Poly Dr.
406/656-5501

Yesteryears
114-118 N. 29th St.
406/259-3314

Buy the Book
2040 Rosebud Dr., #5
406/652-1188

A-1 Attic Dreams Antiques
901 Terry Ave.
406/256-3051

Rose Petal Antiques
726 Grand Ave.
406/248-5801

Depot Antique Mall
2223 Montana Ave.
406/245-5955

4 BOZEMAN

Visitors will find a small town atmosphere with big city amenities in Bozeman. This town, beautifully situated at the base of the Bridger Range, blends spectacular recreation with art galleries, museums, symphony, opera, history and many one-of-a-kind Western stores. Walk through the South Wilson Historic District, a residential area featuring houses that range from large mansions to small cottages. Visit the Gallatin Pioneer Museum for area history and artifacts.

Country Mall Antiques
8350 Huffine Lane
406/587-7688

Cellar 105 Antiques & Gifts
105 W. Main St.
406/587-3013

Country Charm
612 E. Main St.
406/587-5281

The Attic
212 S. Wallace
406/587-2747

Sack's of Bozeman
138 W. Mendenhall
406/587-7283

Rocky Mountain Rug Gallery
628 W. Main St.
406/585-7900

Take 2
7 S. Tracy Ave.
408/586-8324

Davis Torres Furniture Collect
14 W. Main St.
406/587-1587

The Antique Mall
612 E. Main St.
406/587-5281

Antiques, Etc.
25 N. Willson Ave.
406/587-9306

The Brass Monkey
370 Lodgepole Lane
406/586-6855

Brass Monkey The Sandman
370 Lodgepole Lane
406/586-6855

Swenson's Furniture
702 E. Main St.
406/587-8701

Old World Antiques
1530 W. Main St.
406/582-1848

Great Places to Stay

Fox Hollow Bed & Breakfast
545 Mary Road
406/582-8440 or 1-800-431-5010
Open: Year-round

At Fox Hollow Bed & Breakfast, the wonder of Montana's big sky awaits. Sunsets are spectacular from the wraparound porch of this country-style

Montana

home. Settle into an oversized guest room, each with a private bath. Soak in the hot tub while gazing into the cool starlit Montana night. Wake to the aroma of coffee brewing and a delicious gourmet breakfast.

Torch and Toes Bed and Breakfast
309 S. Third Ave.
406/586-7285 or 1-800-446-2138

This 1906 Colonial Revival home, found in the Bon Ton Historic District, was built for Wilbur F. Williams, vice-president of the Bozeman Milling Company. Today, the Torch and Toes Bed and Breakfast retains its original high ceilings, oak wainscoting, and leaded-glass windows. Turn-of-the-century furnishings accentuate the house's original elements. Collections of gargoyles, mousetraps, and old postcards create a fanciful atmosphere. Each of four guest rooms (with private baths) presents an individual setting. During winter, a full breakfast is provided before the fireplace in the dining room. In summer, breakfast is served on the redwood deck.

5 BUTTE

Once known as "the richest hill on earth," Butte is steeped in mining history. Copper, gold, silver were all found here, and Butte became a melting pot of ethnic diversity as immigrants flocked to the mines for employment. The Anselmo Mine Yard in uptown Butte is the best surviving example of surface support facilities that once served the mines. Butte is the home of Montana Tech of the University of Montana, which grew out of Butte's mining heritage. Its Mineral Museum displays 1,500 specimens, including a 27.5 ounce gold nugget. Walking tour brochures of this historic city are available at the Butte Chamber of Commerce. This is also the place to catch a tour of Butte on a replica of an early-day streetcar, "Old No. 1." Three-story, 34-room Copper King Mansion, home of former copper king/politician William A. Clark, has been preserved as it was in the 1880s.

Antiques on Broadway
45 W. Broadway
406/782-3207

Rediscoveries Vintage Clothing
55 W. Park St.
406/723-2176

Debris, Ltd.
123 N. Main St.
406/782-9090

Someplace Else
117 N. Main St.
406/782-2864

Donut Seed Consignments
120 N. Main St.
406/782-7123

Rustic Montana Interiors
27 W. Park St.
406/723-1500

D & G Antiques
16 N. Montana St.
406/723-4552

Great Places to Stay

The Scott Bed and Breakfast
15 W. Copper
406/723-7030 or 1-800-844-2952

Built in 1897, this former boarding house for miners overlooking Butte's Historic Landmark District is today The Scott Bed and Breakfast. Extensively renovated, this historic setting offers the modern comforts of seven rooms, each with private baths. Explore nearby Copper King Mansion, as well as the World Museum of Mining.

6 COLUMBIA FALLS

A stop in this gateway city to Glacier National Park brings family fun and exploration. Enjoy championship golf in the summer; cross country skiing, ice skating and snowmobiling in the winter. The city also boasts a popular waterslide and whitewater rafting.

Charmaine's Antiques & Collectibles
35 5th St. W.
406/892-3121

Pony Circus Antiques
527 Nucleus Ave.
406/892-1965

Great Places to Stay

Bad Rock Country Bed & Breakfast
480 Bad Rock Dr.
406/892-2829 or 1-800-422-3666

Bad Rock Country Bed & Breakfast is an elegant and charming home filled with Old West antiques, minutes from Glacier Park, on 30 acres in a gorgeous farming valley. Enjoy spectacular views of the 7200-foot-high Columbia Mountain, only 2 miles away. Experience the magic of quiet in the country and be pampered in the Bad Rock Bunny way. Soak in the secluded spa in a time reserved exclusively for you. Relax in one of the four new rooms made of hand-hewn square logs, with fireplaces and handmade lodgepole pine furniture, or settle into one of the four rooms in the home, all with private baths. Fantastic breakfasts are only one portion of the superb hospitality.

7 CORAM

Great Places to Stay

Heartwood
400 Seville Lane
406/387-5541

The "Little Cabin" at Heartwood (a family homestead) is a cheerful, 1930s log cabin nestled among tall pines on 215 acres of secluded

Montana

meadows and woodlands - completely surrounded by majestic mountains including views of the famous "Park Mountains" and located just seven miles from Glacier National Park. The "Little Cabin" is tastefully decorated with vintage furniture and accessories - yet remains very cozy and comfortable. The original (working) wood cookstove still occupies its place in the fully modern country kitchen. Accomodations include three bedrooms, living room, kitchen and large bathroom. Take advantage of nature trails, trout pond, nightly campfire, or just rest and relax.

8 GLENDIVE

Helen's Stuff
716 E. Bell St.
406/365-3405

Alley Antiques
616 N. Kendrick
406/365-3330

Antiques & Such
614 N. Meade
406/365-3018

Tin Shed
112½ Country Club Road
406/365-4553

Montana Antiques & Collectibles
1111 W. Bell St.
406/365-4691

9 GREAT FALLS

Great Falls is Montana's second-largest city, located on the Missouri River among the five falls that were both a magnificent spectacle and formidable barrier to early river travel. This area held significance for the Lewis and Clark Expedition. The explorers were forced to spend nearly a month portaging around the falls in June, 1805. Much of the Missouri River in this area remains as it was when Lewis and Clark first viewed it 190 years ago. The "Great Falls" of the Missouri is now the site of Ryan Dam, but may still be visited. Great Falls was also home of cowboy artist, Charlie Russell (1864-1926), whose original home and log studio are now part of the C. M. Russell Museum Complex. Soak up some local culture at the Montana Cowboys Bar and Museum or at Mehmke's Steam Engine Museum.

Browser's Corner
117 Central Ave.
406/727-5150

The Bet Art & Antiques
416 Central Ave.
406/453-1151

Mary Beth Shop
500 4th Ave. N.
406/452-4522

Bull Market Antique Mall
202 2nd Ave. S.
406/771-1869

G.P. Trading Company
405 Central Ave.
406/727-0369

Accents & Antiques
1015 14th St. S.
406/727-6049

Bill's Time Center
827 9th St. S.
406/761-1074

Lucky Lee's
8½ 7th St. S.
406/452-0358

Now & Then Shop
718 13th St. N.
406/452-0671

Janet's General Store
115 Central Ave.
406/761-1655

Far Out Antiques
301 24th St. N.W.
406/452-5211

DeCoy Antiques
500 5th Ave. S.
406/761-4684

10 HAMILTON

Located in the heart of the Bitterroot Valley, Hamilton is Montana's gateway to the Selway-Bitterroot Wilderness and a number of other recreational and historic attractions, including the Ravalli County Museum and Daly Mansion. Built in 1890 by Irish immigrant, Marcus Daly, one of Montana's colorful "copper kings," Daly Mansion with 42 rooms, 24 bedrooms, 15 baths and 5 Italian marble fireplaces, presides over 50 planted acres in Montana's scenic Bitterroot Valley.

Clothes Tree
301 Main St.
406/363-7003

Magpie Nest
247 State St.
406/363-3167

Hamtana
Pennsylvania Ave.
406/363-2482

Howdy Antiques
383 Owings Lane S.W.
406/363-2186

Great Places to Stay

Deer Crossing
396 Hayes Creek Road
406/363-2232 or 1-800-763-2232

Relax on the deck with a steaming cup of coffee and watch the sun rise over the Sapphire Mountains at Deer Crossing, a bed and breakfast with Old West charm. Enjoy a luxury suite with double jacuzzi tub, one of the three gracious guest rooms or the bunk house. The hearty ranch breakfast features garden fresh vegetables. Nearby adventures include fly fishing, rafting, hiking, horseback riding, skiing and snowmobile riding.

11 HELENA

An 1864 gold strike touched off a boom era that transformed Helena into "Queen City of the Rockies" and Montana's capital city. Trace its history along Main Street, still known as Last Chance Gulch. View historic buildings and mansions dating back to the 1870s such as the Original Governor's Mansion built in 1888. This Victorian mansion was the official residence of nine governors between 1913 and 1959. Enjoy the Last Chance Tour Train, a one-hour narrated tour of Historic Downtown Helena.

MT Antique Mall
4528 U. S. Hwy. 12 W.
406/449-3334
Open: Mon.–Sun. 10–5:30
Directions: Located approximately 2 miles west of Helena on U. S. Hwy. 12 toward Missoula. From I-15, go through Helena following the signs for Hwy. 12 W. and Missoula.

Listed on the National Register of Historic Places, Wassweiler Hotel and Bath House, built in 1883, is home to MT Antique Mall. Over 30 dealers display a wide selection of antiques and collectibles offering a variety of quality furniture, accessories, glassware, pottery, plus much more inside this former stopover for the cattle drovers, gold dust rovers, and "strike-it-rich" elite of Helena's boom days.

Missouri River Chronicle Antiques
1125 Helena Ave.
406/442-7887

Days of Yore
25 S. Last Chance Gulch St.
406/443-7947

Quigleys Antiques
5944 U.S. Hwy. 12 W.
406/449-8876

12 HUNGRY HORSE

Grandpa's Attic
8760 Hwy. 2 E.
406/387-4166

13 KALISPELL

Founded in 1891, Kalispell is now a bustling small city and home to much history, culture, commercial activity and outdoor recreation. The city's natural beauty and pleasant lifestyle draw a wide variety of residents and tourists. Get acquainted with the city on a walking tour of historic buildings and enjoy regional culture at the Hockaday Center for the Arts.

Wander through Conrad Mansion's Victorian elegance, built in 1895 as the home of C. E. Conrad, Montana pioneer, Missouri River trader, freighter and founder of the city of Kalispell.

End of the Trail Trading Post
1025 W. Center St.
406/756-3100

Idaho St. Antiques
110 E. Idaho St.
406/755-1324

Kalispell Antiques Market
48 Main St.
406/257-2800

Arts & Antiques Mall
40 2nd St. E.
406/755-1801

Bazaar
154 2nd Ave.
406/257-1878

Antiques of Kalispell
175 6th Ave.
406/257-4415

Southside Consignments
2699 U.S. Hwy. 93 S.
406/756-8526

Glacier Antique Mall
3195 U.S. Hwy. 93 N.
406/756-1690

White Elephant
3258 U.S. Hwy. 93 S.
406/756-7324

Demersville Mercantile
4010 U.S. Hwy. 93 S.
406/755-0917

Stageline Antiques
2510 Whitefish Stage Road
406/755-1044

Mom's Place
227 Main St.
406/257-4333

Four Corners Country Collectibles
105 Welf Lane
406/756-6541

Somers Second Hand & Antiques
210 Montana Hwy. 82
406/857-3234

Great Places to Stay

Creston Country Willows Bed & Breakfast
70 Creston Road
406/755-7517 or 1-800-257-7517

Near Glacier Park, wonder at the majestic mountain views and quiet charm of Creston Country Willows' rural setting. This bed & breakfast provides four guest rooms with private baths. In addition, head for area recreations, such as golfing, fishing or hiking, after the complimentary full country breakfast.

Stillwater Inn Bed & Breakfast
206 4th Ave. E.
1-800-398-7024

Relax in the comfort of this lovely historic home built at the turn of the century. The Stillwater Inn offers four guest bedrooms, two with private bathrooms and two that share a bathroom. Start the day dining on the delicious gourmet breakfast. Within walking distance are antique shops, art galleries and the Charles Conrad Mansion.

14 LAUREL

Located at the junction of great rivers and highways, Laurel is a convenient stop for travelers. The Chief Joseph Statue and Canyon Creek Battlefield Marker in downtown Fireman's Park commemorate the 1877 battle between the Nez Perce Indians, led by Chief Joseph, and the U.S. Cavalry under the command of Col. Samuel Sturgis.

Blue Bell Antiques
210 E. Main St.
406/628-2002

Huff Antiques
405 Maple Ave.
406/628-4493

Lind Antique Mall
101 W. 1st St.
406/628-1337

Montana

15 LIVINGSTON

Downtown Livingston, a designated Historic District on the National Register, encompasses 436 buildings, most within walking distance of one another. With the Yellowstone River flowing through town, Livingston is anglers' heaven, providing excellent floating and fishing access. Visit Park County Museum which is housed in a turn-of-the-century schoolhouse, featuring household displays, Indian artifacts, a stagecoach, sheep wagon and caboose. Located in a restored Northern Pacific Railroad station, Depot Center houses railroad and western history exhibits and art shows.

Save The Pieces
119 W. Callender St.
406/222-8131

Island Antiques
1500 E. Park St.
406/222-8025

Livingston Mercantile & Trade Co.
W. Park St.
406/222-3334

Doris Loomis Antiques
E. River Road
406/222-0427

Cowboy Connection
108 N. 2nd St.
406/222-0272

Authentic & Old Antiques
5237 Hwy. 89 S., Suite 3
406/222-9571

Grandma's Treasures
211 S. Main St.
406/222-2177

Jeannie's Alley Antiques
118½ N. Yellowstone St.
406/222-1617

Krohne Island Antiques
1500 E. Park St.
406/222-8025

Save the Pieces
119 W. Callender St.
406/222-8131

Vik's Antiques
Off Hwy 89 S. at Merrill St.
406/222-0128

16 MISSOULA

Montana's cultural superstar and third largest city, Missoula presides over the north end of the Bitterroot Valley. Best known as the home of the University of Montana, Missoula is an eclectic mix of students, independent business people, professors, foresters, artists and writers. At the head of five scenic valleys and the junction of three great rivers, Missoula has no shortage of recreational opportunities. Missoula is home to the Montana Repertory theatre, Missoula's Children's Theatre, String Orchestra of the Rockies and Garden City Ballet. Take a Trolley Tour through the historic downtown/university area or a carousel ride at A Carousel for Missoula in Caras Park beside the Clark Fork River. Soak up some western Montana history at the Historical Museum at Fort Missoula. Wonder with admiration at St. Francis Xavier Church, built in 1889, the year Montana became a state, outstanding for its graceful steeple, paintings and stained glass.

Ovilla
115 W. Front St.
406/728-3527

Jem Shoppe Jewelers
105 S. Higgins Ave.
406/728-4077

Bird's Nest
219 N. Higgins Ave.
406/721-1125

Mr. Higgins Vintage Clothing
612 S. Higgins Ave.
406/721-6446

1776 Antiques
214 E. Main St.
406/549-5092

Mountain Mama's Antiques
2002 S. Reserve St.
406/549-9281

Opportunity Resources Inc.
2821 S. Russell St.
406/721-2930

Magpie Antiques
109 S. 3rd St. W.
406/543-4428

Fran's Second Hand Store
601 Woody St.
406/549-0440

Ma & Pa's Second Hand Store
531 N. Higgins Ave.
406/728-0899

Herman's on Main Vintage Clothing
137 E. Main St.
406/728-4408

Montana Antique Mall
331 Railroad St. W.
406/721-5366

Horse Trader Antiques
1920 S. Russell St.
406/549-6280

Montana Craft Connection
1806 South Ave. W.
406/549-4486

Third Street Curiosity Shop
2601 S. 3rd St. W.
406/542-0097

17 RED LODGE

This historic mining town has roots that reach back to the European homes of its diverse founders. Situated at the base of the Beartooth Mountains, Red Lodge is one of Montana's premier ski destinations in winter; in summer, it draws hikers, anglers, campers, sightseers and Yellowstone Park visitors via the nearby Beartooth Highway. Enjoy native North American animals and the children's petting zoo at the Beartooth Nature Center. Take in the area's history at the Carbon County Museum, housed in the homestead cabin of John Garrison, subject of the movie Jeremiah Johnson. Explore buildings and houses on and off Main Street that were built between 1883 and 1910 during the coal mining boom. Remnants of the ethnic groups that settled Red Lodge are preserved in "Hibug" Town, Finn Town and Little Italy, whose ethnic traditions are celebrated every August during the 9-day Festival of Nations.

Flower Shop
20 N. Broadway Ave.
406/446-2330

Mama Bear
217 S. Broadway Ave.
406/446-2207

Whispering Pines
12 S. Broadway Ave.
406/446-1470

Cabin
105 S. Broadway Ave.
406/446-3386

Montana Chinook
6 S. Broadway Ave.
406/446-1810

Montana

18　SOMERS

Laurie Levengood's Antiques
4834 Hwy. 93 S.
406/857-3499

Somers Second Hand & Antiques
210 Montana Hwy., #82
406/857-3234

19　ST. REGIS

Cold Creek Antiques
Cold Creek Road
406/649-2675

Discover a fine array of antique furniture, collectibles, glassware as well as a pleasing assortment of accessories and other items in Cold Creek Antiques, a cozy shop.

The Place of Antiques
Downtown St. Regis
406/649-2397
Open: Mon.–Sun 9–5
Directions: From I-90, take Exit #33 into St. Regis.

Featuring original finish and refinished antique oak furniture, The Place of Antiques prepares all of its refinished pieces. In addition to furniture, Red Wing items, depression glassware and advertising memorabilia enhance the shop's offerings brought together by over 70 dealers.

Someplace in Time
Hwy. 135
406/649-2637

For a nostalgic stroll, Someplace In Time offers antique dolls, furnishings, in addition to many other delightful and attractive items.

20　VICTOR

Named for a Flathead Indian chief and nestled in the Bitterroot Valley, Victor offers endless recreational opportunities. Explore the Victor Heritage Museum, housed in the railroad depot.

Antique Sellar
275 Dinger Lane
406/642-3386

Red Willow Dry Goods
111 Main St.
406/642-3130

Nebraska

Mileage
0 _____ 40

Omaha
Lincoln

19 20 Papillion
22 Waterloo
21 Wahoo
7 Fremont
13 Lyons
17 Norfolk
4 Columbus
3 Central City
23 York
12
16 Nebraska City
1 Auburn
2 Beatrice
6 Fairbury
8 Grand Island
5 Doniphan
9 Hastings
15 Minden
10 Kearney
11 Lexington
18 North Platte
14 McCook

75
77
20
81
92
275
281
6
77
136
2
92
26
20
80
6

Nebraska

1 AUBURN

Bobbi-Jon Antique Mall
923 Central Ave.
402/274-5548

Auburn Antique Center
900 Central Ave.
402/274-3056

2 BEATRICE

Bert's Bargains
515 Ella St.
402/228-2670

Riverside Antiques
321 N. 9th St.
402/228-2673

Third Street Antiques
123 N. 3rd St.
402/228-2200

Attic Treasures
400 Court
402/228-2288

Rowdy's Relics
821 N. 11th St.
402/223-2807

3 CENTRAL CITY

Hitching Post Antiques
1607 16th St. (Hwy. 30)
308/946-2211

Time and Again
1401 15th St.
No Phone Listed

4 COLUMBUS

Cottonwood Antique Mall
2423 11th St.
402/564-1099

Memory Lane Antiques
1164 23rd Ave.
402/564-1870

5 DONIPHAN

Robb Mercantile Company
Main St.
402/845-2784

Stars 'n' Stripes
Main St.
402/845-6900

6 FAIRBURY

Stagecoach Mall

510 E St.
402/729-4034
Open: Mon.–Sat. 9–6, Sun. 12–5
Directions: Stagecoach Mall is located 45 miles south of I-80 on Hwy.
15, at the intersection of Hwy. 136 and Hwy. 15.

Located in historic downtown Fairbury, award-winning Stagecoach
Mall offers antiques, collectibles, crafts, gifts and goodies! They've been
featured in *Midwest Living Magazine* and the book *Day Trips in the
Heartland: A Get-Away Guide to Unique Places and Fun in the
Heartland*. Don't miss them!

Linda's Attic
522 D St.
402/729-5180

Great Places to Stay

Personett House Bed and Breakfast Inn

615 6th St.
402/729-2902
Rates: From $35

This bed and breakfast takes its name from Susie Personett, who ran a
boarding house in the home from 1916 to 1941. During World War II the
Jefferson County Chapter of the Red Cross acquired the house and used it
for various war-related purposes, such as assembling clothing and first
aid articles to be sent to England.

Offering guests seven lovely rooms with shared baths, the Personett
House is just one block from downtown Fairbury.

7 FREMONT

Visit historic downtown Fremont, eastern Nebraska's Antique Capital!
There are seven antique shops within walking distance. Fremont is home
of the May Museum that has a general store, a historic school room, an
1860 settler's log cabin, and a 25-room mansion filled with antiques.
Fremont also is the home station of the Fremont and Elkhorn Railway's
Fevr Dinner Train (402/727-0615).

John C. Antique Mall
544 N. Main
402/727-7092

C & E Antiques
530 N. Main
402/721-2101

Antique Alley
105 E. 6th Street
402/727-9542

Dime Store Days
109 E. 6th St.
402/727-0580

Memories Antiques
225 E. 6th St.
402/753-0578

Yankee Peddler West
141 E. 6th St.
402/721-7800

Hen House Gallery
3305 N. Broad St.
402/721-5275

Park Avenue Antiques
515 Park Ave.
402/721-1157

8 GRAND ISLAND

Great Exchange Flea Market

N.E. Corner of Hwy. 34 & S. Locust St.
308/381-4075
Open: Mon.–Sat.10–5, Sun. 12–5
Directions: Eastbound on I-80, Exit 312, go 4 ½ miles north on Hwy.
281 to Hwy. 34, east 2 miles to S. Locust St. Westbound I-80, exit 318,
go 4 miles north to Hwy 34, west 6 miles to Locust St.

The Great Exchange Flea Market has over 12,000 sq. ft. of well lighted,
clean floor area to browse. Certain areas are kept for specific themes,
such as "The Paper Route" where you'll find new, used and collectible

Nebraska

books, plus vintage magazines, newspapers, cookbooks, comics and tear sheets covering most of the paper collecting arena. A large area is set aside for furniture, mainly antique and collectible. A feature area of the market is Abby's Emporium which is the only craft area in the store. In this shop is a trip down memory lane including the tin roofs and picket fences. You'll find everything here from cabinets to doilies. Shelves and benches are loaded with treasures to decorate your home or put a smile on a friend's face.

Billed as the finest flea market in Nebraska, the Great Exchange Flea Market has 60 dealers offering everything from Hummels to handcuffs, depression glassware, pottery, primitives, toys, collectibles and more.

Lana's Antique Mall
112 W. 2nd St.
308/384-9876
Open: Mon.–Sat. 10–5, Sun. 12–5
Directions: From I-80, take Exit 281. Lana's is located 8 to 10 miles from I-80 on Highway 30 in Grand Island.

Nine dealers fill this two-story mall that specializes in country and primitive furnishings and accessories. It's easy to see how a piece will look in your home, since the individual rooms are set up as actual furnished areas with items from the mall.

Point of Interest: People from all over the country come to Grand Island from March through the first week of April to watch the sandhill cranes on their migratory route.

H & S Refinishing & Antiques
327 N. Cleburn St.
308/381-8737

Keith's Red Lamp Antiques & More
108 W. 3rd St.
308/384-6199

Clutter Bug Antiques
219 W. 3rd St.
308/382-0369

Chantilly Lace
327 N. Cleburn St.
308/381-8737

Prairie House
2536 Diers Ave.
308/381-8838

Time After Time
324 W. 3rd St.
308/384-7009

Heartland Antique Mall
216 W. 3rd St.
308/384-6018

Treasure Chest
216 S. Wheeler
308/382-8817

Fantasy Ceramics & Antiques
106 W. 3rd St.
308/381-6454

Country Trader
505 N. Pine
308/384-8277

9 HASTINGS

VIP Antiques
1733 W. 2nd St.
402/463-5055
Fax: 402/463-3038
Open: Mon.–Fri. 8–5, Sat. 12–4
Directions: Traveling I-80, take Exit 312 to South Hwy. 281. Go 16 $^6/_{10}$ miles to 2nd and Burlington St. and turn right (west) on 2nd St. Go exactly $^8/_{10}$ of a mile to the Total Convenience Store, which is on the left. Look up and you will see the VIP Antiques marquee. Turn left and go 1 short block and you are there.

Vicki and Paul Bergman love to cater to antique dealers and collectors, and their 5,000-square-foot warehouse is filled with a full line of antiques and other treasures especially suited for both groups. The selection is varied, the quality is excellent and the price is right! Sounds like my kind of shop.

Antiques And
706 W. 2nd St.
402/463-8010

Centra Warehouse Antiques
1733 W. 2nd St.
402/463-3455

Country Market Antiques
RR 1
402/462-6349

Katie's Nearly Nu
708 E. South St.
402/462-2000

Berdina's Treasure Trove
406 S. Maple
402/462-6596

The Antic Shop
3555 S. Baltimore
402/643-8002

Geranium Hill Antiques
214 S. Burlington
402/463-4354

Great Places to Stay

Grandma's Victorian Inn Bed & Breakfast
1826 W. 3rd St.
402/462-2013
Rates: From $60

An 1886 Victorian with a beautiful staircase and outstanding woodwork, Grandma's offers guests five rooms, each with private bath. The house is filled with antiques, with an accent on rocking chairs and queen-size beds in each guest room. Enjoy such simple, old-fashioned pleasures as sipping lemonade on the beautiful balcony, or relaxing on the front porch swings. Breakfast is served in the dining room, or, for an additional charge, can be served to you in bed!

10 KEARNEY

Kaufmann's Antique & Collectible Emporium
2200 Central Ave.
308/237-4972
Open: Mon.–Sat. 10–5, Sun. 1–5
Directions: Conveniently located off I-80. Go right 2 blocks from first stop light—over railroad overpass.

Kaufmann's Antique & Collectible Emporium is Kearney's largest antique mall with over 65 dealers displaying fine glassware, furniture, vintage jewelry, dolls, early American pieces and much more. Plan to spend at least two to three hours to browse this 8,000-square-foot former '20s variety store. One of our *favorite* antiquing spots.

Great Plains Art & Antique
131 S. Central Ave.
308/234-5250

Antique Co-op
229 Central Ave.
308/236-6990

Dady's Antiques & Collectibles
1809 Central Ave.
308/236-8319

11 LEXINGTON

Kugler Antiques
311 S. Washington St.
308/324-4267
Open: Daily 10–6
Directions: From I-80, take the Lexington exit, turn north and go 2 miles.

Located in a town that claims the title of "Antique Center of Nebraska," Kugler Antiques is unique in its inventory of antique furniture, primitives, glassware, pottery, crocks, silver, coins and old guns. The shop prides itself on providing shoppers with authentic antiques and is well known for its unusual collections.

One of the most interesting is a collection of old mannequins that might remind you of the old department store days, when window dressing was an art in itself.

Bargain John's Antiques
700 S. Washington St.
308/324-4576
Open: Mon.–Sat. 8–7, Sun. 12–6
Directions: Traveling I-80, take the Lexington exit to Hwy. 283. Follow Hwy. 283 into Lexington and turn left at the Pizza Hut off of Hwy. 283. The shop is located in the blue building.

Bargain John's has been Nebraska's largest supplier of quality antique furnishings since 1968. They specialize in Victorian furniture from the

1840s to 1910. They also carry a small quantity of Mission oak pieces and a grand selection of Victorian art glass and cameo glass.

Richardson Bargain Shed
951 W. Walnut
308/324-4786

Tinder Box
909 N. Grant St.
308/324-3585

Youngs Furniture & Auction
1108 N. Adams St.
308/324-4594

Leif's Antique Mall
Van Buren St.
308/324-2242

Memories Bed & Breakfast & Antqs.
900 N. Washington St.
308/324-3290

Memories Antique Shop
900 N. Washington St.
308/324-3290

Hofaker's Antiques
Hwy. 283
308/324-4719

Trinkets & Treasures
E. Hwy. 30 & Jefferson St.
308/324-5344

12 LINCOLN

Burlington Arcade
210 N. 7th St.
402/476-6067
Open: Mon.–Wed. and Sat. 10–6, Thurs.–Fri. 10–8, Sun. 1–5
Directions: From I-80, take the 9th Street Exit to the Historic Hay Market District, where Burlington Arcade is located.

Voted "Lincoln's Best Antique Mall" in 1996, Burlington Arcade Antique Mall is housed in the old Taxi Cab Building in Lincoln's Historic Hay Market District. The 30-plus dealers fill the 7,000-square-foot building with a mix of fine furniture, glassware, linen and jewelry. Great restaurants in the immediate area, combined with Burlington's treasures, make a day's outing a must for avid antiquers and history buffs.

B B & R Antique Mall
1709 O St.
402/474-7505
Open: Mon.–Fri. 10–6, Sat. 10–5, Sun. 12–5
Directions: From I-80, take the exit to 27th St. and travel south to O St. Turn right and the shop is located approximately 10 blocks down, near the intersection of O St. and 17th St. Parking is available behind the shop.

This 42-dealer mall is celebrating its third anniversary this year. They have a large variety of antiques ranging from jewelry to furniture to collectibles from the 1930s to the 1960s — just a big mix of everything.

Conner's Architectural Antiques
701 P St.
402/435-3338
Open: Mon.–Sat. 9:30–6, Sun. 1–5
Directions: From I-80, take the 9th St. Exit. Conner's is located in the

Historic Hay Market District of Lincoln, across the street from the old train depot.

Housed in the old Beatrice Creamery building, Conner's Architectural Antiques offers 20,000 square feet of any and everything you'll need to decorate your home. You'll find lighting, stained glass windows, doors, fireplace mantles, old hardware, garden accents, fencing, wrought iron tables and much, much more.

Additionally, the shop offers a matching service with over 20,000 pieces of china and crystal patterns.

Country Store
2156 S. 7th St.
402/476-2254

Indian Village Flea Market Emporium
3235 S. 13th St.
402/423-5380

Pack Rats A Cooperative
1617 S. 17th St.
402/474-4043

Continental Furniture, Ltd.
400 N. 48th St.
402/464-0434

Scherer's Architectural Antiques
6500 S. 56th St.
402/423-1582

Bittersweet Antiques & Gifts
2215 N. Cotner Blvd.
402/466-4966

Second Wind
1640 O St.
402/435-6072

Q Street Mall
1835 Q St.
402/435-3303

Bailey Antiques, Inc.
710 B St.
402/476-8422

Eastman's Antiques
2236 Bradfield Dr.
402/475-6669

Vel-Roy Antiques & Collectible
648 N. 31st St.
402/477-7062

Aardvark Antique Mall
5800 Arbor Road
402/464-5100

Antique Corner Cooperative
1601 S. 17th St.
402/476-8050

Coach House Antiques, Inc.
135 N. 26th St.
402/475-0429

Applebee's Antiques
3911 S. 48th St.
402/489-6326

Gatherings Antiques & Gifts
100 N. 8th (Haymarket)
402/476-1911

Capitol Beach Antique Mall
1000 W. O St.
402/474-1125

Cornhusker Mall Antiques
2120 Cornhusker Hwy.
402/438-5122

13th Street Antiques
915 S. 13th
402/477-3662

Burnham House Antiques
4600 J St.
402/489-1803

Treasures & Tropics
3845 S. 48th St.
402/486-3960

13 LYONS

Kristi's Antiques, Inc.
Hwy. 77
402/687-2339
Open: Mon.–Sat. 10–5, by appointment for dealers

Dealers, take note! Kristi's caters to you, as well as to the general shopper. They specialize in wholesaling, with over 1,000 pieces of original finish oak and walnut furniture. They also handle quilts, graniteware, stoneware, country store items, and thousands of smalls.

14 McCOOK

Kenny's Country Gifts & Antiques
N. Hwy. 83
308/345-2817

Huegels Hutch
401 Norris Ave.
308/345-7564

Accents, Etc.
307 Norris Ave.
308/345-7720

The Glass House
1503 W. Fifth St.
308/345-2547

15 MINDEN

Minden could be the ideal picture of sweet, romantic middle America: all old town square charm with antique stores and little businesses surrounded by Victorian mansions on manicured lawns, surrounded yet again by rolling, lush farmland.

It really is a cozy little Nebraska prairie town with an old and imposing courthouse complete with a big white dome! There are lots of prosperous businesses in the downtown district, including four antique shops.

Minden also has the Harold Warp Pioneer Village, one of the top museums of its kind in the country. This is an award-winning museum with 26 buildings holding 50,000 items that trace the development of everything from lighting and bathtubs to motorcycles and musical instruments from 1830 onwards. Among the buildings are seven historic structures, including an original livery stable complete with harness shop, and an authentic replica of a sod house. The museum also presents daily weaving, broom-making and other craft demonstrations.

House of Antiques
124 E. 5th St.
308/832-2200

Vinegar Hill Antiques
1161 25 Road
308/743-2445

16 NEBRASKA CITY

Nebraska City Antique Mall
800 Central Ave.
402/873-9805

Carriage House
512 Central Ave.
402/873-7410

Peppercricket Farm Antiques
Hwys. 2 and 75
402/873-7797

Grandma Lu's
117 S. 7th St.
402/873-5799

Nebraska

Cindy's Dream Shop
705 Central Ave.
402/873-5799

The Antique Shop
820 Central Ave.
402/873-3937

17 NORFOLK

Norfolk Market Place

207 Norfolk Ave.
402/644-7824
Open: Mon.–Sat. 10–5, closed Sun.
Directions: Norfolk Market Place is located directly on Business Hwy.
275. Actually, Norfolk Ave. is Business 275!

This is a year-round indoor flea market, so browsing doesn't have to
wait for good weather! They specialize in antiques, collectibles, furniture,
and (here's an unusual one!) old saddles, tack and buckles.

Buck-A-Roo Antiques
308 Northwestern Ave.
402/371-1240

Antique Arcade
Hwy. 81
402/379-0533

Reals Clock Repair & Antiques
127 Norfolk Ave.
402/371-4966

Main Street Antiques
715 Norfolk Ave.
402/371-6400

Double "S" Antiques
212 Northwestern Ave.
402/371-5404

18 NORTH PLATTE

The Hayloft

2006 E. 4th St.
308/532-1300
Open: Mon.–Fri. 10–5:30, Sat. 10–5, Sun. 1–5
Directions: Traveling I-80, take Exit 177 or 179 to East 4th St.

The Hayloft (sounds like a wonderful Nebraska name) offers a nice
selection of antiques, collectibles, handcrafts, art and gift items.

Antique Emporium
2019 E. 4th St.
308/532-9003

Dynamic Perfection
120 Rodeo Road
308/532-7420

Steele's Antique Depot
620 N. Vine St.
308/532-8173

19 OMAHA

Kirk Collection

1513 Military Ave.
1-800-398-2542 or 402/551-0386
Fax: 402/551-0971
Open: Tues.–Sat. 10–5, Mon. by appointment
Directions: Take I-80 to I-480 North to 75 North to the Hamilton St.
Exit. Go left on Hamilton 15 blocks to Military Ave. Take a right on
Military Ave., and the shop is the second building on the right.

The next time you're watching a movie like *Forrest Gump* or *Titantic*,
pay special attention, you may be looking at fabric purchased from The
Kirk Collection.

The Kirk Collection started dealing in antique quilts and only moved
into antique fabrics when owner Bill Kirk brought two trunkloads of fabric
home from an auction and the Kirks had to find a market for it.

After a textile show in L.A., Bill visited the set of "Thirty-Something"
where the designer bought $500 in fabric in under a minute and the
Kirks realized costume designers us a lot of fabric. That led to a four-year
relationship with *Quantum Leap*, plus a lot work with *Homefront* and
Brooklyn Bridge on television. Nancy Kirk jokes "we don't lose customers,
they get canceled." Movie work followed with feature films including
Little Women, *Wyatt Earp*, *Forrest Gump* and the Tom Hanks film *That
Thing You Do* and *Titanic*.

"When setting the time period for a film or TV show, directors know
that men recognize the cars on the street, and women recognize the fabric
in the costumes," says Nancy.

It took the National Quilting Association show in Lincoln to teach the
Kirks that quilters also use a lot of fabric — but in little tiny pieces. They
would come by the booth and ask for a quarter yard of fabric, and we
would say "sorry, we don't cut fabric, because the costume designers
wanted the longest lengths possible."

By the end of that three day show, we realized a quilter could spend
$500 in nothing flat, but wanted it all in quarter yards. Needless to say,
we cut fabric now. So much so, that the Kirks no longer do regular antique
shows, but travel only for major quilt shows. They also send trunk shows
of antique fabrics to quilt guilds and shops around the country. "That
way the fabric can travel while we stay home." says Bill.

Now the majority of their business is done through their mail order
catalog both nationally and internationally, and now on the World Wide
Web at http://www.auntie.com/kirk, but customers can shop in their real
live shop in Omaha.

McMillan's Old Market Antiques
509 S. 11th St.
402/342-8418

Finders Keepers of Omaha
423 S. 13th St.
402/346-1707

A & A Antiques Co-Op Mall
1244 S. 13th St.
402/346-2929

Joe's 13th St. Co-op Antiques
1414 S. 13th St.
402/344-3080

Standing Bear Antiques
1904 S. 13th St.
402/341-4240

Cobweb Corners
1941 S. 13th St.
402/334-2091

Oberman's Furniture
4832 S. 24th St.
402/731-8480

Katelman Antiques
39th & Farnam
402/551-4388

Treasure Mart
8316 Blondo St.
402/399-8874

Omaha Auction Center
7531 Dodge St.
402/397-9575

Blue Ribbon Flea Market & Antique Mall
6606 Grover St.
402/397-6811

Honest John's Emporium
1216 Howard St.
402/345-5078

Ana's Attic
4833 Leavenworth St.
402/556-7366

Anderson O'Brien Gallery
8724 Pacific St.
402/390-0717

Meadowlark Antique Mall
10700 Sapp Brothers Dr.
402/896-0800

A to Z Antiques
4224 Leavenworth St.
402/553-1860

Bag Lady
2630 N St.
402/738-8916

Big Bear Refinishing & Antiques
1524 Military Ave.
402/553-3011

Country Corner
6621 Railroad Ave.
402/731-8707

Morgan's Place Antiques
2351 S. 27th Ave.
402/346-1688

Life's Luxuries
3127 N. 60th Street
402/554-0993

Anchor Harbor Antiques & Cllbls.
4815 S. 24th St.
402/731-0558

A Bit of the Past
6620 S. 36th St.
402/733-8832

Cherishables
1710 N. 120th St.
402/493-2948

City Slicker Antiques & Such
4973 Dodge St.
402/556-8271

Franx Antiques & Art, Inc.
3141 Farnam St.
402/345-5266

Antiques & Fine Art
1215 Howard St.
402/341-9942

Cosgrove Auction Furn. & Antiques
3805 Leavenworth St.
402/342-5254

Antiques Plus
6570 Maple St.
402/556-9986

Brass Armadillo Antique Mall
1066 Sapp Brothers Dr.
800/896-9140

Vinton Street Antique Mall
1806 Vinton St.
402/345-4499

Antiques Thee Upstairs
4832 S. 24th St.
402/731-8480

Barb's Recollections
2212 S. 13th St.
402/346-6111

Candy's Finders Keepers
423 S. 13th St.
402/346-1707

Collector's Paradise
7006 Maple St.
402/571-0879

Once upon a Time
5007 Underwood Ave.
402/553-8755

S W Antiques
4339 S. 87th St.
402/593-0403

Trader Todds
1902 S. 13th St.
402/341-2475

20 PAPILLION

Country at Heart
114 N. Washington St.
402/339-5988

21 WAHOO

Country Antiques
526 N. Linden
402/443-3646

Wahoo Mercantile
1 Mi. N.E. of Wahoo on 92-77
402/443-4305

Hart & Hand
521 N. Broadway
402/443-3135

22 WATERLOO

Venice Antiques
26250 W. Center Road
402/359-5782

Black Horse Antiques
301 3rd St.
402/779-2419

23 YORK

I-80 & 81 Antique Mall
2 Mi. N. Of I-80 on Hwy. 81
402/362-1975

Second Chance Antiques
1125 Jackson St.
402/346-4930

Homestead Antiques
122 N. Washington St.
402/339-1339

Wahoo Bob's Antique Emporium
7th & Linden
402/443-5084

The Trading Post
326 W. 11th
402/443-4474

Nevada

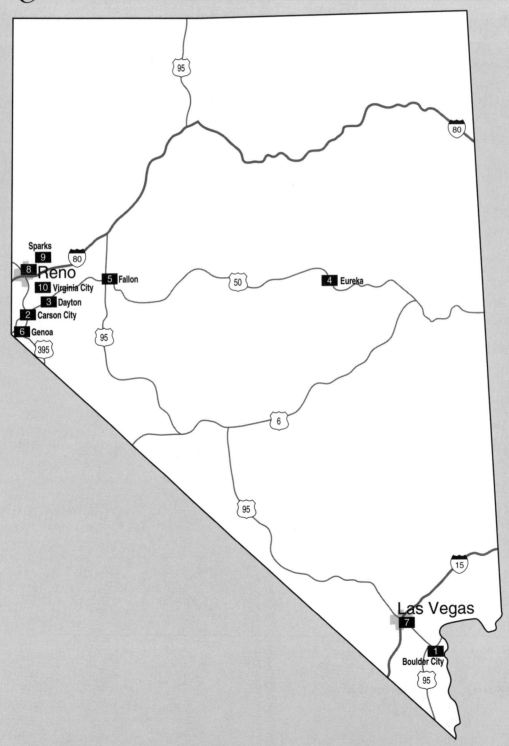

- Sparks **9**
- **8** Reno
- **10** Virginia City
- **3** Dayton
- **2** Carson City
- **6** Genoa
- **5** Fallon
- **4** Eureka
- Las Vegas **7**
- **1** Boulder City

95

80

50

95

395

6

95

15

95

Nevada

1 BOULDER CITY

Acks Attic
530 Nevada Hwy.
702/293-4035

Janean's Antiques
538 Nevada Hwy.
702/293-5747

2 CARSON CITY

Country Castle
314 S. Carson St.
702/887-7447

Bargain Barn
2106 N. Carson St.
702/883-3124

Gasoline Alley
5853 S. Carson St.
702/883-1183

Inglo Antiques & Collectibles
224 S. Carson St.
702/885-0657

Chapel Antiques
112 N. Curry St.
702/885-8511

Callis Corner
202 N. Curry St.
702/885-9185

Harrington's Hall Closet
206 N. Curry St.
702/883-7707

Frontier Antique Mall
221 S. Curry St.
702/887-1466

Art & Antiques
201 W. King St.
702/882-4447

Second Hand Rose
5891 U.S. Hwy. 50 E.
702/883-6575

Primrose Lane Antiques
10112 U.S. Hwy. 50 E.
702/246-3372

Great Places to Stay

Deer Run Ranch Bed & Breakfast
5440 Eastlake Blvd.
Washoe Valley
702/882-3643
Rates: $80-95

An Excerpt From the Archives of Deer Run Ranch

The original ranch, called the Quarter Circle J P, was purchased in 1937 by Emily and Jim Greil (Muffy's parents) for back taxes of $2,400. It and the "Goat Ranch" at the foot of Jumbo Grade two miles north of here were the only residences on the one-lane dirt road around this side of Washoe Lake. All the children in the valley went to the one-room schoolhouse in Franktown, directly across the lake, grades 1-8, one teacher.

Legend has it that the ranch springs, including our spring and pond, watered small truck gardens, the produce being carried by wagon up "Deadman's" (our main driveway) and Jumbo Grades to Virginia City during the height of the mining boom on the Comstock in the late 1800s.

Sometime after the end of World War I, prohibition became the law of the land, and the "Moonshiners" gravitated to isolated lands with plenty of water to set up their stills. The spring tunnels here on the ranch were used for that purpose, and at some point before the repeal of prohibition

in 1933, government agents blew up the stills, destroying the tunnel at our spring. Excavations for our house unearthed pipes and other distillery relics, as well as some of the old shoring from the original spring.

(Your hosts, David, an architect-builder, and Muffy Vhay, a professional artist-potter, are both longtime Nevada residents, and are knowledgeable about local lore and activities.)

Deer Run Ranch As It Is Known Today

Step out of the urban life, and into the peace and tranquility of one of the most idyllic spots in Nevada. Deer Run Ranch Bed and Breakfast is the perfect hideaway for a private, secluded getaway any time of the year. Alfalfa fields surround the complex, which has spectacular views of Washoe Lake and the Sierra Nevada mountains to the west. Tall cottonwoods shade the pond deck, a favorite spot for watching the abundant wildlife that call Deer Run home.

The private guest wing has two comfortable guest rooms with queen beds and private baths, and guest sitting room with private entry. In these tranquil guest rooms you can sit on the window seats and look out at the Sierras: or you might want to sit by the cozy fireplace in the sitting room, which is decorated with Navajo rugs and paintings, and enjoy the extensive library collection.

A full ranch breakfast, served at the handmade table in the sitting room, might include house specialties like omelets Florentine or Provencal. Enjoy fresh-brewed coffee and imported teas, home-baked specialty breads and muffins. Breakfast is served on pottery plates made on the ranch in the studio.

3 DAYTON

Wild Horse Trading Co.
45 Main St.
702/246-7056

4 EUREKA

Interesting Side Trip

Situated on the "Loneliest Road in America," Eureka is the best preserved town on Highway 50 through Nevada. A stroll down Main Street in Eureka will take you back 100 years ago when Eureka was a thriving mining camp. Visit the historic courthouse, the Eureka Opera House, and the Eureka Sentinel Newspaper Building (now a fine museum). Explore the side streets and discover dozens of historic buildings, each with its own fascinating story.

5 FALLON

Fallon Antique Mall
1951 W. Williams Ave.
702/423-6222

Just Country Friends
727 W. Williams Ave.
702/423-3315

6 GENOA

Did you know Genoa is the home of the famous "Genoa Candy Dance?"

The "Candy Dance" originated in 1919 as an effort to raise money to purchase street lights for the community of Genoa. Lillian Virgin Finnegan, native born Genoan, and daughter of Judge D. W. Virgin, suggested a dance with midnight supper at the Raycraft Hotel. As an added fundraiser, she encouraged the Genoa ladies to make a variety of candies to sell by the pound with samples passed around during the evening. The delicious candies proved to be the highlight of the evening and for the tiny town of Genoa, street lights became a reality.

The "Candy Dance" became an annual event, and each year the proceeds were used to keep Genoa's street lights burning. The dance and fair are held each year on the last full weekend in September.

Today, approximately 30,000 people attend this once-a-year, two-day event when the Genoa candy makers and friends whip up approximately 3,000 lbs. of delicious candies such as nut fudge, plain fudge, turtles, almond roca, brittle, dipped chocolates, divinity and mints, to name a few.

The "Genoa Candy Book," featuring prize winning candy recipes and a touch of Genoa's candy making history, is sold at the Candy Gazebo during the event.

Antiques Plus
2242 Main St.
702/782-4951

Dake House Antique Emporium
2242 Main St.
702/782-4951

Great Places to Stay

Genoa House Inn
Jacks Valley Road
702/782-7075
Rates: $115–$130

The Genoa House Inn is an authentic Victorian home on the National Register of Historic Places. Built in 1872 by A. C. Pratt, the town's first newspaper editor, the inn has a rich history of ownership.

The rooms here are distinct in their charm and individuality. One offers a private balcony, another a jacuzzi tub, yet another, a covered porch. All have private baths and are graced with period antiques and collectibles.

To add to the hospitality of the inn, innkeepers Linda and Bob Sanfilippo serve refreshments upon arrival. Early in the morning, coffee is delivered to your door, followed by a full breakfast served in the sunlit dining room; or if you prefer, in the privacy of your own room.

Genoa, the oldest settlement in Nevada, is nestled against the Sierra foothills with a panoramic view of Carson Valley. Activities such as soaring, ballooning, or cycling are always available. For those who prefer to keep their feet on the ground, there are casual walks in the old town, tours of the various Victorian homes and buildings, or visits to Nevada's oldest

saloon. There are also attractions in nearby Lake Tahoe and Virginia City.

Capture the charm of a simpler time in the place where Nevada began, at the Genoa House Inn.

7 LAS VEGAS

The Sampler Shoppes Antiques
6115 W. Tropicana Ave.
702/368-1170
Open: Mon.–Sat. 10–6, Sun. 12–5
Directions: Taking Exit #37 from I-15 for Tropicana, go west on Tropicana 2 ½ miles to Jones Blvd. Located on the southwest corner.

Just minutes from the Las Vegas "Strip" is the largest indoor antique mall in the state of Nevada. Occupying 40,000 square feet of floor space, this emporium displays a vast selection of quality furniture and antiques, books, toys, dolls, jewelry, and other collectibles.

With 200 dealers of distinction already represented, the mall is continuing to fill its available spaces, so there will be even more to delight the collector.

The "Pablo Picasso," located in the shoppes, serves coffee and light meals.

Yesteryear Mart
1626 E. Charleston Blvd.
702/384-6946

Josette's
1632 E. Charleston Blvd.
702/641-3892

Fields of Dreams
1647 E. Charleston Blvd.
702/385-2770

Silver Horse Antiques
1651 E. Charleston Blvd.
702/385-2700

Corner House Antiques
1655 E. Charleston Blvd.
702/387-0334

Fancy That
2032 ½ E. Charleston Blvd.
702/382-5567

Antonio Nicholas Antiques
2016 E. Charleston Blvd.
702/385-7772

Yanas Junk
2018 E. Charleston Blvd.
702/388-0051

Antiques by Sugarplums, Etc.
2022 E. Charleston Blvd.
702/385-6059

Nicholson & Oszadlo
2016 E. Charleston Blvd.
702/388-1202

A Estate Antiques
2026 E. Charleston Blvd., Suite A
702/388-4289

Old Times Remembered
2032 E. Charleston Blvd.
702/598-1983

Judy's Antiques
2040 E. Charleston Blvd.
702/386-9677

Antiques by Sara
3020 W. Charleston, Suite 4
702/877-4330

Maudies Antique Cottage
3310 E. Charleston Blvd.
702/457-4379

Red Rooster Antique Mall
1109 Western Blvd.
702/382-5253

Ratliff's Antiques
2532 E. Desert Inn Road
702/796-9686

House of Antique Slots
1236 Las Vegas Blvd. S.
702/382-1520

Victorian Casino Antiques
1421 S. Main St.
702/382-2466

Romantic Notions
6125 W. Tropicana Ave., Suite F
702/248-1957

Valentinos Zootsuit Connection
906 S. Sixth St., Suite B
702/383-9555

Academy Fine Books
2026 E. Charleston Blvd.
702/471-6500

Antique Warehouse
4175 Cameron St., #B1
702/251-3447

B. Bailey & Co. Antiques
1636 E. Charleston Blvd.
702/382-1993

Buzz & Company
2034 E. Charleston Blvd.
702/384-2034

Sunshine Clocks Antiques
1651 E. Charleston Blvd.
702/363-1312

Vintage Antique Mall
3379 Industrial Road
702/369-2323

Antiquities International
3500 Las Vegas Blvd. S.
702/792-2274

Kathy's Antiques
1115 Western Ave.
702/366-1664

American Collectibles
6125 W. Tropicana Ave., Suite F
702/248-1957

VeNette's Table
2040 E. Charleston Blvd.
702/386-9677

Antique Plus
6105 W. Tropicana Ave.
702/221-0903

Antiques & Collectors Gallery
6125 W. Tropicana Ave., #A
702/889-1444

Bonnie's Antiques & Collectibles
2030 E. Charleston Blvd.
702/385-3010

Las Vegas Antique Slot Machine
4820 W. Montara Circle
702/456-8801

Great Places to Eat

Country Star American Music Grill
On the Strip at Harmon between Tropicana and Flamingo
702/740-8400

Food and drink lovers will find a delightful choice of exciting new menues at the Country Star. This restaurant, backed by Vince Gill, Reba McIntire, and Wynonna, offers high-quality American cuisine at moderate prices and features country music memorabilia, a huge video wall, and CD "listening post" where guests can check out the latest country hits.

8 RENO

Karen Hillary Antiques & Appraisals
418 California Ave.
702/322-1800

All R Yesterday
125 Gentry Way
702/827-2355

Antique Collective
400 Mill St.
702/322-3989

Antique Mall 1
1215 S. Virginia St.
702/324-1003

Reno Antiques
677 S. Wells Ave.
702/322-5858

Grant's Tomb
721 Willow St.
702/322-6800

Briar Patch Antiques
634 W. 2nd St.
702/786-4483

Antique Mall III
1251 S. Virginia St.
702/324-4141

9 SPARKS

Victorian Square Antique Mall
834 Victorian Ave.
702/331-2288

Unique Antiques
2160 Victorian Ave.
702/355-0133

10 VIRGINIA CITY

Comstock Antiques
408 N. A St.
702/847-0626

Peach House
263 N. C St.
702/847-9084

Wells Avenue Antiques
719 E. 2nd St.
702/324-0100

Antique Marketplace
1301 S. Virginia St.
702/348-6444

Times Past Antiques
855 S. Wells Ave.
702/329-0937

Past & Present Antiques
128 E. Sixth St.
702/329-4370

Antique Mall II
1313 S. Virginia St.
402/324-1980

Heartfelt Handmade & Antiques
1434 Victorian Ave.
702/356-8677

Lynch House Antiques
Main St. (Gold Hill)
702/847-9484

Great Places to Stay

Gold Hill Hotel
Hwy. 342
702/847-0111
Rates $35–$135

Gracing the western countryside with quiet charm and elegance, Nevada's oldest hotel, Gold Hill Hotel, built in the late 1850s surrounds guests with period antiques. History and beauty combine in this setting where guests can relax in spacious rooms and soak in an antique claw foot tub. Some rooms have fireplaces—great for those chilly Nevada nights.

A wine list, with over 160 selections, complements the wonderful meals served at the Gold Hill Hotel.

New Mexico

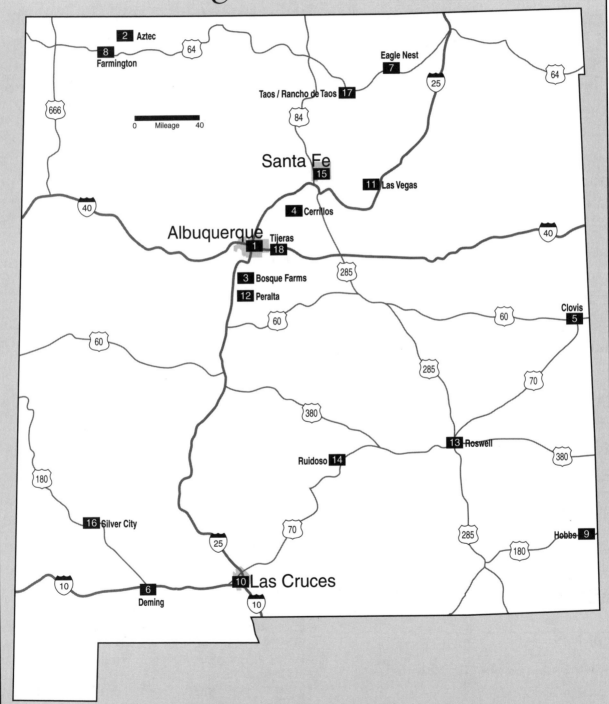

2 Aztec	64
8 Farmington	

Eagle Nest
7

666

25

0 Mileage 40

Taos / Rancho de Taos 17

84

64

Santa Fe
15

11 Las Vegas

40

4 Cerrillos

Albuquerque Tijeras
1 18

40

285

3 Bosque Farms

12 Peralta

60

60

Clovis
5

285

70

380

13 Roswell

60

Ruidoso 14

380

180

16 Silver City

70

285

Hobbs 9

25

180

10 Las Cruces
10

6 Deming

10

New Mexico

1 ALBUQUERQUE

Classic Century Square
4616 Central Ave. S.E.
505/255-1850
Open: Mon.–Sat. 10–6, Sun. 12–5, closed for Thanksgiving, Christmas and Easter
Directions: West of San Mateo

Classic Century Square is New Mexico's largest antiques and collectibles marketplace. With over 40,000 square feet of showroom space on three floors, one can only imagine the variety of treasures from which to choose. Filled to the rafters (literally), the mall has everything; music boxes, quilts and linens, glassware, pottery, advertising items, cast iron, framed prints and oils, war memorabilia, European dolls and Barbie dolls, fifties kitchen items, American Indian artifacts, furniture from every style and period, Star Wars collectibles and the list goes on and on.

An added draw to Classic Century Square has been the building's history and architectural features. Built in 1955 (art deco in design) the entire north side of the building is made of glass windows — shedding light on the spacious interior. In addition, the three-story stairwell is a landmark in the Albuquerque area, as well as historical tidbits like the drums of sterile water stockpiled in the basement from the building's days as a fallout shelter. A train museum located on the third floor is another popular attraction, especially for children.

Serious collectors often shop the market due to its outstanding inventory of "hot" collectibles. Decorators find it a good source for unique and interesting items not commonly found in other shops. Even set decorators for the movie industry have found wonderful props at Classic Century Square. Marketing to the movie industry has generated interest and numerous inquiries over the years. One of their vendor's old trunks was purchased and tossed out of a window in a scene from *Billy the Kid*. With so much to look at, people can sometimes get overwhelmed, but the helpful and knowledgeable staff can quickly help folks find what they are looking for. "We stress service and pleasing the customer," says Bob Sloan. "There is something here for everyone. We know we are the biggest, but we also think we are the best."

Furniture on Consignment
701 Candelaria Road N.E.
505/344-1275

Old Oak Tree Antique Mall
111 Cardenas Dr. N.E.
505/268-6965

Antiques & Alike
3904 Central Ave. S.E.
505/268-1882

Cowboys & Indians Antiques
4000 Central Ave. S.E.
505/255-4054

Antiques on Central
4009 Central Ave. N.E.
505/255-4800

Ailene's & Donna's Antique Mall
4710 Central Ave. S.E.
505/255-1850

Anna's Grapevine Furniture
5517 Central Ave. N.E.
505/268-3427

Lawson's Antiques & Element of Time
2809 Chanate Ave. SW
505/877-0538

Antique Manor
1701 Eubank Blvd N.E.
505/299-0151

Scottsdale Village Antiques
3107 Eubank Blvd. N.E., Suite 7
505/271-1522

Anglo American Antiques, Ltd.
2524 Vermont St. N.E.
505/298-7511

Antiques Consortium
7216 4th St. N.W.
505/897-7115

Antiques & Treasures, Inc.
4803 Lomas Blvd. N.E.
505/268-6008

Chatterelys Antiques & Natural Goods
901 Rio Grande Blvd. N.W., D128
505/242-4430

Adobe Gallery
413 Romero St. N.W.
505/243-8485

Lindy's Ltd
2035 12th St. N.W.
505/244-3320

A Perfect Setting
5901 Wyoming Blvd. N.E., Suite Y
505/821-7601

Aah Such a Deal Antique Furniture
7901 4th St. N.W.
505/898-1501

Dan's Place Antique Clocks
3902 Central Ave. S.E.
505/268-1010

Morningside Antiques
4001 Central Ave. N.E.
505/268-0188

Antique Specialty Mall
4516 Central Ave. S.E.
505/268-8080

Somewhere in Time
5505 Central Ave. N.W.
505/836-8681

Antique Connection
12020 Central Ave. S.E.
505/296-2300

Good Stuff the SW Antiques
2108 Charlevoix N.W.
505/843-6416

B's Antiques/Marie's Collectibles
3107 Eubank Blvd. N.E., Suite 8
505/298-7205

Consignment Interiors, Etc.
5850 Eubank Blvd. N.E.
505/293-0765

Seddon's Rancho Chico Antiques
6923 4th St. N.W.
505/344-5201

Antique Co-op
7601 4th St. N.W.
505/898-7354

John Isaac Antiques Rio Grande
2036 S. Plaza St. N.W.
505/842-6656

Lawrence's
4022 Rio Grande Blvd N.W., Suite D
505/344-5511

Hanging Tree Gallery — Old Town
416 Romero St. N.W.
505/842-1420

Timeless Treasures
2035 12th St. N.W.
505/891-8183

White Dove Gallery
2005 San Felipe Patio Market, #10
505/243-6901

Eddie's Antique Shop
119 Dartmouth Dr. S.E.
505/268-6153

New Mexico

Finders Keepers Antiques
3902 Central Ave. S.E., #A
505/256-7684

Granny's Attic
4807 Lomas Blvd. N.E.
505/266-7607

J & L Antiques & Gifts
6305 Candelaria Road N.E.
505/884-2139

Gertrude Zachary's Antiques
416 2nd St. S.W.
505/244-1320

I-40 Antique Mall
2035 12th St. N.W.
505/243-8011

Route 66 Antique Connection
12815 Central Ave. N.E.
505/296-2300

Great Places To Stay

The Ranchette Bed and Breakfast
2329 Lakeview Road S.W.
505/877-5140 or 1-800-374-3230
Rates: $55–$85
Directions: Call ahead for specific directions from your locations.

Just fifteen minutes from historic old town Albuquerque, The Ranchette Bed and Breakfast seems a world away from the hustle and bustle of the city. With panoramic views of the Sandia and Manzano Mountains, the glorious Western sunsets, and the distant twinkle of the city lights, a sense of calm and beauty descends.

Whether you are lazing in the hot tub under the arbor, or riding the range on one of the majestic Arabian horses in residence, the atmosphere just naturally draws you in and calms you. If you like, you may bring and board your own horse. For those who prefer a more mechanical mode of transportation, walking and bicycle paths are adjacent to the property (bicycles are furnished by The Ranchette), but you'll have to bring your own Nikes!

Inside, all guest rooms are furnished with original art and antiques, writing desks, telephones, and terry robes. The living area offers a grand piano, a cozy fireplace and plenty of space to play games, plan the next day's activities, or just do nothing.

The food here is gourmet vegetarian fare, but if you have specific dietary needs, they'll be happy to accommodate you. They'll even provide picnic lunches or candlelight dinners upon request.

Whether you are on a family vacation or a romantic getaway, The Ranchette Bed and Breakfast offers its own special brand of recreation and relaxation in a smoke-free and alcohol-free environment.

2   AZTEC

Rocky Mountain Antiques
107 S. Main St.
505/334-0004

Aztec Furniture Art & More
201 E. Chaco
505/334-0033

Downtown Antiques
301 S. Main St.
505/334-5818

3   BOSQUE FARMS

Behind the Barn Antiques
1435 Bosque Farms Blvd.
505/869-5212

4   CERRILLOS

What-Not Shop Antiques
15 B First St.
505/471-2744
Open: Daily 10–5

Situated on the Turquoise Trail and built in 1890 by Mr. Griffith, the shop offers Native American jewelry, rugs, pottery, jewelry, pocket watches and exquisite cut glass.

5   CLOVIS

Marlene's Antiques & Gifts
1011 N. Norris St.
505/763-1396
Open: Mon.–Fri. 9:30–5:30

Inside discover antique furniture, collectibles and a gift selection with limited edition collector items.

Prairie Peddler Antiques
100 S. Main St.
505/763-7392
Open: Mon.–Sat. 10–5

Housed in the 1931 former Raton Creamery, you'll find antique furniture, Depression glass, primitives, Carnival, Roseville, elegant glassware, as well as cast iron pieces.

Endless Trail
201 W. Grand Ave.
505/769-1839
Open: Mon.–Fri. 10–5, Sat. 10–6

For the young-at-heart collector, check out the toys, Pez and magazines.

New Mexico

Stitches of New Mexico—Antiques
927 N. Main St.
505/763-5018
Open: Mon.–Fri. 10–5, Sat. 10–4

Inside Stitches of New Mexico, located in the Historic District of downtown, you'll find china, crystal, primitives, old books and records, RS Prussia, Carnival, cut glass, Depression glass, toys, linens, furniture, old pictures and wonderful tapestries.

Furniture Corner 123 W. Grand Ave. 505/762-1113	**Three Keys Antique Mall** 1709 Mabry Dr. 505/763-1740

6 DEMING

Antique Bank of Deming 122 E. Pine 505/544-4150	**Victorian Parlor** 105 S. Silver 505/546-2112
Ox Yoke 115 S. Silver 505/546-4077	**Historical Hotel Antiques** 124 S. Silver 505/544-7747
Sanders Trading Post 204 S. Gold 505/544-3482	

7 EAGLE NEST

Enchanted Circle Co., Antiques & Accommodations
124 E. Main St. (Highway 64)
505/377-3382
Open: Daily 10–5 from May 15–Oct. 15. Call for winter hours.
Directions: Traveling I-25 South from Raton, take Hwy. 64 West through Cimarron to Eagle Nest.

Located along The Enchanted Circle, a 100-mile scenic drive surrounding Wheeler Peak. Enchanted Circle offers antique shopping and overnight accommodations. Housed in the Main Street facility is the antique shop (the area's largest) specializing in china, silver, crystal, quilts, furniture and Southwestern artifacts. Apartments and suites on the second floor over the antique shop have antique furnishings and wood-burning stoves.

8 FARMINGTON

Browsery
1605 E. 20th St.
505/325-4885
Open: Mon.–Sat. 9:30–6

In business for 21 years, featuring furnishings such as antique wardrobes, chests, dressers, pianos and a full line of new Amish-made furniture.

Antique Trove 309 W. Main St. 505/324-0559	**Somewhere In Time** 115 W. Main St. 505/564-2711
Dusty Attic 111 W. Main St. 505/327-7696	**Sentimental Journey** 218 W. Main St. 505/326-6533

9 HOBBS

Estelle's Collectibles
3621 S. Eunice Hwy.
505/393-8633
Open: Mon.–Sat. 9–5

This old house holds antique collectibles, furniture and primitives including irons, skillets, and churns.

Antiques Unique
2420 N. Dal Paso St.
505/392-8527
Open: Mon.–Fri. 8–5

An assortment of antiques including Depression glassware, pottery, primitives (such as irons, crocks, churns), crystal and some furniture will be found in this shop.

Crafters Cottage & Antique Mall
801 E. Bender Blvd.
505/397-4481

10 LAS CRUCES

La Vieja 2230 Avenida De Mesilla 505/526-7875	**Jones & Co. Jewelers** 1160 El Paseo St. 505/526-2809
Main Street Antique Mall 2301 S. Main St. 505/523-0047	**Things For Sale** 606 W. Picacho Ave. 505/526-7876
S.O.B.'s Antiques 928 W. Picacho Ave. 505/526-8624	**Coyote Traders** 1020 W. Picacho Ave. 505/523-1284

New Mexico

Ross Bell Antiques
1144 W. Picacho Ave.
505/523-2089

High Class Junk Joint
1150 W. Picacho Ave.
505/524-4314

11   LAS VEGAS

Plaza Antiques
1805 On the Plaza
505/454-9447
Open: Thurs.–Mon. 10–6, Sun. 12–4

Located on the historic Old Town Plaza, ten dealers display antique furniture, collectibles, primitives, glassware, pottery, vintage clothing and jewelry, western artifacts and much more.

Virginia West Antiques & More
150 Bridge St.
505/454-8802

Twentieth Century Store
514 Douglas Ave.
505/425-3180

12   PERALTA

Past & Present Treasures
3617 Hwy. 47
505/869-4546

13   ROSWELL

Monterey Antique Mall
1400 W. 2nd St.
505/623-3347
Open: Daily 10–6

Ten-thousand square feet and thirteen dealers provide the gamut of antique items—jewelry, furniture, dolls, coins, plus much more.

Byegones
500 W. 2nd St.
505/622-1995

Pedlar Way Upholstery & Antiques
4506 W. 2nd St.
505/624-2521

14   RUIDOSO

Camel House
714 Mechem Dr.
505/257-7479
Open: Daily 9:30–5:30

Features Southwestern artifacts, antique beds, wagons, dressers, buffets, secretaries, pie and whiskey cabinets, tobacco cases, a wide selection of clocks, as well as bronzes. The shop offers Southwestern and Western artists including G. Harvey.

House of Antiques
2213 Sudderth Dr.
505/257-2839

Victorian furniture, lamps, glassware and art glass are the specialties of this shop located in the walking tour section of midtown.

Yesteryear Antiques
122 N. Hwy. 7
505/378-4667

Joyce's Junque
650 Sudderth Dr.
505/257-7575

Auntie Bo's
2314 Sudderth Dr.
505/257-3683

15   SANTA FE

Antique Warehouse
530 S. Guadalupe
505/984-1159

Pachamama
223 Canyon Road
505/983-4020

Scarlett's Antiques
225 Canyon Road
505/983-7092

Casa Ana
503 Canyon Road
505/989-1781

Morning Star Gallery, Ltd.
513 Canyon Road
505/982-8187

Claiborne Gallery
608 Canyon Road
505/982-8019

Kania-Ferrin Gallery
662 Canyon Road
505/982-8767

Tiqua Gallery
812 Canyon Road
505/984-8704

Architectural Antiques
1117 Canyon Road
505/983-7607

The Bedroom
304 Catron St.
505/984-0207

American Country Collection
620 Cerrillos Road
505/984-0955

La Puerta
1302 Cerrillos Road
505/984-8164

Pegasus Antiques & Collectibles
1372 Cerrillos Road
505/982-3333

Stephen's — A Consign Gallery
2701 Cerrillos Road
505/471-0802

Doodlet's Shop
120 Don Gaspar Ave.
505/983-3771

Mary Corley Antiques
215 N. Guadalupe St.
505/984-0863

Santa Kilim
401 S. Guadalupe St.
505/986-0340

Rio Bravo
411 S. Guadalupe St.
505/982-0230

Foreign Traders
202 Galisteo St.
505/983-6441

El Colectivo
556 N. Guadalupe St.
505/820-7205

Foxglove Antiques
260 Hyde Park Road
505/986-8285

In Home Furnishings
132 E. Marcy St.
505/983-0808

New Mexico

Peyton-Wright
131 Nusbaum St.
505/989-9888

Adams House
211 Old Santa Fe Trail
505/982-5115

James Reid, Ltd.
114 E. Palace Ave.
505/988-1147

Susan Tarman Antiques & Fine Art
923 Paseo De Peralta
505/983-2336

El Paso Import Company
418 Sandovol
505/982-5698

Things Finer
100 E. San Francisco St.
505/983-5552

William R. Talbot Fine Arts
129 W. San Francisco St.
505/982-1559

Canfield Gallery
414 Canyon Road
505/988-4199

Hampton Gallery
236 Delgado
505/983-9635

Henry C. Monahan
526 Canyon Road
505/982-8750

Reflection Gallery
201 Canyon Road
505/995-9795

Umbrello Showroom
701 Canyon Road
550/984-8566

Antiques on Grant
126 Grant Ave.
505/995-9701

American Country Collection
620 Cerrillos Road
505/984-0955

Arrowsmiths Relics of the Old West
402 Old Santa Fe Trail
505/989-7663

Wiseman & Gale & Duncan
940 E. Palace Ave.
505/984-8544

Hands of America
401 E. Rodeo Road
505/983-5550

Dewey Galleries, Ltd.
76 E. San Francisco St.
505/982-8632

Vivian Wolfe Antiques
112 W. San Francisco St.
505/982-7769

Bizaare Bazaar Company
137 W. Water St.
505/988-3999

Economos Work of Art
500 Canyon Road
505/982-6347

Moondance Gallery
707 Canyon Road
505/982-3421

Ron Messick Fine Arts
600 Canyon Road
505/983-9533

Jane Smith
550 Canyon Road
550/988-4775

Nedra Matteucci Fenn Galleries
1075 Paseo de Peralta
550/982-4631

Great Places to Stay

Guadalupe Inn
604 Agua Fria St.
505/989-7422
Open: Daily 8–9
Directions: From I-25, take St. Francis Drive exit and stay on St. Francis Drive for 3.7 miles to Agua Fria Street. Turn right onto Agua Fria; proceed 3 blocks until the "604" sign then turn right.

Pampered with family hospitality, enjoy a "truly Santa Fe" experience. Built on family property, the inn offers quiet, privacy and unique charm. Katchine, Hopi spirit dolls, enhance the local flavor of the decor. Fireplaces, patios and whirlpool tubs are available with some rooms. To the rear of the inn, a small garden makes a cozy nook for an outdoor breakfast.

The Don Gaspar Compound
623 Don Gaspar
505/986-8664
Open: Year-round
Rates: $85–$220
Directions: From east & south along I-25, take the Old Pecos Trail exit and go all of the way into town. Turn left on Paseo de Peralta, then left on Don Gaspar. The Compound is 1½ blocks on the left. OR from the north via 285, take St. Francis, turn left on Alameda and follow it to Don Gaspar. Turn right on Don Gaspar and go 4½ blocks to the Compound.

Built in 1912 in Santa Fe's Don Gaspar Historic District, the Compound is a classic example of Mission and Adobe architecture. Six private suites offer wood and gas-burning fireplaces (one is an adobe fireplace), saltillo and Mexican-tiled floors. Step into the secluded adobe-walled garden courtyard and relax to the trickle of the fountain while breathing in the scent of brilliant heirloom flowers.

16 SILVER CITY

The Silver City Trading Co. Antique Mall
205 W. Broadway
505/388-8989
Open: Mon.–Sat. 10–6, Sun. 12–4
Directions: From Lordsburg on I-10, take NM-90 north 42 miles. From Deming on I-10, take US-180 northwest 52 miles. From the north on I-25, you can take NM-152 south of Truth or Consequences, through Hillsboro, Kingston, and the Mimbres Mountains, joining US-180 eight miles east of Silver City (Inquire about road conditions in winter). The alternative is to take NM-26 from Hatch (the chile capital) to Deming and US-180. The antique mall is two blocks west of Hudson Street (NM-90) in Silver City's Historic District and near the campus of Western New Mexico University.

The Silver City Trading Co. is housed in a 12,500-square-foot building erected in 1897. The pressed tin ceilings testify to its longevity. Outstanding among the offerings of the 31 dealers are objects of art, utility and decoration associated with the Old West, as well as contemporary Native American craft production from both sides of the border. Other offerings include objects associated with mining, railroading, and ranching. Collectibles include coins, currency, dolls, toys, jewelry, vintage clothing, china, pottery, and glassware.

Silver Creek Antiques
614 N. Bullard St.
505/538-8705

17 TAOS/RANCHO DE TAOS

Maison Faurie
On The Plaza
505/758-8545

Dwellings Revisited
10 Bent St.
505/758-3377

The Barn
506 Kit Carson Road
505/758-7396

Annabel's Strictly by Accident
4153 State Road 68
505/751-7299

Patrick Dunbar Antiques
222 Paseo Del Tueblo Norte
505/758-2511

Horsefeathers, Etc.
109 Kit Carson Road
505/758-7457

Prints Old & Rare
4155 State Road 68
505/751-4171

Haciendo De San Francisco
Saint Francis Plaza
505/758-0477

18 TIJERAS

Another Place N Time
Just South of I-40 on S S
505/281-1212

North Dakota

Williston 11
2
85

2
Minot 8
83
52

52

Devils Lake 2
2
281

Harvey 6
52

Grand Forks 5
29

Fargo 4
29
94

Valley City 10

Jamestown 7
281

Bismarck 1
83

83

Dickinson 3
22

New England 9

94
85

0   Mileage   30

1 BISMARCK

Antique Interiors
200 W. Main Ave.
701/224-9551
Open: Mon.–Sat. 10:30–5, Sun.1–4
Directions: Downtown Bismarck

Located in the Historic International Harvester Building, this shop specializes in interior design through the use of antiques. Fabrics to complement any decor are also available.

Wizard of Odds 'N Ends
1523 E. Thayer Ave.
701/222-4175
Open: Mon.–Sat. 10–5
Directions: Find this shop near downtown Bismarck.

"We're off to see the wizard, the wonderful Wizard of Odd 'N Ends." Located near downtown Bismarck, this shop offers such a stunning array of antiques and collectibles, you'll think you "really" are in the Emerald City.

Antique and Coin Exchange
722 Kirkwood Mall
701/222-8859
Open: Mon.–Fri. 10–9, Sat. 10–6, Sun. 12–6
Directions: Exit I-94 at State St. Travel south on State St. It curves to Boulevard Ave. Go south on 7th Street to Kirkwood Mall. Shop is located in the mall.

Specializing in "pack in your car" antiques. Large selection of smalls including dishes, coins, jewelry, etc.

Antique Gallery
1514 E. Thayer Ave.
701/223-8668

Antique Mall
200 W. Main Ave.
701/221-2594

Country Home Sweet Home
1144 Summit Blvd.
701/223-4897

Downtown Furniture Co.
117 N. 4th St.
701/255-6061

Wood & Tiques
1514 E. Thayer Ave.
701/255-4912

2 DEVILS LAKE

Garden Gate
410 4th St.
701/662-6388

Antique Exchange
By Appointment
701/662-8801

Buds N Blossoms
405 4th St.
701/662-8166

3 DICKINSON

Carol's Antiques & Collectibles
14 1st St. W.
701/225-4509

Jackie's Antiques & Collectibles
1331 Villard E.
701/227-1027

Barry's 2nd H "Antiques"
2221 Main St. S.
701/225-3701

Collectors Corner
14 1st St. W.
701/227-8411

4 FARGO

Bonanzaville
W. Hwy. 10 (Main Ave.)
701/282-2822
Open: Daily June 1–Nov. 1, call for museum hours
Directions: Tune into 530 AM radio for specific information.

Relive the pioneer days in Bonanzaville. Antique cars, planes, farm machinery, school, church, stores, log and sod homes, dolls, Indian artifacts, museum and much, much more.

Baker's Place Antiques
114 Broadway
701/235-5334

Grandpa's Antiques & Collectibles
3041 Main Ave.
701/237-4569

North Dakota Antiques Mall
1024 2nd Ave. N.
701/237-4423

Market Square Mall
1450 25h St.
701/239-9814

Lifetime Antique Furnishings
18 8th St.
701/235-3144

Fargo Antique Mall
14 Roberts St.
701/235-1145

Gramma's Antiques & Collectibles
314 10th St. N.
701/239-4465

A Place Called Traditions
1201 S. University Dr.
701/280-1864

Great Places to Stay

La Maison des Papillons Bed and Breakfast

423 8th St. S.
701/232-2041
Open: Year-round
Rates $45–$55
Directions: From west on I-94: Take Exit 343 to Main Ave. (downtown), follow Main Ave. to 8th St. Take a right on 5th Ave. south. From north or south on I-29: Take Exit 65 to Main Ave.; once on Main Ave. follow previous instructions. From east on I-94: Take Exit 1 A (in Moorehead, Minnesota); follow 8th St. taking a right on 5th Ave. south.

La Maison des Papillons Bed and Breakfast occupies a house built in 1899 on Historic 8th Street South of Fargo. If it could talk it would share many stories of the history of Fargo such as the fire that consumed most of downtown and raged only blocks away. When walking in the front door, visitors are struck with the warmth and friendliness of days gone by. The cozy grandeur of the ground floor and the intimate privacy of the second-floor bedrooms give a restful welcome invitation to the weary of mind, body, and soul.

La Maison des Papillons has four guest rooms (three of which are ready for occupancy) on the second floor. Each room is named after a butterfly that is native to North Dakota. The Monarch is a double room with a half bath located on the north side of the house for lots of quiet. The Swallowtail is a double room with a beautiful stained glass window and bay window. The Fritillery is a single room overlooking the front yard and nearby park. All rooms share a large old fashioned bathroom occupied by a cast iron tub/shower with clawed feet.

5 GRAND FORKS

Back Porch Antiques and Gifts

205 DeMers Ave.
701/746-9369
Open: Tues.–Sat. 10–6
Directions: From I-29, take the DeMers Ave. exit (140). Go east on DeMers Ave. 3 ½ miles. The shop is 1 block from Red River.

The quaint name of the shop, Back Porch Antiques and Gifts, reveals a cozy, casual atmosphere. Potted red geraniums greet you at the door. Inside you will find a good representation of antique furniture, from headboards to foot stools; in oak, mahogany, walnut, cherry and other woods. Various periods and styles are included; such as Victorian, primitive and Art Deco. You will also discover antique linens, glassware, kitchen items, sewing implements and accessories. Fishing collectibles will catch the fancy of anglers. You can take home unusual gifts and decorative accessories as well.

City Center Antique Mall

16 City Center Mall
701/780-9076

Victoria's Rose Antique Shop

214 DeMers Ave.
701/772-3690

Sanne's Antiques

1020 Cottonwood Ave.
701/772-0541

6 HARVEY

Penny Pinchers

604 Brewster St. E.
701/324-2551

7 JAMESTOWN

The city of Jamestown is known as the Buffalo City, thanks to its 60-ton giant, "The World's Largest Buffalo," a sculpture standing watch on a hill over I-94. Two dozen live buffalo roam the draws below this huge statue, and the National Buffalo Museum shares the high ground at the Frontier Village Complex.

Jamestown is the birthplace for some famous folk: torch singer Peggy Lee, Anne Carlsen, renowned for her work with the disabled, and the best-selling author of all time, writer Louis L'Amour.

Treasure Chest

213 1st Ave. S.
701/251-2891
Open: Mon. 10–7, Tues.–Sat. 10–5, or by appointment.
Directions: Exit 2nd Jamestown exit off I-94. Travel north on 1st Ave. South.

The name given to this antique shop could be considered synonymous with the name used by its former occupants in 1906, First Federal Savings "Bank". The Treasure Chest, as it is called today, holds a wealth of valuable antiques and collectibles, such as, Roseville, Rosemeade, Hull, Carnival, primitives and more.

Antique Attic

219 1st Ave. S.
701/252-6733
Open: Mon.– Fri. 12:30–5:30, Sat. 10–4
Directions: Exit 2nd Jamestown exit off I-94. Travel north on 1st Ave. South

There are 42 dealers offering, oak furniture, fine china, lamps, books & catalogs, fine glassware, dolls, linen & silver, as well as one-of-a-kind items.

North Dakota

On The Countryside
Hwy. 281 S. & 25th St. S.W.
701/252-8941
Open: Mon.–Fri. 10–9, Sat.10--6, Sun. 12–5
Directions: I-94 take 2nd exit, travel south to 25th St and. take a right.

On The Countryside specializes in antique country furnishings, primarily cupboards. Other antique pieces along with decorative accessories are also available here. The Espresso Bar serves pastries, soups, salads and ice cream.

Wilma's Antiques
221 7th St. N.E.
701/252-5145
Open: Mon. 10–7, Tues.–Sat. 10–5 or by appointment
Directions: Exit I-94 at Jamestown. Take Main to 7th N.E.

Wilma's Antiques offers a large variety of antiques and collectibles specializing in everything old and wonderful.

Antiques & Uniques
Park Plaza Mall
Home phone after 5 p.m.
701/252-6682 (No phone in shop)

8 MINOT

Home Sweet Home
103 4th Ave. N.W.
701/852-5604
Open: Mon.–Sat. 9:30–5, Sun. 12–4
Directions: Situated near downtown Minot.

Antiques in a historic setting. Home Sweet Home is located in an old house built in 1899. They offer "everything" (as the owner says) in the way of antiques and collectibles.

Granny's Antiques & Gifts
16 Main St. S.
701/852-3644
Open: Mon.–Sat. 10–5:30
Directions: Granny's is located in downtown Minot.

Granny's Antiques offers furniture, glassware and collectibles along with a nice selection of Victorian items.

Dakota Antiques
8 4th St. N.E.
701/838-1150

Downtown Mall
108 Main St. S.
701/852-9084

Minot Antiques
1326 S. Broadway
701/852-6550

9 NEW ENGLAND

Country Treasures
Hwy. 22
701/579-4746
Open: Lives on premises and is open most of the time
Directions: Located on Hwy. 22 on the east end of New England.

This small, quaint shop specializes in quality smalls. Cookie jars, carnival, depression and pressed glass are represented here.

Main Attractions
709 Main St.
701/579-4419
Open: Mon.–Sat. 10–4
Directions: Exit from Hwy. 22 into New England. Located on Main St.

At this shop, the "Main Attractions" are antique furniture, cookie jars, carnival glass and Dakota pottery.

10 VALLEY CITY

E & S Antiques
148 E. Main St.
701/845-0369
Open: Mon.–Sat.9–5
Directions: Located in downtown Valley City.

Located in the old 1890s Opera House in downtown Valley City, this shop prides itself on offering exceptional antique furnishings and accessories.

Unique Antiques
164 E. Main St.
701/845-3549

Kathleen's Kurio Kabinet
114 3rd St.
701/845-3569

11 WILLISTON

Collectors Corner
109 Main St.
701/572-9313

Larry Lynne Antiques
715 3rd Ave. E.
701/572-3642

Elizabeth's on Broadway
12 E. Broadway
701/774-3835

Oklahoma

Miami 29
Grove 23
412
Locust Grove
Pryor 28
Muskogee 30
40
Vaillant 48
66
Chouteau 12
69
Dewey
Bartlesville
Claremore 13
Broken Arrow 9
69
17
4
75
Tulsa 47
Jenks 26
Okmulgee
Henryetta 25
Skiatook 43
Sapulpa 40
Bristow
75
35
64
Cushing 15
66
8
Okemah 33
Ada
Ponca City
Stroud
44
1
1
Blackwell 6
Perry 36
Stillwater 44
10
Chandler
Seminole 41
Sulphur 46
35
Davis 16
177
Enid 22
Guthrie 24
Edmond 19
Oklahoma City
Shawnee 42
Noble
Purcell 39
Ardmore 3
183
Yukon 66
Norman 32
Blanchard 7
Duncan 18
El Reno 20
81
Chickasha 11
Lawton 27
Clinton 14
183
Altus 2
Elk City 21
40
62
66
183

Mileage 40
0

Oklahoma City

44
66
35
240
Edmond 19
Norman 32
77
35
34
3
Bethany 5
66
44
Yukon 49
40

64

Oklahoma

ROUTE 66

From its official beginning in 1926 through the heyday of auto travel in the '50s and '60s, Route 66 was the road for dreamers. It exemplifies the open road, beckoning adventure with the promise of freedom. It carried families, vagabonds, and untold others through bustling cities and into neon-lit small towns in the heart of America.

During the depression of the '30s, it was the road of hope for "Okies": poor Oklahoma farm families who abandoned their drought-ravaged homes and headed west for a better way of life. Their plight was made famous by John Steinbeck's novel *The Grapes of Wrath*.

Route 66 is "still the place to get your kicks" thanks to dozens of Route 66 cities who have kept their downtowns vibrant. Many today boast a diverse assemblage of shops featuring antiques, collectibles and Route 66 memorabilia. Movie theaters and building facades are being restored to the splendor of time past. Businesses are returning to their downtown districts, and those who remember the Mother Road during its heyday are proudly embracing their heritage. Route 66 is rich in Oklahoma, and it looks like the Main Street of America is here to stay.

1 ADA

Alford Warehouse Sales
217 S. Johnston St.
580/332-1026

Ada Antique Mall
222 E. Main St.
580/332-9927

Treasures in Time
211 E. Main St.
580/436-1200

Granny's Attic
715 E. Main St.
580/436-4241

2 ALTUS

The Enchanted Door
111 W. Commerce St.
580/477-0004

The Enchanted Door offers an "enchanting" shopping experience. Here you'll find antiques, crystals, decorative accessories as well as gift baskets and specialty toys.

Granny's Antiques
905 E. Broadway St.
580/477-1565

Yesterdaze Treasures
113 E. Commerce St.
580/482-1229

Sue's Collectibles & Antiques
110 Falcon Road
580/482-4461

Catch All
1500 S. Main St.
580/482-6950

Designs for the Goodtimes
Bunker Hill Shopping Center
580/477-0298

Remember When
103 N. Hudson St.
580/482-3773

North Main Antique Mall
601 N. Main St.
580/477-1991

Al's Antiques
720 S. Spurgeon St.
580/482-2022

3 ARDMORE

Surrell's
318 Lake Murray Dr. E.
580/223-3799

Antique Sampler
15 Sam Noble Pkwy.
580/226-7643

Honey Creek Emporium
212 E. Main St.
580/369-3524

Peddlers Square Mall
15 N. Washington St.
580/223-6255

Ardmore Furniture
15 Sam Noble Pkwy.
580/226-2090

Portico
21 N. Washington St.
580/223-4033

Main Antique Mall
1 W. Main St.
580/226-4395

Watermark Antiques & Interiors
19 N. Washington St.
580/223-7900

4 BARTLESVILLE

Lace & Such
502 S. Cherokee Ave.
918/336-8000

Piper Furniture
110 S.W. Frank Phillips Blvd.
918/336-1300

Gans Mall
3801 S.E. Kentucky St.
918/335-1046

Good Earth
101 E. Frank Phillips Blvd.
918/336-6633

Depot Corner Antiques
127 S.W. 2nd St.
918/336-9313

Aunt Lou's Collectibles
1205 S.W. Frank Phillips Blvd.
918/337-0033

Media Futures Bookstore
Road 2400
918/333-3695

Vineyard's Vintages
615 Delaware
918/336-4165

Apple Tree Mall
3900 E. Frank Phillips Blvd.
918/335-2485

Victorian Memories
310 S.W. Frank Phillips Blvd.
918/336-2952

Hog Shooter Antiques, Etc.
3922 Nowata Road
918/333-3333

Country Store
Route 3 Box 8970
918/336-0351

Alayne's Doll Boutique
1609 Oklahoma
918/337-0366

Keepsake Candles Factory
Route 3, Box 8970
918/336-0351

Normandy Antiques
117 S.E. Frank Phillips Blvd.
918/338-0818

Yocham's Custom Leather
Nowata Road (4 mi. E. of Hwy. 75)
918/335-2277

5 BETHANY

Before travelers even realize they've left Oklahoma City, 39th St. suddenly looks like a small-town Main St. again. It courses past old gas stations, the Route 66 Trading Post (boasting the "best collection in the nation" of memorabilia) and Oklahoma Southern Nazarene University. A stretch of the old highway curves by the north edge of Lake Overholser and along a rusty steel truss bridge. The old route can be followed around to the west to Yukon, where State Hwy. 66 takes over.

Oklahoma

Judy's Antiques Collectibles & Gifts
6722 N.W. 39th Expressway
405/787-2366

Ancient Tastes & Treasures
3921 N. College Ave.
405/495-3239

Bethany Antiques Mall
3901 N. College Ave.
405/495-7091

Ewok Shop
6632 N.W. 36th St.
405/495-8565

Antique Garden
3926 N. College Ave.
405/495-9117

Cobblestone Gifts & Interiors
6716 N.W. 39th Expressway
405/495-7446

6 BLACKWELL

Ashby's Antique Mall
110 N. Main St.
580/363-4410

Larkin Gallery
201 N. Main St.
580/363-0645

Rowe's Antique Mall
116 N. Main St.
580/363-2233

Time Worn Antiques Mall
112 S. Main St.
580/363-3262

7 BLANCHARD

Janet's Eats & Sweets
100 N. Main St.
405/485-2638

Merctl Antiques & Collectibles
113 N. Main St.
405/485-3131

Shade Tree Antiques
115 N. Main St.
405/485-9600

Yesterday's Best Antique Mall
109 N. Main St.
405/485-2550

Main Street Antiques
114 N. Main St.
405/485-3688

Aged to Perfection
114 2nd St.
405/485-3449

8 BRISTOW

Trash & Treasures
112 N. Main St.
918-367-6201

Joe Mounce Antiques
9th & Main St.
918/367-6492

9 BROKEN ARROW

Picket Fence
1000 N. Elm Place
918/258-2969

Antique Centre
412 S. Main St.
918/251-7092

Riverhill Antiques
19285 E. 131st St.
918/455-7530

Medicine Man Mercantile
222 S. Main St.
918/251-1229

Nailbenders
1819 S. Main St.
918/258-4644

Memory Lane Antique Mall
211 S. Main St.
918/251-9060

10 CHANDLER

Chandler is headquarters for the Oklahoma Route 66 Association. Delightful styles of vintage gas station architecture and twelve buildings on the National Historic Register survived citywide destruction after an 1897 tornado. The Museum of Pioneer History tells the story of Chandler's early days. Three miles west of town is the often-photographed metal barn advertising Meramac Caverns in Stanton, Missouri.

Treasure Barn
1112 W. 15th St.
405/258-3115

Fine Things on the Corner
923 Manvel Ave.
405/258-5101

Outskirts
1909 E. 1st St.
405/258-2902

Brown Furniture
920 Manvel Ave.
405/258-1717

Days of Yesteryear
1214 Manvel Ave.
405/258-2217

11 CHICKASHA

Artistic Expressions Mall
309 W. Chicasha Ave.
405/224-9199

Dangie's Antiques
524 W. Chickasha Ave.
405/224-9019

Ersland Antiques
1124 S. 17th St.
405/224-2049

Yellow Rose Antique Mall
516 W. Chickasha Ave.
405/222-2112

Rocky's Ole Time Shoppe
1002 S. 4th St.
405/224-6945

Collector's Corner
2001 S. 6th St.
405/224-3819

12 CHOUTEAU

Black Star Antiques
702 S. Chouteau Ave. (Hwy. 69 S.)
918/476-6188
Open: Mon.–Sat. 10–6, Sun. 12–6
Directions: Traveling Hwy. 412 take Chouteau Exit. Go north 1 mile. Chouteau Avenue is Hwy. 69 S.

Space galore and jam-packed with items, this 14,000-square-foot shop houses antique clocks, tobacco tins, grocery store memorabilia, carnival chalkware (Kewpie dolls, Betty Boop, various figures). In addition, antique furniture, primitives, art and advertising collectibles are also available.

Frailey's Antiques
Hwy. 69 S.
918/476-6581

13 CLAREMORE

Claremore is home of the world-famous Will Rogers Memorial and Roger's burial site. Visitors can drive by the boarded-up Will Rogers Hotel, once resplendent with radium water baths on its top floor and a street level cafe. On the Rogers State College campus is the Lyon Riggs Memorial honoring the playwright for *Green Grows Like the Lilacs*, from which

came the beloved Rogers and Hammerstein musical *Oklahoma!* Great antique browsing in dozens of shops, many of which are within expansive malls. J. M. Davis Gun Museum features more than 20,000 guns and related items, plus steins, swords, musical instruments and more.

Warden's Antique Clock Shop
105 N. Boling St.
918/341-1770

Milk Barn Antiques
220 N. Missouri Ave.
918/342-1116

Frontier General Store & Antique Mall
318 W. Will Rogers Blvd.
918/341-3442

Peachtree Antiquary
409 W. Will Rogers Blvd.
918/341-1360

Hoover's Have All Mall
714 W. Will Rogers Blvd.
918/341-7878

Antique Peddlers Mall
422 W. Will Rogers Blvd.
918/341-8615

Chamwood Antique Mall
2409 N. Hwy. 20
918/341-7817

Custom Frames & Collectibles
101 S. Seminole Ave.
918/341-2900

Shadows of Time
404 W. Will Rogers Blvd.
918/342-2633

Sanbear Antique Mall
508 W. Will Rogers Blvd.
918/341-6227

A Place in Time Antiques & Cllbls.
1215 W. Will Rogers Blvd.
918/343-9800

14 CLINTON

In 1899, two men, waiting for a train at a station house, climbed on a box car to look over the countryside. Their eyes traveled over the Washita River Valley, and one of them said, "There's the place to build a town." The men were J. L. Avant and E. E. Blake. They were looking at the site where the town of Washita Junction would spring up, almost overnight, some four years later. However, before the dream could become a reality, there was a political fight that reached as far as the United States Congress, and the start of a feud between Arapaho and Washita Junction. The postal department refused to accept the name Washita Junction for the new town. Therefore, "Clinton" was chosen in honor of the late Judge Clinton Irwin.

Antique Mall of Clinton
815 Frisco
580/323-2486

Mohawk Lodge Indian Store
1 mi. E. on Old 66 Hwy.
580/323-2360

15 CUSHING

Friday Store
112 W. Broadway St.
918/225-3936

The Full Moon
120 W. Broadway St.
918/225-3936

16 DAVIS

Nelson's Cottonwood Corner
Hwy. 77 S.
580/369-3836

D & D
206 E. Main St.
580/369-2398

Miss Sarah's
201 E. Main St.
580/369-2092

The New Dusty Steamer Mall
222 E. Main St.
580/369-2959

Bric-A-Brac House
509 E. Main St.
580/369-3916

Davis General Store
112 N. Third St.
580/369-3409

Honey Creek Emporium
212 E. Main St.
580/369-3524

Somethin Old Somethin New
503 E. Main St.
580/369-3418

Country General
1 mi E. of 1/2 Mile Road N.
580/369-3954

17 DEWEY

Dewey Antique Mall
202 N. Osage Hwy. 75
918/534-2660
Open: Mon.–Sat. 10:30–5:30, Sun. 1–5

A collector's paradise! Thirty dealers offer an amazing array of old Ertle banks, Western memorabilia, primitives, glassware and much, much more.

Treasures Are We
306 E. Don Tyler Ave.
918/534-3878

Campbell's Antiques
418 Don Tyler Ave.
918/534-3068

Lighthouse
115 S. Osage
918/534-0662

Linger Longer Antiques
814 N. Shawnee Ave.
918/534-0610

Susie's Miniature Mansion
623 E. Don Tyler
918/534-2003

The Right Place Too
301 S. Osage - Hwy. 75
No phone listed

Something Different
319 E. Don Tyler Ave.
918/534-3645

Bar-Dew Antiques
Hwy. 75 N.
918/534-0222

Forget Me Not
305 S. Osage
918/534-3737

Chancellor Antiques
400 E. Don Tyler
918/534-3338

The Right Place
810 N. Wyandotte
No Phone # Listed

18 DUNCAN

Company's Comin
9 N. 8th St.
580/252-1844

The Ginger Jar Antiques
1609 N. Hwy. 81
580/252-2329

Duncan Antique Mall
920 Main St.
580/255-2552

Decors of Duncan
1898 N. Hwy. 81
580/252-9090

Brass Rail Antiques
5051 N. Hwy. 81
580/252-7277

Nancy's Antiques
Hwy. 70 (Waurika)
580/228-2575

Antique Market Place & Tea Room
726 W. Main St.
580/255-2499

K-Rider Co.
806 W. Main St.
580/255-2211

Aunti Msl
832 W. Main St.
580/252-3945

Red Rose
5051 N. Hwy. 81
580/225-4925

Ace High Pawn
112 E. Main St.
580/252-7296

2 Bs Closet
806 W. Main St.
580/255-2211

Pat's Corner Mall
809 W. Main St.
580/255-4988

19 EDMOND

The city actually began in 1887 when the Santa Fe Railroad built a watering station at the highest point between the Cimarron and North Canadian rivers. The town sprang to life as homesteaders staked their claims around the station during the great Land Run on April 22, 1889.

The founders embodied the true spirit of pioneers—they were trailblazers who worked hard to ensure the best for their families and their futures. This is evident in the "firsts" they accomplished. Edmond was the first town in Oklahoma Territory to have a public school house as well as the first church. The territory's first library was organized in Edmond and the "Normal School" for teachers was established here. The Normal School is now the University of Central Oklahoma.

Country Collectibles
15 N. Littler Ave.
405/359-7210

Edmond Antique Mall
907 S. Broadway St.
405/359-1234

Broadway Antique Mall
114 S. Broadway St.
405/340-8215

Courtyard Antique Market
3314 S. Broadway St.
405/359-2719

20 EL RENO

Motorists may notice something odd about the aged-looking broken neon sign in front of the Big Eight Motel; it boastfully proclaims the place as "Amarillo's Finest." Looks can be deceiving though—the sign is a leftover prop from the movie Rain Man, which was filmed in part in Oklahoma, and Dustin Hoffman and Tom Cruise really slept here. El Reno was a major rail center for the Rock Island years ago, but a ghostly rail yard is all that remains today. Carnegie Library has archived photos of the famed Bunion Derby and paving of Route 66. On the west edge of town is old Fort Reno, where World War II German prisoners are among those buried in its windswept cemetery.

The Old Opera House
110 N. Bickford
405/422-3232
Open: Mon.–Sat. 10–5, Sun. 1–5

This renovated opera house features antiques and crafts. Furniture and accessories, collectibles, art and rugs offer a sampling of the items presented within the charming elegance of this massive and historic structure.

Route 66 Antique Mall
1629 E. State Hwy. 66
405/262-9366
Open: Tues.–Sat. 10–6, Thurs. 10–8, Sun. 1–5, closed Mon.

On the west end of the city, 120 booths display varied and interesting pieces. Primitives are well represented. Other booths offer all types and descriptions of glassware and Americana.

21 ELK CITY

Old 66 Antique Mall
401 E. 3rd St.
580/225-9695

Country Creations Craft & Antique Mall
114 S. Main St.
580/225-7312

Kandie's Kreations & Kollectibles
2424 W. Third (Old Route 66)
580/225-6900

22 ENID

Mini-Mall
129 E. Broadway Ave.
580/233-5521

Down Memory Lane Antiques
101 S. Grand St.
580/242-2100

Tommy's This 'n' That
104 N. Independence
580/233-5642

Ben's Antiques
1205 S. Van Buren
580/237-5968

Cher-Dan's
827 W. Maine Ave.
580/237-6880

The Trolley Shop
910 W. Broadway Ave.
580/242-3123

Olden Daze Antique Mall
117 N. Grand St.
580/242-5633

Cherokee Strip Antiques
124 S. Independence
580/234-7878

Enid Flea Market
S. Van Buren
580/237-5352

23 GROVE

Flour Sack
307 S. Grant St.
918/786-4075

Precious Things
311 S. Grand St.
918/786-7044

Crystal's Antiques
Hwy. 59
918/786-9220

TBN Antiques & Uniques
3650 Hwy. 59 N.
918/786-7721

Donna's Antiques and Collectibles
2124 Hwy. 59 N.
918/786-3534

Old Homestead
6 W. 3rd St.
918/786-8668

Sister's Trading Co.
Hwy. 59
918/786-9511

Don's Swap Shop
5525 Hwy. 59 N.
918/786-9590

Village Barn Antiques
Main St.
918/786-6132

24 GUTHRIE

On a single day in April, 1889, a city was born … a new capital for a new territory. Overnight, 10,000 pioneers turned an open prairie into a sprawling array of crude tents, wagon beds, and rough-hewn wooden buildings. From that first day of chaos, an elegant Victorian city evolved with remarkable architecture and expressive character to become the capital of the 46th state, Oklahoma.

When the capital was moved south, this majesty of the plains fell by the wayside. Today, through careful restoration, this rich architectural legacy has been preserved in all its grandeur. Visitors can shop the numerous boutiques, antique malls and specialty shops downtown and also see the homes of governors, editors, law men, and outlaws in Guthrie's residential district.

Historic walking and trolley tours, jubilant festivals, cowpunching rodeos, live professional theatre, captivating museums, exquisite dining and a charming community make Guthrie a turn-of-the-century destination.

Elk's Alley
210 W. Harrison
405/282-6100

Antiques, Etc.
113 W. Oklahoma Ave.
405/282-9610

Recollections Antique Mall
124 N. First
405/260-0101

Vic's Place
124 N. 2nd St.
405/282-5586

King's Antiques
107 W. Oklahoma Ave.
405/282-0534

Aunt Bea's Attic
114 W. Oklahoma Ave.
405/282-4548

89er Antique Mall
119 W. Oklahoma Ave.
405/282-2661

Red Earth Antiques
103 S. 2nd St.
405/260-1030

25 HENRYETTA

B & Jays Antiques
214 W. Main St.
918/652-7552

Country Violet Antiques
1202 W. Main St.
918/652-4211

Attic Treasures Mall
115 N. 2nd St.
918/652-2484

26 JENKS

Jenks, like many other towns in Indian Territory originated around a railroad. It started as a Midland Valley Railroad Depot along a route between Tulsa and Muskogee.

Adhering to the provisions of the treaty concluded on February 14, 1833, between the Creek Indians and the United States of America, the final Roll of Citizens and Freedmen of the Five Civilized Tribes in Indian Territory had been completed. Those Indian citizens and Freedmen (formerly slaves) received allotments. (In 1904, the land that became the townsite of Jenks, Indian Territory was on the allotment of three Freedmen.) The Midland Valley Railroad Company purchased about 130 acres for the town. In 1907, Jenks became a town with 150 people. The city of Jenks, OK, now consists of nearly 8,800 people.

There are various stories as to the origin of the town name. Some report that it honored a Midland Valley Railroad engineer or conductor; others say the name was that of a carpenter named Jenks who built the depot. Still others believe the town was named for Dr. Jenks who was an early day resident. The agent for the Midland Townsite Company says the name "Jenks" came from a director in the Philadelphia corporation that built the Midland Valley Railroad.

Cornerstone Memories
102 S. 1st St.
918/298-6255

Linda's Things
105 N. 5th St.
918/299-5350

Abbey Road Antiques
107 E. Main St.
918/299-4696

Paradise Found Antiques
109 E. Main St.
918/299-2691

Miss McGillicutty's
203 E. Main St.
918/298-4287

Jenks House
410 E. Main St.
918/299-9100

Ancestors' Antiques
610 W. Main St.
918/298-3080

Niche in Tyme/Radio City Mus. Hall
112 S. 1st St.
918/298-1957

Main Street Antique Mall
105 E. Main St.
918/299-2806

Bittersweet Antiques
108 E. Main St.
918/298-9408

Kracker Box
116 E. Main St.
918/299-5353

Serendipity
207 E. Main St.
918/298-5628

Auntie Em's Victorian Village
101 W. Main St.
918/299-7231

Jenkins Guild Shops
Main St.-General Info
918/299-5005

27 LAWTON

Johnson's Furniture Repair
915 S.W. A Ave.
580/357-7307

Pickering Antiques
2 S.E. B Ave.
580/357-3276

Yesterday's Antique Mall
423 S.W. C Ave.
580/353-6005

Okie's Antiques
1706 N.W. Cache Road
580/355-4104

Wooden Windmill
5224 N.W. Cache Road
580/357-9697

Pickles Antique Mall
620 S.W. D Ave.
580/353-5050

Antiques by Helen
1002 S.W. D Ave.
580/357-1375

Another Time Antiques
709 S.W. E Ave.
580/353-0639

Antiques & Crafts by Cathy
404 S.W. 10th St.
580/355-0710

28 LOCUST GROVE

Pap's Country Market
607 N. Hwy. 82
918/479-5541

McFarland's Unique Antiques
111 E. Harold Andrews Blvd.
918/479-6311

Great Places to Eat

Country Cottage
608 N. Hwy. 82
918/479-6439

Buffet style or changing menu. The specialty is fried chicken.

29 MIAMI

Wind along Main Street to the grand old Coleman Theater, a 1929 Spanish Mission-style structure built with profits from the Turkey Fat Mine in Commerce. The Coleman, once a regular stop on the vaudeville circuit, is now undergoing a $1.5 million renovation project. Visitors may stop by the Chamber office to arrange a tour. Miami's downtown features retail shops and a cafe, and a block away is the Dobson Museum, which houses pioneer and mining artifacts.

Ole Shoppe
301 B St. S.E.
918/540-2961

Gramma's Antique Mall
417 D St. N.E.
918/542-1585

Classy Brass Antiques
31 S. Main St.
918/542-2203

Box Office Antiques
105 N. Main St.
918/540-0557

Magnolia Manor
107 N. Main St.
918/542-2046

Antiques & Uniques
113 N. Main St.
No Phone # Listed

Charlotte's C & T Bargain Center
123 S. Main St.
918/540-0543

30 MUSKOGEE

Collectible Corner & Antique Mall
30 W. Broadway St.
918/682-4335

Beaver's Antiques
540 Court St.
918/682-5503

Mr. Haney's Treasures
210 N. Edmond St.
918/687-6276

Yellow Brick Road
120 S. Main St.
918/686-8704

You Never Know
120 S. Main St.
918/682-8506

Old America Antique Mall
Hwy. 69 S.
918/687-8600

Antiques Galore
2225 W. Shawnee St.
918/683-3281

Mid-American Antique Mall
2251 S. 32nd St. W.
918/683-2922

Main Street USA Antique Mall
2426 N. 32nd St. W.
918/687-4334

31 NOBLE

Remember When
119 S. Main St.
405/872-8484

Vintage Village Antiques
1722 N. Main St.
405/872-7062

32 NORMAN

The Company Store Antique Mall
300 E. Main St.
405/360-5959
Open: Mon.–Fri. 10–6, Sat. 10–5, Sun. 1–5
Directions: From I-35, take the Main St. exit east. Go 2 miles. Shop located on the corner of Main and Crawford St.

When you reach the old green and red buckboard overflowing with colorful flowers, you've found The Company Store. This 7,000-square-foot building is a local landmark (the old Palace Garage) built c. 1900. Inside, 60 dealers present an outstanding variety of distinctive antiques including Flow Blue, Roseville and Rookwood along with exceptional stained glass pieces. Superb furnishings, unusual collectibles and elegant costume jewelry are also available.

Kensington Market Antique Mall
208 W. Gray St.
405/364-8840

Olde Town Market Place
219 E. Gray St.
405/447-8846

Whispering Pines Antiques
Hwy. 9
405/447-8297

Gallery Nouveau
1630 W. Lindsey St.
405/321-8687

Hope Chest Antiques & Collectibles
1714 W. Lindsey St.
405/321-8059

Peddler's Shop
209 W. Main St.
405/360-1015

Hoover Antique Galleries
210 36th Ave. S.W.
405/360-4488

33 OKEMAH

Pioneer Mall
215 W. Broadway St.
918/623-9124

34 OKLAHOMA CITY

The old route is sometimes hard to follow as it jogs down Lincoln Boulevard, past the State Capitol (note the oil wells on the Capitol grounds), then west along Northwest 23rd and 39th Streets. Look for a retro-style McDonald's restaurant at 23rd and Pennsylvania. Not far from the National Cowboy Hall of Fame and the Western Heritage Center on the city's northeast side, an old speakeasy once known as the Kentucky Club now welcomes all as a barbecue restaurant called the Oklahoma County Line. The eclectic Route 66 store at 50 Penn Place Mall injects local flavor into modern folk art, books and other symbols of the Main Street America. West on 39th Street, past Portland is Route 66 Bowl, the oldest still-operating bowling alley in Oklahoma City. A cool purple and green sign outside Meike's Route 66 Restaurant at Meridian Ave. hints of the nostalgic decor inside. A Texaco clock, old gas pump, and an assortment of metal toys give customers a feast for their eyes while they enjoy hearty home style Italian food.

Carolyn's Keepsakes
1116 N.W. 51st St.
405/842-1296

Pat & Barb's Antiques
1120 N.W. 51st St.
405/840-1220

My Daughter's Place
2648 S.W. 44th St.
405/685-5784

Abalache Book & Antique Shop
311 S. Klein Ave.
405/235-3288

Star Antiques
311 S. Klein Ave.
405/232-5901

Top of the Mart
311 S. Klein Ave.
405/239-8325

Lorri Ann's Antiques
3417 Sooner Fashion Mall
405/321-8633

Theo's Marketplace
3720 W. Robinson St.
405/364-0728

Colonies
1120 N.W. 51st St.
405/842-1279

What-Not Shelf Antiques
1120 N.W. 51st St.
405/842-7176

Michael's Antique Clocks
5920 W. Hefner Road
405/722-3300

Raggedy Anne's Market Antiques
311 S. Klein Ave.
405/239-2273

Trader Jean
311 S. Klein Ave.
405/232-8044

Country Temptations
4801 N. Macarthur Blvd.
405/789-8876

Bricktown Antique Shop
100 E. Main St.
405/235-2803

Antique Co-Op
1227 N. May Ave.
405/942-1214

23rd Street Antique Mall
3023 N.W. 23rd St.
405/947-3800

Spivey's Antiques
2500 N. May Ave.
405/947-5454

Return Engagement
7423 N. May Ave.
405/843-6363

Antique House
4409 N. Meridian Ave.
405/495-2221

Antique Centre, Inc.
1433 N.W. Expressway
405/842-0070

Architectural Antiques
By appointment only
405/232-0759

Crow's Nest
2800 N.W. 10th St.
405/947-6655

Apple Orchard
2921 N.W. 10th St.
405/946-3015

English Tea Co.
4405 S.E. 28th St.
405/672-0484

Oodles & Aah's
7622 N. Western
405/848-7099

Etta's Gift Gallery
6017 N.W. 23rd St.
405/495-1048

Antiques & Design
4512 N. Western
405/524-1969

Scranton Uniques
7512 N. Western
405/521-8715

Jody Kerr Antiques
7908 N. Western
405/842-5951

Mike's Antiques
1008 N. May Ave.
405/949-0707

Buckboard Antiques & Quilts
1411 N. May Ave.
405/943-7020

Unique Antiques & Collectibles
2125 N. May Ave.
405/943-0404

Villa Antique Mall
3132 N. May Ave.
405/949-1185

Apple Tree Antique Mall
1111 N. Meridian Ave.
405/947-8999

Pine Shop
12020 N.E. Expressway (I-35)
405/478-0220

Southern Antq. Mall/Treas. House
2196 S. Service Road
405/794-9898

Coca-Nuts Antiques
3234 E. I-240 Service Road
405/672-5600

Bare Necessities Mall
2842 N.W. 10th St.
405/943-2238

Apple Barrel Antique Mall
4619 N.W. 10th St.
405/947-7732

Easley's Touch of Class Antiques
4633 S.E. 29th St.
405/672-9010

Collectibles, Etc.
1516 N.W. 23rd St.
405/524-1700

Top Hat Antiques
4411 N. Western
405/557-1732

Covington Antique Market
6900 N. Western
405/842-3030

Discoveries
7612 N. Western
405/842-9555

Painted Door Gallery, Ltd.
8601 S. Western
405/632-4410

Langhorne Place Antiques
9115 N. Western
405/848-3192

Nothing but the Best
By Appointment Only
405/842-2545

A Family Tree Antique Mall
2422 S. Agnew Ave.
405/634-1159

35 OKMULGEE

Kate's Antiques
107 S. Grand Ave.
No Phone

Starr Collectibles
100 S. Morton Ave.
918/756-0736

36 PERRY

Georgia's Fine Furniture
611 Delaware St.
405/336-4501

Cherokee Strip Antique Mall
645 Delaware St.
405/336-4598

Memories of Yesteryear
317 N. 7th St.
405/336-5650

Hazel's Antiques
817 Wakefield
405/336-4794

37 PONCA CITY

Terri's Toys & Nostalgia
419 S. 1st St.
580/762-8697

Christy's
3005 N. 14th St.
580/765-3800

Grand Avenue Antique Mall
206 E. Grand Ave.
580/762-5221

38 PRYOR

Wacky Jackie
118 S. Adair St.
918/825-6125

Rustiques
207 S. Adair St.
918/825-6151

Sampler Antiques & Wood Works
9201 N. Western
405/848-7007

Antique Hardware
1920 Linwood Blvd.
405/236-5662

Ye Olde Lamp Post
113 S. Grand Ave.
918/756-4539

Legacy Antiques
218 E. 6th St.
918/756-0567

Antiques on the Square
615 Delaware St.
405/336-3327

The Antique Spot
902 11th St.
405/336-5290

The Antique Station
625 6th St.
405/336-5743

Early Attic
510 N. 1st St.
580/762-5142

Granary
218 W. Grand Ave.
580/762-5118

West End Interiors
223 W. Grand Ave.
580/765-8864

Heritage Antique Mall
122 S. Adair St.
918/825-5714

Mary's Whatnots
103 E. Graham Ave.
918/825-3757

39 PURCELL

T's Antiques Mall
116 W. Main St.
405/527-2766

Butler Antiques
202 W. Main St.
405/527-9592

Auntie Mae's Antiques
127 W. Main St.
405/527-5214

40 SAPULPA

Home of Frankoma Pottery, Sapulpa is a popular stopping-off place for travelers seeking diversion. Tours are offered weekdays, and the gift shop is open all week. In town, the Sapulpa Historical Museum is open afternoons except Sunday. Since the 1950s, locals have gathered at Norma's Diamond Cafe, and the Hickory House Restaurant serves up great barbeque and the only live music in town. A three-mile stretch of original Route 66 signed as the Ozark Trail can be found west of town, where venturesome motorists will cross the steel-and-brick Ozark bridge, under an old concrete Frisco railroad bridge, and go by the Teepee Drive In, which still operates in summer.

Antiques 'n' Stuff
15 E. Dewey Ave.
918/224-8049

A Moment in Time
205 E. Dewey Ave.
918/224-7158

Foote & Son Antique Investment Co.
15 N. Elm St.
918/227-0250

Schwickerath Furniture
Main St.
918/224-5396

Homespun Treasures
209 E. Dewey Ave.
918/227-4508

Neat Stuff
1115 E. Dewey Ave.
918/224-6097

Sara's Country Corner
1 S. Main St.
918/224-6544

Great Places to Eat

Freddie's
1425 Sapulpa Road
918/224-4301

For more than 30 years, loyal Freddie's customers have been enjoying its famous barbecue, perfect steaks and super seafood selections, served with Freddie's special tabouli, hummus and cabbage rolls.

This full-service restaurant is a favorite for a friendly, comfortable atmosphere, generous portions and reasonable prices.

41 SEMINOLE

Country Road Antique Market
Exit 200 I-40
405/382-1133

Memory Lane
217 N. Main St.
405/382-8200

Lil's
State Hwy. 3 – 1 ½ mi. N. of Seminole College
405/382-7716

Another Man's Treasures
300 W. Broadway Ave.
405/382-0651

42 SHAWNEE

Crafters Showplace
115 E. Main St.
405/273-7985
Open: Mon.–Sat. 10–5:30, Jan.–March, closed Mon.

In Historic Downtown Shawnee, antiques such as furniture and collectibles will catch your attention. But, the shop's main focus is smaller bric-a-brac pieces and kitchen accessories. In addition, crafts persons will enjoy the array of supplies and completed craft projects for sale.

Antiques of Distinction
111 N. Broadway
405/878-9839
Open: Mon.–Sat. 10–5 , closed Sun.

Fine antiques with an elegant air line your stroll through this shop. Furniture stripping and refinishing are an added specialty.

Legends
124 N. Beard
405/878-0066

With the name hinting fine, quality pieces, antiques and collectibles serve as the basis of the selection. Furniture and accessories are in large part responsible for the singular style of this shop.

Kickapoo Korner
1025 N. Kickapoo St.
405/275-6511

Groves
602 E. Highland St.
405/878-9919

Oliver-Hardin Antiques
313 Macarthur St.
405/273-5060

Main St. Gifts
16 E. Main St.
405/275-1088

OK Territory Antiques Ltd. Co.
214 E. Main St.
405/878-0214

Sante Fe Trading Post
524 E. Main St.
405/275-5900

Green's Corner
723 E. Main St.
405/273-2021

Grandma Had It Antiques
36700 W. Old High #270
405/275-7766

43 SKIATOOK

Ford's Antiques & Collectibles
100 E. Rogers Blvd.
918/396-4268

Christi's Unlimited
112 E. Rogers Blvd.
918/396-0248

Third Time Around
120 E. Rogers Blvd.
918/396-3144

Rogers Blvd. Antiques
101 W. Rogers Blvd.
918/396-0065

Antique Mall of Skiatook
2200 W. Rogers Blvd.
918/396-1279

44 STILLWATER

Jeanne's Antiques
520 S. Knoblock St.
405/372-8567

Delores Antiques
4224 N. Washington St.
405/372-1455

Antique Mall of Stillwater
116 & 122 E. 9th Ave.
405/372-2322

The Myriad
119 E. 9th Ave.
405/372-6181

Mrs. Brown's Attic
211 N. Perkins Road
405/624-0844

Rock Barn Relics
1623 S. Perkins Road
405/372-2276

45 STROUD

City streets are bustling these days, thanks to the Tanger Outlet Mall that opened just a few years ago. Good restaurants are open throughout town, but the Rock Cafe is a truly Route 66 relic. Open since 1939, the eatery was once billed as the busiest truck stop along the old road. Its original owner paid $5 for the stones dug up during the construction of Old 66, and those stones were used to build the cafe. Tasty smoked meats, buffalo, and delectable Swiss/German cuisine are the bill o' fare, and the owner speaks German, Italian, French, English, and Swiss.

Antique Alley Mall
309 W. Main St.
918/968-3761

Memory Lane
405 W. Main St.
918/968-3491

Friends Arts & Antiques
404 W. Main St.
918/968-2568

Great Places to Stay

Stroud House Bed and Breakfast
110 E. Second St.
918/968-2978 or 1-800-259-2978
Rates: $65–$100

When you need a break from the hassles of life (which I do after writing this book), visit the Stroud House Bed and Breakfast, a nationally recognized historic Victorian home. The Stroud House was constructed by J.W. Stroud in 1900 and renovated by the hosts in 1992. Four beautifully decorated guest rooms offer rest and relaxation. Each guest gets a "famous" Stroud House cookie. (I need a care package sent to me now!)

46 SULPHUR

Memory Lane Antiques & Collectibles
820 W. 12th St.
580/622-2090
Open: Mon.–Sat. 10–5, Sun. 12–5
Directions: Traveling I-35 south, take Hwy. 7 east approximately 12 miles. In Sulphur, turn right ½ block at the traffic light on 12th St. (If going I-35 North, take Exit 51.)

A stroll among pieces from yesteryear inside this 2-building, 4,000-square-foot collector's treasure chest reveals fine porcelains such as Haviland, Limoges, Old Ivory and R.S. Prussia. Antique furniture, wall pockets, kitchen collectibles plus collector plates add to the harvest of goods.

Gettin Place
100 W. Muskogee St.
580/622-3796

Quail Hollow Depot
20 Quail Hollow Road
580/622-4081

Great Places to Eat

Bricks Restaurant
2112 W. Broadway
580/622-3125
Open: Sun.–Thurs. 11–9, Fri. & Sat. 11–9:30

Specialties are barbecue and home cooking.

47 TULSA

Heart of Tulsa
Exposition Center at Expo Square
1-800-755-5488
Call for dates

Over 600 exhibitors from Oklahoma and the Midwest gather to display antiques, collectibles, arts and crafts.

Great American Antique Mall
9216 E. Admiral Place
918/834-6363

Browsery
3311 E. 11th St.
918/836-4479

White Bear Antiques & Teddy Bears
1301 E. 15th St.
918/592-1914

Spectrum
1307 E. 15th St.
918/582-6480

Antiquary
1325 E. 15th St.
918/582-2897

Colonial Antiques
1329 E. 15th St.
918/585-3865

Charles Faudree
1345 E. 15th St.
918/747-9706

Sophronia's
1515 E. 15th St.
918/592-2887

Lamppost Silver Co.
13012 E. 21st St.
918/438-3636

Zoller Iqbal Designs & Antiques
1603 E 15th St.
918/583-1966

Amir's Persian Imports
2204 E. 15th St.
918/744-6464

Kay's Antiques
2814 E. 15th St.
918/743-5653

Deco to Disco
3213 E. 15th St.
918/749-3620

Sam Spacek's Antiques
8212 E. 41st St.
918/627-3021

Estate Furniture
1531 S. Harvard Ave.
918/743-3231

Centrum
8130 S. Lewis Ave.
918/299-3400

And Then
4717 S. Mingo Road
918/622-9447

Consignment Treasures
3807 S. Peoria Ave.
918/742-8550

Tulsa Card Co.
4423 E. 31st St.
918/744-8020

Jared's, Inc.
1602 E. 15th St.
918/582-3018

Cisar-Holt, Inc.
1605 E. 15th St.
918/582-3080

Tulsa Antique Mall
2235 E. 51st St.
918/742-4466

Paula's Antiques & Estate Furniture
2816 E. 15th St.
918/742-6191

Glasstique
1341 E. 41st St.
918/742-3434

Brass Buff
1124 S. Harvard Ave.
918/592-1717

Side Door Antiques
1547 S. Harvard Ave.
918/742-5912

Snow's Consignment Store
909 S. Memorial Dr.
918/266-7446

Flowers, Interiors, Antqs. by Phillip
3740 S. Peoria Ave.
918/748-9450

Zelda's Antiques
1701 E. 7th St.
918/583-5599

Country Charm Antiques & Gifts
3316 E. 32nd St.
918/743-3656

48 VALLIANT

Vicki's Antiques, Collectibles & Crafts
Hwy. 70
405/933-5220

49 YUKON

Eagle Crest Antiques
430 W. Main St.
405/350-7474

Grandma's Treasures
453 W. Main St.
405/350-1415

Yukon's Yunique Antique
456 Main St.
405/354-2511

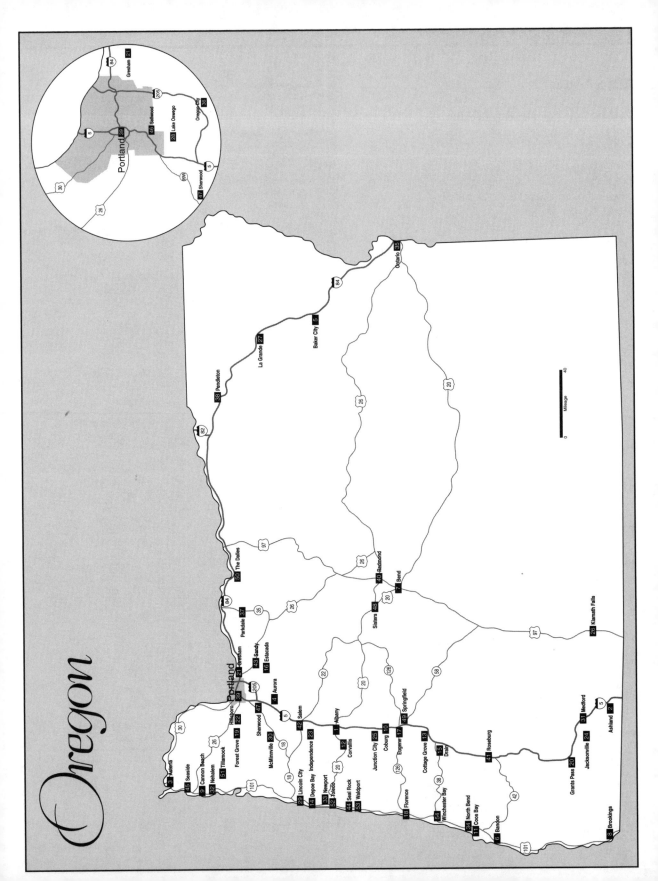

1 ALBANY

A drive east along the Wilamette River on Hwy. 20 takes you back in time to Albany. Here, historic charm is evident in more than 700 beautifully preserved buildings, churches and homes, including the Monteith House, Albany's oldest frame-built home. While you're here discover antique shops, Victorian gardens and a farmers' market via a downtown trolley or horse-drawn wagon tour.

Feather Tree
121 Broadalbin St. S.W.
541/967-9381

Mitsch's Antiques
131 Broadalbin St. S.W.
541/926-724

Antique Traditions
122 Ferry St. S.W.
541/926-0380

Peabody's Antiques-Gifts
238 1st Ave. W.
541/926-3654

Arlene's Victorian Rose
244 1st Ave. S.W.
541/928-4203

Byers Antiques
305 1st Ave. W.
541/928-3195

Pastimes Antiques
317 1st Ave. W.
541/926-0303

First and Ferry Antiques
343 1st Ave. W.
541/928-8774

Albany Book Co.
1425 Pacific Blvd. S.E.
541/926-2612

Clockwise
211 2nd Ave. S.W.
541/926-8507

B and E Antiques and More
223 2nd Ave. S.W.
541/928-2174

2 ASHLAND

As the southernmost town in the I-5 corridor, Ashland is the gateway for many Oregon visitors. The main attraction is the Tony Award-winning Oregon Shakespeare Festival. From mid-February through October, it presents 11 plays on three unique stages. Tickets and bed and breakfast reservations can be hard to come by on weekends and in the summer months, so plan in advance if you can. Better yet, schedule your visit for spring or fall.

While in town, take the Backstage Tour. Visit the Exhibit Center, where you can try on old costumes, then explore some of the other features that play a leading role in the character of Ashland such as antique shops, boutiques, and unusual art galleries.

Rita's Relics
93 Oak St.
541/482-0777

Perry S. Prince Asian Antiques
349 E. Main St.
541/488-1989

3 ASTORIA

Named after John Jacob Astor, the North Coast city of Astoria, at the mouth of the Columbia, is the site of the first permanent United States settlement west of the Rockies. Its historic charm and Victorian ambiance have provided the settings for movies such as *Free Willy* and *Kindergarten Cop*.

Phog Bounder's Antique Mall
1052 Commercial St.
503/325-9722

River's Edge Decorators
1145 Commercial St.
503/325-7040

Fort George Trading Co.
1174 Commercial St.
503/325-1690

Commercial Street Collectibles
1227 Commercial St.
503/325-5838

Marine Drive Antiques
2093 Marine Dr.
503/325-8723

Uppertown Antiques & Gallery
2911 Marine Dr.
503/325-5000

Persona Vintage Clothing
100 10th St.
503/325-3837

4 AURORA

Impressions of Aurora
Hwy. 99 E. & Main St.
503/678-5312

Old Miller Place
21358 Hwy. 99 E.
503/678-1128

Aurora Crossing Antiques
21368 Hwy. 99 E.
503/678-1630

Aurora Antique Mall
21418 Hwy. 99 E.
503/678-2139

Gary's Antiques
21627 Hwy. 99 E.
503/678-2616

Antique Colony
21581 Main St. N.E.
503/678-1010

Main Street Mercantile
21610 Main St. N.E.
503/678-1044

Time After Time
21611 Main St. N.E.
503/678-5463

Cottage Antiques
21631 Main St. N.E.
503/678-5911

Jacobs House
21641 Main St. N.E.
503/678-3078

Aurora State Bank Antiques
21690 Main St. N.E.
503/678-3060

Craig's Four Seasons Antiques
14979 2nd St.
503/678-2266

5 BAKER CITY

Mr. G's
2175 Broadway St.
541/523-2376

Windfall Antiques
2306 Broadway St.
541/523-7531

Baker City Collectibles
2332 Broadway St.
541/523-3592

Franciss Memory House Antiques
1780 Main St.
541/523-6227

Do Overs Antiques
2658 10th St.
541/523-5717

6 BANDON

Country Cottage Antiques
Morrison Road & Hwy. 42 S.
541/347-3800

Big Wheel General Store
130 Baltimore Ave. S.
541/347-3719

Angle's Nest
735 3rd St. S.E.
541/347-1414

Wild Angel Wholesale Antiques
735 3rd St. S.E.
541/347-1717

7 BEND

Buffet Flat

64990 Deschutes Market Road
541/389-9797
Open: Daily 10–6 except Christmas Day
Directions: Situated halfway between Bend and Redmond at Deschutes Junction. From Hwy. 97, travel approximately 500 feet to the northeast corner of Deschutes Junction, turn at the "Big White Wagon." Ask for further directions upon arrival as a new overpass was constructed in 1997.

Featured in *Self Magazine*, on PBS' "The Collectors" and The Learning Channel's "Neat Stuff," Buffet Flat houses a remarkable antique, souvenir and "re-use it" store. Among the extraordinary collection of wares are pieces from the 1800s to 1950s including Victoriana, Art Nouveau, Art Deco, Moderene and Atomic. The shop serves as the jumping off point for The Funny Farm, a private park and playground which is open to the public, no admission. Mind-boggling adventure awaits as you gaze upon such sights as the Bowling Ball Garden, The Love Pond and Cupid's Arrow, or the rare Punk Flamingo to name a very few.

Icehouse Trading Post
20410 N.E. Bend River Mall Dr.
541/383-3713

Homespun Antiques
856 N.W. Bond St.
541/385-3344

Bond Street Antiques
1008 N.W. Bond St.
541/383-3386

Iron Horse Second Hand Store
210 N.W. Congress St.
541/382-5175

Trivia Antiques
106 N.W. Minnesota Ave.
541/389-4166

Cottage Collectibles
210 S.E. Urania Lane
541/389-2075

Farm Antiques
838 N.W. Bond St.
541/382-8565

Enchantments Fine Antiques
1002 N.W. Bond St.
541/388-7324

Deja Vu Experienced Furniture
225 S.W. Century Dr.
541/317-9169

Sally's Antiques & Collectibles
61360 S. Hwy. 97
541/385-6237

605 Antiques
604 N.W. Newport Ave.
541/389-6552

8 BROOKINGS

Old Town Collectibles & Misc.
547-Chetco Ave.
541/469-0756

Van's Antiques
15714 Hwy. 101 S.
541/469-3719

9 CANNON BEACH

Tolovana Antiques
3116 S. Hemlock
503/436-0261

Blue Door
Sandpiper Square
503/436-9542

Pat & Mike's Antiques
148 S. Monro Road
503/436-1843

10 COBURG

Coburg Inn Antique Shops
91108 N. Willamette St.
541/343-4550

Dotson's Coburg Antiques
91109 Willamette St.
541/342-2732

Jolene's Antiques
32697 E. Pearl St.
541/302-3310

Mathew House Antiques
32702 Pearl St.
541/343-3876

Big Wheel Antiques
1091 Coburg Road
541/344-7300

Willow Tree Antique Mall
Coburg Road
541/465-4817

Coburg Road Antiques
90934 Coburg Road
541/683-3310

Iron Kettle Antiques
1359 Goodpasture Island Road
541/683-1267

Joseph's Antiques
32697 E. Pearl St.
541/345-0092

Ages Ago
90999 S. Willamette St.
541/343-6363

Ollie's Oldies
90559 Coburg Road
541/343-9989

Schram's Antiques
3699 Coburg Road
541/683-4965

Cara's Antiques
155 N. Willamette St.
541/345-2142

11 COOS BAY

Auction Company of Southern Oregon

Call ahead for Auction Dates
541/267-5361

When an auction bills itself as a "full service" country auction, you never know what to expect. Anything from antiques to the family farm could be up for grabs. That's what makes it so interesting, Granny could have stuffed a lot of things away in the old barn.

Marshfield Mercantile Annex
145 S. Broadway
541/267-7706

Maddie's Antiques & Collectibles
1161 Cape Arago Hwy.
541/888-9214

Apple Blossom Consignments
285 S. Broadway
541/269-0153

Marshfield Mercantile Antq. Emp.
145 Central Ave.
541/267-4636

Charleston Mall
8073 Cape Arago Hwy.
541/888-8083

Boat Basin Plaza Antiques
5005 Boat Basin Dr.
541/888-8024

12 CORVALLIS

Finders Keepers
5820 N.W. Hwy. 99
541/745-5848

Beekman Place
635 S.W. Western Blvd.
541/753-8250

Gold Dust
1413 N.W. 9th St.
541/758-7427

Corvallis Antiques Co.
3207 N.W. Polk Ave.
541/752-8004

13 COTTAGE GROVE

Rose Garden Mall Antiques & Gifts
501 E. Main St.
541/942-5064

Apple Pie Antiques
811 E. Main St.
541/942-0057

Preston's Treasure Hunt
820 W. Main St.
541/942-3763

Mike & Bev's Antiques
637 E. Main St.
541/942-3664

Petersen's Antiques
818 E. Main St.
541/942-0370

14 DEPOE BAY

What Not Shop
362 S.E. Hwy. 101
541/765-2626

Recollections
Hwy. 101
541/765-2221

15 DRAIN

Nana's Oldies and Goodies
301 N. 1st St.
541/836-7363

16 ESTACADA

Petals N Treasures
398 N. Broadway St.
503/630-4411

Tole Barn
22597 S. Day Hill Road
503/630-4680

17 EUGENE

Fifthpearl Antiques
207 E. 5th Ave.
541/342-2733

The Antique Heart
409 High St.
541/465-1158

Antique Clock Shop
888 Pearl St.
541/683-1349

Nostalgia Collectibles
527 Willamette St.
541/484-9202

Copper Penny Antiques
1215 Willamette St.
541/686-2104

18 FLORENCE

Bay Window
1308 Bay St.
541/997-2002

Divine Decadence
129 Maple St.
541/997-7200

Fine Timed Collectibles
513 Hwy. 101
541/997-6430

Brian's Furniture Farm Antiques
115 N. Seneca Road
541/689-3358

Goodness Gracious
767 Willamette St.
541/345-4517

Collectors Corner
1623 15th St.
541/902-8077

Old Town Treasures
299 Maple St.
541/997-1364

19 FOREST GROVE

Sentimental Journey Antiques
2004 Main St.
503/357-2091

Collections In The Attic
2020 Main St.
503/357-0316

Days Past Antiques & Collectibles
1937 Pacific Ave.
503/357-5405

Acanthus Antiques
2011 Main St.
503/357-3213

Rachel's
1930 Pacific Ave.
503/357-2356

Verboort Village Antiques
39690 N.W. Verboort Road
503/359-0454

20 GRANTS PASS

Black Swann
100 Lewis Ave.
541/474-2477

Blue Moon Antiques Gifts
220 S.W. 6th St.
541/474-6666

6th Street Antique Mall
328 S.W. 6th St.
541/479-6491

Grant's Pass Antique Mall
224 S.W. 6th St.
541/474-5547

Daniel Boone's Trading Post
470 Redwood Hwy.
541/474-2992

Elegance
321 S.E. 6th St.
541/476-0570

Grandma's Attic
122 S.E. H St.
541/479-7363

21 GRESHAM

Antiques by Renee
17 N.W. 1st St.
503/665-4091

By Request
101 N. Main Ave.
503/661-4994

Oregon

Nostalgia Antiques & Collectibles
19 N.E. Roberts Ave.
503/661-0123

22 HILLSBORO

Q's Shoppe
2437 S.E. Brookwood Ave.
503/648-4785

Lestuff & Floral Too
230 E. Main St.
503/640-9197

Country Crossroads Antiques
8750 N.W. Old Cornelius Passroad
503/645-9025

Sniders Hill Theatre Antique Mall
127 N.E. 3rd Ave.
503/693-1686

Stratford House
207 E. Main St.
503/648-7139

Heinrich's Antiques & Collectibles
136 E. Main St.
503/693-7457

Old Library Antiques
263 E. Main St.
503/693-7324

Jill's Cottage
23483 S.W. Rosedale Road
503/591-8970

Snider's Main Street Antique
247 E. Main St.
503/693-0417

23 INDEPENDENCE

Main Street Antiques
144 S. Main St.
503/838-2595

Joni's Antiques
194 S. Main St.
503/838-5944

River Bend Antiques & Used Goods
184 S. Main St.
503/838-4555

Mostly Quilts Vintage
235 Main St.
503/838-5261

24 JACKSONVILLE

J. Bailey's Antiques
120 W. C St.
541/899-1766

Three Gables Antiques
305 S. Oregon
541/899-1891

L & K Antiques
660 N. 5th St.
541/899-7143

Trash Pile Antiques & Collectibles
650 N. 5th St.
541/899-1209

Abigail's Corner
160 W. C St.
541/899-7537

Pickety Place
130 N. 4th St.
541/899-1912

25 JUNCTION CITY

Offering a number of excellent antique shops through which to roam, modern Junction City began with a western flavor. In 1871, the railroad had reached the settlement drawing many citizens from nearby Lancaster to relocate to Junction City. The town's name was conceived along with the notion that a west railroad line would join the main line at this point. Due to finances, no west line was constructed until 1910. Even so, the railroad town grew.

Railroad crew members found Junction City a suitable second home

with its numerous rooming and boarding houses and, of course, saloons. Travelers had money to spend, and a boom time with its accompanying businesses and reputation thrived. Unfortunately, fires ravaged the business section between 1878 and 1882 with the last of the great fires burning out in 1915. The town physically changed direction after this fire as its expansion began to the west.

Today travelers return to Junction City in mid-August as the Scandinavian Festival sprinkles downtown with the appearance of a Scandinavian village while citizens outfit themselves accordingly. Tasty Scandinavian foods are the feature of this event.

Brimhall's Antiques
595 Ivy St.
541/998-2770

Lingo's Sheepbarn Antiques
27579 High Pass Road
541/998-2018

Roberta's Collectibles
1480 Ivy St.
541/998-8782

26 KLAMATH FALLS

Country Mercantile
1833 Avalon St.
541/882-8808

Linkville Antique Co.
1243 Kane St.
541/883-1285

Assistance League Findables
1330 E. Main St.
541/883-1721

Carson's Old West
1835 Oregon Ave.
541/882-4188

White Pelican Antique Mall
229 S. 6th St.
541/883-7224

Shades of the Past
417 N. Spring St.
541/884-1188

Ant Mini Antiques & Mini Barns
1633 Division St.
541/882-9429

Cat's Meow
825 Main St.
541/885-3933

Petri's Interiors of Yesterday
125 N. 9th St.
541/882-8543

Always Antiques & Art Gallery
915 Pine St.
541/882-8700

Armour Antiques & Collectibles
7341 S. 6th St.
541/882-0263

Crafters Market
3040 Washburn Way
541/882-5270

27 LA GRANDE

Ten Twelve Adams Antiques
1012 Adams Ave.
541/962-7171

Hills Antiques & Refinishing
1529 Jefferson Ave.
541/963-4223

Jefferson Antiques
1114 Jefferson Ave.
541/963-9358

Wooden Nickel
2212 E. Penn Ave.
541/963-7507

28 LAKE OSWEGO

Frederick E. Squire III
24 A Ave.
503/697-5924

Uncle Albert's Antiques
15964 Boones Ferry Road
503/635-5535

Oregon

Marquess of Granby
16524 Boones Ferry Road
503/635-3544

29 LINCOLN CITY

Portals of the Past
4250 N. Hwy. 101
541/996-2254

Vintage Corner
1520 N.E. Hwy. 101
541/994-7797

Rocking Horse Mall
1542 N.E. Hwy. 101
541/994-4647

Little Antique Store
2826 N.E. Hwy. 101
541/994-8572

Toby Torrance's Pastime
545 N.W. Hwy. 101
541/994-9003

Curio Cabinet Mall
1631 N.W. Hwy. 101
541/994-9001

Jade Stone Gallery
3200 S.E. Hwy. 101
541/996-2580

Snug Harbor Antiques
5030 S.E. Hwy. 101
541/996-4021

Mouse House
6334 S.E. Hwy. 101
541/996-4127

Streetcar Village
6334 S.E. Hwy. 101
541/996-4480

Herself's
1439 S.W. Hwy. 101
541/994-9566

Bush's Antiques
5021 S.W. Hwy. 101
541/994-7363

Beachtime Antiques
5053 S.W. Hwy. 101
541/994-4001

Judith Anne's Antiques
412 S. Hwy 101
541/993-9912

Ron's Relics
1512 S.E. Hwy. 101
541/994-6788

A Change of Seasons
304 Southeast Hwy. 101
541/994-3765

30 McMINNVILLE

Blue Angel Antique Shoppe
228 N.E. 3rd St.
503/434-5784

Old Salon Antique Shop
238 N.E. 3rd St.
503/472-8209

Out of the Blue N.W. Ltd.
620 N.E. 3rd St.
503/650-8665

31 MEDFORD

Downtown Merchants Mall
117 S. Central Ave.
541/779-6640

Micellany
220 N. Fir St.
541/770-9097

Brass Horseshoe
2581 Jacksonville Hwy.
541/772-8466

Mary's Dream
125 W. Main St.
541/857-1132

Jueden's Furniture
220 E. Main St.
541/772-3260

Crafters Blend
2308 Poplar Dr.
541/770-5052

L C Antiques
2312 Poplar Dr.
541/779-1115

Main Antique Mall
30 N. Riverside Ave.
541/779-9490

Jane's Antiques
308 W. 2nd St.
541/535-1315

Medford Antique Mall
1 W. 6th St.
541/773-4983

32 NEHALEM

Nehalem Antique Mall
Hwy. 101
503/368-7190

Pete's Antiques
Hwy. 101
503/368-6018

Three Village Gallery, Inc.
35995 Hwy. 101
503/368-6924

Robin's Reliques
36025 7th St.
503/368-4114

33 NEWPORT

About halfway down the coast, the picturesque Yaquina Head Lighthouse welcomes you to Newport, a town known for its Dungeness crab and glorious harbor under the graceful Yaquina Bay Bridge. The Historic Bay Front offers a mixture of shops, galleries, canneries and restaurants that serve fresh clam chowder, shrimp, oysters, crab and salmon.

Great Places to Stay

Oar House
520 S.W. Second St.
541/265-9571

Formerly a boarding house, bordello, and most recently a bed and breakfast, Oar House has been serving guests since the early 1900s. This Lincoln County Historic Landmark situated in the beautiful Nye Beach area of Newport delights guests with its history, ghost and nautical theme. Each guest room provides a queen-size bed in addition to a view of the ocean. Be amazed by the 360-degree view of the coast area from the lighthouse.

34 NORTH BEND

Granny's Hutch
1964 Sherman Ave.
541/756-1222

Fran Carter
1966 Sherman Ave.
541/756-4333

Wagon Wheel Antiques & Collectibles
1984 Sherman Ave.
541/756-7023

Echoes of Time
1993 Sherman Ave.
541/756-4072

Treasures
1997 Sherman Ave.
541/756-4678

Bric Brac Shack
2048 Sherman Ave.
541/756-2329

Old World Antiques
2072 Sherman Ave.
541/756-2121

Beauty & The Beast Antiques
615 Virginia Ave.
541/756-3670

35 ONTARIO

Back at the Ranch
2390 S.W. 4th Ave.
541/889-8850

Maria's Antiques
364 S. Oregon St.
541/889-3684

Grandma's Cellar Antiques & Furniture
715 Sunset Dr.
541/889-8591

Collectibles Etcetera
166 S. Oregon St.
541/889-4585

Good Ole Days Antique Mall
2601 N.W. 4th Ave.
541/889-3416

36 OREGON CITY

McLoughlin Antique Mall
502 7th St.
503/655-0393

Maija's Antiques and Collectibles
402 S. McLoughlin Blvd.
503/656-9610

Oregon City Antique Co.
502 7th St.
503/657-6527

37 PARKDALE

Parkdale Plain & Fancy
Baseline at 3rd Ave.
541/352-7875
Open: Tues.–Fri. 10:30–4:30, Sat. & Sun. 10:30–5:30, closed Jan. & Feb.
Directions: Traveling I-84, take Exit 64 at Hood River; travel south on Hwy. 35 for 15 miles to Cooper Spur Road. Take a right on Cooper Spur Road going 2 miles to Baseline. Turn right from Baseline to 3rd. OR Traveling north on Hwy. 35, turn left at Parkdale, then exit onto Baseline. Follow Baseline into downtown Parkdale to 3rd Ave.

For a leisurely browse through the finer and everyday items of yesterday, the former 1930s drugstore, now, Parkdale Plain and Fancy offers its eclectic collection. Among the items overflowing in this shop are antique furniture, books, as well as glassware such as Carnival, Depression and crystal. Primitive items (plates, vases, jugs, churns) enliven the selection. Linger over the house specialty — antique bottles.

38 PENDLETON

Pendleton Antique Co.
104 S.E. Court Ave.
541/276-8172

Georgianna's
207 S.E. Court Ave.
541/276-4094

Collectors Gallery
223 S.E. Court Ave.
541/276-6697

Vintage Court Antiques
224 S.E. Court Ave.
541/276-0747

Picket Fences
239 S.E. Court Ave.
541/276-9515

Twice Nice Antiques & Collectibles
815 S.E. Court Ave.
541/278-1407

Frieda 'n' Friends Antique Mall
1400 S.W. Court Ave.
541/276-7172

Lee's Antiques
813 S.E. Frazer Ave.
541/276-4158

39 PORTLAND

Mother Goose Antiques
1219 S.W. 19th
503/223-4493
Open: Mon.–Sat. afternoons — best to call first
Directions: Call for specific directions.

Owner Sigrid Clark has been in the antiques business over twenty years. Wandering through her shop you will find a wonderland of vintage smalls: garment buttons, collectible holiday items, kitchen collectibles including patented items, dollhouse minatures ('50s & older), cookbooks, an impressive array of sewing items, costume jewelry, salt & pepper shakers, silver trinkets, advertising items, spice tins, matchboxes, postcards, and children's toys.

As the owner puts it, "this is a fun place to shop."

Embry & Co. Antiques & Gifts
4709 S.W. Beaverton Hillsdale Hwy.
503/244-1646

Quintana Galleries
501 S.W. Broadway
503/223-1729

Abacus
1224 S.W. Broadway
503/790-9303

Partners in Time
1313 W. Burnside St.
503/228-6299

Enterprises Antiques
2955 E. Burnside St.
503/223-8866

J.K. Hill's Antiques
7807 S.W. Capitol Hwy.
503/244-2708

Le Meitour Gallery
7814 S.W. Capitol Hwy.
503/246-3631

Laurie's and Casey's Antiques
7840 S.W. Capitol Hwy.
503/244-6775

Pagenwood Restoring
7783 S.W. Capitol Hwy.
503/246-6777

Toby's Antiques & Collectibles
7871 S.W. Capitol Hwy.
503/977-2546

Really Good Stuff
3121 S.E. Division St.
503/238-1838

Family Ties
12659 S.E. Division St.
503-761-7047

Old Town Antique Market
32 N.W. 1st Ave.
503/228-3386

New Antique Village Mall, Inc.
1969 N.E. 42nd Ave.
503/288-1051

Antique Alley
2000 N.E. 42nd Ave.
503/287-9848

Foster Road Collectibles
4932 S.E. Foster Road
503/788-9474

Goods Antique Mall & Emporium
5339 S.E. Foster Road
503/777-9919

Alameda Floral Antqs. & Interiors
5701 N.E. Fremont St.
503/288-6149

At The Rainbow End
5723 S.E. Foster Road
503/788-1934

Bucks Stove Palace & Antiques
6803 S.E. Foster Road.
503/771-3374

Antiques by the Wishing Corner
9201 S.E. Foster Road
503/771-1549

Mill Creek Crossing
9209 S.E. Foster Road
503/775-3141

Tony's Antiques and Collectibles
3709 S.E. Gladstone St.
503/788-1223

Maxine Cozzetto's
2228 N.E. Glisan St.
503/232-4656

Glass Works Gifts & Collectibles
10105 S.W. Hall Blvd.
503/246-9897

Ruby's Antiques, Fine Gifts & Interiors
3590 S.E. Hawthorne Blvd.
503/239-9867

Store II
1004 N. Killingsworth St.
503/285-0747

Leighton House Antiques
1226 Lexington
503/233-4248

Noce Antiques
8332 N. Lombard St.
503/286-3560

Tyrell's Antiques
6429 S.W. Macadam Ave.
503/293-1759

Fanno Creek Mercantile
12285 S.W. Main St.
503/639-6963

Stars Antique Malls
7027 S.E. Milwaukie Ave.
503/239-0346

Stars Antique Malls
7030 S.E. Milwaukie Ave.
503/235-5990

Handwerk Shop
8317 S.E. 13th Ave.
503/236-7870

Amy's Antiques
5851 S.E. Foster Road
503/777-1497

Handwerk Shop
8317 S.E. 13th Ave.
503/236-7870

Wishing Corner
9201 S.E. Foster Road
503/771-1549

Amsterdam Trading Co.
536 N.W. 14th Ave.
503/229-0737

Portland Antique Co.
1211 N.W. Glisan St.
503/223-0999

End of the Trail Collectibles
5937 N. Greeley Ave.
503/283-0419

Uncommon Treasures
3530 S.E. Hawthorne Blvd
503/234-4813

Antiques Plus
6403 N. Interstate
503/289-8788

Classic Antiques
1805 S.E. M. L. King Blvd.
503/231-8689

Slot Closet Antiques
5223 N. Lombard St.
503/286-3597

Milwaukie Antique Mall
10875 S.E. McLoughlin Blvd.
503/786-9950

Tigard Antique Mall
12271 S.W. Main St.
503/684-9550

A Child at Heart Antiques
6802 S.E. Milwaukie Ave.
503/234-3807

Old Friends
3384 S.E. Milwaukie Ave.
503/231-0301

Timeless Memories Antiques
7048 Milwaukie Ave.
503/234-3807

David H. Palmrose Antiques
1435 N.W. 19th Ave.
503/220-8253

Habromania
203 S.W. 9th Ave.
503/223-0767

Avalon Antiques
318 S.W. 9th Ave.
503/224-7156

Abundant Life Antiques
1130 S.E. 182nd Ave.
503/665-4301

Vintage Corner Antique Mall
13565 S.W. Pacific Hwy.
503/684-7024

George's Antiques
640 S.E. Stark St.
503/233-7787

Plaid Rabbit Button Exchange
111 N.W. 2nd Ave.
503/224-0678

Polished Image
122 N.W. 10th Ave.
503/228-8347

Renaissance Galleries & Interiors
414 S.W. 10th Ave.
503/226-1982

Richard Rife French Antique
300 N.W. 13th Ave.
503/294-0276

Gold Door Antiques & Art
1434 S.E. 37 th Ave
503/232-6069

Andrew's Antiques
916 S.E. 20th Ave.
503/234-9378

Classic Woods
1108 N.W. 21st Ave.
503/242-1849

Jack Heath Antiques
1700 N.W. 23rd Ave.
503/222-4663

N.W. Collectibles & Antique Paper
7901 S.E. 13th St.
503/234-6061

White Parrot Antiques & Collectibles
7919 S.E. 13th Ave.
503/236-5366

Corner House Antiques
8003 S.E. 13th Ave.
503/235-3749

Palookaville
211 S.W. 9th Ave.
503/241-4751

Stone Fox Gallery
506 N.W. 9th Ave.
503/228-7949

Phone Company
135 S.E. 102nd Ave.
503/253-1124

L.L. Trading Post
12115 S.E. Powell Blvd.
503/761-5960

Antique Slot Machines, Inc.
12037 S.E. Stark St.
503/253-3773

Arthur W. Erickson, Inc.
1030 S.W. Taylor St.
503/227-4710

Jerry Lamb Interiors & Antiques
416 N.W. 10th Ave.
503/227-6077

Retrospection
619 S.W. 10th Ave.
503/223-5538

Cubby Hole Antiques
7824 S.W. 35th Ave.
503/246-8307

Geraldine's
2772 N.W. Thurman St
503/295-5911

Star's N.W. Antique Mall
305 N.W. 21st Ave.
503/220-8180

Shogun's Gallery
206 N.W. 23rd Ave.
503/224-0328

Peter M. Sargent Antiques
2430 S.W. Vista Ave.
503/223-3395

Kathryn's Antiques & Collectibles
7907 S.E. 13th Ave.
503/236-7120

General Store
7987 S.E. 13th Ave.
503/233-1321

Den of Antiquity
8012 S.E. 13th Ave.
503/233-7334

Oregon

Treasure Chest Antiques
8015 S.E. 13th Ave.
503/235-6897

The Sellwood Collective
8027 S.E. 13th Ave.
503/736-1399

Royal Antiques
8035 S.E. 13th Ave.
503/231-9064

Spencer's Antiques
8130 S.E. 13th Ave.
503/238-1737

Consignment Gallery
8133 S.E. 13th Ave.
503/234-6606

American Country Antiques
8235 S.E. 13th Ave.
503/234-8551

The Green Door
8235 S.E. 13th Ave., #11
503/231-2520

The Blue Hen & Company
8309 S.E. 13th Ave.
503/234-3197

Gilt Vintage Jewelry & Antiques
8017 S.E. 13th Ave.
503/231-6395

Farmhouse Antiques
8028 S.E. 13th Ave.
503/232-6757

Sellwood Peddler Attic
8065 S.E. 13th Ave.
503/235-0946

Sellwood Antiques Mall
7875 S.E. 13th Ave.
503/232-3755

Anomaly
8235 S.E. 13th Ave.
503/230-0734

Lily White
8235 13th Ave.
503/234-1630

Ragtime Antiques & Repairs
8301 S.E. 13th Ave.
503/231-4023

Wood Pile Antiques
8315 13th Ave.
503/231-1145

Great Places to Stay

General Hooker's Bed and Breakfast
125 S.W. Hooker
541/222-4435 or 1-800-745-4135
Fax: 503/295-6410
Rates: $70–$115

   As the early morning's misty fog clears from town, General Hooker's bed and breakfast sits in the midst of its tranquil Historic District. The Victorian townhouse, a stroll from downtown, displays a restrained Victorian ornamentation. Much of the casually comfortable atmosphere grows out of the 19th century family heirloom furnishings. Furniture is tasteful and cozy. In addition, Northwestern art provides an interesting flare to the decor. Throughout the house, guests move to the music of Bach and Vivaldi. Guest accommodations include four rooms, two with private baths.

40 REDMOND

Old Farmer's Co-op Antiques
106 S.E. Evergreen Ave.
541/548-7975

Route 97 Trading Post
2424 N. Hwy. 97
541/923-4660

Country Pleasures
502 S.W. Evergreen Ave.
541/548-1021

The Gilbert House
203 S. 6th St.
541/548-1342

World of Treasures
215 S.W. 6th St.
541/923-0226

Memory Shoppe
422 S.W. 6th St.
541/923-6748

The Keeping Room
528 S.W. 6th St.
541/548-7888

41 ROSEBURG

Majestic Antiques
715 S.E. Cass Ave.
541/672-1387

From Days Gone By
630 S.E. Rose St.
541/673-7325

Angles in the Attic
400 S.E. Jackson St.
541/673-7101

42 SALEM

Antique Village
211 Commercial St. N.E.
503/581-0318

A Part of the Past Antique Mall
241 Commercial St. N.E.
503/581-1004

Best Dressed Doll
385 Howell Prairie Road S.E.
503/362-6583

Engelberg Antiks II
148 Liberty St. N.E.
503/363-8155

Nancy Van Zandt Antiques
1313 Mill St. S.E.
503/371-8612

Et Cetera Antiques
3295 Triangle Dr. S.E.
503/581-9850

43 SANDY

Sandy Traders
38905 Proctor Blvd.
503/668-5749

Treasures Antique Mall, Inc.
39065 Pioneer Blvd.
503/668-9042

Past & Presents
418 S.W. 6th St.
541/923-0147

Country by Design Antiques
453 S.W. 6th St.
541/923-3350

Woodtique
2660 N.E. Stephens St.
541/673-8385

Antique Mall & Marketplace
1212 S.E. Stephens St.
541/672-8259

Earle Antique Co.
223 Commercial St. N.E.
503/370-9666

A Touch of Nostalgia
255 Court St. N.E.
503/588-9123

Gingerbread Haus Antiques
145 Liberty St. N.E.
503/588-2213

Icons & Keepsakes
148 Liberty St. N.E.
503/370-8979

Reid's Antiques
2625 Salem Dallas Hwy. N.W.
503/581-1455

Every Bloomin' Thing
615 Wallace Road N.W.
503-378-1821

Something Old Something New
38922 Pioneer Blvd.
503/668-0808

Oregon

44 SEAL ROCK

Antiques, Etc.
Hwy. 101
541/563-2242

A Part of the Past
10841 N.W. Pacific Coast Hwy.
541/563-5071

Granny's Country Store
10261 N.W. Pacific Coast Hwy.
541/563-4899

Purple Pelican Antique Mall
10641 N.E. Pacific Coast Hwy.
541/563-4166

45 SEASIDE

What was once "The End of Lewis & Clark Trail" is now Oregon's largest beach resort community. Seaside's legacy of hospitality dates back to 1873, when railroad baron Ben Holladay built the luxurious Seaside Hotel.

Wesrose's Antiques
3300 Hwy. 101 N.
503/738-8732

Yankee Trader
4197 Hwy. 101 N.
503/738-6633

Cynthia Anderson Antiques
567 Pacific Way
503/738-8484

Ike & Debbie's Red Barn Antiques
3765 Hwy. 101 N.
503/738-0272

Cottage and Castle
501 S. Holladay Dr.
503/738-2195

46 SELLWOOD

Sellwood Bazaar Antiques
7733 S.E. 13th Ave.
503/236-9110

Golden Girls' Antiques
7834 S.E. 13th Ave.
503/233-2160

Sellwood Antique Mall
7875 S.E. 13th Ave.
503/232-3755

N.W. Collectibles & Antique Paper
7901 S.E. 13th Ave.
503/234-4248

The General Store
7987 S.E. 13th Ave.
503/232-1321

Den of Antiquity
8012 S.E. 13th Ave.
503/233-7334

Gilt Antiques
8017 S.E. 13th Ave.
503/231-6395

The Sellwood Collective
8027 S.E. 13th Ave.
503/736-1399

The Raven Antiques & Military
7805 S.E. 13th Ave.
503/233-8075

Misty's Antiques
7825 S.E. 13th Ave.
503/233-9564

Leighton House Antiques, Ltd.
1226 Lexinton
503/233-4248

Kathryn's Antiques & Collectibles
7907 S.E. 13th Ave.
503/236-7120

Corner House/Queen Anne's Lace
8003 S.E. 13th Ave.
503/235-3749

The Treasure Chest
8015 S.E. 13th Ave.
503/235-6897

Farmhouse Antiques
8028 S.E. 13th Ave.
503/232-6757

Royal Antiques
8035 S.E. 13th Ave.
503/231-9064

1874 House
8070 S.E. 13th Ave.
503/233-1874

Sellwood Antiques & Cllbls. Market, Inc.
8132 S.E. 13th Ave.
503/236-9650

The Anomaly, Parlor of Eclectic Art
8235 S.E. 13th Ave.
503/230-0734

Ragtime Antiques
8301 S.E. 13th Ave.
503/231-4023

Woodpile Antiques
8315 S.E. 13th Ave.
No Phone Listed

Sellwood Pedler, Attic Goodies
8065 S.E. 13th Ave.
503/235-0946

R. Soencer Antiques, Inc.
8130 S.E. 13th Ave.
503/238-1737

American Country Antiques
8235 S.E. 13th Ave.
503/234-8551

The Blue Hen and Co.
8309 S.E. 13th Ave.
503/234-3197

The Handwerk Shop
8317 S.E. 13th Ave.
503/236-7870

47 SHERWOOD

Smockville Station Antiques
170 N.W. 1st St.
603/625-5866

Manhattan Trade Post Antique Mall
22275 S.W. Pacific Hwy.
503/625-7834

Railroad Street Antique Mall
260 N.W. Railroad Ave.
503/625-2246

Main Street Crossing
5 N.W. Main St.
503/625-5434

Bare Pockets
230 N.W. Railroad Ave.
503/625-5491

Whistle Stop Antique Mall
130 N.W. Railroad Ave.
503/625-5744

Great Places to Stay

Inn of the Oregon Trail
416 S. McLoughlin
503/656-2089

A stone's throw from the end of the Oregon Trail waits an 1867 Gothic Revival-style home built by E.B. Fellow, Inn of the Oregon Trail. Overlooking the landscaped gardens are three delightfully outfitted guest rooms on the third floor. The ground floor provides another room which offers a private entrance, bath, fireplace and wet bar. Fellows House Restaurant occupies the main floor and is open to the public weekdays, but private dinners for inn guests can be arranged with advance notice. Explore the inn and the surrounding historic Oregon City.

48 SISTERS

Lonesome Water Books
255 W. Cascade
541/549-2203

Country Collections
351 W. Hood St.
541/549-7888

Treasure Trove Craft & Antiques
160 S. Hood St.
541/549-2142

Oregon

49 SPRINGFIELD

Antique Peddlers I & II
612 Main St.
541/747-1259

Pretty Things For You
2142 Main St.
541/747-7718

Country Rose
3000 Gateway St.
541/746-4605

Mare's Place
448 Main St.
541/744-2021

Rolla's Relics & Reusables
868 Main St.
541/741-0838

Rose Moss
214 Pioneer Pkwy. W.
541/741-2411

Glory Days Antique Mall
2020 Main St.
541/744-1112

Paramount Antique Center
143 21st St.
541/747-3881

50 THE DALLES

Klindt's Used Books & Collectibles
319 E. 2nd St.
541/296-4342

Bishop's Antiques Gifts & Collectibles
422 W. 2nd St.
541/298-1804

Clem's Attic
2937 E. 2nd St.
541/296-4448

2nd Street Place
402 E. 2nd St.
541/296-8500

Old Mill Bargain Center
2917 E. 2nd St.
541/296-6706

51 TILLAMOOK

Great Places to Stay

Blue Haven Inn Overflow Shop
3025 Gienger Road
503/842-2265
Rates $60–$75
The inn never closes.
Directions: Turn west off Hwy. 101 at Gienger Road. The inn is located 2 miles south of Tillamook, Ore.

Sitting in the midst of two-acres surrounded by tall evergreens, Blue Haven affords guests country serenity and seclusion. Built in 1916, the country home has been skillfully restored featuring charming antiques and limited edition collectibles throughout. Each of the 3 guest bedrooms provides a unique decor. Tara, overlooking the garden, presents a *Gone With the Wind* theme highlighted by its four poster bed, Civil War chess set and memorabilia from the movie. The queen-size brass bed in La Femme hearkens to the "feminine and frilly" ladies boudoir of earlier days. A nautical atmosphere engulfs Of The Sea, a most comfortable room, with wingback chair and ottoman in addition to a view of the garden. Enjoy a relaxing pause on the country porch to swing. Listen to music from an old radio or antique gramophone in the library/game room. In the mornings, sit down to the complimentary gourmet breakfast served in the formal dining room on fine bone china and crystal. (Dietary preferences are carefully catered to.) Step around to the Overflow

Shop adjacent to the inn offering antiques, glassware, limited edition plates, dolls, sewing machines, as well as clawfoot bathtubs.

Smokehouse Antiques Mall
116 Main St.
503/842-3399

Dekunsam's Second Hand Store
1910 2nd St.
503/842-2299

52 TOLEDO

Sherwood Antiques
112 W. Graham St.
541/336-2315

Antiques 'n' More
199 S. Main St.
541/336-4210

Cedric & Christy Brown Antiques
404 N. Main St.
541/336-3668

Ada's Gifts & Collectibles
123 N. Main St.
541/336-2524

Main Street Antique Mall
305 N. Main St.
541/336-3477

53 WALDPORT

Waldport Mercantile
145 S.W. Arrow St.
541/563-4052

Doug and Mim's
340 N.W. Hemlock Hwy. #-34
541/563-2454

Glass Treats & Antqs. Prcln. & Restoration
332 N. Deer Hill Dr.
541/563-6282

Antiques & Reference Books
Hwy. 101
541/563-2318

Old Maid New
255 S.W. Maple St.
541/563-6411

Family Tree Collectibles
1265 S.W. Range Dr.
541/563-2099

Mim's Whims
340 N.W. Hemlock (Hwy. 34)
541/563-2454

54 WINCHESTER BAY

Winchester Bay offers over 300 camp sites on the Pacific Ocean, Umpqua River or on beautiful Lake Marie. The area provides great fishing opportunities for the guys and kids while mom antiques.

Winchester Bay Trading Company
Corner of Broadway & 8th St.
1 block from Hwy. 101
541/271-9466
Open: Daily 10–4
Directions: Hwy. 101, 2 miles south of Reedsport or 25 miles north of Coos Bay.

The personal touch thrives at Winchester Bay Trading Company. This husband and wife team hand select the shop's merchandise from regional estate sales. Because of their nearness to the bay, a large supply of nautical items can always be found among the rare books, Fitz and Floyd pieces, exquisite glassware and unique items such as an old tin bathtub.

South Dakota

Frederick 8
Aberdeen 1

Milbank 12
29

Watertown 21
212

Volga 20
Brookings 3
14

81
Dell Rapids 7

Sioux Falls 17
Tea 19
Worthing 22
Canton 4
29

90
Yankton 23

Mitchell 13
281

Kimball 11

Pierre 15

83

14

90

Rapid City 16

Belle Fourche 2
Spearfish 18
Deadwood 6
Piedmont 14
Hill City 9
Custer 5
Hot Springs 10

85
212

385

Mileage
0   30

1 ABERDEEN

Aberdeen was once the home of Frank Baum, an 1890s Aberdeen newspaper editor who later wrote the all-time favorite children's story *The Wonderful Wizard of Oz.*

Mother's Antique Mall
117 S. Main St.
605/225-8992

Heirlooms Etc. at the Depot
1100 S. Main St.
605/226-3660

Remember When Antiques
504 S. State St.
605/226-3612

Hitch'n Post Antiques & Collectibles
2601 6th Ave. S.E.
605/229-1655

Bourdon's Furniture Antiques
38497 133rd St.
605/226-0604

Lauinger's Country Store
305 6th Ave. S.W.
605/225-0910

Court Street Lighting
123 Railroad Ave. S.E.
605/229-0359

Meier Antiques
524 State St. & Railroad Ave.
605/229-5453 or 605/225-9592

2 BELLE FOURCHE

Love That Shoppe
515 State St.
605/892-4006
Open: Mon.–Sat. 9–8, Sun. 1–4
Directions: The shop sits in Downtown Belle Fourche at Hwys. 85 and 212.

Located in an historic 9,000-square-foot building, Love That Shoppe's 50 plus dealers' mix of Victorian, primitives, depression glass, heirloom jewelry, crockery and period furniture combine to make an enjoyable day for shopping.

And when you tire of shopping, The Rocking '50s Soda Fountain located in the shop will take you back to the old drug store soda fountain days with their menu of bottled cokes, root beer floats, hot dogs, soft pretzels, ice cream sodas, sundaes and banana splits.

Tri-State Bakery Studio
705 State St.
605/892-2684
Open: Tues.–Sat 9:30–5:30, Mon. 9:30–2
Directions: downtown Belle Fourche at Hwys. 85 and 212

The old Tri-State Bakery building, dating back to 1927, is on the National and State Historical Registers and is truly representative of its early days. All the old equipment once used in creating the delicious confections, pastries and breads is still housed in the building and is available for viewing by interested customers.

Today, it has been converted to the Tri-State Bakery Studio offering a large selection of vintage advertising papers and tins and a limited amount

of furniture. Also located here is the town's only Espresso Bar which features mochas and Italian sodas.

The Old Grizz Trading Post
2207 Fifth Ave. and 512 State St.
605/892-6668
Open: Daily 10–5

This 6,800-square-foot shop specializes in cowboy and western memorabilia, as well as a large variety of antiques and collectibles. The furniture selection mainly consists of, but is not limited to, pieces from the 1870s up through the '30s and '40s.

The Agers live on the premises at the Fifth Street location, a stately old home, dating back to 1892. They are currently in the process of restoring it to its original condition. The house still has 80% of its original wallpaper and an original 50-foot mural in the dining room.

The Agers encourage you to stop in anytime; if they're home; they're open.

Robb House Antiques
By appointment only
605/892-2846

3 BROOKINGS

Threads of Memories Antique Mall
309 4th St.
605/697-7377

Country Peddler
320 Main Ave.
605/697-6292

4 CANTON

Canton Square Antique Emporium
121 E. Fifth St.
605/987-3152
Open: Mon.–Fri. 9–8, Sat. & Sun. 9–5
Directions: Exit 62 from I-29, then 9 miles east.

Antique shop in the atmosphere of an old variety store, now a historical building. The owner says they have anything you want or ever hoped for in the way of antiques and collectibles.

Lincoln County Antique Center
123 W. 5th St.
605/987-4114
Open: Mon.–Sat. 10–5, closed Sun.
Directions: Exit Highway 18 off I-29. Travel east 8 miles to Canton.

Presenting 10,000 square feet of quality Victorian furniture, art and books.

Norma's This 'n' That Shop
109 N. Main St.
605/987-5816
Open: Thurs.—Sat. 10–5 or by appointment (call 605/987-2269 for appointment)
Directions: Located 8 miles off I-29. Take Highway 18 east to Canton.

A general line of antiques and collectibles are featured.

5 CUSTER

Mountain Valley Antiques
3 miles W. on Route 16
605/673-5559

Wild Bill's Antq. Mall & Rock Shop
2 miles W. of Custer on Hwy. 16
605/673-4186

6 DEADWOOD

Aunt Sophia's
By appointment only
800/377-1516

7 DELL RAPIDS

S & L Antiques & More
416/418 4th St.
605/428-4457

8 FREDERICK

Worthy Treasures Antiques
39147 105th St.
605/329-2143

Adeline Antiques
1149 300 91st Ave.
605/329-2112

9 HILL CITY

Orloske Antiques
Deerfield Road (Hwys. 16 & 385)
605/574-2181
Open: Daily 9–5 year-round, and by appointment
Directions: 1½ miles west of Hill City on Deerfield Road and also at the intersection of Highways 16 and 385.

The total combined shopping area of these two shops is 10,000 square feet. 1800s furniture, primitives, glassware, toys, western items (saddles, tack, etc.) and Redwing Pottery are offered throughout the shop.

Big 45 Frontier Gun Shop
23850 Hwy. 385
605/574-4702

10 HOT SPRINGS

Fargo Mercantile
321 N. River St. (Across from foot bridge)
605/745-5189

Pioneer Trading Co.
143 S. Chicago
605/745-5252

11 KIMBALL

Mentzer Antiques
Main St.
605/778-6688

Great Places to Stay

Red Barn Inn
Rural Route 2, Box 102
605/778-6332
Open: Year-round
Rates: $32.50 and up
Directions: From I-90 eastbound traffic: Take Exit 272; then travel ½ mile south, 7½ miles east, and 3 miles south on a gravel road. From I-90 westbound traffic: Take Exit 284; then go 4 miles west and 3 miles south on a gravel road.

American know-how triumphs again in this 70-year-old horse barn. No longer do steel bits, leather harnesses or hay decorate the interior. Today, a rustic decor outfitted with antique furniture and accessories celebrates the barn's reincarnation. Four rooms with separate baths serve as accommodations. Complimentary breakfast is served.

12 MILBANK

5th Street Antiques
902 S. 5th St.
605/432-5326

Bleser House Bed & Breakfast
311 S. 4th St.
605/432-4871

Reflections in Time
W. Hwy. 12
605/432-9495

13 MITCHELL

Second Impression Palace
412 N. Main St.
605/996-1948
Open: Spring–summer Mon.–Sat. 8:30–6:30, Sun. by chance; Fall–winter Mon.–Sat. 9–6, closed Sun.
Directions: Located only 1½ blocks south of the World's Only Corn Palace! Eastbound on I-90: Take Exit 330 north to Havens, east to Sanborn, north to 1st Avenue, east to Main Street, north to 412 North Main Street. Westbound on I-90: From Exit 332, go north to 1st Avenue, west to Main Street, north to 412 North Main Street.

This unique antique mall is a fascinating layout of old storefronts built from reassembled antique wood, glass, metal and tin. The award-winning display has been acclaimed from New York to San Francisco, and is a museum in itself.

Behind the doors of this indoor "Main Street" are more than 40 dealers

South Dakota

and 50 consignors with enough selection to satisfy everyone.

Walk down the boardwalk of time to the General Store and find trunks, dressers and Hoosier cabinets. For a more elegant variety of furniture try the Undertaker's. If vintage clothing and accessories are what you seek, you'll want to check into the Brothel. At the Sheriff's Office/Jailhouse, you'll find old tools, car accessories, and horse gear.

Cellar
400 N. Main St.
605/996-0515

14 PIEDMONT

James O. Aplan Antiques & Arts
I 90 Exit 40 Tilford Road
605/347-5016

15 PIERRE

Capital City Antiques
819 N. Euclid Ave.
605/224-4971

16 RAPID CITY

Traders Corner
3501 Canyon Lake Dr.
605/341-4242

Country Estates Heritage House
2255 N. Haines Ave.
605/348-5994

Antique & Furniture Mart
1112 W. Main St.
605/341-3345

Gaslight Antiques
13490 Main St.
605/343-9276

Hidden Treasures
1208 E. North St.
605/342-7286

Big K
805 E. Denver St.
605/343-1221

Coach House Antiques
Hwy. 79
605/399-3838

Country Lane Furniture Brian Peck
2332 W. Main St.
605/343-9401

St. Joe Antique Mall & Gifts
615 Saint Joseph St.
605/341-1073

Antiques & Collectibles
225 Omaha St.
605/342-8199

Great Places to Stay

das Abend Haus Cottages & Audrie's Bed and Breakfast
23029 Thunderhead Falls Road
605/342-7788
Open: Year-round

Old World hospitality is thriving in the Black Hills at this enchanting retreat for couples only. Rich in the Abend Haus tradition, the spacious suites and log cottages are furnished with the largest collection of European antiques anywhere in the state.

17 SIOUX FALLS

Architectural Elements
818 E. 8th St.
605/339-9646

Kolbe's Clock & Repair Shoppe
1301 S. Duluth Ave.
605/332-9662

Eight St. Treasure Chest
1002 E. 8th St.
605/338-6878

Maxwell House Antiques, Inc.
612 W. 4th St.
605/334-3640

Recycled Treasures
801 N. Main Ave.
605/330-9473

Chopping Block Antiques, Ltd.
207 S. Phillips Ave.
605/334-1469

Cliff Ave. Flea Vendors
3515 N. Cliff
605/338-8975

The Patina
26th & Western Park Ridge Mall
605/357-8884

The Book Shop
223 S. Phillips Ave.
605/336-8384

D&J Glass & Art Clinic
26707 466th Ave.
605/361-7524

Koenig's Antiques
1103 N. Main Ave.
605/338-0297

Exchange
1512 E. 10th St.
605/338-9155

Antiques Gallery Midwest
1502 W. 10th St.
605/334-3051

Old House Stuff
818 E. 8th St.
605/339-9646

Irish's Garage Antiques
618 S. 5th Ave.
605/334-6540

The Curiosity Shoppe
725 N. Main Ave.
605/334-1412

Antique Mall
828 N. Main Ave.
605/335-7134

Cedar Acres Antiques
"Sebbo's" 3721 N. Cliff
605/334-8689

Off The Hook Phone Service
Phone First
605/334-3151

Prairie Home Antiques
5900 E. 10th St.
605/338-2042

Dakota Weaver
5016 E. 16th St.
605/336-7336

Packaging Store
1404 W. 41st St.
605/332-4789

Antique Furniture Co.
27102 Elbers Ave.
605/368-2112

Dakota Collectables
101 N. Fairfax Ave.
605/338-8797

Emporium
923 S. Grange Ave.
605/334-8813

Midwest Antiques Gallery
1502 W. 10th St.
605/334-3051

Exchange West
1005 W. 11th St.
605/333-0049

18 SPEARFISH

Snowy Creek Antiques
112 W. Illinois St.
605/642-2660
Open: Mon.–Fri. 8–5
Directions: Take the Spearfish exit from I-90. Shop is located in downtown Spearfish off Main Street on Illinois Street.

Oak furniture, old oak file cabinets, African art, western collectibles, primitives, toys, china, glassware are just a few of the many items offered here.

Old Mill Antiques
222 W. Illinois St.
605/642-4704
Open: Winter Mon.–Sat. 10–5, summer Mon.–Sat. 9–6
Directions: Exit I-90. Shop is located in downtown Spearfish off Main Street.

15 dealers — a good general line of antiques and collectibles including late 1800s to '40s furniture, kitchenware, Depression glass, pottery and mining and railroad collectibles.

The Browser Bin
206 Colorado
605/642-7434

Seifert's Country House
RR 1 Box 143K
605/642-4930

Key Antiques
344 N. 5th St.
605/642-7087

Kiefer Consignments
513 Spearfish Canyon Road
605/642-7436

19 TEA

I-29 Antiques & Collectibles Mall
46990 271st St.
605/368-5810
Open: Mon. 9–9, Tues.–Sat. 9–5, Sun. 12–5
Directions: From I-29, take Exit 73, and go ¼ mile west.

Featuring McCoy, Fiesta, Hall pottery and Red Wing stoneware, all 10,000 square feet of this mall have been put to good use by the 75 dealers.

The curious antiquer can also find old toys, antique furniture, pictures, jewelry, glassware, and "tokens." More unusual items such as old signs plus well pumps add a touch of rustic to the collection.

20 VOLGA

Red Barn Antiques
46080 U.S. Hwy. 14
605/627-5394

21 WATERTOWN

Main Street Antiques
6 E. Kemp Ave., uptown Watertown
605/886-1919

Westgate
125 E. Kemp Ave.
605/882-1361

Yellowed Pages Used Books Vol. II
10 E. Kemp Ave.
605/886-3640

22 WORTHING

Antiques & Things
112 Main St.
605/372-4853

23 YANKTON

Kollectible Kingdom
317 W. 5th St.
605/668-9353
Open: Daily (closed Tues.) May–Nov. 9–6, Dec.–April 11–5:30 (some Sun. 12–5)
Directions: Traveling Hwy. 81 (easily accessible from I-29 or I-90). Turn east on 5th Street which is located between Coastal convenience store and Super Lube. Shop is located behind Super Lube.

Red Wing stoneware and Depression glass are the most popular and are featured pieces in this intimate and jam-packed shop. Also notable among the diverse and plentiful selections are unusual glassware and china. For those seeking a delightful challenge, a rummage sale section allows for sifting and digging.

Dakota Antiques & Collectibles
408 W. 11th & Broadway
605/665-7230

Wright's Antique Shop
313 Mulberry St.
605/665-2003

Gingerbread Shack
515 E. 4th St.
605/665-9924

Lewis & Clark Gallery
221 W. 3rd St.
605/665-0129

Texas *Western*

Inset: San Antonio

35
41
10
Converse
410
281
132
San Antonio
35
90
410
10
37
35

Main map:

83
162 Wheeler
83
83
Pampa 117
Clarendon 34
Memphis 103
82
Sweetwater 147
San Angelo 131
Borger 20
60
Snyder 141
20
87
Plainview 123
Big Spring 17
287
Amarillo 3
27
Lubbock 96
84
385
Midland 105
Odessa 114
40
60
82
385

0 Mileage 60

El Paso
10
54

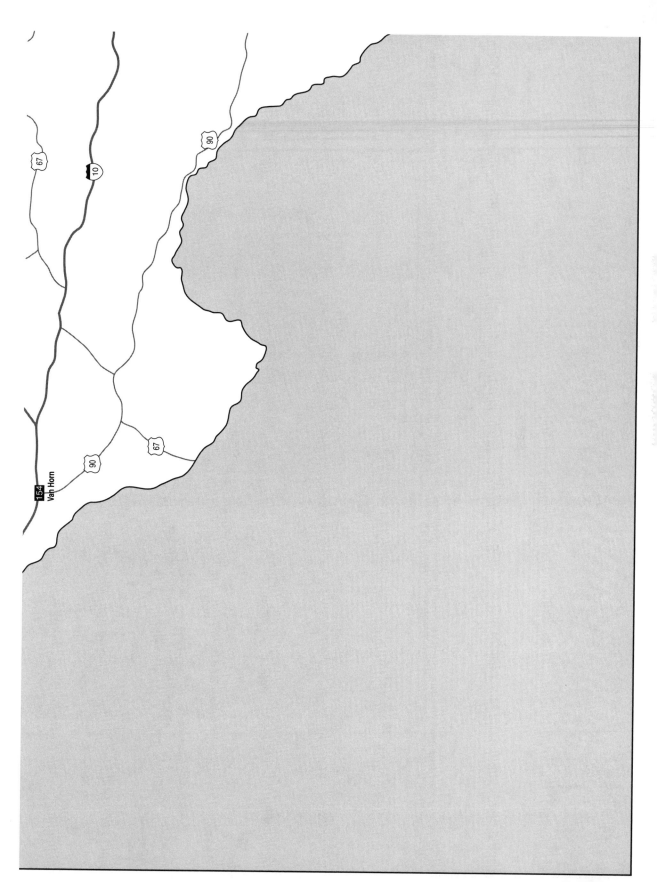

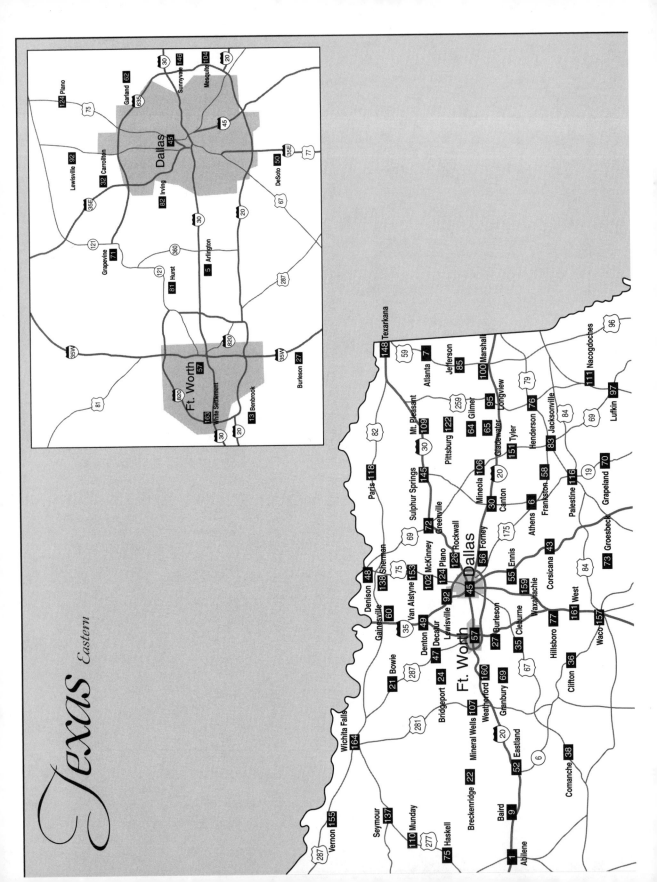

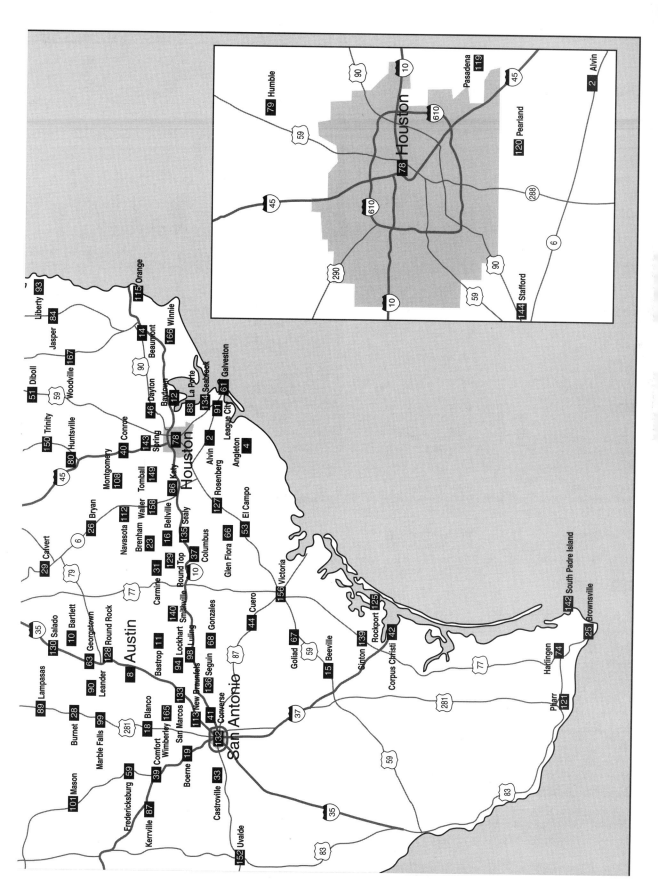

Texas

1 ABILENE

Poppy's Antique Mall & Museum
126 S. Access Road
915/692-7755

Antique & Almost
3146 S. 11th St.
915/695-2423

Sharon Specialties
721 Hickory St.
915/672-1793

Gizzmotique
641 Pecan St.
915/677-0041

One Horse Sleigh Antiques
1009 S. Treadaway Blvd.
915/676-1429

R. Honey's
3301 S. 14th St.
915/698-9696

Antique Gallery
2544 Barrow St.
915/692-2422

Barnard's Antiques
501 Hickory St.
915/677-9076

Yesterdaze Mall
2626 E. Hwy. 80
915/676-9030

McCloskey's
1646 N. 6th St.
915/672-6277

Olde Abilene Treasures
2102 N. 1st St.
915/672-6493

Twin Mill Antiques
350 S. U.S. Hwy. 83
915/692-9578

2 ALVIN

Village Antiques & Shoppes
1200 FM 1462
281/585-1959

Finder's Keepers
312 E. House St.
281/585-0806

Dixieland Antiques
1255 W. Hwy. 6.
281/585-4085

Once upon a Time
1004 W. Hwy. 6
281/331-7676

Country Notions
217 W. South St.
281/585-6582

Sarah's Bypass Antiques
820 N. Hwy. 35 Bypass
281/585-2909

3 AMARILLO

Historic Route 66 at Amarillo

Amarillo is the pride of West Texas, and the pride of Amarillo is the Historic Route 66 District! This one-mile stretch of history was once a trolley car suburb of Amarillo, which has become a regional center for many activities on the hottest stretch of the "Mother Road."

With its quaint shops, galleries, eateries, and historic attractions, Sixth Street has something for everyone.

The Summer Festival, an annual event, takes place on the third weekend in June. Activities include

shopping, eating, street dancing to live music, art displays, and other functions. The town hosts other special events throughout the year. Nightly entertainment is offered at many of the restaurants.

For more information, contact Historical Route 66 Association, P.O. Box 4117, Amarillo, TX 79116 or call 806/372-US66.

Town and Country Antiques Mall

2811 W. Sixth St.
806/373-3607
Open: Mon.–Sat. 10–5:30, Sun. 1–5

A wonderful place for an eclectic assortment of collectibles and antiques. Town and Country specializes in great furniture.

Alex's 66 Antique Mall

2912 W. Sixth St.
806/376-1166
Open: Mon.–Sat. 10–5, Sun. 1–5

18th- and 19th-century antiques plus collectibles.

Country Co-op Mall

2807 W. Sixth St.
806/372-4472
Open: Mon.–Sat. 10–5:30, Sun. 1–5

This 12,000-square-foot mall of 50-plus antique dealers is filled with antiques, collectibles and gift items.

Webb Galleries Amarillo

2816 W. Sixth St.
806/342-4044
Open: Wed.–Sat. 11–5

Regional and Contemporary Art.

Worldwide Antiques

3218 W. Sixth St.
806/372-5288

European and American antiques. Unique antiques and gifts.

No Boundaries Antiques, Gifts and Collectibles

602 S. Carolina St.
806/371-7270
Open: Mon.–Sat. 10–5

A charming house filled with treasures.

Texas

This Olde House
3901 W. Sixth St.
806/372-3901
IN TOUCH INFO LINE 806/376-1000 #6153
Open: Weekdays 10–5:30, Sun. 1–5, closed Tues.

An old craftsman-style house filled with antiques, collectibles and gifts.

Red Door Antiques
3211 W. Sixth St.
806/373-0316
IN TOUCH INFO LINE 806/376-1000 #6150
Open: Mon.–Sat. 10–5:30

A complete line of American and European furniture, as well as glassware including Fiesta and American Fostoria.

Adobe Walls Woodworks
2904 W. Sixth St.
Web site: www.adobewalls.com

Handcrafted Southwest furniture, artworks and home accents.

Puckett Antiques
2706 W. Sixth St.
806/372-3075
Open: Mon.–Sat. 10–5:30

Gifts for everyone, small and large, old and new. From fine china, crystal, furniture to barbed-wire.

The Mustard Seed
3323 W. Sixth St.
806/376-9209
Open: Mon.–Sat. 10–5:30

Specializing in primitives, both large and small. A great selection of linens and gift items.

Clay and Company
604 S. Maryland
806/376-7866

Antiques, collectibles and ladies fine clothing.

Buffalo Gals
2812 W. Sixth St.
806/374-6773
Open: Mon.–Sat. 10–6

Antiques, collectibles and gifts. An assortment of homemade fudge.

Great Places to Eat on Route 66 Amarillo

Golden Light Cafe
2908 W. Sixth St.
806/374-9237
IN TOUCH INFO LINE 806/376-1000 #6158
Open: Serving food 10–10, beverage service until 2 a.m.

The longest continuously-operated restaurant on Historic Route 66. The menu features burgers, fries, chili, sandwiches and many varied beverages.

The Park on Sixth
3315 W. Sixth St.
806/374-7275
Open: Mon. 10–4, Tues.–Sat. 10–10
Dinner Menu: Thurs., Fri., and Sat.

Norman Antiques & Art
1006 S. Adams St.
806/376-7115

Depot Antiques
500 W. Amarillo Blvd.
806/376-6352

Slesick Studio & Gallery
6666 W. Amarillo Blvd.
806/352-8823

Hobbs Street Mall
3218 Hobbs Road
806/356-6552

Phoenix & Co.
3701 Plains Blvd., Suite 83
806/355-4264

Sixth Street Antique Mall
2715 W. 6th Ave.
806/374-0459

Carousel Antiques & Collectibles
2806 W. 6th Ave.
806/373-9142

Timeless Accents
3020 W. 6th Ave.
806/373-5473

Beauford Hill Antiques
500 W. Amarillo Blvd.
806/376-6352

English Rose
6203 W. Amarillo Blvd.
806/359-7905

Cornerstone Consignments
3218 Hobbs Road
806/356-0225

Amarillo Antique Mall
3701 Plains Blvd.
806/355-4264

Galaxy Toys
2461 I-40 W.
806/352-0800

Clockworks
2725 W. 6th Ave.
806/371-7121

Scent and Fantasy Two
2818 W. 6th Ave.
806/371-0773

Antiques Plus
3119 W. 6th Ave.
806/372-3137

Texas

D & N Collectibles
3208 W. 6th Ave.
806/371-8400

Victorianna
3300 W. 6th Ave.
806/374-6568

Don R. Reid, Inc.
2717 Stanley St.
806/356-0903

Minka's Garden
3615 W. 6th Ave.
806/372-1199

Delightful Treasures
3304 W. 6th Ave.
806/379-7107

Rusty and Dusty Antique Shop
3302 W. 6th Ave.
806/374-6568

Antique Amarillo
2700 W. 6th Ave.
806/374-1066

The Nat Antiques & French Bakery
2705 W. 6th Ave.
806/372-8685

Great Places to Stay

Maryland House Bed & Breakfast
600 S. Maryland St.
806/376-7866

4 ANGLETON

Jeter's Old World Antiques
Hospital Dr.
409/849-5452

Yesterdaze
517 E. Mulberry St.
409/849-8834

Bargain Palace
200 S. Velasco St.
409/849-4711

County Seat Antiques
227 N. Velasco St.
409/848-1810

Kelly's Crossroads Antiques
112 W. Mulberry St.
409/849-0308

The Magnolia Tree
724 W. Mulberry St.
409/848-8044

Gallery Antiques & Collectibles
212 N. Velasco St.
409/849-9336

Attic Treasures
125 E. Cedar
409/849-7307

5 ARLINGTON

Antiques by Ellis
1906 W. Park Row
817/275-6761 or 817/274-6879 for special appointments
Open: Tues.–Sat. 11–5:30 or by appointment Sun.–Mon.
Directions: From I-30 take Fielder exit, south 4 miles, right on Park Row, 2 blocks on the left. From I-20 take Cooper Exit, north 5 miles, left on Park Row past Fielder, 2 blocks on the left.

Located in the same spot for the past 20 years, Sue and Asa Ellis specialize in fine American antiques from 1840-1910. If you are searching for true antique furniture, accessories and lighting, then this is one antique "stop" you shouldn't pass up (no reproductions). Their specialty is furniture with an emphasis on quality and the unusual. The inventory is evenly divided between formal Victorian and fancy oak, with approximately 200 exceptional pieces available at all times.

Antique Marketplace Arlington
3500 S. Cooper St.
817/468-0689

Antique Sampler Mall & Tearoom
1715 E. Lamar Blvd.
817/861-4747

Moth Ball
401 E. Randol Mill Road
817/459-2553

Design Center
138 S. Bowen
817/265-0549

Al's Antiques
1543 S. Bowen
817/548-8151

Antiques & Moore Mall & Tearoom
3708 W. Pioneer Pkwy.
817/548-5931

6 ATHENS

Olga Antiques
312 S. Carroll St.
903/677-1733

Eden Antiques
400 N. Prairieville St.
903/677-1560

Alley Antiques & Collectibles
400 N. Prairieville St.
903/675-9292

Wooden Nickel Mall
2001 S. Palestine St.
903/677-9496

7 ATLANTA

Yesterdays Antique Mall
212 N. East St.
903/796-9742

Hiram St. Antique Mall
117 E. Hiram St.
903/796-9474

8 AUSTIN

Lelysee Antiques
5603 Adams Ave.
512/459-1727

Chantal's Antique & Design Center
2525 W. Anderson Lane
512/451-5705

Smith's Antiques & Refinishing
3650 Garner Blvd.
817/265-7048

D Militaria & Collectibles Shop
823 Oram St.
817/274-3515

Helen's Antiques & Used Furniture
2307 Medlin
817/275-2064

Antiques, Etc.
404 E. First St.
817/543-1567

Abram Street Antiques
500 E. Abram
817/460-7250

Waldenwood Country Antiques
504 E. Corsicana St.
903/675-2561

Goode's Imporium
109 E. Tyler St.
903/675-9425

Serendipity
412 N. Prairieville St.
903/675-8335

Atlanta Antiques
113 E. Hiram St.
903/796-4942

Memory Lane Mall
110 E. Main St.
903/796-0485

Mona and Don's Antiques
5617 Adams Ave.
512/458-1661

Antique Outlet
10401 Anderson Mill Road
512/257-1020

Texas

Antique Marketplace
5350 Burnet Road
512/452-1000

The Market
701 Capital of Texas Hwy.
512/327-8866

Rue's Antiques
1500 S. Congress Ave.
512/442-1775

Uncommon Objects
1512 S. Congress Ave.
512/442-4000

Armadillo Antiques & Jewelry
1712 S. Congress Ave.
512/443-7552

Tipler's Lamp Shop
1204 W. 5th St.
512/472-5007

Log Cabin Antiques
9600 W. Hwy. 290
512/288-4037

Craftown Gallery
13945 Hwy. 183
512/331-4252

Accent Antiques
2200 S. Lamar Blvd.
512/441-6656

Lamar Antiques
2058 S. Lamar Blvd.
512/448-3184

Danforth's Antiques & Gifts
1612 Lavaca St.
512/478-7808

Austin Antique Mall
8822 McCann Dr.
512/459-5900

Eradeco Antiques & Collectibles
110 E. North Loop Blvd.
512/450-0861

Robert Gage Antiques
1304 Rio Grande St.
512/472-4760

Jean's Antiques and Gifts
2 Miles south of Wimberly
512/282-1541

Radio Ranch
1610 W. 35th St.
512/459-6855

Halbert Antiques
5453 Burnet Road
512/451-8037

Now & Always Antiques
1413 S. Congress Ave.
512/707-2692

Antigua
1508 S. Congress Ave.
512/912-1475

Off The Wall
1704 S. Congress Ave.
512/445-4701

Turn of the Century Antiques
1703 N. Cuernavaca Dr.
512/263-5460

Antiques by Grace Homan
3303 Glenview Ave.
512/472-7366

House of Harriette & John
12719 W. Hwy. 71
512/263-5103

Capitol Used Furniture & Antiques
11115C N. Lamar Blvd.
512/836-1472

Amelias Retro Vogue and Relics
2024 S. Lamar Blvd.
512/442-4446

Corner Collectors
6539 N. Lamar Blvd.
512/453-4556

Garner & Smith Antiques, Etc.
1013 W. Lynn St.
512/474-1518

Hog Wild Vintage Toys
100A E. North Loop Blvd.
512/467-9453

Hurts Hunting Grounds
712 Red River St.
512/472-7680

Dreyfus Antiques
719 E. 6th St.
512/473-2191

Fancy Finds
1009 W. 6th St.
512/472-7550

Brady's of Austin
1807 W. 35th St.
512/459-8929

Architects and Heroes Antiques
1809 W. 35th St.
512/467-9393

Attal's Galleries
3310 Red River St.
512/476-3634

Austin House Antiques
2041 S. Lamar Blvd.
512/445-2599

James Powell Antiques
715 West Ave.
512/477-9939

Antiques Warehouse
5530 Burnet Road
512/453-6355

Austin Antique Glassware
13107 FM 969
512/276-7793

Durham Trading & Design Co.
1009 W. 6th St.
512/476-1216

Great Places to Stay

Trails End Bed & Breakfast
The B & B Store (gift shop)
12223 Trails End Road #7
512-267-2901 or 1-800-850-2901
Open: B&B open year-round
Rates $55–$170
Gift shop open year-round 1–5 — call for appt.
Directions: From IH 35 two miles out of Georgetown, take RM 1431 and go 11 8/10 miles to Trails End Road. Turn left onto Trails End and go 7/10 of a mile to the gravel road. There will be several mail boxes next to the gravel road. Turn left and go to where the road curves to the right. Keep on going around the curve and the B&B is a large gray house trimmed in white on the left. An appointment is needed. The inn is located on the north side of Lake Travis between Cedar Park, Jonestown, Austin and Leander.

For specific information see Leander #90.

9 BAIRD

The town of Baird, Texas, is a great "comeback" story. The downtown district is only three blocks long, but has five antique malls and over a dozen individual shops with either antiques or collectibles. All of the shops are located either on Market Street (the main street) or within a half block on an intersecting street.

There are several good places to eat and two bed and breakfasts, with a third in progress. More buildings are being restored all the time on the three block historic downtown strip, and the town hopes to  eventually have all of them filled with shops that are either antiques or related businesses.

In 1993 Baird received the designation of "Antique Capital of West Texas" from the Texas Legislature due to their revitalization efforts and the numerous antique businesses, none of which existed prior to 1991. Before they began their revitalization program, there were only two hardware stores and a drug store in the downtown area. It's quite different now, and they draw large numbers of antique shoppers from all over.

Baird is located 20 miles east of Abilene and 120 miles west of Fort Worth.

Henson's Antiques
230 Market St.
915/854-1756
Open: Mon.–Sat. 10–5:30
Directions: Take Exits 306, 307 or 308 off Hwy. 20. Located 20 miles east of Abilene and 120 miles west of Ft. Worth.

If you are an advanced collector of fine quality American antique furniture and accessories or if you are a designer whose clients demand only the best, then you'll be delighted with the personally selected inventory available at Henson's Antiques. The shop specializes in American Victorian period furniture, both walnut and rosewood, ranging from gorgeous matched suites for bedroom, parlor and dining room to striking single pieces such as armoires, secretaries, marble top tables, pier mirrors and hall trees. With no intention of excluding any collectors, Henson's inventory offers styles from other periods including top of the line oak, carved front china cabinets, roll-top desks, bedroom suites and bookcases for home or office.

The shop most recently attracted the attention of *Southern Living Magazine.* An unusual tambour roll filing cabinet was featured in an article entitled "Ticket to Yesterday in Baird." It is not unusual for the elite members of the press or customers for that matter to be drawn to Henson's Antiques. Clients from as far away as New York, California, Florida and Washington flock to Henson's for the outstanding offering of quality merchandise. What is unusual, however, is that the shop is located in a tiny West Texas town.

A few years back, Baird was a railroad town but when the Texas & Pacific Railroad closed shop, the town felt its tomorrow had left the station. For years, only the rustle of leaves and whistle of wind rambled along Baird's Market Street. Then, in 1993 the tiny town of Baird received state recognition when the Texas Legislature declared it the "Antique Capital of West Texas" due to the revitalization efforts and the numerous antique shops.

Betty Henson, owner of Henson's Antiques, was a leader in the town's revitalization. She and her husband, Weldon, have been avid collectors

of formal American antiques for more than 25 years. Betty first became interested in antiques while studying interior design in the late '60s. The antiques found in Betty's shop are selected using the same criteria as is used in the selection of pieces for her own home; excellent quality, condition, uniqueness, function, design, style and age are all considered.

You will often find pieces from well-known American cabinet makers who took great pride in the pieces they produced. In addition to the many fine furnishings available, you'll find decorative accessories including clocks, mirrors, lamps, prints, paintings, china, glass, porcelain, silver and silverplate.

Market Street Mall
212 Market St.
915/854-1408
Open: Tues.–Sat.10–5:30, Sun. 1:30–5:30, closed Mon.
Directions: Take Business 20 to downtown Baird. Market Street intersects.

Market Street Mall is a multi-dealer mall located in a historic building in downtown Baird. With new items arriving weekly, this unique shop offers a wide array of antiques and collectibles. From Victorian through 50s; furniture and a wide variety of smalls, Market Street Mall is an antiquer's delight with wide aisles, good lighting, climate control, and handicap accessibility.

The Antique Market 334 Market St. 915/854-1997	**Creations by Collene** 331 Market St. 915/854-5980
Em's Sweets, Eats, & Antiques 140 Market St. 915/854-5956	**Flashback** 234 Market St. 915/854-1410
Antique Memories 304 Market St. 915/854-2021	**Barbara's Country Tyme Antiques** 300 Market St. 915/854-2424
Callahan County Collectibles 124 E. 2nd St. 915/854-1782	**Odds & Ends** 344 Market St. 915/854-5958
Rags & Riches 128 Market St. 915/854-1084	**Plaza Corner** 245 Market St. 915/854-5972
The Trading Post 346 Market St. 915/854-2655	**Trail's End Antiques** 223 Market St. 915/854-2594
Brigham Livery Stable 127 Market St. 915/854-5952	**The Old Shoppe** 312 Market St. 915/854-1911
Hughes Trading Co. & Antiques 743 W. 4th St. 915/854-1714	

Texas

Bed & Breakfasts/Motel/RV Parks

The Old Conner House B&B
340 Vine St.
915/854-1890

Baird Motor Inn & RV Campground
I-20 @ Exit 307
915/854-2527

10 BARTLETT

Clark St. Antique Shop
Clark St.
254/527-3933

Grumbley's Antiques
Clark St.
254/527-3141

Bartlett Antique Mall
110 E. Clark St.
254/527-3251

Rooms with a View
135 E. Clark St.
254/527-4460

Mary Jane's II
Clark St.
254/527-4445

The Trellis
Clark St.
254/527-4300

Village Antique Mall
16 E. Clark St.
254/527-3234

Major Roome's Emporium
221 Clark St.
254/527-3111

11 BASTROP

Wyldwood Antique Mall
Hwy. 71 W.
512/321-3280

Texas Mercantile
921 Main St.
512/303-1843

Ritz
1005 Main St.
512/321-4326

Old Town Emporium
918 Main St.
512/321-3635

Apothecary's Hall Antiques
505 Main St.
512/321-3022

12 BAYTOWN

Burns Antiques & Trading Emporium
600 N. Alexander Dr.
281/422-7321

Buford's Antiques
3716 Decker Dr.
281/424-4081

Temptations
207 W. De Fee St.
281/422-5693

Bea's Treasure Chest
2 N. Main St.
281/420-3494

Schoolmarm's Attic
1504 E. Texas Ave.
281/427-3914

Baytown Country Shop & Gifts
723 E. Texas Ave.
281/427-0749

The Consignment
2312 N. Alexander Dr.
281/837-1061

Decker Drive Antiques
3716 Decker Dr.
281/424-5211

Goose Creek Emporium
219 W. De Fee St.
281/427-6690

Town & Country Sales
5215 Sjolander Road
281/421-1904

Trash & Treasures
1106 Largo St.
281/422-0618

13 BENBROOK

Great Places to Eat

Cracker Barrel Old Country Store
I-20 & Winscott, Exit 429B
817/249-3360

14 BEAUMONT

McCoy's Antiques
1455 Calder St.
409/835-1764

Calder House
1905 Calder St.
409/832-1955

Time After Time Antiques
2481 Calder St.
409/832-0016

Old Store Antiques
8370 College St.
409/866-2205

The Cottage
2391 Calder St.
409/832-3447

Finders Fayre Quality Antiques
1485 Calder St.
409/833-7000

Select Antiques & Furnishings
2694 Hazel St.
409/833-7610

Old Store Antiques
8319 College St.
409/866-6280

Collage
2470 N. 11th St.
409/899-3545

Old Crockett Street Market
881 Crockett St.
409/832-3209

15 BEEVILLE

Final Touch
207 W. Carter St.
512/358-5808

McKitchens Antiques & Tea Room
401 E. Houston St.
512/358-1442

Delphines
114 W. Hefferman St.
512/362-2144

The Antique Place
1101 N. Washington St.
512/358-2908

16 BELLVILLE

Bellville Antique Mall
11 N. Bell St.
409/865-9620

Julia's Antiques
410 Centerhill Road
409/865-5285

Rafters Antiques
467 Hwy. 36 N.
409/865-3316

Cottonwood Cottage
8 N. Holland St.
409/865-8411

Antiques Etc. Emporium
14 N. Holland St.
409/865-8087

Andy's Candys
11 N. Bell St.
409/865-9620

Barn & Bell
854 FM 529 (Burleigh)
409/865-9648

On The Square
4 S. Holland St.
409/865-2230

Square Trader
12 N. Holland St.
409/865-9305

Frog Hollow
22 N. Holland St.
409/865-3007

Texas

The Country Shop
20 E. Main St.
409/865-9639

Nothing Ordinary Antiques
123 E. Main St.
409/865-8033

17 BIG SPRING

Aunt Bea's Antiques
1711 N. FM 700
915/263-6923

Antique Mall of Big Spring
110 Main St.
915/267-2631

Antique Korner
217 Main St.
915/268-9580

Alamo Antiques
114 E. 2nd St.
915/264-9334

Dahmer's Antiques
204 S. Main St.
915/267-5223

18 BLANCO

Unique Antiques
315 Main St.
210/833-2201 or 1-800-460-1733
Open: Thurs.–Tues. 10–5, closed Wed.
Directions: Unique Antiques is located on Hwy. 281, which is Main Street, on the west side of the old Blanco County Courthouse Square.

Although Unique Antiques handles antiques and collectibles, glassware and gifts in general, they particularly carry American oak furniture and a large selection of Depression glass. They also carry the largest collection of flow blue in Texas hill country. All their items are top quality and shoppers can buy just one piece or a whole estate!

Blanco Flea Market
5th & Pecan St.
210/833-5640

A Step Back
Hwy. 281 S.
210/833-4270

Merchantile
313 Main St.
210/833-2225

Classic Antiques
317 Main St.
210/833-2216

Front Porch on the Park
145 N. Holland St.
409/865-8833

The Country Store
Lamesa Hwy. 1/2 mi. N. Hwy. 20
915/267-8840

Main Street Emporium
113 Main St.
915/263-1212

The Country Store
209 Runnels
915/263-3093

Dahmer's Antiques
7309 N. Service Road
915/393-5537

Blanco Trash & Treasures
313 4th St.
No phone listed

Nannie's Antiques
303 Main St.
210/833-9001

Cranberry Antiques
400 3rd St.
210/833-5596

19 BOERNE

Antiques 'n' Things
106 S. Main St.
210/249-2313

Antiques & Old Lace
146 S. Main St.
210/816-2530

The Rusty Bucket
195 S. Main St.
210/249-2288

Boerne Clock Co.
233 S. Main St.
210/249-6080

Iron Pigtail
470 S. Main St.
210/249-8877

Carousel Antiques & Pickles
118 S. Main St.
210/249-9306

Boerne Emporium
179 S. Main St.
210/249-3390

St. George & The Dragon
210 S. Main St.
210/249-2207

Landmark
404 S. Main St.
210/249-6002

Heyday
615 S. Main St.
210/249-4951

20 BORGER

House of Coffee & Gifts
100 W. Grand
806/274-7375

While antiquing in Borger, Texas, plan to visit the "House of Coffee" located at the corner of South Main and Grand Street in one of the first hotels built in 1926, in the original town of Isom, Texas. Isom was part of the heritage of the Texas Panhandle and the pioneering spirit that changed the Panhandle from a habitat of buffalo and cattle to a land of people.

Housed in this building is a wonderful gift shop featuring a blend of gifts: crystal, handkerchiefs, pewter frames, flower wreaths, all set in a Victorian flair with consignment antiques from Timeless Treasures.

Plan to stay for a cup of Espresso coffee, a spot of tea from 15 varieties or one of many Coco flavors. The summer months offer frozen latte, along with 14 varieties of bagels and cream cheese toppings. If you visit in the fall or winter months, you could be served soup on Tuesday or Thursday at noon.

It took six months to transform the bottom area of the old hotel into this unique coffee house. The owner, Michele Nelson is a Borger native and has fond memories of when this part of the building was Barney's Pharmacy. The soda equipment in the pharmacy was taken out for the Youth Building at First Methodist Church, however, Michele still has the counter bar with the names carved on display as well as other memorabilia. Future plans for the 24 hotel rooms upstairs with original sink, heaters and transom windowed doors is undecided.

The building began as the "Isom Hotel" and was the center of Isom before it became Borger. When leased to John and Pearl Mulkey, the hotel sign read "Mulkey Hotel." They claimed it as their homestead in 1929 even though according to records, it belonged to Agnes Howe. The next owners, Light James and his family named it "St. James." The James brothers lived there until 1940.

The bottom south end of the building was sub-leased to the Hatcher Drug Co. in 1929. In the 1934 phone book it was listed "West Grand." In 1936 Byron Andress leased the space and the building housed Dr. J. R. Walker's office and a barber shop and the Hotel Isom lobby. Later the entire north end was used by Drs. W. G. & M. M. Stephens and Dr. Harvey Hayes. Mrs. Viola Stephens sold the building to Michele and she then opened for business in October 1996. You are welcome to come by and browse awhile, have a cup, and experience Isom, Texas, now known as Borger.

Season's Antiques
120 5th St.
806/274-6130

Timeless Treasures
700 W. Wilson St.
806/273-6802

Four Sisters
416 N. Main St.
806/274-5220

21 BOWIE

Nostalgia Antiques
200 N. Mason St.
940/872-6272

Antique Express
210 N. Mason St.
940/872-4717

Texas Pride Cards & Collectibles
Newport Hwy.
940/872-5114

Treasure House
303 W. Wise St.
940/872-1899

Days Gone By
204 N. Mason St.
940/872-2033

Market Place
216 N. Mason St.
940/872-5011

Martha's Attic
206 Smythe St.
940/872-4705

Chisolm Trail Antique Mall
202 N. Mason St.
940/872-4450

22 BRECKENRIDGE

Antique Shoppe
105 W. Walker St.
254/559-1639

Antique Depot
500 E. Walker St.
254/559-9724

The Pat Rogers Collection
201 W. Walker St.
254/559-6653

23 BRENHAM

Brenham holds a special place in the hearts of romantics because of a colorful piece of history and artwork that is in the town. Brenham is home to one of only 12 antique carousels in Texas, and this particular one is the only example of a C. W. Parker Carousel with Hersehill-Spillman horses. Manufactured prior to 1910, this piece of Americana is at Fireman's Park in Brenham and visitors can ride it anytime.

Brenham is also home to Blue Bell Creameries, said to produce the

best ice cream in the country. They ought to know how to do it — they've been making ice cream since 1911.

Country Co-Op
101 E. Alamo St.
409/830-0679

J. H. Faske Company
114 E. Alamo St.
409/836-9282

Somewhere In Time
204 W. Alamo St.
409/277-9511

K & S Collectibles
Houston Hwy.
409/836-3575

Catherine Newton's Antiques
1302 W. Main St.
409/836-2898

Today & Yesterday
101 W. Alamo St.
409/830-0707

Seek & Find Antiques
115 W. Alamo St.
409/830-1930

Brenham Antique Mall
213 W. Alamo St.
409/836-7231

Nancy's Antiques
1700 Key St.
409/836-7520

24 BRIDGEPORT

Serendipity House
1003 Halsell St.
940/683-3999

Granny's Antiques
1010 Halsell St.
940/683-4043

Our Antiques & Collectibles
1018 Halsell St.
940/683-3959

Once Again Antiques
1105 Halsell St.
940/683-6455

T & L Antique Shop
1004 Halsell St.
940/683-5545

Hidden Away Memories
1016 Halsell St.
940/683-8050

Once Again Antique Mall
1020 Halsell St.
940/683-6717

25 BROWNSVILLE

Pilar's Antiques & Tea Room
302 E. Adams St.
210/541-7450

Second Thought
2265 Boca Chica Blvd.
210/541-7423

26 BRYAN

Attic Antiques
118 S. Bryan Ave.
409/822-7830

Gazebo Antiques
3828 S. College Ave.
409/846-0249

Plantation Shop
2024 S. Texas Ave.
409/822-6220

Old Bryan
202 S. Bryan Ave.
409/779-3245

By Jacs
701 E. Villa Maria Road
409/822-2662

Tin Barn Antiques & Collectibles
3218 S. Texas Ave.
409/779-6573

Texas

By-Mac Collections
202 W. 26th St.
409/775-7875

Amity of Bryan
300 W. 26th St.
409/822-7717

27 BURLESON

Burleson Old Town Collectibles
108 S. Main St.
817/295-3301

28 BURNET

Cobblestone Cottage
212 E. Jackson St.
512/756-7407

A Taile of Two Antiques
212 S. Main St.
512/756-9806

Shoppee
206 E. Polk St.
512/756-7984

29 CALVERT

Front Porch
505 S. Main St.
409/364-2933

Farmer's Wife Antiques
515 S. Main St.
409/364-2489

Calvert Antique Mall
509 N. Main St.
409/364-2089

30 CANTON

The saying that everything is bigger and grander in Texas must have started in Canton. This town, with its regular population of just about 3,000, is the undisputed home of the granddaddy of all trade days!

Canton's First Monday Trade Days are world famous. This unbelievable "happening" dates back at least 150 years, with records existing back to the mid-1800s; most likely it's much older. First Monday Trade Days developed around the circuit court held on the first Monday of each month. In the pioneer days of East Texas, this was a time to set aside work and go into town to the county seat to hear court, buy needed supplies and sell produce and farm animals. In the mid-1960s a progressive-thinking Canton city council saw the monthly market as a potential gold mine and began purchasing land to form the First Monday Park. The park currently encompasses over 300 acres.

Through the years this gathering evolved into today's multi-acre

Brazos Trader Antiques
210 W. 26th St.
409/775-2984

Burleson Antique Mall
2395 S.W. Wilshire Blvd.
817/295-7890

Burnet Antique Mall
206 S. Main St.
512/756-7783

Treasures on the Square
216 S. Main St.
512/756-8514

Boll Weevil Antiques
508 S. Main St.
409/364-2835

S & S Antiques
517 S. Main St.
409/364-2634

grounds with over 6,000 booths offering literally everything: antiques, arts and crafts, clothing, toys, tools, junk, even animals from dogs to zebras! Weather is not a factor, even though a lot of the area is still outdoors. Many of the booths are now inside 14 pavilions, with an additional 35,000 square feet of building devoted strictly to antiques.

Any one of four exits off I-20 will bring you to downtown Canton.

Buffalo Village
202 N. Buffalo St.
903/567-2434

Times Past
114 E. Dallas St.
903/567-5709

Timeless Treasures
111 S. Hwy. 19
903/567-6762

Recollections & Vintage Quilts
138 E. Dallas St.
903/567-6945

Stone's Antiques
Hwy. 120
903/567-6620

Marcella's Antiques
150 E. Terrell St.
903/567-6936

Nearby Antique Shopping (Edgewood)
Edgewood is located 10 miles north of Canton.

Red Door Antiques
111 N.W. Front St.
903/896-1423
Open: Tues.–Fri. 10–5, Sat. 10–3, extended hours during Canton First Monday Trade Days.

As you walk through the Red Door, Juanelle Wright and her dealers have selected a wonderful selection of fine furnishings, glassware such as depression, carnival, pressed and cut, as well as many unique collectibles.

Sadie's
203B Front St.
903/896-4070

Tin Lady Antiques
202 N. Houston
903/896-1889

Great Places to Stay

Humphries House
201 S. Main St.
903/896-4358
Rates: $85–$125 (four guest rooms)

The modest Victorian structure was completed in 1894 by William Henry and Molly Humphries who migrated to Edgewood from Walnut Grove, Miss., in 1890. After purchasing the site from the Texas & Pacific Railroad, they contracted local craftsmen to construct their home where two sons – Eldrige and Shelton – were reared. Throughout the years, ownership has remained

with descendants of the original builder. According to family records, the original owner was instrumental in developing the local business community and constructing the first frame Methodist Church in 1897. Wife, Molly, contributed to the social environment by organizing the first women's organization known as the Civic and Culture Club and she was often hostess to church and civic groups.

This simple two-story house is the only authentic example of Victorian architecture remaining in the area and its design is typical of the modest houses built in Van Zandt County in the 1890s. Painstakingly restored by the grandson of the original owner; the Humphries House has been thoroughly modernized yet its quaint charm has been carefully preserved to give visitors a physical record of a distinct time and place in rural East Texas.

Interesting Side Trip

Founded in 1976 as a bicentennial ongoing project, Edgewood Heritage Park encompasses fourteen restored and furnished structures representing rural life in 1900 Van Zandt County. The outdoor museum preserves the rural culture and architectural heritage for present and future generations.

Turn-of-the-century buildings, such as the "Tomcat" Cafe, The Edgewood Band Stand, Gilliam's Gas Station, a country store, barber shop and print shop help visitors experience a taste of what life was like back then.

Other buildings built in the late 1800s include the Church in the Wildwood, a "dogtrot" cabin and two-room pioneer cabin. The Blacksmith Shop, the Heritage Center and the Carriage House exhibit collections of vintage tools and memorabilia.

31 CARMINE

Antiques & Stuff
Hwy. 290
409/278-3866

Hoppe Store Antiques
Hwy. 290
409/278-3713

32 CARROLLTON

T L C Treasures
1013 S. Broadway St.
972/245-7729

Dolls of Yesterday & Today
1014 S. Broadway St.
972/242-8281

Mary Lou's
1015 S. Broadway St.
972/466-1460

Ten of Arts
1019 S. Broadway St.
972/242-3357

Pleasures Past
1105 S. Broadway St.
972/242-2084

Finishing Touch Antique Mall
1109 S. Broadway St.
972/446-3038

Classic Militaria
1810 N. Interstate 35
972/242-1957

Old Craft Store
1110 W. Main St.
214/242-9111

33 CASTROVILLE

Alice's Antiques
1213 Fiorella St.
210/931-9318

Market Place Antiques
1215 Fiorella St.
210/538-3350

Cottage
413 Lafayette St.
210/538-9713

Castroville Emporium Antiques
515 Madrid St.
210/538-3115

Attic
1105 Fiorella St.
210/931-9602

34 CLARENDON

Curiosity Shop
Hwy. E. 287
806/874-2409

Poor Boys Antiques
206 S. Kearney
806/874-2233

Petty's Antiques & Collectibles
222 S. Kearney
806/874-3875

My Playhouse
300 S. Kearney
No phone listed

S & S Gallery
317 S. Kearney
806/874-5096

35 CLEBURNE

Butch's Treasure Chest
207 E. Henderson
No Phone

A Taste of Time
216 E. Henderson
817/558-2288

Randy's Antiques & More
204 S. Main St.
817/645-1985

Cleburne Antique Mall
215 S. Main St.
817/641-5550

Bettie's Antiques & Mall
216 S. Main St.
817/645-2723

36 CLIFTON

Clifton Antique Mall
206 W. 5th St.
254/675-2300

Hobbyhorse Gifts & Antiques
114 Main St.
254/675-7723

Bosque County Emporium
121 Main St.
254/675-8133

Yankee Clipper Antiques
325 W. 5th St.
254/675-1722

37 COLUMBUS

Hometown Hall
1120 Milam St.
409/732-5425

Double Tree & English Ivy
1237 Bowie St.
409/732-8802

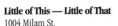

Texas

Little of This — Little of That
1004 Milam St.
409/732-6034

Lasting Impressions
1124 Milam St.
409/732-9700

38 COMANCHE

Comanche is named for the Comanche Indians who once ruled the Southwest Plains. Nestled in the hills of Central Texas, Comanche has friendly people who will help make your visit memorable. There are antique shops, restaurants and over 80 motels and bed and breakfasts. See the historic "Fleming Oak" and "Old Cora Courthouse" on the square. Great fishing, camping, water sports and golf can be found at nearby Lake Proctor.

Furniture Barn
300 N. Austin
915/356-2787

Comanche Trading Post
300 W. Central Ave.
915/356-5022

Antique Country
400 E. Central Ave.
915/356-2248

Sybil's Antiques
410 E. Central Ave.
915/356-3338

Old Tyme Antiques
508 E. Central Ave.
915/356-3550

Quilts & Tops
605 E. Central Ave.
915/356-2047

Red Top Antiques
605 W. Central Ave.
915/356-2173

This Ole House Antiques
706 W. Central Ave.
915/356-2441

Martin's Antiques
804 E. Central Ave.
915/356-5711

Dee Dee's Corner
807 E. Central Ave.
915/356-2118

Culbertson's Custom Quilting
201 W. Grand
915/356-3901

Selections on the Square
127 N. Houston St.
915/356-3153

39 COMFORT

Antiquities, Etc.
702 High St.
210/995-4190

Comfort Common
717 High St.
210/995-3030

Bygone Days Antiques
815 High St.
210/995-3003

Comfort Emporium
607 Hwy. 27
210/995-4000

Faltin & Company
Main St. & 7th St.
210/995-3279

Marketplatz Antique Center
405 7th St.
210/995-2000

Southwestern Elegance
509 7th St.
210/995-2297

40 CONROE

Russ Clanton Antiques
711 W. Dallas St.
409/756-8816

Antique Mall of Conroe
725 W. Davis St.
409/788-8222

Ah Collectables
920 W. Lewis St.
409/539-5122

Edith's Antiques & Gift Shop
910 Cable St.
409/756-3711

Pauline's Antiques
915 Cable St.
409/756-4762

Attic Antiques
1304 FM 2854
409/539-9116

Pamela's Antique Parlor
FM 2854
409/441-6895

Stock Exchange Antique Mall
302 N. Frazier St.
409/760-3800

Heintz Furniture & Antiques
701 N. Frazier St.
409/756-3024

Tizzie's Antiques & Collectibles
916 W. Lewis St.
409/788-2344

Golden Eagle Traders
1908 N. Frazier St.
409/441-7355

41 CONVERSE

De's Oldies 'n' Goodies
209 S. Seguin Road
210/658-2083

Chism Trail Antiques
616 S. Seguin Road
210/659-2104

42 CORPUS CHRISTI

Sand Dollar Hospitality
3605 Mendenhall Dr.
1-800-528-7782

If you are searching for that perfect getaway vacation or just an exceptional place to spend the night, then I suggest contacting Sandy at Sand Dollar Hospitality. The service represents a wide variety of bed and breakfast and guest cottages in Corpus Christi and the surrounding areas.

Lee-Cunningham
3100 S. Alameda St.
512/882-4482

Emma's Arbor
4309 S. Alameda St.
512/985-8309

Betty's Trash to Treasures Too
4315 S. Alameda St.
512/993-1027

Gene's Antiques
4331 S. Alameda St.
512/994-0440

Home Sweet Home Antique Market
4333 S. Alameda St.
512/991-4001

Second Hand Rose Antiques
4343 S. Alameda St.
512/993-9626

Sister Sue's
4323 S. Alameda St.
512/992-5300

Lea's Glass Nook
1911 Ayers St.
512/884-3036

Betty's Trash to Treasures
3301 Ayers St.
512/882-9144

Country Peddlers
4337 S. Alameda St.
512/993-7237

Antiques Downtown
312 N. Chaparral St.
512/882-8865

Victorian Lady
315 N. Chaparral St.
512/883-1051

Texas

Country Peddlers Downtown
317 N. Chaparral St.
512/887-6618

Rucker & Rucker Inc.
451 Everhart Road
512/994-1231

Irene's Antique Flea Market
3906 Leopard St.
512/884-4467

McLaughlin Furniture Shop
1227 12th St.
512/882-3991

Odds & Ends
9841 E. Padre Island Dr.
512/937-8944

Dragonfly Antiques
821 S. Staples St.
512/888-5442

Wild Good Chase
3509 S. Staples St.
512/851-9535

Antiquity, Inc.
318 N. Chaparral St.
512/882-2424

Two J's Antiques
613 Everhart Road
512/994-0788

Yesterday Peddler
3131 McArdle Road
512/851-2141

Objets D'Art II
5858 S. Padre Island Dr.
512/993-2126

Quaint Shop
811 S. Staples St.
512/884-9541

W. Gardner
821 S. Staples St.
512/887-9351

43 CORSICANA

This & That Antiques
101 S. Beaton St.
903/874-6941

Carousel Crafts & Antiques
118 S. Beaton St.
903/872-4141

Jim's Clock Shop
127 W. Collin St.
903/874-5141

CSL Antiques & Collectibles
106 W. 6th Ave.
903/874-8333

Home Town Antiques
110 N. Beaton St.
903/874-8158

Merchant's
320 N. Beaton St.
903/872-6445

Traders Outpost
105 W. 7th Ave.
903/872-5392

44 CUERO

Gallery of Memories
121 N. Esplanade St.
512/275-9226

Country Collectibles
Hwy. 87
512/275-2011

45 DALLAS

Forestwood Antique Mall
5333 Forest Lane
972/661-0001
Web site: www.antiquelandusa.com
Open: Mon.–Sat. 10–7, Sun. 12–6
Garden Tea Room open: Mon.-Sat. 11-3

At Forestwood Antique Mall, you'll experience one of the most impressive, bustling antique malls in the country. Furniture enthusiasts will find an extensive selection of antiques ranging from 18th and 19th century American, English and French to an unusual collection of primitives, art deco and '50s pieces. Other specialties from the 250 plus dealers include depression and cut glass, Majolica, crystal, sterling and silverplate, china, art pottery, Oriental rugs, airplane memorabilia, perfume bottles (including Factice), books, paintings, rugs, estate and costume jewelry, toys advertising and movie posters, and much more.

The Boulevard Emporium
1010 N. Industrial Blvd.
214/748-1860
Open: Mon.–Sat. 10–5

Quality Antiques and Design Accessories.

Clements Antiques and Auction Gallery
1333 Oak Lawn Ave.
214/747-7700
Open: Mon.–Fri. 9–5

Specializing in 18th and 19th Century Antiques.

Country Garden Antiques
147 Parkhouse
214/741-9331
Open: Daily 11–5 or by appt.

Furnishings for Home and Garden.

The Estate Warehouse
905 Slocum St.
214/760-2424
Open: Mon.–Sat. 9–6 or by appt.

Monthly estate liquidations.

Farzin Designs
1515 Turtle Creek Blvd. (at The Gathering)
214/747-1511
Open: Mon.–Sat. 10–6 or by appt.

Decorative antiques, rugs, and accessories.

The Gathering
1515 Turtle Creek Blvd.
214/741-4888
Open: Mon.–Sat. 10–6 or by appt.

Over 100 international-quality antiques, art, and design dealers.

Jaime Leather and Fabric Upholstery
1100 N. Industrial Blvd.
214/742-8700
Open: Mon.–Fri. 8–6, Sat. 9–3

Specializing in the upholstery of antique furniture.

Liberty and Son Designs
1506 Market Center Blvd.
214/748-3329
Open: Mon.–Sat. 10–6, Sun. by appt.

Extensive selection of antique and decorator furnishings.

Lots of Furniture
910 N. Industrial Blvd.
214/761-1575
Open: Mon.–Sat. 10–5, Sun. 12–5

12,000 square feet of antique furniture and exotics.

Mama's Daughters' Diner
2014 Irving Blvd.
214/742-8646
Open: Mon.–Fri. 6–3, Sat. 7–3

Homemade breakfast and lunch.

Parkhouse Antiques
114 Parkhouse
214/741-1199
Open: Wed.–Sun. 11–6

For home and garden.

The Rocket Restaurant
1838 Irving Blvd.
214/741-1324
Open: Mon.–Sat. 5–2:30

Full breakfast and lunch.

Sandaga Market African Imports
1325 Levee
214/747-8431
Open: Mon.–Fri. 9–6 or by appt.

Selection of ceremonial & decorative art.

Silver Eagle
1933 Levee
214/741-2390
Open: Tues.–Sat. 10:30–5

Unusual and affordable antiques.

Special Consideration by Pettigrew & Associates, Inc.
1715 Market Center Blvd.
214/475-1351
Open: Mon.–Fri. 9–5

New, old, odd lot furniture & decorative items.

White Elephant Antiques Warehouse
1026 N. Industrial Blvd.
214/871-7966
Open: Mon.–Sat. 10–5

18,000 square feet, 75 dealers, & 90 vignettes.

The Wrecking Barn
1421 N. Industrial Blvd., Suite 102 at Glass St.
214/747-2777
Open: Mon.–Fri. 9–5, Sat. 10–3

Architectural salvage.

Designing Men
4209 Avondale, Suite 308
214/599-0029

Antiques Antiques
5100 Belt Line Road, Suite 218
972/239-6124

The Emporium at Big Town
Big Town Mall (Mesquite)
214/320-2222

Sample House
122 Casa Linda Plaza
214/327-0486

Kornye Gallery
2200 Cedar Springs Road
214/871-3434

Love Field Antique Mall
6500 Cedar Springs Road
214/357-6500

Ken Riney Antiques
500 Crescent Court
214/871-3640

Beckie's Antiques & Gifts
1005 W. Davis St.
214/942-8626

Gregor's Studios
1413 Dragon St.
214/744-3385

Heritage Collection Ltd.
2521 Fairmount St.
214/871-0012

Three Graces Antiques
2603 Fairmount St.
214/969-1922

Eagles Antiques
2711 Fairmount St.
214/871-9301

Sam's Antique Rugs
5333 Forest Lane
972/233-9777

Trinkets & Treasures
10244 Garland Road
214/320-3794

Antique Bahr
1801 Greenville Ave.
214/826-1064

House of Prokay Antiques
1807 Greenville Ave.
214/824-7618

Atrium
3404 Belt Line Road
972/243-2406

Consignment Store
5290 Belt Line Road
972/991-6268

Mary Cates & Co.
2700 Boll St.
214/855-5006

Ornaments & Heirlooms
2512 Matton St.
214/871-2020

Roxy
3826 Cedar Springs Road
214/827-8593

Cathy's Antiques
500 Crescent Court, Suite 140
214/871-3737

Sample House & Candle Shop
9825 N. Central Expressway
214/369-6521

Corner Shop
Decorative Center
214/741-1780

Joe Cooner Gallery
1605 Dragon St.
214/747-3603

Les Antiques, Inc.
2600 Fairmount St.
214/720-0099

Uncommon Market, Inc.
2701 Fairmount St.
214/871-2775

Forestwood Antique Mall
5333 Forest Lane
972/661-0001

Curiosity Corner
8920 Garland Road
214/320-1752

Lone Star Bazaar
10724 Garland Road
214/324-1484

A S C Deco
1805 Greenville Ave.
214/821-8288

Linda's Treasures & Tea Room
1929 Greenville Ave.
214/824-7915

Lula B's Antique Mall
2004 Greenville Ave.
214/824-2185

Allison Daughtry Antiques
2804 Greenville Ave.
214/823-8910

Anna's, Etc.
3424 Greenville Ave.
214/828-9393

Nicole's Antiques
3611 Greenville Ave.
214/821-3740

Ivy House
5500 Greenville Ave.
214/369-2411

Connie Williamson Antiques
2815 N. Henderson Ave.
214/821-4134

Nick Brock Antiques
2909 N. Henderson Ave.
214/828-0624

Canterbury Antiques
2923A N. Henderson Ave.
214/821-5265

Whimsey Shoppe
2923 N. Henderson Ave.
214/824-6300

Beaux-Arts
1505 Hi Line Dr.
214/741-5555

Gameroom Express
141 Howell St.
214/747-3232

Garrett Galleries
1800 Irving Blvd.
214/742-4343

Knox Street Antiques
3319 Knox St.
214/521-8888

The British Trading Co./Pine Shoppe
4518 Lovers Lane
214/373-9071

Lovers Lane Antique Market
5001 W. Lovers Lane
214/351-5656

Market Antiques
5470 W. Lovers Lane, Suite 335
214/352-1220

Lower Greenville Antique Mall
2010 Greenville Ave.
214/824-4136

Chique & Shabby
2915 Greenville Ave.
214/828-0500

Waterbird Traders
3420 Greenville Ave.
214/821-4606

Copper Lamp
5500 Greenville Ave.
214/521-3711

Albert Copeland Continental
11117 Harry Hines Blvd.
214/241-9686

Brant Laird Antiques
2901 N. Henderson Ave.
214/823-4100

Kent-Stone Antiques
2819 N. Henderson Ave.
214/826-7553

Richard Alan Antiques
2923 N. Henderson Ave.
214/826-1588

On Consignment, Inc.
2927 N. Henderson Ave.
214/827-3600

Del Saxon Fine Arts & Antiques
1525B Hi Line Dr.
214/742-6921

Market Antiques
430 N. Park Center
214/369-7161

Notable Accents
8204 Kate St.
214/369-5525

William Little Antiques
7227 Lakehurst Ave.
214/368-8230

Park Cities Antique Mall
4908 W. Lovers Lane
214/350-5983

Le Passe
5450 W. Lovers Lane, Suite 227
214/956-9320

Consignment Galleries
5627 W. Lovers Lane
214/357-3925

Texas

Silver Vault
5655 W. Lovers Lane
214/357-7115

Antique Galleries
2533 McKinney Ave.
214/871-1516

El Paso Import Co.
4524 McKinney Ave.
214/559-0907

Mews
1708 Market Center Blvd.
214/748-9070

Unlimited Ltd. — The Antique Mall
15201 Midway Road
972/490-4085

Antique Shop
5616 E. Mockingbird Lane
214/823-7718

Millennium
3601 Parry Ave.
214/824-7325

507 Antiques
10755 Preston Road
214/368-1100

Saint Johns Silver
2603 Routh St.
214/871-2020

Pearle Dorrace Antiques
2736 Routh St.
214/855-0008

Adam & Eve Antiques
3121 Routh St.
214/871-0225

Modern & Antique Clock Repair
10435 Springhaven Dr.
972/216-9514

Maison De France
1007 Slocum St.
214/742-1222

East & Orient Company
1123 Slocum St.
214/741-1191

Pittet Co.
1215 Slocum St.
214/651-7033

Oriental Rugs, Inc.
1404 Slocum St.
214/748-8891

Windsor Antique Mall
6126 Luther Lane — Preston Center
214/750-8787

McKinney Ave. Antique Market
2710 McKinney Ave.
214/871-1904

Loyd-Paxton
3636 Maple Ave.
214/521-1521

Trains & Toys
109 Medallion Center
214/373-9469

Englishman's Antiques
15304 Midway Road
972/980-0107

Antique Angie
603 Munger Ave.
214/954-1864

China Cupboard
718 N. Paulus Ave.
214/528-6250

HMI Architectural
1811 Rock Island St.
214/428-7774

Drew Ltd. Antique Gallery
2722 Routh St.
214/880-0009

Collage 20th Century Classics
3017 Routh St.
214/880-0020

Antiques Unique
180 Spring Creek Village
972/386-5477

Southwest Gallery
4500 Sigma @ Welch
972/960-8935

Gary Elam & Associates
1025 Slocum St.
214/747-4767

Somerset Galleries
1205 Slocum St.
214/760-7065

Oriental Treasures
1322 Slocum St.
214/760-8888

Le Louvre French Antiques
1313 Slocum St.
214/742-2605

Louis Rosenbach Antiques, Inc.
1518 Slocum St.
214/748-0906

Old Wicker Garden
6606 Snider Plaza
214/373-8241

Rosedale House
6928 Snider Plaza
214/369-6646

Remember When Shop
2431 Valwood Pkwy.
972/243-3439

Odds and Ends Shop
210 W. Yarmouth St.
214/942-9326

Shalanes Antique Gallery
5811 S R L Thornton Freeway
214/374-7455

46 DAYTON

The Old School
111 W. Houston
409/258-9342 or 1-800-491-9342
Open: Wed.–Sat. 9:30–5:30, Mon.–Tues. by appointment
Directions: Dayton is midway between Houston and Beaumont on Hwy. 90. Houston St. is one block south of Hwy. 90. The shop is directly behind the Sonic Drive-in.

Anyone care to guess why Ann Westmoreland's shop is called The Old School? I'll give you a hint: it used to house teachers and students and was a place of learning for the community. The building was constructed somewhere in the late 1800s, and was last used as a school in 1908. Ann carries furniture, glassware, primitives, jewelry, coins, some Southwestern artifacts along with other antiques and collectibles.

Charlette's Web
FM 1960
409/258-5933

General Store
212 N. Main St.
409/258-8928

47 DECATUR

Sisters Four Collectibles
115 W. Main St.
940/627-3177

Red Pepper Trading Post
121 N. State St.
940/627-7959

Y.C. King & Sons
1528 Slocum St.
214/698-1977

Samplers
6817 Snider Plaza
214/363-0045

Snider Plaza Antiques
6929 Snider Plaza
214/373-0822

Days of Olde
2901 Valley View Lane
972/247-2417

Bettyann & Jimbo's Antique Market
4402 W. Lovers Lane
214/350-5755

Main Street Bazaar
312 N. Main St.
409/258-4049

Charles Antiques
408 W. Main St.
940/627-2485

Memory Lane Antiques
104 N. Trinity St.
940/627-1121

Crossroads Antiques Mall
301 S. Washburn St.
940/627-7047

48 DENISON

Antique Showroom

421 W. Main St.
903/465-2253 or 903/465-2211
Email: antiqueshwrm@texoma.net
Open: Mon.–Sat. 10–5:30

Would you like to buy antique furniture and small goods direct from Europe at dealer prices? If so, you should make a special effort to attend the monthly "Tag Sale" held in Denison, Texas, the third Thursday of each month. The Antique Showroom imports 40 foot containers of antique furniture to the United States and every month a full container load of furniture and small goods arrives from a different country; England, Scotland, Northern Ireland, France and Italy are some of the countries that are represented at the sale. The sale is conducted as a "Tag Sale," meaning that each and every item is individually priced and marked with a two-part perforated price tag.

The pricing is based on "Cost Plus" (usually 20-25%), this helps keep the sale a no-hassel event, which can provide everyone with great bargains. The Antique Showroom is entering its third year of presenting full container loads of antiques for sale. The concept of the "Tag Sale" has been extremely successful and received very well by the general public and antique dealers alike. It allows everyone to browse through the entire load being offered and make buying decisions without the pressure and confusion associated with auctions.

The Antique Showroom also offers full containers for sale to individuals, antique malls or auction houses seeking to buy in volume or in large quantities. A full container load can have as many as 200 furniture pieces and up to 50 or 60 lots of small goods. Auctioneers have found container loads to be very profitable and a great way to build a regular following of customers.

Group buying trips are another service offered by the Antique Showroom. Every April, August and December you have the opportunity to travel with the buyers from the Antique Showroom to purchase antiques in any one of five countries throughout the United Kingdom and Europe. A buying trip can be a great way to find that special piece of furniture you have been searching for and have the opportunity to visit some of the most interesting and beautiful cities in the world.

Antiques & Cars by Bob Taylor
213 W. Heron St.
903/463-9924

Katy Antique Station
104 E. Main St.
903/465-7352

Hart Place Mall
500 W. Main St.
903/463-1230

Wright's Antiques
1030 W. Main St.
903/465-9392

Castaway Furniture
1500 W. Johnson St.
903/463-9855

Tucker Furniture
422 W. Main St.
903/465-3630

Manor House Antiques & Cllbls.
611 W. Main St.
903/465-2601

Blue Moon Antique Mall
410 W. Main St.
903/463-7505

49 DENTON

Memories So Special
105 Hickory St.
940/484-8560

Downtown Mini Mall
108 N. Locust St.
940/387-0024

Antique Warehouse
809 N. Locust St.
940/565-0666

Courthouse Collection
111 W. Hickory St.
940/381-1956

Cooks Red Barn Antiques
212 E. Hickory St.
940/382-5004

Carriage Hill Collectibles
105 W. Hickory St.
940/484-6194

50 DeSOTO

Great Places to Eat

Cracker Barrel Old Country Store
I-35 E. & Wintergreen Blvd., Exit 416
972/224-3004

51 DIBOLL

Quaint Shop
Route 3, Box 601
409/829-3466

The Dusty Attic
910 N. Temple Dr.
409/829-2743

Village Antiques
Hwy. 59 S.
409/829-4500

Live Oak Antiques & Collectibles
1443 N. Temple Dr.
409/829-3554

52 EASTLAND

House of Antiques
908 S. Bassett
254/629-1124

Antiques & Uniques
114 W. Commerce St.
254/629-2143

Kountry Korner
112 S. Seaman St.
254/629-2214

Hogs 'n' Clover Antiques Gifts
109 E. Commerce St.
254/629-2755

I-20 Antiques
Exit 343
254/629-8682

Texas

53 EL CAMPO

Rose Garden
123 S. Mechanic St.
409/543-1097

Prairie Antiques & Collectibles
708 N. Mechanic St.
409/543-9511

54 EL PASO

Posada San Miguel
9618 Socorro Road
915/858-1993

Grapevine Antiques & Collectibles
5024 Doniphan Dr.
951/584-3981

Ye Olde Antiques
5024 Doniphan Dr.
915/584-7630

Marketplace at Placita Sante Fe
5034 Doniphan Dr.
915/585-9296

Raquel's
5372 Doniphan Dr.
915/584-7861

Another Man's Treasure
6016 Doniphan Dr.
915/581-0077

Rosebud Antiques & Gifts
6016 Doniphan Dr.
915/584-7227

Ruby's
6016 Doniphan Dr.
915/581-0077

Stephen's Antiques
6016 Doniphan Dr.
915/585-0028

P & L Trading Post
6020 Doniphan Dr.
915/581-0287

A J's
6022 Doniphan Dr.
915/833-3432

Mary McNellis Antiques
6022 Doniphan Dr.
915/584-6878

Swan's Antiques
6022 Doniphan Dr.
915/585-7358

C R V Enterprises
6184 Doniphan Dr.
915/581-6416

Stars & Stripes Antiques
6458 Doniphan Dr.
915/833-6228

Antique Borderland
6465 Doniphan Dr.
915/584-3230

Caldarella's Furniture, Inc.
5660 El Paso
915/859-4777

Eastside Antique Mall
7924 Gateway Blvd. E.
915/594-0673

Rings Antiques & Collectibles
7924 Gateway Blvd. E.
915/594-0673

Antiques Etcetera
8022 N. Mesa St.
915/833-4712

Wooden Horse Antiques
132 W. Redd Road
915/581-1976

Eagle's Nest
7410 Remcon Circle
915/584-0868

Mesa Street Antique Mall
7410 Remcon Circle
915/584-0868

Nana's Treasures
7410 Remcon Circle
915/585-0940

55 ENNIS

On The Corner
101 S. Dallas St.
972/875-8825

Magnolia Station Antiques
201 S. Dallas St.
972/875-7360

Deedee's Antiques Collectibles & More
808 E. Ennis Ave.
972/875-2011

Good Time Charlies Antiques
114 W. Knox St.
972/875-9737

56 FORNEY

Pavillion Antiques
4 Forney Industrial Park
972/222-8902

Wholesale Antiques
5 Forney Industrial Park
972/564-4433

Snooper's Paradise
6 Forney Industrial Park
972/564-4214

Deridder Antiques Corp.
Forney Industrial Park
972/226-8407

Star Antique Mall
Forney Industrial Park
972/564-1055

Doc's Antiques
107 Hwy. 80
972/552-4305

Philbeck's Antiques
119 E. Hwy. 80
972/564-9842

Clement's Antiques of Texas, Inc.
121 E. Hwy. 80
972/564-1520

Bowling Antiques
10512 W. U.S. Hwy. 80
972/564-1433

Little Red's Antiques
Hwy. 80
972/226-2304

Cotton Gin Mall
210 Hwy. 688
972/564-1220

Aires Limited
E. 125 Hwy. 80
972/564-4913

57 FORT WORTH

Rufe Snow Antique Mall
6801 N.E. Loop 820
North Richland Hills
817/498-0733
Web site: www.antiquelandusa.com
Open: Mon.–Thurs. 10–6, Fri.–Sat. 10–8, Sun. 12–6

At Rufe Snow Antique Mall, you'll experience one of the largest, most impressive antique malls in the country. See thousands of antiques (furniture, crystal, pottery, jewelry, silver, books and collectibles) creatively displayed throughout 40,000 square feet of individual showrooms and attractive vignettes.

The unique landmark location has been home to 200 of the area's finest antique dealers since 1994. A distinctive reputation for quality and selection attracts shoppers, designers and collectors from all over the world.

Texas

Cowtown Antiques, The Trading Post
2400 N. Main St.
817/626-4565
Open: Tues.–Thurs. 10–5, Fri.–Sat. 11–6, Sun. 12–5, closed Mon.

Cowtown Antiques and The Trading Post are two different shops located almost together and owned by the same folks. Both are open the same hours (listed above) so you can get double your shopping time in here. The shops are in the historic Fort Worth Stockyards … "Where the West Begins," and shoppers can experience the old time atmosphere and rich heritage of this Fort Worth landmark.

With the sounds of cowboy music filling the background, shop for Western collectibles and memorabilia, pocket watches, Western wear, mounts, and hides. In addition, there is furniture, stained glass and advertising memorabilia.

Harris Antiques & Imports
7600 Scott St.
817/246-8400 or 817/246-5852
Directions: Harris Antiques & Imports is located in West Fort Worth, in a suburb called White Settlement. The shop is at I-30 West, Cherry Lane Exit (north), then right on Scott St.

Carolyn Harris and company sells both wholesale and retail, with about 95% of their sales being to dealers, auctioneers and designers. Anyone who loves antiques should go to the showroom just to look and be impressed. Their new location is an air-conditioned mall that is the length of three football fields - a total of 440,000 square feet of antiques and accessories! Harris Antiques & Imports has been in business in Fort Worth for over 35 years, and offers merchandise to shoppers world-wide. Besides all the furniture, they offer bronzes, oil paintings, cut glass and porcelain. It's no wonder they hold the title of "the world's largest home furnishings, accessories and antiques store."

Black Orchid
3801 Camp Bowie Blvd.
817/731-8611

Leigh-Boyd
4632 Camp Bowie Blvd.
817/738-3705

Antique Colony, Inc.
7200 Camp Bowie Blvd.
817/731-7252

Antique Shop
5401 Jacksboro Hwy.
817/740-9966

Yabba Dabba Doo Antiques
6517 E. Lancaster Ave.
817/654-4100

Flories Antiques
3915 Camp Bowie Blvd.
817/763-5380

Fort Worth Antiques
4909 Camp Bowie Blvd.
871/731-4220

From The Hide
117 W. Exchange Ave.
817/624-8302

Doll House
1815 E. Lancaster Ave.
817/332-8674

Drew's Antiques & Primitives
7113 E. Lancaster Ave.
817/451-8822

Antique Connection
7429 E. Lancaster Ave.
817/429-0922

Lake Worth Bazaar
4024 Merrett Dr.
817/237-8064

Cornish Antiques & Collectibles
320 S. Oakland Blvd.
817/536-9975

Lemon Tree Antiques Art & Books
804 Pennsylvania Ave.
817/332-5519

Harris's Antiques
7600 Scott St.
817/246-5852

Norma Baker Antiques
3311 W. 7th St.
817/335-1152

Butler's Antiques & Uniques
514 W. Seminary Dr.
817/921-3403

Quilters Emporium
3526 W. Vickery Blvd.
817/377-3993

Hidden Treasures Antiques
8906 White Settlement Road
817/246-8864

Stockyard Antiques
1332 N. Main St.
817/624-2311

Montgomery St. Antique Mall
2601 Montgomery St.
817/735-9685

Choices on Park Hill
2978 Park Hill
817/927-1854

Nick's Frame & Antique Shop
2616 Scott Ave.
817/534-3601

Sample House
1540 S. University Dr.
817/429-7857

Market
3433 W. 7th St.
817/334-0330

Lambert Antiques
2812 Stanley Ave.
817/926-3450

Newton's Antiques
5216 White Settlement Road
817/737-7009

Great Places to Stay

Azalea Plantation Bed and Breakfast
1400 Robinwood Dr.
1-800-68-RELAX

Azalea Plantation is a stately plantation style home reminiscent of Tara, nestled in a quiet residental neighborhood near downtown's restored Sundance Square and only ten minutes from the Stockyards Historic District. The bed and breakfast sits amidst one and a half acres of oak trees highlighted with rock terracing, gazebo and fountains. Guest rooms and cottages are spacious, furnished with antiques and very private with private baths. The Magnolia Cottage/Suite is the perfect honeymoon/anniversary romantic getaway spot, with its Texas size whirlpool for two, cozy bedroom and charming parlor.

58 FRANKSTON

Pandora's Box
102 W. Main St.
903/876-5056
Open: Mon.–Sat. 9–5:30, closed Sun.
Directions: Pandora's Box is located on the square in Frankston, one block west of Hwy. 155 and one block south of Hwy. 175.

Here's a true junque store that's not afraid to say so! That's their description of themselves: a 4,000-square-foot true junque store with architectural antiques and a garden shop, all housed in an old automobile dealership building.

59 FREDERICKSBURG

Watkins Hill
608 E. Creek
210/997-6739 or 1-800-899-1672
Open: Year-round, business hours Mon.–Fri. 8–5, Sat.–Sun. 8–2

Watkins Hill Guest House is so perfectly suited for the scenic area in which it is located. Visitors are attracted to the European atmosphere, historic landmarks and the bread and pastries for which Fredericksburg is famous. Watkins Hill is conveniently accessible from Austin, San Antonio, Houston and Dallas/Fort Worth. Mr. Edgar Watkins, the innkeeper, will provide excellent directions to the Guest House from your location.

Watkins Hill is an unusual — and unusually elegant — bed and breakfast complex in Fredericksburg, Texas.

Dreamchild of native Texan Edgar Watkins, Watkins Hill began life just a few years ago when Watkins gave up a career in product design and public relations to return to his home state and buy the 1855 Basse House, now the centerpiece of his inn. He knew he wanted something out of the ordinary for his bed and breakfast, and he knew what he didn't like about other B&Bs, so he designed Watkins Hill with these things in mind.

One of his pet peeves is sitting down to breakfast with a group of strangers in the custom of traditional B&Bs. So he decided to serve his guests with breakfast by room service at the guest's requested time. He also doesn't like the term "bed and breakfast," instead preferring to call his accommodation a "guest house."

Another concept from the start was not to fill the inn with Texas farm furniture. Instead Watkins created an imaginary scenario, and went from there, "I fantasized that a stylish bachelor had moved here in the 1850s from the East, and had brought his family's furniture with him." Following that fantasy, the Basse House is furnished with upscale antiques from the mid-18th century to the mid-19th century, including a rare little steel bathtub from a Paris hotel.

The entire complex currently spans two acres, with seven buildings, four of which are historic 19th century structures (1835, 1840, 1855 and 1890). Twelve guest rooms are available, with a total sleeping capacity of about 40 guests. All of this is located just two blocks from Fredericksburg's Main Street and its shops, yet longhorn cattle graze across the way on the opposite side of the street and along the creek that runs beside it.

All but two rooms have fireplaces and porches or balconies. Every room has a butler's pantry with a refrigerator stocked with complimentary wine, two kinds of coffee and several kinds of tea, distilled water, fruit juice and apples. Guests also get four kinds of snacks, current magazines, and recommendations of places to dine.

There are so many little touches of elegance, luxury and whimsey that guests could spend all their time just wandering around looking for these surprises. Beeswax tapers and potted candles glow beside a mid-19th-century faux bamboo French daybed. One living room wall is covered floor to ceiling with a circa 1870 theatrical backdrop. It's a scarred canvas painting of a forest, but the creases and nicks in it fit beautifully with the combination of primitive and elegant decors that swirl throughout the house. The frayed edges of the canvas are disguised at the top behind a pressed tin valance dipped in brass, and along both sides by a pair of 19th century pilasters from New York state. Doors at either end open onto the porches, with the open front door offering a view of a Victorian cast-cement fountain and an expansive meadow. Luxury and style with the unusual make wonderful weekend or week-long companions for guests who like to be pampered and intrigued.

Texas Trading Co.
109 N. Adams St.
210/997-1840

American Hiddledy Piggledy
411 S. Lincoln St.
210/997-5551

Idle Hours
411 S. Lincoln St.
210/997-2908

Antique Haus
107 S. Llano St.
210/997-2011

Cornerstone Market
201 E. Main St.
210/997-3204

Jabberwocky Antiques
207 E. Main St.
210/997-7071

Lauren Bade Antiques
229 E. Main St.
210/997-9570

Der Alte Fritz Antiques
409 E. Main St.
210/997-8249

Room No. 5
239A W. Blvd. #5
210/997-1090

Homestead Warehouse Store
411 S. Lincoln St.
210/997-0954

Wild Goose Chase Antiques
105 S. Llano St.
210/997-4321

Showcase Antiques Shop
119 E. Main St.
210/997-5505

Remember Me
203 E. Main St.
210/997-6932

Red Baron's Antiques
215 E. Main St.
210/997-6368

Main St. Antiques
234 W. Main St.
210/997-8913

Rustic Styles
414 E. Main St.
210/997-6219

Three Horse Trader
609 W. Main St.
210/997-6499

60 GAINESVILLE

Recollection Antiques
105 W. California St.
940/668-2170

Miss Pitty Pats Antique Porch
111 W. California St.
940/665-6540

Lindsay House
318 E. California St.
940/665-7171

Carousel Antique Mall
112 S. Dixon St.
940/665-6444

Old West Traditions
107 W. California St.
940/665-7503

Shady Oak Gallery
111 S. Commerce St.
940/665-0275

Naughty Lady Antiques
108 N. Chestnut St.
940/668-1767

Gainesville Antique Mall Main
1808 N. IH-35
940/668-7798

61 GALVESTON

Madame Dyer's Bed & Breakfast
1720 Postoffice St.
409/765-5692
Open: Year-round
Directions: Take I-45 South from Houston to Galveston. When you cross over the Causeway onto the island, the interstate highway becomes Broadway. Travel about 50 blocks to 18th St. Make a left turn onto 18th St. and go 5 blocks to Postoffice St. Turn right onto this one-way street. Madame Dyer's is the second house on the left. Park in front.

This elegant 1889 Victorian mansion is located in the East End Historic Homes District, which is one of the most beautiful and best preserved areas of Victorian homes in the country. It is within walking distance of The Strand Historic District, where restored vintage buildings house specialty shops, galleries, museums, restaurants, outlet shops and antique malls; and is two blocks away from Gallery Row, where upscale antique and gallery shops abound. In other words, it's location is perfect! Guests can even have a horse drawn carriage pick them up at the B&B's front door, or they can catch the historic trolley just two blocks away.

The ornate, two-store mansion has been faithfully restored to its turn-of-the-century glory, with two wrap-around porches, high airy ceilings, wooden floors and lace curtains.

Each room is furnished with antiques, including the three guest rooms. Ashten's Room, with private bath, is furnished with a queen size bed of carved oak and antique accent pieces. Blake's Room, with a queen size bed set in a bay window, is decorated in English antiques and antique rug beaters, shoe lasts and sewing memorabilia. The private bath just down the hall holds a claw-foot tub. Corbin's Room holds a king size bed, a tiled fireplace with an oak mirrored mantel, antique dolls,

whimsical old hats, and a pedestal sink and claw-foot tub in the adjoining bath.

There is a coffee/tea buffet provided each morning upstairs for early risers, a full breakfast every morning in the dining room, homemade cookies in the dining room at all times, and complimentary snacks and beverages available in the kitchen round the clock.

Jewels & Junque
2715 Broadway St.
409/762-3243

Collectors Gallery
2222 Postoffice St.
409/765-6443

Old Peanut Butter Warehouse
100 20th St.
409/762-8358

Somewhere in Time Antiques
124 20th St.
409/762-1094

Off The Wall Antiques
1811 23rd St.
409/765-9414

B.J.'s Antiques
2111 Postoffice St.
409/763-6075

Hendley Market
2010 Strand
409/762-2610

Yesterday's Best
120 20th St.
409/765-1419

La Maison Rouge
418 22nd St.
409/763-0717

62 GARLAND

Chase & James Furniture
1817 S. Garland Ave.
942/864-0092

Old South Antiques & Auction
1413 N. I Hwy. 30
942/240-4477

Treasure Chest of Antiques
115 N. 6th St.
942/276-6075

Old Garland Antique Mall
108 N. 6th St.
942/494-029

The Cabbage Patch
901 Jupiter
942/272-8928

The Ritz
Main St.
942/494-0083

Farm House Antiques
509 W. State St.
942/487-8262

63 GEORGETOWN

Cobblestone
708 S. Austin Ave.
512/863-9607

Rust & Dust
113 E. 7th St.
512/863-6463

Georgetown Antique Mall
713 S. Main St.
512/869-2088

Poppy Hill Marketplace
820 S. Austin Ave.
512/863-8445

On The Square
712 S. Austin Ave.
512/869-0448

Georgetown Emporium
114 E. 7th St.
512/863-6845

Texas Sampler
101 River Hills Dr.
512/863-7694

Texas

64 GILMER

Old Town Mall
201 Henderson St.
903/843-2359

Corner Store Antiques
203 W. Tyler St.
903/843-2466

65 GLADEWATER

Gladewater Antique Mall
100 E. Commerce Ave.
903/845-4440

Jade Junction
106 E. Commerce Ave.
903/845-3876

Now & Then Antique Mall
109 W. Commerce Ave.
903/845-5765

Bygone Tymes Mall
109 N. Main St.
903/845-2603

B & B Bygones Antiques
111 S. Main St.
903/845-2655

Old Tyme Antiques & Collectibles
111 S. Main St.
903/845-4708

Antiques
112 S. Main St.
903/845-6493

Carlyne's Collectibles
112 N. Main St.
903/845-3923

Main Street Treasures
113 N. Main St.
903/845-6671

Good Old Stuff
114 S. Main St.
903/845-8316

K D Wayside Shop
119 S. Main St.
903/845-4093

Mel's Country Classics
120 S. Main St.
903/845-2519

The Loft
121 S. Main St.
903/845-4429

Country Girl Collection
124 S. Main St.
903/845-6143

Dru's Knick Knacks
125 S. Main St.
903/845-5635

Country Carousel Mall
201 S. Main St.
903/845-4531

Studio
201 N. Main St.
903/845-6910

Bishop's Antique Mall
202 S. Main St.
903/845-7247

Saint Clair Antique Emporium
104 W. Pacific Ave.
903/845-4079

Heritage Antiques & Collectibles
112 W. Pacific Ave.
903/845-3021

66 GLEN FLORA

Glen Flora Emporium
103 S. Bridge St.
409/677-3249
Open: Wed.–Sun. 10–6
Directions: Glen Flora is five miles north of U.S. Hwy. 59 at Wharton, Texas. Take the Eagle Lake exit and travel north on FM 102 until you reach the small town of Glen Flora. Bridge St. is FM 960, which intersects with FM 102. The shop is at the intersection of FM 102 and FM 960. Turn left into the parking lot. You can't miss the emporium - it's the largest building for miles.

The town of Glen Flora was founded in 1900 and is currently undergoing restoration and reconstruction. The building that houses the emporium was built in 1912. This 20 plus dealer mall handles furniture, glassware, pottery, jewelry, vintage clothing and so on.

67 GOLIAD

Goliad is one of the three oldest municipalities in Texas and was the site of the Aranama Indian village named Santa Dorotea. In 1749 the Spanish government transferred The Royal Presidio (fort) of Nuestra Senora De Loreto De La Bahia De Expiritu Santo to this location along with the Mission Nuestra Senora Del Espiritu Santo De Zuniga. A small villa grew up around the walls of the fort and was called La Bahia. This area was occupied by the Spanish until 1821 when Mexico became an independent nation. In 1829 the name "Goliad" was officially adopted. It is an anagram of the name "Hidalgo" in honor of the patriot priest of the Mexican Revolution.

In what was termed the first offensive action of the Texas Revolution, local colonists captured Goliad on October 9, 1845. The First Declaration of Texas Independence was signed here on December 20. Along with it was raised the "Bloody Arm Flag", the first flag of Texas independence. During the 1836 campaign, Col. James Fannin's Texans were defeated at the Battle Of Coleto and were massacred one week later on March 27, 1836 at the Presidio La Bahia. The Goliad Massacre represents the largest single loss of life (352) in the cause of Texas independence and inspired the battle cry "Remember The Alamo - Remember Goliad."

The Honeycomb Antiques
122 N. Courthouse Square
512/645-2331

The Christmas Goose
136 N. Courthouse Square
512/645-8087

68 GONZALES

Catty Corner Antiques
501 N. Saint Joseph St.
210/672-2975

Dub's Antique Mall
517 N. Saint Joseph St.
210/672-7917

Bowden's Antiques
620 N. Saint Joseph St.
210/672-7770

Violet's Treasures
712 N. Saint Joseph St.
210/672-9744

Laurel Ridge Antiques
827 N. Saint Joseph St.
210/672-2484

Polly's House Flowers & Antiques
830 Saint Paul St.
210/672-2013

69 GRANBURY

Brazos River Trading Co.
115 E. Bridge St.
817/573-5191

Sugar & Spice Antiques
117 W. Bridge St.
817/579-1224

Antique Emporium
116 ½ N. Crockett St.
817/573-1939

Wagon Yard Antiques
213 N. Crockett St.
817/573-5321

Scarlet Thread
3018 Fall Creek Hwy.
817/326-3430

Classic Antiques
4316 Hwy. 377
817/579-5658

Trading Company
109 N. Houston St.
817/573-3800

Pearl St. Antiques & Treasures
503 E. Pearl St.
817/279-1270

70 GRAPELAND

Bobbye's
315 S. Market St.
409/687-4979

Flo's Antiques
210 Main St.
409/687-4778

71 GRAPEVINE

Guests Main Street Antiques
201 E. Franklin St.
817/488-3647

Air Nostalgia
420 S. Main St.
817/481-9005

Grapevine Antique Mall
415 N. Northwest Hwy.
817/329-6946

72 GREENVILLE

Better Days Antiques
2402 Lee St.
903/455-3035

Downtown Tradin' Days
2801 Lee St.
903/454-9908

Country Craft Mall
2814 Terrell Road
903/455-7736

Greenville Village
2316 Johnson St.
903/455-1887

73 GROESBECK

Groesbeck Antiques Mall
105 N. Ellis St.
254/729-3443

Antique Mall of Granbury
4303 N. Hwy. 37
817/279-1645

The Bazaar
4318 E. Hwy. 377
817/579-9295

Hightower Antiques & Uniques
130 N. Houston St.
817/573-4488

Witherspoon's Antiques
600 E. Pearl St.
817/573-5254

Echoes of Texas
924 N. Market St.
409/687-2070

Julia's Antiques & Tearoom
210 N. Main St.
817/329-0622

Collectors Exchange
415 N. Northwest Hwy.
817/329-6946

Courthouse Square Antiques
2512 Lee St.
903/455-0557

Billie Taggart's 1800 Shop
2417 Oneal St.
903/455-4151

Greenville Antiques
2605 Halifax St.
903/454-2488

Texan Antiques & Gifts
2712 Lee St.
903/455-6246

Bonds Store & Gallery
217 W. Navasota St.
254/729-5511

74 HARLINGEN

Tejas Finders
Paul C. Moon Jr.
Route 1, Box 695 Wilson Road
210/423-6870

He's only 21 years old, but already well on his way to establishing a solid professional name for himself in the antique trade. "He" is Paul C. Moon, Jr., and he is what's known as a "picker" in the antique world.

"I search for whatever the buyer is looking for," says Moon. "When I locate the piece, I send the buyer photographs of the piece, if possible, and, if he is completely satisfied, we come to an agreement and I expedite the deal."

Moon began his interest in antiques when he was managing an antique shop in the Harlingen, Texas area. He was fascinated by the Victorian style and era, and now specializes in Victorian pieces; however, he will search for whatever style and pieces a buyer wants to find. He's been a picker for two years, and business is good.

Working out of his home in Harlingen, Moon generally limits his travels and searches to the valley area around Harlingen. Situated in the very southeastern tip of Texas, Harlingen is conveniently located in the coastal region of east Texas, where the Victorian style abounds, left over from the influence of the steamboat and paddlewheeler days, plus the influence of changing styles that were easily accessible by water routes.

The next time you need a certain piece and style, call Moon. If it's Victorian in Texas, he probably knows right where to look.

Hilites
107 E. Jackson St.
210/412-7573

Frank's Collectibles & Antiques
123 E. Jackson St.
210/423-4041

Antique Furniture Warehouse
2710 S. F St.
210/425-3131

Somewhere in Time Antiques
111 E. Jackson St.
210/412-2577

Youngblood Interiors & Antiques
302 E. Jackson St.
210/412-1155

75 HASKELL

Hub of the rolling plains, Haskell was named after Charles Ready Haskell, a Revolutionary soldier who fell with Fannin at Goliad. Haskell was incorporated in 1885 and known in pioneer days as "Willow Pond Springs" and later as "Rice Springs." Today Haskell offers a beautiful city park, overnight RV parking, fishing, hunting and, of course, antiquing.

Texas

Nemir's Antiques

510 N. 2nd St.
940/864-2258
Open: Mon.–Fri. 10–5
Directions: Nemir's is located at the corner of 2nd Street and North
Avenue F. From Hwy. 380, turn north 1 block west of the main red light,
which is Avenue F. Go 1 block to 2nd Street and turn east. The shop is
right on the corner. From Hwy. 277, turn west 1 block north of the
main red light. This will be 2nd Street and the shop is on the corner.

Nemir's Antiques is a large, family-owned store with a grand selection
of quality antiques and collectibles. The 5,000-square-foot store offers
something for everyone including, but by no means limited to, a variety
of old toys and pottery.

Peddlers Village
304 S. 1st St.
940/864-2878

Old Stuff Antiques & Gifts
300 S. Ave. E.
940/864-2430

76 HENDERSON

Ms. Patty's Attic
501 Kilgore Dr., Hwy. 259 N.
903/657-1146

Sweet Lorraine's
501 1/2 Kilgore Dr., Hwy. 259 N.
903/657-1163

Trunks & Treasures
123 E. Main St.
903/657-8879

Emporium on the Square
102 N. Marshall St.
903/657-3854

Nelda's Nook
112 N. Marshall St.
903/657-2332

Four Oaks Gallery
709 State Hwy. 43 E.
903/657-8207

77 HILLSBORO

Veranda's Interiors & Antiques
114 S. Covington St.
254/582-9995

Old Citizens Emporium
50 W. Elm St.
254/582-1995

Dee Dee's Gifts & Tiques
106 E. Elm St.
254/582-0355

Arnold's Country Charm
110 W. Elm St.
254/582-5201

Franklin St Antiques
55 W. Franklin St.
254/582-0055

Antique Village, Inc.
116 E. Franklin St.
254/582-8632

Rainbow Gems Jewelers & Antique Mall
75 N. Waco St.
254/582-8430

Hillsboro Antique Mall
114 S. Waco St.
254/582-8330

78 HOUSTON

Carolyn Thompson's Antique Center of Texas

1001 W. Loop N.
713/688-4211
Open: Daily 10–6
Directions: 1001 W. Loop N., just 2 miles north of The Galleria.

No trip to, or near, Houston would be complete without a visit to Carolyn
Thompson's Antique Center. David and I spent an entire day browsing
throughout the store. Fortunately for us, the Center has a Texas Tea Room
(David is not a happy shopper when he's hungry). The food was wonderful.
Our choice was the special of the day offered from a menu of soups,
salads, sandwiches or hot entree (the special) along with desserts and
cookies for munching as you shop.

The Antique Center is the kind of store every antique shop or mall
should be. The inventory is very diverse, offering something for everyone.
For me this makes for a very pleasant shopping experience. May selections
are usually primitive, early American painted pieces and I was thrilled to
find a nice offering of such pieces among the exquisite formal furnishings
found throughout the store. If your decor requires massive, finely crafted,
artfully detailed furnishings, then look no further than Carolyn
Thompson's where you'll find the absolutely the best in the nation.
Accessories of comparable quality are also available to complete an
outstanding room setting. Below is a partial listing of the items available
from over 200 dealers at Carolyn Thompson's Antique Center of Texas:
rugs, clocks, china, bronze, cabinets, chandeliers, art glass, French,
Italian, American furnishings, stained glass, porcelain (one dealer
specializes in Haviland), flow blue, silver, lace, paintings, architectural
pieces, religious items, vintage hunting and fishing equipment, jewelry,
dolls, and a large selection of collectibles.

Trade Mart Antiques

Sam Houston Tollway @ Hammerly
713/467-2506
Open: Fri–Sun. 10–6
Directions: Located at Sam Houston Tollway @ Hammerly, 2 miles
north of I-10.

This 70,000-square-foot building is an antique lovers paradise.
Consisting of over 100 unique shops, you can find anything from
exceptional antique furniture and unique collectibles to unusual gift
items. Each shop is staffed with helpful and knowledgeable dealers to
assist you with your questions and
purchases. When it's time to take a
break, you can relax at the cafe for
a delicious meal or snack.

Fine antiques and collectibles from England, Europe, Asia, China and
America are available in mahogany, walnut, pine, oak, cherry, and other

woods. Custom furniture makers can help you design and will construct a piece of furniture to your specifications. Persian rugs, old coins, stamps, books, Civil War and western memorabilia are just a few of the specialty shops in the market. China, Depression glass, stemware, silverware, paintings, and decorative items for the home and office are in great supply at The Trade Mart. Many of Houston's finest interior decorators stop by The Trade Mart for unusual items for their clients.

The Trade Mart has a vast selection of gift shops to visit. There are specialty shops featuring estate and designer jewelry, Goebel figurines, chandeliers, light fixtures, tools and tapestries.

L R Antiques

2230 Bissonnet
713/524-3272
Open: Mon.–Sat. 10–6
Directions: Located between Greenbriar and Shepherd off Hwy. 59.

Since 1987, LR Antiques has been know in Houston, Texas for offering the finest in European antiques of the best craftsmanship, design, and beauty.

The owners of LR Antiques travel all over Europe to personally select an exceptional assortment of investment quality 18th, 19th, and 20th century furnishings and accents. Their goal is to bring the discriminating collector beautiful one-of-a-kind pieces that they will enjoy and cherish throughout the ages.

LR Antiques brings four or five 40-foot containers a year from France, Belgium, Holland, Ireland and England. All items are unique in a variety of styles from Art Deco to Renaissance, Art Nuevo to Louis III-VI.

These and other items are always available for viewing and sale at 2230 Bissonnet St.

Gallery Auctions, Inc.

243 Blue Bell
281/931-0100 or 1-800-764-8423

Auction each Monday morning at 10 a.m. and Tuesday night at 7 p.m. Call for special auction schedules.

Sherry Kelley's Antiques

2323 Woodhead St.
713/520-7575
Open: Mon.–Sat. 10–6
Directions: From Hwy. 59, the Southwest Freeway, exit Shepherd and go north on Shepherd to Fairview. Turn east (right) on Fairview and go to the first stop sign, which is Woodhead. Sherry Kelley's Antiques is at the corner of Fairview and Woodhead. From I-10, exit Shepherd and go south to West Gray and turn left. Go east to Woodhead and turn right. Proceed south to 2323 Woodhead and Fairview. The shop is two blocks north of Westheimer and 7 blocks east of Fairview.

Sherry Kelley is a direct importer of European antiques, making up to five trips a year to Europe, hand picking each item. Sherry specializes in mahogany Georgian style furniture, prints, books, crystal and decorative items.

Knight's Gallery
1320 W. Alabama St.
713/521-2785

Lynette Proler Antique Jewelers
2622 W. Alabama St.
713/521-1827

Dorothy Mostert Antiques
404 Avondale St.
713/523-9165

Warren Antique Collection
2121 N. West Belt
713/465-2985

Carl Moore Antiques
1610 Bissonnet St.
713/524-2502

Gilded Monkey
2314 Bissonnet St.
713/526-8661

Silver Shop
2348 Bissonnet St.
713/526-7256

R & S Antiques
2402 Bissonnet St.
713/524-9178

Southwest Antiques & Collectibles
6735 Bissonnet St.
713/981-6773

H. Karl Scharold Antiques, Inc.
5243 Buffalo Speedway
713/661-3466

Back Porch Antiques
17715 Clay Road
713/345-9238

Cleary's Antiques
10817 Craigheard Dr.
713/664-6643

Odeon Gallery
2117 Dunlavy St.
713/521-1111

Brian Stringer Antiques
2031 W. Alabama St.
713/526-7380

Almeda Antique Mall
9827 Almeda Genoa Road
713/941-7744

Barziza's Antiques
2121 N.W. Belt Dr.
713/467-0628

Simone Antique & More II
11723 W. Bellfort
713/561-7403

Madison Alley Antiques
1720 Bissonnett St.
713/526-6146

Britannia Antiques
2338 Bissonnet St.
713/529-3779

Antiques Antiques
14546 Carol Crest St.
713/527-0841

Southwest Antiques Too
6727 Bissonnet St.
713/981-6633

Simpson's Galleries
4001 Main St.
713/524-6751

Gabriel Galleries of Houston
7600 Burgoyne
713/528-2647

Crescent Enterprises Antiques
9229 Clay Road
713/462-4880

Antiques Houston
3200 W. Dallas Ave.
713/523-4705

J. Silver Antiques
3845 Dunlave St.
713/526-2988

Inside Outside
510 W. 18th St.
713/869-6911

Four Roses Antiques
7979 N. Eldridge Pkwy.
713/897-0507

Adkins Architectural Antiques
3515 Fannin St.
713/522-6547

Made in France
2912 Ferndale St.
713/529-7949

Ferndale Gallery & Antiques
2935 Ferndale St.
713/527-8358

The Market-Champion Village
5419 W. FM 1960
713/440-8281

French Antique Exchange
3301 Fondren Road
713/785-0785

Carriage House
10609 Grant Road
713/469-4840

T's Antiques
10609 Grant Road
713/890-8899

Cobblestone Antiques
7623 Louetta
713/251-0660

Campbell & Co. Antiques
3110 Houston Ave.
713/880-8178

Picket Fence
3010 Hwy. 146
713/474-4845

Woodlands Antique Mall
26710 N. IH 45
713/364-8111

Timely Treasures Antiques
11503 Jones Road
713/897-9577

Bediko Antiques & Refinishing
3402 Laura Koppe Road
713/692-3008

Gillespie's Antiques
4113 Leeland St.
713/247-9604

Candlelight Cottage
7979 N. Eldridge Pkwy.
713/469-4210

Sander's Antiques
315 Fairview St.
713/522-0539

James A. Gundry, Inc.
2910 Ferndale St.
713/524-6622

Phyllis Tucker Antiques
2919 Ferndale St.
713/524-0165

McLaren's Antiques & Gifts
3225 FM 1960
713/893-0432

White & Day Antiques
6711 FM 1960
713/444-3836

Ann's Creative Framing & Antiques
1928 Fountain View Dr.
713/781-7772

Look
5110 Griggs Road
713/748-6641

Burton's Antiques
9333 Harwin Dr.
713/977-5885

Silvi's Antiques Etc.
2223 Hwy. 6 S.
713/597-8557

Once upon a time
1004 W. Hwy. 6
713/331-7676

Gypsy Savage
1509 Indiana St.
713/528-0897

Meg's Cottage, Inc.
2819 W T C Jester Blvd.
713/956-2229

Nelly's Porch
16300 Kuykendahl Road
713/893-4659

Stevens Antique Furniture
5301 Laura Koppe Road
713/631-3196

Annie's Art & Antiques
1415 Murray Bay St.
713/973-6659

Richard's Antiquites, Inc.
3500 Main St.
713/528-5651

Once in a Life Time
12454 Memorial Dr.
713/465-8828

Thistle Antiques
12472 Memorial Dr.
713/984-2329

Happenings
4203 Montrose Blvd.
713/524-1507

Old Katy Road Antiques
9198 Old Katy Road #B
713/461-8124

Market Place Antiques
10910 Old Katy Road
713/464-8023

Sitting Room
2402 Quenby
713/523-1932

Baca Antique
2121 W. Sam Houston Pkwy. N.
713/984-0228

Hurta's Historics
2121 W. Sam Houston Pkwy. N.
713/468-1680

Antique Panache
9137 Spring Branch Dr.
713/464-2022

Country Home Antiques
14916 Stuebner Airline Road
713/440-1186

Reeves Antiques
2415 Taft St.
713/523-5577

Flashbacks Funtiques
1626 Westheimer Road
713/522-7900

Rosen Kavalieriques
1715 Westheimer Road
713/527-0660

Pride and Joy Antiques
1727 Westheimer Road
713/522-8435

The Emporium Architectural Antiques
1800 Westheimer Road
713/528-3808

Norbert Antiques
3617 Main St.
713/524-4334

Darby's Off-Memorial
12460 Memorial Dr.
713/465-0245

Antiques at Rummel Creek
13190 Memorial Dr.
713/461-9110

Antiques on Nineteenth
345 W. 19th St.
713/869-5030

C & H Antiques
10910 Old Katy Road
713/465-1120

Max Miller Antiques
10910 Old Katy Road
713/467-0450

Norman
2425 Ralph St.
713/521-1811

British Emporium
2121 W. Sam Houston Pkwy. N.
713/467-3455

General Mothers Antiques
2121 W. Sam Houston Pkwy. N.
713/984-9461

Cabin Creek Lodge
1703 Spring Cypress Road
713/350-5559

Mattye's This and That Antiques
14916 Stuebner Airline Road
713/580-4222

Abelar Antiques
6008 W. 34th St.
713/683-8055

Antq. Warehaus/Trash & Treasures
1714 Westheimer Road
713/522-6858

Old Blue House Antiques
1719 Westheimer Road
713/521-2515

Westheimer Antique Center
1738 Westheimer Road
713/529-8585

Past Era Antique Jewelry
2311 Westheimer Road
713/524-7110

Howard Graetz Antiques
1844 Westheimer Road
713/522-5908

Kay O'Toole Antiques
1921 Westheimer Road
713/523-1921

Antique Pavilion
2311 Westheimer Road
713/520-9755

David Lackey Antiques & China
2311 Westheimer Road
713/942-7171

Margaret K. Reese Antiques
2233 Westheimer
713/523-8889

Wicket Antique
2233 Westheimer Road
713/522-0779

Brownstone Gallery
2803 Westheimer Road
713/523-8171

The Market
4060 Westheimer Road
713/960-9084

Joyce Horn Antiques
1008 Wirt Road
713/688-0507

Carol Gibbins Antiques
1817 Woodhead St.
713/524-9011

John Holt Antiques & Primitives
2416 Woodhead St.
713/528-5065

House of Glass
3319 Louisiana St.
713/528-5289

Hillingham Antiques
1848 Westheimer Road
713/523-4335

River Oaks Antiques Center
2119 Westheimer Road
713/520-8238

Crow & Company
2311 Westheimer Road
713/524-6055

M. J. Fine Things
2311 Westheimer Road
713/529-6960

Florian Fine Art
2323 Westheimer Road
713/942-9919

R.N. Wakefield & Co.
2702 Westheimer Road
713/528-4677

Lewis & Maese Arts Antiques
3738 Westheimer Road
713/960-1454

Belgravia Antiques
11195 Westheimer Road
713/785-4797

Cottage Antiques
2233 Westheimer Road
713/523-8889

Golden Eye
2121 Woodhead St.
713/528-3379

Las Cruces Antiques
2422 Woodhead St.
713/524-2422

Studio
3951 San Felipe St.
713/961-7540

Historical Houston Heights

Whether you are seeking affordable antiques, an outstanding playground for the kids, or turn-of-the-century showplace homes, Houston Heights is the place to come. Founded in 1887, this planned streetcar community, designed to be a rural sanctuary from Houston, is located just four miles from downtown. A landmark for over a century, its main thoroughfare, Heights Boulevard, was modeled after Boston's Commonwealth Avenue and has been designated by the City of Houston as a "Scenic Right-of-Way." Victorian and early 20th century homes, churches, and a public library still line the Boulevard, and today an excellent walking trail exists along the esplanade where the trolley once ran. The spectacular new Heights Playground, a Robert Leathers design,

complete with a depot and Victorian castle, plus Marmion Park with its majestic gazebo, and the Victorian Rose Garden are all on the Boulevard. All three are maintained by Heights' neighborhood organization, the Houston Heights Association. In addition to the beauty and historical attractions of this area, the Heights also provides shoppers with a wealth of antique stores, clothing stores, folk art shops, and casual eateries.

Old Fashioned Things

811 Yale St.
713/880-8393
Email: harelec@swbell.net
Directions: Exit off I-10 West or 610 North Loop West - From I-10W take the Yale/Heights Blvd. exit and go north. From 610 N. Loop, take the Yale St. exit and go south.

Located in a cottage built in 1906, in the heart of the Historic Houston Heights, Old Fashioned Things is just four blocks north of Interstate 10, between downtown Houston and the Galleria area. Old Fashioned Things offers a truly unique shopping experience. Upon entering, you'll be greeted by the wonderful aromas of scented candles, potpourri, sachets, and oils that grace the tops and shelves of vintage curio cabinets, linen presses, and washstands from the turn of the century. The shop also features collectible furniture, lighting fixtures, textiles, French lace, frocks, glassware, and costume jewelry. A special section is reserved for infants and children, which includes garments, furniture, books, and toys. You'll find romantic gift items that complement the historic atmosphere, such as English friendship balls and Forever soaps.

Note from the proprietors: Laura and Dennis Virgadamo invite you to stop by and visit Monday through Saturday 10 a.m. to 6 p.m. or Sunday by appointment. They accept MasterCard, Visa, Discover and personal checks with proper identification. Layaways are welcome.

R & F Antiques

912 Yale St.
713/861-7750
Open: Sun.–Tues. by chance of appt., Wed.–Sat. 10–5:30
Directions: Located approximately 7 blocks north of I-10 at the Heights and Yale exit.

In this "barn" red building, you will find seven rooms brimming with American furniture. For more than 25 years, Gary & Jennifer Baroski have brought the finest quality antiques to the Houston area. The shop features curved glass china cabinets, tables, chairs, secretaries, beds, chests and an outstanding selection of fireplace mantels. The shop specializes in American antiques.

Note: I personally have not visited this shop, but I have been told by several serious collectors that it is one of the best shops in the country.

Texas

11th Street Antiques
720 W. 11th St.
713/802-2719

Chippendale Eastlake in Heights
250 W. 19th St.
713/869-8633

Byers Original Finishes
115 W. 13th St.
713/868-5937

Heights Antique Co-op
321 W. 19th St.
713/864-7237

Homestyle Resale
215 E. 11th St.
713/868-3400

John's Flowers & Antiques
373 W. 19th St.
713/862-8717

Sugar's Collectibles
249 W. 19th St.
713/868-7006

Twenty Second Second
611 W. 22nd St.
713/864-0261

Past Connections & Collectibles
235 West 19th St.
713/802-1992

Heights Country Store
801 Heights Blvd.
713/862-4161

Heights Collection
3617 White Oak Dr.
713/880-8203

On The Corner
837 Studewood St.
713/863-9143

Heights Antiques on Yale
2110 Yale
No phone listed

Alabama Furniture & Accessories
2200 Yale St.
713/862-3035

Antiques on Nineteenth
345 W. 19th St.
713/869-5030

Charm of Yesteryear Antiques
355 W. 19th St.
713/868-1141

Historic Heights Antqs. & Interiors
249 W. 19th St.
713/868-2600

Inside Outside
510 W. 18th St.
713/869-6911

Laroy Antqs. & Refurbishing, Inc.
632 W. 19th St.
713/862-5051

Stardust Antique
1129 E. 11th St.
713/868-1600

William & Mary's Antiques
605 W. 19th St.
713/864-7605

August Antiques
803 Heights Blvd.
713/880-3353

Everything Special
1906 Ashland
713/869-6906

Heights Station Antiques
121 Heights Blvd.
713/868-3175

Jubilee
242 W. 19th St.
713/869-5885

Edie's Sales, Unlimited
701 E. 20th St.
No phone listed

Great Places to Stay

Angel Arbor Bed and Breakfast Inn

848 Heights Blvd.
1-800-722-8788
Web site: www.angelarbor.com

Located on a tree-lined boulevard with jogging trails, this elegant Georgian-style inn is a local historic landmark. To visit Angel Arbor is to be magically returned to the early 1920s, to the stately brick residence

built originally for John and Katherine McTighe. The first floor of the inn boasts an antique filled parlor, reading room, formal dining room, and a sunroom for games or casual dining. A wicker furnished solarium overlooks the backyard garden, and artfully placed angel statue. Upstairs, three spacious bedrooms each contain queen bed and private bath. Also, a separate outside suite provides seclusion with a sitting room and deck.

79 HUMBLE

Spruce Goose Shoppes
620 2nd St.
281/540-7766

Granny Jean's Antiques
212 Charles St.
281/548-3020

80 HUNTSVILLE

Bluebonnet Square Antique Mall
1110 11th St.
409/291-2800

Fisher's Antiques
Hwy. 190
409/295-7661

Scottie's
1110 Sam Houston Ave.
409/291-9414

The Raven Antiques & Gallery
1204 Sam Houston Ave.
409/291-2723

Avalon Antiques
1215 Sam Houston Ave.
409/291-6097

Victorian House Antiques
Hwy. 19
409/295-3904

Good Old Days
604 S. Sam Houston Ave.
409/291-8407

Stone Wall Antiques
1202 Sam Houston Ave.
409/291-3422

Sam Houston Antique Mall
1210 Sam Houston Ave.
409/295-7716

81 HURST

Antiques Et Al
208 W. Bedford Euless Road
817/282-8197

Hurst Antique Mall
416 W. Bedford Euless Road
817/282-2224

Whistle Stop
1350 Brookside
817/282-3224

Country Express
245 W. Bedford Euless Road
817/282-9335

Antique Flea
431 W. Bedford Euless Road
817/285-8859

Antique Homestead
750 W. Pipeline Road
817/268-1527

82 IRVING

Antiques on Main Street
105 S. Main St.
972-259-1093

Timeless Treasures
111 S. Main St.
972-254-9007

Ken's Discount Antiques & Gifts
108 W. 6th St.
972/259-5505

Irving Antique Mall
129 S. Main St.
972/254-0339

Texas

Oliver's Used Books & Things
130 S. Main St.
972/253-1299

Patsy B
136 S. Main St.
972/254-1086

Kimberley's Antiques
247 Plymouth Park
972/986-5733

Nostalgia, Etc.
1120 Senter Road, Suite 102
972/554-6781

Debby's Emporium
929 E. 6th St.
972/438-5895

Ye Olde Shoppe
135 S. Main St.
972/254-0615

Yesterdaze Collectibles
304 W. Pioneer Dr.
972/253-6473

Moss Rose
510 E. 2nd St.
972/579-7491

B & E Ventures
410 E. 6th St.
972/253-7615

83 JACKSONVILLE

Treasure Cove Mall
2027 N. Jackson (Hwy. 69 N.)
903/586-6140
Open: Mon., Thurs.–Sat. 10–6, Sun. 12–5, closed Tues. & Wed.
Directions: Located on Hwy. 69 North approximately 2 miles from the intersection of Hwys. 69 & 79.

Treasure Cove Mall is an exceptional shop in the wares that it presents and for one very unique service. For seven years the mall has specialized in refinishing and restoring grand pianos! Three staff refinishers complete the "huge" task of turning your 1800s grand into a true masterpiece. Additionally, the shop provides caning and wicker repair. For those of you just wanting to shop, the mall offers an outstanding selection of quality antiques within its 10,000 square feet; Roseville, Weller, glassware, quilts, clocks, Coke collectibles, Blue Ridge, old tools and furnishings from formal to primitive are just a few of the items available from the mall's 50 dealers.

Smith Barret Antiques
531 N. Bolton St.
903/586-5123

Jackson Street Merchantile
1201 S. Jackson St.
903/586-0282

Ruffles
114 E. Commerce St.
903/586-0141

84 JASPER

The Cottage
337 College
409/384-7862

Past Time Antiques
Hwy. 96 S.
409/384-6440

Nancy Jane's
403 College
409/384-4781

Hwy. 63 Antiques
Hwy. 63
409/384-7324

Hearts & Flowers
209 E. Houston
409/384-2462

Hancock Drug Store
165 N. Main St.
409/384-2541

Treasures of Old
2573 N. Wheeler St.
409/384-9580

The Heart Of Things
126 E. Lamar
409/384-9374

S.E. Texas Antique Mall
2034 S. Wheeler St.
409/384-7078

85 JEFFERSON

Maison-Bayou Bed & Breakfast Plantation
300 Bayou St.
903/665-7600
Web site: www.maisonbayou.com
Open: Year-round
Rates $59–$135

This place is so wonderful we decided to use more text than usual — so therefore we opted to omit the directions. For specific directions from your location, please call Jan or Pete.

On the surface of your mind, it's sort of hard to connect Texas with Louisiana swamps and bayous — unless you live in east Texas — but if you think about it, or if you look at a map, you realize that east Texas butts right up to Louisiana and the two states sort of blur the lines between them for quite a ways into Texas. That's why you end up with such an anomaly like Maison-Bayou in Jefferson, Texas. Just over the Texas/Louisiana state line and northwest a bit from Shreveport, Jefferson itself sits on a river beside the Big Cypress Bayou.

Maison-Bayou, a Creole plantation, is located on the ancient riverbed of the Big Cypress, in the middle of 55 wooded acres, yet it is only a short walk or a very short drive to the center of historic downtown Jefferson. The main house is an authentic reproduction of an 1850s Plantation Overseer's House, which features heart of pine floors, pine walls and ceilings, natural gas burning lanterns in each room, and period antiques and fabrics. A full breakfast is served in the dining room. The cabins are architecturally styled after authentic slave quarter cabins, with modern amenities carefully mixed in. All cabins have private baths, and yes, they all have indoor plumbing — although the toilets are the old-fashioned pullchain variety — and individually controlled heat and air conditioning. Each cabin is located on the cypress alligator pond with a full view. Alligators are often spotted during the summer, while beaver and otters cavort in the pond during the winter.

Cabin One is the most authentically reproduced example of a slave cabin on the plantation, with cypress shake shingle roof, high pitched ceiling, wood walls and heart of pine floors. The hand-made four poster bed is full size and features a hand-made quilt. The cabin also provides a wood burning fireplace and a pier with a canoe.

Cabin Two features whitewashed walls, heart of pine floors and old-

Texas

style tin roof. The Mission style full-size wooden bed dates to the turn of the century and is adorned with a traditional quilt. Youth-size bunk beds are included in the cabin as well. Relax in the rocking chair and watch the beaver pond from the cabin.

Cabins Three and Four are built in the "dog trot" architectural style: two independent cabins having a common roofline, sharing a full-length front and back porch, separated by a six-foot-wide breezeway that runs the entire width between both cabins. Each cabin holds a primitive four-poster wooden bed, rocking chairs and tables with reading lamps.

Next choice for guests is the Robert E. Lee replica steamboat paddlewheeler, moored along the bank of the cypress pond. Guests sleep in a queen-size sleigh bed, and relax downstairs on the bow under a cooling ceiling fan. Or, they can climb the spiral staircase to the pilot's house and go outside for a view of the cypress pond, then stretch out for a sunbath on the deck!

Don't feel quite comfortable sleeping with the gators? For all you landlubbers, there are two railroad cars and three bunkhouses still available. First is the authentic private rail car. Here guests are surrounded by beautifully varnished wood walls and ceiling, accented by 20 windows and 2 skylights, giving a panoramic view of the woods and Big Cypress Bayou.

The riverfront caboose sits directly on the banks of Big Cypress Bayou. This old Frisco line caboose offers a full-size iron bed and a view of the river from the bed or from the observation windows.

The three bunkhouses are built on the old Jefferson to Marshall stagecoach road and, appropriately, overlook the corral where horses, a burro and a llama make their homes. Buck, doe and fawns graze in nearby pastures.

As if these unusual accommodations aren't enough to hold your interest, there are a multitude of activities for guests to enjoy. On-site events and catering include pig roasts, crawfish boils, barbecues, trail rides and hayrides, weddings and receptions, company outings, family gatherings, camp and church groups and birthday parties. Wonderful nature trails and excellent fishing holes are a favorite with guest.

Maison-Bayou is a one-stop pleasure destination in a setting that's like a page out of history or a good novel. Don't miss it!

Pride House
409 Broadway
1-800-894-3526
Rates $85–$110

Myth America lives in this former steamboat port of 2,200; in antique houses, behind picket fences, along brick streets and on Cypress Bayou. Step into 19th century small-town America as you walk through the doors of the finest homes in town, chug through the lillypads on the paddlewheel steamer, cheer the newlyweds leaving the church, listen to the gossip over catfish at the cafe, and find things at the hardware you haven't seen in years.

Located in the 19th century antique capital of Texas, Pride House Bed & Breakfast invites you to shop in dozens of antique shops by day and sleep in one at night!

Guests will find 10 rooms with private baths in this turn-of-the-century home with its 12-foot ceilings, stained glass windows, family steamboat memorabilia, antiques and heirlooms, original art, footed bathtubs and fireplaces. Their enticements include some statements that anyone would be hard-pressed to ignore: "Come on the weekend — we'll bake you a cake. Weekdays, we'll cut your rate. Every day we'll treat you like family — with hot or cold drinks whenever you like and breakfasts you'll never forget." These legendary breakfasts include things like their own Jefferson Pecan Coffee, Pears Praline, Not Eggsactly Benedict, Texas Bluebonnet Muffins and Strawberry Butter.

River City Mercantile
111 Austin St.
903/665-8270

Old Mill Antiques
210 E. Austin St.
903/665-8601

Country Corner
Hwy. 59 S.
903/665-8344

Jefferson Bottling Works
203 Polk St.
903/665-3736

Three Rivers Antiques
116 N. Walnut St.
903/665-8721

The Old Store I & Jefferson Fudge Co.
123 N. Walnut St.
903/665-3562

Golden Oldies
203A N. Polk
N/A

Petticoat Junktion
120 Polk
903/935-7322

Sweet Memories
Corner Walnut & Hwy. 49 E.
903/665-3533

Choices Antiques Mall
215 Polk
903/665-8504

Gold Leaf
207 N. Polk
903/665-2882

Jefferson General Store
113 E. Austin St.
903/665-8481

Liz-Beth's Antiques
216 W. Austin St.
903/665-8781

Granny Had It
114 N. Polk St.
903/665-3148

Old Store II
226 N. Polk St.
903/665-2422

Walnut Street Market
121 N. Walnut St.
903/665-8864

Old House Antiques
304 N. Walnut St.
903/665-8852

Jefferson Arts
607 E. Broadway
903/665-3174

Robbie's Music Machines
215 Polk
903/665-8533

Turner's Place
Hwy. 59 N.
903/665-2282

Cypress Cargo
120 W. Lafayette
903/665-1414

86 KATY

From Rags to Riches
5714 1st St.
281/391-8200

Country Village
5809 Hwy. Blvd.
281/391-2040

Limited Editions
2nd St.
281/391-1994

Classic Home Furnishings
5305 Hwy. Blvd.
281/391-7515

Decorative Treasures
5626 2nd St.
281/391-2299

87 KERRVILLE

Corner Post
1518 Broadway
830/792-3377

Grandma's House
200 S. Sidney Baker
830/896-8668

Water Street Antique Co.
820 Water St.
830/257-5044

Five Points Antiques
607 E. Lane
830/257-8424

Pampell's Antiques
701 Water St.
830/257-8484

88 LA PORTE

A Unique Store
300 W. Main St.
281/471-5551

Through The Ages
324 W. Main St.
281/470-6614

Roelof's Antiques
301 W. Main St.
281/471-3807

L & B Antiques
312 W. Main St.
281/470-8533

89 LAMPASAS

Country Collectables
1900 S. Hwy. 281
512/556-5686

Ashley's Antiques & Collectibles
523 E. 3rd St.
512/556-6555

Antique Emporium
406 S. Live Oak St.
512/556-6843

90 LEANDER

Trails End Bed & Breakfast
The B & B Store (gift shop)
12223 Trails End Road #7
512-267-2901 or 1-800-850-2901
Open: B & B open year-round
Rates $55–$170
Gift shop open year-round 1–5 — call for appointment
Directions: From IH 35 two miles out of Georgetown, take FM 1431 and go 11 8/10 miles to Trails End Road. Turn left onto Trails End and go 7/10

of a mile to the gravel road. There will be several mail boxes next to the gravel road. Turn left and go to where the road curves to the right. Keep on going around the curve and the B&B is a large gray house trimmed in white on the left. An appointment is needed. The inn is located on the north side of Lake Travis between Cedar Park, Jonestown, Austin and Leander.

This is the perfect place to go for a getaway weekend or vacation. Trails End is a country retreat located in the unique central Texas Hill Country. As innkeepers JoAnn and Tom Patty say, "There is nothing immediate you have to do at Trails End Bed & Breakfast." That means guests get to kick back and enjoy the porches, decks, the gazebo, the refreshing pool, walking in the woods or riding bikes.

Make it a family vacation — there's a private guesthouse for six and bring the boat or water toys for a splashing good time on nearby Lake Travis. For golfing guests, a number of golf courses are convenient. When the urge to explore hits, downtown Austin is just 35 minutes away, and Georgetown, Round Rock, Cedar Park, Lago Vista, Leander, Burnet and Salado are an easy drive.

Hitching Post
18643 FM 1431
512/267-9125

91 LEAGUE CITY

Hole in the Wall Antiques
447 Hwy. 3 S.
281/332-3953

Lee Holley's Antiques
1824 E. Main St.
281/332-5823

Past & Presents
809 E. Main St.
281/332-1517

92 LEWISVILLE

After Glow Antiques
417 E. Church St.
972/221-6907

Rare Bits Antiques
310 Lake Haven
972/420-4222

Corner Home Antique & Gallery
101 W. Main St.
972/219-0887

String of Pearls
104 W. Main St.
972/436-9337

Buttermilk Flats Antiques
565 E. Church St.
972/221-1993

Antiques, Etc.
180 Lewisville Plaza
972/436-5904

Victorian Rose Antiques
102 W. Main St.
972/221-7266

Old Red Tractor Antiques
109 W. Main St.
972/221-4022

Texas

Pepper Tree
112 W. Main St.
972/221-6345

Sample House
2403 S. Stemmons Freeway
972/315-0212

93 LIBERTY

Trinity River Trading Post
818 Commerce St.
409/336-3652

Liberty Bell Antique Co-Op
2040 Trinity St.
409/336-5222

94 LOCKHART

Royals Antiques
401 S. Commerce St.
512/398-6849

Lockhart Antique Emporium
119 W. San Antonio St.
512/398-4322

95 LONGVIEW

Blue Door Antiques
1311 Alphine St.
903/758-7592

Petticoat Lane Antiques
208 N. Center St.
903/757-8988

Betty's Antiques
414 E. Cotton St.
903/753-8204

Jean's Antiques
2111 S.E. Man Road
903/234-9011

Classic Collections
409 W. Loop #281
903/663-1028

Jean's Antiques
1809 E. Marshall Ave.
903/234-9010

Alice's Wonderland
3712 W. Marshall Ave.
903/295-1295

Link to the Past
100 W. Tyler St.
903/758-6363

Looking Glass Antique Mall
788 S. Mill
972/221-4022

Beverly's Then & Now
1806 Sam Houston St.
409/336-9005

Archway Antiques
113 N. Main St.
512/398-7001

George Preston's Antiques
205 N. Center St.
903/753-8041

Turner Antiques
211 E. College St.
903/758-2562

Antiques Traders
207 N. Court St.
903/758-9707

Frederick-Nila Jewelers
306 N. 4th St.
903/753-2902

Consignments by Carolyn
1003 E. Marshall Ave.
903/758-7211

Linda's Best of Both Words
2713 W. Marshall Ave.
903/759-4422

Gifts of Distinction
4005 W. Marshall Ave.
903/759-6055

Treasures at Uptown Mall
106 W. Tyler St.
903/757-4425

Christie's Collectibles
113 W. Tyler St.
903/234-0816

96 LUBBOCK

Antique Mall of Lubbock
7907 W. 19th St.
806/796-2166
Directions: From I-27 take Loop 289 to West 19th St. (Levelland Hwy. 114W). Continue west on 19th Street 3 miles and look for the Big Yellow Awning on the south side of the highway.
General Information: "The Source For Dealers" open 7 days a week from 10–6 with over 24,000 square feet with 150 quality showcases and 80 fabulous booths specializing in "Hard to Find" Americana antiques and collectibles.

If you're an Antique Lover, this is one antique mall you truly don't want to miss! No brag, but they are told almost daily by dealers who travel the country that the Antique Mall of Lubbock is the BEST MALL they have ever been to. In addition, the Lubbock area has exploded with 5 malls and over 40 shops in the immediate area. Here are some of the collectibles you will find at the Antique Mall of Lubbock.

*Booth 7 - "Jennie Lee's Red Wing Shop" specializing in all types of pottery and stoneware especially some of the most fantastic pieces of Red Wing you will ever find!

*Booth 8 - "Dick Tarr's Treasures" specializes in a general line of furniture and collectibles including fine porcelain, carnival glass and one of the largest selections of Ertl banks in the Southwest!

*Booth 14 - Emma Ward's "Collectors Corner" specializes in all types of glass and dinnerware, including Depression and Elegant Glassware, Franciscan, Fiesta and Coors Rosebud.

*Booth 29 - Joyce Cheatham's "Bagladi's" booth has 1000s of small collectibles of every description imaginable.

*Booth 36 - "Chris' Collectibles" booth includes dolls of every description plus hundreds of toys and figures from the baby boom era.

*Booth 28 - "Ray Summer's Western Booth" has anything western related plus tools, farm and ranch related items.

*Booth 55 - "DR & Co. Collectibles" carries a general line of all types of furniture, toy trains, fountain pens, tins, toys, books, sports memorabilia, black memorabilia and much more.

*Booth 59 - "RB's General Store" specializing in quality advertising, old store stock and anything unusual and hard to find. Expect to be impressed with quality and quantity! Catering to Quantity Buyers!!

*Booth 99 - "Nina's Treasures" has a HUGE quantity of general line antiques and collectibles of every description from small to large that are fabulous!

The booths listed above are just a few mentioned, but you can't miss "Papa's Pharmacy" which includes old drug store merchandise in pristine condition, "Shane's General Store" that has thousands of old store stock merchandise that are unbelievable - A MUST TO SEE, "Clay's Cowboy Hideaway," "Cory's Sport Booth," "Nina's Elegant Booth," "Kristy's Kitchen," "Logan's Blue Room," "Matt's Oil Booth," "Timmy's Coke Collectibles," and many more.

The Antique Mall has been voted by the people of Lubbock and the Lubbock area as the BEST ANTIQUE MALL four years in a row! This speaks volumes — so don't miss out!

Garden Patch
1311 Alcove Ave.
806/793-0982

Mandrell's Antiques & Collectibles
5628 Brownfield Hwy.
806/799-0172

Carey Me Away Antiques
2309 E. 50th St.
806/765-0160

Antiques and More
3407 50th St.
806/791-1691

Flea Market
2323 K Ave.
806/747-8281

Glass Hut
7323 W. 19th St.
806/791-1260

Lucky's World Antique Market
3612 P Ave.
806/744-2524

Clark's Collectibles
2610 Salem Ave.
806/799-4747

Vintage Rose
2610 Salem Ave.
806/793-7673

Antiques Galleria
1001 E. Slaton Road
806/745-3336

Antiques Lubbock
2217 34th St.
806/763-5177

Pat's Antiques
2257 34th St.
806/747-4798

As Time Goes By
4426 34th St.
806/795-0840

Bobo's Treasures
202 S Ave.
806/744-6449

Treasure Chest Antiques
2226 Buddy Holly
806/744-0383

Katz in the Alley
2712 50th St.
806/795-9252

Finishing Touch
1401 N. Gary Ave.
806/762-2754

Train Station Antiques
6105 19th St.
860/788-0603

As Time Goes By
4426 34th St.
806/795-0840

Chaparral Antique Mall
2202 Q Ave.
806/747-5431

Old Time Clock Shop
2610 Salem Ave.
806/797-8203

Ruth Little Art & Antiques
3402 73rd St.
806/792-0485

J. Patrick's Antiques & Collectibles
2206 34th St.
806/747-6731

The Cottage
2247 34th St.
806/744-3927

Antique Marketplace
2801 26th St.
806/785-1531

97 LUFKIN

Lufkin Antique Mall
118 N. 1st St.
409/634-9119

Paul Nerren's Junk Barn
4500 U.S. Hwy. 59 N.
409/632-2580

Warehouse Antiques
Hwy. 59 N.
409/632-5177

Carousel Antiques
302 N. Raguet & Frank St.
409/639-4025

98 LULING

Cripple Creek Mine
517 E. Davis St.
210/875-5062

Welcome Back Antiques
711 E. Davis St.
210/875-3738

99 MARBLE FALLS

Antiques Plus
1000 W. Hwy. 1431
830/693-3301

Main Street Emporium
204 Main St.
830/693-7037

Carol's Cottage
108 Main St.
830/693-7668

100 MARSHALL

La Trouvaille
203 W. Austin St.
903/938-2006

101 MASON

Country Collectibles
Hwy. 87 N.
915/347-5249

Antique Emporium
106 S. Live Oak
915/347-5330

Angelina Antique Gallery
205 Herndon St.
409/634-4272

Kinard's Antiques & Collectibles
5151 U.S. Hwy. 59 N.
409/634-6933

Wishing Well Antiques & Gifts
901 S. John Redditt Dr.
409/632-4707

Trinkets, Treasures & Trash
519 E. Davis St.
210/875-9100

Natures Nest Unique Gift Shop
946 E. Pierce St.
210/875-2383

Wise Owl
3409 Hwy. 281
830/693-3844

Past & Presents
700 Main St.
830/693-8877

Antiques 'n' Things
214 S. Lafayette St.
903/935-3339

Underwood's Antique Mall
100 N. Live Oak
915/347-5258

P.V. Antiques
Ft. McKevett
915/347-5496

102 McKINNEY

Iron Kettle Antiques
Hwy. 5
972/542-4903

Affordable Antiques & More
719 N. Kentucky St.
972/562-5551

Antique House
212 E. Louisiana St.
972/562-0642

Remember This Antiques
210 N. Tennessee St.
972/542-8011

Pat Parker's Art Antiques
108 W. Virginia St.
972/562-6571

Treasures from the Past
115 E. Virginia St.
972/548-0032

The McAllister Collection
101 N. Kentucky St.
972/562-9497

One of a Kind
214 N. Kentucky St.
972/542-7977

Duffy's Antiques
202 E. Louisiana St.
972/542-5980

McKinney Antiques
112 N. Tennessee St.
972/548-8044

Victorian Corner
100 W. Virginia St.
972/548-9898

Town Square Antiques
113 E. Virginia St.
972/542-4113

Antique Company Mall
213 E. Virginia St.
972/548-2929

103 MEMPHIS

Grandmaw's Attic
5th & Main St.
806/259-2575

Crafts & Collectibles
315 Hwy. 287 N.
806/259-3817

Ivy Cottage
121 N. 5th St.
806/259-3520

104 MESQUITE

Antique Plus
2611 N. Belt Line Road
972/226-6300

The Dusty Attic
3330 N. Galloway Ave.
972/613-5093

Sharon's Main St. Antiques
120 E. Main St.
972/329-3147

Emporium at Big Town
950 Big Town Shopping Center
214/690/6996

Missing Pieces
109 W. Main St.
972/288-3513

105 MIDLAND

ABC Antiques
110 Andrews Hwy.
915/682-4595

Geri's Antiques & Fine Linens
307 Dodson St.
915/687-2660

Cat's Meow
408 Andrews Hwy.
915/687-2004

Antiques by Josephs
325 Dodson St.
915/687-3040

Old Town Antiques
329 Dodson St.
915/570-0588

Antiques, Etc.
2101 W. Wadley Ave.
915/682-9257

Motif
2101 W. Wadley Ave.
915/683-4331

Craft's Bazaar
3712 W. Wall St.
915/689-8852

106 MINEOLA

Places in the Heart
111 E. Broad St.
903/569-9096

Unique Mall
124 E. Broad St.
903/569-9321

Heirloom Shoppe
119 E. Commerce St.
903/569-0835

Country Girls Antiques
110 S. Johnson St.
903/569-6007

The Brownstone Mall
408 S. Pacific St.
903/569-6890

107 MINERAL WELLS

Wynnwood Village Antiques Mall
2502 U.S. Hwy. 180 E.
940/325-9791

Down Memory Lane
201 E. Hubbard St.
940/328-0609

Richey's Antiques & Uniques
1201 E. Hubbard St.
940/325-5940

Wild Rose Antiques
213 N. Oak Ave.
940/325-9502

Anita's Antiques
307 N. Oak Ave.
940/325-1455

Judy Jackson's Bargain Barn
2420 W. Front St.
915/682-0227

Laura's Things Finer
2101 W. Wadley Ave.
915/683-4422

Yesterdays News Antique Mall
3712 W. Wall St.
915/689-6373

Broad Street Mall
118 E. Broad St.
903/569-0806

Beckham Hotel Antique Mall
115 E. Commerce St.
903/569-0835

Main Street Emporium
102 S. Johnson St.
903/569-0490

Roses and Relics
219 N. Newsom St.
903/569-9890

Durham Antiques
1823 N. Pacific St.
903/569-2916

Thurmon's Bargain Barn
3703 N. Hwy. 281
940/325-1695

Mama Jo's Treasures
800 E. Hubbard St.
940/328-0043

Sarah Jane's Antiques & Crafts
115 N. Oak Ave.
940/325-3005

Century Corner Antiques
225 N. Oak Ave.
940/325-2525

108 MONTGOMERY

Antique Emporium
404 Eva
409/597-6903

Westlake Antqs. & Old Book Shop
25400 Hwy. 105 W.
409/582-6829

Liberty Bell Antiques
207 Liberty
409/597-4606

Olde Towne Montgomery
208 Liberty
409/597-5922

The Old Post Office & Drugstore Antiques
210 Liberty
409/597-4400

109 MOUNT PLEASANT

Odds and Ends Shop
100 W. Alabama St.
903/572-2802

Browns Country Attic
1705 W. Ferguson Road
903/577-9240

Classic Place
2000 W. Ferguson Road
903/572-6667

Antiques & Uniques
109 N. Madison Ave.
903/572-1545

Grand Nanny's Attic II Antiques
115 N. Madison Ave.
903/572-7081

A Little Bit of Country
Union Hill Road
903/572-3173

Jo's Antiques
Union Hill Road
903/572-3173

110 MUNDAY

Memories of Munday Mall
110 E. Main St.
940/422-5400
Open: Mon.–Sat. 10–6, Sun., 1–5
Directions: Memories of Munday is located at the intersection of Hwy. 277 and Hwy. 222 in downtown Munday, Texas, which is approximately midway between Abilene and Wichita Falls (75 miles).

Located in the early 1900s community of Munday, the Memories of Munday Mall offers a varied selection of items from ten area dealers. Furniture, glassware, costume jewelry, and collectibles as well as a nice selection of vintage linens are displayed for your appeal.
News Alert: The shop features Ty Beanie Babies and will ship to you anywhere in the world!

Schoolmarm Antiques
210 W. Main St.
940/422-4474

111 NACOGDOCHES

Bremond Doll Shoppe
416 Bremond St.
409/569-9676

K.H. Newman Antiques
7144 Center Road
409/564-0820

Sparks Antiques
276 Community Road
409/564-4838

Aubrey's Main Shoppe
1523 E. Main St.
409/569-7962

Antique Market
412 E. Main St.
409/564-8294

Moth Nest Vintage Clothing
2012 E. Main St.
409/560-5114

Laurel's Antiques
4705 North St.
409/569-6290

Old Pillar St. Antiques
108 E. Pillar St.
409/564-6888

Nanny's Antiques
Hwy. 259
409/564-2433

Squash Blossom Colony Mall
209 E. Main St.
409/560-1788

Sloane's Antiques
413 E. Main St.
409/559-0013

Pineapple Post
102 North St.
409/564-8285

Xavier Sanders Antiques
116 N. Pecan St.
409/560-3131

112 NAVASOTA

Past & Present
119 E. Washington Ave.
409/825-7545

Twin Oaks Antique Mall
716 E. Washington Ave.
409/825-1837

Downtown Antique Mall
207 E. Washington Ave.
409/825-8588

113 NEW BRAUNFELS

Hopes Carousel
147 E. Faust St.
830/629-8113

Lee's Antiques
125 Hwy. 81 W.
830/629-7919

Gruene Antique Company
1607 Hunter Road.
830/629-7781

Hampe House
1640 Hunter Road
830/620-1325

New Braunfels Log Haus Antiques
469 IH 35 S.
830/629-3774

New Braunfels Emporium Nostalgia
209 W. San Antonio St.
830/608-9733

Downtowner Antique Mall
223 W. San Antonio St.
830/629-3947

Palace Heights Antiques Mall
1175 Hwy. 81 E.
830/625-0612

Second Time Around
870 S. State Hwy. 46
830/629-6542

Gruene General Store
1610 Hunter Road
830/629-6021

Cactus Jack's Antiques, Etc.
1706 Hunter Road
830/620-9602

Front Porch Antiques & Gifts
471 Main Plaza
830/629-0660

Good Pickins
219 E. San Antonio St.
830/625-9330

Voigt House Antiques
308 E. San Antonio St.
830/625-7072

Texas

Vicky's Antiques
719 W. San Antonio St.
830/625-2837

Dan's Collectables
921 S. Seguin Ave.
830/629-3267

114 ODESSA

A Antique Shoppe
402 E. 8th St.
915/333-1718

Chez La Nae Fine Furnishings
5701 Austin Ave.
915/550-3106

The Brass Lamp/Antique Auto Museum
709 S. Grandview
915/332-9875

115 ORANGE

Nana & Poppie's Antiques
3834 W. Park Ave.
409/883-6941

Pat's This & That
2490 Martin Luther King Jr. Dr.
409/883-7215

Country Porch
521 S. Hwy. 87
409/883-6503

116 PALESTINE

Linda's Antiques
3913 W. Oak St.
903/729-1448

Vintage House
616 W. Palestine Ave.
903/729-7133

Shelton Gin Antiques & Sandwich Shop
310 E. Crawford St.
903/729-7530

117 PAMPA

L & P Interiors
110 S. Cuyler
806/665-3243'

Call Antiques
620 W. Francis Ave.
806/665-1391

Trash & Treasure Shop
1425 N. Hobart St.
806/669-6601

Headrick Country Home Antiques
697 S. Seguin Ave.
830/625-1624

Be-Bops
1077 S. Seguin Ave.
830/625-6056

D & D Antiques
2210 W. 416 46th St.
915/367-9427

Country Mercantile
6108 Ector Ave.
915/363-8909

Wagon Wheel Antiques
6070 W. University Blvd.
915/381-6638

Antiques & Uniques
2207 Macarthur Dr.
409/883-7989

This Ol' House Co-Op
3433 Martin St.
409/883-3991

Parlours
902 10th St.
409/886-0146

Barbara Hardens Antiques
Hwy. 84 E.
903/729-6604

J's Music & Antiques
400 N. Queen St.
903/729-3144

Yesterday's Treasures
618 W. Francis Ave.
806/665-9449

J&B Antiques & Used Books
302 W. Foster Ave.
806/665-8415

Collectors Corner
2216 N. Hobart St.
806/665-3246

Cottage Collection
922 W. 23rd Ave.
806/665-4398

118 PARIS

Kaufman Korner Mall
134 1st St. S.W.
903/784-6012

Curiosity
101 Grand Ave.
903/739-2716

Blackburn's Antiques
Hwy. 82 E.
903/785-0862

Reflections of Ducharme
6335 Lamar Ave.
903/784-3823

Junk Lady Antiques
286 N.E. Loop #286
903/785-2513

119 PASADENA

Heritage Collectables & Antiques
3207 Preston Road
281/998-2775

Stuff and Such
1615 Richey
281/473-6144

Country Roads Antiques
1415 Southmore Ave.
281/473-2092

Stephanie's Antique Furniture
5220 Spencer Hwy.
281/487-3900

120 PEARLAND

Cole's Antique Village
1014 N. Main St.
281/485-2277

Country Merchant Antiques
14602 Suburban Garden Road
281/997-1319

121 PHARR

Eva's Antiques
508 N. Cage Blvd.
210/787-6457

Socorros Antiques
620 W. Ferguson St.
210/702-0494

Antiques by Winona
138 Clarksville St.
903/784-4862

Paris Antique Mall
Hwy. 19/Hwy. 24
903/785-0872

Great Expectations
7 Lamar Ave.
903/784-4499

Reno Antique Mall
6720 Lamar Ave.
903/737-9904

Saffle Antique Mall
20 N. Plaza
903/785-8446

Collectors Corner
701 Houston Ave.
281/473-9345

A-1 Antiques
1905 Shaver St.
281/472-3777

Antique Junction
111 W. Southmore Ave.
281/473-9824

A Dream Come True
2316 N. Main St.
281/997-6468

Bygones by Guy Antiques
119 W. Park St.
210/702-4661

Memories Antiques & Mall
1311 W. Hwy. 495
210/781-4881

122 PITTSBURG

Charlotte's Market St. Antiques
1 Market St.
903/856-2577

All Occasions Mall
122 & 128 Quitman St.
903/856-3285

Rick's Antiques Safari
121 Quitman St.
903/856-6929

123 PLAINVIEW

Old World Antiques
431 Broadway St.
806/293-3118

Antiques by Billie
609 Broadway St.
806/293-9407

Shoppe
707 Broadway St.
806/296-2201

Moore's Lantern Antiques
1406 Joliet St.
806/296-6270

Horton Antiques & Collectibles
607 Broadway St.
806/293-7054

Uniques and Antiques
615 Broadway St.
806/293-7826

Harman-Y House Antiques
815 Columbia St.
806/296-2505

Second Story Antiques & Cllbls.
403 Yonkers St.
806/296-5444

124 PLANO

Antiqueland
1300 Custer Road
972/509-7878

Blue Goose
1007 E. 15th St.
972/881-9295

Main Street Gifts & Antiques
1024 E. 15th St.
972/578-0486

Sherwood House
3100 Independence Pkwy.
972/519-0194

History House Antiques
1408 J Ave.
972/423-2757

The Market
4709 W. Parker
972/596-2699

Blue Goose
3308 Preston Road, Suite 315
972/985-5579

English Pine Co.
3000 Custer Road, Suite 220
972/596-4096

Simple Country Pleasures
1013 E. 15th St.
972/422-0642

Ann's Place
1025 E. 15th St.
972/422-5306

Cobwebs Antiques Mall
1400 J Ave.
972/423-8697

Nanny Granny's Antique Museum
1408 J Ave.
972/423-3552

Sample House
1900 Preston Road
972/985-1616

125 ROCKPORT

Bent Tree Galleries
504 S. Austin St.
512/729-4822

Harcrows
S. Hwy. 188
512/729-1724

Moore Than Feed
902 W. Market St.
512/729-4909

Mary Ann's Antiques
1005 E. Main St.
512/729-1945

126 ROCKWALL

Lakeview Lodge Antiques
706 S. Goliad St.
972/722-0219

Rockwall Antiques
212 E. Rusk St.
972/722-1280

Bountiful
708 S. Goliad St.
972/722-1313

Past Times Antiques & Collectibles
214 E. Rusk St.
972/771-8100

127 ROSENBERG

Back When Antiques
2615 Ave. H
281/342-0601

Walgers Cottage
1030 Lawrence
281/232-6421

Memory Shoppe
931 3rd St.
281/232-7353

Baker's Woods & Wares
3117 Ave. I
281/232-7733

Old Town Antiques
828 3rd St.
281/232-2125

Nearby Antique Shopping (Wallace)
Wallace is located 18 miles from Rosenburg.

Country Rose
6321 Commerce
409/478-6193

Third Generation Antiques
6405 Commerce
409/478-6884

Dolly's
6417 Hwy. 36
409/478-7563

J.J.'s Stuff 'n' Such
6535 Commerce
409/478-7232

Encore and More
Old City Meat Market
409/478-6373

Wallace Flea Market
6715 Hwy. 36
409/478-6126

128 ROUND ROCK

Antique Mall of Texas
1601 S. I-35
512/218-4290

Wooten & Son
1401 Sam Bass Road
512/255-1447

129 ROUND TOP

Emma Lee Turney's Antiques Productions
P.O. Box 821289
Houston, TX 77282-1289
281/493-5501 or 281/293-0320
Email: turnyshows@aol.com

Twice each year Emma Lee Turney brings outstanding antiques shows to the Round Top area. Billed as one of the largest antiques fairs in the

Texas

nation, the show attracts dealers and buyers from across the United States and abroad. Emma Lee has recently written a book on her antiquing adventures.

Royers Round Top Cafe
"On the Square"
1-800-624-PIES

Cut through the backroads between Houston and Austin to find the tiny town of Round Top and one of the smallest town squares in America. Here you'll find three antique shops and Royers' Cafe which serves some of the best "sophisticated" food in the country.

My favorite—the ribs, along with buttermilk pie (the best I've ever eaten). The cafe also offers fresh salmon, grilled quail, chicken and a variety of pasta dishes.

130 SALADO

Antique Jewelry & Collectables
N. Main St.
254/947-9161

Fletcher's Books & Antiques
Main St.
254/947-5414

Hutchens House
369 N. Main St.
254/947-8177

Recollection Antiques
Royal & Center
254/947-0067

Red Barn Antique Center
90050 B Royal
254/947-1050

Main Street Place
3 Salado Square
254/947-9908

Classic Antiques
N. Main St.
254/947-0604

Salado Country Antiques
Main St.
254/947-8363

Salado Antique Mall
550 N. Main St.
254/947-1010

Royal Emporium
Royal & Main St.
254/947-5718

Spring House Antiques
Royal
254/947-0747

131 SAN ANGELO

Consignments, Etc.
109 S. Chadbourne St.
915/658-6480

June's Folly
202 S. Chadbourne St.
915/655-9459

Hard Time Post
915 N. Chadbourne St.
915/657-0905

Jewel of the Concho
10 E. Concho Ave.
915/653-8782

Grammy's Corner
117 S. Chadbourne St.
915/655-8400

Arclight Antiques
230 S. Chadbourne St.
915/653-8832

S & R Trading Post
4736 N. Chadbourne St.
915/655-5087

J. Wilde
15 E. Concho Ave.
915/655-0878

Sassy Fox
34 E. Concho Ave.
915/658-8083

Cactus Patch
108 E. Concho Ave.
915/655-1456

Hodgepodge Antiques
114 Hardeman Pass
915/655-5148

Centerpiece Antiques
Municipal Airport Lobby
915/949-9078

Treasure Trunk
37 W. Twohig Ave.
915/658-6697

132 SAN ANTONIO

Plantiques
1319 Austin Hwy.
210/824-2634

Pristine Peacock Estate Jewelry
555 W. Bitters Road
210/494-6230

Halfmoon Antique Mall, Inc.
112 Broadway St.
210/212-4401

Land of Was
3119 Broadway St.
210/822-5265

Pat Pritchard Antiques & Folkware
5405 Broadway St.
210/829-5511

Hugh Lackey Antiques
3505 Broadway St.
210/829-5048

Marshall's Brocante
8505 Broadway St.
210/804-6320

Chicago Connection
8505 Broadway St.
210/804-6322

Affordable Antiques
8934 Broadway St.
210/822-9600

Lasting Impressions
600 & 606 W. Hildebrand Ave.
210/737-9130

Abbey's Antiques
1503 W. Hildebrand Ave.
210/732-5266

Confetti Antique Mall
42 E. Concho Ave.
915/655-3962

Traders Mall
79 E. 14th St.
915/655-9617

American British Antiques
746 U.S. Hwy. 87 S.
915/651-4873

Vi's Country Village
5270 Old Christoval Road
915/651-9088

Washington Square
230 W. Washington
915/658-5765

Charlotte's Antiques & Clocks
2015 Austin Hwy.
210/653-3672

Blanco Fulton Antiques
1701 Blanco Road
210/737-7208

Alamo Antique Mall
125 Broadway St.
210/224-4354

Lion & Eagle
3511 Broadway St.
210/826-3483

Christo's
5921 Broadway St.
210/820-0424

J. Adelman Antiques & Art
7601 Broadway St.
210/822-5226

Center for Antiques
8505 Broadway St.
210/804-6300

San Antonio's Center for Antiques
8505 Broadway St.
210/804-6300

Bobs Gifts & Antiques
3461 Fredericksburg Road
210/734-9007

Antiques on Hildebrand
521 W. Hildebrand Ave.
210/734-9337

Barn Haus
26610 U.S. Hwy. 281 N.
210/980-7678

Antiques Downtown Mall
515 E. Houston St.
210/224-8845

Antique Connection
4119 McCullough Ave.
210/822-4119

J. Adelman Antiques & Estate Jewelry
Mengu Hotel at Alamo Plaza
210/225-5914

Gas Light Antique Shoppe
208 E. Park Ave.
210/227-4803

Dear Things
8324 Pat Booker Road
210/590-3003

River Square Antiques, Gifts & Collectibles
514 River Walk St.
210/224-0900

Accents Antiques & Design
119 W. Sunset Road
210/826-4500

Different Drummer
1020 Townsend Ave.
210/826-3764

Echoes from the Past
517 E. Houston St.
210/225-3714

Timeless Treasures, Inc.
4343 McCullough Ave.
210/829-7861

Main Place for Antiques
102 W. Mistletoe Ave.
210/736-4900

York's Furniture Annex
306 E. Park Ave.
210/226-1248

Greenlight Antiques
13316 O'Connor Road
210/590-6107

Moran Antiques & Appraisals
2119 San Pedro Ave.
210/734-5668

Treasures & Trifles, Inc.
210 W. Sunset Road
210/824-9381

Ivy Cottage Antiques & Collectibles
407 8th St.
210/224-2597

Great Places to Stay

The Columns on Alamo
1037 S. Alamo St.
210/271-3245 or 1-800-233-3364
Open: Daily 8–9
Directions: From I-37, take Exit #140B (Durango Street) at the Alamodome, and go 2 blocks from the freeway westbound on Durango to Alamo St. Turn right and go south on Alamo five blocks to the corner of Sheridan St. and Alamo.

Innkeepers Ellenor and Art Link decided to open their elegant and stunning home as a bed and breakfast in 1994. The massive house is an 1892 Greek Revival home and they also use the adjacent 1901 guesthouse as part of the inn. Located in the historic King William District near the trolley, the inn offers 11 guest rooms, all with private baths, furnished with Victorian antiques and period reproductions. Guests can share the common areas in both houses and on the landscaped grounds.

The Links are resident innkeepers and are always ready and able to suggest excursion itineraries, dining and shopping forays for guests, and to help in planning which cultural and seasonal events to attend. They prepare their guests for the day's adventures with a full breakfast served in the main house.

When staying at The Columns, guests will be within easy walking distance to the River Walk, the Alamo, the Convention center, Southtown

restaurants and shops, La Villita, German Heritage Park and Rivercenter Mall. It's only a short drive from The Columns to the Spanish Mission Trail, San Antonio Alamodome, Sea World, Fiesta Texas and the Lone Star Brewery and Hall of Horns.

Falling Pines Inn
300 W. French Place
210/733-1998
Rates: $100-150

This is an interesting place in an already interesting city — a purely luxurious bed and breakfast in an historic home that caters to the upscale crowd. Construction of Falling Pines began in 1911, under the plans and directions of famed architect Atlee Ayeres. Pine trees, not native to San Antonio, tower over the mansion on a one-acre, park-like setting in the Monte Vista Historic District, one mile north of downtown San Antonio.

The house itself is a combination of brick and limestone, with a green tiled roof, shuttered windows, and a magnificent limestone archway entrance and veranda on the front facade. The entry level has six rooms with quarter-cut oak paneling, wood floors, oriental carpets, fireplaces and a tiled solarium where breakfast is served. The large and elegantly appointed guest rooms are on the second level. The third level is entirely one suite, the 2,000 square foot Persian Suite that commands a grand view of downtown San Antonio and the nearby Koehler Mansion, home of a beer baron. The Persian Suite has two large, private balconies and a luxurious private bath, and is draped in miles and miles of material, reminiscent of exotic Persian tents.

133 SAN MARCOS

Ashley's Attic
2201 Hunter Road
512/754-0165

Antique Outlet Mall
4200 IH 35 S.
512/392-5600

Paper Bear Heartworks Co.
214 N. LBJ Dr.
512/396-2283

Partin's Second Tyme Furniture
2108 RR 12
512/396-4684

Centerpoint Station
3946 IH 35 S.
512/392-1103

Maudie's Antiques
202 N. LBJ Dr.
512/396-8999

Anchor Antiques
360 S. LBJ Dr.
512/353-3995

Partin's II
2300 RR 12
512/396-2777

Texas

Great Places to Stay

Crystal River Inn
326 W. Hopkins
512/396-3739
Open: Year-round
Directions: Crystal River Inn is located in San Marcos, off I-35 at Exit #205. Exit #205 is Hopkins Street

With 13 guest rooms to choose from, visitors will enjoy this Texas inn that has garnered three stars in the Mobil Travel Guide. The inn itself is a romantic, luxurious Victorian mansion set in the middle of Texas hill country. It's close to the headwaters of the crystal clear San Marcos River — hence the name — and is filled with antiques, fireplaces and fresh flowers. There are gardens and fountains, a wicker-strewn veranda, and the beautiful outdoors. Gourmet breakfasts and brunches include such delectable items as stuffed French toast and bananas Foster crepes. Mystery weekends, river trips and romantic getaways are the hosts' specialty.

134 SEABROOK

Glory to God Antiques
1417 Bayport Blvd.
281/474-3639

Another Era
909 Hardesty Ave.
281/474-7208

Picket Fence
3010 Hwy. 146
281/474-4845

Old Seabrook Antique Mall
1002 Meyer Road
281/474-4451

Victorian Rose
909 Hall Ave.
281/474-1214

Town & Country Antiques
913 Hardesty Ave.
281/474-2779

Carousel Antiques
1002 Meyer Road
281/474-4451

Marilyn's Antiques
1402 2nd St.
281/474-4359

135 SEALY

Sealy Sampler Antiques
419 Hardeman St.
409/885-3349

Country Antiques
121 Meyer Road
409/885-7976

Sealy Antique Center
663 Hwy. 90 E.
409/885-6556

Classic Collections
223 Fowlkes St.
409/885-7930

Antique Shop
413 Meyer St.
409/885-0285

Lillys Antiques
502 N. Meyer St.
409/885-4040

136 SEGUIN

Art-Iques by Ken Miller
106 N. Austin St.
210/379-3209

A Wild Hare
112 W. Court St.
210/372-4822

Antique Trading Post
1530 N. State Hwy. 46
210/303-2037

Blue Hills Antique Mall
6832 N. State Hwy. 123
210/379-2059

Affordable Antiques
6771 N. State Hwy. 123
210/303-3135

137 SEYMOUR

Granny's Stuff
101 S. Main St.
940/888-2213

See More Antiques & Collectibles
910 N. Main St.
940/888-2689

Hogues
300 S. Main St.
940/888-2511

Classics
1620 Main St.
940/552-0672

138 SHERMAN

A Touch of Class Antique Mall
118 W. Lamar St.
903/891-9379 or 972/529-5206
Open: Mon.–Sat. 9:30–5:30, Sun. 12:30–5
Directions: From Hwy. 75, take exit #58 (Lamar Street). Go to the second stoplight on the southwest corner of the downtown square, across from the Courthouse.

A Touch of Class Antique Mall offers fine antique furniture, quality glassware, and a large variety of collectibles and primitives in this historic furniture store which was the pride of the Red River Valley for over 100 years.

From the top dealers in the Southwest, you will find a large selection of tin toys, fire department, railroad, fishing and golf memorabilia. Imported antiquities from China, England, France and more complete the exquisite offerings at A Touch of Class Antique Mall.

Elm House Antiques
710 N. Elm St.
903/892-4418

Bobby Denes Antiques & Vintage
333 W. Jones St.
903/892-4272

Kelly Square Antiques
115 S. Travis
903/868-1771

Ray Bob Antiques
220 W. Houston
903/892-8745

Donna's Corner
308 E. Houston St.
903/813-0044

Sherman Antique Mall
221 S. Travis
903/892-1225

Pieces of the Past
901-B E. Lamar
903/868-2253

Texas

139 SINTON

Country Cornerstone Co-Op
207 W. Sinton St.
512/364-5756

Gwen's Antiques
223 E. Sinton St.
512/364-1165

140 SMITHVILLE

Alum Creek Antique Center
W. Hwy. 71
512/237-3817

Cedar Chest Antiques
W. Hwy. 71
512/237-3817

Silver Fox Antiques
W. Hwy. 71
512/237-4825

House of Antiques
116 Main St.
512/237-4393

Century House
119 Main St.
512/237-5549

Crystal's Corner
204 Main St.
512/237-3939

Main St. Village
216 Main St.
512/237-2323

Simply Country
106 N.E. 2nd St.
512/237-2038

Wild Rose Antiques
108 N.E. 2nd St.
512/237-5122

141 SNYDER

Known as the "Land of the White Buffalo," Snyder is where buffalo hunter J. Wright Mooar killed one of only seven white buffalo ever seen in the U.S. The original hide is on display at the ranch home of Mooar's granddaughter Judy Hays, who hosts the huge White Buffalo Festival annually in October. Another favorite for visitors to Snyder is the "Legends of Western Swing Festival" in June at the Scurry County Coliseum with the biggest names in western swing music. Sights in Scurry County include fields of snow-white cotton, herds of Texas cattle, miles of bobbing pump jacks bowing to past and present, oil rigs highlighting the terrain like magnificent monuments, rustic canyons full of the plants and animals that add to the beauty and mystery of West Texas and the most beautiful sunsets and starry nights your mind can imagine.

Timber and Threads
1801 25th St.
915/573-4018

Nathalie's
1803 25th St.
915/573-9680

House of Antieks
4008 College Ave.
915/573-4422

142 SOUTH PADRE ISLAND

Padre Antiques & Collectibles
104 E. Hibiscus St.
956/761-7440

Peddlers Co-Op
5813 Padre Blvd.
956/761-7585

Island Emporium
1900 Padre Blvd.
956/761-4529

143 SPRING

AntiqueLand USA
21127 Springtown Dr.
281/350-4557
Web Site: www.antiquelandusa.com
Open: Mon.–Sun. 10–6

At AntiqueLand, USA you'll enjoy one of the most impressive antique malls in the country. See thousands of antiques and collectibles creatively displayed throughout 85,000 square feet of attractive showrooms. The convenient location is home to over 300 unique shops and over 100 showcases representing the area's finest antique dealers.

Keepsakes & Kollectables
219 A Gentry St.
281/353-9233

The Doll Company
315 Gentry St.
281/350-4904

A Place in Time
315 Gentry St., Suite A
281/353-6323

Diane's Spring Emporium
324 Gentry St.
281/288-9202

Gentry Square Galleries
315 Gentry St.
281/353-5568

The Doll Hospital
419 Gentry St.
281/350-6722

Cobblestone Antiques
7623 Louetta Road, Suite 121
281/251-0660

Brenda's Attic
134 Main St.
281/288-0223

The Spotted Pony
202 Main St.
281/355-1880

Buffalo Spirit
215 Main St.
281/355-8100

Antiques & More on Main
302 Main St.
281/350-1214

The Wild Goose Chase
118 B Midway
281/288-9501

Friends
214 Midway St.
281/353-2255

Robyn's Nest Antiques
200-1 Noble St.
281/288-7252

Southern Charm
26303 Preston E.
281/288-4933

Lana Williams Gallery
26407 Preston
281/288-4043

Krystal Lain Antiques, Etc.
130 Spring Cypress
281/353-7442

Granny's Odds & Ends
219 B Spring Cypress
281/288-6530

Pete & Sue's Antique Clocks
1408 Sue Ann Lane
281/288-7188

Spring Antique Mall
1426 Spring Cypress Road
281/355-1110

Cabin Creek Lodge Antique Mall
1703 Spring Cypress Road
281/350-5559

Antique Mall
21127 Spring Town Dr.
281/350-4557

144 STAFFORD

Simone Antiques & More
11723 W. Bellfort St.
281/561-7403

Elegant Junk
Main St. (Hwy. 90)
281/242-3424

Antiques, Etc.
3202 S. Main St.
281/499-9669

145 SULPHUR SPRINGS

Bright Star Antique Mall
102 College St.
903/885-4584

Granny's Attic
105 N. Davis St.
903/885-5042

Burrow's Antiques
725 Davis St. N.
903/885-5173

Old Town Antique Mall
101 Gilmer St. N.
903/885-5646

Sanderson Antique Mall
109 Linda Dr.
903/439-0259

Victorian Rose
206 Main St.
903/885-2482

146 SUNNYVALE

East Fork Mall Antiques
613 E. Hwy. 80
972/226-2704

Jot Um Down Store
613 E. Hwy. 80
972/226-0974

Accent Antiques
616 E. Hwy. 80
972/226-9830

Fischer's Antiques
536 Long Creek
972/226-1445

147 SWEETWATER

Sweetwater, established in the 1870s, was a trading post with the name derived from "Mobeetie," the Kiowa word for "sweet water" to describe the water in a nearby creek. Today, Sweetwater is a very modern small city. Annual events include the famous Rattlesnake Round-up and the AJRA National Finals Rodeo.

Rat Rows Antiques
113 Oak St.
915/235-8651

Second Hand Rose
122 Oak St.
915/235-1504

Arlene's Book House
124 Oak St.
915/235-1504

Raspberry Corner Antique Mall
301 Oak St.
915/235-3885

Lone Star Antiques Mall
318 Oak St.
915/235-8177

Vernon's Antiques
401 Oak St.
No phone listed

148 TEXARKANA

Oak Tree
123 E. Broad
501/773-1588

M & M Antiques Mall
401 E. Broad
501/773-1871

Dun Sailin Oldes
611 Burma Road
903/838-9430

Jennie's Antique Mall
1901 College Dr.
903/792-2333

Red Wagon Antiques
Hwy. 59
903/832-6841

Nick's Antiques
213 Wood St.
501/772-6194

Pot Luck Antique Shop
I-30 W. Exit #218
903/832-1151

Garden Gate Antiques
603 E. 9th
501/773-1147

State Line Antique Mall
1104 State Line Road
501/772-8414

Green Country
1216 Trexler Road
903/671-2521

J. Brown Antiques
817 Walnut
903/793-4114

149 TOMBALL

Whistle Stop Tearoom
107 Commerce St.
281/255-2455

Victoria Station Antiques
111 Commerce St.
281/357-0555

Precious Temptations
115 Commerce St.
281/351-2119

Tender Touch
115 Commerce St.
281/351-2119

Antique Station
119 Commerce St. & Walnut
281/351-7887

Maggie Mae's
121 Commerce St.
281/255-8814

Blue Caboose
104 N. Elm St.
281/255-8788

Country Harbor
106 N. Elm St.
281/255-2330

Patchwork Blue
605 Mason
281/351-5301

Tomball Antique Co-op
208 W. Main St.
281/351-4160

Tomball Haus
216 W. Main St.
281/255-8282

314 East Main Antiques
314 E. Main St.
281/351-9488

Faye's Antiques
315 W. Main St.
281/255-3844

Three Sisters Antiques
330 W. Main St.
281/351-4725

The Owl's Nest
408 W. Main St.
281/351-1103

Just Passin' Time
418 W. Main St.
281/255-2999

J.T. Texas Co.
611 W. Main St.
281/351-2202

Antique Press
701 W. Main St.
281/255-8855

Texas

Past & Present
701 W. Main St.
281/255-8855

150 TRINITY

Teddie Bear's Antiques and Collectibles
Route 4
(four miles south on Hwy. 19)
409/594-6321 or 1-888-TED-DY88
Open: Daily 9–7
Email: www.teddiebears.com
Directions: Teddie Bear's is located 19 miles east of Huntsville, Texas (I-45) on Hwy. 19, just across the Trinity River Bridge, or 4 miles south of Trinity, Texas on Hwy. 19.

A true country market, Teddie Bear's may just very well be the most intriguing and most fun place to visit that we've discovered! Two acres of antiques and uniques to browse through is only part of the reason you should stop in if you are in the area. The variety of items stuffed onto these two acres range from neat "stuff" on outside sales tables to indoor highly collectible treasures.  Dealers can ask for a private tour of the huge barn full of early American primitives on the Garrisons' farm just four miles away.

Ted "the Teddy Bear" and Victoria Garrison are always available to greet old and new friends alike. Ted will gladly help load things in your car or even make a free delivery if you live in the vicinity. One of the reasons people keep coming back to visit Teddie Bears is for the genuine friendliness they find there. Victoria explains it this way: "We always have something new to surprise our customers. We're a two-acre mini-flea market that keeps expanding with a life of its own! One stop to another, if for nothing else than to see what we've started next at Teddie Bear's!"

151 TYLER

Antiques & Uniques
433 S. Vine Ave.
903/593-2779
Open: Tues.–Sat. 10–5, Sun.–Mon. by chance or appointment
Directions: Traveling I-20, take the exit to Hwy. 69 and follow to downtown Tyler.

This is another shop that is very important to know. If you are into lamps, these folks can help you in every way. Not only do they buy and sell antiques, handle appraisals and estate sales, carry gift items and reproductions, they also custom build, rewire and repair lamps, and sell lampshades. They keep over 500 lampshades in stock at all times!

John R. Saul's Antiques
108 S. Broadway Ave.
903/593-4668

Rose Tyler Antiques
202 S. Broadway Ave.
903/592-6711

Barham's Antiques
308 S. Broadway Ave.
903/593-3863

Brass Lion Antiques
5935 S. Broadway Ave.
903/561-1111

Front Street Antiques
202 W. Front St.
903/531-0008

Old City Antique Mall
302 E. Locust St.
903/533-1110

Crossroads Gallery Antiques
114 W. 6th St.
903/597-3021

Glass Owl Antiques
428 S. Vine Ave.
903/595-0251

Tyler Square Antiques & Tearoom
117 S. Broadway Ave.
903/535-9994

V.J.'s Antique Mall
236 S. Broadway Ave.
903/595-3289

Hudson House Interiors
2301 S. Broadway Ave.
903/593-2611

Mary's Attic
417 S. College Ave.
903/592-5181

Latifs Antiques
13819 U.S. Hwy. 69 N.
903/882-6031

Special Effects
4517 Old Bullard Road
903/509-0020

Grey Pony
12663 State Hwy. 31 W.
903/593-8905

152 UVALDE

Loessberg's
524 E. Pecos St.
830/278-3958

Market Square Antiques
103 N. West St.
830/278-1294

Open House Antiques
100 W. North St.
830/278-9380

Way Out West Antiques
103 N. West St.
830/278-3648

153 VAN ALSTYNE

Yellow Rose Drug Store Antique Mall
210 E. Marshal St.
903/482-6167

Great Places to Stay

The Durning House Bed & Breakfast and Restaurant
205 W. Stephens
903/482-5188
Open: Bed & Breakfast open daily, restaurant open for lunch Wed.–Fri. 11:30–2, dinner (Fri.–Sat. only) 6–9
Directions: From Hwy. 75, take Exit #51. After exiting toward town (east), go 6 blocks and the B&B is on the right at 205 West Stephens. If you come to a red light (the only one in town), you've gone a block too far. Van Alstyne is 50 miles north of Dallas, 15 miles north of McKinney and 15 miles south of Sherman, Texas.

When the Hixes purchased this wonderful little Victorian home, it housed their antique shop called "Elderly Things Antiques." The house is totally decorated in antiques, and some of the pieces scattered throughout the B&B and restaurant are for sale.

Guests are first greeted by three concrete pigs lolling in the front garden area, sporting hats befitting the seasons and holidays.

Diners have enjoyed the food so much that many of the recipes offered here have been included in a cookbook called Hog Heaven — Recipes from the Durning House. As an added incentive, if you mention The Antique Atlas, you will receive a 10% discount!

154 VAN HORN

Great Places to Stay

Los Nopales
1106 W. Broadway
915/283-7125
Open: Daily 2–6
Directions: Traveling I-10 East, take Exit #138 and continue 1 3/10 miles on Business Loop 10. Traveling I-10 West, take Exit #140B and continue 1 1/2 miles on Business Loop 10. From the intersection of U.S. 90, U.S. 54 and Business Loop 10, travel 8/10 mile west. Los Nopales is located next to Chuy's Mexican Food Restaurant.

Los Nopales is, indeed, different! They carry antiques and collectibles, art and rare books, including Texana, and there is a refinishing and upholstery shop adjoining the antique shop. They also sell Southwest native plants, and that's also connected to the name of the shop, as owner Joy Scott explains: "When I purchased a commercial lot with an abandoned building on it here in Van Horn, I was searching for an unusual business name that might truly represent our uniqueness. As we set about cleaning up the place, we discovered a prickly pear — in Spanish a "nopal" — growing on the roof amid all the debris that had accumulated there for years. There were prickly pear plants already growing in front of a fence on one part of the property. It seemed like destiny to name the business Los Nopales. For a multi-faceted business like ours, with a Southwestern flair, there just couldn't be a more appropriate name."

155 VERNON

Jailhouse Village
1826 Cumberland
940/553-4004

Yellow Rose Antique Mall
1516 Main St.
940/553-1511

Hall Hardware & Furniture
1512 Fannin St.
940/552-5391

Yesterdaze Antiques & Collectibles
1519 Main St.
940/552-6727

PMH Enterprises
1601 Main St.
940/552-1660

156 VICTORIA

Victoria Antique Shop
804 Berkman Dr.
512/575-2203

Laurent Street Antique Mall
1602 N. Laurent St.
512/578-0813

Homestead
106 W. Rio Grande St.
512/572-9666

Blue Moon Antique Mall
1520 E. Rio Grande St. (Hwy. 59)
512/575-3233

Antique Attic
1401 S. Laurent St.
512/575-5043

Victoria's House of Lamps
1042 N. Main St.
512/575-6200

Mundine Antiques
601 E. Rio Grande St.
512/576-9445

157 WACO

Crystal Palace Antiques
618 Austin Ave.
254/756-7662

Antiques on Austin
1525 Austin Ave.
254/753-1795

Laverty's
600 N. 18th St.
254/754-3238

Show & Tell Antiques
1525 Morrow Ave.
254/752-5372

Victoriana Antiques & Gifts
561 Westview Village
254/772-7704

Cottage Shop
708 Austin Ave.
254/756-0988

Courtyard Classic Antiques
4700 Bosque Blvd.
254/751-7077

Saint Charles Shops
600 Austin Ave.
254/753-5531

Goodie Mill
2300 Washington Ave.
254/753-9616

158 WALLER

Autumn's Morn
40142 Hempstead Hwy.
409/372-5415

Queenie's Antiques & Co-Op
2611 Washington St.
409/372-9346

Clark's Collectables & Antiques
3106 Taylor
409/921-2960

Bluebonnet Antiques
2510 Hempstead Hwy.
409/931-2951

159 WAXAHACHIE

Courthouse Antiques
200 S. Rogers
972/938-2777 or 1-888-983-5144
Open: Mon.–Fri. 10–5:30, Sat. 10–6, Sun. 12:30–5:30
Directions: Located in Historic Downtown Waxahachie.

Courthouse Antiques, Collectibles, and Gifts is situated in the very shadow of the beautiful and famous Ellis County Courthouse located in Waxahachie, Texas. The 102-year-old courthouse and this charming Victorian town have been featured in numerous movies, and located right on the Historic Courthouse Square you'll find the store. In keeping with the surroundings, they offer vintage clothing, Haviland china, including chocolate pots and tea sets; Wedgewood, Noritake, Johnson Bros. and various European china; vintage baby items such as wicker strollers and baby scales and ceramic baby feeders; furniture dating back to the early 19th century, some in its original condition and some beautifully and faithfully restored; toys and dolls, some dating back to the '20s and '30s and some highly collectible such as Madame Alexander dolls, Gund plush toys, Ideal and Matchbox cars and planes, stained glass and other architectural pieces; books, linens and lace; jewelry and watches; clocks; glassware, atomizers, decanters and bottles; bedroom and dining suites; trunks and luggage. They also buy antiques and are especially interested in buying Haviland, vintage clothing, children's items and toys.

Gingerbread Antique Mall
310 S. College
972/937-0968

Briarpatch
404 W. Main St.
972/937-7717

Old Town Village Antiques
307 S. Rogers St.
972/938-9515

Barbara's Antiques
113 N. College
972/935-9338

Links to the Past
512 N. College
972/937-1421

Gran's Antiques
208A S. Rogers St.
972/923-2207

Waxahachie Crafters & Antiques
315 S. Rogers St.
972/938-1222

160 WEATHERFORD

Wanda's Antiques
2206 E. Bankhead Dr.
817/594-6222

Horton House
1103 Ft. Worth Hwy.
817/599-8945

Age Before Beauty
209 N. Main St.
817/596-8550

On The Level Antique Mall
1716 Blair Dr.
817/594-8991

Dresser Drawer Antiques
118 S. Main St.
817/594-1191

Patty's Country Memories
219 N. Main St.
817/594-9303

Sparks Antiques & Collectibles
220 Main St.
817/598-0089

The Land of Aah's
315 E. Oak
817/598-0101

Texas Treasures
1124 Palo Pinto St.
817/599-9505

Miss B's
311 N. Main St.
817/596-0902

Wanda's Antiques
1116 Pala Pinto St.
817/599-4112

Granny's Attic
127 York
817/613-9011

161 WEST

Molly B's Antiques
415 S. George Kacir Dr.
254/826-3052

Huaco Antiques
20818 N. I-35
254/826-7262

West Mercantile
126 N. Main St.
254/826-4461

Way Out West
105 E. Oak St.
254/826-3924

Rasberry's Consignor Antiques
2481 IH 40 W.
254/355-5181

Heritage Antiques
I-35
254/826-3042

Olde Czech Corner Antiques
130 N. Main St.
254/826-4094

162 WHEELER

Antique Cupboard
103 W. Texas St.
806/826-3741
Open: Mon.–Sat. 9:30–5, Sun. by appointment
Directions: From I-40 at Shamrock, Texas, take Hwy. 83 North for 16 miles to downtown Wheeler.

Here's a shop that lists itself as having "a little bit of everything" including a large selection of depression glass, elegant glass, kitchen collectibles, quilts and primitives.

163 WHITE SETTLEMENT

Harris Antiques & Imports
7600 Scott St.
817/246-8400 or 817/246-5852
Open: Mon.–Sat. 8:30–5:30
Directions: Harris Antiques & Imports is located in West Fort Worth, in a suburb called White Settlement. The shop is at I-30 West, Cherry Lane Exit (north), then right on Scott Street.

This store gets my vote for being the largest antique shop in America. Carolyn Harris and company sells both wholesale and retail, with about 95% of their sales being to dealers, auctioneers and designers. But anyone

Texas

who loves antiques should go to the showroom just to look and be impressed. Their new location is an air-conditioned mall that is the length of three football fields — a total of 440,000 square feet of antiques and accessories! Harris Antiques & Imports has been in business in Fort Worth for over 35 years, and offers merchandise to shoppers world-wide. Besides all the furniture, they offer bronzes, oil paintings, cut glass and porcelain. It's no wonder they hold the title of "the world's largest home furnishings, accessories and antiques store."

164 WICHITA FALLS

Sue's Antique Mall
609 7th St.
940/322-9552
Open: Tues.–Sat. 10–5
Directions: From I-44 and Hwy. 287, take 8th Street east to Ohio Street, turn left one block to 7th Street, then turn left again and go ¹/₂ block to the shop.

Few antique shops are fortunate enough to be able to display their goods in an antique building. Sue's Antique Mall occupies a 100+ year old building that is still being researched. You won't have to research the items you find here however, as there is something for everyone who has a love for antiques and collectibles.

The Hand Place
4304 Call Field Road
940/691-4563

Colonial House Antiques I & II
1510 Monroe St.
940/761-2280

Johnson's Junction
1514 Monroe St.
940/723-5332

Corner Cupboard Antiques
1518 Monroe St.
940/767-6583

King Albert's Antiques & Interiors
1827 Pearl Ave.
940/761-4226

Depot Square Antiques
620 Ohio Ave.
940/766-6321

Depression Glass by Bonnie
1032 Covington St.
940/855-1591

The Market on Monroe
1512 Monroe St.
940/723-4997

Village Antique Mall
1516 Monroe St.
940/322-6255

Monroe St. Antique Mall
1523 Monroe St.
940/761-4151

Griffis Antiques
5521 Northwest Freeway
940/855-7711

Potts Antique Shop
1310 10th St.
940/322-3488

165 WIMBERLEY

O'Neal's Antiques
100 Lange Road
512/847-3148

Jeans Antiques, Gifts & Boutique
11552 Ranch Road 12 S.
512/487-2307

Old Mill Store
Wimberley Square
512/847-3068

166 WINNIE

Just What You Need
344 Broadway
409/296-3099

Winnie Antique Mall
Hwy. 124 & Cedar St.
409/296-2701

Old Time Trade Days
I-10 & 1663
409/296-3300

167 WOODVILLE

Family Tree
304 W. Bluff St.
409/283-2116

Another Time
104 Charlton St.
409/283-8222

Family Affair Antiques
Hwy. 190 W.
409/283-5685

Pine Country Antiques
511 W. Bluff St.
409/283-3183

Yvonne's Antiques
112 S. Charlton St.
409/283-2119

Utah

84
15
89

10 Ogden

84   80

3 Bountiful

80

14 Salt Lake City

9 Murray

11 Park City

Midvale **8**

5 Draper

1 American Fork

12 Pleasant Grove

13 Provo

15 Springville

40

0   Mileage   40

7 "Heritage Valley"
- Fairview
- Mt. Pleasant
- Spring City
- Ephrom
- Manti

89

15

70

Teasdale **17**

24

2 Boulder

4 Cedar City

6
Escalante

89

12

15

St. George

16

9

89

1 AMERICAN FORK

Lake City Antiques
143 N. 200 W.
801/756-9149

Flamingo Road
35 North Barratt Ave.
801/763-8142

2 BOULDER

Great Places to Stay

Boulder Mountain Ranch and Bed & Breakfast

Hells Back Bone Road
801/335-7480
Open: All the time
Directions: Located 3 ½ miles off Scenic Byway 12. Just seven miles from rural Boulder.

This working cattle ranch offers the urban cowboy an opportunity to participate in the "western experience." One to six day excursions are available offering horseback riding along with other adventures for a taste of the true west. Set out on a five day ride from Bryce Canyon to the ranch along the Great Western Trail or if you're a "true cowboy" try trail riding and cattle working. For relaxation, fish in the nearby streams. Lodge rooms or cabins are available. Breakfast is available each morning.

3 BOUNTIFUL

Newman's Antiques & Art
44 S. 400 RR 2
801/298-2884

Bountiful Antiques
399 N. Main St.
801/295-7227

4 CEDAR CITY

Grey Wolf's Antiques & Collectibles
223 N. 100 W.
801/865-1973

Betty's Antiques & Collectibles
1181 S. Main St.
801/586-7221

5 DRAPER

Treasures Unlimited
132 81 S. Minuteman Road
801/576-8626

6 ESCALANTE

Situated in the heart of Scenic Byway 12, Escalante and its environs were among the last frontiers to be explored in the continental United States. In the 1700s, two Spanish priests, along with their expedition, came through the area looking for a passable trail to Los Angeles. The town was eventually named for one of these priests. In 1876, Mormon pioneers settled here because of its mild climate, good grazing land, and abundance of minerals and water.

One of the few places that can still boast clean air, Escalante is surrounded by the mysteries of the past. Little is known about the civilization that lived here centuries ago, and visitors will want to explore the cliff-dwellings and artifacts left by the ancients who once occupied the mountains and canyons. The wildlife is plentiful for hunters and fishermen, and the sweeping vistas are ideal for photographers. The town itself offers modern accommodations, as well as a variety of gift and specialty shops in which to roam. The restaurant and cafes promise anything from sandwiches to steaks to satisfy even the hungriest explorer.

Serenidad Gallery — Fine Art and Antiques

360 W. Main St.
801/826-4810
Open: Mon.–Sat. 8–9, Sun. 1–8
Directions: Go 60 miles from Hwy. 89 to the west, and 65 miles from Hwy. 24 to the northeast. The town is in the heart of Scenic Hwy. 12.

With an eye for quality, this shop carries a fine selection of art and antiques with a Western theme.

Great Places to Stay

Rainbow Country Tours and Bed & Breakfast

586 E. 300 S.
1-800-252-8824 or 801/826-4567
Fax: 801/826-4557
Directions: Located on the east end of Escalante. Turn behind the Chevron Station, go ¼ mile to the first house on the right.

This bed and breakfast offers you an idyllic place to unwind. Comfortable and peaceful, it provides all the amenities of a traditional bed and breakfast — private rooms and hearty food — plus hot tub and wrap-around sun deck with sweeping vistas of mountain and desert.

For your entertainment, they provide off-the-beaten-path jeep and/or hiking tours, as well as overnight camping. Owner Gene Windle can also take you safely and comfortably in his 8-passenger wagon to see "some of the most beautiful, remote places in the American West." Ask him to show you the petrified forests and the 3000-year-old Indian rock art.

7 HERITAGE VALLEY

By the time Utah became a state in 1896, the population had comfortably settled in nearly every corner of its boundaries. In fact, settlers had been colonizing likely townsites for nearly fifty years.

Such is the case with the historic towns of, Spring City, Fairview, Mt. Pleasant, Ephraim, and Manti. This string of communities was settled during the 1850's by industrious and determined Mormons from the United States and Europe.

Today, these towns form Utah's "Heritage Valley". In a state where history is preserved with pride, these central Utah towns stand out for their uncommon devotion to preserving their 19th century origins with architectural integrity and continuing pioneer spirit.

Spring City is one of Utah's finest examples of preservation. Laid out using the strict grid design considered ideal by early Mormons, the entire town of Spring City is on the National Historic Register. Spring City is architecturally eclectic. Some homes are styled with the Scandinavian designs favored by early settlers, and other structures are built in Greek and Romanesque Revival and classic Victorian styles. Heritage Days, a celebration held each spring, includes tours of historic homes, and artists' studios, wagon rides, a turkey barbecue, and much more. A self-guided walking tour is available year-round.

Fairview was settled in 1859, and many of the buildings from this era remain. The Fairview Museum of History and Art offers an excellent collection of items evocative of pioneer days including hand-crafted household implements. The museum also exhibits the remnants of ancient Pueblo cultures common to the area, and modern-day paintings and sculpture.

Mt. Pleasant was also settled permanently in 1859. Its colorful Main Street is a model of community pride and hard work. The majority of the streets' structures were built between 1880 and 1905. Mt. Pleasant's rich history includes the signing of the treaty between central Utah settlers and the Ute Indians. Mt. Pleasant hosts a pioneer pageant each summer.

Settled by a few determined families in the 1850s, Ephraim's quiet streets are lined today with carefully preserved buildings and homes, both common and ornate. The renovated "Ephraim Cooperative Mercantile Association" building is one Main Street example. Guided tours of historic sites are available. Ephraim is the home of Snow College, founded in the 1880s. Today's enrollment is about 2,500 students. A Scandinavian Festival held each Memorial Day weekend pays homage to the Mormon convert settlers.

Manti was one of the first five towns incorporated into the "State of Deseret," as early Mormons hoped their territory would someday be known. The town's most famous structure is the Mormon Temple constructed between 1877 and 1888, and still in use today. The grounds of the cream-colored oolite limestone edifice are the location of the Mormon Miracle Pageant each July. Drawing thousands of spectators nightly, it tells the story of the founding of the LDS Church, and of the early pioneers who settled this area.

For more information about ways to enjoy Utah's Heritage Valley, Contact: Sanpete Economic Development, P. O. Box 59, Ephraim, Utah 84627, 801-283-4321.

Antique Shops

Antiques Etc.
58 N. Main St.
Manti
801/835-1122

Pherson House Antiques & Bed and Breakfast
244 S. Main St.
Ephraim
801/283-4197

Bed & Breakfast

Ephraim Homestead
135 W. 100 N.
Ephraim
801/283-6367

Heritage House
498 N. 400 W.
Manti
801/835-5050

Larsen House
298 S. State St.
Mt. Pleasant
801/462-9337

Legacy Inn
337 N. 100 E.
Manti
801/835-8352

Mainti House Inn
401 N. Main St.
Manti
801/835-0161

Yardley Inn
190 S. 200 W.
Manti
801/835-1861

Museums

Mon.–Sat. 10–5, summer 10–6, Sun. 2–6

Fairview Museum
86 N. 100 E.
Fairview
801/427-9216

Mt. Pleasant Museum
150 S. State
Mt. Pleasant
801/462-2456

8 MIDVALE

Bingham Junction Antiques
23 N. Main St.
801/255-0330

Antiques Emporium
32 N. Main St.
801/565-0242

First Class Antiques & Collectibles
7615 State St.
801/568-7878

Amusement Sales
127 N. Main St.
801/255-4731

9 MURRAY

Lyn Annes Collectables
4844 S. State St.
801/263-2293
Open: Mon.–Fri. 11–5:30, Sat. 11–5

This is a unique shop that specializes in vintage wearables, including accessories. They also carry a selection of costume jewelry and glassware.

After Glow
4844 S. State St.
801/263-2293
Open: Mon.–Fri. 11–5:30, Sat. 11–5
Directions: From I-15 take the 53rd South Exit #303. Go east to State St.

Offering the largest selection of glassware in the area, this shop also features a variety of fine china, primitives, costume jewelry, and paper.
The shop gladly offers dealer discounts and appraisal services.

Sherry's Antiques
4859 S. State St.
801/266-3145

Notions
4838 S. State St.
801/263-7733

Rare Necessities
4967 S. State St.
801/288-0518

10 OGDEN

Boom Town Antiques
406 Canyon Road
801/621-6778

Young's General Store
109 Historic 25th St.
801/392-1473

Painted Lady
115 Historic 25th St.
801/393-4445

Lilt of Yesteryear
3638 Jackson Ave.
801/394-1896

Country Way Gifts & Antiques
460 Second St.
801/392-0332

Abby's Antique Mall
134 31st St.
801/394-9035

Curio Shop
241 25th St.
801/393-0926

Erika Martin Antiques
3480 Washington Blvd.
801/393-5963

Cowboy Trading Post
268 25th St.
801/399-9511

Country Antiques
118 24th St.
801/394-4934

Ginger Jar Antiques
424 29th St.
801/399-4901

Reflections Antiques & Collectibles
2386 Wall Ave.
801/392-4904

11 PARK CITY

Southwest Indian Traders
550 Main St.
801/645-9177

Great Places to Stay

Angel House Inn
713 Norfolk Ave.
1-800-ANGEL-01 or 801/647-0338
Open: Year-round
Directions: From Salt Lake City, take I-80 to Route 224. This becomes Park Ave. At town lift, turn right on 8th St.; go two blocks, then left onto Norfolk.

Set in historic Park City, with the rugged Wasatch Mountains as a backdrop, an exquisite Victorian mansion has been transformed into the Angel House Inn. Built in 1889, during an era of elegance and service, proprietors Joe and Jan Fisher Rush have restored this historical house to its former grandeur and welcome you to experience one of its 9 romantically designed and themed rooms. Highlights of its amenities include its immediate access to Park City resorts for world class skiing in the winter and adventurous hiking and mountain biking in the summer.
Each of its 9 designer appointed rooms are named after angels who represent and embody the essence of romance and pleasure of the natural world. The inn also features an elegant sitting and breakfast area that ensures your stay is one reminiscent of the Victorian era.

Old Miners' Lodge-A Bed and Breakfast Inn
615 Woodside Ave.
1-800-648-8068 or 801/645-8068
Fax: 801/645-7420
Open: Year-round

Situated in the Historic District, this 1889 lodge was once a boarding house for fortune seeking miners. Besides the three suites and ten antique-filled guest rooms (complete with down comforters and pillows) there is a large fireplace in the living room and an outdoor hot tub available to guests all year round. Other amenities include terry cloth robes in all guest baths and a full breakfast each morning.
With the Park City ski area just a stone's throw away, this inn can easily accommodate groups or family gatherings.

Utah

12 PLEASANT GROVE

Collector's Cottage
100 E. State Road
801/785-6782

Rosebud Antiques
15 S. Main St.
801/796-0108

13 PROVO

Kristi & Joseph Antiques
260 N. University Ave.
801/375-1211

This 'n' That Antiques
1585 W. Center St.
801/375-3133

14 SALT LAKE CITY

Brass Key Antiques
43 W. Broadway
801/532-2844

Generations Antiques
2085 S. 900 E.
801/466-0456

Beehive Collectors Gallery
368 E. Broadway
801/533-0119

Ec-Lec-Tic
380 Pierpont Ave.
801/322-4804

Trolley Antique & Unique
602 S. 500 Ave. (Trolley Square)
801/575-8060

Sugar House
2144 Highland Dr., Suite 130
801/487-5084

Temptations Plus
3922 Highland Dr.
801/272-6222

Ken Sanders Rare Books
268 S. 200 E.
801/521-3819

Antique Shoppe
2016 S. 1100 E.
801/466-2171

Elemente
353 Pierpont Ave.
801/355-7400

Jitter Bug-Toy Dealers
243 E. 300 S.
801/537-7038

Squires Antiques
357 W. 200 S.
801/363-1191

Wasatch Furniture Co.
623 S. State St.
801/521-8845

Briar Patch Antiques
407 E. 300 S.
801/322-5234

Bearcat Antiques
43 W. 300 S.
801/532-2844

Gary Thompson Antiques & Art
43 W. 300 S.
801/532-2844

Kennard Antiques
65 W. 300 S.
801/328-9796

Olympus Cove Antiques
179 E. 300 S.
801/532-1070

Antiques Gallery
217 E. 300 S.
801/521-7055

Antoinette's
247 E. 300 S.
801/359-2192

Copper Cowboy Antiques
268 S. 300 E.
801/328-4401

Carmen Miranda's
270 S. 300 E.
801/359-7741

Due Time
279 E. 300 S.
801/521-4356

Thomson & Burrows Antiques
280 S. 300 E.
801/521-0650

Cobwebs
1054 S. 2100 S.
801/485-9295

Honest Jon's Hills House
126 S. 200 W.
801/359-4852

Great Places to Stay

Wildflowers Bed & Breakfast
936 E. 1700 S.
801/466-0600

Built in 1891, this beautiful Victorian home is surrounded by an array of wonderful colors, one of which is evident in the blue spruce trees which surround the grounds, and more so in the wildflowers of all different shades of the rainbow. Listed on the National Register of Historic Places, the Wildflowers Bed & Breakfast is gorgeously enhanced with original chandeliers, stained glass windows, Oriental rugs, antiques, and an astonishing hand-carved staircase.

A gourmet breakfast is served to the guest, making the stay at Wildflowers a complete and enjoyable one.

15 SPRINGVILLE

PJ's Antiques
211 N. Main St.
801/489-9137

Pioneer Antiques
391 N. Main St.
801/489-6853

T.C. Antique Barn
2310 S. State St.
801/489-9623

16 ST. GEORGE

Holland House
70 N. 500 E.
801/628-0176

Bentley's House of Antiques
46 N. 100 W.
801/674-1812

Dixie Trading Post
111 W. Saint George Blvd.
801/628-7333

Butterfield's Antiques
248 E. Saint George Blvd.
801/673-8333

General Store Antiques
640 E. Saint George Blvd.
801/628-8858

17 TEASDALE

The Old House
417 S. 500 W. (Loa) 20 mi. from Teasdale
801/836-2382

Great Places to Stay

Cockscomb Inn Bed & Breakfast
97 S. State St.
801/425-3511
Open: Daily year-round.

This quaint inn is only minutes from Capitol Reef National Park. The charming rooms all have private baths. Hiking and biking information is available. Excellent full breakfast is served.

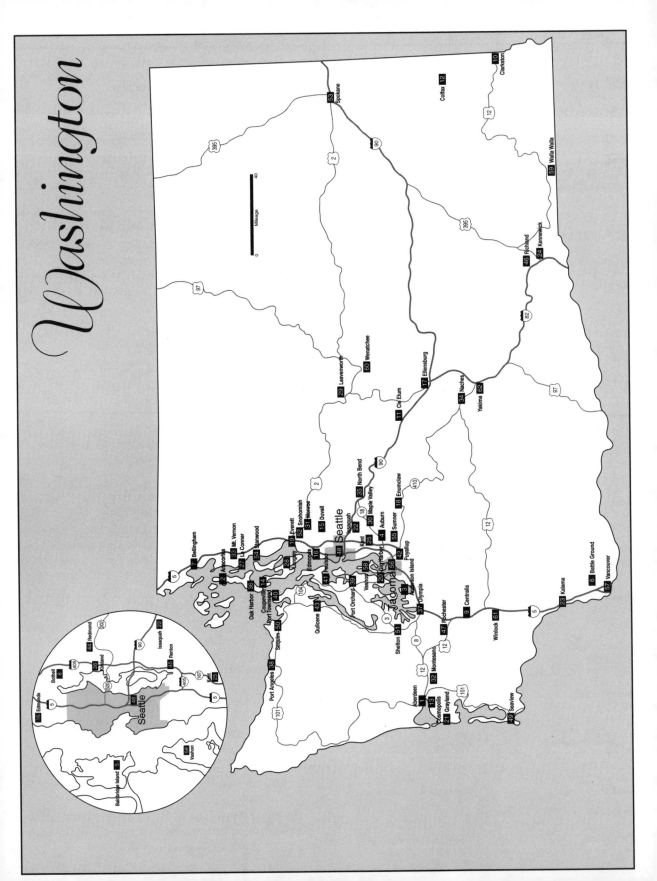

Washington

1 ABERDEEN

Clevenger's Antique Mall
201 S. Broadway St.
360/533-1317

Judy's Antiques & Collectibles
401 W. Market St.
360/532-4359

Karrie's Furnishings
110 W. Wishkah St.
360/533-7330

Grand Heron
200 E. Heron St.
360/532-5561

Central Park Antiques
6617 Olympic Hwy.
360/538-1173

Antique Co-Op
112 W. Wishkah St.
360/533-6516

2 ANACORTES

The Business
1717 Commerical Ave.
360/293-9788

Home Sweet Home Antiques
2701 Commercial Ave.
360/293-1991

15th St. Antiques & Gallery
1012 15th St.
360/299-3120

Left Bank Antiques
1904 Commercial Ave.
360/293-3022

Days Gone By
3015 Commercial Ave.
360/299-2222

Anacortes Junk Co.
202 Commercial Ave.
360/293-4014

3 ANDERSON ISLAND

Oro Bay Merchantile
12312 Eckenstam Johnson Road
253/884-1700

Great Places to Stay

Hideaway House Bed and Breakfast

11422 Leschi Circle
253/884-4179
Open: Daily around the clock
Rates: $55–$75
Directions: From I-5 either north or south: Take Exit 119 and follow the signs to Steilacoom. After about 3½ miles the road leads to the ferry, with parking on the left. It is a beautiful 20-minute ferry ride to Anderson Island. Proceed west off the ferry and veer to the left at the "Y" in the road. Pass the store on the right, turn left onto West Josephine Boulevard. Go one mile, turn right onto Leschi Circle, and go to the blue house.

This description of Hideaway House and innkeepers Hank and Faye Lynn Hollenbaugh makes you appreciate that old-fashioned common courtesy and genuine desire to help others is not entirely dead.

The Hollenbaughs started their B&B unintentionally. The ferry schedule to the island is often confusing to tourists, which used to result in frequently stranded travelers. They often came to the Island General Store, where Hank works, looking for a solution. Many of them were without funds, and things only got worse when they discovered they were stranded on the island until the next morning's ferry at 6:30 a.m. Out of compassion, Hank and Faye Lynn found themselves saying, "Well, we have a room...things will look better in the morning."

And things did look better, after a good night's sleep, hot shower, hearty breakfast and directions back to the ferry dock. Unfortunately, accepting this freely given gift of hospitality from strangers was a source of embarrassment to some guests. Eventually, Hank and Faye Lynn decided to accept donations, if the guests insisted.

This happened often enough that they decided to do some major remodeling. Under the canopy of giant fir trees that surround the house, they added a large, open deck that opens into a suite decorated in garden/sunflower motif (the Sunflower Room). The focal point of the suite is a bright sunflower quilt created by Hank's 82-year-old mother in Pennsylvania. The suite includes a kitchenette and private bath, and children are welcome.

The deck also leads into the Angel Room. This suite holds a tulip quilt, created by the late, well-known islander Lois Scholl and offers a double spa tub. Both suites have access to the upstairs of the main house and to the dining area, where guest are graciously and amply fed wonderful, home-cooked meals.

4 AUBURN

Maw's Antiques and Collectibles
121 E. Main St.
253/939-3740

Lynn's Antiques & Refinishing
130 W. Main St.
253/939-6799

Cedar Chest
119 E. Main St.
253/833-4165

Auburn Main Street Antiques
124 E. Main St.
253/804-8041

Back by Popular Demand
33620 135th Ave. S.E.
253/939-1239

5 BAINBRIDGE ISLAND

Rose Gulch Antiques
11042 Forest Lane N.E.
206/842-5002

Bad Blanche Antiques
133 Winslow Way E.
206/842-1807

Sow's Ear & Friends
554 Winslow Way E.
206/842-1203

Now and Then Shoppe
901 S.W. 152nd St.
206/242-8238

Discoveries Downstairs
155 Winslow Way E.
206/842-5873

6 BATTLE GROUND

Rock Creek Antiques
31902 N.E. Lewisville Hwy.
360/687-1892

Jo's Antiques
612 E. Main St.
360/687-0251

Washington

Main Street Antiques
706 E. Main St.
360/687-2365

Secret Treasures
186 E. Bakerview Road
360/734-5057

Fairhaven Antiques & Art
1200 Harris Ave.
360/734-7179

Bristol Antiques & Books
310 W. Holly St.
360/733-7809

Pink Flamingo
407 W. Holly St.
360/671-2789

Old Town Antique Mall
427 W. Holly St.
360/671-3301

Cheryl Leaf Antiques & Gifts
2828 Northwest Ave.
360/734-2880

I-5 Antique Mall
4744 Pacific Hwy.
360/384-5955

8 BOTHELL

Farmhouse Antiques
23710 Bothell Everett Hwy.
425/483-3354

Town Hall Antique Mall
23716 Bothell Everett Hwy.
425/487-8979

Red Barn Loft
23929 Bothell Everett Hwy.
425/485-6582

9 CENTRALIA

Common Folk Company
125 E. High St.
360/736-8066

Elderly Things Antiques
918 W. Locust St.
360/736-8927

Centralia Square Antique Mall
201 S. Pearl St.
360/736-6406

Old Post Office Antique Mall
718 E. Main St.
360/687-1805

American Antiques
2330 Elm St.
360/650-9037

Urban Archeologist Antique Mall
214 W. Holly St.
360/676-0695

Bellingham Bay Collectibles
314 W. Holly St.
360/676-9201

Aladdin's Lamp Antique Mall
427 W. Holly St.
360/647-0066

Jacks by the Tracks
705 W. Holly St.
360/647-9422

Glass Affair
4392 Northwest Dr.
360/734-0382

Wynne Associates
4744 Pacific Hwy.
360/384-5955

White House Antique Mall
23712 Bothell Everett Hwy.
425/483-0676

Red Barn Antq. Collectibles & Gifts
23929 Bothell Everett Hwy.
425/486-7309

Wrecking Bar Ranch Antiques
24323 Lockwood Road
425/486-3203

Q's Country Shoppe
Centralia Square — 202 W. Locust St.
360/330-2844

Cranberry Bog
920 W. Locust St.
360/330-0594

Collector's Showcase
201 S. Pearl St.
360/736-6026

Maxine's Antiques
201 S. Pearl St.
360/736-1699

Irresistibles
113 N. Tower Ave.
360/330-0338

Rob Duffy's Antiques
310 N. Tower Ave.
360/736-1282

A & D Antique Mall
405 N. Tower Ave.
360/330-5240

Centralia Antique Furniture Market
120 S. Tower Ave.
360/736-4079

10 CLARKSTON

Hangar Old Tyme Photos
935 Port Way
509/758-0604

Dan's Antiques
823 6th St.
509/758-6223

11 CLE ELUM

Many Visions
113 E. First St.
509/674-2568

Rose Blue
111 N. Tower Ave.
360/736-0370

Hidden Treasures
302 N. Tower Ave.
360/736-7572

Timeless Treasures & Co.
314 N. Tower Ave.
360/736-3898

American Antique Furniture Market
120 S. Tower Ave.
360/330-0427

Rick's Wholesale Antiques
120 S. Tower Ave.
360/736-2529

Bric-A-Brac Mall
834 6th St.
509/758-7772

Great Places to Stay

Aster Inn & Antiques

521 E. 1st St.
509/674-2551
Open: Daily 10–10 except Christmas, New Year's and Thanksgiving
Directions: From the west, from I-90: Take Exit 84 straight for approximately 10 blocks (five blocks east at the only stoplight). The inn is on the left at the opposite end of the block from Cle Elum's Gourmet Bakery and Meat Market. From the east, from I-90: Take Exit 85. Turn left on Hwy. 903 and follow the signs to Cle Elum. It is exactly 1$7/_{10}$ miles from the freeway exit on the right.

A visit to Aster Inn & Antiques is a chance to experience firsthand some living history and hear about life early in the century in the Washington area from people who have literally experienced it. There are two interconnected parts of this living history saga: Aster Inn and Aster Antiques.

The antique store, which is attached to the inn, sells everything from collectibles to primitives, mostly in "as is" condition. This is a family-owned business, established at the turn of the century and now running continuously for more than 90 years. Innkeeper and third generation family member Patrecia Starbird says, "We can almost guarantee every shopper will be entertained by stories of the local bordellos (now extinct), coal mines, early one-room school houses, arranged brides, etc. The stories aren't even secondhand, but are the experiences of the two proprietors!"

These two proprietors are still working at the store and in the inn's office every summer – Theresa, age 93 and the matriarch of the family, and her brother, Dominic, age 88. The 1885 "store" has been at various times a schoolhouse, saloon, grocery store, gift shop, and for the last thirty years, an antique shop.

Aster Inn was build in 1934 and has been remodeled recently, retaining and maintaining a 1930s atmosphere with some "thoroughly Modern Millie" rooms! Jacuzzi, clawfoot tubs and mini-stocked kitchens are favorites.

12 COLFAX

Bryan's Antiques
Hwy. 195
509/397-3259

Quail Crossing
707 N. Main St.
509/397-6026

Whitman Mall
121 S. Main St.
509/397-2522

13 COSMOPOLIS

Cooney Mansion
1705 Fifth St.
360/533-0602

14 COUPEVILLE

Front Street Antiques
7 N.W. Front St.
360/678-7514

Salmagundi Farms
185 S. State Hwy. 20
360/678-5888

Elkhorn Trading Co.
15 N.W. Front St.
360/678-2250

Country & Victorian Treasures
2531 W. Libbey Road
No phone listed

San De Fuca Old Store
694 N. State Hwy. 20
360/678-3626

15 DUVALL

McCoy's Mercantile
15515 Main St. N.E.
425/788-7920

Liberty's Lighthouse
15720 Main St. N.E.
425/788-8683

Duvall's Trading Post
15906 Main St. N.E.
425/788-9455

Country Collections
15525 Main St. N.E.
425/788-2939

Tuxedo's Junction
15904 Main St. N.E.
425/788-9678

Old Memories
15925 Main St. N.E.
425/788-7508

16 EDMONDS

E & E Collectibles at Beeson House
116 4th Ave. N.
425/774-3431

Edmonds Antique Mall
201 5th Ave. S.
425/771-9466

Added Touch Antiques & Collectibles
23428 7th Ave. W.
425/778-3108

Country Cove Antiques
527 Dayton St.
425/672-9277

Rosa Mundi's Antiques
318 Main St.
425/771-6598

Valhalla Antiques & Collectibles
508 Main St.
425/771-1242

Wally's World
519 Main St.
425/774-0040

Waterfront Antique Mall
190 Sunset Ave. S.
425/670-0770

Heaton House Gallery
122 5th Ave. S.
425/771-7855

Old General Store
201 5th Ave. S., #12
425/771-2561

Amaryllis Antiques
18606 7th Ave. W.
425/775-2252

Aurora Antique Pavilion Inc.
24111 Hwy. 99
425/744-0566

Edmonds Sports Collectibles
508 Main St.
425/672-7892

Glorious Treasures Antique Shop
518 Main St.
425/775-5753

Mam's Vintage Linens & Things
537 Main St.
425/771-5310

Mainly Antiques
519 Main St.
425/774-0040

17 ELLENSBURG

Etcetera Shoppe
115 E. 4th Ave.
509/962-2578

Main Street Market Antique Mall
308 N. Main St.
509/925-1762

Meadowlark Farm
606 N. Main St.
509/962-3706

Edsel Antiques
213 W. 4th Ave.
509/962-5295

Anchor in Time
310 N. Main St.
509/925-7067

Hub Antiques & Estate Sales
307 N. Pearl St.
509/925-6581

Washington

Showplace Antique Mall
103 E. 3rd Ave.
509/962-9331

Attic
109 E. 3rd Ave.
509/925-7467

18 ENUMCLAW

Enumclaw Antique Mall
1501 Cole St.
360/825-4546

Country Peddler
19428 S.E. 400th St.
360/825-8313

19 EVERETT

Simply Victorian
1911 Hewitt Ave.
425/303-0760

Timeless Antiques
1922 Hewitt Ave.
425/258-9350

Maxine's Antiquities & Curios
2715 Hewitt Ave.
425/252-7812

20 GIG HARBOR

Barber Shop Antiques
1617 Stone Dr. N.W.
253/858-2922

Pandora's, Inc.
3801 Harborview Dr.
253/851-5164

21 GRAYLAND

Dittos Antiques & Gifts
1634 State Route 105
360/267-4644

Pregnant Onion Antiques
2399 Tokland Road
360/267-6914

22 ISSAQUAH

Haus of Antiques
157 1/2 Front St. N.
425/392-3424

Washington Antiques & Restorations
685 N.W. Gilman Blvd.
425/391-7947

Fogarty's Antiques
107 E. 3rd Ave.
509/962-3476

Delee's Antiques & Accents
1717 Cole St.
360/825-9112

Irene's Archives
1917 Hewitt Ave.
425/258-1881

Country Peddler
2114 Hewitt Ave.
425/258-1557

Grand Central Antique Mall
2804 Grand Ave.
425/252-1089

Hide & Sea
3306 Harborview Dr.
253/858-8971

Key Center Trading Post
15510 92nd St. KPN
253/884-2220

Olde Merchantile
1820 State Route 105
360/267-0121

Grandma's Treasure Chest Antiques
2190 State Route 105
360/267-1616

Gillman Antiques Gallery
625 N.W. Gilman Blvd.
425/391-6640

23 KALAMA

River Town Antique Mall
155 Elm St.
360/673-2263

Drew & Davis Antiques
222 N.E. 1st St.
360/673-4029

Memory Lane Antique Mall
413 N. 1st St.
360/673-3663

24 KENNEWICK

Sloping M Antiques Collectibles
W. Kennewick Ave.
509/582-1631

Carmichael's Antiques
3900 S. Oak St.
509/582-8216

Lea's Last Place Antiques
302 N. Union St.
509/735-4305

25 KENT

Robin's Antique Mall
201 1st Ave. S.
253/854-6543

The Shop
223 1st Ave. S.
253/852-5892

Now 'n' Then
218 W. Meeker St.
253/852-5890

Stagg's Coins Baseball Cards
317 W. Meeker St.
253/854-6340

Accrete Antiques
24526 104th Ave. S.E.
253/854-8916

26 KIRKLAND

Mambo
205 Kirkland Ave.
425/889-8787

Alexander McCallum Toppin
215 Lake St. S.E.
425/827-6593

Antiques at Park Lane
128 Park Lane
425/803-0136

Heritage Square
176 N. 1st St.
360/673-3980

Columbia Antiques & Collectibles
364 N. 1st St.
360/673-5400

Nostalgia Revisted
323 W. Kennewick Ave.
509/586-7250

Appleseed Gallery & Shops
108 Vista Way
509/735-2874

Crown Collectibles
109 N. Washington St.
509/586-6501

Lace Legacy, Etc.
220 1st Ave. S.
253/852-0052

Fanny Jean's Antiques & Things
213 W. Meeker St.
253/852-2053

Joy's Collectables
304 W. Meeker St.
253/854-6403

Mad Hatter Antiques
25748 101st Ave. S.E.
253/859-9293

Anniebelle Countryside Antiques
218 1st Ave. S.
253-852-6094

Danish-Swedish Antiques
207 Kirkland Ave.
425/822-7899

Woodshed Antiques
5918 Lake Washington Blvd. N.E.
425/822-8600

Bettina's
128 Park Lane
425/889-0234

Kirkland Antique Gallery
151 3rd St.
425/828-4993

27 LA CONNER

Nasty Jack's Antiques
103 E. Morris St.
360/466-3209

Cameo Antique Mall
511 E. Morris St.
360/466-3472

Morris Street Antiques
503 E. Morris St.
360/466-4212

Great Places to Stay

Katy's Inn-A Victorian Bed and Breakfast

503 S. Third
360/466-3366 or 1-800-914-7767
Open: Year-round
Rates: $69–$99
Directions: From I-5 going north from Seattle: Take Exit 221. Go west (left) over the freeway and take the first right to Conway/La Conner. Travel a country road for 10 minutes that leads to La Conner (signs are posted). Enter La Conner on Morris Street. Go left (south) on Second 1 block, then left up the hill on Washington 1 block. Katy's Inn is on the corner of Third and Washington — 1 ¼ hours drive from Seattle; 1 ½ hours from Vancouver, B.C.

Katy's Inn is first in several things: first-rate in location — within walking distance of everything in town, the first house in La Conner (built in 1876), and the first bed and breakfast in town (begun in 1984). This 1876 Victorian sits on a hillside two blocks above historic La Conner, which is filled with shops, galleries, antique stores, and waterfront cafes. Captain John Peck built this charming country Victorian for his wife and four daughters. It is filled with antiques, and the gardens are a blaze of Victorian glory. The inn offers five guest rooms: four upstairs (two with private baths), with French doors that open onto a wraparound porch with a beautiful view of the town and the Swinomish Channel, and a suite with private bath downstairs and a private entrance that opens into the garden.

If guests want a little activity before hot-tubbing or rocking and reading at the inn, they can feed the sea gulls on the waterfront; sail, raft or canoe down the Swinomish Channel; fish from the pier; take a cruise on the San Juan Islands ferry; ride a bike through the world-famous tulip fields of the Skagit Valley; or take a bird watching/whale watching cruise.

28 LANGLEY

Whidbey Island Antiques
Anthes Ave. at 2nd Ave.
360/221-2393

Lowry-James Fine Antiques
101 Anthes
360/221-0477

Virginia's Antiques & Gifts
206 1st St.
360/221-7797

29 LEAVENWORTH

Cabin Fever Rustics
923 Commercial St.
509/548-4238

Happy Wanderer
833 Front St.
509/548-6584

30 MAPLE VALLEY

Maple Valley Trading Post
12400 Renton Maple Valley Road S.
425/413-0277

Saratoga Antiques
221 1st St.
360/221-4363

Country Things Antiques & Gifts
221 8th St.
509/548-7807

Antique Loft
25531 S.E. 240th St.
425/432-0669

Great Places to Stay

Maple Valley Bed and Breakfast

20020 S.E. 228th
425/432-1409
Open: Daily — reservations required

For specific directions, please call the innkeeper who will be happy to direct you from your location.

If you have a hankering to be in the woods, in the quiet of the Pacific Northwest, this is your place. Innkeepers Clarke and Jane Hurlbut have turned their rustic cedar cottage into the Maple Valley Bed and Breakfast, complete with turret and especially built second floor suites. The hand-hewn cottage offers cedar walled guest rooms, one of which was actually built around its special bed! The bed, a handcrafted cedar piece created by Clarke out of logs cut from a nearby woods, is a prized family possession. French doors lead from each guest room onto a spacious balcony. Mint laced jugs of water and chocolate cookies await guests in each suite, and "hot babies" are quietly slipped between the sheets at night. Sounds intriguing, doesn't it? In fact, these "hot babies" have, on more than one occasion, given many guests an unexpected thrill as toes make contact with the warm, shifting lump tucked discreetly between the covers. According to the Hurlbuts, more than one person has sprung from the bed wondering if they had gotten closer to nature than they had ever intended! (Just for the record: "hot babies" are sand-filled bed warmers placed at the foot of the beds at night.)

Breakfast at the inn features Jayne's house specialty hootenanny oven pancakes, an old family recipe; or she might serve any of a number of her other specialties, like omelets, eggs benedict, or waffles. The rustic inn is not only a bed and breakfast, but an almost mythical destination for cyclists, foreign visitors and neighbors, and bed and breakfast guests mingle freely with whomever comes to share the Hurlbuts special kind of hospitality.

31 MONROE

Antique Boutique
119 W. Main St.
360/805-0325

Cobweb Antiques
21928 Yeager
360/794-4256

Antiques
110 E. Main St.
No phone listed

Great Places to Stay

The Frog Crossing Antiques & Collectibles, Bed & Breakfast
306 S. Lewis
206/881-7089 or 360/794-7622
Directions: ¼ mile south from Hwy. 2 and directly on State Route. 203 (Lewis St.)

The home of The Frog Crossing Antiques & Collectibles, Bed & Breakfast was built in 1913 and sits on ¾ of an acre near old Main Street in Monroe.

Monstrous old maple trees and gorgeous rhododendrons surround the house giving it the feel of walking through a park. Carriage tracks from the wagon trains which crossed its path in the olden days can still be see in the front yard.

Romantic rooms with fireplaces set the stage for the perfect getaway vacation. A beautiful Victorian bed with appropriate accessories from the same time period complete the decor.

The bed and breakfast houses an antique shop offering wonderful pieces from which to choose a memento of your stay at The Frog Crossing.

For those of you wanting to explore, The Frog Crossing is only a hop, skip and jump away from Snohomish — The Antique Capital of the Northwest.

32 MONTESANO

Fox's Den
124 Brumfield Ave.
360/249-5850

Great Places to Stay

The Abel House Bed and Breakfast
117 Fleet St. S.
360/249-6002
Open: Year-round
Rates: Begin at $55
Directions: Montesana is at the intersection of State Highways 12 and

107, about 40 miles west of Olympia and 10 miles east of Aberdeen. In-town signs direct you to the Abel House Bed and Breakfast.

People should visit the Abel House just to see it! You don't often see houses (this one built in 1908) with nine bedrooms on three of the four floors! The main floor is conveniently a common area, with the living room and library boasting "box beamed" ceilings and unique fireplaces. The entry, staircase, and dining room feature the original natural wood with a genuine Tiffany chandelier in the dining room. As the inn's brochure says, "Alas, as with many vintage homes, one bathroom per floor was considered "quite adequate." Fortunately for guests, the Abel House has recently added an addition that has eased the situation somewhat and provided some private baths. There is a game room on the upper floor, and the three lower floors are serviced by an elevator. The mansion's grounds have been lovingly and meticulously maintained and are open for guests' strolling pleasures. Breakfast and tea are served in the garden, the country English dining room, or in the privacy of the guest's room, whichever is preferred. As innkeeper Victor Reynolds says, "Eight years of repeat business indicates the house and staff are first-rate for even the most discriminating B&B goer!"

33 MOUNT VERNON

Old Movie House Antique Mall
520 Main St.
360/336-8919

D.B.'s General Store
1670 Old High #99 S.
360/424-5908

Posh
312 Pine St.
360/336-2728

34 NACHES

Bales Antiques
81 Locust Lane
509/653-2090

Country Kitchen Antiques
224 Naches Ave.
509/653-2008

Hobbit Shop Antiques
2450 S. Naches Road
509/965-0768

Wayside Antiques
10000 U.S. Hwy. 12
509/653-2120

35 NORTH BEND

Shoebox Antiques
108 W. North Bend Way
425/888-4949
Email: shoebox@snovalley.com
Open: Wed.–Sun. Noon–6:30

Felix and Randi Slette own (truly) the cutest antique shop in town. The shop has no dealers so the Slettes' hand pick each and every item in the store. Located in an old 1925 historic building, one would never expect to see such a large offering of antiques in such a small space (800 square feet). The couple has a special fancy for Jadeite glassware. So obviously this is a must stop for Martha Stewart. You will find at least 200 pieces in stock on any day such as McKee, Fire King, Jeanette and others.

California pottery from the '30s, '40s and '50s is another favorite of the owners along with a nice selection of advertising items, "guy stuff," railroad items, furniture and more.

If you are looking for something special you can email the Slettes' to be added to their search list. Once they locate the item, they then email photos back to you for your approval or selection. Looks like antique shopping on the net is here to stay.

Thanks, Felix and Randi, for taking such a special interest in your shop and your customers. It's very refreshing. Wishing you much continued success.

Bad Girls Antiques
42901 S.E. North Bend Way
425/888-1902
Open: Wed.–Sat. 11–5, Sun. 12–5
Directions: From eastbound I-90: Take Exit 27, take a left off the exit, and stay on the road straight through the town of North Bend. Bad Girls is on the right, 4+ miles from the exit and 1 mile from the stoplight in town. From westbound I-90: Take Exit 32, take a right off the exit, and follow the road until you must turn. Turn left. The shop is about ¹/₂ mile on the left.

These "bad girls" offer a 4,000-square-foot building filled to the brim for your shopping pleasure! Browsers and buyers can take their pick from quality furniture, antique and not-so-old items, unique collectibles, art pottery, fine glass, and 1940s dinnerware.

As is common with most antique dealers, their customers often create some very funny moments. Such is the case in this story as told by Jeanne Marie Klein. "A customer came into the store one day with a lamp that she wanted to know more about. She showed it to my partner," says Jeanne Marie Klein, a Bad Girl owner, "claiming it was made (and signed) by someone named 'Art Newvoo.' 'Who was this man?' she wanted to know. My partner was quizzically examining the lamp when I entered the room. She was very puzzled and asked if I recognized the name as a designer. Frowning, I thought 'Art Newvoo?' The light dawned, and I exclaimed, "You mean Art Nouveau — that's not a person, it's a style!" The poor lady was mystified until we explained further. After she left, we had a good laugh and decided that 'Art Newvoo' must have a sister called 'Arlene Deco!'"

Zara's Collectables
401 Ballarat Ave. N.
425/888-0271

Snoqualmie Valley Antique Co.
116 W. North Bend Way
425/888-5900

Jaclyn Rose Antiques
107 W. North Bend Way
425/831-5403

---

36 OAK HARBOR

Joseph's Antiques
28 E. Fakkema Road
360/679-3242

Aladdin's Antiques/DB's General Store
780 S.E. Pioneer Way #101
360/679-4744

Lorenzo's Lighting & Antiques
770 W. Pioneer Way
360/675-7619

Oak Harbor Antique Mall
1079 W. Pioneer Way
360/679-1902

37 OLYMPIA

Mike Cook Antiques & Collectibles
106 1/2 4th Ave.
360/943-5025

Lamplight Antiques
2906 Capitol Blvd. S.
360/943-9841

Once upon a Time
7141 Old High #101 N.
360/866-4050

Summit Lake Antiques & Restorations
10724 Summit Lake Road N.W.
360/866-0580

Second Hand Rose
9243 Yelm Hwy. S.E.
360/459-0954

Hexen Glass
1015 4th Ave. E.
360/705-8758

Homespun Craft & Antique Mall
5729 Little Rock Road S.W.
360/943-5194

R. Vernon's
2724 Pacific Ave. S.E.
360/705-0108

Old Bank
404 Washington St. S.E.
360/786-9234

Sherburne Antiques & Fine Art, Inc.
100 E. 4th Ave.
360/357-9177

38 PORT ANGELES

Marion's Port Angeles Antiques
220 W. 8th St.
360/452-5411

Corps Shop
222 N. Lincoln St.
360/457-7041

Waterfront Antique Mall
124 W. Railroad Ave.
360/452-3350

Mouse Trap Antiques & Gifts
128 W. 1st St.
360/457-1223

Springtime Robins & Rainbows
719 S. Lincoln St.
360/452-4019

Retro-Ville Antiques & Collectibles
118 W. 1st St.
360/452-1429

39 PORT ORCHARD

Side Door Mall
701 Bay St.
360/876-8631

Harbor Antique Mall
802 Bay St.
360/895-1898

Owl in the Attic Antiques
5637 S.E. Mile Hill Dr.
360/871-0382

Olde Central Antique Mall
801 Bay St.
360/895-1902

Great Prospects Variety Mall
1039 Bethel Road
360/895-1359

Washington

40 PORT TOWNSEND

Port Townsend Antique Mall
802 Washington St.
360/385-2590

Ancestral Sell
830 Water St.
360/385-1475

April Fool & Penny Too
725 Water St.
360/385-3438

Starrett House Antiques
802 Washington St.
360/385-2590

Undertown
211 Taylor St.
360/379-8069

Antique Company
1133 Water St.
360/385-9522

41 POULSBO

Abigail's Attic Antiques
2300 N.W. Vinland
360/697-7077

Bad Blanche
18890 Front St.
360/779-7788

Cat's Meow
18940 Front St. N.E.
360/697-1902

Granny & Papa's Antique Mall
19669 7th Ave. N.E.
360/697-2221

Hiding Place Antiques
18830 Front St. N.E.
360/779-7811

Front Street Antiques
18901 Front St. N.E.
360/697-1899

Antique Junction
122 N.E. Moe St.
360/779-1890

Great Places to Stay

Edgewater Beach Bed & Breakfast
26818 Edgewater Blvd.
1-800-641-0955
Directions: For specific directions from your location, please call the Innkeepers.

The Edgewater Beach Bed & Breakfast is a charming and peaceful retreat ideally suited for those who want to get away from the hustle and bustle of everyday life and commune with nature. The unassuming front of this two-story cottage-style home conceals a large 4,800-square-foot structure of which 3,000 square feet are dedicated to the guests.

The house was built in 1929 by Dr. Mayme MacLafferty, a Seattle physician and surgeon who selected the beautiful land to be the site of her weekend home in the country.

The guest area includes a warm, 670 square foot Great Room with surrounds an impressive, two-sided granite fireplace. Off of the Great Room is a large, bright Sun Room that opens onto an immense 2,800-square-foot deck overlooking Puget Sound's fjord (Hood Canal), an inlet of the ocean that flows in a channel carved by a glacier. The views from the Sun Room and the deck are awe inspiring. From the deck or Sun Room, the vast panoramic vista of the Olympic Mountains behind the fjord is simply breath-taking.

A family of Great American Bald Eagles lives on the edge of the fjord, and their flights are beautiful to watch. Many birds including crows and herons make their homes here; and sometimes the guests are visited by otters, sea lions and deer. On rare occasions, a whale has been spotted swimming in the fjord.

The Edgewater Beach Bed & Breakfast has accommodations for three parties. In addition to the Great Room and Sun Room, guests have access to a glass-enclosed dining room and a spacious, old-fashioned kitchen. The home is furnished in a relaxed, eclectic and sometimes whimsical manner that puts guests at ease while lightening their spirits. Many antiques and treasures from all over the United States create a delightful melange of beauty and playfulness.

Guests are treated to a bountiful breakfast basket that includes: smoked salmon, smoked turkey, cheeses, fresh fruit, pastries, cereal and sparkling beverage and juice.

42 PUYALLUP

Heier Echelon
107 W. Meeker
253/841-3187

Real Oldies of Yesteryears
110 S. Meridian
253/845-4471

Traditions Antiques
202 S. Meridian
253/840-8732

Carnaby Antique Mall
8424 River Road
253/840-3844

Antique City
103 S. Meridian
253/840-4324

Pioneer Antique Mall
113 S. Meridian
253/770-0981

Anderson's Edgewood Mall
10215 24th St. E.
253/952-5295

Puyallup Antique Mall
201 3rd St. S.E.
253/848-9488

43 QUILCENE

Granny's House of Glass
Hwy. 101 N.
360/765-3230

Ju Ju Junque
11 Old Church Road
360/765-3500

Gay Lees Bowser Beads
11 Old Church Road
360/765-3545

Quilcene Art & Antiques
11 Old Church Road
360/765-4447

44 REDMOND

Olde Stuff Antiques
16545 N.E. 80th St.
425/869-1697

Golden Days
8058 161st Ave. N.E.
425/883-0778

Valley Furniture & Interiors
8200 164th Ave. N.E.
425/885-4222

Edwardian Antiques, Inc.
7979 Leary Way N.E.
425/885-4433

Washington Antiques
8309 165th Ave. N.E.
425/881-7627

45 RENTON

Park Avenue Antiques
101 Park Ave. N.
425/255-4255

Relics Antiques
229 Wells Ave. S.
425/227/6557

Antique Palace Too
807 S. 3rd St.
425/235-9171

Antique Country Station
926 S. 3rd St.
425/235-6449

Downtown Renton Antique Mall
210 Wells Ave. S.
425/271-0511

St. Charles Place Antiques
230 Wells Ave. S.
425/226-8429

Cedar River Antique Mall
900 S. 3rd St.
425/255-4900

46 RICHLAND

Carel's Antiques
1119 S.E. Columbia Dr.
509/783-1775

Richland Antiques Mall
1331 George Washington Way
509/943-6762

Collector's Emporium
1315 George Washington Way
509/943-2841

Uptown Antiques Mall
1340 Jadwin Ave.
509/943-1866

47 ROCHESTER

Up The Creek Antiques
474 Ingalls Road
360/736-3529

Honest Don's Antiques
19225 Joselyn Road S.W.
360/273-8114

48 SEATTLE

Eileen of China
624 S. Dearborn St.
206/624-0816
Open: Daily 10–6

This 30,000-square-foot showroom is filled with exquisite, elegant and unique Asian Antiques and Arts. Enhance your home with traditional Chinese furniture; Zitan, Haunghwali, Hardwood and Rosewood. Simplicity of workmanship.

G.C.C. Gallery
408 Occidental Ave.
206/344-5244

G.C.C. Gallery is a family-opened business which has been producing top-of-the-line replica antique furnishings in Seoul, Korea, since 1976. The Gallery specializes in authentic oriental styles in such finishes as oyster oliver, burr elm, zelkova, paulownia as well as veneers.

Lyon's Antique Mall
4516 California S.W.
206/935-9774
Web site: www.lyonsam.com
Open: Mon.–Sat. 10–6, Sun. 11–5
Directions: Located in the old JC Penney, one block north of Alaska Junction in West Seattle

This large antique mall offers a wide variety of antiques and collectibles, including art deco, books, crystal, pottery, dolls and Barbies, furniture, jewelry, primitives, silver, toys, records and porcelain.

Antique Importers
640 Alaskan Way
206/628-8905

Seattle Antique Market, Inc.
1400 Alaskan Way
206/623-6115

Cascade Mall
9530 Aurora Ave. N.
206/524-9626

Rhinestone Rosie
606 W. Crockett St.
206/283-4605

Hunters Antiques
106 Denny Way
206/285-9172

Bogart Bremmer & Bradley Antiques
8000 15th Ave. N.W.
206/783-7333

M. Maslan Photos, Postcards & Ephemera
214 1st Ave. S.
206/587-0187

Flury & Company, Ltd.
322 1st Ave. S.
206/587-0260

Kagedo Japanese Antiques
520 1st Ave. S.
206/467-9077

Azuma Fine Art & Gallery
530 1st Ave S.
206/622-5599

Legacy, Ltd.
1003 1st Ave.
206/624-6350

Asia Gallery
1220 1st Ave.
206/622-0516

Antique Warehouse
1400 Alaskan Way
206/624-4683

Dragers Classic Toys
4905 Aurora Ave. N.
206/545-4400

Japanense Antiquities Gallery
200 E. Boston St.
206/324-3322

Greg Davidson Antiques
1307 First Ave.
206/625-0406

Campbell Antiques & Collectibles
13027 Des Moines Memorial Dr.
206/243-6807

Mandrakes
8300 15th Ave. N.W.
206/781-2623

Carolyn Staley Fine Prints
313 1st Ave. S.
206/621-1888

Antiquarius
514 1st Ave. N.
206/282-5489

Clarke and Clarke
524 1st Ave. S.
206/447-7017

Pioneer Square Mall
602 1st Ave.
206/624-1164

Antique Elegance
1113 1st Ave.
206/467-8550

Rudy's Vintage Clothing & Antq. Watches
1424 1st. Ave.
206/682-6586

Washington

Isadora's Antique Clothing
1915 1st Ave.
206/441-7711

Village Manor
17651 1st Ave. S.
206/439-8842

The Junk Shop
1404 14th Ave.
206/329-4148

Fremont Antique Mall
3419 Fremond Place N.
206/548-9140

Johnson & Johnson Antiques
6820 Greenwood Ave.
206/789-6489

Hobby Horse Antiques
7421 Greenwood Ave.
206/789-1574

Pelayo Antiques
8421 Greenwood Ave.
206/789-1333

Jean Williams Antiques
115 S Jackson St.
206/622-1110

Daily Planet
11046 Lake City Way
206/633-0895

Antique Galleria
17171 Lake Forest Park N.E.
206/362-6845

First Hill Collectibles
1004 Madison St.
206/624-3207

Apogee
4224 E. Madison St.
206/325-2848

Stuteville Antiques
1518 E. Olive Way
206/329-5666

Auntie Shrews Antiques
816 S.W. 152nd St.
206/242-0727

Antique Junktion Mall
23609 Pacific Hwy. S.
206/878-3069

Raven's Nest Treasure
85 B Pike St.
206/343-0890

Jukebox City
1950 1st Ave. S.
206/625-1950

David Weatherford Antiques
133 14th Ave. E.
206/329-6533

Chelsea Antiques
3622 N.E. 45th St.
206/525-2727

Private Screening
3504 Fremont Place N.
206/548-0751

Goode Things
7114 Greenwood Ave.
206/784-7572

Pelayo Antiques
7601 Greenwood Ave.
206/789-1999

Hurds Antiques, Etc.
8554 Greenwood Ave.
206/782-2405

Honeychurch Antiques
1008 James St.
206/622-1225

Gens Antiques & Dolls
12518 Lake City Way N.E.
206/365-5440

Hotel Lobby Antiques
4105 Leary Way N.W.
206/784-5340

Veritables
2816 E. Madison St.
206/726-8047

Michael Reed Black Antiques
125 W. Mercer St.
206/284-9581

Antiques of Burien
209 152nd St. S.W.
206/431-0550

My Granny's Attic
901 S.W. 152nd St.
206/243-3300

Spindrifters
Pike Place Market, #321
206/623-6432

B & W Antiques
311 E. Pike St.
206/325-6775

Wrinkled Bohemia
1125 Pike St.
206/464-0850

Great Western Trading Co.
1501 Pike Place
206/622-6376

Old Friends Antiques
1501 Pike Place
206/625-1997

N B Nichols & Son
1924 Post Alley
206/448-8906

Curbside Collectibles
7011 Roosevelt Way N.E.
206/522-0882

Kobo
814 E. Roy St.
206/726-0704

Ruby Montana's Pinto Pony, Ltd.
603 2nd Ave.
206/621-7669

Partners in Time
1332 6th Ave.
206/623-4218

Silhouette Antiques & Gifts
1516 N.E. 65th St.
206/525-2499

Craniums Cool Collectibles
12331 32nd Ave. N.E.
206/364-8734

Carriage House Galleries
5611 University Way N.E.
206/523-4960

Fairlook Antiques
81 1/2 Washington
206/622-5130

Reba's Classic Ceramics
222 Westlake Ave. N.
206/622-2459

Antique Liquidators
503 Westlake Ave. N.
206/623-2740

Turner Helton Antiques
2600 Western Ave.
206/322-1994

The Antlers
15214 9th Ave. S.W.
206/242-3304

Antique Touch
1501 Pike Place Market, #318
206/622-6499

Mugs Antiques
1501 Pike Place
206/623-3212

Inside Out
Westlake Center/400 Pine St.
206/292-8874

Broadway Clock Shop
2214 Queen Anne Ave. N.
206/285-3130

Vintage Costumers
7011 Roosevelt Way N.E.
206/522-5234

Shahlimar
217 2nd Ave. S.
206/447-2570

Laguana Vintage Pottery
609 2nd Ave.
206/682-6162

Ageing Fancies
308 N.E. 65th St.
206/523-4556

Pacific Galleries
2121 3rd Ave.
206/441-9990

Porter Davis Antiques
103 University St.
206/622-5310

Oasis Antique Oriental Rugs
5655 University Way N.E.
206/525-2060

Downtown Antique Market
2218 Western Ave.
206/448-6307

222 Westlake Antique Mall
222 Westlake Ave. N.
206/628-3117

Antique Distributors
507 Westlake Ave. N.
206/622-0555

Madame & Co. Vintage Fashions
117 Yesler Way
206/621-1728

Great Places to Stay

Beech Tree Manor
1405 Queen Anne Ave. N.
206/281-7037
Open: Year-round 9–8
Directions: Beech Tree Manor is located at the northwest corner of the intersection of Queen Anne Avenue North and Lee Street. It has on-street parking. Electric trolleys link the Manor to downtown Seattle and, by transfer, to the entire Metro area.

Nestled on historic Queen Anne Hill, adjacent to downtown Seattle, this turn-of-the-century mansion has been beautifully restored. Its name comes from the rare and massive Copper Beech tree on the property that has, so far, withstood nature, man, and progress. This bed and breakfast has been described as "an excellent bed and breakfast" by the *New York Times*, and "stunning" by *Seattle's Best Places*. Winning such praises as these comes from the inn's attitude about itself, which is described in its brochure as "organized for the enjoyment of those who require a genteel atmosphere for their temporary housing and special celebrations." To achieve this "genteel atmosphere," the inn offers a very proper English decor, with seven guest rooms (some with private bath). The mansion is filled with a lifetime collection of antiques and offers "all the modern amenities a seasoned traveler expects," plus a few extras, like pure white cotton sheets and a shady porch with wicker rockers. So if proper English is your style, we suggest a stay at the Beech Tree.

49 SEAVIEW

Dory's Antiques & Collectibles
48th at Pacific Hwy.
360/642-3005

Stagecoach Antiques
4005 Pacific Hwy., #103
360/642-4565

Sea-Tryst Antiques
48th Place
360/642-4888

Gollywobbler Antiques
4809 Pacific Hwy. S.
360/642-8685

50 SEQUIM

Bramble Cottage Antiques, Ltd.
305 W. Bell St.
360/683-1724

Lighthouse Antique
261321 Hwy. 101
360/681-7346

Gardiner Antiques
10417 Hwy. 101
360/797-7728

Queen's Cabinet Antiques
157 W. Cedar St.
360/681-2778

Anne's Sequim Antiques
253 W. Washington St.
360/683-8287

51 SHELTON

Frontier Antiques
317 S. 1st St.
360/426-7795

Second Floor Antiques
107 S. 4th St.
360/427-9310

Carole's Jewelry
221 W. Railroad Ave.
360/426-7847

Olympic Gateway Coins & Cllbls.
106 S. 4th St.
360/426-0304

Red Rose Antiques
1209 Olympic Hwy. S.
360/426-1290

52 SNOHOMISH

Ranee-Paul Antiques
900 1st St.
360/568-6284

Rick's Antiques
916 1st St.
360/568-4646

Black Cat Antique Mall
923 1st St.
360/568-8144

River City Antique Mall
1007 1st St.
360/568-1155

Snohomish Antiques Company
1019 1st St.
360/563-0343

Victoria Village
1108 1st St.
360/568-4913

Michael's 1st Street Antique Mall
1202 1st St.
360/568-9735

Collectors Book Store
829 2nd St.
360/568-9455

Casablanca Antiques
104 C Ave.
360/568-0308

Sharon's Antique Mall
111 Glen Ave.
360/568-9854

Brenda's Antiques & Collectibles
118 Glen Ave.
360/568-2322

Star Center Mall
123 Glen Ave.
360/402-1870

Remember When Antique Mall
908 1st St.
360/568-0757

Old Store Antiques
922 1st St.
360/568-1919

Another Antique Shop
924 1st St.
360/568-3629

First Bank Antiques
1015 1st St.
360/568-7609

Antique Station
1108 1st St.
360/568-5034

Antique Palace
1116 1st St.
360/568-2644

Egelstad's Clock Shop
809 2nd St.
360/568-3444

Star Center Mall Antiques
829 2nd St.
206/402-1870

Faded Glory, Ltd.
113 C Ave.
360/568-5344

Antique Gallery Mall
117 Glen Ave.
360/568-7644

Collector's Showcase
118 Glen Ave.
360/568-1339

Louis C. Wein Antiques & Art
102 Union St.
360/568-8594

Washington

Great Places to Stay

Redmond House Bed and Breakfast

317 Glen Ave.
360/568-2042
Rates: $85–$100
Directions: Snohomish is located on Hwy. 9, just east of Everett, Washington. Traveling from I-5 either north or south: use the Wenatchee-Stevens Pass exit to Hwy. 2. Cross the "Trestle" and stay to the right. The first exit will take you right into town and onto Avenue D. Turn east on 4th Street and right on Glen.

The Redmond House is another "must" for dyed-in-the-wool antique junkies. It's located in the Victorian era town of Snohomish, within easy walking distance of the "Antique Capital of the Northwest"— 400 antique dealers, gift shops, and restaurants. For the better halves who don't want to spend every minute poking through "old stuff," there are all types of outdoorsy things to do, like exploring the Centennial Trail and the walking tour of Snohomish, plus other hiking, boating, golfing, skiing, hot air ballooning, parachuting, and visits to wineries and sports events all right there in town or within easy driving distance.

The inn greets guests with wonderful gardens and a wraparound porch complete with wicker furniture and a porch swing. The house itself is furnished with period antiques and quilts for everyone's comfort. There's a sunroom with games and a hot tub, a ballroom with big band music, bedrooms with featherbeds, and some even with clawfoot tubs for soaking, plus complimentary tea or sherry at the end of a hard day.

53 SPOKANE

Persnickey's Antiques & Collectibles
408 N. Argonne Road
509/891-7858

B.J.' Books 'n' Brew
1320 W. Francis Ave.
509/327-2988

Luminaria & La Tierra
154 S. Madison St.
509/747-9198

Aunt Bea's Antiques
5005 N. Market St.
509/487-9278

United Hillyard Mall
5016 N. Market St.
509/483-2647

Benson's Antiques
5215 N. Market St.
509/487-3528

Duprie's Antiques
920 W. Cora Ave.
509/327-2449

Vintage Post Cards & Stamps
1908 N. Hamilton St.
509/487-5677

Cloke & Dagger Antiques
4912 N. Market St.
509/482-2066

Hillyard Variety Consnmt Store
5009 N. Market St.
509/482-3433

Collectors Showcase Antique Mall
5201 N. Market St.
509/482-7112

Monroe St. Bridge Antique Market
604 N. Monroe St.
509/327-6398

Antique Gallery
620 N. Monroe St.
509/325-3864

Worthington Discontinued China
2217 N. Monroe St.
509/328-7072

Wooden Rail
818 N. Pines Road
509/922-3443

Ben's Antiques
2130 E. Sprague Ave.
509/535-4368

Spokane Antique Mall
12 W. Sprague Ave.
509/747-1466

Antiquex
28 W. 3rd Ave.
509/624-6826

Schade Brewery Antique Mall
528 E. Trent Ave.
509/624-0272

Spokane Book Center
626 N. Monroe St.
509/328-2332

Vintage Rabbit Antique Mall
2317 N. Monroe St.
509/326-1884

Spokane Valley Antique Mall
23 S. Pines Road
509/928-9648

N.W. Collector Arms
12021 E. Sprague Ave.
509/891-0990

Larsen's Antique Clock Shop
953 E. 3rd Ave.
509/534-4994

Timeless Treasures Antiques
10309 E. Trent Ave.
509/928-0819

No Place Like Home
13409 E. Wellesley Ave.
509/922-4246

54 STANWOOD

Apple Barrell Antiques
1415 Pioneer Hwy., #530
360/652-9671

Yo Mama's Attic Antiques
8617 271 St. N.W.
360/629-3995

55 SUMNER

The Blue Lantern
1003 Main St.
253/863-5935

Whistle-Stop Antique Mall
1109 Main St.
253/863-3309

Cobwebs Removed, Inc.
1008 Main St.
253/863-1924

56 TACOMA

Abigail's Antiques
8825 Bridgeport Way S.W.
253/588-9712

Victoria's
702 Broadway
253/272-5983

Freighthouse Antiques Emporium
728 Broadway
253/627-8019

Memory Mall
744 Broadway
253/272-6476

Treasure Chest
11605 Bridgeport Way S.W.
253/581-2454

Mimi's Antique Furniture
3813 N. 26th St.
253/759-0506

Sanford & Son Antiques
743 Broadway
253/272-0334

Time Machine
746 Broadway
253/272-7254

Washington

Lily The Pad
756 Broadway
253/627-6858

Collector's Nook
213 N. I St.
253/272-9828

European Antique Imports
1930 Pacific Ave.
253/272-8763

Pacific Run Antique Mall
10228 Pacific Ave. S.
253/539-0117

Aries Antiques
16120 Pacific Ave.
253/582-9029

Claudia Smith's Antiques
5101 N. Pearl St.
253/759-6052

Anchor Antiques Co.
5129 N. Pearl St.
253/752-1134

Teri's Curiosity Shop
760 Saint Helens Ave.
253/383-3211

Museum Antiques
5928 Steilacoom Blvd. S.W.
253/584-3930

Katy's Antiques & Collectibles Mall
602 E. 25th St.
253/305-0203

Woodward's Antiques
12146 C St.
253/531-1005

Bellocchio Antiques & Bistro
1926 Pacific Ave.
253/383-3834

Ramlawn Antiques
1936 Pacific Ave.
253/272-5244

Parkland Parish Antique Mall
12152 Pacific Ave. S.
253/537-0978

Valentino's Antiques & Books
4931 N. Pearl St.
253/759-3917

Ruston Antique Galleries
5101 N. Pearl St.
253/759-2624

Curtright & Son Gallery
759 Saint Helens Ave.
253/383-2969

Key Antiques
5485 Steilacoom Blvd S.W.
253/588-0569

Mandarin Oriental Antiques
5935 Steilacoom Blvd. S.W.
253/582-6655

Great Places to Stay

The DeVoe Mansion Bed & Breakfast
208 E. 133rd St.
206/539-3991
Open: Daily 8–9
Rates: $80–$90
Email: devoe wolfenet.com
Web site: www.wolfenet.com/~devoe/
Directions: From Seattle or Tacoma: Take I-5 south (from Olympia take I-5 north) to Exit 127. Go east on Hwy. 512 approximately two miles to the Pacific Avenue exit (signs also say Mt. Rainier, State Route 7, Parkland, Pacific Lutheran University). Go south on Pacific Avenue approximately 2 miles, and turn left on 133rd Street South. Continue two blocks and the DeVoe Mansion is on the corner of 133rd Street and B Avenue.

Ladies, this one's for you! The 1911 DeVoe Mansion was named to the National Historic Register in 1993 in honor of a tireless pioneer in the women's suffrage movement. The home was built for John and Emma Smith DeVoe, who moved into the mansion one year after Emma had successfully helped the women of Washington State achieve the right to vote. It would be another 10 years before all women in the United States were granted that same right. Emma's home was named to the National Historic Register as a tribute to her devoted efforts to the suffrage cause on both national and state levels.

To understand and appreciate the mansion's history and decor, guests need to know a little about Emma, because Emma's life's work in the suffrage movement is the decorating basis for each of the mansion's guest rooms. Emma's dedication to the suffrage cause began when she was eight years old, when she and her sister attended a rally featuring Susan B. Anthony. When Emma came to Washington State in 1906, she found a very disorganized, unmotivated suffrage association. Her first winter on the West Coast saw her elected as president of the Washington State Equal Suffrage Association, and she spent the next four years traveling the state, rejuvenating and revitalizing the association. On November 8, 1910, Washington became the fifth state in the union to pass women's suffrage.

Each of the guest rooms is named for someone who was significant in Emma's life. The Susan B. Anthony Room features an 1880s hand-carved oak bedroom set, private sitting area and private bath. The Carrie Chapman Catt Room is highlighted by a queen-size, four-poster mahogany rice bed with an old growth Alaskan cedar tree just outside the window. The John Henry DeVoe Room is named for Emma's most devoted supporter — her husband. It holds an antique queen-size 1860s pine bedroom set. Guests are also treated to two porches for rocking and relaxing, a hot tub on the deck, landscaped grounds for strolling, and breakfast.

57 VANCOUVER

Yesterday's Treasures
707 Grand Blvd.
360/695-2330

Downtown Main Antique Mall
1108 Main St.
360/696-2253

Something Nice Antiques & Collectibles
2310 Main St.
360/694-2948

Henker's
14013 S.E. Mill Plain Blvd.
360/256-5620

Vendors Outlet Mall
7907 N.E. Hwy. 99
360/574-6674

Main Street Trader
1916 Main St.
360/695-0295

Country Peddler
2315 Main St.
360/695-6792

Jadestone Gallery
10922 N.E. St. Johns Road
360-573-2580

58 VASHON

Lawing's Antiques & Textiles
16619 Westside Hwy. S.W.
206/463-2402

Owens Antiques & Decorative Arts
19605 Vashon Hwy. S.W.
206/463-5193

Sandy's Antiques & Jewelry
17607 Vashon Hwy. S.W.
206/463-5807

Washington

59 WALLA WALLA

Bonnie's Antiques
2815 E. Isaacs Ave.
509/529-2009

Country Collectors
226 E. Main St.
509/529-6034

Shady Lawn Antiques & Espresso
711 N. Rose St.
509/529-2123

General Store
211 W. Main St.
509/522-8663

Antique Mall at Vintage Square
315 S. 9th Ave.
509/525-5100

60 WENATCHEE

Pretentious Antique Co.
328 N. Chelan Ave.
509/663-8221

Village Mall Antiques
611 S. Mission St.
509/662-9171

Antique Mall of Wenatchee
11 N. Wenatchee Ave.
509/662-3671

Collectors Gallerie
928 N. Wenatchee Ave.
509/663-5203

Adams Supply Co.
509 S. Mission St.
509/662-2210

Early American Light Lamps
1206 Okanogan Ave.
509/662-0386

Dimitri's Antiques & Seconds
810 S. Wenatchee Ave.
509/662-2920

Treasures of the Heart
20 S. Wenatchee Ave.
509/663-8112

61 WINLOCK

Kattywampus Antique Mall
405 1st St. N.E.
360/785-4427

Old Hatchery
707 N.E. 1st St.
No Phone

62 YAKIMA

Somewhere in Time
3911 S. 1st St.
509/248-7352

Shopkeeper
807 W. Yakima Ave.
509/452-6646

Mt. Mommie's General Store
225 Naches Ave.
509/653-2556

Churchill's Books & Antiques
125 S. 2nd St.
509/453-8207

Antiques, Etc.
5703 Tieton Dr.
509/966-2513

Yesterday's Village
15 W. Yakima Ave.
509/457-4981

Depot
32 N. Front St.
509/576-6220

Antique Alley Mini-Mall
1302 W. Lincoln Ave.
509/575-1499

Calico Barn Antiques
1471 S. Naches Road
509/966-1462

Antiques & Decor, Ltd.
108 S. 3rd Ave.
509/457-6949

Lantern Antiques
8507 Tieton Dr.
509/966-1396

Green Gables
302 E. Yakima Ave.
509/577-0744

Wisconsin

58 Superior

2

53

9 Cable

23 Hayward

69 Webster

7 Boulder Junction

0   Mileage   40

73 Woodruff

35

63

Minocqua 36

48 Rhinelander

8

49 Rice Lake

60 Turtle Lake

51

141

43 Osceola

Hwy. 141 24

20 Gills Rock

17 Egg Harbor

12

41

42

51 River Falls

94

15 Eau Claire

29

67 Wausau

Shawano

52

6 Bonduel

55 Sturgeon Bay

10

10

Algoma 1

35

Stevens Point 54

Green Bay 21

53

Wisconsin Rapids 72

66 Waupaca

41 New London

12

51

70 Wild Rose

2 Appleton

33

Menasha

10

Manitowoc 32

40 Necedah

Wautoma 68

21

44 Oshkosh

59

5 Berlin

Tomah

90

46 Princeton

Sheboygan 53

27 La Crosse

14

71 Wisconsin Dells

43

62 Viroqua

28 Lake Delton

151

41

35

50 Richland Center

12

Columbus 11

3 Beaver Dam

Cedarburg 10

Hartford 22

61

14

57 Sun Prairie

Madison

Milwaukee

Fennimore

Mt. Horeb

31

Lake Mills

30

94

42

34

19

18

14 Dodgeville

38

Oconomowoc

65 Waukesha

18

39 Mukwonago

35 Mineral Point

14

90

43

64 Waterford

47 Racine

16 Edgerton

12

45

151

Platteville

Janesville 25

Delavan

Elkhorn

8

61

56 Sturtevant

Monroe 37

13

18

Burlington

Union Grove

26 Kenosha

12 Darien

Beloit 4

63

29 Lake Geneva

Walworth

Wisconsin

1 ALGOMA

Algoma Antique Mall
300 4th St.
920/487-3221

Granny's Attic Antiques
1009 Jefferson St.
920/487-3226

Gaslight Antiques
1000 Freemont
920/487-5705

White Pine Antiques
720 3rd St.
920/487-7217

2 APPLETON

Audios Antiques
1426 N. Ballard Road
920/734-2856

Avenue Coins & Jewelry
303 E. College Ave.
920/731-4740

Memories Antique Mall
400 Randolph Dr.
920/788-5553

Am. Heritage Antique & Appraisal
6197 W. City Tk. Kk
920/734-8200

Harp Gallery Antiques & Furniture
2495 Northern Road
920/733-7115

Fox River Antique Mall
1074 S. Van Dyke Road
920/731-9699

3 BEAVER DAM

Added Touch
108 Front St.
920/887-2436

Crosswalk Antiques
124 Front St.
920/887-9586

Tree City Antiques
114 Front St.
920/885-5593

General Store Antique Mall, Inc.
150 Front St.
920/887-1116

4 BELOIT

Nest Egg, Ltd.
816 E. Grand Ave.
608/365-0700

Caple Country Antiques
309 State St.
608/362-5688

Riverfront Antiques Mall
306 State St.
608/362-7368

5 BERLIN

Abe Old Antiques
166 Huron St.
920/361-0889

Picture That Antiques Mall
107 W. Huron St.
920/361-0255

Picture That
102 E. Huron St.
920/361-0255

6 BONDUEL

Hearthside Antique Mall
129 S. Cecil St.
715/758-6200

7 BOULDER JUNCTION

Joan's Antiques
10377 Main St.
715/385-2600

Fisherman's Wife
10382 Main St.
715/385-9205

8 BURLINGTON

Gingham Dog Antiques
109 E. Chestnut St.
414/763-4759

Antique Alley Mall
481 Milwaukee Ave.
414/763-5257

Hemenway House Antiques
N5503 State Road 120
414/723-2249

Gingham Dog Antiques
120 E. Chestnut St.
414/763-2348

Alby's Antiques & Amusements
216 N. Pine St.
414/767-1191

9 CABLE

Cottage Shop
Box #113
715/798-3077

Honey Creek Antiques
RR 1 #73
715/798-3958

Nordik Sleigh Antiques
Hwy. M
715/798-3967

10 CEDARBURG

Creekside Antiques
N69 W6334 Bridge Road
414/377-6131

Robin's Nest Antiques & Gifts
N70 W6340 Bridge Road
414/377-3444

Antiquenet
6920 Kingswood Dr.
414/375-0756

Antique Loft
576 62 Ave.
414/377-9007

American Country Antiques
W61 N506 Washington Ave.
414/375-4140

Nouveau Antique & Jewelry Parlor
W62 N594 Washington Ave.
414/375-4568

Stonehouse Antiques
2088 Washington Ave.
414/675-2931

Cedar Creek Antiques
N70 W6340 Bridge Road
414/377-2204

Spool N Spindle Antiques
N70 W6340 Bridge Road
414/377-4200

Don's Resale & Antique Shop
N57 W6170 Portland Road
414/377-6868

Crow's Nest
6404 66 St.
414/377-3039

Heritage Lighting
W62 N572 Washington Ave.
414/377-9033

Patricia Frances Interiors
W62 N634 Washington Ave.
414/377-7710

11 COLUMBUS

Antique Shoppes of Columbus Mall
141 W. James St.
920/623-2669

Antique Shops of Columbus
902 Park Ave.
920/623-3930

Columbus Antique Mall & Museum
239 Whitney St.
920/623-1992

12 DARIEN

Ice Cream Shoppe
18 S. Beloi St.
414/724-5060

13 DELAVAN

Geneva Lakes Imports & Antiques
2460 N. County Tk. O S.
414/728-8887

Treasure Hut Florist
6551 State Road 11
414/728-2020

Antiques of Delavan
229 E. Walworth Ave.
414/728-9977

Beall Jewelers
305 E. Walworth Ave.
414/728-8577

Remember When
313 E. Walworth Ave.
414/728-8670

Beall Jewelers Clock Gallery
306 E. Walworth Ave.
414/728-8577

Buttons & Bows
312 E. Walworth Ave.
414/728-6813

Delavan Antique & Art Center
230 E. Walworth Ave.
414/740-1400

14 DODGEVILLE

Carousel Collectibles & Antiques
121 N. Iowa St.
608/935-5196
Open: May–Dec. 7 days a week, Jan.–Apr., Mon.–Sat. Call ahead to be sure shop is open. Hours vary.
Directions: *Traveling north from Dubuque on Hwy. 151*, exit to Hwy. 23 North into downtown Dodgeville. *Traveling west from Madison on 151-18*, take Exit 60 (18 W.) to Hwy. 23. At stoplight turn left to downtown Dodgeville. *From Spring Green*, stay on Hwy. 23 South to downtown Dodgeville.

Carousel Horses have been a big part of the Reynolds family's lives for the past 20 years. Virginia Reynolds began painting carousel horses at The House On The Rock. She learned a very unique method of painting, and after five years passed this knowledge on to her daughter Cherie. During the next 15 years, the two worked together painting hundreds of carousel horses in all sizes. The painting of each horse is one-of-a-kind. In 1985 Carousel Collectibles and Antiques was opened. Through her creativity and artistic talents, Virginia passed on her love of carousels to many people who came to the shop. Virginia died unexpectedly in January 1995, which was a great loss to all those who knew her and admired her

work. Cherie continues the painting of carousel horses with the hopes of carrying on her mother's memory and her love of carousels.

In addition to beautifully handpainted carousel horses, the shop carries a wide variety of collectibles — stunning glassware, handpainted dishes, pottery, primitives, furniture, paper collectibles, pictures, books and more. The shop also carries many carousel gift items including the handpainted carousel horses ranging from 12 to 60 inches in size.

Rustic Floreral Antiques
101 W. Leffler St.
608/935-5564

Woodshed
RR 1
608/935-3896

15 EAU CLAIRE

Rice's Antiques
202 S. Barslow St.
715/835-5351

Piney Hills Antiques
5260 Deerfield Road
715/832-8766

Antique Emporium
306 Main St.
715/832-2494

Molly's Mercantile
2807 E. Hamilton Ave.
715/839-8535

16 EDGERTON

Mildred's Antiques
4 Burdick St.
608/884-3031

Antiques & Art Gallery
104 W. Fulton St.
608/884-6787

Sisters Act
114 W. Fulton St.
608/884-6092

Edgerton Resale Mall
204 W. Fulton St.
608/884-8148

17 EGG HARBOR

Basil Sweet, Ltd.
7813 Egg Harbor Road
920/868-2300

Country Bumpkin
6228 State Hwy. 432
920/743-8704

Door County Antiques
7150 State Hwy. 42
920/868-2121

Bay Trading Co.
7367 State Hwy. 42
920/868-2648

Olde Orchard Antique Mall
7381 State Hwy. 42
920/868-3685

CJ's Antiques, Etc. & CJ's Too
7899 State Hwy. 42
920/868-2271

Shades of the Past
8010 State Road 42
920/868-3800

Cupola House
7836 Egg Harbor Road
920/868-3941

18 ELKHORN

Powell's Antique Shop
14 W. Geneva St.
414/723-2952

Front Parlor Antiques
6696 Millard Road
414/742-3489

Wisconsin

Twin Pines Antique Mall
5438 State Road 11
414/723-4492

Loveless Antiques
7091 U.S. Hwy. 12
414/742-2619

Dave's Antiques
W6610 N. Lakeshore Dr.
414/742-2416

Bits of the Past & Present
5691 State Road 11
414/723-4763

Heirlooms
12 S. Wisconsin St.
414/723-4070

Van Dyke's Apple Basket
20 S. Wisconsin St.
414/723-4909

19 FENNIMORE

Tuckwood House
1280 10th St.
608/822-3164

20 GILLS ROCK

Great Places to Stay

Harbor House Inn
12666 Hwy. 42
920/854-5196

This 1904 Victorian bed and breakfast is located in Gills Rock, a fishing village on the northern tip of beautiful Door County. The original home has been in the Weborg family since its inception, and has recently been restored to its original elegance. A Scandinavian wing has been added with large rooms, each with kitchenettes and decks overlooking the harbor. Cottages are also available (one with a woodburning fireplace). A 35-foot lighthouse has recently been erected, providing a romantic luxury accommodation with fireplace and Jacuzzi. All rooms feature private baths. Enjoy a continental-plus breakfast each morning.

21 GREEN BAY

American Antiques and Jewelry
1049 W. Mason St.
920/498-0111

Towne Trader Antiques & Auction Service
914 Main St.
920/435-8070

Yesteryear's Antique Mall
611 9th St.
920/435-4900

Ginny's Antiques & Collectable
3808 Riverside Dr.
920/336-3666

Antique Collectors Corner
898 Elmore St.
920/497-7141

Meadow Suite
630 E. Walnut St.
920/432-1733

Red's-Shirley Antiques
1344 Main St.
920/437-3596

Packer City Antiques
712 Redwood Dr.
920/490-1095

Sue's Antiques & Collectibles
1231 S. Military Ave.
920/497-2033

J & S Antique Mall
3110 Kewaunee Road
920/863-3203

22 HARTFORD

Sharron's Antiques
135 N. Main St.
414/673-2751

Erin Antiques
1691 State Road (Hwy. 835)
414/673-4680

Hartford Antique Mall
147 N. Rural
414/673-2311

Great Places to Stay

Jordan House Bed and Breakfast
81 S. Main St.
414/673-5643
Open: Year-round. Reservations required
Rates: $65 Private Bath, $55 Shared bath
Directions; From Hwy. 41, take Hwy. 60 exit west 7 miles to downtown Hartford (intersection of Highways 60 and 83). Turn left on Main St., go 1 ¹/₂ blocks.

Built at the turn-of-the-century the Jordan House was designed by Mr. Jacob Jacoby, a noted Milwaukee architect. The original building plans are still intact and reflect the care and substance of construction. Four spacious guest rooms decorated with period furniture await your arrival. A hearty country breakfast is served each morning.

Convenient to all major highways in southeastern Wisconsin, antique malls and shops abound in the area. Hartford is also the home of the Kissel automobile. Built from 1906 until the Depression in 1931, the Kissel was a high caliber custom built car. The Hartford Heritage Auto Museum, within walking distance of the Jordan House, provides a rare opportunity to see the largest assembled group of these rare luxury cars as well as over ninety other vintage cars and other automobile memorabilia.

23 HAYWARD

Red Shed Antiques
County Road, #B
715/634-6088

Hill's Antiques
RR 2
715/634-2037

Main Street Curiosity Shop
214 Main St.
715/634-1465

Remember When
114 N. Dakota Ave.
715/634-5282

Nelson Bay Antiques
RR 3
715/634-2177

Great Places to Stay

Edgewater Inn B&B
Route 1, Box 1293
715/462-9412

The fieldstone foundation and fireplace offer a hint of history from this turn-of-the-century home. Records show Arthur White and his wife

Lillian purchased 147 acres in the township of Spider Lake on August 15, 1905. They later added more tracts of land totaling 300 acres. On this lakefront property, Art, a lumberman and entrepreneur, built one of the area's largest farms.

24 HWY. 141

These shops are located within a few miles of each other throughout the small towns of Lena, Coleman, Middle Inlet, Wausaukee, Amberg, Pembine and Niagra along Hwy. 141.

The White Rabbit Collector's Mall
135 N. Rosera (Hwy. 141)
(Lena)
920/892-6290

Collector's Paradise Antique Mall
N9205 Hwy. 141
(Middle Inlet)
715/854-3187

Amberg Antiques & Sweets
N15450 Hwy. 141
(Amberg)
715/759-5343

Woodsong Gallery
N18360 Hwy. 141
(Pembine)
715/324-6482

Up Nort Antiques
202 N. Hwy. 141
(Coleman)
920/897-4900

McNeely's Old Store
723 Main St. (Hwy. 141)
(Wausaukee)
715/856-5831

Serendipity Shop
W7510 County Z (1 mi. east on Z)
(Pembine)
715/324-5556

Niagra Emporium
1049 Main St. (Hwy. 141)
(Niagra)
715/251-4190

25 JANESVILLE

Carousel Consignments
31 S. Main St.
608/758-0553

Pipsqueak & Me
220 W. Milwaukee St.
608/756-1752

General Antique Store
8301 N. U.S. Hwy. 1 St.
608/756-1812

Another Antique Shop
419 W. Milwaukee St.
608/754-5711

Foster Lee Antiques
218 W. Milwaukee St.
608/752-5188

Franklin Stove Antiques
301 W. Milwaukee St.
608/756-5792

Yesterdays Memories Antique Mall
4904 S. U.S. Hwy. 51
608/754-2906

Just Between Friends
904 Rockport Road
608/758-4783

26 KENOSHA

Sara Jane's Antiques & Collectibles
627 58th St.
414/657-5588

Cypress Tree
722 50th St.
414/652-6999

Dairy Land Antiques
5220 120th St.
414/857-6802

A Miracle on 58th Street
706 58th St.
414/652-3132

Country Cove Antiques
710 57th St.
414/654-0738

Greta's
4906 7th Ave.
414/658-1077

Laura's Resale & Collectibles
6013 Sheridan Road
414/657-1810

Hyden Seec Antiques
5623 6th Ave.
414/654-8111

Memory Lane Antiques
1942 22nd Ave.
414/551-8452

Red Barn Antique
12000 Sheridan Road
414/694-0424

Helen's Remember When Antiques
5801 6th Ave.
414/652-2280

Apple Lane Antiques
5730 Burlington Road
414/859-2017

27 LA CROSSE

Caledonia Street Antique Mall
1213 Caledonia St.
608/782-8443

Hornet's Nest Antiques
1507 Caledonia St.
608/785-2998

4th St. Antique Gallery
119 4th St.
608/782-7278

Antique Center — La Crosse Ltd.
110 3rd St. S.
608/782-6533

Plantique
115 7th St. S.
608/784-4053

Wild Rose
1507 Caledonia St.
608/785-2998

Manon's Vintage Shop
535 Main St.
608/784-2240

Vintage Vogue
115 5th Ave. S.
608/782-3722

28 LAKE DELTON

Old Academy Antiques & Gift Mall
Hwy. 12
608/254-4948

Braun's Happy Landing Antique Shop
30 N. Judson
608/253-4613

Our Gang Antique Mall
Hwy. 23
608/254-4401

29 LAKE GENEVA

Sign of the Unicorn
233 Center St.
414/248-1141

Steffen Collection
611 W. Main St.
414/248-1800

Lake Geneva Antique Mall
829 Williams St.
414/248-6345

Antiques International
611 W. Main St.
414/248-1800

Cedar Fields
755 W. Main St.
414/248-8086

Great Places to Stay

T. C. Smith Historic Inn B&B
865 Main St.
1-800-423-0233

This stunning 1845 mansion features 19th century light fixtures, converted from gas lights. Parquet floors, magnificent hand tooled black walnut balustrades and staircase, and the hand painted walls with miniature oil paints and original trompe oeil, all by famed Chicago artist John Bullock, are just a hint of what you'll experience at this historic inn.

30 LAKE MILLS

Old Mills Market
109 N. Main St.
920/648-3030
Open: Winter Sun.–Sat. 10-5, Tues. by chance, summer daily 10–5
Directions: Located 24 miles east of Madison on I-94 or 64 miles west of Milwaukee on I-94. From I-94, exit onto Hwy. 89 South; go ¾ mile. In Lake Mills, shop is located across from the Commons Park.

Tucked inside the turn-of-the-century Historic Luetzow Meat Market building, the eclectic selection of antiques and collectibles includes furniture, vintage clothing, jewelry, heirloom gifts, linens and one-of-a-kind jackets fashioned from vintage materials. Appraisals, by on-staff qualified appraiser, and estate services are provided. A treat for the tummy while shopping comes in the shop's special hand-dipped chocolates.

Opera Hall Antique
211 N. Main St.
920/648-5026

Gwen's Antiques
102 Church St.
920/648-6183

31 MADISON

Broadway Antiques Mall
115 E. Broadway
608/222-2241

Bethel Parish Shoppe
315 N. Carroll St.
608/255-9183

Antiques Mall of Madison
4748 Cottage Grove Road
608/222-2049

Janet's Antiques
815 Fern Dr.
608/238-4474

Hopkins & Crocker, Inc.
807 E. Johnson St.
608/255-6222

Florilegium
823 E. Johnson St.
608/256-7310

Vintage Interiors
2615 E. Johnson St.
608/244-3000

Antique Gallery
6608 Mineral Point Road
608/833-4321

Chris Kerwin Antiques & Interiors
1839 Monroe St.
608/256-7363

Mapletree Antique Mall
1293 N. Sherman Ave.
608/241-2599

Kappel's Clock Shop
2250 Sherman Ave.
608/244-6165

Rick's Olde Gold
1314 Williamson St.
608/257-7280

Stony Hill Antiques
2140 Regent St.
608/231-1247

Great Places to Stay

Mansion Hill Inn
424 N. Pinckney St.
608/255-3999
Web site: www.mansionhillinn.com

Mansion Hill Inn is an 1858 Romanesque Revival home that was lovingly restored by the Alexander Company in 1985. Eleven exquisite guest rooms are filled with period antiques, hand carved Italian marble fireplaces, and floor to ceiling arched windows. All guest rooms have private baths, many with whirlpool tubs.

32 MANITOWOC

Ebert's Antiques
5712 Country Trunk JJ
920/682-0687

Washington St. Antique Mall
910 Washington St.
920/684-2954

Antique Mall of Manitowoc
301 N. 8th St.
920/682-8680

Viking Antiques
314 N. 8th St.
920/682-0100

Pine River Antiques
7430 Hwy. Cr.
920/726-4440

Larco Resale & Antiques
2204 N. Rapids Road.
920/682-9066

Medley Resale & Antiques
1114 S. 10th St.
920/682-8400

Wheeler on the River Antiques
436 N. 10th St.
920/682-3069

Timeless Treasures
112 N. 8th St.
920/682-6566

33 MENASHA

About Time/Red Barn/Menasha Jack's Antiques
68 Racine
920/725-4880
Open: Tues.–Sat. 10–4:30 March–Jan., Sat. 10–4:30 only in Feb.
Directions: Take Hwy. 441 to Menasha, exit at Racine St. Go south approximately 1 mile.

Three stores in one offer not only a wide variety, but also a large quantity of antiques such as furniture, fixtures, lamps, jewelry, primitives, graniteware, stoneware and pottery. In addition to great selections, the shops buy and appraise antique pieces.

Anderson Resale Shop
922 Appleton Road
920/725-5599

Country Goose My
1018 Appleton Road
920/722-1661

Not New Now
212 Main St.
920/725-5545

Wood Shed
746 3rd St.
920/725-3347

34 MILWAUKEE

Wishful Things
207 E. Buffalo St.
414/765-1117

Noah's Ark
7153 W. Burleigh St.
414/442-1588

Capital City Comics
2565 N. Downer Ave.
414/332-8199

Fifth Avenue Antiques
422 N. 5th St.
414/271-3355

Antique Center — Walkers Point
1134 1st St.
414/383-0655

Architectural Antiques
804 W. Greenfield Ave.
414/389-1965

Past Presence Collectibles
7123 W. Greenfield Ave.
414/774-7585

Peter Bentz Antiques & Appraisals
771 N. Jefferson St.
414/271-8866

Milwaukee Antique Center
341 N. Milwaukee St.
414/276-0605

Echols Antiques & Gifts
6230 W. North Ave.
414/774-5556

Eileen's Warehouse Antiques
325 N. Plankinton Ave.
414/276-0114

Town & Country Shop, Inc.
8822 N. Port Washington Road
414/352-6570

Tony's Resale
949 N. 27th St.
414/931-0949

Lights of Olde
203 N. Water St.
414/223-1130

Centuries Antiques
326 N. Water St.
414/278-1111

Antique Cupboard Sterling Matching
3712 N. 92nd St.
414/464-0556

Time Traveler Book Store
7143 W. Burleigh St.
414/442-0203

Chattel Changers, Inc.
2520 E. Capitol Dr.
414/961-7085

Village Bazaar
2201 N. Farwell Ave.
414/224-9675

Brass Light Gallery
131 S. 1st St.
414/271-8300

Carter's on Delaware
2466 Graham St.
414/482-0014

Collectors Toystop
6026 W. Greenfield Ave.
414/771-7622

Celebrity Coin & Stamp
4161 S. Howell Ave.
414/747-1888

American Estates
2131 S. Kinnickinnic Ave.
414/483-2110

D & H Antiques Toys & Trains
501 W. Mitchell St.
414/643-5340

Military Relics Shop
6910 W. North Ave.
414/771-4014

Legacies, Ltd.
7922 N. Port Washington Road
414/352-8114

Colonel's Choice
2918 S. 13th St.
414/383-8180

American Victorian
203 N. Water St.
414/223-1130

Water St. Antiques
318 N. Water St.
414/278-7008

D & R International Antiques, Ltd.
137 E. Wells St.
414/276-9395

Elizabeth Bradley Antiques
1115 W. Greentree Road
414/352-1521

Shorewood Coin Shop
4495 N. Oakland Ave.
414/961-0999

35 MINERAL POINT

Livery Antiques
303 Commerce St.
608/987-3833

Green Lantern Antiques
261 High St.
608/987-2312

36 MINOCQUA

Island City Antique Market
8661 Hwy. 51 N.
715/356-7003

Hildebrand's Antiques
7537 U.S. Hwy. 51 S.
715/356-1971

Finder's Keepers
7 Hwy. W.
715/356-7208

37 MONROE

New Moon Antiques
1606 11th St.
608/325-9100

Garden Gate Floral & Antiques
1717 11th St.
608/329-4900

Bevs Attic Treasures
1018 17th Ave.
608/325-6200

Breezy Acres Li Antiques
1027 16th Ave.
608/325-1201

It's a Bunch of Crock Antiques
1027 16th Ave.
608/328-1444

Luecke's Diamond Center, Inc.
1029 16th Ave.
608/325-2600

Log Cabin Antiques
W5848 County Road B
608/325-7795

38 MOUNT HOREB

First Street Antiques
111 S. 1st St.
608/437-6767

Hoff Mall Antique Center
101 E. Main St.
608/437-4580

Main Street Antiques
126 E. Main St.
608/437-3233

Isaac's Antiques
132 E. Main St.
608/437-6151

Lucy's Attic
520 Springdale St.
608/437-6140

Yapp's Antique Corner
504 E. Main St.
608/437-8100

39 MUKWONAGO

Country Junction
101 N. Rochester St.
414/363-9474

Indian Creek Antiques
214 S. Rochester St.
414/363-7015

40 NECEDAH

Northland Collectors Mart
211 S. Main St.
608/565-3730
Open: Spring/summer Mon.–Sat. 10–5, Sun. 10–4; Nov. & Dec. daily 10–4; Jan.-Mar. Thurs.–Sun. 10–4
Directions: Necedah is situated at the intersection of Highways 21 and 80.

Across from the town gazebo sits a collector's haven crammed with antiques and collectibles. Among the extraordinary array of styles, periods, textures, and functions, antiquers roam among furniture, glassware, figurines, pottery, jewelry and artifacts.

41 NEW LONDON

Studio Antiques
1776 Division St.
920/982-4366

42 OCONOMOWOC

Mapleton Antiques
W360 8755 Brown St.
920/474-4514

Old Homestead Lighting
514 Silver Lake St.
920/567-6543

Marsh Hill, Ltd.
456 N. Waterville Road
920/646-2560

Ye Old Antiques — Rural
N880 W38726 McMahon Road
920/474-4380

Gathering Place
5780 359 St.
920/567-5123

43 OSCEOLA

Osceola Antiques
117 Cascade St.
715/294-2886
Open: Mon.–Sat. 10–5, Sun. Noon–5
Directions: Downtown Osceola is on Wisconsin Hwy. 35. From I-94, go north at Hudson on Hwy. 35.

Osceola Antiques is Northwest Wisconsin's largest antique shop. With over 11,000 square feet for prime antique hunting you're sure to find just what you're looking for here. The shop displays furniture of all eras, linens to accent, art, jewelry, loads of glassware and more. For collectors and the curious, over 800 antique reference books are available. Enjoy ice cream, homemade candy or cappuccino while you shop.

Old Mill Stream Antiques
105 Cascade St.
715/755-2344

44 OSHKOSH

A Blend of the Past Antiques
738 N. Oakwood Road
920/235-0969

Wagon Wheel Antiques
2326 Oregon St.
920/233-8518

Impressions-Antiques, Etc.
1773 S. Washburn St.
920/235-3899

Cat's Meow Antiques & Collectibles
807 Ohio St.
920/231-6369

Originals Mall of Antiques
1475 S. Washburn St.
920/235-0495

Treasure Shop
2968 Jackson St.
414/231-5551

45 PLATTEVILLE

Marilee's Main Street Mall
70 E. Main St.
608/348-6995

Milly McDonnell's
5946 U.S. Hwy. 151
608/348-8500

Platteville Antiques
5924 State Road 80 #-81
608/348-4533

46 PRINCETON

River City Antique Mall
328 S. Fulton St.
920/295-3475

Melcherts Antiques
605 S. Fulton St.
920/295-4243

Victorian House Antiques
330 W. Water St.
920/295-4700

Parkside Antique Mall
501 S. Fulton St.
920/295-0112

Merry's Little Toy Shop
615 W. Water St.
920/295-6746

Princeton Antique Mall
101 Wisconsin St.
920/295-6515

47 RACINE

Fair Trader
1801 Douglas Ave.
414/637-2222

Travel Through Time Antiques
1859 Taylor Ave.
414/637-7721

Now & Then Gifts & Antiques
1408 Washington Ave.
414/634-8883

Avenue Antiques
1436 Washington Ave.
414/637-6613

Antique Mall of Racine
310 S. Main St.
414/633-9229

Ace & Bubba Treasure Hunters
218 6th St.
414/633-3308

Another Man's Treasure
1354 Washington Ave.
414/633-6869

D & J's Junque
1428 Washington Ave.
414/633-9884

Americana Antique Shop
2330 Airline Road
414/886-0416

Midwest Antiques
2504 Douglas Ave.
414/637-6562

Wisconsin

48 RHINELANDER

Jane's Country Cottage
3961 Indian Lake Road
715/272-1444

Second Hand Rose Antiques
1309 Lincoln St.
715/369-2626

Demitra Lane Antiques & Gifts
432 Lincoln St.
715/362-2206

49 RICE LAKE

Country Antique Shop
1505 Fencil Ave.
715/234-4589

Victorian Cottage
601 N. Main St.
715/234-3482

Bits of Yesteryear Antiques
2237 Lakeshore Dr.
715/234-4641

Portals to the Past
613 N. Main St.
715/234-7530

50 RICHLAND CENTER

Valley Antiques
186 S. Central Ave.
608/647-3793

Memory Lane Antique Mall
177 E. Haseltine St.
608/647-8286

Antiques & Etc.
194 E. Court St.
608/647-4732

Ray's Trading Post
RR 1
608/536-3803

51 RIVER FALLS

Chicken Coop Antiques
7086 N. 820th St.
715/425-5716

Homestead Antiques
208 N. Main St.
715/425-9522

Little River Antiques
363 Cemetery Road
715/425-5522

County Line Antiques
RR 3 #-148A
715/425-9118

52 SHAWANO

Zurko's Midwest Promotions
211 W. Green Bay St.
715/526-9769

A-C Antiques
Route 2
715/524-5254

Yesterdays Antique Mall
712 E. Green Bay St.
715/524-6050

53 SHEBOYGAN

Craftmaster Antiques & Restoration

2034 N. 15th St.
920/452-2524
Open: Mon.–Sat. 10–4, closed Sun.
Directions: Take Hwy. 23, exit east to 14th St. Make a left turn on 14th St., Make a right turn on 15th St. or exit Hwy. 42 into Sheboygan. Make a left turn on Geele Ave., make right turn on 15th St.

Enjoy an old mill setting and browse on three floors full of antiques and collectibles. Discover fine furniture, primitives, china, glassware, stoneware, light fixtures, collectibles and a little bit of everything for everyone. The shop holds true to its slogan: Variety at a reasonable "take home" price!

Sheboygan Antiques
336 Superior Ave.
920/452-6757

Sheridan Park General Store
632 S. 14th St.
920/458-5833

Hiding Place
1219 Michigan Ave.
414/452-4566

Treasure Gardens
1327 N. 14th St.
920/458-8232

Three Barns Full-Two
7377 State Road 42
920/565-3050

54 STEVENS POINT

Downtown Antiques Shops
1100 Main St.
715/342-1442

Second Street Antiques
900 2nd St.
715/341-8611

Sweet Briar
1157 Main St.
715/341-8869

Memory Market
2224 Patch St.
715/344-2026

Kurtzweil Antiques
1652 Burgundy Lane
715/344-0874

55 STURGEON BAY

Westside Antiques
22 S. Madison Ave.
920/746-9038

Cottage Antiques and Quiltry
820 Egg Harbor Road
920/746-0944

Antiques of Institute
4530 State Hwy. 57
920/743-1511

Great Places to Stay

Whitefish Bay Farm B&B

3831 Clark Lake Road
920/743-1560
Web site: www.whitefishbayfarm.com

Enjoy the quiet rural atmosphere of this restored 1908 farmhouse and eighty acre farm. Light filled, spacious guest rooms are decorated in contemporary country furnishings, handmade quilts, handwoven wool rugs and throws, and original artwork. An abundant homemade breakfast is served at the dining room table where guests meet to share conversation and experiences.

Wisconsin

Scofield House B&B
908 Michigan St.
1-888-463-0204

A stay at the Scofield House is a true bed and breakfast experience. Afternoon "sweet treats" on the buffet, with complimentary gourmet drinks, has become a Scofield House ritual. Oven fresh cookies and baked goods are something to come home to after a long day of "recreational shopping" or enjoying other more natural pursuits the county has to offer.

56 STURTEVANT

Revival
9410 Durand Ave.
414/886-3666

Carridge House Antiques
9525 Durand Ave.
414/886-6678

School Days Mall
9500 Durand Ave.
414/886-1069

Antique Castle Mall
1701 S.E. Frontage Road
414/886-6001

Tree of Life
2810 Wisconsin St.
414/886-1601

57 SUN PRAIRIE

Circa Victoriana
104 E. Main St.
608/837-4115

Coffee Mill Antique Mall
3472 Hoepker Road.
608/837-7099

58 SUPERIOR

Superior Collectible Inv.
1709 Belknap St.
715/394-4315

Port of Call Superior Marketplace
4101 E. 2nd St.
715/398-5030

Berger Hardware & Antiques
525 Tower Ave.
715/394-3873

Curious Goods
1717 Winter St.
715/392-7550

Doherty's Antiques
207 39th Ave. E.
715/398-7661

59 TOMAH

Antique Mall of Tomah
I-94 and Hwy. 21 East
608/372-7853
Open: Apr.–Dec., Mon.–Sat. 8–8, Sun. 9–5; Jan.–Mar. 9–5 daily
Directions: From I-94 and Hwy. 21 East, take Exit 143 to Tomah.

The 60-plus dealers of quality antiques and collectibles specialize in "smalls." Primitives, jewelry, glassware, plates and dishware, in addition to a large assortment of lamps make up the pleasing selection. The stock of furniture is limited but offers fine workmanship and good condition.

Oakdale Antique Mall
Route 3
608/374-4700

Esther's Antiques
RR 4
608/372-6690

60 TURTLE LAKE

Memories Antiques and Collectibles
231 W. U.S. Hwy. 8
715/986-4950

Country Side Antiques
12 W. U.S. Hwy. 8
715/986-2737

61 UNION GROVE

Storm Hall Antique Mall
835 15th Ave.
414/878-1644

House on Main
1121 Main St.
414/878-1045

Ye Olde Red Barn Antiques
20816 Durand Ave.
414/878-2044

62 VIROQUA

Golden Comb & Etc.
124 W. Court St.
608/637-7835

Main Street Antique Mall
207 N. Main St.
608/637-8655

Etc. Antiques & Collectibles
124 W. Court St.
608/637-6429

Antiques Cellar
205 N. Main St.
608/634-2749

Lam's Ear Country Gifts
608/637-2099

Small Ventures
608/637-8880

63 WALWORTH

On The Square Antique Mall
109 Madison
414/275-9858

Bittersweet Farm
114 Madison
414/275-3062

Van's Antiques
1937 U.S. Hwy. 14
414/275-2773

Raggedy An-Tiques
216 S. Main St.
414/275-5866

64 WATERFORD

Freddy Bear's Antique Mall
2819 Beck Dr.
414/534-2327

Heavenly Haven Antique Mall
318 W. Main St.
414/534-4400

Afternoon Tea Antiques & Furniture
411 E. Main St.
414/534-3664

Dover Pond Antiques
28016 Washington Ave.
414/534-6543

65 WAUKESHA

Just A Little Bit of Country
N4 W22496 Bluemont Road
414/542-8050

Babbling Brook
416 E. Broadway
414/544-4739

Store
301 N. Grand Ave.
414/547-2740

James K Beier Antique Maps
2312 N. Grandview Blvd
414/549-5985

Susan H. Kruger Antiques
401 Madison St.
414/542-7722

Bix Stripping & Refinishing
850 Martin St.
414/542-3185

A Dickens of a Place
521 Wisconsin Ave.
414/542-0702

Gift Sampler
275 W. Main St.
414/544-1343

Fortunate Finds
124 E. Saint Paul Ave.
414/542-8110

Great Places to Stay

Mill Creek Farm Bed and Breakfast
S47 W22099 Lawnsdale Road
414/542-4311
Office hours: Daily 7–11
Rates: $65–$75
Directions: From I-43 going west, take Racine Ave. (Exit 54) north 2 miles to County 1 (Lawnsdale Road). Turn left on County 1, go 1 6/10 miles. The farm is on the left. Located 7 miles southeast of Waukesha, 20 miles southwest of Milwaukee.

Located on 160 acres in Waukesha County, you'll find one of the area's loveliest, private retreats. Mill Creek Farm offers two special rooms adorned with fine linens and all the amenities to make your stay a pleasant one. Guests share a fully renovated, skylit bath, elegantly decorated for comfort and convenience right down to the heated towel rack! The reading/television room offers a subdued atmosphere for curling up with a good book or watching a romantic movie.

This wooded Shangri-la offers a variety of outdoor activities to help you escape. You can head out on a paddle boat and absorb the serenity of Mill Creek Pond, or fish for bass and bluegills in this one-acre spring-fed pond.

For the more active relaxer, there are 3 miles of groomed trails to hike, jog, or cross-country ski.

This amusing anecdote was submitted by the Mill Creek Farm Bed and Breakfast: "Last summer we had as our guests a young family from the Chicago area. Mother, father, and two sons came for a three-day period planning to enjoy the Milwaukee Zoo, Wisconsin State Fair, Old World Wisconsin, and several other attractions in the area. However, when they got here they discovered our pond for which we provided them with fishing poles and paddle boat. The boys began to catch fish, frogs, and all manner of pond life. As the first day progressed, they decided to stay on the farm and not venture out for other sights. The second day, the same decision. Third day, same decision. So it turned out, they never left the farm for the whole three-day stay! And as they were leaving on the morning of the fourth day, Noah, who is 7, turned to his father and said, 'Dad, how much would it cost to buy this place?' We concluded that Noah was the youngest sale prospect we've ever had!"

66 WAUPACA

Grey Dove Antiques & Resale
118 S. Main St.
715/258-0777

Danes Home
301 N. Main St.
715/256-0693

67 WAUSAU

Kimberly's Old House Gallery
1600 Jonquil Lane
715/359-5077
Open: Thurs., Fri. & Sat. 10–5, and by chance or appointment

Roam 10,000 square feet packed with antique architectural pieces. Fireplaces, lighting, plumbing, and millwork represent some of the finds. Building salvage, cross-country delivery and locating services also available.

Kasens Bittersweet Antique Furniture
8705 Bittersweet Road
715/359-2777

Rib Mt. Antique Mall
3300 Eagle Ave.
715/848-5564

Stoney Creek Antiques & Jewelry Shop
4307 State Hwy. 52
715/842-8354

Ginny's Antiques & Consignments
416 3rd St.
715/848-1912

68 WAUTOMA

Coach's Corner Antiques
2192 Hwy. 152
920/787-3845

Silver Lake Antique Mall
W. 7853 State Road 21
920/787-1325

Finishing Touch Antiques
502 W. Main St.
920/787-2525

69 WEBSTER

Lake Country Mall
Hwy. 35
715/866-7670

Old House Antiques
7419 Airport Road
715/349-7289

70 WILD ROSE

Finder's Keepers Antiques
526 Front
920/622-3077

Sampler
N6571 State Road 22
920/622-4499

Oakwood Farm Antiques & Crafts
Alp Road
920/622-3165

71 WISCONSIN DELLS

Antique Mall of Wisconsin Dells
720 Oak St.
608/254-2422

Days Gone By Antique Mall
729 Oak St.
608/254-6788

Wisconsin

72 WISCONSIN RAPIDS

Kellner Pioneer Shop
8620 County Trunk W.
715/424-2507

Whetstones Antiques
322 State Hwy. 73 S.
715/325-5139

Hi Button Shoe
9420 State Hwy. 13 S.
715/325-2444

Antique Heaven
3620 8th St.
715/423-3599

Aunt Nancy's Antiques Collectibles
6421 State Hwy. 13 S.
715/325-2800

73 WOODRUFF

Mill
1405 1st Ave.
715/356-5468

Town 'n' Travel Antique Shop
237 U.S. Hwy. 51 N.
715/358-2535

Roxane's Antiques & Gifts
189 U.S. Hwy. 51 N.
715/356-7718

Wyoming

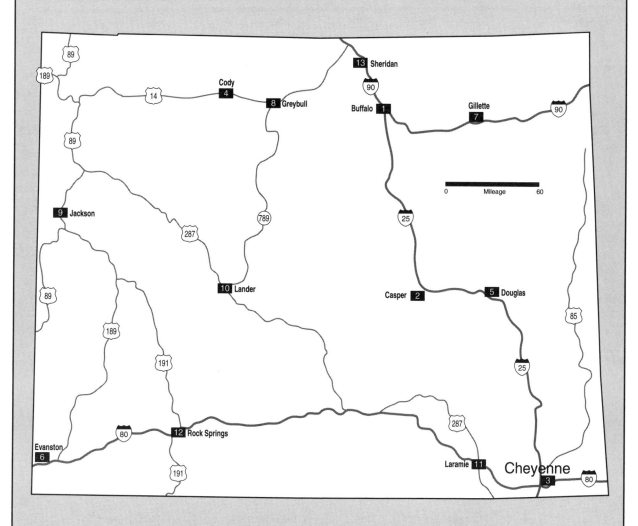

89

189

89

89

89

189

191

191

14

Cody **4**

8 Greybull

9 Jackson

287

789

10 Lander

13 Sheridan

90

Buffalo **1**

Gillette
7

90

25

Casper **2**

5 Douglas

85

25

80

12 Rock Springs

Evanston
6

287

Laramie **11**

Cheyenne

3

80

0   Mileage   60

Wyoming

1 BUFFALO

Yesterday's Treasures
100 E. Hart St.
307/684-7318

Heritage Antiques
22 S. Main St.
307/684-2326

Rock Bottom Country Store
29448 Hwy. 196
307/684-2364

2 CASPER

Doubletree Antiques & More
146 S. Elk
307/472-4858
Open: Tues.–Sat. 10–5, closed Sun. and Mon.
Directions: Exit off I-25 at McKinley St. Go south on McKinley to First St. Turn east on First then south on Elk.

This shop has a constantly changing inventory, which means business is good. On a regular basis, they stock 1800s through Art Deco furniture, a wide selection of oak furniture, glassware such as Depression, carnival and much more. An additional bonus; there is a furniture refinisher on site who gives free estimates. What more can you ask for?

Carriage House Antiques
830 W. 15th St.
307/266-2987
Open: Tues.–Sat. 10–5, Fri. 11–5, closed Sun. and Mon.
Directions: Take Poplar St. Exit off I-25. Travel south on Poplar to CY Ave. Turn left on CY then immediately right on 15th St.

Carriage House has a complete line of antiques including glassware, pottery, jewelry, toys, Cowboy and Indian collectibles.

Mary's
341 W. Yellowstone Hwy.
307/577-5206

What's in Store
211 W. Collins Dr.
307/237-8137

Antique Lighting Inc.
1514 S. Kenwood St.
307/265-4614

Accents
227 E. 1st St.
307/473-1781

Lotsa Stuff
1023 E. 2nd St.
307/473-2212

Yellow Horse Antiques
107 Jonquil St.
307/235-1457

Great Places to Stay

Durbin Street Inn Bed & Breakfast
843 S. Durbin St.
307/577-5774

Combine the comfort and friendliness of a bed and breakfast with the excitement of the Old West. The Durbin Street Inn was built in 1917 and is a comfortable two-story American Foursquare. Located in what is now an historical residential area known as the "big tree" area, it is within blocks of downtown shopping, good restaurants, museums, and just minutes from Casper Mountain. The area offers about everything you could desire in cultural events, the nearby historical sites of Old Ft. Casper and Independence Rock.

3 CHEYENNE

Sidekick Antique Mart
1408 S. Greeley Hwy.
307/635-3136
Open: Daily 10–6
Directions: Exit south on Greeley Hwy. off I-80. Located one to two miles on the right.

This multi-dealer market (70-80 dealers) with its 10,000 square feet of space is filled with primitives, old tools, barnwood furniture, 1800s to 1950s oak, walnut and mahogany furniture, Fenton, Cambridge and Imperial glassware, porcelains, black powder guns, brewery, Coke, sports and Indian memorabilia and Persian rugs. The inventory is limitless. If you can't find it here, you'll probably have a hard time finding it anywhere.

Old Gold Antiques
1309 W. 8th St.
307/632-8557

Tee Pee
3208 S. Greeley Hwy.
307/635-8535

Tomorrow's Treasures Antiques
903 W. Lincoln Ave.
307/634-1900

Bart's Flea Market
Lincolnway & Evans
307/632-0063

Collectibles Corner
2622 Pioneer Ave.
307/634-7706

Antiques Central
2311 Reed Ave.
307/638-6181

Grandma's Attic
113 W. 17th St.
307/638-6126

Frontier Antiques
1715 Carey Ave.
307/635-5573

Downtown Flea Market
312 W. 17th St.
307/638-3751

The Avenue Flea Market
315 1/2 E. 7th Ave.
307/635-5600

Treasures from the Heart
1024 E. Pershing Blvd.
307/638-6736

Bart's Flea Market
Lincolnway & Tomes
307/632-0004

Collectibles Corner
2622 Pioneer Ave.
307/634-7706

Old Gold Antiques
1309 W. 18th St.
307/632-8557

Wyoming

Great Places to Stay

Porch Swing Bed and Breakfast

712 E. 20th St.
307/778-7182
Rates: $43–$66

The Porch Swing Bed and Breakfast in its charming authentically restored 1907 two-story cottage is filled with antiques. Handmade quilts are on every bed. Summer gardens are fragrant with flowers and herbs. Edible flowers are served as well as a full breakfast by the fire in the winter and on the back porch in the summer. Located within walking distance is downtown Cheyenne where you may enjoy museums and restaurants as well as other forms of entertainment. Not far from the bed and breakfast, mountain parks for hiking, bicycling, and cross-country or downhill skiing are available.

4   CODY

Olde General Store

1323 Sheridan Ave.
307/587-5500
Open: Summer 9-9 (7 days a week), June-August; Winter 9-6, Mon.-Sat., 12-4 Sun.
Directions: Hwy. 14 is the main street in Cody. Shop is located on Hwy. 14 which is also Sheridan Ave.

The two floors of this shop specialize in mostly oak furniture including a few pieces of Mission Oak. They also have added a line of handmade Wyoming log furniture. Throughout the store, you'll find primitives, collectibles, western memorabilia as well as gifts and decorative accessories.

Old West Antiques
1215 Sheridan Ave.
307/587-9014

Cottage Antiques
1327 Rumsey Ave.
307/527-4650

The Wiley House
913 Sheridan Ave.
307/587-6030

Bear Tooth Floral & Gifts
1316 Beck Ave.
307/587-4984

Great Places to Stay

Parson's Pillow Bed & Breakfast

1202 14th St.
307/587-2382
1-800-377-2348
Directions: Located just off Hwys. 14, 16, 20 and 120. For specific directions from your location please call the innkeepers, Lee & Elly Larabee.

Put on your boots and amble down "Main Street" Cody, visiting fine restaurants, shops, and galleries. After a hard day on the antique trail, have an old-fashioned ice cream soda ... or saddle up old tin lizzy and head out to the Cody Nite Rodeo, Old West Trail Town or visit the Buffalo Bill Museum.

Then, after a short ride out of town watching the buffalo roam and the antelope play, knock the dust off your boots at Parson's Pillow Bed and Breakfast, a wood framed church dedicated in 1902 as a Methodist Episcopal Church. Prior to that, Mr. Beck, one of William F. Cody's closest friends who helped Buffalo Bill in the founding and building of Cody, was involved in a poker game one evening. The pot grew to a whopping $500!!! At that point, Mr. Beck and his opponent agreed that the winner would use the money to build Cody's first church building. Mr. Beck won and built an Episcopal Church. However, even in losing, the Methodists built their own church at the corner of 14th and Beck Avenue! The former bell tower with its magnificent bell, which was donated by a cousin of Buffalo Bill's (herself an Episcopalian), was the envy of Mr. Beck and all the Episcopalians!

Today, comfort, elegance and the sense of coming home are yours to enjoy as a guest of Parson's Pillow B & B. Filled with antiques and turn of the century lace, this 1902 former church has been caringly restored so that all who enter it might experience western homestyle hospitality. Choose from four themed guest rooms: the Rose — filled with Barbara Cartland novels to enhance your romantic fantasies; the Garden — provides a private vintage pedestal tub; the Western — rustic simplicity with a private oak-framed prairie tub; and the Memories — featuring an antique bed with fluffly feather pillows. Breakfast is served in the dining room.

5   DOUGLAS

Antiques, Etc.
404 S. 4th St.
307/358-2253

Briar Patch
115 N. 3rd St.
307/358-4437

Country Touch
421 S. 4th St.
307/358-3641

6   EVANSTON

The story of Evanston is largely a story of the Union Pacific Railroad, which was, at that time laying track through the country at a rate of seven miles per day. One November, the graders had reached Bear River City, about 90 miles west of Green River.

The Bear River City Riot of November 21, 1868, was instigated by the rough element which preyed on the railroad workers. The riot has served as the prototype for nearly every Western movie ever made, the good guys against the bad guys. Soldiers from Fort Bridger were called to quell the disorder, but the good guys had things well in hand by the time they arrived.

Bear River City eventually grew into Evanston, which was named for the surveyor who platted the town, and Evanston became the commercial and shipping center of the area.

Sheila's Memories Antiques and Collectibles

900 Main St.
307/789-0638
Open: Mon.–Sat. 10–5
Directions: Take Front St. Exit off I-80. Go 3 blocks; turn left at 9th St. Go one block to Main St. Located at the corner of 9th and Main. An alternative: Exit I-80 at Harrison Drive. Go to Main St.; turn left and store is at the corner of 9th and Main.

Collectors listen up! Inside this 7,200-square-foot shop, boasting to have a large selection of everything, sit two rare and in good condition 1950s pinball machines. Hummel figurines grace tabletops as well. Grandeur and beauty increase with prints from Parrish, Fox and Thompson. Additional pieces include Victorian furniture and accessories, old dolls and toys, as well as vintage jewelry. Appraisal services are offered.

Eliza Doolittle's
944 Main St.
307/789-5656

Blue Moon Collectibles
221 10th St., #101
307/789-6268

7 GILLETTE

Doc's Swap Shop Antiques
950 Chandler Lane
307/682-1801

Flower Boutique
1001 S. Douglas Hwy.
307/682-4569

Collectors
1612 E. U.S. Hwy. 1416
307/682-8929

8 GREYBULL

Established in 1909 as a railroad town, Greybull is named for the Greybull River, which itself was derived from a legendary grey bison bull said to be sacred to the Indians. Currently a center for bentonite mining, Greybull is also a region rich in Indian relics, fossils and semiprecious stones. The Greybull Museum (free admission) is just one block east of the Post Office on Greybull Ave. Displayed are Indian apparel and artifacts, old weapons and pioneer utensils. There are outstanding agate collections dating back millions of years. Don't miss the largest fossil ammonite in the world.

9 JACKSON

Samuel's Continental Imports

745 W. Broadway
307/733-4794
Open: Mon.–Sat. 10–9, Sun. by appointment only
Directions: Jackson Hole is considered the kickoff point when approaching the Grand Tetons and Yellowstone National Park from the south, Samuel's is easy to find. Just follow the signs on I-80 or I-15 and you will arrive at the doorsteps at 745 West Broadway as you enter the town of Jackson, Wyo., Samuel's is the large green building just opposite the Virginia Lodge. You can't miss it. The American and Italian flags are always flying outside the door.

Samuel's Continental Imports had its beginning in 1993, when two people, Sam Galano and Molly Morgan, with a love for fine old European and American furniture felt that there was a lack of the same in the ever increasing number of antiques and designer stores in Jackson Hole, Wy., and the surrounding areas. So they decided to bring "the stuff" they loved to this western town through overseas buyers in addition to their own finds in barns, estate sales, auction houses, and private homes. They imported the graceful lines of many eras and styles and rejoiced in the warm patinas of the quality wood that European and American craftsmen have used to create decorative and practical furniture for generations. They even have an "in house doctor" for the pieces. Sam Galano, part owner of the business, has a highly trained eye and years of knowledge and expertise in restoration. Samuel's Continental Imports also offers custom framing and uses only conservation materials to preserve the quality of each piece being framed. Sam is responsible for this work and takes an artistic approach to insure the art work is complemented, not overwhelmed. They haven't ignored the smalls, offering everything from art glass and fine china to nail kegs and horseshoes. The store carries an extensive line of antique lighting fixtures and showcases original artwork.

Showcase Antiques
115 W. Broadway Ave.
307/733-4848

Bear Print
140 N. Cache
307/733-1558

Fighting Bear Antiques
35 E. Simpson
307/733-2669

Beyond Necessities Antiques
335 S. Millward
307/733-7492

Back Porch
145 E. Pearl Ave.
307/733-0030

Cheap Thrills
250 W. Pearl Ave.
307/739-9266

Antiques of Jackson Hole
745 W. Broadway St.
307/733-0311

Cottage Antiques
155 W. Pearl Ave.
307/733-0849

10 LANDER

Village Store
23 Shrine Club Road
307/332-2801

Annie's Attic
523 Garfield
307/332-2279

Great Places to Stay

Blue Spruce Inn

677 S. 3rd St.
1-888-503-3311
Web site: rmisp.com/bluespruce

Built in 1920, the Blue Spruce Inn is surrounded by giant blue spruce trees and flower gardens. Throughout the inn, magnificent oak crown molding and woodwork prevail as outstanding examples of the Arts and Crafts period of the early 20th Century.

Piece of Cake B&B

P.O. Box 866
307/332-7608

Butch Cassidy never had such luxury! Lodge with two rooms and three cabins — all private large baths, Egyptian cotton linens. Breathtaking views — 10,000 plus open acres, yet five minutes to Main St. Free loop tour package and picnic lunch with two-night or longer stay. Miss the other world? Come into the lodge great room and view the projection screen television with all major networks at three different time zones or relax with your selection of videos or books.

11 LARAMIE

The city of Laramie is noted as playing a definite role in the testing of many of Wyoming's unique laws. Reporters flocked to the Gem City of the Plains to witness the first woman in the world to serve on a jury in March, 1870. In the fall of 1871, another first occurred in Laramie when "Grandma" Louiza Swain went to the polls and was the first woman in the world to vote in a general election.

Golden Flea Gallery

725 Skyline Road
307/745-7055
Open: Daily 10–6
Directions: On the south side of Laramie near the Holiday Inn and Motel 6. Once on Skyline Road, go 4/10 mile as it bends to the left, Golden Flea is on the left side of the street. Getting to Skyline Road: From I-80 heading east: take Exit 313 (Third St.). Turn left onto Skyline Road (at Holiday Inn). From I-80 heading west: take Exit 313 (Third St.). Turn left onto Third St. Go 2/10 miles then turn left as though to get on I-80 E., but then immediately turn right onto service road (Skyline Road) by Holiday Inn. From Hwy. 287 N. from Fort Collins, Colorado: turn right as if to get on I-80 E., then immediately turn right onto service (Skyline) road.

The "great wide open" of Wyoming has come indoors at this 20,000-square-foot gallery. Inside, among the wares of over 140 dealers, you can wander among antique furnishings and accessories, collectibles, old records and books. An interesting and surprising assortment of gift items adds to the greatness of this showcase named after such a small creature (the flea).

Country Antiques The 2nd Story
105 E. Ivinson Ave.
307/745-4423

Curiosity Shoppe
206 S. 2nd St.
307/745-4760

Under One Roof
1002 S. 3rd St.
307/742-8469

Granny's Attic
1311 S. 3rd St.
307/721-9664

Victoria's Treasures
408 S. 2nd St.
307/742-6062

12 ROCK SPRINGS

Olde Towne Antiques

426 S. Main St.
307/382-3207
Open: Mon.–Sat. 10–5
Directions: Exit I-80 at Elk St. Travel south to old downtown Rock Springs.

This eight dealer shop offers a large selection of Depression glass, pottery, kitchen collectibles, advertising and railroad items, 1920s and '30s furniture, stoneware and toys. Big selection, great prices!

Antique Mall
411 N. Front St.
307/362-9611

Tynsky's Rock Shop
706 Dewar Dr.
307/362-5031

13 SHERIDAN

Raven's Nest Antiques

1617 N. Main St.
307/672-8171
Open: Mon.–Sat. 10–5, closed Sun.
Directions: Traveling east on I-90 exit Sheridan Main St. Downtown. Shop is about eight blocks from I-90 across from Kentucky Fried Chicken.

This five-dealer, 3,000-square-foot shop features high boys, oak and pine Hoosiers as well as other fine pieces of furniture. From days of yore you will find elegant glassware, Fiesta, sheet music, vintage clothing, costume jewelry and western memorabilia.

Pack Rat
157 W. Brundage St.
307/672-0539

Interior Images
200 W. Brundage St.
307/674-7604

Best Out West Antiques & Collectibles
109 N. Main St.
307/674-5003

Q Man Music & Antiques
528 N. Main St.
307/672-9636

North Main Antiques
1135 N. Main St.
307/672-3838

Largest Malls

ARIZONA

Glendale
The Town of Glendale
80 antique and speciality shops

Mesa
Antique Plaza
114 W. Main St.
602/833-4844
20,000 sq. ft. — 100 dealers

Phoenix
Brass Armadillo
12419 N. 28th Dr.
1-888-942-0030
700 dealers

Scottsdale
Antiques Super-Mall
1900 N. Scottsdale Road
602/874-2900
60,000 sq. ft. — 250 dealers

Antique Trove
2020 N. Scottsdale Road
602/947-6074
125 dealers

Antique Centre
2012 N. Scottsdale Road
602/675-9500
125 dealers

Tucson
Antique Mall
3130 E. Grant Road
520/326-3070
100 dealers

ARKANSAS

Alma
Days Gone By
400 Heather Lane
501/632-0829
27,000 sq. ft. — 175 dealers

Sisters 2 Too Antique Mall
702 Hwy. 71 N.
501/632-2292
130 dealers

Benton
Jerry Van Dyke's Den & Attic Antiques
117 S. Market St.
501/860-5600
25 rooms in historic downtown building

Camden
Downtown Antique Mall
131 South Adams St. S.E.
870/836-4244
18,000 sq. ft.

Clinton
Antique Warehouse of Arkansas
Hwy. 65 N. & 110
501/745-5842
5 buildings full of antiques

Eureka Springs
Yesteryears Antique Mall
Hwy. 62/412 at Rock House Road
501/253-5100
125 dealers

Keo
Morris Antiques
306 Hwy. 232 W.
501/842-3531
50,000 sq. ft. — 8 large buildings

Little Rock
Fabulous Finds Antiques
1521 Merrill Drive, Ste. D175
501/224-6622
17,000 sq. ft. — 80 dealers

North Little Rock
Crystal Hill Antique Mall
I-40 & Crystal Hill Road
501/753-3777
12,000 sq. ft. — 60 dealers

Rogers
Shelby Lane
719 W. Walnut
501/621-0111
300 booths

Searcy
Frances Antiques
701 W. Race Ave.
501/268-2154
3 buildings full

Texarkana
M & M Antique Mall
401 E. Broad St.
870/773-1871
100 dealers

Van Buren
Antique Warehouse of Arkansas
402 Main St.
501/474-4808
20,000 sq. ft.

CALIFORNIA

Aptos
Village Fair Antiques
417 Trout Gulch Road
408/688-9883
17,000 sq. ft. — 20 shops

Bakersfield
5 & Dime Antq. Mall & Luncheonette
1400 19th St.
805/323-8048
22,000 sq. ft. — 70 dealers

Beaumont
Nelson's Giant Antique Showcase & Booth Mall
630 California Ave.
909/769-1934

Carlsbad
Carlsbad Antique District
Three Blocks of Shops
9 shops

Carson
Memory Lane Antique Mall
20740 S. Figueroa St.
301/538-4130
20,000 sq. ft. — 250 dealers

Chico
Eighth & Main Antique Center
745 Main St.
916/893-5534
25,000 sq. ft.

Clovis
Clovis Antique Mall
530 & 532 Fifth St.
209/298-1090
100 dealers

Dana Point
The Landmark Antiques
34241 Coast Hwy.
714/489-1793
100 dealers

El Cajon
Magnolia Antique Mall
456 N. Magnolia Ave.
619/444-0628
12,000 sq. ft. — 85 dealers

Glendora
The Orange Tree Antique Mall
216 N. Glendora Ave.
626/335-3376
40 shops in a quaint village

Healdsburg
Vintage Plaza Antiques
44 Mill St.
707/433-8409
19,000 sq. ft.

Loma Linda
Loma Linda Antique Mall
24997 Redlands Blvd.
909/796-4776
55 air conditioned shops

Long Beach
Julie's Antique Mall
1133 East Wardlow Road
562/989-7799
17,000 sq. ft. — 120 dealers

Sleepy Hollow Antique Mall
5689 Paramount Blvd.
562/634-8370
17,000 sq. ft. — 180 dealers

Los Angeles
The Antique Guild
3225 Helms Ave.
310/838-3131
130 showcases and booths

Westchester Faire
8655 S. Sepulveda Blvd.
310/670-4000
30,000 sq. ft. — 75 dealers — 3 cafés

Modesto
Antique Emporium
1511 J. St.
209/759-9730
1208 Ninth St.
209/527-6004
17,500 sq. ft. — 70 dealers

Napa
Riverfront Antique Centre
705 Soscol Ave.
707/253-1966
24,000 sq. ft. — 100 dealers

Ontario
Treasures 'n' Junk Antique Mall
215 S. San Antonio
909/983-3300
15,000 sq. ft. — 70 dealers

Orange
Country Roads Antiques & Gardens
204 W. Chapman
714/532-3041
15,000 sq. ft. — 5,000 sq. ft. garden

Orange Circle Antique Mall
118 S. Glassell
714/538-8160
125 dealers

Orinda
The Family Jewels
572 Tahos Road
510/254-4422
Over 100,000 pieces of vintage jewelry

Pasadena
The Pasadena Antique Center & Annex
444-480 S. Fair Oaks
626/449-7706
33,000 sq. ft. — 130 dealers

Largest Malls

Paso Robles

Heritage House Antique Gallery
1345 Park St.
805/239-1386
12,000 sq. ft.

The Antique Emporium Mall
1307 Park St.
805/238-1078
12,000 sq. ft. — 55 dealers

Petaluma

Vintage Bank Antiques
101 Petaluma Blvd.
707/769-3097
3 floors

Pomona

Pomona's Antique Row
100-200 block of E. 2nd St.
400 dealers, 20 stores

Robbins Antique Mart
200 E. 2nd St.
909/623-9835
27,000 sq. ft. — 110 dealers

Rancho Cordova

Antique Plaza
11395 Folsom Blvd.
916/852-8517
75,000 sq. ft. — 250 dealers

Redlands

Emma's Trunk Antique Mall
1701 Orange Tree Lane
909/79-TRUNK
100 dealers

**Illa's Antiques & Collectibles
and The Packing House Mall**
215 East Redlands Blvd.
909/793-8898
30,000 sq. ft. — 80 dealers

**Precious Times Antique
Mall of Redlands**
1740 Redlands Blvd.
909/792-7768
150 dealers

Sacramento

River City Antique Mall
10117 Mills Station Rd.
916/362-7778
20,000 sq. ft. — 70 dealers

San Bernardino

The Heritage Gallery
1520-A S. E St.
909/888-3377
25,000 sq. ft.

Treasure Mart Antique Mall
293 E. Redlands Blvd.
909/825-7264
90 dealers

San Carlos

Laurel St. Antiques
671 Laurel St.
650/593-1152
10,000 sq. ft.

The Antique Trove
1119 Industrial Way
650/593-1300
30,000 sq. ft.

San Diego

T & R Antiques Warehouse
4630 Santa Fe St.
619/272-2500
15,000 sq. ft.

San Francisco

San Francisco Antique Design Mall
701 Bayshore Blvd.
415/656-3530
36,000 sq. ft.

San Jose

West San Carlos St.
Over 200 dealers in a one-mile strip

San Marcos

San Marcos Antique Village
983 Grand Ave.
760/744-8718
12,000 sq. ft. — 65 dealers

Santa Monica

Santa Monica Antique Market
1607 Lincoln Blvd.
310/314-4899
20,000 sq. ft. — 150 dealers

Sebastopol

The Antique Society
2661 Gravenstein Hwy. S.
707/829-1733
20,000 sq. ft. — 100 dealers

Sherman Oaks

Sherman Oaks Antique Mall
14034 Ventura Blvd.
818/906-0338
95 shops

Solvang

Solvang Antique Center
486 First St.
805/686-2322
100+ galleries & showcases

Soquel

Historic Soquel Village
Soquel Drive
5 multidealer shops, 9 single shops

Studio City

The Cranberry House
12318 Ventura Blvd.
818/506-8945
15,000 sq. ft.

Sutter Creek

Water St. Antiques
78 Main St.
209/267-0585
35,000 sq. ft.

Ventura

35 shops within a one-mile radius
Visitor's Information: 800/333-2989

Visalia

**Antiques at The Works
Showcase Mall**
26644 S. Mooney
209/685-1125
16,000 sq. ft. — 100 dealers

Whittier

King Richard's Antique Center
12301 Whittier Blvd.
562/698-5974
100,000 sq. ft.

COLORADO

Denver

Antique Market
1212 S. Broadway
303/744-0281

Architectural Salvage, Inc.
1215 Delaware St.
303/615-5432

**The Gallagher Collection
at the Antique Guild**
1298 S. Broadway
303/756-5821
Located on Denver's Antique Row

Littleton

Colorado Antique Gallery
5501 S. Broadway
303/794-8100

IDAHO

Boise

Collectors Choice I & II
5284 Franklin Road
208/336-2489
5150 Franklin Road
208/336-3170
Two large locations — 75+ dealers

Coeur D'Alene

Coeur D'Alene Antique Mall
3650 N. Government Way
408 W. Haycraft Ave. #11
208/667-0246
125+ dealers — 2 large locations

ILLINOIS

Chicago

Lincoln Antique Mall
3141 N. Lincoln Ave.
773/244-1440
11,000 sq. ft.

Wrigleyville Antique Mall
3336 N. Clark St.
773/868-0285
10,000 sq. ft.

Coal Valley

Country Fair Mall
504 W. 1st Ave. (Hwy. 6)
309/799-3670
20,000 sq. ft.

Divernon

Lisa's I & II Antique Malls
I-55 & Route 104
217/628-1111
40,000 sq. ft.

East Peoria

Pleasant Hill Antique Mall
315 S. Pleasant Hill Road
309/694-4040
30,000 sq. ft. — over 200 dealers

El Paso

El Paso Antique Mall
I-39 & Rt. 24
309/527-3705
16,000 sq. ft. — 200 dealers

Grayslake

Antique Warehouse
2 S. Lake St.
708/223-9554
65 dealers — no reproductions

Greenup

**Historic Western Style Town
Antique Mall**
113 E. Kentucky St.
217/923-3514
14,000 sq. ft.

Kankakee

Indian Oaks Antique Mall
N. Route 50 & Larry Power Road
815/933-9998
18,000 sq. ft. — 170 dealers

Orland Park
Beacon Avenue Antique Row
708/460-8433
Five shops on one block.

Princeton
Sherwood Antique Mall
1661 N. Main, I-80, Exit 56 S.
815/872-2580
40,000 sq. ft.

Sandwich
Sandwich Antiques Market
U.S. 34 Fairgrounds
773/227-4464
550 quality dealers

Springfield
The Barrel Antique Mall
5850 S. 6th St.
217/585-1438
27,000 sq. ft. — 138 dealers

Wheeling
Antiques Center of Illinois
1920 S. Wolf Road
847/215-9418
50 shops under one roof

IOWA

Ames
Memories on Main
203 Main St.
515/233-2519
11,000 sq. ft. — 80+ dealers

Cedar Rapids
Wellington Square Antique Mall
1200 2nd Ave. S.E.
319/368-6640
17,000 sq. ft. — 118 dealers

Davenport
Antique America Mall
702 W. 76th St.
319/386-3430
23,000 sq. ft. — 150 dealers

Des Moines
Brass Armadillo Inc.
701 N.E. 50th Ave.
515/282-0082
36,000 sq. ft. — 450 dealers

KANSAS

Augusta
White Eagle Antique Mall
10187 S.W. U.S. Hwy. 54
316/775-2812
100 dealers

Lawrence
Quantrill's Antique Mall & Flea Market
811 New Hampshire St.
913/842-6616
20,000 sq. ft. — 150 dealers

Leavenworth
Caffee's Leavenworth Antique Mall & Tea Room
505 Delaware
913/758-0193
3 floors

Ottawa
Ottawa Antique Mall & Restaurant
202 S. Walnut St.
785/242-1078
17,000 sq. ft. — 100 dealers

Prairie Village
Mission Road Antique Mall
4101 W. 83rd St.
913/341-7577
40,000 sq. ft., 2 floors — 250 dealers

Topeka
Antique Plaza of Topeka
2935 S.W. Topeka Blvd.
913/267-7411
18,000 sq. ft.

Wichita
White Eagle Antique Mall
10187 S.W. U.S. Hwy. 54
316/775-2812
100 dealers

Wooden Heart Antiques
141 S. Rock Island St.
316/267-1475
Large two-story warehouse

LOUISIANA

Baton Rouge
AAA Antiques
9800 Florida Blvd.
504/925-1644
80,000 sq. ft. — 75 dealers

Landmark Antique Plaza Inc.
832 St. Phillip St.
504/383-4867
55,000 sq. ft.

Westmoreland Antique Gallery
3374 Government St.
504/383-7777
55,000 sq. ft.

Denham Springs
Benton Brothers Antique Mall
115 N. Range Ave.
504/665-5146
12,000 sq. ft.

New Orleans
New Orleans Antique District
"Magazine St."
Over 80 shops

Shreveport
Heirloom Antiques
3004 Highland Ave.
318/226-0146
10,000 sq. ft.

Nigel's Heirloom Antique Gallery
421 Texas St.
318/226-0146
22,000 sq. ft., 5 floors

Washington
O'Conner's Antiques
210 S. Church St.
318/826-3580
15,000 sq. ft.

West Monroe
Antique Alley
Located Downtown
Trenton St.
14 shops

MINNESOTA

Maple Plain
Country School House Shops
5300 U.S. Hwy. 31
612/479-6353
3-story schoolhouse — 100+ dealers

Stillwater
Mid Town Antique Mall
301 S. Main St.
612/430-0808
11,000 sq. ft. — 75 dealers

More Antiques
312 N. Main St.
612/439-1110
11,000 sq. ft.

The Mill Antiques
410 N. Main St.
612/430-1816
20,000 sq. ft. — 80+ dealers

MISSOURI

Bonne Terre
Bonne Terre Antiques
1467 State Hwy. 47
573/358-2235
3 large buildings

Columbia
Ice Chalet Antique Mall
3411 Old Hwy. 63 S.
573/442-6893
28,000 sq. ft. — 200+ dealers

Eureka
Ice House Antiques
19 Dreyer
314/938-6355
14 shops on 4 floors

Wallach House Antiques
510 West Ave.
314/938-6633
3 levels of quality shopping

Greenwood
Greenwood Antiques & Country Tea Room
5th & Main St.
816/537-7172
15,000 sq. ft. — 70 shops

Independence
Country Meadows
4621 Shrank Dr.
816/373-0410
40,000 sq. ft. — 400 dealers

Ozark
Antique Emporium
1702 W. Boat St.
417/581-5555
12,000 sq. ft. — 100+ dealers

Finley River Heirlooms
105 N. 20th St.
417/581-3253
18,000 sq. ft. — 300 dealers

Maine Streete Mall
1994 Evangel St.
417/581-2575
27,000 sq. ft.

Ozark Antiques & Collectibles
200 S. 20th St.
417/581-5233
17,000 sq. ft. — 100+ dealers

Riverview Antique Center
909 W. Jackson
417/581-4426
20,000 sq. ft. — 100+ dealers

Platte City
I-29 Antique Mall
Junction I-29
816/858-2921
12,000 sq. ft. — 80+ dealers

St. Charles
St. Charles Antique Mall
#1 Charlestowne Plaza
314/939-4178
30,000 sq. ft. — 450 dealers

St. Louis
South County Antique Mall
13208 Tesson Ferry Road
314/842-5566
1 acre — 650 dealers

Largest Malls

Warson Woods Antique Mall
10091 Manchester Road
314/909-0123
25,000 sq. ft. — 350+ dealers

MONTANA

Billings
Depot Antique Mall
2223 Montana Ave.
406/245-5955
60+ dealers

Bozeman
Country Mall Antiques
8350 Huffine Lane
406/587-7688
65+ dealers

St. Regis
The Place of Antiques
Downtown St. Regis
406/649-2397
70+ dealers

NEBRASKA

Grand Island
Great Exchange Flea Market
N.E. Corner of Hwy. 34 & Locust St.
308/381-4075
12,000 sq. ft. — 60 dealers

Lincoln
Aardvark Antique Mall
5800 Arbor Road
402/464-5100
25,000 sq. ft.

Omaha
Meadowlark Antique Mall
10700 Sapp Brothers Dr.
1-800-730-2135
400+ dealers

NEVADA

Las Vegas
Red Rooster Antiques
1109 Western Ave.
702/382-5253
25,000 sq. ft.

Sampler Shoppes Antiques
6115 W. Tropicana @ Jones
702/368-1170
40,000 sq. ft. — 200 dealers

Reno
Antique Mall I
1215 S. Virginia St.
702/324-1003
12,000 sq. ft. — 60 dealers

NEW MEXICO

Albuquerque
Classic Century Square
4616 Central S.E.
505/265-3161
40,000 sq. ft.

Silver City
Silver City Trading Co.
205 W. Broadway
505/388-8989
12,500 sq. ft.

NORTH DAKOTA

Jamestown
Treasure Chest
213 1st Ave. S.
701/251-2891
Located in 1900s early bank

Valley City
E & S Antiques
148 E. Main St.
701/845-0369
Located in 1890s opera house

OKLAHOMA

Ada
Alford Warehouse Sales
217 S. Johnston St.
580/332-1026
2 large buildings

Ardmore
Black Star Antiques
702 S. Chouteau Ave.
918/476-6188
14,000 sq. ft.

El Reno
Rt. 66 Antique Mall
1629 E. State Hwy. 66
405/262-9366
120 booths

Muskogee
Old America Antique Mall
Hwy. 69 S.
918/687-8600
27,000 sq. ft.

Oklahoma City
Oklahoma City Antique District
"Over 400 dealers"

OREGON

Lincoln
Lincoln City Antique District
16+ shops on Highway 101

North Bend
Sherman Avenue Antique Shops

Portland
Antique Capital of Oregon
Over 100 shops

Sellwood
Sellwood Antique District
13th St.
26+ shops

SOUTH DAKOTA

Mitchell
Second Impression Palace
412 N. Main St.
605/996-1948
2 full floors

Tea
I-29 Antiques & Collectibles
46990 271st St.
605/368-5810
10,000 sq. ft. — 75 dealers

TEXAS

Abilene
Poppy's Antique Mall
126 S. Access Road
915/692-7755
10,000 sq. ft.

Amarillo
Historical Route 66
Sixth Street
806/372-3901
Numerous shops located between Western and Georgia on Sixth Street on Historical Route 66.

Baird
More than 20 antique shops and related businesses.

Dallas
Unlimited Ltd.
The Antique Mall & Tea Room
15201 Midway Road
972/490-4085
175 antique and collectible shops

White Elephant Antiques Warehouse
1026 N. Industrial Blvd.
214/871-7966
18,000 sq. ft. — 75 dealers

Fort Worth
Harris Antiques & Imports
7600 Scott St.
817/246-8400
440,000 sq. ft.

Houston
Almeda Antique Mall
9837 Almeda Genoa
713/941-7744
100 shops and showcases

Carolyn Thompson's Antique Center of Texas
1001 W. Loop N.
713/688-4211
200+ dealers

Trade Mart
Sam Houston Tollway @ Hammerly
713/467-2506
70,000 sq. ft.

Lubbock
Antique Mall of Lubbock
7907 W. 19th St.
806/796-2166
24,000 sq. ft. — 150 booths

Trinity
Teddie Bears Antiques & Collectibles
Hwy. 19 S., Route 4
409/594-6321
Two acres of antiques and junque to browse

WASHINGTON

Centralia
Centralia Square Antique Mall
201 S. Pearl St.
360/736-6406
2 large buildings, 90 dealers

Kalama
Kalama Antique District
1st St.
150 dealers

WISCONSIN

Appleton
Fox River Antique Mall
1074 S. Van Dyke Road
920/731-9699
20,000 sq. ft. — 165 dealers

Sheboygan
Craftmasters Antiques & Restorations
2034 N. 15th St.
920/452-2524
Three full floors of merchandise

WYOMING

Laramie
Golden Flea Gallery
725 Skyline Road
307/745-7055
140 dealers